To Christine
and John

Wishing you a happy life
in your new house – and
hoping that this will have some
practical application when you
tear yourself away from it !!

Love Helen and Barry Tyers
xxxx
October 1997.

WHERE TO WATCH BIRDS IN SPAIN

To D. Francisco Bernis Madrazo

WHERE TO WATCH BIRDS IN SPAIN

Sociedad Española de Ornitología
SEO / BirdLife

General Coordinator
Eduardo de Juana A.

Secretary
Bernardo Arroyo

Introductory texts
Eduardo de Juana A.

Maps
Mónica Martinoy

Illustrations
Juan Varela

First edition: December 1994

Translation: *Victoria Ennion*

Revision: *Sheila Hardie*

Design: *Xavier Ruiz*

Cover Photograph: Bearded Vulture (*Gypaetus barbatus*), *Jorge Puig*

Printed by: *Printer Industria Gráfica, S.A.* (Barcelona, Spain)

Dipòsit Legal: B-35034-94

ISBN: 84-87334-14-8

CONTENTS

FOREWORD

A visit to Spain offers magnificent opportunities for birdwatching and, with 360 species catalogued within the Peninsula, there are birds to suit the most varied ornithological tastes. By visiting any of the 309 selected sites recommended here, accompanied by practical tips on access, accomodation, information on ecology and on the type of birds to be found in the area, you are guaranteed to delight in the splendour of the unique and extraordinary countryside, flora and fauna, components of a fragile natural paradise which must be protected and treated with the greatest care and respect. No information is given on the Balearic or the Canary Islands since, owing to the fact that the surface area of these archipelagos —which are in general visited in specific expeditions— is quite limited, it is easier to count on local help when planning birdwatching trips.

From the Ptarmigan and the Capercaillie, symbols of the boreal forest, to the Spanish Imperial Eagle and the Black Vulture of the Mediterranean mountains, the Great Bustard of the dry cereal farming areas, the Trumpeter Finch of the arid gullies or the Purple Gallinule and the Marbled Teal of the Andalusian wetlands, one can enjoy the common and the rare, the large and the small, whilst helping to ensure that nature conservation always remains the top priority. Another advantage of the Iberian Peninsula is that all seasons of the year have something to offer: nestbuilding in spring, migratory birds on passage in summer and autumn along with the highest numbers of sedentary species, and, in winter, lots of winter visitors such as the Crane which occupies the warm regions inland.

The information contained in this book, dear visitor, will allow you to be enthralled by the outstanding geographical features, people and bird populations which are to be found in the Iberian Peninsula. We stretch forth a helping hand to enable you to get to know and to protect this heritage. We bid you a warm welcome and would like to receive the support which you judge most appropriate to protect, and to spread the news about, our bounteous natural heritage.

Let me just end by quoting the words of Abel Chapman and Walter J. Buck, British travellers who, in 1910, described Unexplored Spain: "As naturalists —that is merely as born lovers of all that is wild, and big, and pristine— we thank the guiding destiny that early directed our steps toward a land that is probably the wildest and certainly the least known of all in Europe —a land worthy of better cicerones than ourselves".

Francisco J. Purroy
President of SEO–BIRDLIFE

INTRODUCTION

This book is a collective work by members of the Sociedad Española de Ornitología (Spanish Ornithological Society) aimed at making things easier for those who wish to go birdwatching in Spain.

There are currently many books on the market giving details about the shapes, colours and behaviour of the birds in Spain. There is plenty information too on the distinguishing features which permit them to be identified in the field, but, except for some specific regions or provinces, up to now there has been no book which indicated exactly where one should go to see a particular species. It is doubtless hard to acquire this type of information, often only known by small groups of experts who normally only divulge their knowledge orally and to people they trust. We should, therefore, be grateful for the collaboration of the 225 or so ornithologists who accepted to share with us their wealth of knowledge, gained in many cases as a result of many years of fieldwork, and many long hikes.

This book has been written with both Spanish birdwatchers and those who are visiting from other countries in mind. Birdwatching is, in fact, a hobby shared by thousands of people all over the world and Spain is fortunately a country with a lot to offer in the way of ornithological abundance and diversity. It is in fact essentially in order to maintain, or to increase, the value of our avifauna that we have written this guidebook, in the conviction that helping others to get to know and to enjoy birds is a good way of obtaining support in the desperate and vital struggle for the conservation of nature and birds in Spain.

For many people, however, this is a double edged sword: revealing the whereabouts of certain places can be the first step towards their deterioration or destruction. In this respect, we have tried our hardest to be careful by avoiding choosing those areas which might be particularly sensitive and, in contrast, giving preference to those which benefit from some type of protection. Despite this, it is essential that, as requested in the foreword to this book, readers adopt the most basic conservationist code of behaviour when out birdwatching.

The idea of, where possible, avoiding the reader unnecessary complications has also prevailed in the choice of sites. In particular, preference has generally been given to the most easily reached spots and the shortest and simplest routes. Moreover, bearing in mind that the majority of those using this book will probably be travelling by car, distances are given in kilometres, when necessary information is given on the state of the roads or tracks and possible parking places are also indicated. Some places, however, are best visited on foot or by public transport, for example those situated in large urban parks or in the outskirts of cities, areas which can be of particular interest to novice ornithologists. For this reason, in this type of site more complete information is given on the species which can be observed, including birds which are very common and widespread in the territory and which would otherwise have been ommitted.

The structure of the book is defined by the Autonomous Regions. In the chart below one can see the number of sites corresponding to each Region. Although the numbers logically vary substantially in accordance with the large differences in surface area, the smaller Regions tend to be represented by a relatively larger number of sites.

	(1)	(2)	(3)
Andalusia	44	14.2	17.7
Aragon	40	12.9	9.7
Asturias	10	3.2	2.1
Cantabria	9	2.9	1.1
Castile–La Mancha	21	5.8	16.1
Castile–León	48	15.5	19.1
Catalonia	22	7.1	6.5
Extremadura	26	8.4	8.4
Galicia	26	8.4	6.0
Madrid	11	3.6	1.6
Murcia	8	2.6	2.3
Navarra	12	3.9	2.1
País Valenciano	16	5.2	4.7
País Vasco (Basque Country)	8	2.6	1.5
Rioja	8	2.6	1.0

(1) total number of sites per Autonomous Region.
(2) as percentage of total number of sites in book (309).
(3) surface area of the Autonomous Region as percentage of total surface area of peninsular Spain (429.463 km^2).

On a whole, the extent covered, both by the total number of sites (309), and their distribution over peninsular Spain, is more than satisfactory. Replies to the offers to collaborate were normally both affirmative and enthusiastic and only on very few occasions did the editorial team have to write on sites which were considered virtually indispensable; cases in which it was fortunately easy to find the necessary published information. Following more geographic than political criteria, the book encompasses Andorra and the Rock of Gibraltar, and not the Balearic or Canary Islands. In general, these islands are visited on separate journeys from those made to the Iberian Peninsula and, furthermore, in the case of the Canary Islands, the avifauna

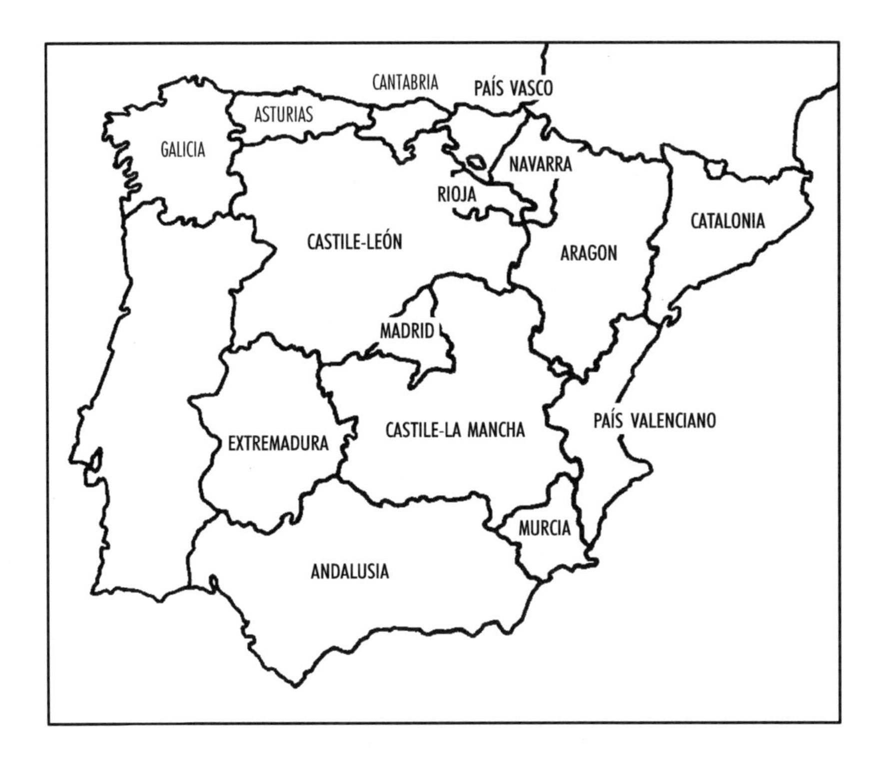

is quite peculiar to the region. As for the Balearic Islands, there are several publications which give detailed information on the birds to be found there.

At the start of each of the chapters dedicated to the Autonomous Regions, there is a general map illustrating the chosen sites and the basic river network. Following on from this, information is provided on the avifauna most typical of the region as well on the geographical and ecological features of the terrain. By reading through these sections, one can get an idea of the type of environment predominant in each Region —for example sea cliffs, mountain forests or lagoons— and the species of birds characteristic of the area, with precise details being given on which place or places are the most representative in each case. Thus, it is hoped that the reader can rapidly form an overall idea about each area and, with the help of this information, make more accurate and better-informed decisions about the route to take. The chapters dedicated to each Autonomous Region are thereafter divided into several sections, of which the first three (General characteristics, Main species and Access), also aim to orientate the readers' decisions, especially regarding the most fundamental question of all, whether or not to visit the locality in question. The second part of each chapter (Description, Recommended routes, Accomodation and Comments) provides information which is above all useful once actually in the area.

We sincerely hope that with this guidebook we will have succeeded in achieving a result worthy of the enthusiasm and hard work put into its creation. We apologize in advance for any possible errors that might have crept in. On this subject, with possible future editions in mind, we would be really grateful if you could let us know about any omissions or errors you detect by writing to the following address:

SEO / BirdLife,
("Where to Watch Birds in Spain")
Carretera de Humera, 63, 1°
28224 Pozuelo de Alarcón
(Madrid)
Spain

ACKNOWLEDGEMENTS

A big thank you, first of all, to each and every one of the ornithologists who participated in this book and whose names appear below the corresponding locality sections. The coordinator also wishes to highlight the help given by several people who, to a great extent, took on the roles of provincial or regional coordinators: Pepe Guitián, Chol Ramón (HABITAT) and Jorge Mouriño (ERVA) in Galicia; Fernando Alvarez-Balbuena (Coordinadora Ornitolóxica d'Asturies) in Asturias; José María Cereza in Huesca and José Luis Lagares in Teruel; Francisco Blanco (ADENEX) and 'Angel Sánchez in Extremadura; Ramón Prades in Castellón; José Ignacio Dies in Valencia and Franciso Robledano (Departamento de Biología y Ecología de la Universidad de Murcia) in Murcia. He is also very grateful to LYNX EDICIONS, and in particular to Josep del Hoyo and Jordi Sargatal, both ornithologists, members of the SEO and participants in this book, for their constant hard work and enthusiasm. Last, but by no means least, he would like to thank the Servicio Geográfico del Ejército for their kind cooperation in permitting the use of the topographic maps.

ANDALUSIA

White-headed Duck
Oxyura leucocephala

Andalusia, without a doubt one of the best known and most attractive areas of Spain, is also probably the one most visited by birdwatchers from other countries. There are many reasons for this. The considerable size of Andalusia, measuring 87,000 km^2, makes it the second largest Autonomous Region in Spain. The landscape is very varied, with continuously alternating plains and mountains; a wide variety of climatic conditions and of vegetation; a long coastline lying on both the Atlantic and the Mediterranean, and, perhaps above all, an impressive series of wetland areas from which we have no choice but to single out the wonderful marshland at the mouth of the Guadalquivir. On the other hand, the fact that the area lies so far to the south gives rise to the presence of a series of species, such as Crested Coot, White-rumped Swift and Trumpeter Finch, which in biogeographical terms are African species rather than European ones. To all these can be added an excellent tourist infrastructure as well as an ambitious policy for conservation which in recent years has meant that over 17 percent of Andalusia has been turned into protected areas.

The geography of Andalusia consists of three main sections: the Sierra Morena, the Guadalquivir river basin and the Cordilleras Béticas, each of these areas having individual characteristics in terms of bird population. The first is an extensive series of mountains running for over 400 km through the northern provinces of Huelva, Seville, Cordoba and Jaén, and the southern provinces of Badajoz (Extremadura) and Ciudad Real and Albacete (Castile-La Mancha). These correspond to the southern edge of the Central Meseta of Spain, a Paleozoic core characterized by siliceous rock types such as quartzite, slate and granite. This area is relatively rolling with many low altitude ranges running parallel and quite close together. The climate is Mediterranean with oceanic influence, giving rise to well-developed vegetation. This includes woodland of holm oak (*Quercus rotundifolia*) and cork oak (*Quercus suber*), areas of cistus and other Mediterranean shrubs, and, on northern slopes, woods consisting of Lusitanian oak (*Quercus faginea*) and Pyrenean oak (*Quercus pyrenaica*). In many places, pine and eucalyptus plantations have made an unwelcome appearance. Population in the area is very sparse, and the land is mainly used for stock farming —large areas of *dehesa*, wooded grazing land— and for hunting big game. What has been said of the areas of Extremadura and Castile-La Mancha is also true of the Sierra Morena, which perhaps should only be mentioned here for the size of its population of birds of prey (Goshawk, Buzzard, Golden Eagle, Booted Eagle, Bonelli's Eagle, Eagle Owl...) and the occasional appearance of nesting species such as Black Stork, Black Vulture and Span-

AN

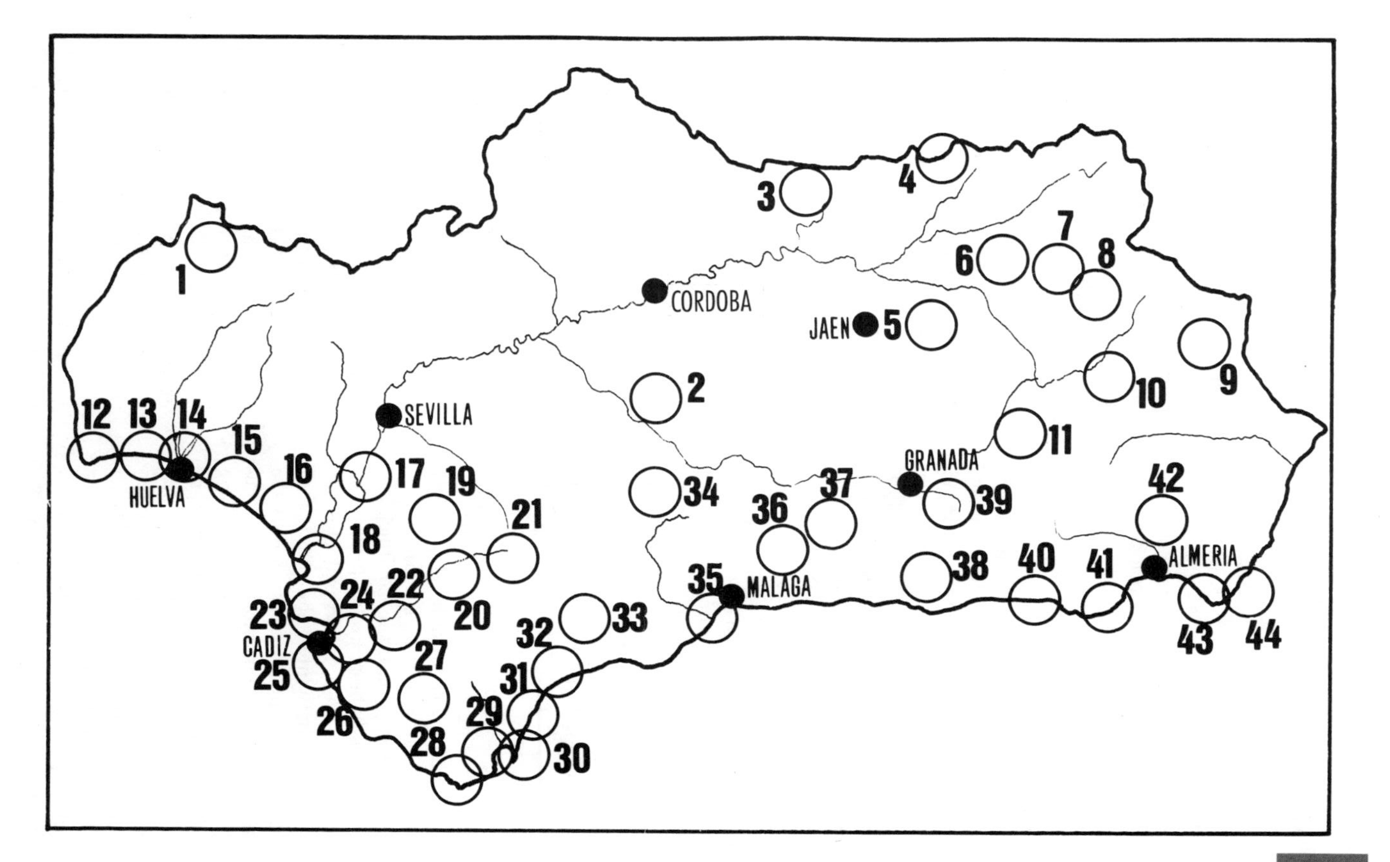

HUELVA
SEVILLA
CORDOBA
JAEN
GRANADA
MALAGA
ALMERIA
CADIZ
1
2
3
4
5
6
7
8
9
10
11
12
13
14
15
16
17
18
19
20
21
22
23
24
25
26
27
28
29
30
31
32
33
34
35
36
37
38
39
40
41
42
43
44

ish Imperial Eagle, birds seldom seen in other areas of Andalusia. In addition, part of the province of Cordoba lies on the far side of the range. This occurs in the region of Los Pedroches, which differs little from the neighbouring areas of Extremadura. As in Extremadura, in Los Pedroches you should see Black-shouldered Kite, Great Bustard, large numbers of wintering Crane and Spanish Sparrow. We have only selected three representative areas in the Sierra Morena: Aracena-Aroche (AN.1), Andújar (AN.3) and Despeñaperros (AN.4). The latter two are easily reached via the main road, but there are wonderful sites in many other places, some of which are very close to the cities of Seville (Parque Natural de la Sierra Norte) and Cordoba (Parque Natural de la Sierra de Hornachuelos).

Lying in the centre of Andalusia, the Guadalquivir river basin is very different, being for many centuries the most populated and cultivated part of Andalusia. The rolling inland countryside has, more than anywhere else, lost virtually any remaining natural vegetation to olive groves and cereal crops. Thus birdlife is relatively sparse. The olive groves, frequently stretching over vast areas, are the site of large numbers of Serin and Greenfinch, along with Turtle Dove, Great Tit, Short-toed Treecreeper, Goldfinch, Chaffinch and other slightly more exotic species such as Rufous Bush Robin and Orphean Warbler. In winter, the number of species present increases, as does the number of individuals, which reach impressive figures in the case of Song Thrush, Blackcap and Chaffinch. Agriculture on the open land is highly intensive, thanks to the extremely fertile soil, meaning that it is no longer possible to see Great Bustard or even Montagu's Harrier, Little Bustard or Stone Curlew. However, it is still possible to see White Stork, Lesser Kestrel, Red-legged Partridge, Quail, Barn Owl, Little Owl, Bee-eater, Hoopoe, Calandra Lark, Short-toed Lark, Crested Lark, Black-eared Wheatear, Fan-tailed Warbler, Spotless Starling, Tree Sparrow, Linnet and Corn Bunting.

The banks of the river Guadalquivir and some of its tributaries add variety at any time of the year with Little Bittern, Night Heron, Mallard, Moorhen, Stock Dove, Scops Owl, Kingfisher, Sand Martin, Nightingale, Cetti's Warbler, Reed Warbler, Great Reed Warbler, Olivaceous Warbler, Melodious Warbler, Sardinian Warbler, Penduline Tit and Golden Oriole among other nesting species. Stretches of the river which have been dammed —Marmolejo, Cordobilla, Malpasillo, Doña Aldonza, Pedro Marín, Puente de la Cerrada (AN.6) and the Bornos reservoir (AN.20), among others— some of the original lagoons that have miraculously survived until the present day include Zoñar (AN.2), Rincón, Espera, Lebrija, Las Cabezas (AN.19), Medina (AN.22), Puerto de Santa María (AN.23), Chiclana (AN.26), Campillos and the largest of all, Fuentedepiedra (AN.34), are the best and virtually only places which can be fully recommended to the birdwatcher in the midst of the open country. In these places you will have opportunities of seeing Great Crested Grebe, Cattle Egret, Purple Heron, Greater Flamingo (Medina and Fuentedepiedra), Gadwall, Marbled Teal, Red-crested Pochard, Pochard, White-headed Duck, Marsh Harrier, Purple Gallinule, Crested Coot, Black-winged Stilt, Whiskered Tern, Savi's Warbler and, in winter, various ducks, waders and passerines such as Bluethroat.

By contrast, the part of the Guadalquivir basin which gives onto the

Atlantic is full of attractions in terms of birdwatching and wildlife in general. This low and sandy area is swept by offshore currents circulating eastwards which tend to silt up the inlets and river mouths, giving rise to wetland areas of great interest strung along the coast. These often lie on the far side of attractive strings of dunes, surrounded by scrubland and pine woods. The largest and best known are, of course, those making up the Marismas del Guadalquivir, with the world-famous Coto de Doñana (AN.16 and AN.17) where, in addition to water birds, you will also have opportunities of seeing birds of prey in large numbers (Black Kite, Red Kite, vultures, Short-toed Eagle, Spanish Imperial Eagle, Booted Eagle, Hobby, Peregrine Falcon), Mediterranean woodland species (Great Spotted Cuckoo, Red-necked Nightjar, Orphean Warbler, Azure-winged Magpie) and species dwelling on open land (Stone Curlew, Pin-tailed Sandgrouse, Lesser Short-toed Lark, Spectacled Warbler). However, the mouths of the rivers Guadiana (Ayamonte-Isla Cristina, AN.12), Piedras (AN.13), Tinto and Odiel (AN.14) should not be forgotten. Likewise the lagoons of Palos and Las Madres (AN.15), the Bonanza salt pans (Sanlúcar de Barrameda, AN.18) or the huge complex of inlets, channels, salt pans and fish ponds present in the bay of Cádiz (AN.24 and AN.25). Among the water birds not mentioned yet which you may see in these wetland areas are the following: during the breeding season, Black-necked Grebe, Squacco Heron, Little Egret, Spoonbill, Avocet, Collared Pratincole, Little Ringed Plover, Kentish Plover, Lapwing, Redshank, Black-headed Gull, Slender-billed Gull, Yellow-legged Gull, Gull-billed Tern, Little Tern and Baillon's Crake; in winter, Cormorant, Grey Heron, Glossy Ibis, Greylag Goose, Shelduck, Widgeon, Red-breasted Merganser and Caspian Tern; and during the migration periods, Black Stork, Garganey, Osprey, Common Tern and many other species, particularly waders.

Moving south from Cádiz towards the Straits of Gibraltar, the coastline suddenly becomes steep and occasionally features cliffs (for example the well-known Tajo de Barbate near Cabo Trafalgar) as we enter the third of the geographical units mentioned above, the Cordilleras Béticas. Given their position, these are also responsible for the fact that the Mediterranean coastline has similar characteristics with mountains running directly down to the sea and only a few small flat areas suitable for cultivation (around Gibraltar, Málaga, Vélez-Málaga, Motril, Adra, Dalías, Almería...). The rivers in this area are short, only giving rise to small deltas (river Palmones, AN.29; river Guadiaro, AN.31; river Guadalhorce, AN.35; Albuferas de Adra, AN.40), which cannot compare in interest to the estuaries and marshes on the Atlantic coast. To these can be added two salt works on the coast of Almería (Roquetas-Punta Entinas, AN.41 and Cabo de Gata, AN.44), which are the southernmost salt pans in the whole of Mediterranean Spain.

It is possible to watch sea birds at all points on the Andalusian coast, but particularly around the Straits of Gibraltar (Tarifa, AN.28, and Gibraltar, AN.30). Cory's Shearwater, Manx Shearwater, Yelkouan Shearwater, Storm Petrel, Leach's Storm-petrel, Gannet, Shag, Arctic Skua, Great Skua, Little Gull, Mediterranean Gull, Audouin's Gull, Lesser Black-backed Gull, Lesser Crested Tern, Sandwich Tern, Razorbill and Puffin are some of the species usually seen, although they are easier to spot during migration or after big storms out to sea. What is more, as is well known, the Straits of Gibraltar also provide opportunities for watching the active migration of many inland birds, particularly storks and gliding birds of prey (White Stork, Honey Buzzard, Black Kite, Egyptian Vulture, Griffon Vulture, Short-toed Eagle, Booted Eagle). Especially in autumn, the sight of hundreds or thousands of large birds fighting the strong winds prevailing in the area as they try to cross the stretch of sea separating them from Africa is quite unforgettable. To this can be added the flight of numerous diurnal migrants: Bee-eater, swifts, swallows, wagtails, sparrows and various finches, as well as the possibility of large numbers of nocturnal migrants (warblers, flycatchers) which come to rest in the areas of scrubland and thickets around the straits.

From the Campo de Gibraltar to the boundaries with Murcia and Albacete a complex mountain region extends, usually known by the generic name of Cordilleras Béticas. These ranges present a wide variety of structures and rock types, as well as very varied climatic conditions and vegetation. Precipitation is at its highest at the western end near the Atlantic —the Sierra de Grazalema, with over 2,000 mm of rain per year, is the rainiest part of Spain. This is also true of the northern slopes of some of the more exposed ranges such as Cazorla, but rapidly decreases as one moves east and south. Vegetation therefore also changes, with woodland consisting of oak, cork oak and Spanish fir (*Abies pinsapa*) in the west, and just Aleppo pine (*Pinus halepensis*) at the far east of the ranges. Logically enough, this also gives rise to rapid changes in birdlife present, with the absence in dry habitats of forest-dwelling species such as Great Spotted Woodpecker, Robin, Blackcap, Bonelli's Warbler, Chiffchaff, Nuthatch and Hawfinch. In the same way, the presence of birds of prey also faithfully reflects the general impoverishment of the drier ranges, where Griffon Vulture, Egyptian Vulture, Sparrowhawk, Buzzard, Booted Eagle and several other species tend to disappear, leaving only Bonelli's Eagle and Kestrel. Altitude and rock type are other factors which inevitably condition birdlife in these mountains. In general terms the highest mountains and those composed of limestone rock are the best sites for birds. We feel that the sites chosen give a fair representation of the wide range of possible habitats: Grazalema (AN.21), Bermeja and Crestellina (AN.32), Sierra de las Nieves (AN.33), Tejeda and Almijara (AN.34), gorges of the river Cacín (AN.37), gorges of Los Vados (AN.38), Sierra Nevada (AN.39), Mágina (AN.5), Cazorla (AN.7), La Sagra-Seca-Castril (AN.8) and Sierra de María (AN.9). The highest ranges, such as the Sierra Nevada, La Sagra and Cazorla, give rise to a wider range of habitats in terms of plant and birdlife, although altitudes (3,481 m in the case of the Sierra Nevada, the highest peak in mainland Spain) do not fully compensate for the fact that the ranges are very southern and far removed from other mountain chains. The only true alpine species, Alpine Accentor, only appears on the summits of the Sierra Nevada, while it is possible to see species such as Tawny Pipit, Whitethroat or Ortolan Bunting at very high levels. On the other hand, the limestone ranges of Mágina, Cazorla, Tejeda or Grazalema usually have more gorges and cliffs, suitable nesting places for species such as Griffon Vulture, Peregrine Falcon, Rock Dove, Eagle Owl, Pallid Swift, Alpine Swift, Crag Martin, Black Redstart, Blue Rock Thrush or Chough.

At the driest eastern end of the Cordilleras Béticas is an extremely arid subregion straddling the provinces of

Granada and Almería. Located in the rain shadow of the mountains, this area frequently receives less than 300 mm of precipitation per year. This rain falls extremely irregularly, with torrential downpours followed by long periods of drought. This area also runs into the provinces of Murcia (see relevant section) and the País Valenciano, constituting what has become known as Southeast Spain. The landscape has North African characteristics and, in terms of birdlife, has a very marked personality with relatively high numbers of steppe-dwelling species (Little Bustard, Stone Curlew, Black-bellied Sandgrouse, Dupont's Lark, Short-toed Lark, Lesser Short-toed Lark, Thekla Lark, Black-eared Wheatear, Spectacled Warbler) and species to be found in rocky areas and bare river gorges (Bonelli's Eagle, Black Wheatear, Blue Rock Thrush, Trumpeter Finch). This area includes the valleys of Guadix (AN.11), Baza (AN.10) and Huéscar-La Puebla de Don Fadrique (Murcia, MU.2), in conjunction with the spectacular Desierto de Tabernas (AN.42), the coastal steppe of Punta Entinas (AN.41) and Las Amoladeras (AN.43) as well as the fascinating range at Cabo de Gata (AN.44).

AN.1
ARACENA - AROCHE

A low mountain area with extensive dry grazing lands.

Main species

Residents: Black Vulture, Goshawk, Buzzard, Golden Eagle, Bonelli's Eagle, Eagle Owl, Sardinian Warbler, Crested Tit, Hawfinch, Rock Bunting.

Summer visitors: Black Stork, Short-toed Eagle, Booted Eagle, Great Spotted Cuckoo, Red-necked Nightjar, Red-rumped Swallow, Orphean Warbler, Golden Oriole, Woodchat Shrike.

Access

From the N-630 between Seville and Mérida, at Venta del Alto take the N-433 which traverses the area and brings you to Portugal (El Rosal de la Frontera). About 18 km after Aracena you will come the junction with the N-435 which runs northwards to Higuera la Real and Fregenal de la Sierra, both in the province of Badajoz.

Description

An extensive section of the western Sierra Morena, with low mountains (500 to 900 m a.s.l), largely taken up by dry grazing lands with cork oak given over mainly to pig farming. There are also areas of Mediterranean scrubland, large plantations of pine and eucalyptus, small woods of chestnut, and by the rivers and riverbeds, alders and thickets of oleander. In places, there are granite outcrops such as the Peñas de Aroche.

The area has been declared a Natural Park and covers a surface area of 184,000 ha.

Recommended routes

From the N-433 and the N-435 it is possible make a series of trips by car, using the existing road network. A

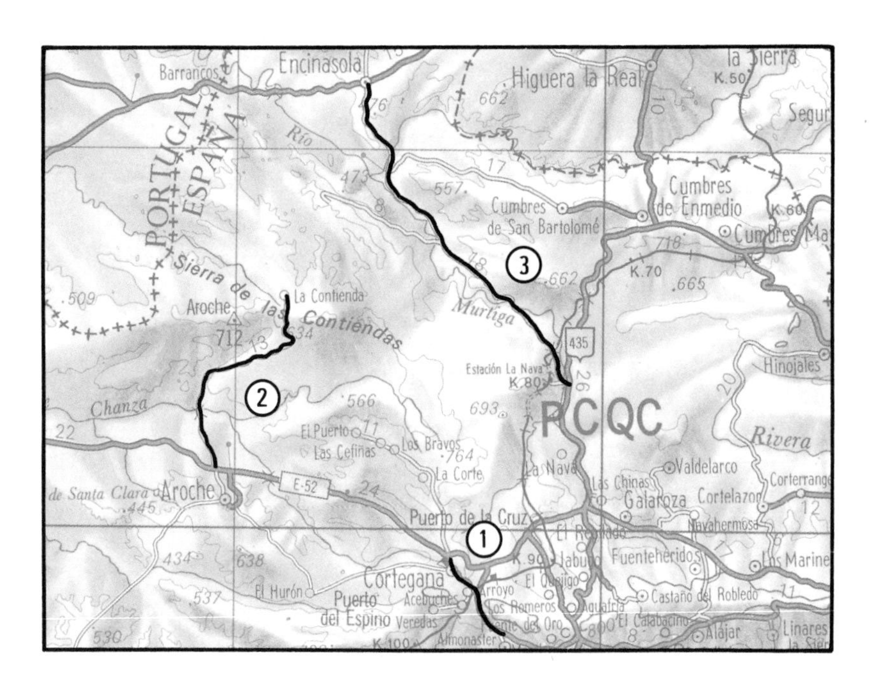

small road leads off southwards from Cortegana; this road climbs 3 km up to a small pass beside the peak of Almonaster (1). This peak, at 915 m, is the highest in the area and enables you to gain a general impression of the region. Also recommended is the road joining Aroche with La Contienda (2) which, near the railway station at La Nava, links Encinasola to the N-435 (3).

Accommodation

There is some accommodation available in the main towns of the area, and especially in Aracena, a tourist site.

Eduardo de Juana Aranzana

■ AN.2 ZÓÑAR LAGOON

Wetland area: a small lagoon lying among fields.

Main species

Residents: Little Grebe, Great Crested Grebe, Mallard, Red-crested Pochard, White-headed Duck, Marsh Harrier, Purple Gallinule, Coot, Kingfisher.

Summer visitors: Little Bittern, Reed Warbler, Great Reed Warbler.

Winter visitors: Widgeon, Teal, Pintail, Shoveler, Pochard, Tufted Duck.

Access

From Lucena, take the N-331 towards Cordoba and stop in Aguilar de la Frontera (22 km). Here, take the C-329 towards Puente Genil and you will see the lagoon to the right of the road, midway between the two towns.

Description

The Zóñar lagoon, measuring 37 ha and containing slightly saline water, is

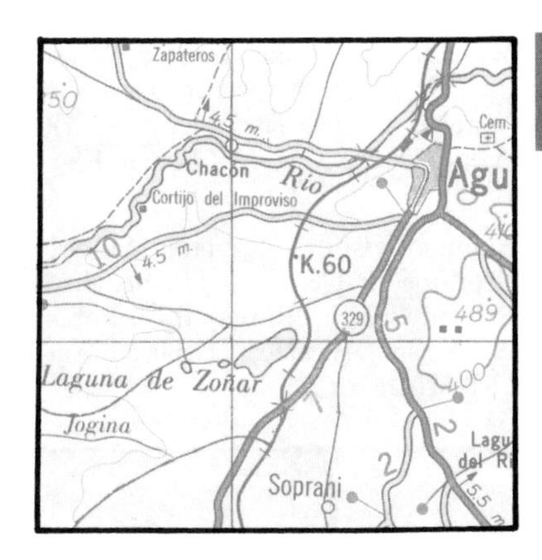

surrounded by a fringe of reeds and reedmace. It lies among fields, olive groves and vineyards. There is plentiful underwater vegetation. It is an Integral Reserve measuring 66 ha.

Recommended routes

The network of farm tracks running around the lagoon gives you a series of opportunities to approach the lagoon and watch the water birds most characteristic of this wetland area. A further point of interest, giving a general impression of the area, is the railway bridge lying beside the lagoon.

Accommodation

You will find accommodation in the nearby towns of Lucena, Montilla and Puente Genil.

Bernardo Arroyo

■ AN.3 ANDÚJAR RANGE

A mountain area with extensive areas of Mediterranean woodland and scrubland.

Main species

Residents: Black Vulture, Griffon Vulture, Goshawk, Golden Eagle, Spanish Imperial Eagle, Eagle Owl, Green

Woodpecker, Great Spotted Woodpecker, Black Wheatear, Sardinian Warbler, Crested Tit, Long-tailed Tit, Azure-winged Magpie, Chough, Hawfinch.

Summer visitors: Egyptian Vulture, Short-toed Eagle, Booted Eagle, Great Spotted Cuckoo, Rufous Bush Robin, Black-eared Wheatear, Orphean Warbler, Woodchat Shrike.

Winter visitors: a large number of wintering passerines including Dunnock, Robin, Song Thrush, Redwing, Blackcap, Chiffchaff and Chaffinch.

Access

From Andújar on the N-IV, take the road for the Santuario de Santa María de la Cabeza. Alternatively, this point can be reached from La Carolina, also on the N-IV, via a long, narrow surfaced road which passes through interesting areas of the Sierra Morena via the villages of El Centenillo, Selladores and Las Viñas. Access is also possible from Puertollano, in the province of Ciudad Real, via Solana del Pino.

Description

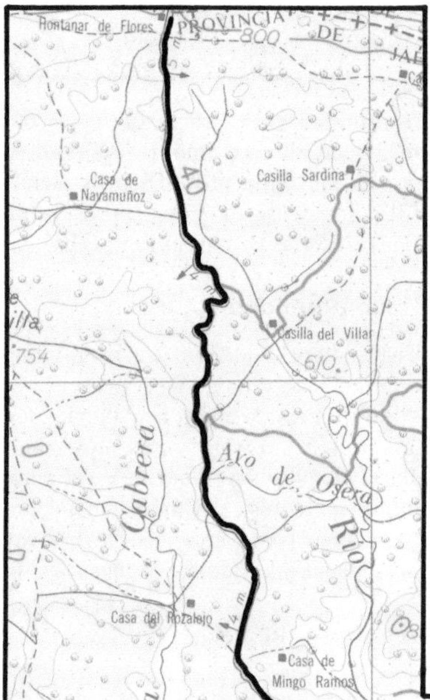

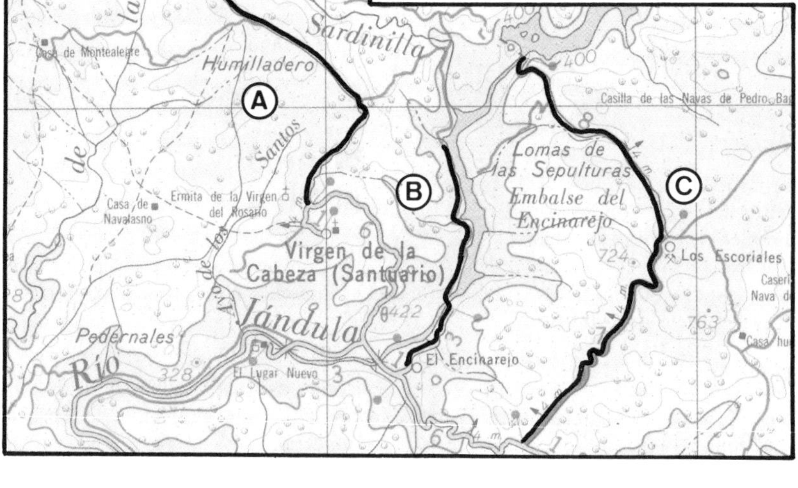

A series of ranges of mountains of moderate height (500–1,290 m a.s.l.) with numerous valleys and gorges in the midst of the Sierra Morena. Vegetation consists of typical Mediterranean woodland; it is unspoiled and is constituted by holm oak, Lusitanian oak, cork oak, umbrella pine and the occasional Pyrenean oak. There are also areas of dry grazing land and extensive areas of scrubland with strawberry tree (*Arbutus unedo*), mastic tree (*Pistacea lentiscus*), *Phillyrea media*, myrtle (*Myrtus communis*) and cistus (*Cistus* spp.). There is a lot of big game in the area, and hunting is one of the main uses the land is put to.

It is a Natural Park (60,800 ha).

Recommended routes

Route A consists of a car journey from the Santuario de la Virgen de la Cabeza, a monastery, in the direction of Puertollano, until reaching the provincial boundary with Ciudad Real, which runs through the middle of the Sierra Madrona. Make stops at will to watch the many birds of prey and to contemplate beautiful landscapes.

Route B has its starting point on the same road a little farther to the south, on the bridge over the river Jándula. From here take the forestry track which leads upstream to the Encinarejo reservoir and subsequently to its far ends. The area has a wide variety of habitats and therefore many species of birds.

Route C runs along the road from Las Viñas to the La Lancha dam (Embalse del Jándula), taking you through areas of dry grazing land and scrubland.

Accommodation

A wide variety of accommodation is available in Andújar, La Carolina and Bailén. Within the Park itself it is possible to stay at the monastery, Santuario de la Virgen de la Cabeza.

Comments

The best times of year for visiting the area are from mid-September to late November, and from mid-March to late May.

You should remember that petrol stations are sparse in the area, being located at La Carolina, Andújar and Solana del Pino.

It is worthwhile obtaining information from the offices of the Agencia de Medio Ambiente de Jaén (environmental department in Jaén) or from the information centre in the Park.

Alfonso M. Sánchez-Lafuente,
Joaquín Muñoz-Cobo,
Pedro Rey Francisco Valera
and José Eugenio Gutiérrez.

■ AN.4 DESPEÑAPERROS

A mountain area with Mediterranean woodland, scrubland and many rocky areas.

Main species

Residents: Griffon Vulture, Goshawk, Spanish Imperial Eagle, Golden Eagle, Bonelli's Eagle, Eagle Owl, Great Spotted Woodpecker, Crag Martin, Black Wheatear, Blue Rock Thrush, Crested Tit, Long-tailed Tit, Azure-winged Magpie, Chough, Hawfinch, Rock Bunting.

Summer visitors: Great Spotted Cuckoo, Rufous Bush Robin, Red-rumped Swallow, Golden Oriole, Woodchat Shrike.

Access

The N-IV runs through this area.

Description

The river Despeñaperros creates a natural corridor through one of the steepest areas of the Sierra Morena, dividing the Southern Meseta from the Guadalquivir river valley. The mountains are of average height (500-1,290 m a.s.l.), with numerous valleys and gorges, forested with typical Mediter-

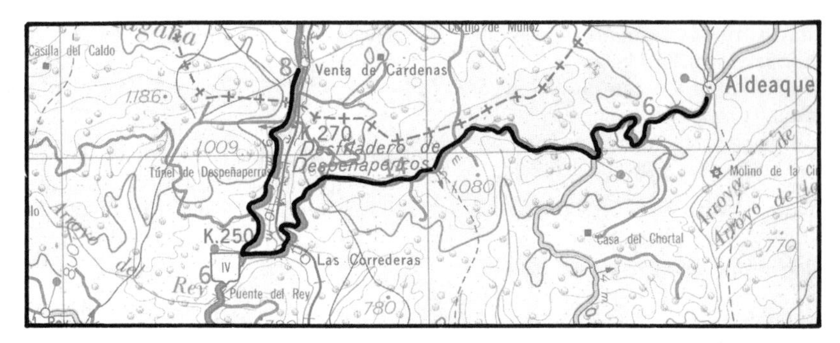

ranean mountain flora such as holm oak, cork oak, Lusitanian oak and, in some places, Pyrenean oak. Although there are degenerate areas (dry grazing lands and conifer plantations), there are also many areas of well-conserved natural vegetation.

This area is a Natural Park of 6,000 ha, of great wealth in terms of fauna and hunting.

Recommended routes

From the car parks located along the main road it is possible to see the high quartzite rock faces known as Los Organos (translates as organ pipes), with associated birdlife.

Alternatively, the road crossing the Park to Aldeaquemada is also interesting with habitats of Mediterranean scrubland, dry grazing lands and pine plantations. Once in Aldeaquemada, it is worth visiting the nearby waterfall known as La Cimbarra.

Accommodation

Accommodation is available year round in La Carolina, Santa Elena and Aldeaquemada.

Comments

The best times of year for visiting the Park are from mid-September to late November and from mid-March to late May.

It is worth obtaining information from the offices of the Agencia de Medio Ambiente in Jaén (environmental department) or from the information centre in the Park.

Alfonso M. Sánchez-Lafuente, Joaquín Muñoz-Cobo, Pedro Rey Francisco Valera and José Eugenio Gutiérrez.

AN.5 MÁGINA RANGE

A mountain area with many cliffs and large numbers of birds of prey.

Main species

Residents: Golden Eagle, Bonelli's Eagle, Peregrine Falcon, Eagle Owl, Skylark, Firecrest, Crested Tit, Chough, Rock Sparrow.

Summer visitors: Tawny Pipit, Wheatear, Rock Thrush, Whitethroat, Spotted Flycatcher.

Winter visitors: Ring Ouzel.

Access

As the N-IV passes through Bailén, take the N-323 to Jaén and continue in the direction of Granada until at the 340 km marker post you join the N-321. Continue along the N-321 to Mancha Real and from there take the C-328 to Bedmar.

The southern side of the range can best be reached via the road from Jaén to Granada; at the 360 km marker post, take the turning for Cambil and Huelma (N-324).

Description

The Sierra de Mágina forms part of the Cordilleras Subbéticas. The range reaches its greatest height in the province of Jaén at 2,167 m. The height difference allows for a series of bioclimatic levels and thus a remarkably wide variety of habitats: woodland consisting of holm oak, Lusitanian oak, pine, Phoenician juniper (*Juniperus phoenicea*), screes, and high-altitude pastures and scrubland. Limestone cliffs abound. The area is mainly used for stock farming, forestry and handcrafts.

The area is a Natural Park (19,900 ha).

Recommended routes

Route A starts in Bedmar, on the northern slopes of the range, and climbs up to Pico de Mágina via the track to Ermita de Cuadros, a chapel. The route takes you through areas of holm oak and pine woodland, mountain streams and, on the highest ground, Phoenician juniper.

Route B climbs from Bélmez de la Moraleda along the course of the river Gargantón, crossing a valley with huge rock formations.

Route C takes you from Cambil towards Pico de Cárceles (2,052 m), passing through Cortijo de los Prados. This spot abounds in pine woods, alpine meadows and areas of low-growing Phoenician juniper.

Accommodation

Accommodation is easy to find year round in all of the villages near the range (Torres Bedmar, Cambil, Huelma, Bélmez de la Moraleda, Albánchez de Ubeda).

Comments

It is a good idea to ask for information in the offices of the Agencia de Medio Ambiente (environmental department)

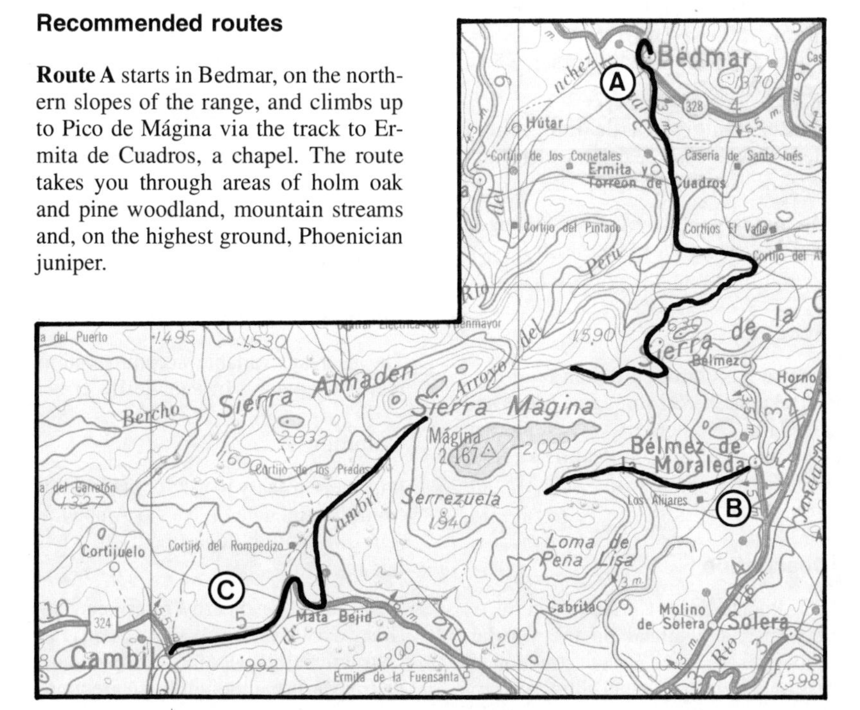

in Jaén. This information will provide you with details of existing facilities or necessary permits for entering the Natural Park.

Alfonso M. Sánchez-Lafuente, Joaquín Muñoz-Cobo, Pedro Rey, José E. Gutiérrez and Francisco Valera.

AN.6 PUENTE DE LA CERRADA RESERVOIR

A dammed stretch of river.

Main species

Residents: Gadwall, Mallard, Pochard, Purple Gallinule, Black-winged Stilt, Avocet, Redshank, Penduline Tit.

Summer visitors: Little Grebe, Great Crested Grebe, Little Bittern, Purple Heron, Marsh Harrier, Kingfisher, Savi's Warbler, Reed Warbler, Great Reed Warbler.

Winter visitors: Cattle Egret, Grey Heron, Widgeon, Teal, Shoveler, Lapwing, Snipe, Bluethroat.

On passage: Osprey, Little Ringed Plover, Ringed Plover, Kentish Plover, Dunlin, Black-tailed Godwit, Curlew.

Access

As you pass through Bailén on the N-IV, take the N-322 through Linares and Ubeda to Torreperogil, where you then take the local road to Peal de Becerro and Cazorla. The reservoir is 15 km from Torreperogil.

Description

The Puente de la Cerrada reservoir is an artificial wetland on the Guadalquivir river. Since its construction, it has undergone a gradual silting-up pro-

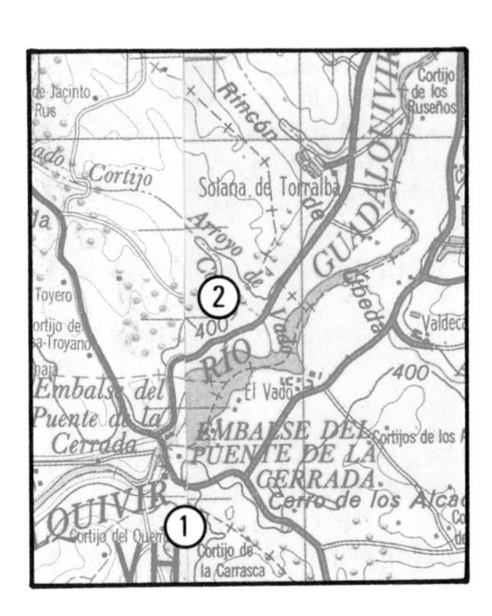

cess caused by river detritus. This process has allowed for the establishing of an extensive belt of marsh vegetation, consisting mainly of reedmace and reeds, which is much used by water birds as shelter and as a nesting ground.

It has been declared a Paraje Natural or Site of Natural Interest (663 ha).

Recommended routes

From the dam (1) and the road to Solana de Torralba (2), you can see various parts of the reservoir. These points are also good vantage points for watching water birds.

Accommodation

The nearest available accommodation is in Torreperogil or Peal de Becerro.

Comments

It is not necessary to ask for permission from the Agencia de Medio Ambiente (environmental department) to visit this reservoir.

There are other nearby reservoirs farther downstream with similar characteristics (Doña Aldonza and Pedro Marín), although these are more problematic since access to them is across private land and roads leading to them are not suitable for ordinary cars.

The best time of day for watching birds is early in the morning.

Alfonso M. Sánchez-Lafuente,
Joaquín Muñoz-Cobo,
Pedro Rey, José E. Gutiérrez
and Francisco Valera.

■ AN.7 CAZORLA RANGE

A mountain area with extensive pine forests and many cliffs.

Main species

Residents: Red Kite, Bearded Vulture (virtually extinct), Griffon Vulture, Goshawk, Sparrowhawk, Golden Eagle, Bonelli's Eagle, Peregrine Falcon, Rock Dove, Eagle Owl, Great Spotted Woodpecker, Woodlark, Crag Martin, Wren, Robin, Black Redstart, Black Wheatear, Blue Rock Thrush, Mistle Thrush, Sardinian Warbler, Blackcap, Firecrest, Long-tailed Tit, Crested Tit, Nuthatch, Azure-winged Magpie, Chough, Raven, Rock Sparrow, Crossbill, Cirl Bunting, Rock Bunting.

Summer visitors: Egyptian Vulture, Short-toed Eagle, Booted Eagle, Alpine Swift, Red-rumped Swallow, Wheatear, Black-eared Wheatear, Rock Thrush, Spectacled Warbler, Subalpine Warbler, Orphean Warbler, Bonelli's Warbler, Chiffchaff.

Access

Cazorla is perfectly located to be the starting point for visits to this area. Another interesting site is Pozo Alcón, located on the southern slopes of the range 55 km from Cazorla.

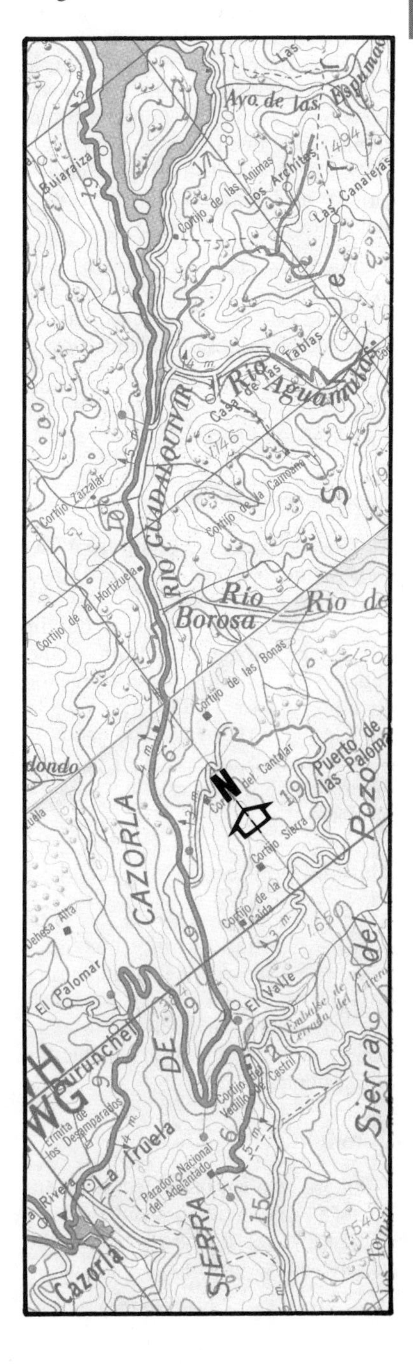

Description

The Cazorla range forms part of the Cordilleras Subbéticas. It is an impressive limestone massif which reaches a maximum height of just over 2,000 m. There are great differences in height with deep gorges and large cliffs. The heads of the rivers Guadalquivir and Segura lie in these mountains.

Although vegetation is varied, pine forests generally dominate, forming dense and extensive areas of woodland. There are also a lot of endemic flora.

The area is a Natural Park (Sierra de Cazorla, Sierra de Segura and Sierra Las Villas, 214,000 ha).

Recommended routes

At Torre del Vinagre, 18 km from Cazorla on the road leading to the Tranco de Beas reservoir, there is an information centre where you can obtain information on signed footpaths or the options for walking, horse riding or travelling in a four-wheel drive vehicle with specialized guides. You can also gain a general impression of the area by driving along the existing network of roads.

Accommodation

Although Cazorla has a wide variety of hotel accommodation, it is also possible to stay in the neighbouring villages. There is a Parador Nacional, campsites and, in addition to this, every year areas are made suitable for wild camping.

Comments

For those who are interested, there are botanical gardens at Siles and Torre del Vinagre; these contain most of the woody species growing in the area.

Bernardo Arroyo

■ AN.8 LA SAGRA, SECA AND CASTRIL RANGES

A mountain area with rocky areas and pine woods.

Main species

Residents: Griffon Vulture, Buzzard, Golden Eagle, Eagle Owl, Tawny Owl, Great Spotted Woodpecker, Thekla Lark, Dipper, Black Wheatear, Blue Rock Thrush, Nuthatch, Chough, Crossbill.

Summer visitors: Short-toed Eagle, Booted Eagle, Alpine Swift, Bee-eater, Tawny Pipit, Black-eared Wheatear, Spectacled Warbler, Subalpine Warbler, Woodchat Shrike.

Winter visitors: Hen Harrier, Merlin, Woodcock, Water Pipit, Dunnock, Alpine Accentor, Ring Ouzel.

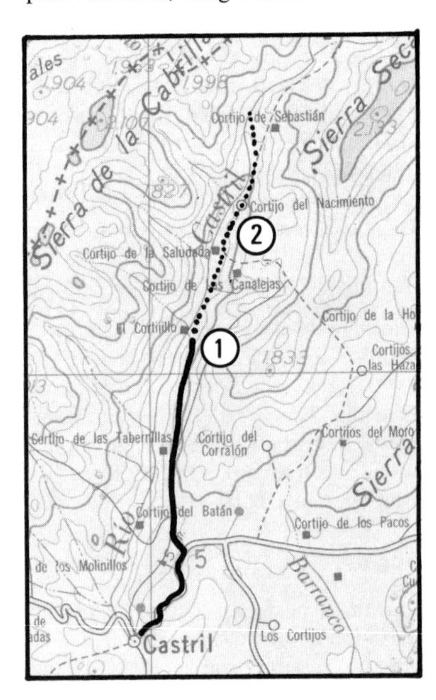

Access

From Baza, take the N-342 (Vélez Rubio–Granada) towards Murcia until reaching Cúllar de Baza (21 km). Here, join the C-3329 for Huéscar (27 km); in Huéscar turn onto the C-330 for Castril (27 km) or Puebla de Don Fadrique (24 km). Alternatively, in Huéscar, take the minor road for La Losa and Santiago de la Espada, which runs between the ranges of Seca and La Sagra.

Description

Steep mountains forming part of the Cordilleras Béticas, reaching their highest point with the peak of La Sagra (2,383 m). The valley sides are quite steep and are occupied by many rocky areas. Pine woodland forms the main kind of vegetation.

The Sierra de Castril is a Natural Park of 14,135 ha.

Recommended routes

Driving along the roads between Castril, Huéscar, Puebla de Don Fadrique and Santiago de la Espada will be extremely useful in terms of gaining a general impression of this area. A second route is proposed through the Sierra de Castril, beginning 3.5 km from Castril on the road to Huéscar. From here, take a track which runs down to the river and then follows the river to El Cortijillo (1), where you can leave your car and continue on foot until reaching the farm of El Nacimiento (2). En route you may see Sparrowhawk, Firecrest, Ring Ouzel, Nuthatch and Crossbill. El Nacimiento farm is also a good place for seeing a series of cliff-dwelling species such as Griffon Vulture, Golden Eagle, Alpine Swift and Chough. The route finishes at the head of the river Castril, lying in a deforested area where you may have sightings of Tawny Pipit, Water Pipit and Alpine Accentor. The whole trip takes a total of 5 hours.

Accommodation

There are hostels in all the villages in the area, and particularly in Huéscar; here, some rooms are available at Hostal El Cortijillo which is particularly beautiful, lying as it does on the river Castril.

José María González Cachinero

■ AN.9 MARÍA RANGE

Mountain area.

Main species

Residents: Goshawk, Golden Eagle, Peregrine Falcon, Little Bustard, Stone Curlew, Black Wheatear, Long-tailed Tit, Treecreeper, Great Grey Shrike.

Summer visitors: Short-toed Eagle, Scops Owl, Bee-eater, Roller, Wheatear, Black-eared Wheatear.

Winter visitors: Dunnock, Alpine Accentor, Ring Ouzel.

Access

From Vélez Rubio on the N-342, take the C-321 towards Orce. Stop at María (15 km).

Description

A limestone and dolomite range lying within the Cordilleras Béticas. The main peaks reach some 2,000 m in height. Because of the great altitudinal differences, vegetation is very widely ranging and includes woodland of pine and holm oak and various kinds of scrubland.

The area is a Natural Park (18,962 ha).

Recommended routes

As you leave María in the direction of Orce, after 2 km turn left onto a track leading to the *ermita* or chapel of La

Virgen de la Cabeza. From here, a footpath climbs to the top of the range and the pass of Portachico. This route, which enables one to visit the most important habitats of the Sierra María, takes some 4 hours.

Accommodation

Vélez Rubio, Vélez Blanco and María all avail of hotel accommodation.

Comments

You are required to have permission to visit the area from the Agencia de Medio Ambiente (Centro Residencial Oliveros; Bloque Singular, 2ª planta; 04001 Almería; telephone: 951-237680).

Segundo Cañadas Albacete, Hermelindo Castro Nogueira, Juan Manrique Rodríguez, José Manuel Miralles García and Juan Carlos Nevado Ariza

■ AN.10 HOYA DE BAZA

Steppe area.

Main species

Residents: Little Bustard, Stone Curlew, Black-bellied Sandgrouse, Green Woodpecker, Thekla Lark, Dupont's Lark, Black Wheatear, Great Grey Shrike, Chough, Rock Sparrow.

Summer visitors: Red-necked Nightjar, Bee-eater, Lesser Short-toed Lark, Short-toed Lark, Tawny Pipit, Black-eared Wheatear, Olivaceous Warbler, Spectacled Warbler, Golden Oriole.

Access

The city of Baza, lying on the N-342, is the centre of this region.

Description

The Hoya de Baza is a depression lying between the mountains of the Cordilleras Béticas, which reach an average height of 700-800 m a.s.l. Slopes are not very steep and the whole is dominated by sparse, open, halophytic scrubland in the flat areas, esparto grassland on the hillsides and riparian vegetation beside the river courses.

Recommended routes

In Baza, take the minor road to Benamaurel and after 7.5 km turn right onto a track. The route takes you along this track on foot. To begin with, the track crosses a flat area with halophytic

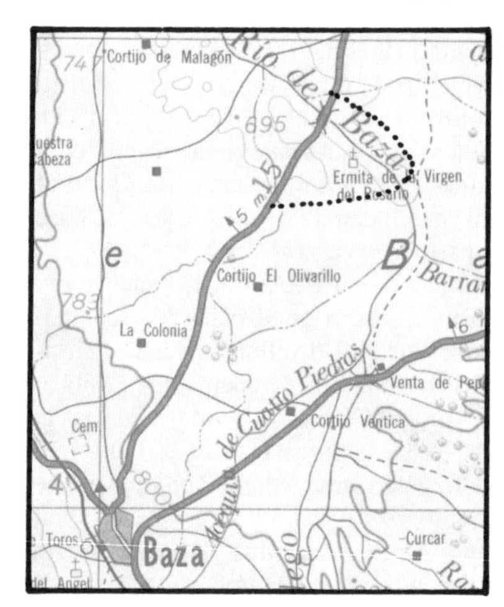

vegetation where you may see Stone Curlew, Red-necked Nightjar, Dupont's Lark and Lesser Short-toed Lark. After 3 km you will come to the river Baza where you can climb the hillsides lying along the right bank. Here you will be able to see Little Bustard, Black-bellied Sandgrouse, Thekla Lark and Spectacled Warbler, while the small clay gullies running down to the river are a good spot for seeing Black Wheatear, Rock Sparrow, Bee-eater and Chough. To return, either retrace your steps or continue downstream where you may find Golden Oriole and Olivaceous Warbler. Eventually you will come out on the Benamaurel road.

Between the 160 and 170 km marker posts on the N-342, a series of tracks lead off across interesting steppe areas, although some of these tracks are in bad condition. It is easy to get lost, and to avoid this you should always use the main road as a reference point.

Accommodation

A series of hotels and restaurants lie on the main road as it passes through Baza. Near the area and on the road itself is Cúllar de Baza, where the Venta del Angel offers good value for money.

Juan Manuel Pleguezuelos and Manuel Soler

AN.11 HOYA DE GUADIX

Steppe area.

Main species

Residents: Sparrowhawk, Peregrine Falcon, Little Bustard, Stone Curlew, Rock Dove, Black-bellied Sandgrouse, Long-eared Owl, Green Woodpecker,

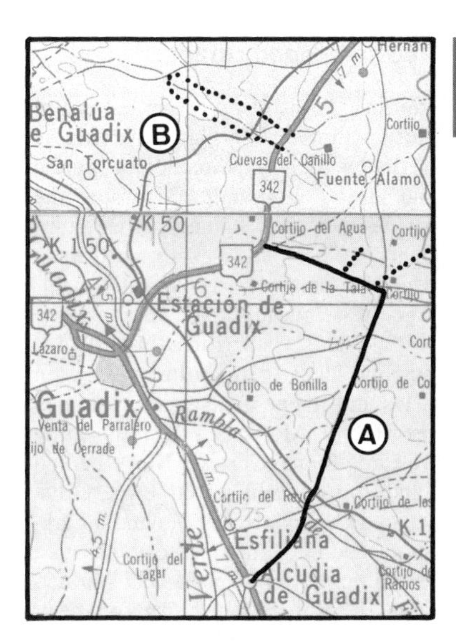

Calandra Lark, Thekla Lark, Crag Martin, Black Wheatear, Dartford Warbler, Great Grey Shrike, Chough, Raven, Rock Sparrow.

Summer visitors: Montagu's Harrier, Hobby, Great Spotted Cuckoo, Red-necked Nightjar, Bee-eater, Roller, Short-toed Lark, Red-rumped Swallow, Black-eared Wheatear, Spectacled Warbler, Golden Oriole, Woodchat Shrike.

Access

Guadix, 59 km from Granada on the N-342, is the main town of the region.

Description

An extensive depression lying at an average height of 1,050 m. It is rolling and crisscrossed by numerous dry riverbeds with screes and steep banks. The area is mostly taken up by cereal crops with a large proportion of fallow land. There are also areas of broom and esparto grass, expanses of dry grazing land with holm oak woodland and almond tree groves.

Recommended routes

Route A consists of a car journey combined with walks. To start, leave Guadix on the N-342 in the direction of Murcia and after 4 km, before crossing the bridge over the Agua riverbed, turn right onto a broad, well-surfaced track which eventually brings you to the village of Alcudia de Guadix on the N-324. This track runs through dry grazing lands with holm oak, grain fields and steppe areas where you may see Hobby, Montagu's Harrier, Little Bustard, Stone Curlew, Black-bellied Sandgrouse, Long-eared Owl, Great Spotted Cuckoo, Roller, Calandra Lark, Short-toed Lark and, on the slopes with sparse vegetation, Spectacled Warbler. Some of the abandoned farms are nesting sites for Black Wheatear.

Route B consists of a walk along the Grao river bed, which can be reached by continuing for a farther 3 km along the N-342. You can leave your car beside the bridge. From here, work your way downstream along the middle of the riverbed for some 4 km until you reach some big caves used as shelters for livestock, which can easily be seen on the right. En route you may see Kestrel, Peregrine Falcon, Crag Martin, Black Wheatear, Chough, Raven, Rock Sparrow and also Green Woodpecker, which in this area burrows its nest in the clay screes. Return via the plains lying on the left bank of the riverbed, staying close to the edge of the river course. Here you may see Montagu's Harrier, Little Bustard, Stone Curlew, Black-bellied Sandgrouse, Calandra Lark and Short-toed Lark.

Accommodation

There is plenty of accommodation available in Guadix.

Manuel Soler
and Juan Manuel Pleguezuelos

■ AN.12 AYAMONTE – ISLA CRISTINA

Coastal marshland.

Main species

Residents: Cattle Egret, Little Egret, Grey Heron, White Stork, Mallard, Red Kite, Buzzard, Marsh Harrier, Black-winged Stilt, Avocet, Little Ringed Plover, Kentish Plover, Great Grey Shrike.

Summer visitors: Purple Heron, Spoonbill, Black Kite, Montagu's Harrier, Collared Pratincole, Little Tern, Bee-eater, Yellow Wagtail, Woodchat Shrike.

Winter visitors: Cormorant, Red-breasted Merganser, Oystercatcher, Ringed Plover, Golden Plover, Grey Plover, Little Stint, Dunlin, Black-tailed Godwit, Bar-tailed Godwit, Whimbrel, Curlew, Spotted Redshank, Redshank, Greenshank, Common Sandpiper, Turnstone, Little Gull, Lesser Black-backed Gull, Caspian Tern, Sandwich Tern.

On passage: waders, gulls, Common Tern, Arctic Tern, Whiskered Tern, Black Tern.

Access

The areas to be visited are located close to the towns of Ayamonte and Isla Cristina. From Huelva, the N-431 will take you to Ayamonte.

Description

A complex of marshes with the particularly interesting lagoon of El Prado and the marshes on the river Carreras, in Isla Cristina and on the river Guadiana.

The El Prado lagoon is shallow and measures some 50 ha. It is virtually entirely covered with marsh vegeta-

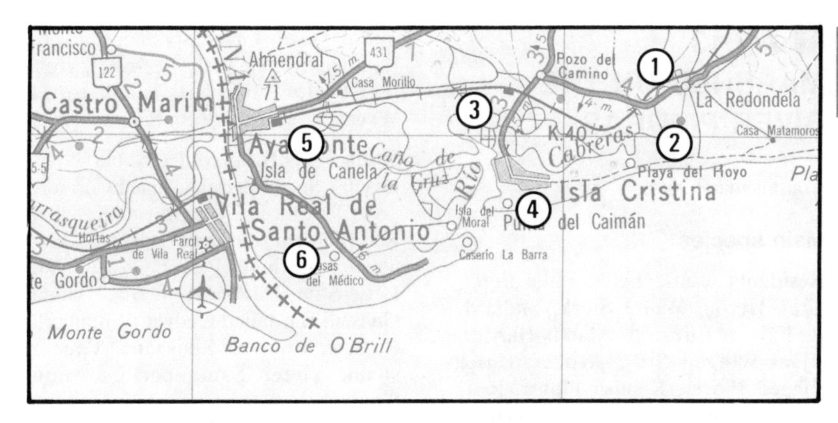

tion. It is an important area used by many birds for shelter and as a feeding ground.

The marshland on the river Carreras is old, and although some channels with water run through it, the area has now turned into a large hypersaline pond which has become badly degenerated.

The marshes of Isla Cristina are in fact the mouth of the river Carreras where it joins the sea. Much of the marshland has been changed into fish farms and traditional salt pans, although there are still some areas which are well-conserved. This applies to the sandbars which have formed at the river mouth (Punta del Caimán).

The marshes at Ayamonte have virtually all been changed into fish farms, although some parts of the Isla Canela and the mouth of some of the tributaries upstream on the river Guadiana have remained intact.

The marshes at Isla Cristina and parts of those at Ayamonte have been declared a Paraje Natural or Site of Natural Interest (2,145 ha).

Recommended routes

A series of approaches to the most interesting parts of this marshland complex will enable us to gain a general impression of the area and the birdlife present. The El Prado lagoon is opposite the old railway station at La Redondela, 6 km from Isla Cristina (1). The marshes of the river Carreras (2) lie in this area; here you will see large numbers of Black-winged Stilt and Collared Pratincole.

The most interesting section of the Isla Cristina marshes is that lying on either side of the road joining Isla Cristina with Pozo del Camino (3). Other interesting spots are the harbour and Punta del Caimán (4), the latter being favourable for watching gulls.

As for the Ayamonte marshes, it is worth visiting the fish farms at El Pinillo (5) which can be reached via a dirt track running off to the left, about 3 km from Ayamonte if you are coming from Huelva.

You can also visit the nearby marshes at Isla Canela (6), although they may well have been destroyed by the time this book is published.

Accommodation

There is plenty of hotel accommodation available in Ayamonte and Isla Cristina.

Comments

It is worth taking a telescope.

Héctor Garrido

AN.13 MARSHES ON THE RIVER PIEDRAS

Coastal marshland.

Main species

Residents: Cattle Egret, Little Egret, Grey Heron, White Stork, Mallard, Red Kite, Buzzard, Marsh Harrier, Black-winged Stilt, Avocet, Little Ringed Plover, Kentish Plover, Redshank, Black-headed Gull, Yellow-legged Gull, Dartford Warbler, Sardinian Warbler, Great Grey Shrike.

Summer visitors: Purple Heron, Spoonbill, Black Kite, Short-toed Eagle, Montagu's Harrier, Booted Eagle, Collared Pratincole, Little Tern, Turtle Dove, Great Spotted Cuckoo, Red-necked Nightjar, Bee-eater, Roller, Yellow Wagtail, Black-eared Wheatear, Woodchat Shrike.

Winter visitors: Manx Shearwater, Leach's Storm-petrel, Gannet, Cormorant, Pochard, Common Scoter, Red-breasted Merganser, Osprey, Oystercatcher, Ringed Plover, Grey Plover, Little Stint, Dunlin, Ruff, Black-tailed Godwit, Bar-tailed Godwit, Whimbrel, Curlew, Spotted Redshank, Greenshank, Green Sandpiper, Common Sandpiper, Turnstone, Arctic Skua, Little Gull, Lesser Black-backed Gull, Caspian Tern, Sandwich Tern, Razorbill, Bluethroat.

On passage: waders, Audouin's Gull, Common Tern, Arctic Tern, Whiskered Tern.

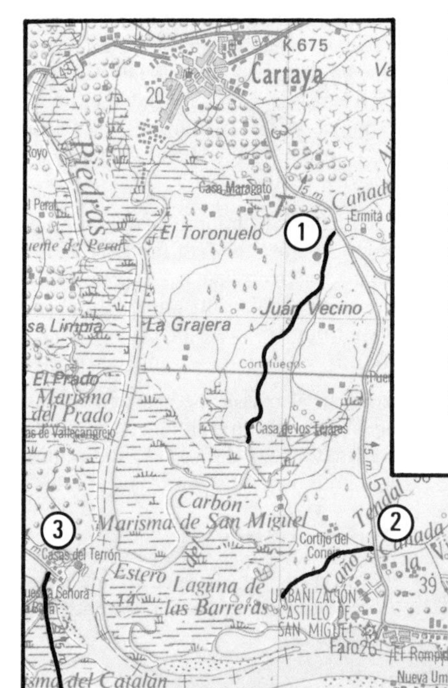

Access

From Huelva, take the N-431 towards Ayamonte and stop in Cartaya (34 km).

Description

The El Rompido sandbar, some 12 km long, closes off the mouth of the river Piedras and promotes the sedimentation of the detritus brought down by the current, giving rise to the formation of this marshland. Until a few years ago, the area was well-conserved, but the spread of fish farming has considerably altered its original qualities. These farms attract large quantities of birds, giving rise to serious problems since the birds are in conflict with the interests of those exploiting the areas.

The marshes of the river Piedras and the Barra del Rompido have been declared a Paraje Natural or Site of Natural Interest (2,530 ha).

Recommended routes

If you wish to watch marshland birds, take any of the tracks leading to the fish farms located to the right of the road from Cartaya to El Rompido. However, those which lead to the points of greatest interest are the following: one which starts beside a butane gas storage area 2 km from Cartaya (1); and a second, a wide gravel track which leads off some 6 km from Cartaya (2) and leads not only to the fields on the Isla del Vinagre but also to the San Miguel marshes, an area of intact marshland of great interest.

Access to the El Rompido sand bar is on foot from the hamlet of El Terrón (3), near Lepe. Drive down the road to the beach and from there, continue on foot to the end of the sand bar. This spot is of great interest in terms of seabirds in winter and during the migration periods.

Accommodation

Accommodation is available in Cartaya and Lepe, although a wider variety is to be had in nearby Huelva, Ayamonte and Isla Cristina.

Comments

To reach the fish farms you should ask permission from the owners and, since the area has recently been declared a protected area, you will soon have to apply for permission from the Agencia de Medio Ambiente de la Junta de Andalucía (environmental department), Av. Sanlúcar de Barrameda, 3, 2°; 21001 Huelva; telephone: 955-24 54 67.

It is worth using a telescope on these itineraries.

Héctor Garrido

■ AN.14 MARSHES ON THE RIVER ODIEL

Coastal marshland.

Main species

Residents: Cattle Egret, Little Egret, Grey Heron, Spoonbill (large breeding colony), White Stork, Greater Flamingo, Mallard, Pochard, Red Kite, Marsh Harrier, Black-winged Stilt, Avocet, Stone Curlew, Kentish Plover, Little Ringed Plover, Yellow-legged Gull, Fan-tailed Warbler, Sardinian Warbler, Azure-winged Magpie.

Summer visitors: Little Bittern, Purple Heron, Black Kite, Montagu's Harrier, Purple Gallinule, Little Tern (over 500 pairs), Purple Gallinule, Scops Owl, Red-necked Nightjar, Pallid Swift, Bee-eater, Roller, Red-rumped Swallow, Yellow Wagtail, Black-eared Wheatear, Golden Oriole.

Winter visitors: Black-necked Grebe, Cormorant, Shelduck, Widgeon, Teal, Pintail, Shoveler, Common Scoter, Red-breasted Merganser, Osprey, Peregrine Falcon, Coot, Oystercatcher, Ringed Plover, Grey Plover, Knot, Sanderling, Curlew Sandpiper, Dunlin, Ruff, Black-tailed Godwit, Bar-tailed Godwit, Whimbrel, Curlew, Spotted Redshank, Redshank, Greenshank, Common Sandpiper, Grey Phalarope, Little Gull, Lesser Black-backed Gull, Caspian Tern, Sandwich Tern, Razorbill, Short-eared Owl, Kingfisher.

On passage: waders, Audouin's Gull, Common Tern, Arctic Tern, marsh terns.

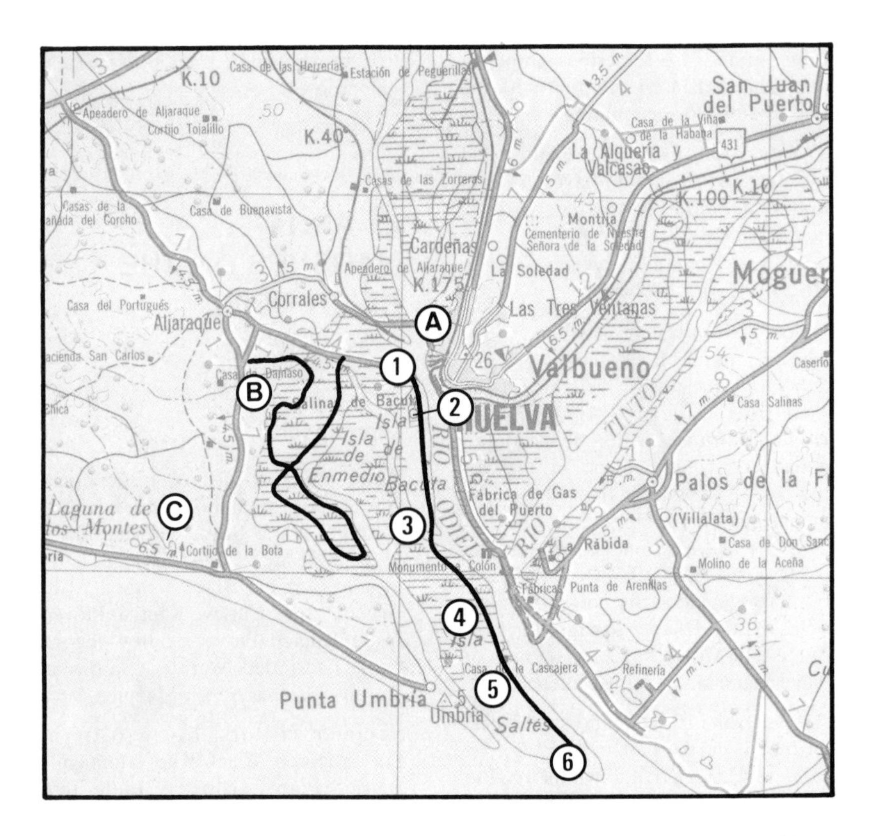

Access

Leave Huelva via the road to Punta Umbría and having crossed the bridge known as Sifón de Santa Eulalia, turn left onto the road to Las Islas, known locally as the *Carretera del Espigón* and signed as Dique Juan Carlos I. 3 km after the crossroads you will find an information centre, currently under construction, with car parks and facilities for the public.

Description

The marshes of the river Odiel are tidal. A sandbar closing the mouth of the rivers Tinto and Odiel has played an important role in the formation of these marshes. Although they have been partly transformed into salt pans, there are still many islands linked by a complicated maze of canals.

The area has been declared a Paraje Natural de Interés Nacional or Natural Site of National Interest (7,185 ha) and is also a Biosphere Reserve.

Recommended routes

Route A runs along the road known as Carretera El Espigón or Carretera Las Islas. It is a car journey of some 25 km, and the points of greatest interest are the following:

1) Information Centre at Calatilla. The Centre may be completed by the time this book is published. The centre will provide information, enable you to make reservations for guided visits and also provide permits for visiting pro-

tected areas. Until the Centre is functioning, enquiries should be addressed to the Agencia de Medio Ambiente (Av. Sanlúcar de Barrameda, 3, 2°, 21001 Huelva).

2) Bacuta salt pans. Traditional salt pans where you can see Spoonbill, herons, Greater Flamingo, waders, ducks and gulls.

3) Burro Bridge. Leave your vehicle in the car park located before the bridge on the right-hand side. By climbing to the highest point of the bridge you will gain a good view over the whole area. At low tide during the migration periods, thousands of waders are present.

4) Woodland on the Isla de Saltés. Isolated stands of woodland located on an island which cannot be visited without permission.

5) Sand flats. Sand flats which are uncovered at low tide. Of greatest interest is the Bajo del Bengalés, the last one to the left of the road, where you will see terns and gulls.

6) El Espigón lighthouse. A good spot for watching scoters, Razorbill, skuas, shearwaters, etc.

Route B consists of a car journey taking you to the inland salt pans and lagoons, where in autumn and winter you will see large numbers of a great variety of water birds. This route should be done with a guide or having first obtained a special permit.

Route C takes you to the lagoon of El Portil, which can be reached via the housing estate of the same name on the road from Huelva to El Rompido. You can walk around the lagoon, although you should find out first at the information centre in Calatilla whether you need a permit.

Accommodation

Tourism in the area is highly developed, although in summer you may have problems finding somewhere to stay.

Comments

It is worth using a telescope in this area.

Héctor Garrido

■ AN.15 PALOS AND LAS MADRES LAGOONS

Natural lagoons.

Main species

Residents: Little Grebe, Cattle Egret, Little Egret, Grey Heron, Mallard, Water Rail, Purple Gallinule, Coot, Kentish Plover, Redshank, Kingfisher.

Summer visitors: Little Bittern, Purple Heron, White Stork, Little Tern, Whiskered Tern, Great Spotted Cuckoo, Roller, Yellow Wagtail, Reed Warbler, Great Reed Warbler, Golden Oriole.

Winter visitors: Black-necked Grebe, Cormorant, Glossy Ibis, Pochard, Common Scoter, Red-breasted Merganser, White-headed Duck, waders, gulls, Razorbill.

On passage: Great Crested Grebe, Night Heron, Osprey, Greater Flamingo, Widgeon, Teal, Garganey, Shoveler.

Access

From Huelva, take the C-442 towards Mazagón. About 10 km after crossing the bridge over the river Tinto you will find the first of the lagoons to the left of the road. The three lagoons making

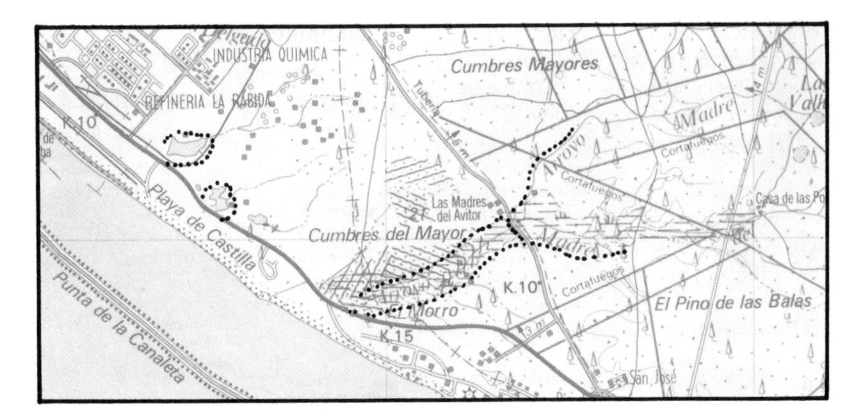

up this area are all visible from the road, but since there are no signs you should keep a close lookout.

Description

The lagoons of Primera de Palos, Jara and Las Madres are the only remaining examples of the string of lagoons which used to run parallel to the beach of Castilla. They were once surrounded by pine woods, although these are now being replaced by strawberry fields.

The lagoons have been declared a Paraje Natural or Site of Natural Interest.

Recommended routes

A walk around the lagoons will be enough to see the main species of birds present. It is easy to find a place to park your car near the lagoons. It is recommended that you undertake the route in an anticlockwise direction.

The Primera de Palos lagoon has a perimeter of some 3 km which can be walked in 2 hours. The shore nearest the road can be seen in its entirety, and on the far shore there is a small beach where you will be able to see various waders.

La Jara lagoon has similar dimensions to Primera de Palos. It is the site of Little Bittern, Purple Gallinule, warblers, ducks and, with luck, crakes. The surrounding land becomes flooded in winter, which may cause problems in terms of access to the area.

The Las Madres lagoon is the largest of the three, with a perimeter of about 5 km. In winter this lagoon is the site of Cormorant and various ducks and gulls, while in summer its most frequent inhabitants are Purple Gallinule, Little Bittern, grebes and warblers. On reaching the Madre del Avitor stream, turn round to walk along the far side of the lagoon, or alternatively walk up alongside the stream in the hope of seeing Glossy Ibis, Grey Heron, Purple Heron, Snipe and Curlew. It is also worth walking through the nearby pine woods to see various birds of prey as well as Great Spotted Cuckoo, Roller and Golden Oriole.

Once you have visited the three lagoons, it is worth going to the beach of Castilla to watch wintering Common Scoter, Red-breasted Merganser, Razorbill and Osprey.

Accommodation

There is plenty of accommodation available in Mazagón, Huelva and Palos de la Frontera.

Comments

The best times of year for visiting the area are autumn and winter.

José Ramón Magro Montiel

■ AN.16 DOÑANA NATIONAL PARK AND SURROUNDING AREA

Marshland, Mediterranean woodland and beaches with shifting dunes. This area is of outstanding ornithological importance.

Main species

Residents: Little Grebe, Black-necked Grebe, Cattle Egret, Little Egret, Grey Heron, Greater Flamingo, Gadwall, Mallard, Marbled Teal, Red-crested Pochard, Pochard, Red Kite, Marsh Harrier, Buzzard, Spanish Imperial Eagle, Peregrine Falcon, Purple Gallinule, Coot, Crested Coot, Black-winged Stilt, Avocet, Stone Curlew, Kentish Plover, Redshank, Pin-tailed Sandgrouse, Calandra Lark, Lesser Short-toed Lark, Thekla Lark, Cetti's Warbler, Fan-tailed Warbler, Dartford Warbler, Sardinian Warbler, Azure-winged Magpie.

Summer visitors: Great Crested Grebe, Little Bittern, Night Heron, Squacco Heron, Purple Heron, White Stork, Spoonbill, Garganey, Black Kite, Short-toed Eagle, Montagu's Harrier, Booted Eagle, Hobby, Collared Pratincole, Slender-billed Gull, Gull-billed Tern, Little Tern, Whiskered Tern, Great Spotted Cuckoo, Red-necked Nightjar, Bee-eater, Short-toed Lark, Red-rumped Swallow, Savi's Warbler, Spectacled Warbler.

Winter visitors: Leach's Storm-petrel (with storms out at sea), Cormorant, Greylag Goose, Shelduck, Widgeon, Teal, Pintail, Shoveler, Common Scoter, Hen Harrier, Crane, Golden Plover, Black-tailed Godwit, Razorbill, Kingfisher, Penduline Tit.

On passage: Glossy Ibis, Griffon Vulture, Merlin, waders in general, Audouin's Gull, Caspian Tern, Sandwich Tern, Common Tern, Black Tern, Black-eared Wheatear, Subalpine Warbler.

Access

From the motorway between Seville and Huelva (A-49), come off at the exit for Bollullos Par del Condado and from there take the minor road for Almonte, El Rocío and Matalascañas (39 km). In El Rocío, the Sociedad Española de Ornitología (SEO) or Spanish Ornithological Society and the Almonte Town Council have recently opened an information centre designed specifically for birdwatchers (Casa de Cultura, c/ El Ajolí, 44; telephone: 955-442310). Just after El Rocío, you will cross the course of the river Rocina, and the first turn to the right will bring you to the information centre of the same name. Continue along the road towards Matalascañas and about 12 km from El Rocío, another signed track runs off to the right to the El Acebuche Information Centre (Centro de Recepción).

The La Rocina Information Centre avails of car parking space, an information office and audiovisual facilities providing information on the La Rocina stream. It is also the departure point for a footpath running along the edge of the stream. From the centre a surfaced road runs off to the Palacio del Acebrón where there is an exhibit called El Hombre y Doñana (Man and the Doñana region). From the Palacio another circular footpath runs off.

The information centre at El Acebuche avails of car parking space, information service, an audiovisual show and an exhibit regarding the National Park. From here a footpath runs off. This is where you can reserve seats in the vehicles which visit the interior of the Park (see Route D).

The timetable for the Centres and footpaths is 08:00-19:00 from October to March, and 08:00-20:00 from April to September. For further information, telephone: 955-442340.

For information on trips into the interior of the Park with a four-wheel drive vehicle, call 955-430432.

Description

The Parque Nacional de Doñana, established in 1969 and reclassified and extended in 1978, consists of three main habitats. The largest is marshland, which annually undergoes flooding and draining and is used by a vast quantity of water birds as a place to breed, rest on their migratory journeys and as a wintering ground.

The *cotos*, an area of stabilized sand, are covered with various kinds of scrub, stands of cork oak and pine woodland. In the *vera* or transitional area where the sand borders the marshes, there are some cork oaks collectively known as the *pajarera* (heronry) which provide nesting sites for Spoonbill, White Stork and various species of heron.

Finally, the third habitat is formed by the system of shifting dunes with their corresponding lagoons and *corrales* (hollows lying between the dunes which are occupied by umbrella pines (*Pinus pinea*)), which exist in close relation to the beach.

The farm of El Acebuche lies in the area of *cotos* in the west of the Park. There is a complex of lagoons, and the protected area of the La Rocina stream consists of the river course and neighbouring riverside woodland.

Ensuring that water existing above ground is kept in reasonable condition and preventing depletion of the amount of underground water are the two main problems affecting the conservation of the Doñana region.

Recommended routes

Route A starts at the information centre in La Rocina. The first section is a 2.5 km walk along a footpath which takes you to the area around the La Rocina stream, a broad water course surrounded by well-conserved riverside woodland. It is worthwhile undertaking this walk during the afternoon. There are 3 hides from which, in winter, you can see roosts of herons and various ducks and, in summer, large numbers of storks and Spoonbill. At the relevant times of year you will be able to see or hear Marbled Teal, Black Kite, Booted Eagle, Savi's Warbler, Penduline Tit and Azure-winged Magpie.

The second section of the route is 2.5 km long and can be done on foot or by car. It takes you along the road skirting the Marismas (marshes) or Playas (beaches) of El Rocío and the village of the same name, bringing you to the

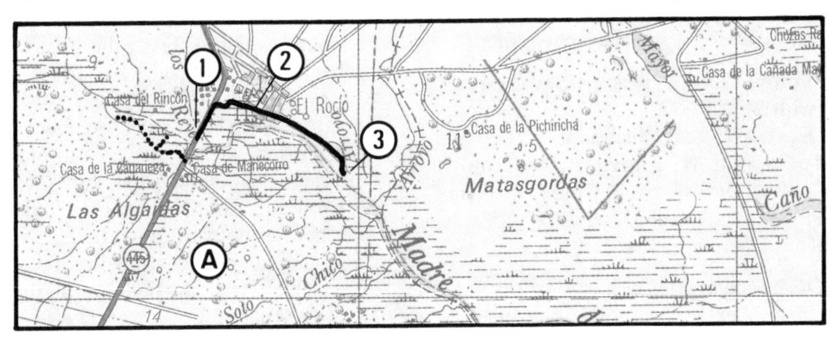

sewage works at Boca del Lobo. The La Canariega bridge (1) over the course of the La Rocina river, the Paseo Marismeño in El Rocío (2) and the Boca del Lobo (3) are the three classic vantage points over the marshes, and from them it is possible to see a multitude of water birds. Herons, Spoonbill, Greater Flamingo and Black-winged Stilt are present all year round. In autumn and winter Glossy Ibis, White-headed Duck, Ferruginous Duck and many other ducks are present, as are Crested Coot and Little Gull. Waders are present in larger numbers and in greater variety during the migration periods, but nonetheless there are large numbers of Black-tailed Godwit and Avocet during the winter. In the cork oaks near La Boca del Lobo, you will frequently see Black Kite, Red Kite, Egyptian Vulture, Griffon Vulture, Black Vulture, Short-toed Eagle, Buzzard, Spanish Imperial Eagle and Booted Eagle, while on the fence posts running across the marshes, every winter you will see Spotted Eagle.

The starting point for **route B** is the Puente del Ajolí, a bridge you will encounter as you leave El Rocío in the direction of the Muro de la Confederación Hidrográfica del Guadalquivir, a dyke.

The route runs along the Raya Real until reaching the Cañada Mayor stream, where you take the track to the house of the same name until reaching the beginning of the Muro de la Confederación. Drive along the dyke to its end. When you reach the Muro de Entremuros, another dyke, turn right bringing you to the gate across the entrance of the National Park, the end of the route.

The route is 27 km long and the first 5 km will take you through a sandy area. Access to the bridge of El Ajolí from El Rocío may be problematic, and during the rainy season it is only accessible with a four-wheel drive vehicle, providing rainfall has not been too extreme. It is not difficult to move along the Muro, although the vast num-

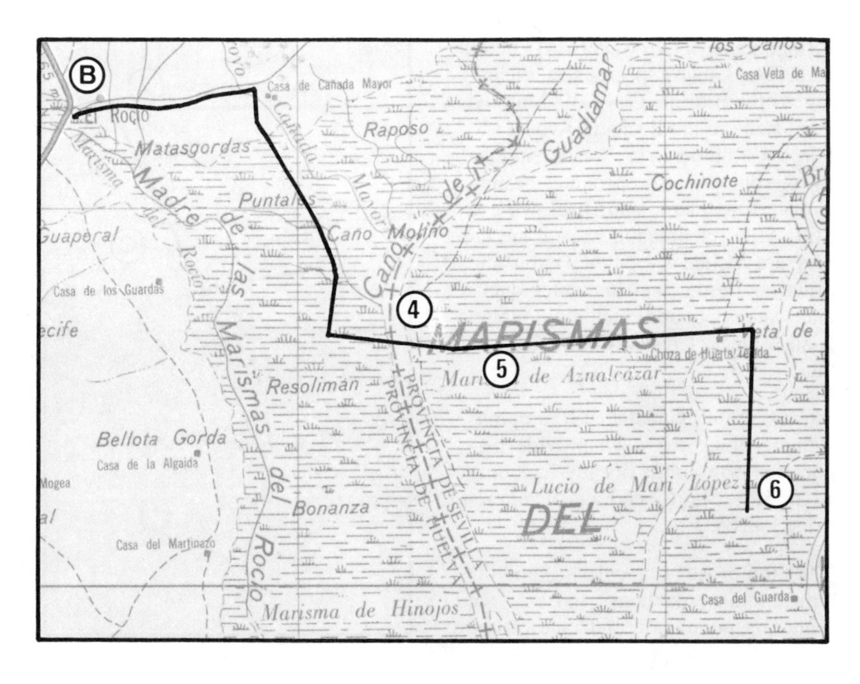

ber of potholes and ruts mean that you should drive with care.

On reaching the Muro, you begin to move across the marshes, where any of the water birds cited for Doñana can be seen at the right time of year. For this reason we have limited ourselves to mentioning the most important species and those which are easiest to see at each point on the route. On the first stretch, from the beginning of the Muro to the so-called "Lucios de la F.A.O." (*lucio* is a more or less permanent lagoon within the marshes) (4) you will see, together with thousands of Greylag Goose, the occasional Pink-footed Goose, Snow Goose, White-fronted Goose, Bar-headed Goose, Canada Goose and Barnacle Goose. There are also huge groups of wintering ducks, the main species being Widgeon, Teal and Shoveler.

The Marisma de Hinojos is usually the site of a roost for several thousands of wintering gulls, and in winter and during the migration periods you will often see Dunlin, Little Stint, plovers, Ruff and many other waders. At Lucios de la F.A.O. many species nest, including Little Bittern, Gadwall, Marbled Teal, Red-crested Pochard, Avocet and Purple Gallinule. In the area around the dyke, you will also encounter nesting Collared Pratincole and Black-winged Stilt. After the breeding season the *lucios* are visited by Night Heron and Squacco Heron, and in winter ducks and waders abound, including White-headed Duck, Crested Coot and Little Gull.

After Caño de Guadiamar, the pylons running along the dyke provide perches for many birds of prey including Black Kite, Short-toed Eagle and Peregrine Falcon.

The farm of Los Caracoles (5) and the surrounding area house most of the wintering population of Crane on the lower reaches of the Guadalquivir. White Stork and Greylag Goose are regular visitors, along with Montagu's Harrier and Hen Harrier. This is also a wonderful spot for watching Calandra Lark, Lesser Short-toed Lark and other members of the lark family as well as pipits.

At the Lucio del Cangrejo Grande and the surrounding area (6) you should see Great Crested Grebe, Little Bittern, Purple Gallinule, Purple Heron, Marbled Teal, White-headed Duck and Crested Coot. The islands provide nesting grounds for Avocet, Slender-billed Gull, Gull-billed Tern and Little Tern. In winter you will see, in addition to ducks and waders, Cormorant, Marsh Harrier, Little Gull and Kingfisher.

Route C consists of a walk along the footpath at El Acebuche. Before setting out, survey the lagoon of La Soriana (7) beside the road, where you will see

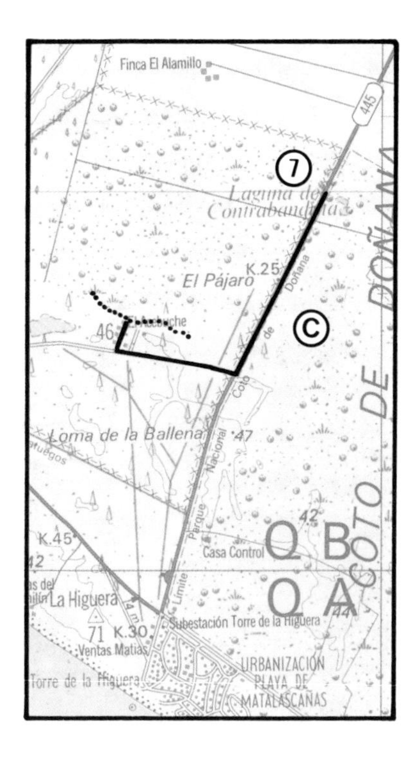

the birds of prey which inhabit the Park and also the nesting sites of various water birds. The path is 1 km long and skirts the lake. There are eight hides. From these hides you will be able to see nesting Great Crested Grebe, Little Grebe, Little Bittern, Purple Gallinule and various types of duck. In one of the islands covered with pine trees, a colony of Cattle Egret and Little Egret took over in 1990, with some pairs of Night Heron and Grey Heron. Finally, among the species which are relatively frequently seen are Squacco Heron and Ferruginous Duck.

Route D is that undertaken with four-wheel drive vehicles belonging to the Cooperativa de Guías (a body of official guides), taking you inside the area of the Park. The trip takes about four hours and enables you to visit the beach, the shifting dune system, Las Marismillas and El Pinar del Faro, skirting the southernmost edge of the marshes. The list of species which can be seen is vast, although you should always bear in mind the logical limitations of this kind of trip. On the beach (8), you should be able to see, virtually all year round, Peregrine Falcon, Oystercatcher, Kentish Plover, Sanderling, gulls, Caspian Tern, Sandwich Tern and Raven. During the migration periods there is a wide variety of species, especially gulls and waders, with frequent sightings of Little Egret, Osprey, Black-winged Stilt, Avocet, Grey Plover, Bar-tailed Godwit, Whimbrel, Slender-billed Gull, Audouin's Gull, Common Tern, Little Tern and Black Tern. In summer and autumn there is a constant stream of Gannet migrating down the coastline, and subsequently the beach becomes the site of wintering Common Scoter and Razorbill. Finally, after big storms out at sea you may encounter large numbers of dead Leach's storm-petrel, sometimes accompanied by bodies of Storm Petrel, Gannet, Kittiwake, Puffin, etc.

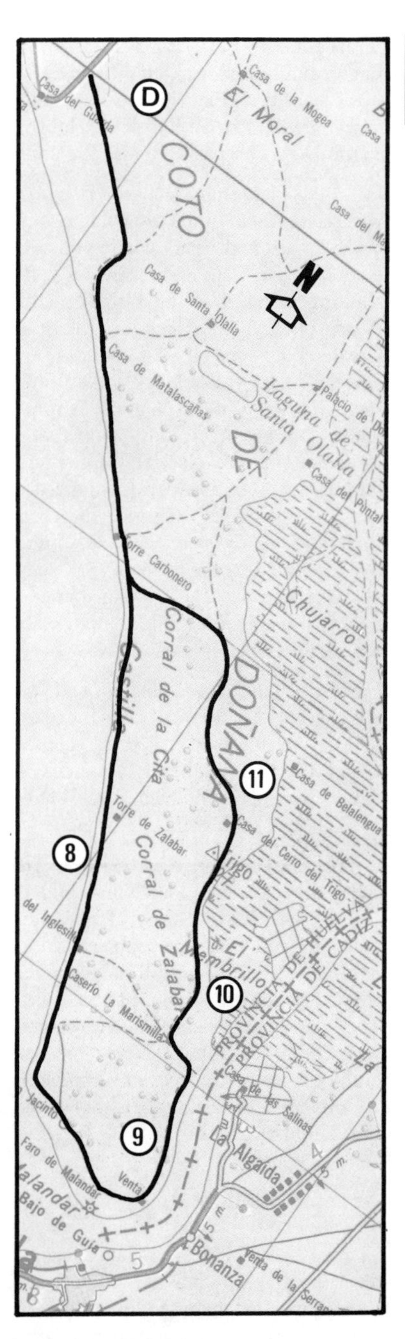

From Pinar del Faro (9) you will have no difficulty in seeing Black Kite,

Short-toed Eagle, Buzzard, Booted Eagle and Azure-winged Magpie. At Los Llanos de la Plancha and Marismillas, you will also see Red Kite, Hobby, Turtle Dove (on passage) and Raven.

From the El Membrillo hide (10), you will see the *lucio* of the same name, one of the largest in the Park where you will be able to see many of the species constituting marsh-dwelling birdlife. This is one of the best places for watching Greater Flamingo all year round, as is also the case with Shelduck. Other birds frequently seen in the *lucio* are herons, ducks, Black-winged Stilt, Avocet, etc. In winter you may also see Osprey and during the migration periods there are numerous waders. Spanish Imperial Eagle frequently perches in the pine trees surrounding the *lucio* and you may also see Crested Coot moving among the groups of Coot which congregate before the breeding season.

From the house at Vetalengua (11), you will be able to see the same range of birdlife and some other species such as Great Crested Grebe, Black-necked Grebe, Spoonbill, Marbled Teal, White-headed Duck, Whiskered Tern, etc.

Finally, Raven and Short-toed Eagle frequently fly over the dunes, and if you are visiting the area of a winter morning, you will be able to see Greylag Geese around the hill named after them, the largest dune in the Park. They come to the dune to swallow sand in order to be able to digest the sea club-rush roots (*Scirpus maritimus*) on which they feed during their stay in the Guadalquivir marshes.

Accommodation

There are many hotels in Matalascañas, as well as apartments and chalets, although most of them tend to be closed out of season. There are also several campsites lying along the coast road to Huelva. Finally, there are hostels and pensions in El Rocío. To obtain more information, ring 955-245753.

Comments

A really interesting route would be one which included Veta La Palma and the Preparque Este (an area lying just to the east of the Park proper), although currently this area is not open to the public. Another outstanding location is the Caño de Guadiamar, a water channel which can be seen by walking along a track running parallel to it, starting off from the dyke near the F.A.O. Finally, before long it will also be possible to put together a route taking you to some of the lagoons belonging to the Abalario group, a system of natural lagoons running westwards and constituting the continuation of the El Acebuche lagoons.

Manuel Máñez and Luis García

■ AN.17 BRAZO DEL ESTE

Wetland area: marshes, fields and an abandoned river arm lying on the edge of Doñana National Park.

Main species

Residents: Little Grebe, Night Heron, Cattle Egret, Little Egret, Glossy Ibis, Red Kite, Marsh Harrier, Buzzard, Water Rail, Purple Gallinule, Black-winged Stilt, Avocet, Stone Curlew, Kentish Plover, Lapwing, Redshank, Black-bellied Sandgrouse, Pin-tailed Sandgrouse, Kingfisher, Lesser Short-toed Lark.

Summer visitors: Little Bittern, Squacco Heron, Purple Heron, Marbled Teal, Montagu's Harrier, Baillon's Crake, Collared Pratincole, Whiskered Tern, Black Tern, Bee-eater, Black-eared Wheatear, Savi's Warbler, Olivaceous Warbler.

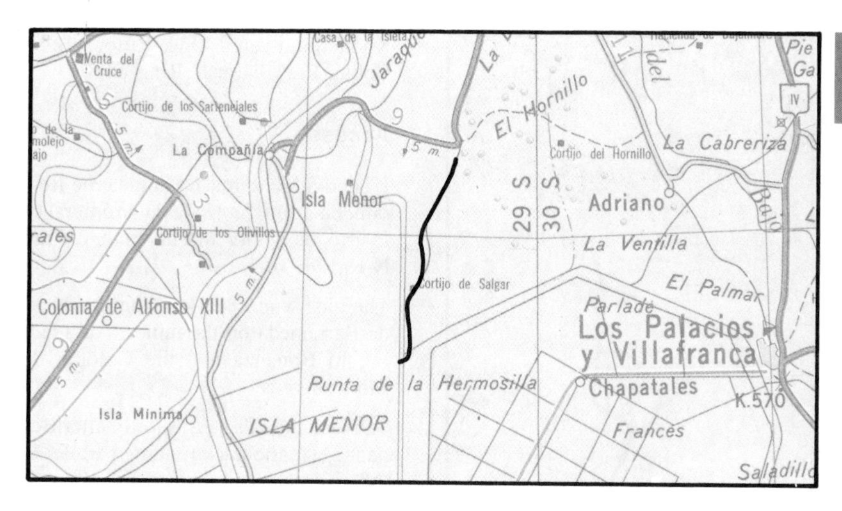

Winter visitors: Grey Heron, Greylag Goose, Gadwall, Shoveler, Red-crested Pochard, Hen Harrier, Spotted Crake, Little Bustard, Ringed Plover, Grey Plover, Short-eared Owl, Wryneck, Water Pipit, Bluethroat, Penduline Tit.

On passage: Black Stork, Crane, waders in general.

Access

From Seville, take the N-IV towards Cádiz. At the 549 km marker post turn right onto the minor road for Isla Menor and, when you see the Bar Acebuche after 14 km, turn onto a surfaced service road which runs into the marshes. Continue along this road for 2 km until reaching a clay wall, which you follow to the right until reaching the Brazo del Este.

Description

The marshland lying next to the old course of the river Guadalquivir has been subjected to a series of transformations in an attempt to convert it into farmland, meaning that its surface area has now been reduced to some 300 ha.

It has been declared a Paraje Natural or Site of Natural Interest (1,336 ha).

Recommended routes

The network of farm tracks in the area makes it extremely accessible, and also unnecessary to specify a specific route.

Accommodation

In Seville and the surrounding towns there is plenty of hotel accommodation as well as several campsites.

Comments

Pay attention to where you are going, since it is rather easy to become lost in this area.

Alfonso Barragán and Francisco Domínguez (GOSUR)

■ AN.18 LA ALGAIDA AND SALT PANS AT SANLÚCAR DE BARRAMEDA

Pine woodland and salt pans lying very close to Doñana National Park.

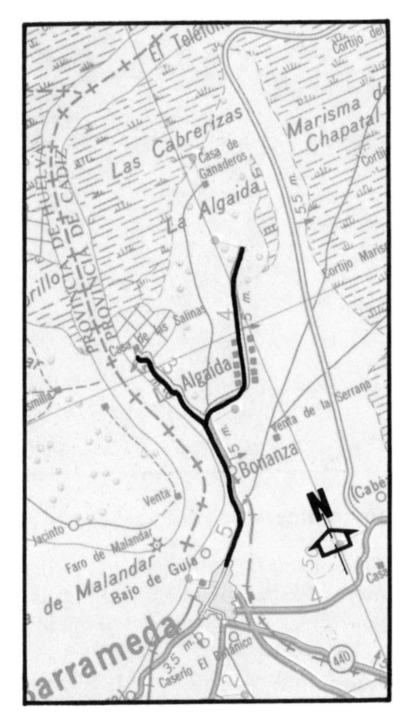

Main species

Residents: Greater Flamingo, Red Kite, Marsh Harrier, Spanish Imperial Eagle, Water Rail, Avocet, Stone Curlew, Pin-tailed Sandgrouse, Calandra Lark, Lesser Short-toed Lark, Great Grey Shrike, Azure-winged Magpie.

Summer visitors: Night Heron, Purple Heron, Spoonbill, Marbled Teal, Short-toed Eagle, Montagu's Harrier, Booted Eagle, Hobby, Spotted Crake, Collared Pratincole, Slender-billed Gull, Great Spotted Cuckoo, Red-necked Nightjar, Roller, Wryneck, Short-toed Lark, Spectacled Warbler, Golden Oriole.

Winter visitors: Greylag Goose, Shelduck, Osprey, Peregrine Falcon, Woodcock, Caspian Tern, Bluethroat, Fieldfare, Goldcrest, Reed Bunting.

On passage: Black Stork, Honey Buzzard, Ruff, Red-necked Phalarope, Knot, Short-eared Owl, Rufous Bush Robin, Rock Thrush, Ring Ouzel.

Access

It is possible to reach Sanlúcar de Barrameda from Jerez de la Frontera or Puerto de Santa María, both on the N-IV.

The pine wood is 8 km from Sanlúcar de Barrameda on the minor road leading to Bonanza and the Colonia de Montealgaida.

To reach the salt pans, shortly after Bonanza take the track running parallel to the river Guadalquivir. The salt pans are private property and you should ask for permission to enter them.

La Algaida lies within the Parque Natural del Entorno de Doñana (Natural Park including the surroundings of Doñana).

Description

A wood of umbrella pines measuring some 700 ha. It is located on an old dune, the last and southeasternmost of the Doñana dune system.

The salt pans are part of the marshes of the river Guadalquivir, which have been transformed for this purpose. The salt pans are flooded year round and form a complex of lagoons, canals, inlets and channels of varying depths and salinities. In summer, when the marshland dries out, they act as a collecting ground for water birds.

Recommended routes

A forestry road runs from north to south through the pine wood. A number of tracks lead off from this road, enabling you to visit virtually the whole of the pine wood.

At the salt pans there is a network of tracks which make for easy access.

Accommodation

There are several hotels in Sanlúcar de Barrameda. Hotel Los Helechos, in the town centre, is recommended.

Comments

Permission to visit the salt pans should be sought in the offices lying beside the access gate to the pans (APROMASA). Avoid the midday hours in summer, when the heat may become unbearable.

The best times of year for visiting the salt pans are during the spring and autumn migration periods. Remember to take insect repellent.

Javier Hidalgo

■ AN.19 ESPERA AND LEBRIJA LAGOONS – LAS CABEZAS

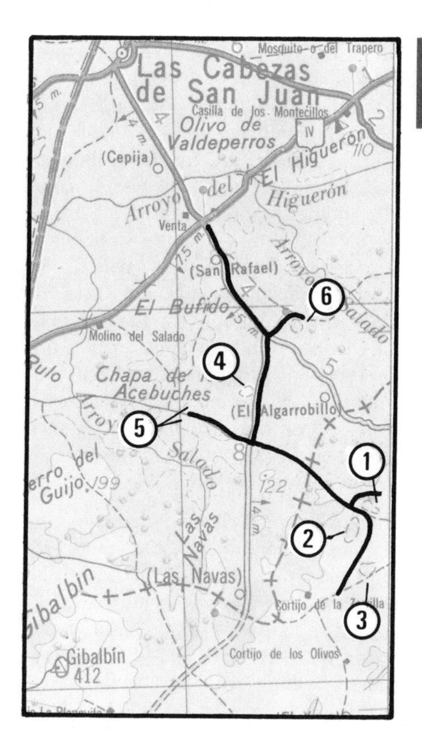

Freshwater lagoons.

Main species

Residents: Cattle Egret, Gadwall, Red-crested Pochard, Pochard, White-headed Duck, Purple Gallinule, Crested Coot, Cetti's Warbler, Fan-tailed Warbler, Sardinian Warbler.

Summer visitors: Black-winged Stilt, Great Reed Warbler.

Winter visitors: Greater Flamingo (also large groups in summer), Teal, Shoveler, Marbled Teal (above all in autumn).

On passage: waders, mainly Black-tailed Godwit.

Access

From Jerez de la Frontera (N-IV) take the N-342 to Arcos de la Frontera, where you join the C-343 for Espera (43 km).

Description

A complex formed by a series of small lagoons lying amidst the farmlands between Cádiz and Seville, surrounded by fields and areas of mastic tree, wild olive tree (*Olea europaea*) and kermes oak (*Quercus coccifera*). The lagoons are semi-permanent and during long periods of drought water remains only in the lagoons of El Taraje and La Dulce. Tamarisks form a belt around most of the lakes, although others are surrounded by bulrush (*Scirpus lacustris*), reedmace (*Typha latifolia*) and reeds.

They have been designated Reservas Naturales or Nature Reserves covering a total of 402 ha in a protected area measuring 1,595 ha.

Recommended routes

Go through the village of Espera and turn left for Las Cabezas de San Juan.

After less than 2 km, turn left again onto a surfaced road leading to the Hondilla lagoon (1). A little farther on, you will come across the Salada de Zorrilla lagoon (2), and from there a track will take you to Dulce de Zorrilla (3), another lagoon. Continuing from La Salada, you will come to a junction; by turning right you will reach the El Pilón lagoon (4). Opposite El Pilón are the lagoons of La Galiana, La Cigarrera and La Peña, which all lie very close together (5). Continue from El Pilón lagoon and the track will come out on the road from Espera to Las Cabezas de San Juan, close to El Taraje lagoon (6).

Given the small size of the lagoons, visiting each one will enable you to see the most typical birds of the area. It is worth making use of the high ground around the lagoons as an observation point to overcome the difficulties caused by high-growing vegetation.

The lagoons of Hondilla, Salada de Zorrilla and Dulce de Zorrilla are most interesting, being the site of Greater Flamingo, White-headed Duck, Marbled Teal, Crested Coot and Purple Gallinule. You will also see some of these species on the other lagoons, particularly White-headed Duck and other ducks, waders and grebes.

Accommodation

There is a Parador Nacional in Arcos de la Frontera. In Jerez de la Frontera plenty of accommodation is available.

Comments

Landowners may prevent you from visiting some of the lagoons. It is therefore worthwhile asking permission beforehand.

Francisco Hortas, Carlos Martínez Ortega and Iñigo Sánchez García

■ AN.20 ARCOS DE LA FRONTERA AND THE BORNOS RESERVOIR

A stretch of river which has been dammed and is surrounded by riverine woodland and high cliffs.

Main species

Residents: Great Crested Grebe, Cattle Egret, Little Egret, Marsh Harrier, Purple Gallinule, Stone Curlew, Kingfisher, Cetti's Warbler, Fan-tailed Warbler, Sardinian Warbler.

Summer visitors: Night Heron, Squacco Heron, Purple Heron, White Stork, Montagu's Harrier, Lesser Kestrel, Black-winged Stilt, Collared Pratincole, Pallid Swift, Bee-eater, Red-rumped Swallow, Olivaceous Warbler.

Winter visitors: Cormorant, Grey Heron, ducks, Osprey.

On passage: Spoonbill, gulls and waders.

Access

Take the N-IV to Jerez de la Frontera. Here, join the N-342 and drive to Arcos de la Frontera, 32 km away.

Description

The middle reaches of the river Guadalete are characterized by the fact that they run through agricultural land and are dammed by the reservoirs of Arcos and Bornos. The ends of both reservoirs contain shallow water where abundant marsh vegetation grows, which in the case of the Bornos reservoir consists of an extensive area of tamarisks growing on flooded land. Some stretches of the river accommodate relatively well-conserved riverine

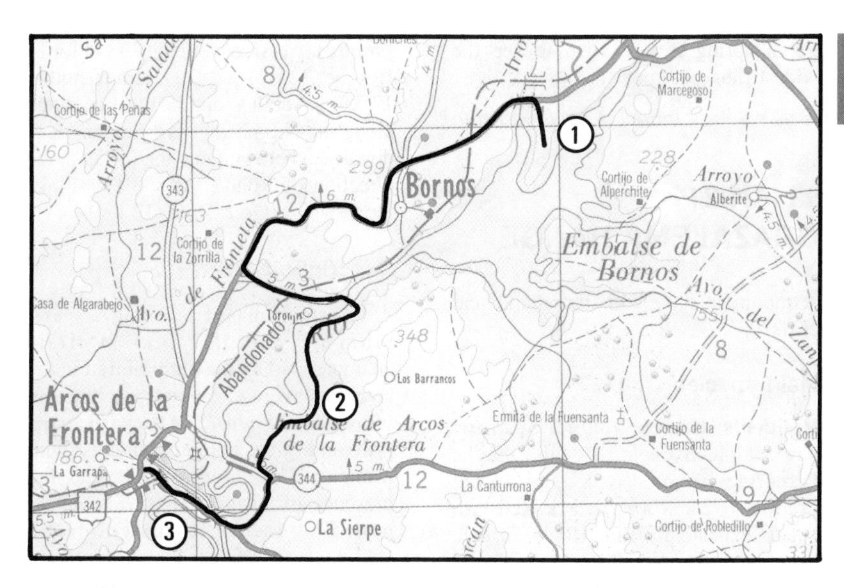

woodland. The town of Arcos de la Frontera lies on top of a high river cliff.

The ends of the Arcos reservoir (120 ha) and the Bornos reservoir (630 ha) have both been declared Parajes Naturales, Sites of Natural Interest.

Recommended routes

Since the stretch of river to be covered is relatively long, we recommend a single car journey taking you to the most interesting points:

1) End of the Bornos reservoir. From here you can gain a good view of the area surrounding the Pitas farm, which lies on the right bank of the reservoir. This point can be reached by a dirt track leading off from Coto de Bornos, a village lying near the 48.2 km marker post on the N-342. The tamarisks are the site of a large colony of Cattle Egret and Little Egret, with some pairs of Purple Heron, Night Heron and Squacco Heron. In some years another colony establishes itself upstream from the Villamartín bridge; this place is also easier to watch from, since it is highly accessible. It is also a habitual wintering place for Osprey.

2) End of the Arcos de la Frontera reservoir. This area can be commanded from the surfaced tracks running along the left bank of the reservoir (El Santiscal). You will have no difficulty in seeing Great Crested Grebe, Grey Heron, Marsh Harrier, Osprey and Cetti's Warbler.

3) River cliffs at Arcos de la Frontera. These lie on the outskirts of the town and are the home of a large colony of Lesser Kestrel. The river, which runs at the foot of the cliffs, floods in some sections, giving rise to abundant vegetation where you may see Purple Gallinule.

Accommodation

There is not a vast amount of accommodation available in Arcos de la Frontera, although there is a Parador Nacional. There is a campsite near the Arcos reservoir.

Comments

Visiting the area will be rewarding at any time of year, although you should go in spring if you wish to see the widest range of species.

Julio J. Ceballos Benito

AN.21 GRAZALEMA RANGE

A mountain area with woodland and cliffs.

Main species

Residents: Griffon Vulture, Sparrowhawk, Golden Eagle, Bonelli's Eagle, Peregrine Falcon, Rock Dove, Crag Martin, Wren, Robin, Black Redstart, Black Wheatear, Blue Rock Thrush, Sardinian Warbler, Firecrest, Crested Tit, Chough, Raven, Rock Sparrow, Hawfinch, Rock Bunting.

Summer visitors: Egyptian Vulture, Short-toed Eagle, Booted Eagle, Red-necked Nightjar, Alpine Swift, Bee-eater, Red-rumped Swallow, Rock Thrush, Blackcap, Bonelli's Warbler, Chiffchaff.

Access

Take the N-IV to Jerez de la Frontera, and from there the N-342 to Arcos de la Frontera. At Arcos join the C-344 for El Bosque (32 km) and Grazalema (another 12 km). Another option is to continue along the N-342 until just before Algodonales, where you join the C-339 in the direction of Ronda. After 19 km, take the C-344 to Grazalema (12 km).

Description

A limestone massif reaching a maximum height of 1,655 m. It is characterized by the high rainfall in the area (an average annual precipitation of over 2,000 mm). The rock is karstic, providing great botanical interest with numerous endemic species and the presence of Spanish fir (*Abies pinsapo*). The latter form woodland stretching for 400 ha on the northern slopes of the Sierra del Pinar, with other small stands of trees elsewhere. There are also areas of holm oak, cork oak, Lusitanian oak, mountain pine and varied Mediterranean scrub. Cliffs and rocky areas abound.

The area is a Natural Park (51,695 ha) and a Biosphere Reserve.

Recommended routes

The roads joining El Bosque with Grazalema and Grazalema with Zahara de

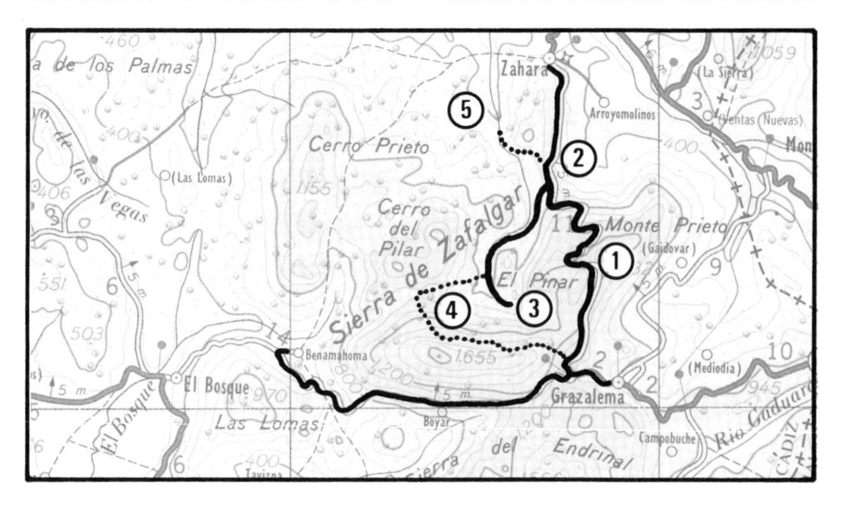

la Sierra will enable you to gain a general impression of the area, to see wonderful landscapes and to spot many of the species of greatest interest. On the second of these roads the mountain passes of Las Palomas (1) and Los Acebuches (2) can be used as starting points for smaller routes. Between these two passes a road climbs up to the Spanish fir wood (3). For those wishing to walk farther in the range, it is well worth climbing up to the pass of Las Cumbres (4) following the northern side of the San Cristóbal range and visiting the spectacular river gorge known as Garganta Verde (5).

Accommodation

The villages in the area (Grazalema, Zahara, Ubrique) provide various options, but possibilities are greater in Ronda, a place of great historical and artistic interest located some 30 km from Grazalema. There are also campsites and areas for wild camping in several places (Grazalema, Benaocaz, Benamahoma and El Bosque).

Comments

There is a visitors' centre in El Bosque where among other things you should find out whether areas of the Spanish fir woodland are closed. This wood is sometimes extremely crowded with people.

Eduardo de Juana Aranzana

■ AN.22 MEDINA LAGOON

A freshwater lagoon.

Main species

Residents: Great Crested Grebe, Cattle Egret (roost in the summer months), Gadwall, Red-crested Pochard, White-headed Duck, Marsh Harrier, Purple

Gallinule, Crested Coot, Cetti's Warbler, Fan-tailed Warbler, Sardinian Warbler.

Summer visitors: Black-necked Grebe, Little Bittern, Coot (22,000 individuals in August 1988), Black-winged Stilt, Whiskered Tern, Great Reed Warbler, Subalpine Warbler.

Winter visitors: Greater Flamingo (in large numbers in summer), Greylag Goose, Widgeon, Teal, Pintail, Shoveler, Marbled Teal (large numbers in autumn), Shelduck.

On passage: waders in general.

Access

From Jerez de la Frontera, on the N-IV, take the C-440 towards Medina Sidonia. The lagoon is 10 km after turning onto the C-440 and the entrance, lying to the left of the road, is well-marked. There is also a car park.

Description

A freshwater lagoon lying between hillsides used for stock farming. The lagoon is surrounded by a belt of reeds, tamarisks and sea club-rush. The north shore is the site of sand and gravel extraction, which contributes to the acceleration of the silting process.

Although the lagoon sometimes dries out in summer, it usually maintains its water, leading to the presence of many water birds coming from other areas and the nearby marshes of the Guadalquivir river.

The area is an Integral Reserve (121 ha with a protection area of 254 ha).

Recommended routes

Only one route is practicable. This consists of a walk along the southern shore of the lagoon beside a drainage channel. You are not allowed to enter other areas.

Accommodation

There are several hotels and many hostels in Jerez de la Frontera. However, these become full during the Easter Week, the Feria del Caballo (a horse fair taking place in May) and when motor racing and motorbike racing occurs on the nearby race circuit. There is a campsite at Puerto de Santa María, 14 km from Jerez de la Frontera.

Francisco Hortas,
Iñigo Sánchez García
and Carlos Martínez Ortega

■ AN.23 EL PUERTO DE SANTA MARÍA LAGOONS

Freshwater lagoons.

Main species

Residents: Little Grebe, Great Crested Grebe, Black-necked Grebe, Gadwall, Mallard, Red-crested Pochard, Pochard, White-headed Duck, Purple Gallinule, Coot, Crested Coot, Cetti's Warbler, Fan-tailed Warbler, Sardinian Warbler.

Summer visitors: Little Bittern, Marbled Teal, Collared Pratincole,

Whiskered Tern, Black Tern, Reed Warbler, Great Reed Warbler.

Winter visitors: Cattle Egret, Greater Flamingo, Widgeon, Teal, Pintail, Shoveler, Tufted Duck, waders in general, Kingfisher, Penduline Tit.

On passage: Night Heron, Purple Heron, Garganey.

Access

The area can be reached from El Puerto de Santa María on the N-IV running towards Jerez de la Frontera. After 3 km turn left onto the road for Casino Bahía de Cádiz and on the first bend turn right, following an irrigation channel for 1.5 km until reaching the Juncosa lagoon. It is recommended that you leave your car at this point and continue on foot.

Description

A complex of three natural lagoons. The surface of La Juncosa is entirely covered with a dense mass of rushes, while at the Laguna Chica reeds and rushes form a belt around the lake. The Laguna Salada is the largest of the three and is surrounded not only by reeds, reedmace and rushes but also by isolated stands of tamarisk and wild olive trees. There are also two artificial islets.

It is a Nature Reserve (228 ha of protected land).

Recommended routes

The three lagoons lie very close together and can be visited in turn to see the birds most characteristic of the area.

Accommodation

There is a range of accommodation available in Puerto de Santa María, including a campsite.

Comments

To visit the lagoons you must first ask for permission from the Agencia de Medio Ambiente de Cádiz (Av. Ana de Viya, 3; telephone: 956-274629). There, they will also inform you of the water level, which may be at zero during the summer, depending on rainfall.

Rafael García Costales

AN.24 LA TAPA SALT PANS

Marshes which have been turned into salt pans.

Main species

Residents: Little Egret, White Stork, Avocet, Kentish Plover, Yellow-legged Gull, Fan-tailed Warbler, Sardinian Warbler.

Summer visitors: Black-winged Stilt, Little Ringed Plover, Common Tern, Little Tern, Yellow Wagtail.

Winter visitors: Grey Heron, Greater Flamingo, Shelduck, ducks, waders, gulls, Kingfisher.

On passage: Spoonbill, Osprey, waders, Caspian Tern, marsh terns.

Access

The salt pans lie near El Puerto de Santa María on the N-IV, and can be reached by two routes. One consists of taking the turn at the 653.8 km marker post on the N-IV next to the RENAULT garage, which takes you directly to the salt pans. The other option is to continue along the N-IV and having crossed the San Alejandro bridge over the river Guadalete, leave your vehicle and continue on foot, crossing the railway line.

Description

The La Tapa salt pans are the remains of the old marshes of the river Guadalete, which have now been drained for agricultural purposes. At the salt pans you will see some shallow lagoons designed to obtain salt and a series of channels and swampy areas, bordered with abundant halophytic vegetation, which are used for intensive fish farming.

The salt pans lie within the Parque Natural de la Bahía de Cádiz and make

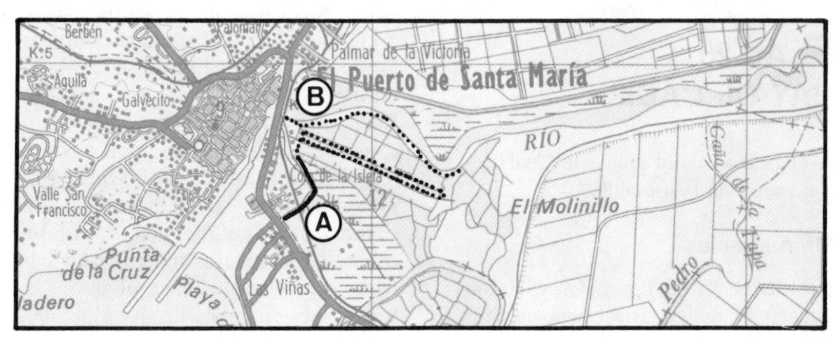

up 402.5 ha of the total area of this Natural Park.

Recommended routes

Route A consists of a walk around the inside of the salt pan area, for which you should obtain permission from the company operating the pans. A walk of some 4 km will take you past the lagoons, channels and swampy areas, these latter being at the end of the route; this should be enough to see the most important water birds residing in the area.

Route B consists of a walk running between the edge of the salt pans and the river Guadalete. It is also about 4 km long and has the added attraction of enabling you to see a series of species such as Oystercatcher, Turnstone, plovers, etc. which are only present in the river.

Accommodation

El Puerto de Santa María provides a wide variety of accommodation including a campsite.

Comments

The best time of year for visiting the area is from August to October, when the number and variety of birds are at their greatest. It is better not to undertake route A during the spring, when many of the birds will be nesting on the dividing walls.

Rafael García Costales

■ AN.25 BAY OF CÁDIZ

A coastal wetland area with marshes, salt pans and fish ponds.

Main species

Residents: Little Egret, Grey Heron, Greater Flamingo, Black-winged Stilt, Avocet, Kentish Plover, Redshank, Fan-tailed Warbler, Sardinian Warbler.

Summer visitors: Little Tern, Black-eared Wheatear, Woodchat Shrike.

Winter visitors: Cormorant, Widgeon, Oystercatcher, Grey Plover, Sanderling, Dunlin, Bar-tailed Godwit, Whimbrel, Greenshank, Turnstone.

On passage: Osprey, Ringed Plover, Knot, Little Stint, Curlew Sandpiper.

Access

The main towns in the area of the Bay of Cádiz are Cádiz, San Fernando and Puerto Real.

Description

The Bay of Cádiz is a stretch of coastland which has sunk as a consequence of tectonic movements and has been submitted to frequent invasions by the sea. The area includes marshes, intertidal zones, channels and swampy areas, although much of the marsh area has been lost as a result of population increase and the creation of salt works and fish farms.

The area is a Natural Park stretching for around 10,000 ha, including two Parajes Naturales or Sites of Natural Interest (Isla del Trocadero and Marisma de Sancti-Petri, measuring a total of 695 ha).

Recommended routes

Route A consists of a car journey some 5 km long through the marshes of Los Toruños. Leave Puerto de Santa María on the N-IV in the direction of Puerto Real and by the Camping Guadalete (a campsite at the 655 km marker post), turn right for the beach of Valdelagrana, subsequently taking the second left. From this road the beach can be reached via several tracks, with car parks at the end of each of these. In winter these points will give sightings

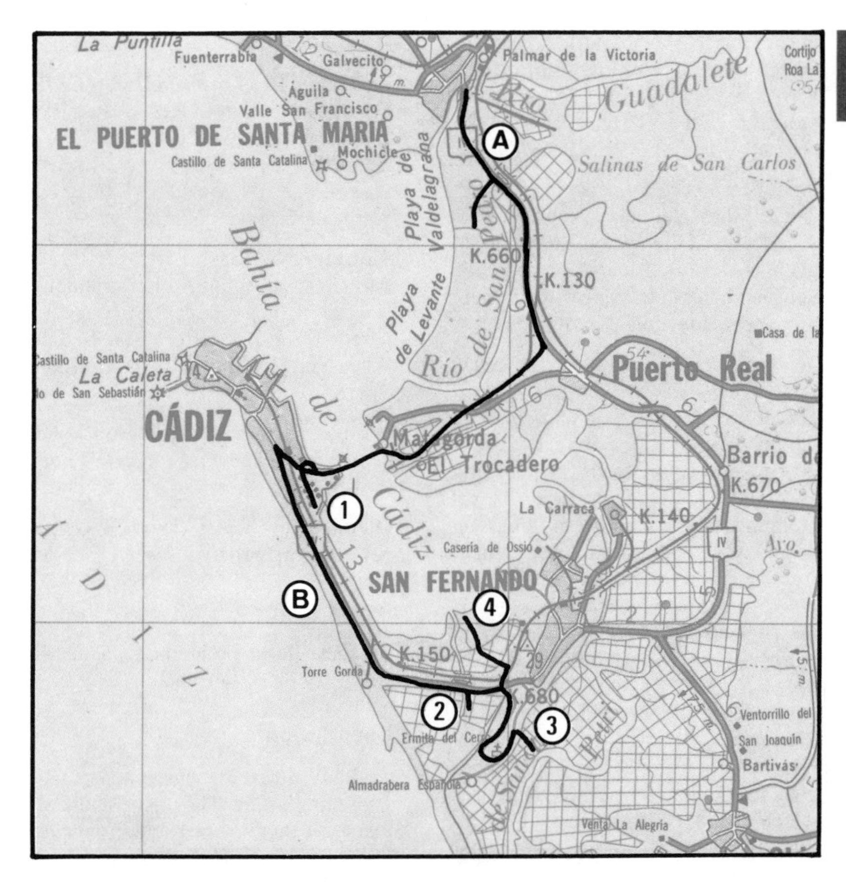

of Oystercatcher, Sanderling, Turnstone, plovers and gulls. During the breeding season you will be able to see Little Tern, although their numbers are dropping because of the many people who use the beach in summer. It is worth visiting the San Pedro river channel, where you may see Curlew.

Route B takes you through the areas of greatest interest in the Bay of Cádiz proper.

To reach point 1, cross the bridge known as Puente de León de Carranza (on the road from Puerto Real to Cádiz) and take a right turn signed for Zona Franca. You will pass a hypermarket called Hipercádiz, and shortly after that turn left to pass underneath the road. Continue for some 800 m, parallel to the railway line, until you reach a vantage point. This looks over an area of intertidal mud flats which have been affected by the dumping of rubbish but nonetheless make for close-range sightings of Bar-tailed Godwit, Kentish Plover, Ringed Plover, Turnstone and other waders. In summer you may also see Curlew Sandpiper, Knot and Little Stint.

To reach point 2, leave Cádiz in the direction of San Fernando and park your car by the river Arillo. Just after crossing the river you will find some abandoned salt pans to the right, which you can walk through. Depending on water levels you will see Greater Flamingo, Avocet, Black-tailed Godwit, Grey Plover, Black-winged Stilt, plovers and, occasionally, Cormorant. In summer Little Tern will also be present.

Point 3 can be reached from San Fernando, where you take a right turn for the Muelle Gallinera, a wharf lying on the Sancti-Petri estuary. At low tide you will be able to see a wide variety of waders including Whimbrel.

To reach point 4, return to the N-IV. Leave your car by a barracks located next to the petrol station and continue on foot in the direction of Seville. After 900 m you will see a dirt track leading off to the left, taking you across a level crossing without barriers and bringing you to some salt pans. Subsequently, take the second right and the next left, making your way towards some fishermen's houses. After 200 m turn right along a track ending beside an electricity pylon. From here, you will be able to see the intertidal mud flats where you will have sightings of Grey Heron, Little Egret, Osprey and Widgeon in addition to waders. Other birds which you may see en route are Sardinian Warbler, Black-eared Wheatear and Fan-tailed Warbler.

Accommodation

The surrounding villages and towns avail of plenty of accommodation, although there may be no vacancies in summer and during the Carnival period (late February).

Francisco Hortas
and Alejandro Pérez-Hurtado

■ AN.26 CHICLANA DE LA FRONTERA LAGOONS

Freshwater lagoons.

Main species

Residents: Black-necked Grebe, Cattle Egret, Little Egret, Red-crested Pochard, White-headed Duck, Marsh Harrier, Purple Gallinule, Kentish Plover, Cetti's Warbler, Fan-tailed Warbler, Sardinian Warbler.

Summer visitors: Little Bittern, Purple Heron, White Stork, Montagu's Harrier, Black-winged Stilt, Whiskered Tern, Bee-eater, Black-eared Wheatear, Melodious Warbler, Woodchat Shrike.

Winter visitors: Grey Heron, Widgeon, Pintail, Shoveler, Avocet, Golden Plover, Kingfisher.

On passage: Greater Flamingo, Garganey, Osprey, waders in general.

Access

Chiclana de la Frontera is on the N-340, very close to Cádiz.

Description

Shallow natural lagoons which change with the seasons. They have abundant marsh vegetation, particularly in the case of La Paja. They lie in an area of agricultural land.

The lagoons of Jeli and Montellano are Nature Reserves (49 ha with a protection area of 518 ha).

Recommended routes

The La Paja lagoon lies beside the N-340, 3 km outside Chiclana de la Frontera in the direction of Algeciras.

To reach the lagoons of Jeli and Montellano, in Chiclana take the C-346 in the direction of Medina Sidonia and after 2 km turn left towards the cycle track stadium (*velódromo*). Having passed the stadium, turn right onto a dirt road which after 5.8 km will bring you to an unmarked junction. Turn right to reach the Jeli lagoon; 100 m farther on, another track running off perpendicularly to the right will bring you to the Montellano lagoon.

Although all three lagoons can be reached by car, we recommend that you walk to the lagoons of Jeli and Montellano. This walk starts at the 7 km marker post on the C-346, where the Cañada Real, a drove road, crosses the main road at right angles. Leave your vehicle here and after an hour of walking along the road you will come to the Jeli lagoon where you will be able to see Black-necked Grebe, Marsh Harrier, Purple Gallinule, Whiskered Tern and, with luck, White-headed Duck. Continue along the drove road for another 45 minutes until you come to a relatively well-surfaced farm track. Turn right onto this track and continue walking. Shortly after, turn right again to come to the Montellano lagoon, which is small and holds less attractions for birdwatchers, although it has a more attractive setting than the previous lagoon. To return, retrace your steps. The walk will take a total of some 6 hours.

Accommodation

Plenty of accommodation is available in Chiclana de la Frontera. Hotel Fuentemar and Hotel Ideal are both recommended.

Comments

To visit the Jeli and Montellano lagoons, you should first ask permission from the Agencia de Medio Ambiente de la Junta de Andalucía (Av. Ana de Viya, 3; telephone: 956-274629).

The best time of year for visiting the area is from December to May, although you should bear in mind that heavy rainfall may make some tracks impassable.

Julio J. Ceballos Benito

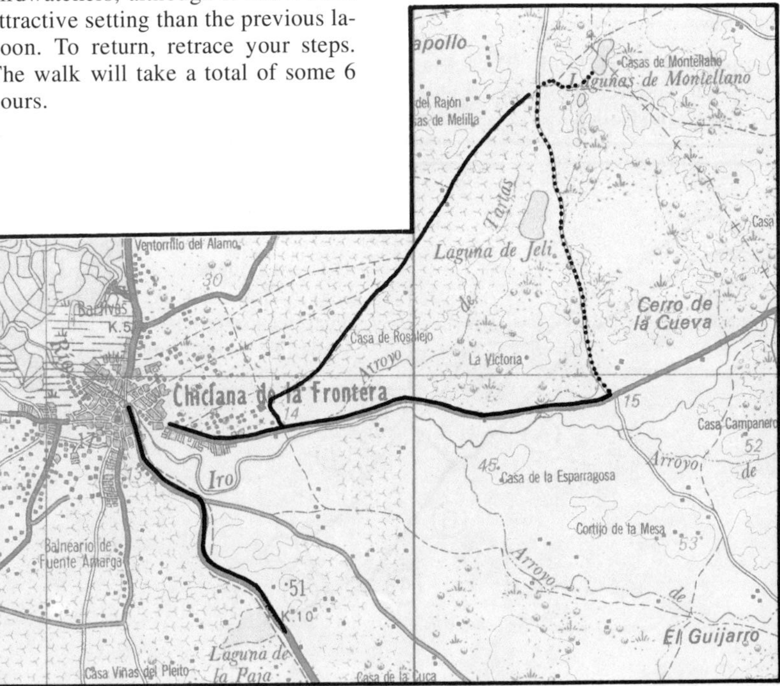

AN.27 LA JANDA (TAHIVILLA)

Fields and grazing land, sometimes flooded, located on the site of a former lake, now drained.

Main species

Residents: Cattle Egret, Little Egret, Little Bustard, Great Bustard, Stone Curlew, Calandra Lark, Thekla Lark, Fan-tailed Warbler.

Summer visitors: White Stork, Montagu's Harrier, Collared Pratincole, White-rumped Swift, Bee-eater, Short-toed Lark, Red-rumped Swallow, Rufous Bush Robin.

Winter visitors: Grey Heron, Black-shouldered Kite, Marsh Harrier, Hen Harrier, Spanish Imperial Eagle, Crane, Golden Plover, Green Sandpiper, Woodpigeon, Penduline Tit, Spanish Sparrow.

On passage: Black Stork, Black Kite, Egyptian Vulture, Short-toed Eagle, Booted Eagle, Roller.

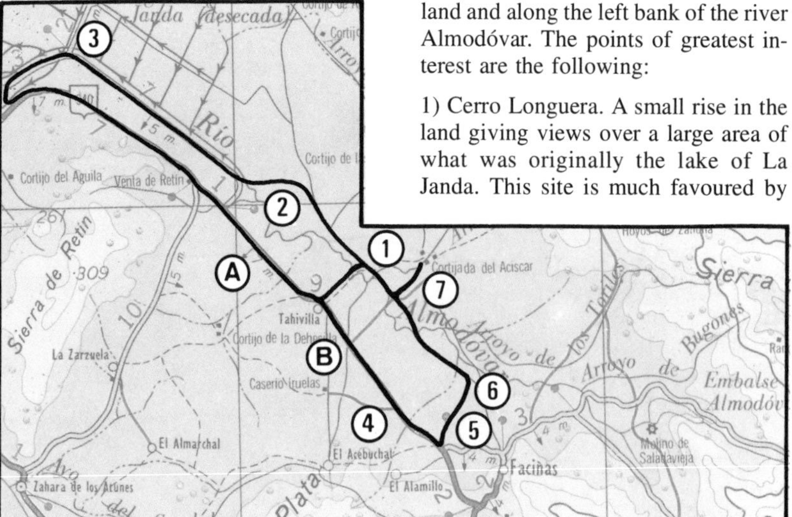

Access

Take the N-340 from Cádiz to Algeciras and stop in Tahivilla (49 km from Chiclana de la Frontera).

Description

When the former lake was dried out, La Janda became an extensive area of fields and winter grazing land. Generally the land is flat and with the characteristics of a steppe habitat, although the area becomes flooded after heavy winter rainfall. The area is criss-crossed by an extensive network of river courses, drains and sumps which retain water during the summer. Towards the north, where the area borders with the surrounding hills, there are areas of dry grazing land with groves of wild olive trees.

Recommended routes

Given the large size of the area and the nature of the land, it is worth undertaking these trips by car, although you should not leave the main tracks during the rainy season.

Route A leaves Tahivilla and takes you northwards through farmland, pastureland and along the left bank of the river Almodóvar. The points of greatest interest are the following:

1) Cerro Longuera. A small rise in the land giving views over a large area of what was originally the lake of La Janda. This site is much favoured by

Great Bustard, Crane and Hen Harrier. If you are very lucky, in winter you will see Black-shouldered Kite.

2) Tapatana bridge. From this point the river Almodóvar runs through an artificial channel. You will have frequent sightings of Little Egret, Grey Heron, Marsh Harrier and Collared Pratincole.

3) Bridge over the Canal Colector. In winter this is frequently the site of ducks, Golden Plover and Little Bustard. It is not rare to see the occasional juvenile Spanish Imperial Eagle, which frequent the area.

Route B consists of taking the N-340 out of Tahivilla towards Tarifa. At the entrance to the Iruelas farm (4), there are some areas of dry-land farming where you may see Montagu's Harrier and Great Bustard. Continue along the road until reaching the turning for Facinas, and from there take the track leading to the hamlet of La Herrería (5) where you will see some nests belonging to White Stork in the prickly pear cacti. Continue along the Cañada Real (drove road) until reaching the farm of Arraez (6), a place frequented by small groups of Crane and where, as with most of the other places mentioned, Calandra Lark, Thekla Lark and Short-toed Lark abound. The next stop is Cortijada de Aciscar (7) where the famous Laja looms up, an impressive rocky cliff with a substantial vulture breeding colony. There is also a large area of wild olive trees where, among other species, you will see Rufous Bush Robin and Woodchat Shrike. Returning to the Cañada Real, continue until reaching the road to La Haba, which will bring you back to the N-340.

Accommodation

Between Facinas and Tarifa, on the N-340, there are several hotels and a number of campsites.

Comments

To enter other areas, in addition to those described above, you should first obtain permission from the landowners.

The best time of year for visiting the area is winter, although it is also interesting during the autumn migration.

Julio J. Ceballos Benito

■ AN.28 TARIFA

Beaches, pastures, woodland and mountains lying in an area, the Straits of Gibraltar, which is of great importance for migratory birds.

Main species

Residents: Cattle Egret, Griffon Vulture, Peregrine Falcon, Little Bustard, Great Bustard, Kentish Plover, Eagle Owl, Calandra Lark, Short-toed Lark, Thekla Lark, Stonechat, Fan-tailed Warbler, Cetti's Warbler, Corn Bunting.

Summer visitors: White Stork, Egyptian Vulture, Short-toed Eagle, Montagu's Harrier, Booted Eagle, Lesser Kestrel, Collared Pratincole, Turtle Dove, Scops Owl, Red-necked Nightjar, Pallid Swift, White-rumped Swift, Bee-eater, Red-rumped Swallow, Tawny Pipit, Rufous Bush Robin, Black-eared Wheatear, Olivaceous Warbler, Woodchat Shrike.

Winter visitors: Grey Heron, Hen Harrier, Sanderling, Dunlin, Lesser Black-backed Gull, Crane, Crag Martin, Meadow Pipit, finches.

On passage: Cory's Shearwater, Manx Shearwater, Yelkouan Shearwater, Storm Petrel, Leach's Storm-petrel (after storms), Gannet, Black Stork, diurnal raptors in general, Common

Scoter, Little Ringed Plover, Ringed Plover, Knot, Little Stint, Curlew Sandpiper, Ruff, Black-tailed Godwit, Bar-tailed Godwit, Whimbrel, Redshank, Common Sandpiper, Turnstone, Audouin's Gull, Lesser Crested Tern, Sandwich Tern, Little Tern, Black Tern, Razorbill, Puffin, Swift, Alpine Swift, Bee-eater, numerous passerines.

Access

Tarifa, on the N-340 between Cádiz and Algeciras, is the main starting point for trips in the area.

Description

Tarifa is strategically positioned, commanding the Straits of Gibraltar and just 14 km from the African continent. It is a perfect spot for watching birds on migration, particularly gliding species. In addition, the coastline is relatively unspoiled with long beaches, while the surrounding mountains and hills are the site of substantial areas of cork oak and Lusitanian oak woodland.

A substantial section of the beach to the west of Tarifa is a Paraje Natural or Site of Natural Interest (Playa de Los Lances, 226 ha), and some parts of the mountains lie within the large Parque Natural de los Alcornocales, a Natural Park measuring 170,000 ha.

Recommended routes

Route A runs for several kilometres along the beach of Los Lances, starting from Tarifa itself. Running parallel to this open beach is a depression which can become flooded. It is separated from the beach by a sandbar. This is an interesting spot for watching gulls, including Audouin's Gull, Sandwich Tern and Lesser Crested Tern. Waders also abound. Near the beach are the nesting grounds of Kentish Plover, Calandra Lark, Short-toed Lark and Thekla Lark. This is also a strategic point for watching the migratory movements of birds of prey, swallows and finches.

Route B consists of a car journey along the Santuario valley. This can be reached by turning right off the N-340, 3 km outside Tarifa in the direction of Cádiz. From the sanctuary of Nuestra Señora de la Luz, continue until reaching Cañada de la Jara, where you turn right and continue until coming to the road from Tarifa to Algeciras near the El Cabrito pass. This is a broad and very beautiful valley running between ranges of hills. It acts as a funnel for many of the migrants crossing the Straits of Gibraltar, giving rise to spectacularly large numbers of birds of prey and storks. In the rivers and riverbeds crisscrossing the valley you will be able to see Rufous Bush Robin and other passerines.

Route C will take you through the hills and cork oak woods of the inland area. Continue along the Santuario valley until the end where the road joins the road from Facinas to Los Barrios. From this point it is 25 km to Los Barrios, and along the way you will be able to see Booted Eagle, Sparrowhawk, Peregrine Falcon and Griffon Vulture. It is also worth going for a walk in the cork oak woods to see a wide range of forest-dwelling species. Watch out also for groups of swifts and swallows since you may see the occasional White-rumped Swift.

The main attraction of **route D**, running along the road from Algeciras to Tarifa (23 km), is the possibility of watching birds of prey and storks on migration. The most strategic lookout points (marked on the map) are the following:

1) The isthmus at Tarifa which joins the town with the island of Las Palomas.

2) The Tarifa reservoir.

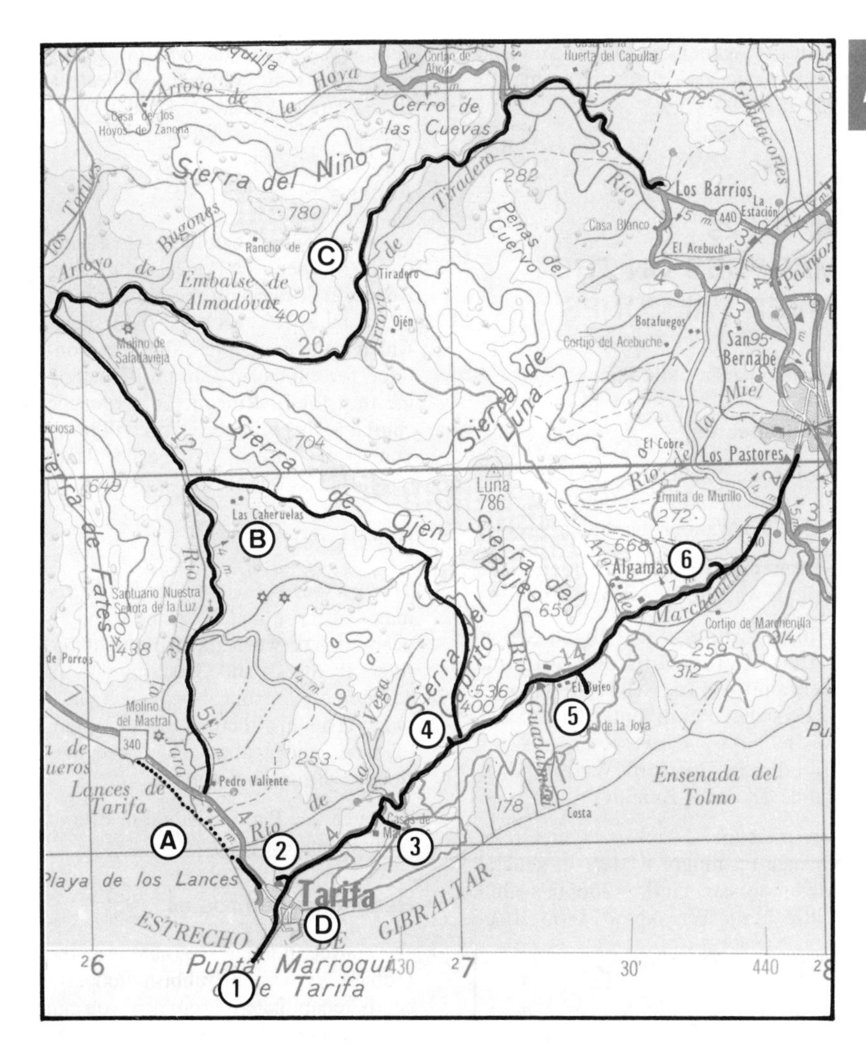

3) Hillside at La Cazalla.

4) The Cabrito pass (a nearby bunker).

5) Hillside at La Hoya.

6) El Algarrobo.

Generally speaking, autumn migration is more intense than spring migration. When the wind is blowing from the east the best spots are those nearest Tarifa, while with winds coming from the west it is best to head for El Algarrobo.

Accommodation

Accommodation is plentiful in the area, both in Tarifa and along the N-340 running towards Cádiz. As for campsites, Río Jara (within the Paraje Natural or Site of Natural Interest of Playa de Los Lances) and La Peña are recommended.

Comments

If you wish to visit the beach of Los Lances you should ask for permission from the Agencia de Medio Ambiente (Av. Ana de Viya, 3, Cádiz; telephone: 956-274629).

Jesús Parody

AN.29 MARSHES ON THE RIVER PALMONES

Coastal marshes and dunes.

Main species

Residents: Water Rail, Little Ringed Plover, Kentish Plover, Cetti's Warbler, Fan-tailed Warbler, Sardinian Warbler.

Summer visitors: Short-toed Lark, Yellow Wagtail, Woodchat Shrike.

Winter visitors: Little Egret, Spoonbill, Greylag Goose, Shelduck, Garganey, Marsh Harrier, Osprey, waders in general, Little Gull, Sandwich Tern, Short-eared Owl, Bluethroat, Dartford Warbler, Penduline Tit, Reed Bunting.

On passage: Black-necked Grebe, Greater Flamingo, waders in general, Mediterranean Gull, Audouin's Gull, Little Tern, Whiskered Tern, Black Tern, Bee-eater, Sand Martin, Tawny Pipit, Tree Pipit, Whinchat, Wheatear, Black-eared Wheatear, Garden Warbler.

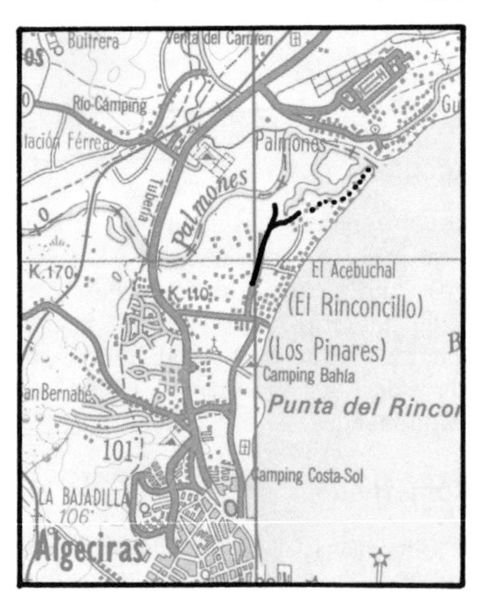

Access

Palmones, which can be reached from the N-340 between Algeciras and San Roque, is located on the left shore of the marshes. To reach the right shore, which is the more interesting part, continue for another 4 km until reaching the turn for El Rinconcillo. From the church in this village, a road will bring you to the base of a large headland, once used as a rubbish dump.

Description

The marshes you see today are the remains of those which existed some 25 years ago between the mouths of the rivers Palmones and Guadarranque. In addition to the marshes, which have many channels, there is also a system of dunes and a plain which becomes flooded during the rainy season.

The area is a Paraje Natural or Site of Natural Interest (58 ha).

Recommended routes

The starting point of the route is on the promontory with the rubbish dump, recently rehabilitated. From here you can gain a panoramic view of the area. On the area which is liable to flooding, in the appropriate seasons you will see Shelduck, Teal and other ducks. The electricity pylons running across the area serve as perches for Osprey. The channels in the marsh are a good spot for seeing waders, gulls and herons.

Continue along the track leading to the rubbish dump; this will take you across an area of irrigated land and subsequently to the coastal dunes, from where you can walk to the mouth of the river Palmones.

Accommodation

There is a wide range of accommodation available in the area. Hotel Terol in Palmones, Hostal Bahía and the El Bahía campsite in El Rinconcillo are all recommended for their proximity to the site.

Comments

Access to the marshes is regulated by the issue of permits from the Agencia de Medio Ambiente (Av. Ana de Viya, 3, Cádiz; telephone: 956-274629).

The best times of year for visiting the area are during the migration periods and in winter (in short, from mid-July through to May).

Jesús Parody

■ AN.30 GIBRALTAR

A large rock strategically located on a crossroads of migratory routes for seabirds as well as storks, birds of prey, passerines and other birds.

Main species

Residents: Shag, Peregrine Falcon, Barbary Partridge, Yellow-legged Gull, Blue Rock Thrush.

Summer visitors: Cory's Shearwater, Yelkouan Shearwater, Pallid Swift.

Winter visitors: Gannet, Arctic Skua, Great Skua, Little Gull, Mediterranean Gull, Razorbill, Crag Martin (roost of up to 3,000 individuals), Alpine Accentor.

On passage: Black Stork, White Stork, Honey Buzzard, Black Kite, Egyptian Vulture, Short-toed Eagle, Marsh Harrier, Hen Harrier, Montagu's Harrier, Booted Eagle, Pomarine Skua, Audouin's Gull, Lesser Crested Tern, Puffin, Wryneck, Rufous Bush Robin, Black Redstart, Redstart, Whinchat, Wheatear, Black-eared Wheatear, Ring Ouzel, Redwing, Fan-tailed Warbler, Melodious Warbler, Dartford Warbler, Spectacled Warbler, Subalpine Warbler, Orphean Warbler, Wood Warbler, Pied Flycatcher, Woodchat Shrike, Siskin, Rock Bunting, Ortolan Bunting.

Access

Access to Gibraltar is from La Línea de la Concepción, which is reached via San Roque on the N-340. You will need a passport to cross the frontier. Despite the small size of Gibraltar, it is worth using a car (or taxi) to reach the most interesting areas.

Description

Gibraltar is a promontory some 6 km long and a maximum of 1 km wide. It is dominated by El Peñón (the Rock), a limestone outcrop rising 425 m above sea level. Although the isthmus and the western side of El Peñón are very built up, the rest of the area is occupied by dense scrubland consisting of wild olive trees and other Mediterranean shrubs. Ornithological interest is derived from its geographical position and the opportunities provided for watching birds of prey, seabirds and other birds on migration. A bird typical of the area is the Barbary Partridge, which was probably introduced from Africa, as were the Barbary Apes of the Rock.

All species of fauna and flora in the area are protected, and hunting of any kind is prohibited.

Recommended routes

The points of greatest interest are the following:

1) Europa Point. This is the southernmost part of Gibraltar and can be reached by bus from the frontier (every 30 minutes until 20:30). Beside the

lighthouse is a good point for watching seabirds including Shag (nesting on the eastern side of the Rock or Peñón) and Audouin's Gull (on migration between July and September).

2) Cable Car Top Station. This can be reached on foot from the car park at St. Michael's Cave or via cable car (open 09:30-19:15). This is the highest point of the Rock and the best place for watching the autumn migration of raptors, particularly when winds are blowing from the west. It is possible to see over 10,000 birds of prey in a single day, as well as vast quantities of Bee-eater, swifts, swallows and finches.

3) Jews Gate. A vantage point lying to the south of the Rock, perfect for watching the spring migration of birds of prey, storks and other birds, but only when the wind is blowing from the west. This area can be reached by car.

4) Upper Rock. This area of scrubland covers the upper half of the Rock. It can be reached from several points; you can leave your vehicle in a series of car parks and take a walk along the paths. This is a good place for seeing the wide variety of passerines which remain during the migration periods, although you may also see Barbary Partridge in the firebreaks and other open areas, particularly in the early morning or at sunset.

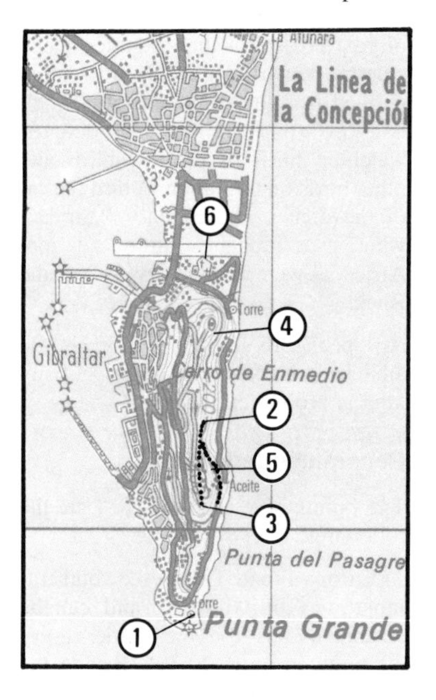

5) Mediterranean Steps. A spectacular walk descending from the top of the Rock along its eastern side. This can be reached by leaving your car at St. Michael's Cave. You may see Barbary Partridge, Blue Rock Thrush, Peregrine Falcon and, in winter, Alpine Accentor.

6) North Front Cemetery. One of the few flat, undeveloped areas of Gibraltar. This is a good place for watching large numbers of passerines during the migration periods. The cemetery is open every day from 08:00 to 18:00.

Accommodation

There are several hotels in Gibraltar, as well as a wide variety of accommodation in Algeciras, La Línea and the surrounding area.

Comments

It is worthwhile avoiding the rush hours when people cross the frontier (08:00-09:00 as you enter Gibraltar and 18:00-20:00 as you leave). At these times, large queues of cars may form.

For watching birds out to sea, you should bear in mind the position of the sun. During sunny summer days the best time is in the afternoon.

It would be appreciated if you would send a list of your most interesting sightings to the Gibraltar Ornithological and Natural History Society (Gibraltar Museum, 18-20 Bomb House Lane).

Ernest F. J. Garcia and Charles Perez

AN.31
ESTUARY OF THE RIVER GUADIARO

A river mouth.

Main species

Residents: Little Grebe, Kentish Plover, Cetti's Warbler, Fan-tailed Warbler.

Summer visitors: Short-toed Lark.

Winter visitors: Little Egret, ducks, Marsh Harrier, Water Rail, waders in general, Kentish Plover, Crag Martin, Water Pipit, Bluethroat, Penduline Tit, Reed Bunting.

On passage: Purple Heron, Greater Flamingo, ducks, birds of prey, waders, Little Gull, Audouin's Gull, Gull-billed Tern, Lesser Crested Tern, Whiskered Tern, Little Tern, Bee-eater, Red-rumped Swallow, Sedge Warbler, Subalpine Warbler, Woodchat Shrike.

Access

Leave San Roque on the N-340 towards Málaga and continue until reaching the turn for Puerto Sotogrande. Go through the checkpoint you will encounter and drive along the right-hand lane. On reaching Sotogrande turn right again along the main street. Cross the bridge over the river and at the first junction turn left onto Paseo del Parque which will bring you to the Playa Sotogrande housing development.

Description

Despite the fact that the estuary of the river Guadiaro lies at the heart of a tourist complex, this estuary is important because, in company with the mouth of the river Guadalhorce, this is the only wetland area which has remained undamaged on the badly spoiled Costa del Sol. The most interesting part of the

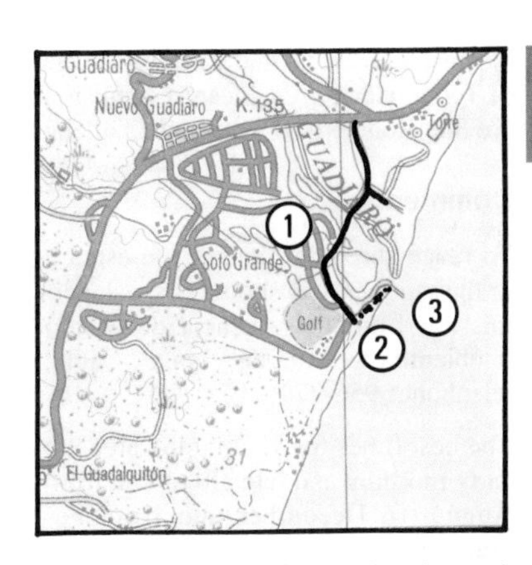

estuary is an island, greatly changed from its natural state but still sustaining reedbeds, cane and tamarisk. This island lies in a fork between two channels which terminate in the river. The area is protected from the sea by a sandbar.

It has been declared a Paraje Natural or Site of Natural Interest.

Recommended routes

The most interesting points on the route are the following:

1) Bridge over the river Guadiaro. From here you can see the mouth of the river and the intertidal zone lying near the island, where you will have no difficulty in seeing gulls and waders. In August and September you should see Audouin's Gull and Lesser Crested Tern.

2) From the holiday houses at Playa Sotogrande you will have a view of one of the channels running beside the island. In the vegetation of the channel you should see herons, crakes and Water Rail.

3) The sandbar closing off the mouth of the river is a good spot for watching seabirds and waders.

Accommodation

There is plenty of accommodation available in Sotogrande (albeit on the expensive side) and in the nearby village of Torreguadiaro. The nearest campsites are San Roque, La Casita and Chullera.

Comments

To reach the inner part of the estuary or the sandbar, you should first ask permission from the Agencia de Medio Ambiente (Av. Ana de Viya, 3, Cádiz; telephone: 956-274629).

The best times for visiting the area are early morning and late afternoon, from August to December and from February to April.

Jesús Parody

■ AN.32 BERMEJA AND CRESTELLINA RANGES

Mountain ranges of average height with high cliffs.

Main species

Residents: Griffon Vulture, Goshawk, Sparrowhawk, Bonelli's Eagle, Peregrine Falcon, Eagle Owl, Tawny Owl, Crag Martin, Green Woodpecker, Dipper, Black Wheatear, Blue Rock Thrush, Chough.

Summer visitors: Egyptian Vulture, Short-toed Eagle, Booted Eagle.

On passage: Above all in autumn, diurnal birds of prey and storks on passage, making for the Straits of Gibraltar.

Access

The best departure point for visiting the area is Estepona on the N-340.

Description

Sierra Bermeja is a massif forming part of the southern edge of the mountains of Ronda. Maximum height is reached with the peak of Los Reales (1,449 m). The valley sides are steep, and plant life features extensive woodlands of pine and Spanish fir (*Abies pinsapo*) on the northern side of Los Reales, the only woodland of this kind to grow on non-limestone soil. The peridotitic rock constituting this range gives the whole a red colour from which the name of the range is derived. This rock type causes soil to be rich in heavy metals, giving rise to the growth of very specialized flora.

Sierra Crestellina is a large limestone spur reaching 905 m in height, backing onto the far westernmost part of the Sierra Bermeja. The northern side of this range is formed by a spectacular cliff, while the southern slopes are taken up by Mediterranean scrubland and some holm oak and carob (*Ceratonia siliqua*).

Recommended routes

The route proposed for this area is a long excursion of 136 km along the roads running through the area. Start in Estepona and take the road for Jubrique until reaching the Peñasblancas mountain pass, from where you will gain an excellent view of the whole range. This is a wonderful place for watching birds of prey on passage. From the pass a track leads off to the summit of the peak of Los Reales; about 3 or 4 km before reaching the peak, you will come across a campsite and restaurant.

Continue along the road towards Jubrique; this road runs through extensive pine woodland where you may see, among other species, Goshawk, Sparrowhawk and Booted Eagle. The route continues to Algotacín, where you take the C-341 to Gaucín. In Gaucín take the minor road for Manilva or Casares. This last stretch runs along the foot of the Sierra Crestellina,

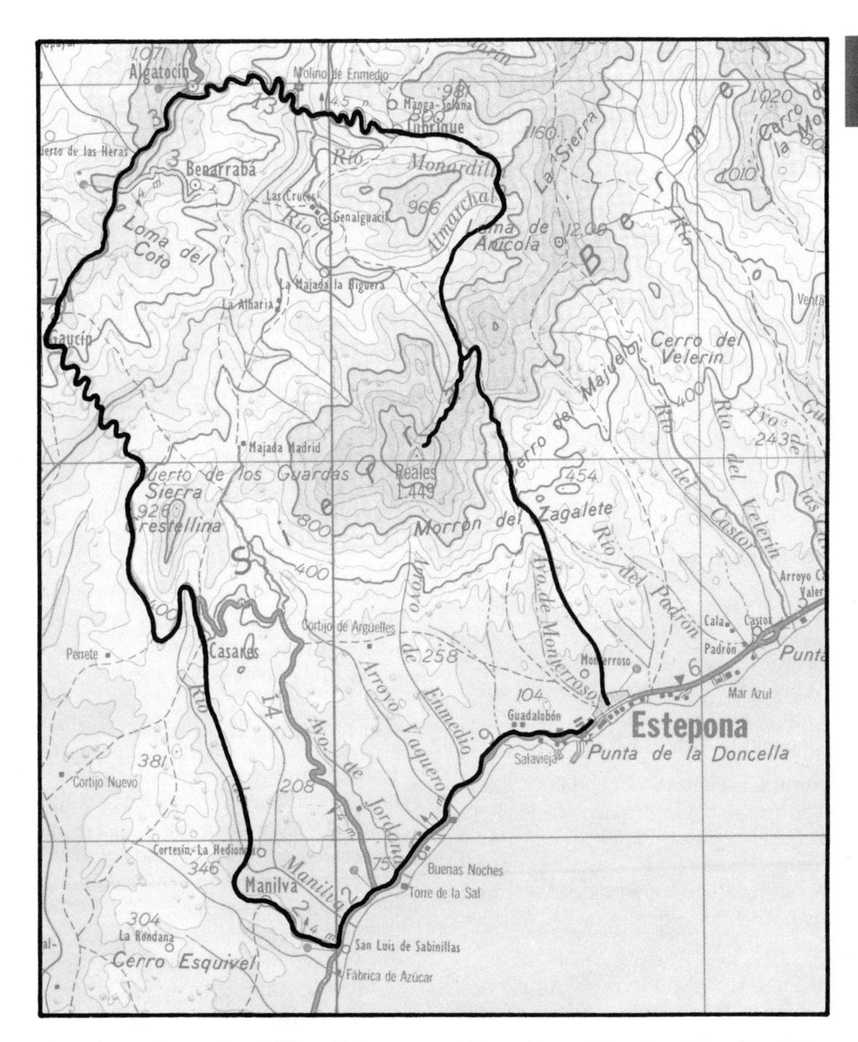

a good spot for seeing Griffon Vulture, Egyptian Vulture, Bonelli's Eagle, Peregrine Falcon, Crag Martin, Chough, Black Wheatear, etc.

Accommodation

The proximity of the Costa del Sol makes for a wide range of accommodation. You can also find accommodation in the villages of Jubrique, Algotacín and Gaucín. There are campsites at Los Reales de Sierra Bermeja and by the river Genal between Jubrique and Algotacín.

Comments

In addition to the route proposed here, there are many alternatives for those who like walking and for those who have vehicles suitable for driving along difficult mountain tracks. What is more, in Jubrique there is a cooperative which organizes ecological trips on horseback (information can be obtained from the Ayuntamiento or town council in Jubrique).

The best times of year for visiting the area are spring and autumn.

Javier Plata Escalona,
Manuel Garrido Sánchez
and Eduardo Alba Padilla.

AN.33 LAS NIEVES RANGE

A mountain area with interesting areas of woodland and high cliffs.

Main species

Residents: Griffon Vulture, Goshawk, Sparrowhawk, Golden Eagle, Bonelli's Eagle, Peregrine Falcon, Eagle Owl, Green Woodpecker, Great Spotted Woodpecker, Thekla Lark, Black Wheatear, Blue Rock Thrush, Firecrest, Crested Tit, Great Grey Shrike, Chough, Crossbill, Rock Bunting.

Summer visitors: Egyptian Vulture, Short-toed Eagle, Booted Eagle, Red-necked Nightjar, Pallid Swift, Alpine Swift, Bee-eater, Roller, Red-rumped Swallow, Redstart, Black-eared Wheatear, Rock Thrush, Spectacled Warbler, Subalpine Warbler.

Winter visitors: Wryneck, Alpine Accentor, Ring Ouzel, Fieldfare, Redwing, Siskin.

On passage: Honey Buzzard and other migratory birds of prey.

Access

The area can be reached from the C-344 between Málaga and Ronda. In Yunquera, between the villages of Coín and El Burgo, take a forest track leading off from the outskirts of the village. After 5 km the track forks; the right fork terminates immediately in a layby where you can leave your car. The left fork continues for some 3 km more and also avails of parking space.

Another access point (**route B**) consists of taking the C-339 out of Ronda for San Pedro de Alcántara. At the 13 km marker post turn left onto a signed track, perfectly passable, which will take you to the farm of Los Quejigales where you can leave your vehicle (10 km).

Description

The Sierra de las Nieves is part of the Serranía de Ronda, which reaches its greatest height with the peak of Torrecilla (1,919 m) in the province of Málaga. This is a steep mountain range abounding in large gorges and cliffs. Vegetation consists of areas of Spanish fir (*Abies pinsapo*), although there are also areas of pine, holm oak and chestnut. Scrubland also takes up a considerable part of the area.

Recommended routes

Route A consists of a climb of some 4 hours to the summit known as Enamorados (1,783 m). Start in Yunquera and on reaching a fork, take the road leading off to the right to continue on foot up the gorge. The route will take you through areas of pine and Spanish fir where you may see Goshawk, Sparrowhawk, Short-toed Eagle, Booted Eagle, Redstart and Crossbill. In the scrubland areas you may see Red-necked Nightjar, Thekla Lark, Spectacled Warbler, Subalpine Warbler and Sardinian Warbler, while the rock gorges will give sightings of Griffon Vulture, Golden Eagle, Bonelli's Eagle, Peregrine Falcon, Alpine Swift and Chough. The high ground is also interesting and you may see Rock Thrush, Blue Rock Thrush, Black Wheatear and Black-eared Wheatear. If you visit the area in autumn and winter, you may also see Fieldfare, Ring Ouzel and Alpine Accentor.

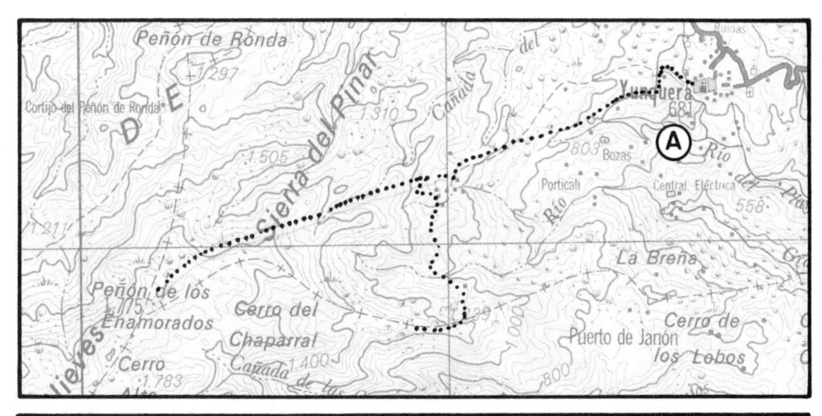

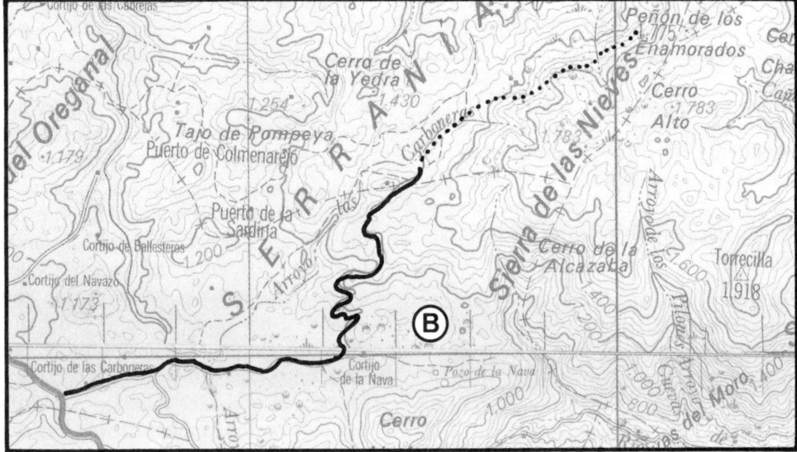

An alternative to this route is to bear left at the fork and walk up the gorge of La Caina.

Route B consists of a two-hour walk. It takes you from the farm of Los Quejigales to the pass of the same name. The birds you will see are largely the same as for **route A**, although the main attractions of this walk are the huge mature specimens of Spanish fir in the Cañada del Cuerno, a gorge. In autumn Ring Ouzel and Fieldfare also abound, since they eat the fruit of the many hawthorn (*Crataegus monogyna*) bushes. Another option is to climb up to the pass of Los Pilones where you may see Rock Thrush in summer and Alpine Accentor in winter.

Accommodation

Plenty of accommodation is available in the area, particularly in Ronda, Tolox and Yunquera. There is also a campsite and a couple of places where wild camping is allowed.

Pedro Díaz Robledo

■ AN.34 FUENTEPIEDRA LAGOON

An extensive inland lagoon with a large breeding colony of Greater Flamingo.

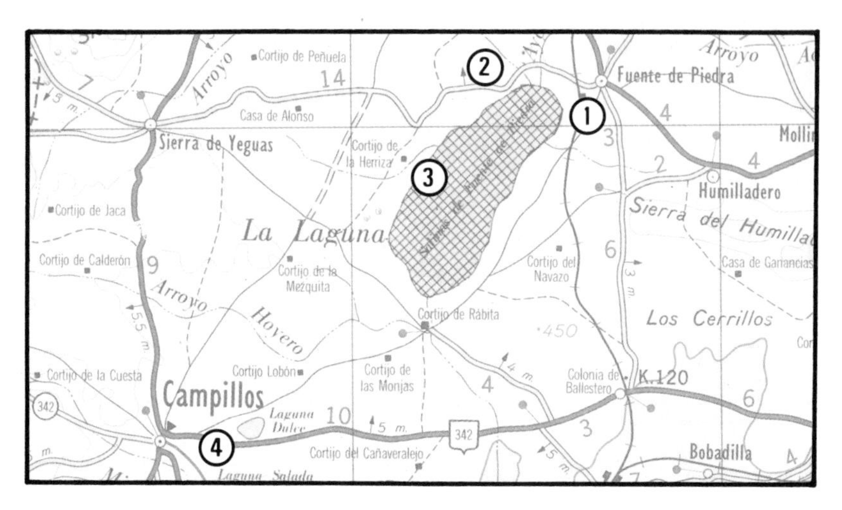

Main species

Residents: Greater Flamingo (up to 14,000 pairs in 1990), Mallard, Stone Curlew, Kentish Plover, Black-headed Gull, Fan-tailed Warbler, Sardinian Warbler.

Summer visitors: Montagu's Harrier, Lesser Kestrel, Red-crested Pochard, Black-winged Stilt, Avocet, Slender-billed Gull, Gull-billed Tern, Bee-eater, Short-toed Lark, Yellow Wagtail, Black-eared Wheatear, Melodious Warbler, Spectacled Warbler, Woodchat Shrike.

Winter visitors: Grey Heron, Greylag Goose, Shelduck, Widgeon, Teal, Pintail, Shoveler, Coot, Crane, Little Bustard, Snipe.

On passage: waders, marsh terns.

Access

The N-334 between Málaga and Seville passes through the village of Fuentepiedra or Fuente de Piedra, which lies beside the lagoon.

Description

A natural lagoon measuring some 1,400 ha; it is elongated and measures some 6.5 km long by 2.5 km wide, lying in a broad basin between cereal crops and olive groves. Its waters are shallow and saline; old salt pans have left the remains of walls and jetties in the lagoon, providing nesting grounds for flamingos, gulls and waders. Water levels vary greatly, both during the course of the year (the lagoon usually dries up completely in summer) and from one year to the next; the presence of greater or lesser numbers of birds depends on the amount of water in the lagoon. Around the shores are extensive areas of halophytic scrub but marsh vegetation is sparse.

The area is a Nature Reserve of 1,364 ha.

Recommended routes

Since this is a strictly protected area you should limit your visit to the bird hides and be guided by the information provided by the rangers, particularly during the breeding season. As you leave Fuentepiedra in the direction of Sierra de Yeguas, just after the railway line, on the Cerro del Palo (1) there is an information centre.

You should also cast an eye over the mouths of the rivers Pueblo (2) and Los

Arenales (3); since these are freshwater streams with some marsh vegetation, you will have no difficulty in increasing the variety of birds seen.

For the same reason it is worthwhile approaching the lagoon of Dulce de Campillos (4), located beside the village of Campillos on the N-342, some 20 km from Fuentepiedra.

Accommodation

Some accommodation is available in Fuentepiedra and other nearby villages, but it is probably worth going to Antequera where a wider range of accommodation is on offer.

Comments

The best months for visiting the area are April and May. It is worth making use of the early morning hours.

Eduardo Alba and Manolo Garrido

AN.35 MOUTH OF THE RIVER GUADALHORCE

Coastal marshes which have become degenerated but include flooded gravel pits.

Main species

Residents: Little Grebe, Water Rail, Cetti's Warbler, Fan-tailed Warbler.

Summer visitors: Little Bittern, Kentish Plover, Pallid Swift, Bee-eater, Short-toed Lark, Yellow Wagtail.

Winter visitors: Yelkouan Shearwater, Cattle Egret, Little Egret, Grey Heron, Marsh Harrier, Sanderling, Snipe, Jack Snipe, Arctic Skua, Mediterranean Gull, Sandwich Tern, Razorbill, Kingfisher, Crag Martin, Bluethroat, Penduline Tit.

On passage: Cory's Shearwater, Gannet, Squacco Heron, Purple Heron, Spotted Crake, waders in general, Little Gull, Audouin's Gull, Common Tern, Little Tern, Whiskered Tern, Black Tern, Sand Martin, reed warblers.

Access

From Málaga, take the N-340 towards Cádiz. After 4 km, just before crossing the bridge over the river Guadalhorce, near the sugar mill, turn right. Continue under the bridge and take the first track running off towards the sea until reaching a fence where you leave your car.

Description

The mouth of the river Guadalhorce is one of the last relicts of the marshland which once abounded in the low-lying floodplains around Málaga. The area now enjoys protection after many years of hard struggle, and the area protected today stretches between the two arms of the river and the sea. In addition to the marshes, which flood in winter, and the coastal strip, there is also an area of riverside woodland and some lagoons which have formed in gravel pits.

Recommended routes

The route proposed for this area is a walk of some 5 km. To begin with, it runs parallel to the riverbed along the left bank and on reaching the beach turns towards the course of the river Viejo, from where you return to your departure point. The points of greatest interest are the following:

1) Course of the river Guadalhorce. Here you will see Cattle Egret, reed warblers and Penduline Tit.

2) Mouth of the river. This area is frequented by waders and gulls including

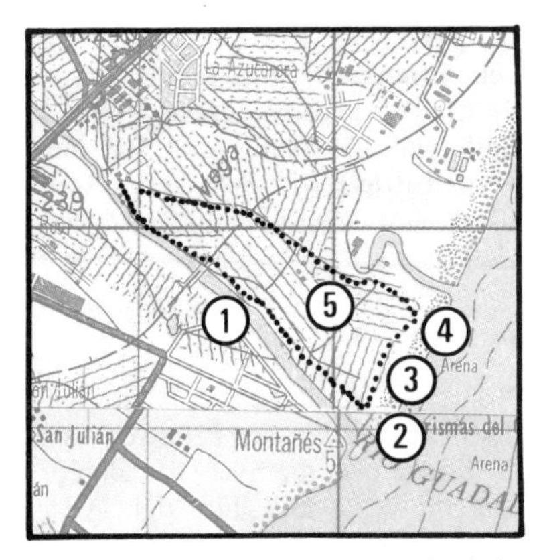

Mediterranean Gull and Audouin's Gull.

3) Salt marshes. During the breeding season, you will see Kentish Plover and Short-toed Lark.

4) Beach. A good spot for seeing Gannet, Sanderling, Sandwich Tern and skuas.

5) River Viejo and lagoons. This is the most interesting area and you will see herons, grebes, ducks, gulls and, in the vegetation, the occasional Bluethroat.

Accommodation

Accommodation in Málaga and the surrounding area is freely available.

Comments

The best time of year for visiting the area is autumn.

Eduardo Alba Padilla, Manuel Garrido Sánchez and Javier Plata Escalona.

■ AN.36 TEJEDA AND ALMIJARA RANGES

An area of very steep mountains.

Main species

Residents: Goshawk, Sparrowhawk, Buzzard, Golden Eagle, Bonelli's Eagle, Peregrine Falcon, Eagle Owl, Tawny Owl, Thekla Lark, Skylark, Crag Martin, Dipper, Black Wheatear, Blue Rock Thrush.

Summer visitors: Short-toed Eagle, Booted Eagle, Scops Owl, Red-necked Nightjar, Nightjar, Alpine Swift, Tawny Pipit, Wheatear, Black-eared Wheatear, Rock Thrush, Spectacled Warbler, Bonelli's Warbler.

Winter visitors: Alpine Accentor, Ring Ouzel.

Access

To reach the Sierra Tejeda, go to Vélez-Málaga on the N-340, and there take the C-335 towards Alhama de Granada. After 10 km turn right onto the local road for Canillas de Aceituno and continue for 5 km until you find another turning to the right for Alcaucín (4 km).

To reach the Sierra Almijara, in Nerja take the minor road to Frigiliana (6 km).

Description

The sweep of mountains formed by the Sierra Tejeda and the Sierra Almijara, both part of the Cordilleras Béticas, marks the boundary between the provinces of Málaga and Granada. The mountains are steep, and valley sides are crisscrossed by deep ravines. The Tejeda range reaches its highest point with the peak of Maroma (2,065 m), and the Almijara range with the peak of Navachica (1,834 m).

The valley bottoms are taken up by vineyards, almond groves and olive groves, while the valley sides are occupied by holm oak, Lusitanian oak and pine plantations with scrubland consisting of whin, cistus and thyme.

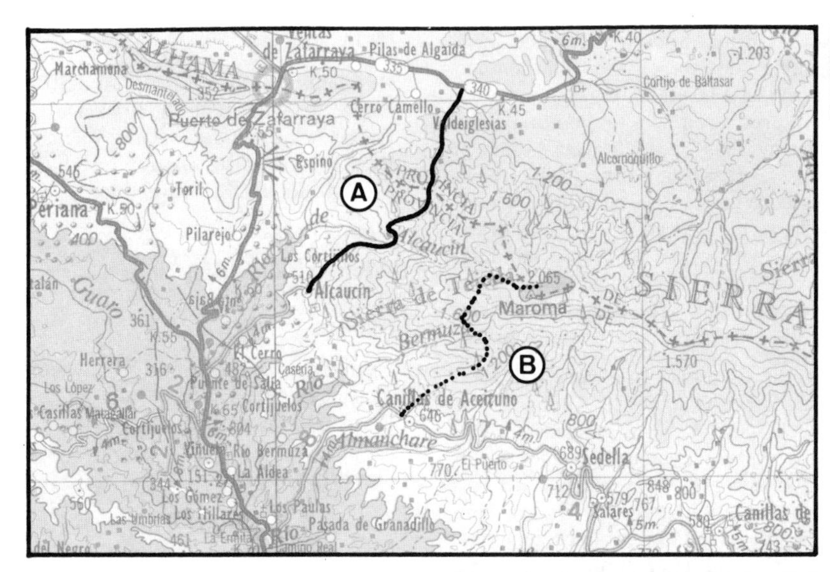

The high ground is covered by scrub, with brooms and junipers.

Recommended routes

Route A consists of a 12 km car journey along the northeastern side of the Sierra Tejeda. Start at the Don Manuel bridge at the crossroads for Alcaucín. The road, narrow and steep, crosses vineyards and fields where you may see Rufous Bush Robin. After the village, take the track to El Alcázar which leads to the riverbed of the same name, where there is a spring and an area for camping. From here you will be able to contemplate the impressive cliffs of Tajo Fuerte, a good place for watching birds of prey and other cliff-dwelling species. Continue along the track, which will take you through oak and Lusitanian oak woodland where a relatively wide variety of forest-dwelling species are present. To return, either retrace your steps or alternatively walk back along the C-335.

Route B is a challenging climb to the peak of Maroma for which a whole day is needed. In Canillas de Aceituno, take a path which after an hour of steep climbing will bring you to the spring of La Rávita, the only place with a water supply at nearly all times of year. Slightly farther up is the Collado de la Rávita, a mountain saddle giving views of the large cliffs on the southern side

of Maroma. Subsequently, the track winds along gorges filled with scrub to reach, at a height of 1,600 m, a broom covered area where you may see Tawny Pipit and Wheatear, which at this level substitute the many Black-eared Wheatear present at lower levels. The path brings you to the ruins of the Casa de las Nieves, an old building; from there it is possible to reach the summit, distinguished by a survey point. To return, retrace your steps.

Route C consists of a walk of some 6 km through the Sierra Almijara. The walk starts at the main square in Frigiliana, taking you along a track which drops steeply between irrigated farmland and fruit orchards. On reaching the river Higuerón, the track gently ascends the riverbed, providing opportunities for seeing a wide range of birds. Continue until the point where the terrain becomes extremely steep, and then turn back.

Accommodation

Towns on the coast offer a wide variety of accommodation, although it is also possible to find somewhere to stay in the inland villages. There are also several campsites.

Comments

The best time of year for visiting the area is in spring, particularly the months of April and May.

Javier Plata Escalona,
Eduardo Alba Padilla
and Manuel Garrido Sánchez.

■ AN.37 GORGES OF THE RIVER CACÍN

A gorge with high cliffs.

Main species

Residents: Golden Eagle, Bonelli's Eagle, Peregrine Falcon, Rock Dove, Eagle Owl, Crag Martin, Grey Wagtail, Blue Rock Thrush, Dartford Warbler, Chough, Raven, Rock Bunting.

Summer visitors: Bee-eater.

Winter visitors: Kingfisher.

Access

From Granada, take the C-340 towards Alhama de Granada and stop at the Los Bermejales reservoir (43 km).

Description

A deep gorge carved by the waters of the river Cacín. The cliffs are extremely high, and the scree slopes are occupied by scrubland consisting of whin, rosemary and halimium bushes.

Recommended routes

The route recommended here is a 5 km walk along the upper edge of the cliffs. It begins at the dam of the Los Bermejales reservoir and runs along the left bank of the river, providing opportunities for seeing a wide range of cliff-dwelling birdlife. It is also possible to follow this route along the

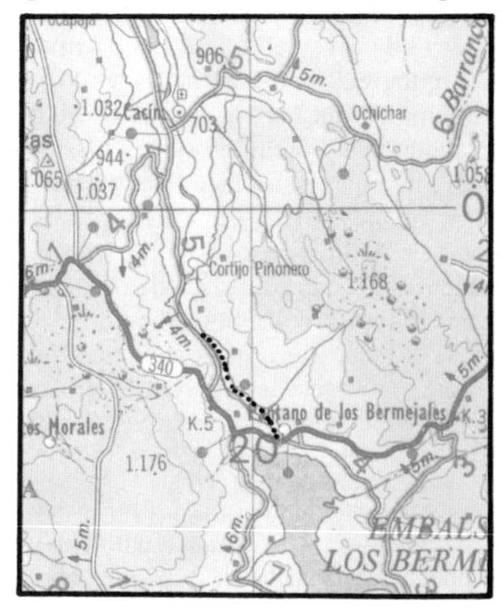

bottom of the gorge, although it is rather more difficult. To return, either retrace your steps or alternatively use the nearby road to Cacín.

The adjoining Los Bermejales reservoir is the site, in winter, of various ducks, Grey Heron, Great Crested Grebe, Cormorant and, more occasionally, Osprey.

Accommodation

Granada, 43 km away from this site, provides a wide range of accommodation. It is also possible to stay in Alhama de Granada.

Manuel Soler
and Juan Manuel Pleguezuelos

■ AN.38 TAJOS DE LOS VADOS

High cliffs.

Main species

Residents: Bonelli's Eagle, Peregrine Falcon, Little Ringed Plover, Rock Dove, Eagle Owl, Crag Martin, Grey Wagtail, Blue Rock Thrush, Black Wheatear, Rock Sparrow.

Summer visitors: Pallid Swift, Alpine Swift, Red-rumped Swallow, Yellow Wagtail, Black-eared Wheatear.

Winter visitors: Common Sandpiper, Kingfisher, Alpine Accentor, Black Redstart.

Access

Coming from Granada towards Motril, the N-323 runs along the bottom of the gorge for the last few kilometres before reaching the coast.

Description

A gorge worked by the waters of the river Guadalfeo. The gorge is some 3 km long and at some points the rock walls reach a vertical height of over 300 m.

Recommended routes

The Tajos de los Vados can be visited via the road, making a series of stops at will to watch the birds present. You can also walk from the junction with the minor road running from Guájar–Faragüit to the dam of Azud, at the end of the gorge. If you decide to do this, it is worth working your way down the right bank of the river to avoid the road, which runs along the left bank. In addition to the Mediterranean cliff-dwelling species (including birds of prey) you may also see, in the gravel pits by the river, Little Ringed Plover and Grey Wagtail. Occasionally, White-rumped Swift is present.

Accommodation

The towns on the coast (Motril, Salobreña and Almuñécar) provide plenty of possibilities for accommodation, al-

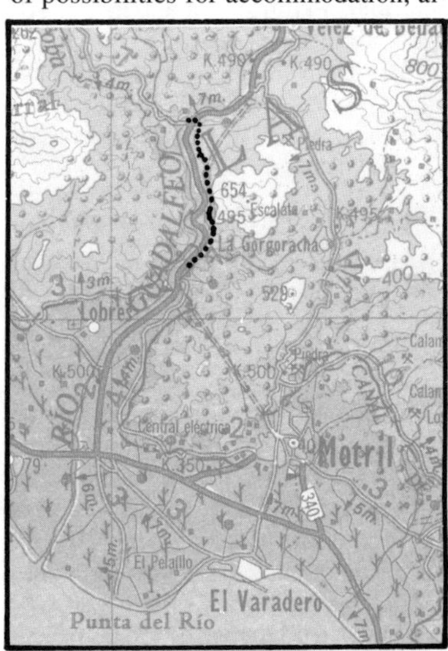

though they may well be full during the summer months. Lanjarón, a famous spa town, also has plenty of hotels which are much quieter than those on the coast and also lie much closer to the routes recommended here.

Juan Manuel Pleguezuelos and Manuel Soler

AN.39 SIERRA NEVADA

An extensive area of mountains.

Main species

Residents: Goshawk, Sparrowhawk, Golden Eagle, Bonelli's Eagle, Peregrine Falcon, Common Sandpiper, Eagle Owl, Scops Owl, Green Woodpecker, Skylark, Thekla Lark, Crag Martin, Grey Wagtail, Dipper, Alpine Accentor, Blue Rock Thrush, Cetti's Warbler, Dartford Warbler, Spectacled Warbler, Crested Tit, Great Grey Shrike, Chough, Rock Sparrow, Crossbill, Hawfinch, Rock Bunting.

Summer visitors: Booted Eagle, Alpine Swift, Wryneck, Tawny Pipit, Rufous Bush Robin, Wheatear, Black-eared Wheatear, Black Wheatear, Rock Thrush, Orphean Warbler, Golden Oriole, Ortolan Bunting.

Winter visitors: Ring Ouzel, Siskin.

On passage: many different kinds of birds of prey.

Access

To undertake routes A and B, in the centre of the city of Granada take the *carretera de la sierra*, the road leading to Pinos Genil and Pico Veleta. After 8 km turn left for Güejar-Sierra (10 km). On reaching this village turn right onto a small surfaced road taking you successively to Maitena, El Charcón and Barranco de San Juan (5.5 km). To reach the start of route B, in El Charcón take a narrow, steep road leading up past Hotel del Duque and taking you after 6.5 km onto the *carretera de la sierra* or mountain road. Turn left onto this road and after 12 km you will reach the *Albergue Universitario*, a youth hostel, and the Peñones de San Francisco.

The starting point for route C involves leaving Granada via the area of El Zaidín (La Hípica) for La Zubia (6 km). Having passed through La Zubia, turn left onto a road climbing up to Cumbres Verdes (in case of doubt, ask somebody for directions). Follow this road for 9 km until the point where it is no longer surfaced.

Description

The Sierra Nevada is an impressive massif some 70 km long, with an average width of 20 km. The highest point is Mulhacén (3,481 m), the highest mountain in the Iberian Peninsula. In addition, there are more than 20 peaks over 3,000 m.

Vegetation is highly diversified because of the range of altitudes, although it is only well-conserved in some places. A series of aggressive activities such as deforestation, overgrazing, vermin poisoning etc. have reduced the amount of fauna present, although it is still abundant.

Recommended routes

Route A consists of a walk starting at the San Juan gorge at the end of the road leading up from Güejar-Sierra. From here, take the La Estrella path which runs parallel to the course of the river Genil along its left bank. The track climbs gently for some 10 km, bring you to the place known as Cueva Secreta. Here the path fades out and the terrain becomes very steep; it is easy

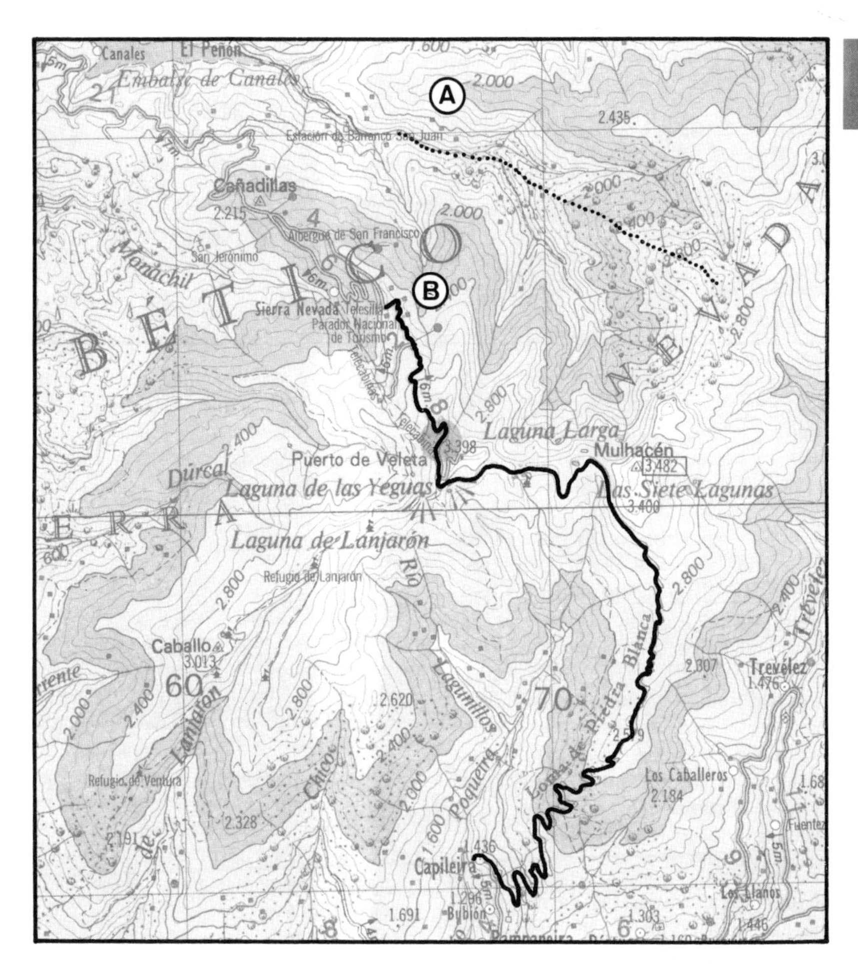

to become lost beyond this point, so it is recommended that you turn back. The first part of the route runs through oak woodland where you may see Hawfinch, Bonelli's Warbler and Golden Oriole, while the second part takes you through an area of thorny scrub where you may, in addition to Ortolan Bunting, also see Golden Eagle, Peregrine Falcon and Eagle Owl.

Route B, running from the Albergue Universitario (youth hostel) to the village of Capileira, is some 45 km long (40 km of unsurfaced track). It is worth doing this journey by car, although your car should be able to cope with problems caused by fuel combustion at heights over 3,000 m. This road is open every year from early July onwards and is kept clear until mid-October when the first autumn snows come (see Comments). The starting point for this route, on the northern slopes of the Sierra Nevada, is a good place for seeing Spectacled Warbler, Ortolan Bunting, Rock Thrush and Chough. After 8 km you will pass the lake of Las Yeguas where, at nearly 3,000 m, Grey Wagtail and Common Sandpiper nest. Shortly afterwards you will come to the Carihuela pass where the asphalt

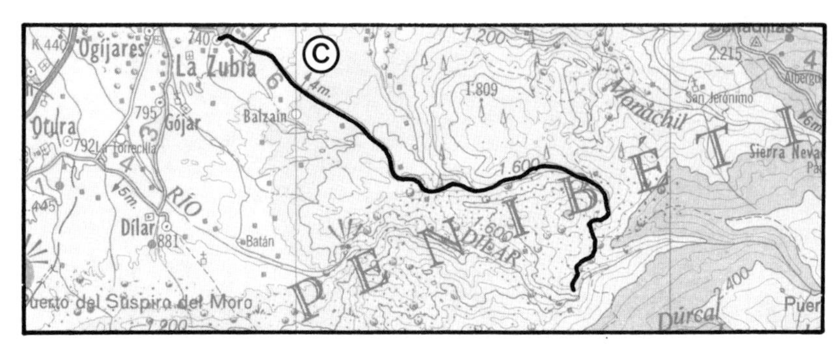

comes to an end and you reach the southern side of the Sierra. On this high ground, lying above 3,000 m, you will see Alpine Accentor; on the plains located below you should see Tawny Pipit, Skylark and Wheatear. The track continues downhill; follow the clearest route and you will reach Capileira. From this village a surfaced road will bring you to Orjiva and the bed of the river Guadalfeo. When you reach this point you will, in 2 hours, have dropped from 3,100 m at the Carihuela pass to 300 m at the latter point. A walk near the river Guadalfeo will allow you to increase the number of birds seen with Red-rumped Swallow, various warblers, Rufous Bush Robin and Olivaceous Warbler.

Route C begins at the farm of La Fuente del Hervidero and brings you to the Ruquino pass. It is 8.5 km long and gently climbs along a track which is suitable either for driving or for walking. The first part of the route takes you through areas of thorny scrub where you will be able to see various kinds of buntings, Dartford Warbler and Chough. Subsequently, the track enters a pine wood where you will be able to see Golden Eagle, Goshawk, Sparrowhawk, Crossbill, Crested Tit and other forest-dwelling species.

Accommodation

Plenty of accommodation is available in Granada. The Albergue Universitario is also recommended since it is well-sited, has a pleasant atmosphere and reasonable prices, although the number of places available is limited. Also recommended is Mesón Poqueira in Capileira.

Comments

If you are undertaking route B, you should take sun cream, sunglasses, warm clothing and an altimeter. If you wish to do this route on foot, a bus leaves Fuente de las Batallas (in the city of Granada) and goes up to the Albergue Universitario every day at 09:00. If you undertake this route in September or October, you should be very aware while on high ground of approaching snowstorms. If this happens, drop down as fast as possible on either side of the range so that you do not become cut off by the snow.

Juan Manuel Pleguezuelos and Manuel Soler

AN.40 ALBUFERA DE ADRA

Two small coastal lagoons.

Main species

Residents: Little Grebe, Great Crested Grebe, Red-crested Pochard, Pochard, White-headed Duck, Marsh Harrier.

Summer visitors: Little Bittern, Black-winged Stilt, Bee-eater.

Winter visitors: Black-necked Grebe, Cormorant, Cattle Egret, Little Egret, Tufted Duck, Bluethroat, Penduline Tit.

On passage: Purple Heron, Ferruginous Duck, Whiskered Tern, Black Tern, White-winged Black Tern.

Access

The lagoons are 6 km from Adra on the N-340 running towards Almería.

Description

The diversion of the river Adra and the construction of a breakwater in the port, both undertaken at the turn of the century, produced changes in the coastline which favoured the accumulation of sandbars and with this, the formation of two lagoons on the land of the former river delta. Around the two bodies of water is a fringe of marsh vegetation constituted by reeds and canes. The surrounding area has been badly degenerated by numerous plastic greenhouses.

The area is a Nature Reserve (153 ha with a buffer zone of 22 ha).

Recommended routes

There are 3 raised hides for birdwatching, from which you can command excellent views of the lagoons.

Accommodation

There is plenty of accommodation available in the nearby towns and villages.

Comments

To use the raised hides you should ask permission from the Agencia de Medio Ambiente (Centro Residencial Oliveros, Bloque Singular, 2ª planta;

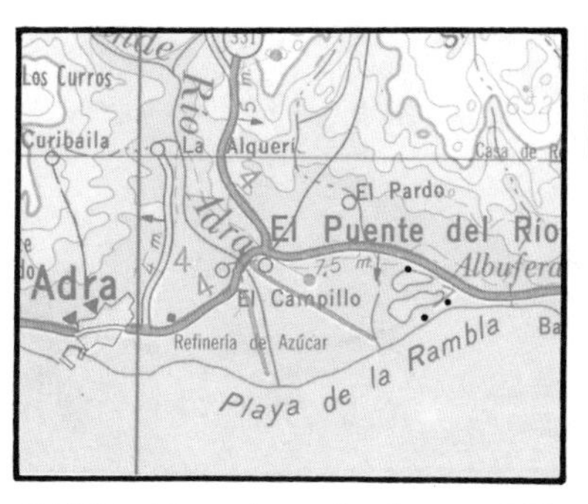

04004 Almería; telephone: 951-237680).

The time of year when the greatest concentration of ducks is present is from October to March.

Segundo Cañadas Albacete,
Hermelindo Castro Nogueira,
Juan Manrique Rodríguez,
José Manuel Miralles García,
Juan Carlos Nevado Ariza

■ AN.41 ROQUETAS – PUNTA ENTINAS

A coastal wetland area with a string of dunes and areas of scrubland.

Main species

Residents: Little Egret, Shelduck, Little Bustard, Kentish Plover, Black-winged Stilt, Avocet, Stone Curlew, Sandwich Tern, Lesser Short-toed Lark, Sardinian Warbler.

Summer visitors: Little Bittern, Montagu's Harrier, Collared Pratincole, Little Tern, Red-necked Nightjar, Bee-eater, Roller, Sand Martin, Yellow Wagtail.

Winter visitors: Black-necked Grebe, Cormorant, Golden Plover, Grey Plover, Lapwing, Whimbrel, Curlew,

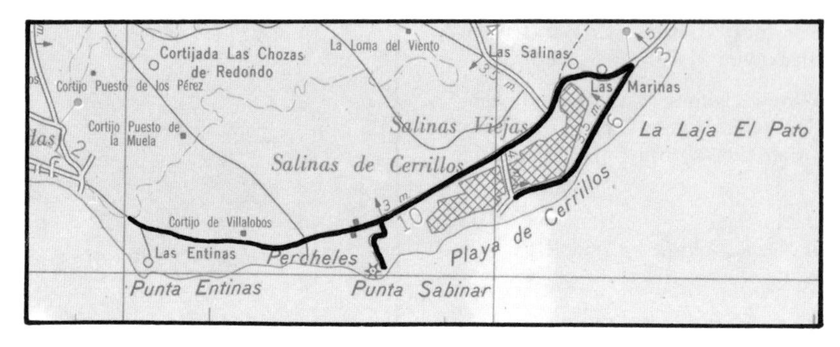

Audouin's Gull, Razorbill, Puffin, Bluethroat.

On passage: Purple Heron, White Stork, Black Stork, Spoonbill, Pochard, Common Scoter, Osprey, Black-tailed Godwit, Redshank, Greenshank, Common Sandpiper, Turnstone, Whiskered Tern, Black Tern, White-winged Black Tern.

Access

Take the N-340 out of Almería in the direction of Málaga. After 14 km turn right for Roquetas de Mar and from there take the track leading to the Urbanización Almerimar, a housing development.

Description

A string of coastal dunes 500 m wide with Phoenician juniper and mastic tree. Inland from here are clay plains subject to flooding, which give way subsequently to coastal steppe. Some areas of these plains were converted into salt pans, which have now been abandoned.

The area is a Paraje Natural or Site of Natural Interest, including a Nature Reserve (1,960 ha).

Recommended routes

The track linking Roquetas de Mar with the Almerimar housing development runs along the edge of the site and, by alternating walks with driving, you will gain a full impression of the area. If you walk around the salt pans, you will find it easier to watch water birds.

Accommodation

The towns in the area provide a good range of accommodation.

Comments

To visit the area you should obtain permission from the Agencia de Medio Ambiente (Centro Residencial Oliveros, Bloque Singular, 2ª planta; 04004 Almería; telephone: 951-237680).

Numbers of birds are at their highest in spring and autumn, during the time of the migration periods.

Segundo Cañadas Albacete,
Hermelindo Castro Nogueira,
Juan Manrique Rodríguez,
José Manuel Miralles García
and Juan Carlos Nevado Ariza.

AN.42 TABERNAS

A typical semidesert landscape with dry riverbeds (*ramblas*) and gullies.

Main species

Residents: Bonelli's Eagle, Kestrel, Peregrine Falcon, Rock Dove, Stone

Curlew, Little Owl, Crag Martin, Black Wheatear, Blue Rock Thrush, Sardinian Warbler, Raven, Rock Sparrow.

Summer visitors: Little Ringed Plover, Turtle Dove, Great Spotted Cuckoo, Scops Owl, Red-necked Nightjar, Alpine Swift, Bee-eater, Roller, Red-rumped Swallow, Rufous Bush Robin, Black-eared Wheatear, Olivaceous Warbler, Spotted Flycatcher, Woodchat Shrike, Trumpeter Finch.

Access

Take the N-340 out of Almería in the direction of Murcia and stop at Tabernas (29 km).

Description

A sub-desertic area lying between the ranges of Filabres and Alhamilla. The landscape is very rugged with dry riverbeds, gullies and gorges. Vegetation on the hillsides is constituted by grasses and small shrubs, while the bottoms of the dry riverbeds are the site of stands of tamarisk and oleander.

This is a Paraje Natural or Site of Natural Interest measuring 11,265 ha.

Recommended routes

The route proposed for this area consists of a 6 km walk taking about 4 hours. Leave your car at the junction of the N-340 with the C-3126 and work your way down to the bottom of the dry riverbed. Walk northwards along this riverbed until reaching the outskirts of the village of Tabernas.

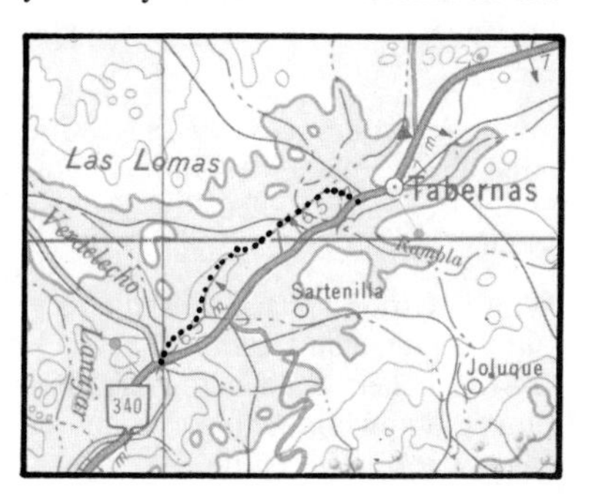

Accommodation

Plenty of accommodation is available in Almería.

Comments

It is worth trying to avoid visiting the area in summer when temperatures are extremely high. On the other hand, in October and November rainfall may be very heavy and dangerous.

To visit the area you should first ask permission at the Agencia de Medio Ambiente (Centro Residencial Oliveros, Bloque Singular, 2ª planta; 04004 Almería; telephone: 951-237680).

Segundo Cañadas Albacete, Hermelindo Castro Nogueira, Juan Manrique Rodríguez, José Manuel Miralles García and Juan Carlos Nevado Ariza.

■ AN.43 LAS AMOLADERAS

Coastal steppe area.

Main species

Residents: Little Bustard, Stone Curlew, Kentish Plover, Black-bellied Sandgrouse, Dupont's Lark, Lesser Short-toed Lark, Thekla Lark, Spectacled Warbler, Sardinian Warbler, Great Grey Shrike, Spanish Sparrow.

Summer visitors: Little Tern, Red-necked Nightjar, Roller, Short-toed Lark, Black-eared Wheatear.

Winter visitors: Whimbrel, Curlew, Audouin's Gull, Trumpeter Finch.

Access

Leave Almería on the N-332 in the direction of Níjar. 4 km after El Alquián, turn right for San José and after 6 km you will come to the steppe area, lying on both sides of the road.

Description

A coastal plain with steppe vegetation and with mastic tree (*Pistacea lentiscus*), jujube (*Ziziphus lotus*) and marram grass (*Ammophila arenaria*) which have colonized the dune areas. It should also be pointed out that plantations of *Agave fourcroides* were established during the 1950s.

The Refugio de Las Amoladeras (900 ha) is a bird reserve administrated by the Spanish Ornithological Society (SEO), and most of this area lies within the Cabo de Gata Natural Park.

Recommended routes

6 km along the San José road, a surfaced track runs off to the left taking you to the landing lights of Almería airport. This track will enable you to visit the whole of the Las Amoladeras area in a couple of hours.

Accommodation

Plenty of accommodation is available in Almería.

Comments

If you wish to visit the reservation area of Refugio de Las Amoladeras, you should ask for permission at the Agencia de Medio Ambiente (Centro Residencial Oliveros, Bloque Singular, 2ª planta; 04004 Almería; telephone: 951-237680).

Segundo Cañadas Albacete, Hermelindo Castro Nogueira, Juan Manrique Rodríguez, José Manuel Miralles García and Juan Carlos Nevado Ariza.

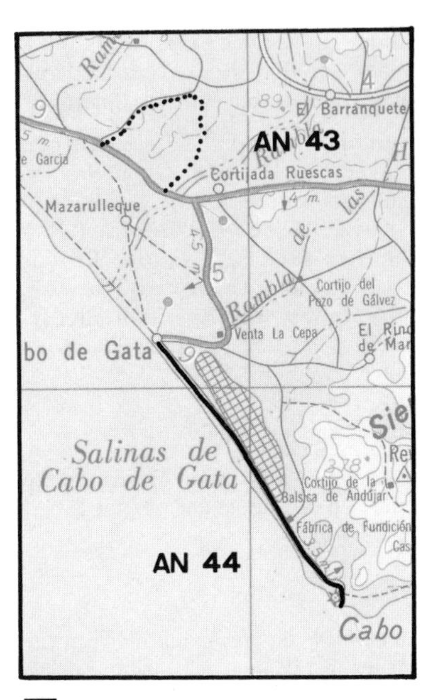

■ AN.44 SALT PANS AT CABO DE GATA AND CABO DE GATA RANGE

Coastal salt pans and a volcanic massif with beaches and cliffs.

Main species

Residents: Shag, Greater Flamingo, Bonelli's Eagle, Peregrine Falcon, Black-winged Stilt, Avocet, Stone Curlew, Yellow-legged Gull, Eagle Owl, Lesser Short-toed Lark, Trumpeter Finch.

Summer visitors: Lesser Kestrel, Collared Pratincole, Little Tern, Alpine Swift, Bee-eater, Roller, Rufous Bush Robin.

Winter visitors: Black-necked Grebe, Little Egret, Grey Heron, Shelduck, Oystercatcher, Golden Plover, Grey Plover, Lapwing, Snipe, Whimbrel, Curlew, Razorbill, Puffin.

On passage: Yelkouan Shearwater, Storm Petrel, Gannet, Purple Heron, White Stork, Black Stork, Spoonbill, Common Scoter, Osprey, Greenshank, Common Sandpiper, Whiskered Tern.

Access

Leave Almería on the N-332 in the direction of Níjar. 4 km after El Alquián turn right onto the road for San José. After a farther 9 km, turn right again for the hamlet of Cabo de Gata.

Description

A stretch of coastline dominated by the Sierra del Cabo de Gata, a range of hills reaching some 500 m in height. The steep hillsides with abundant rocky outcrops are covered with sparse scrubland featuring dwarf fan palm. At the foot of the hills are the salt pans, stretching for some 350 ha.

This area, which has an annual average precipitation of under 200 mm, is the driest place in the Iberian Peninsula.

It is a Natural Park (26,000 ha) with several reserve areas, including the salt pans. These salt pans are managed by an agreement between the salt works (UNESA) and the Agencia de Medio Ambiente (environmental department).

Recommended routes

In the hamlet of Cabo de Gata a road runs parallel to the beach, taking you to the salt pans and subsequently to the Cabo de Gata lighthouse. From this road, a track leaves the buildings of the salt works and takes you to a hide looking out over the salt pans, from where you can see an interesting range of water birds. After the lighthouse, the road is no longer surfaced and will take you to San José, skirting the range of hills and providing opportunities for going for walks in the area.

Accommodation

Plenty of accommodation is available in Almería, and you can also stay in San José.

Comments

To visit the area between the Faro de Vela Blanca (lighthouse) and San José, you should obtain permission from the Agencia de Medio Ambiente (Centro Residencial Oliveros; Bloque Singular, 2ª planta; 04004 Almería; telephone: 951-237680).

Segundo Cañadas Albacete,
Hermelindo Castro Nogueira,
Juan Manrique Rodríguez,
José Manuel Miralles García
and Juan Carlos Nevado Ariza

ARAGON

Ptarmigan
Lagopus mutus

This beautiful inland area takes up the central and largest part of the Ebro valley. It is a region of exceptional variety, and over a distance of a mere 100 km as the crow flies there are alpine meadows and woods of silver fir as well as true semi-desert areas. It is quite a large region, and over half of the small human population lives in Zaragoza. By and large natural surroundings are well conserved, as evidenced by, among other factors, the abundance of birds of prey. The landscapes of Aragon are vast and solitary. For the ornithologist, the groups of birds of greatest interest are undoubtedly those inhabiting the following habitats; woodland and alpine zones in the Pyrenees, and the steppe areas typifying the Ebro valley. Cliffs, mountains, scrubland, riverside woodland, lagoons and fields also help to define and expand the extensive range of birdlife in the area, ensuring that travellers will be well rewarded for their pains.

The 40 selected sites can be combined together into a series of groups. Running from north to south, the first is within the province of Huesca, lying on the spine of the Pyrenees. The mountains are at their lowest on the border with the province of Navarra and their altitudes slowly increase as one moves eastwards towards Catalonia, reaching heights of over 3,300 m with the peaks of Monte Perdido, Posets and Maladeta. In contrast to the French side of the Pyrenees, on the Aragonese side there are very few roads allowing for easy access to these high levels; exceptions to this are the ski resort at Cerler (Benasque valley, AR.12), the spa at Panticosa (AR.6) and the mountain pass of El Portalet (Tena valley, AR.5). In other areas it is necessary to walk for long distances along paths, mostly steep, if you wish to reach the *ibones* (small glacial lakes) and screes; in these areas you will have the company of alpine marmot and chamois, and see birds such as Ptarmigan, Alpine Accentor, Wallcreeper, Alpine Chough and Snow Finch. In addition you will encounter Quail, Skylark, Water Pipit, Black Redstart, Wheatear, Rock Thrush and Linnet, also frequently present at lower levels and in many other mountains in the Iberian Peninsula. This is also the case for certain birds of prey, including Bearded Vulture, Golden Eagle and Kestrel.

In terms of woodland birds, you will find most reward in alpine and subalpine woodland. Beech (*Fagus sylvatica*), silver fir (*Abies alba*), Scots pine (*Pinus sylvestris*) and mountain pine (*Pinus uncinata*) are the preferred habitat for species such as Honey Buzzard, Capercaillie, Woodcock, Tengmalm's Owl, Black Woodpecker, Goldcrest, Treecreeper, Marsh Tit, Crossbill and Bullfinch among others. The high ground, where woods of mountain pine with an undergrowth of

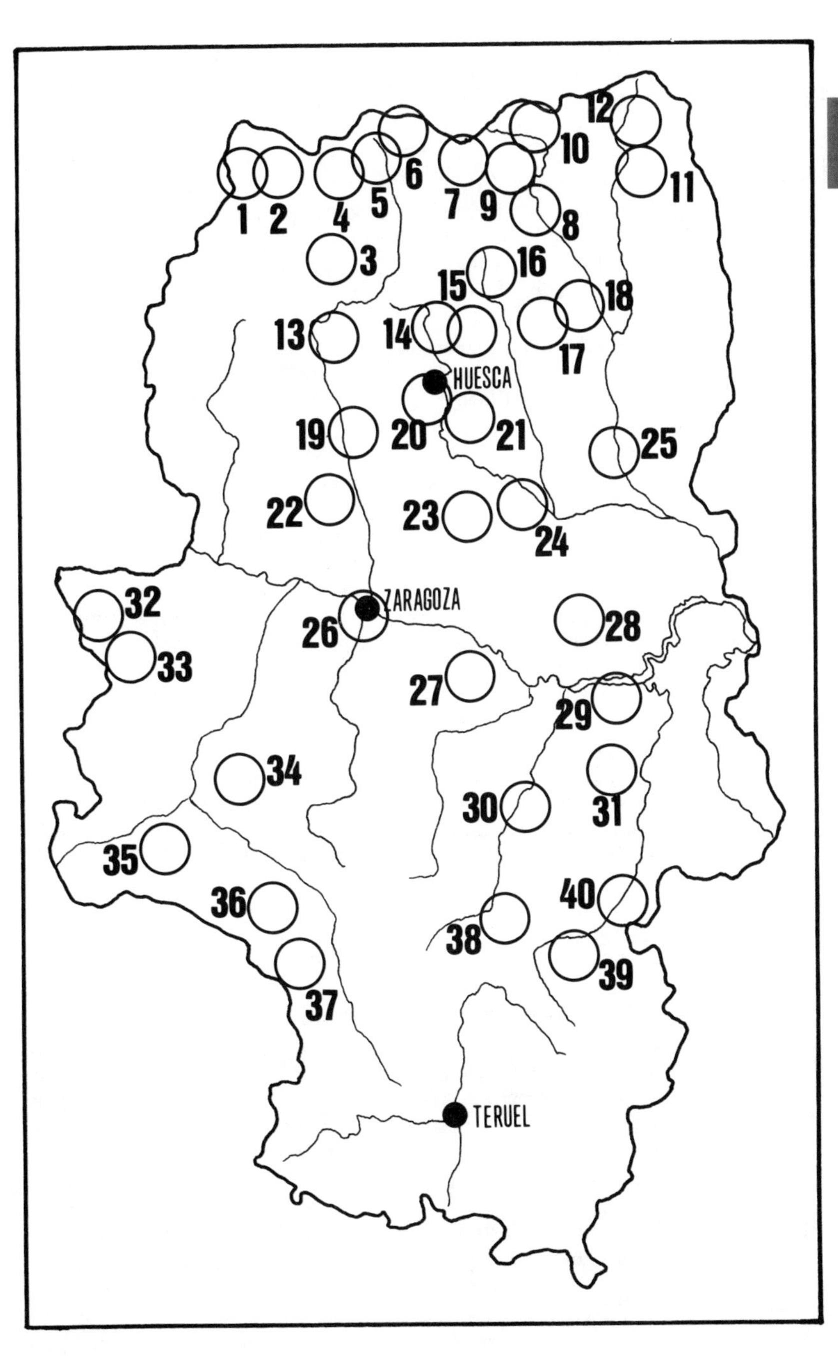

1
2
3
4
5
6
7
8
9
10
11
12
13
14
15
16
17
18
HUESCA
19
20
21
22
23
24
25
ZARAGOZA
26
27
28
29
30
31
32
33
34
35
36
37
38
39
40
TERUEL

alpenrose (*Rhododendron ferrugineum*) and blaeberry (*Vaccinium myrtillus*) give way to heath and alpine meadows, is a good habitat for seeing Grey Partridge, Ring Ouzel and Citril Finch. Particularly highly recommended are the woods at Zuriza (Ansó valley, AR.1), Selva de Oza (Hecho valley, AR.2), Villanúa (AR.4) and various spots in the Benasque valley (AR.12). The central section of the mountains is the site of the Ordesa National Park and the surrounding area (AR.7, AR.9 and AR.10). The area offers tremendous landscapes and many different options, although at certain times of year the area becomes overcrowded.

Valley bottoms in the Pyrenees are also excellent spots for birdwatchers, supporting a wide range of species in which Wryneck, Red-backed Shrike, Whinchat and Yellowhammer coexist with heat-loving species such as Scops Owl, Bee-eater, Golden Oriole and Cirl Bunting. Birds of prey abound, including Red Kite, Egyptian Vulture, Montagu's Harrier and Booted Eagle. During the migration period you may see Black Stork and Crane. The valley of the river Aragón between Puente la Reina and Jaca, known as the Canal de Berdún, and the valley of the river Ara (Ainsa-Bergua, AR.8) are good examples of this kind of habitat.

The ranges lying to the south of the main body of the Pyrenees are known by the generic name of Prepirineo. These include the Las Peñas range (San Juan de la Peña and Peña Oroel, AR.3), the famous *mallos* or needles of Riglos (AR.13), the vast Guara range (AR.14, AR.15, AR.16, AR.17 and AR.18) and the impressive massif of Turbón (AR.11). These places go to make up a world apart, rugged, isolated, spectacular and now dotted with ruined villages, abandoned fields and areas of reestablished woodland, including species running from scrubby holm oak (*Quercus rotundifolia*) and Lusitanian oak (*Quercus faginea*) to silver fir and beech. For the birdwatcher, perhaps the most interesting feature of this area are the narrow ravines carved by mountain streams, along the sides of which roads in the area frequently run. The towering cliffs of the ravines are home to Bearded Vulture, Egyptian Vulture, Griffon Vulture (in large numbers), Golden Eagle, Bonelli's Eagle, Peregrine Falcon, Eagle Owl, Alpine Swift, Crag Martin, Black Redstart, Blue Rock Thrush, Chough, Raven, Rock Sparrow and, in winter, Alpine Accentor and Wallcreeper.

A proportionately larger part of Aragon corresponds to the Ebro basin. The area is more highly populated and cultivated, and not as interesting. The steppe areas of Aragon are very well known; they coincide with the central plains lying on either side of the Ebro, where rainfall is at its lowest. Here meagre dry cereal crops are interspersed with areas of low-lying, very open scrubland, frequently growing on salt marshes and gypsum. These areas, making for impressive landscapes, also support extremely interesting plant life as well as being the habitat of species such as Montagu's Harrier, Lesser Kestrel, Little Bustard, Great Bustard (now very rare), Stone Curlew, Black-bellied Sandgrouse, Pin-tailed Sandgrouse, Little Owl, Dupont's Lark, Calandra Lark, Short-toed Lark, Lesser Short-toed Lark, Crested Lark, Tawny Pipit, Black-eared Wheatear, Fan-tailed Warbler, Great Grey Shrike and Corn Bunting. Other species come in winter, such as Red Kite, Hen Harrier, Merlin and other birds of prey, and during the autumn passage you may come across groups of Dotterel. Of the many possible sites, we would recommend Sasos de Gurrea (AR.19), the areas surrounding the ponds at Alcañiz (AR.31), Belchite (AR.27) and Los Monegros (AR.28).

The extending of irrigation systems all too often poses a serious threat to the survival of these habitats and the birdlife they support.

As soon as you move slightly to the north or south of the steppe area you will inevitably encounter small ranges of hills which are typically relatively flat and badly eroded. On the cliffs, gullies and slopes you will see Egyptian Vulture, Golden Eagle, Kestrel, Peregrine Falcon, Rock Dove, Stock Dove, Eagle Owl, Thekla Lark, Crag Martin, Black Wheatear, Blue Rock Thrush, Dartford Warbler, Spectacled Warbler, Chough, Raven, Rock Sparrow, Rock Bunting, Ortolan Bunting and many other species. Meanwhile, in the Aleppo pine (*Quercus halepensis*) woods, where undergrowth consists of kermes oak (*Quercus coccifera*), rosemary (*Rosmarinus officinalis*) and other Mediterranean shrubs, you may see birds of prey such as Black Kite, Short-toed Eagle, Goshawk, Sparrowhawk, Buzzard, Booted Eagle, Hobby and Long-eared Owl. Other more or less habitual species include Turtle Dove, Great Spotted Cuckoo, Red-necked Nightjar, Woodlark, Subalpine Warbler, Sardinian Warbler, Orphean Warbler, Bonelli's Warbler, Firecrest, Woodchat Shrike, Crossbill and Cirl Bunting. Examples of these areas are the Tramaced range (AR.21), the Zuera-Castejón hills (AR.22), the Sierra de Alcubierre range (AR.23) and the Arcos range (gorges of the river Martín, AR.30).

In the dry regions at hand, the typical irrigation ponds and occasional natural lagoons and ponds not only provide an interesting contrast in the landscape but also widen the range of fauna considerably. Of the many existing wetland areas, we recommend the La Sotonera reservoir (AR.19), the Alberca de Cortés and the Alberca de Loreto, near Huesca (AR.20), the large lagoon at Sariñena (AR.24), the unusual lagoons at Chiprana (AR.29) and the saltwater ponds at Alcañiz (AR.31). Other wetland areas are stretches of the rivers Cinca (AR.25) and Ebro with their abandoned meanders (*galachos*) at Juslibol and La Alfranca, near Zaragoza (AR.26). In these areas, look out for nesting species such as Little Grebe, Great Crested Grebe, Black-necked Grebe, Little Bittern, Night Heron, Cattle Egret, Little Egret, Purple Heron, White Stork, Marsh Harrier, Shelduck (a recent colonizer), Red-crested Pochard, Water Rail, Black-winged Stilt, Little Ringed Plover, Kentish Plover, Kingfisher, Sand Martin, Reed Warbler, Great Reed Warbler and Penduline Tit. In winter and during the migration season many other waterbirds make their appearance, especially ducks and waders.

The southernmost part of Aragon includes a major geographical feature, the Sistema Ibérico or Iberian System. While the ornithological interest of the area is not comparable to that of the Pyrenees, it still has many attractions. To the far northwest is the solitary peak of the Sierra del Moncayo (AR.32 and AR.33) which rises up to 2,135 m, allowing for the growth of residual beech woodland on the northern slopes and the presence of nesting species typical of northernmost Spain such as Grey Partridge, Woodcock, Tree Pipit and Red-backed Shrike. The other mountains in the range scarcely reach 2,000 m with the ranges of Gúdar and Javalambre, both in the Teruel region. Here pine forests dominate and areas above the treeline are very small. Other areas of extensive pine forest which would be worth visiting are the Montes

Universales and the Sierra de Albarracín, both of which lie close to the city of Teruel. The foothills of the Iberian System are more interesting, featuring rivers which have carved gorges. These gorges, sometimes of great length and most spectacular in appearance, always abound with birds of prey and other cliff-dwelling species (Egyptian Vulture, Griffon Vulture, Blue Rock Thrush, Chough, etc). Good examples of this are the gorges of the river Jalón near Calatayud (AR.34), those of the river Piedra near Nuévalos (AR.35), the gorge of the river Martín (AR.30), the source of the river Pitarque (AR.39) and above all the gorge of the river Guadalope (AR.40).

Another characteristic feature of the Sistema Ibérico are the extensive flat or rolling areas lying between mountains at heights usually over 1,000 m. Here vegetation is semi-arid and birdlife is typical of steppe areas, including Skylark and Wheatear as well as Little Bustard, Stone Curlew, Black-bellied Sandgrouse, Short-toed Lark and particularly Dupont's Lark. Examples of these areas are Belmonte de Calatayud (AR.34), the Gallocanta lake (AR.36), the flat-topped plateau at Blancas (AR.37) and those at Sant Just (AR.38), although the latter is of greater interest for observing passerines on autumn passage. Special mention should be made of the lake at Gallocanta, an absolute jewel. It is a large lake and, in the years when water level is high, vast quantities of ducks and Coot congregate there in winter and during the spring it is a breeding ground for species such as Black-necked Grebe, Marsh Harrier, Gadwall, Red-crested Pochard, Pochard, Lapwing, Black-winged Stilt, Avocet, Kentish Plover, Gull-billed Tern and Whiskered Tern. At migration time, it is a resting place for numerous waders and above all Crane, which at times reach numbers of several tens of thousands.

■ AR.1 ANSÓ VALLEY

A high mountain area.

Main species

Residents: Red Kite, Bearded Vulture, Griffon Vulture, Goshawk, Golden Eagle, Grey Partridge, Black Woodpecker, Alpine Accentor, Dartford Warbler, Alpine Chough, Chough, Rock Sparrow, Snow Finch, Citril Finch, Rock Bunting.

Summer visitors: Honey Buzzard, Egyptian Vulture, Short-toed Eagle, Montagu's Harrier, Booted Eagle, Alpine Swift, Crag Martin, Rock Thrush, Subalpine Warbler, Orphean Warbler, Wallcreeper.

Winter visitors: Hen Harrier.

On passage: Black Stork.

Access

Take the N-240 to Berdún which is 8 km from Puente la Reina and 27 km from Jaca.

Description

A narrow, winding valley with large expanses of woodland, above all pine woods and beech woods. There are also rocky gorges and cliffs, and on the higher ground there are alpine pastures.

Recommended routes

The route described here consists of a car journey running all the way along the valley from Berdún to Zuriza. The most interesting points are the following:

1) As you leave Berdún you will see Griffon Vulture, Egyptian Vulture, Red Kite, Black Kite, Booted Eagle and, in the fields between Berdún and Biniés, Montagu's Harrier.

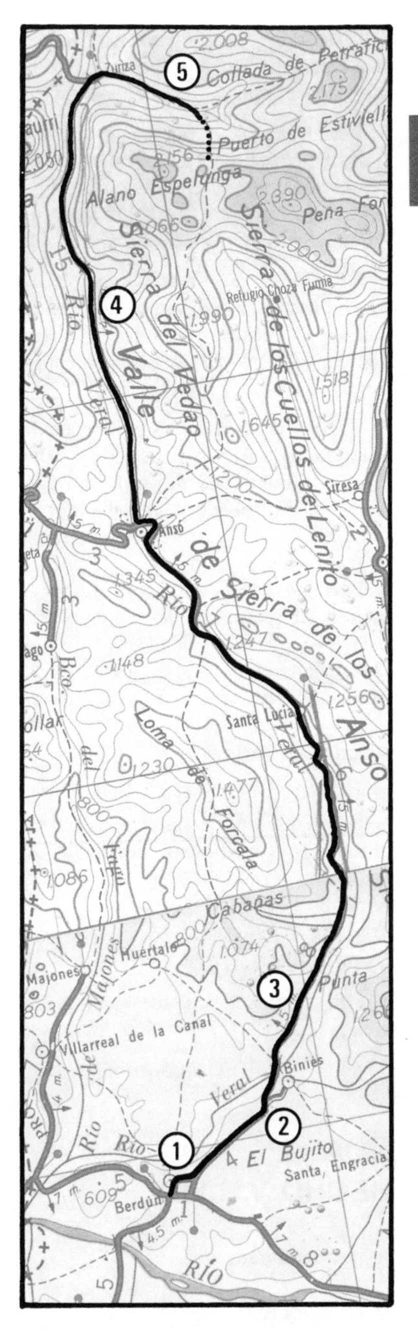

2) Bridge at the entrance to the Biniés ravine: a short walk around the area

near the bridge will enable you to see Bee-eater and various species of warblers and buntings.

3) Foz de Biniés: stopping at the exit from the first tunnel will allow you to see a wide range of cliff-dwelling birdlife, running from birds of prey to Alpine Swift, Crag Martin and Rock Sparrow.

4) The road between Ansó and Zuriza has several interesting places where you can stop at will; among other raptors, you may see Golden Eagle.

5) Zuriza: take the track which leads along the Petrafitxa ravine, crosses the river and continues upwards through the woodland; leave your vehicle in a place which will allow for easy access to the upper edge of the tree line; a walk in the woods will provide opportunities of seeing Black Woodpecker, Citril Finch, Grey Partridge, Ring Ouzel and, in the rocky areas, Rock Thrush, Wallcreeper and Snow Finch.

Accommodation

Tourism is highly developed in the area, giving rise to plenty of possibilities. We recommend El Rincón de Emilio in Berdún and, in Ansó, Fonda Aísa and Posada Magoria.

Comments

The best time of year for visiting the area is spring.

David Serrano Larraz

■ AR.2 HECHO VALLEY

A high mountain area.

Main species

Residents: Red Kite, Bearded Vulture, Griffon Vulture, Golden Eagle, Ptarmigan, Grey Partridge, Black Woodpecker, Alpine Accentor, Marsh Tit, Chough, Alpine Chough, Rock Sparrow, Snow Finch, Citril Finch, Bullfinch, Rock Bunting.

Summer visitors: Egyptian Vulture, Short-toed Eagle, Booted Eagle, Alpine Swift, Crag Martin, Rock Thrush, Ring Ouzel, Red-backed Shrike, Wallcreeper.

Access

Take the C-134 from Jaca to Puente la Reina (19 km), from where you join the minor road for Hecho (26 km).

Description

A large Pyrenean valley, the head of which is formed by a sizeable ravine. The more open parts of the valley are taken up by fields and pastures, while the valley sides are covered by extensive woodland consisting of pine and beech. The high parts of the valley, at over 2,000 m, are taken up by alpine meadows.

Recommended routes

This route consists of a car journey along the road running up the valley. You can make stops along the valley

bottom to watch Red Kite, Short-toed Eagle, Spotless Starling, Dartford Warbler and Red-backed Shrike. After the village of Siresa you will enter the gorge, where you may see Bearded Vulture, Golden Eagle, Egyptian Vulture, Griffon Vulture, Alpine Swift, Alpine Chough, Rock Thrush, etc. Farther up, in the area known as Selva de Oza, you will see forest birds including Black Woodpecker and Marsh Tit.

To reach the high ground, some 4 km after Siresa take the well-marked right turn for Gabardito. From here walk up to the peak of Visuarín; on the way you will have sightings of Alpine Chough, Snow Finch, Wallcreeper, Ring Ouzel, Citril Finch, etc.

Accommodation

There are plenty of hotels and restaurants in the area; examples are Hotel Castillo d'Acher in Siresa or Hotel Lo Foratón and Hostal La Val in Hecho. In Selva de Oza there is a campsite which is open during the summer and for major public holidays. In summer you may find that all accommodation is full.

Manuel Serrano Larraz

■ AR.3 SAN JUAN DE LA PEÑA AND PEÑA OROEL RANGES

A low mountain area.

Main species

Residents: Red Kite, Bearded Vulture, Griffon Vulture, Goshawk, Sparrowhawk, Golden Eagle, Peregrine Falcon, Capercaillie (rare), Black Woodpecker, Goldcrest, Firecrest, tits, Chough, Crossbill.

Summer visitors: Black Kite, Egyptian Vulture, Short-toed Eagle, Booted Eagle, Alpine Swift, Crag Martin.

Winter visitors: Alpine Accentor, Redwing, Marsh Tit, Wallcreeper, Treecreeper, Citril Finch, Bullfinch.

Access

Take the C-125 from Jaca to Bernués (17 km) going over the Oroel mountain pass. A minor road leads from Bernués to San Juan de la Peña (11 km). The stretch of road near the Oroel pass is very winding and badly surfaced, but nonetheless takes you through interesting areas.

Another possibility is to leave Jaca on the C-134 and after 9 km take the turning for Santa Cruz de la Serós, and from there a surfaced track to San Juan de la Peña (12 km).

Description

The Sierra de las Peñas, a mountain range where altitudes do not reach more than 2,000 m, has a complicated system of contours featuring high, rocky cliffs. The valley sides are covered with various kinds of woodland, particularly pine woods, while the surrounding flat land is given over to crops.

Recommended routes

Route A is a car journey which can be undertaken in the course of a morning, although it is worthwhile spending a whole day in the area. The route starts in Jaca and takes you to San Juan de la Peña and Puerto Oroel. The most interesting places are the following:

1) Confluence of the Atarés ravine with the river Aragón: a good area for spotting Short-toed Eagle, Booted Eagle, Red Kite, Black Kite, Goshawk, etc.

2) Santa Cruz de la Serós: from here you can command a view of the north

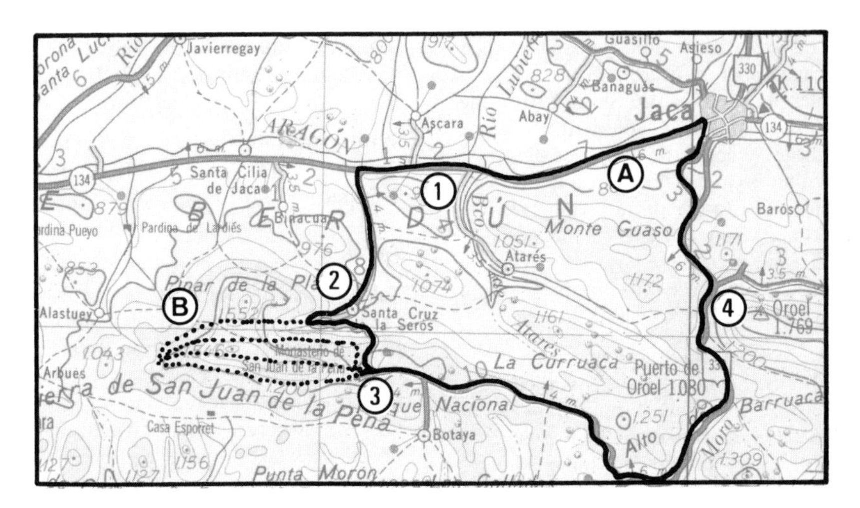

face of San Juan de la Peña, where you will see Griffon Vulture, Egyptian Vulture, Bearded Vulture, Golden Eagle and Peregrine Falcon.

3) Monasterio de San Juan de la Peña: the old monastery building provides nesting sites for Alpine Swift, Crag Martin and Chough. Around both the old monastery and the new monastery you will see some interesting species of woodland birds.

4) Oroel mountain pass: a good place for seeing large numbers of birds of prey, particularly vultures.

Route B is a walk from the new monastery at San Juan de la Peña to the Ermita de San Salvador, a chapel. The route runs along the edge of the rock face, or alternatively along a track running through woods of pine and silver fir. On reaching the chapel, work your way down to the Cuculo mountain saddle and from there walk down the Carbonera ravine to the road. This last stretch takes you through wonderful mixed woodland consisting of beech and silver fir where you may see Black Woodpecker. The whole route can be done in 5 hours, although by using two cars you can save yourself the last 6 km of road walking.

Apart from these routes, you can also take short walks and explore the areas of rock and woodland, since the Sierra de las Peñas provides many alternatives of this nature.

Accommodation

Jaca offers plenty of accommodation in the form of hotels and campsites, although during the summer it is worthwhile booking in advance.

César Pedrocchi Renault

■ AR.4 VILLANÚA – CANFRANC ESTACIÓN

A high mountain area.

Main species

Residents: Bearded Vulture, Griffon Vulture, Golden Eagle, Grey Partridge, Alpine Accentor, Ring Ouzel, Alpine Chough, Chough, Citril Finch, Crossbill, Rock Bunting.

Summer visitors: Egyptian Vulture, Short-toed Eagle, Alpine Swift, Crag Martin, Rock Thrush, Wallcreeper.

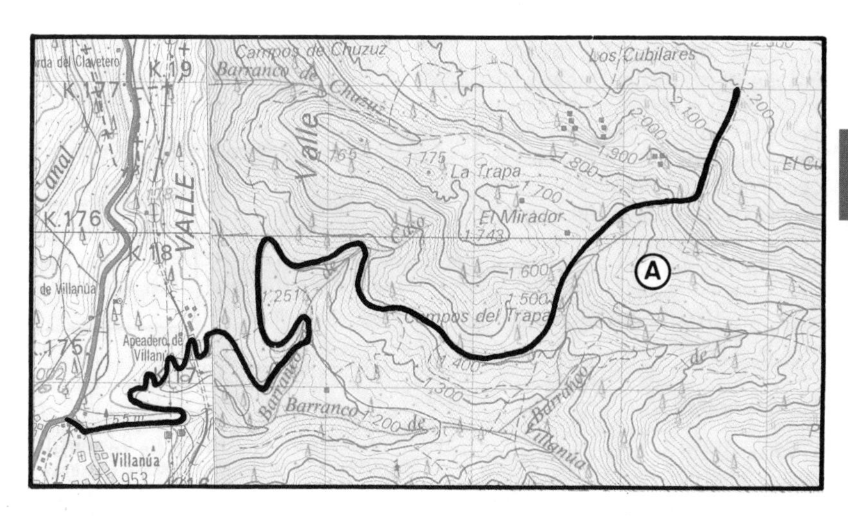

Access

Take the N-330 out of Jaca. Villanúa is 14 km from Jaca, and the Canfranc ski resort 22 km.

Description

A high Pyrenean mountain area, where the steep valley sides are covered with pine woods, giving way to alpine pastures at higher altitudes, where there are also many rocky outcrops.

Recommended routes

Route A begins in Villanúa, close to the bridge over the river Aragón. From here take a surfaced track which immediately becomes a forestry road. After 4 km you will reach a fork; take the left-hand road which after 9 km will bring you to the plains at Trapal. To begin with the track runs across meadows with scattered woodland and subsequently through dense pine woods where you may see Short-toed Eagle, Red Kite, Citril Finch, Crossbill and Rock Bunting. Leave your car on the Trapal plains and from there walk up to Peña Collarada. You will come across a rock wall which can be traversed without difficulty via a breech, bringing you out on the alpine pastures. As you climb, you will see Grey Partridge, Ptarmigan, Alpine Accentor, Snow Finch, Wallcreeper and Alpine Chough. You may also see Bearded Vulture or Golden Eagle, which often fly over the area.

Route B is a walk which can be done in 3 or 4 hours. Between the end of the Ibón de Ip reservoir and Canfranc-Estación (the ski resort), cross a bridge and continue along the track through

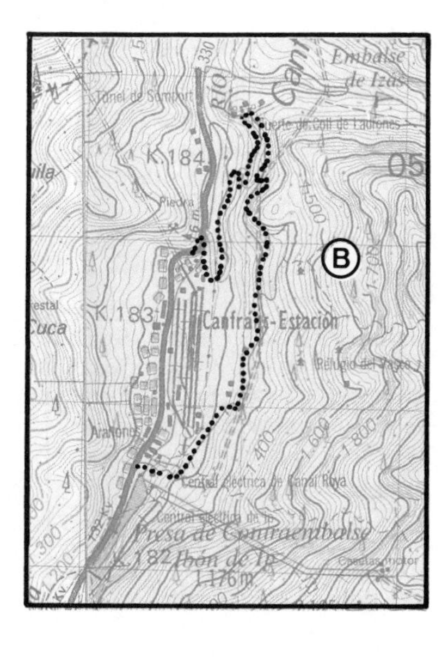

coniferous woodland. The track terminates by some pastures from which a marked path (GR-11) takes you down the steep Coll de Ladrones, skirting the bases of a series of cliffs. Once there take the track leading to Canfranc-Estación (the ski resort), running along the left bank of the river Aragón. This route allows for the exploration of large rock faces and combines sightings of cliff-dwelling birds and woodland birds.

Accommodation

A wide range of accommodation is available in the area. There are also campsites in Canfranc, Jaca and Santa Cilia de Jaca.

José Luis Rivas González and David Serrano Larraz

■ AR.5 TENA VALLEY

A high mountain area.

Main species

Residents: Red Kite, Bearded Vulture, Goshawk, Golden Eagle, Peregrine Falcon, Ptarmigan, Grey Partridge, Woodcock, Tawny Owl, Black Woodpecker, Dipper, Alpine Accentor, Marsh Tit, Wallcreeper, Treecreeper, Alpine Chough, Snow Finch, Citril Finch, Bullfinch.

Summer visitors: Honey Buzzard, Booted Eagle, Water Pipit, Tree Pipit, Ring Ouzel, Whinchat, Whitethroat, Spotted Flycatcher, Yellowhammer.

Access

The C-136 runs the entire length of the Tena valley, covering 45 km between Sabiñánigo and El Portalet.

Description

The Tena valley, located in the central Pyrenees, consists of a mountainous landscape of great beauty. There are many woods, constituted by beech, oak, silver fir and pine, while at higher altitudes there are also hay fields and pastures. Also worth mentioning are the rocky cliffs and tarns, known locally as *ibones*.

Recommended routes

Route A is a car journey of some 30 km going from Biescas to the Puerto del Portalet, a mountain pass. The greatest points of interest are the following:

1) Asieso ravine: a wooded valley where many woodland birds can be seen.

2) Peña Telera slopes: a high mountain setting with pastures and rocky cliffs.

3) Búbal reservoir: it is well worth working your way along the left bank of this reservoir between Hoz de Jaca and El Pueyo.

4) Escarra forest: a walk through this oak wood will enable you to see birds typical of this habitat.

5) Formigal forest: on the edges of this beech wood and the neighbouring fields you may see Honey Buzzard, Grey Partridge, Tree Pipit and Whinchat.

6) El Portalet: alpine meadows and rocky outcrops where you may see Ptarmigan, Snow Finch, Wallcreeper, Alpine Accentor, Alpine Chough, Water Pipit, etc.

Route B is a walk taking you to the high ground of the Tena valley. From Sallent de Gállego work your way up to the La Sarra reservoir, and from there walk along a well-marked path to reach the *ibón* or tarn of Respumoso, currently dammed, in a couple of hours. The most interesting species you will see on this walk are those typical of high altitude habitats.

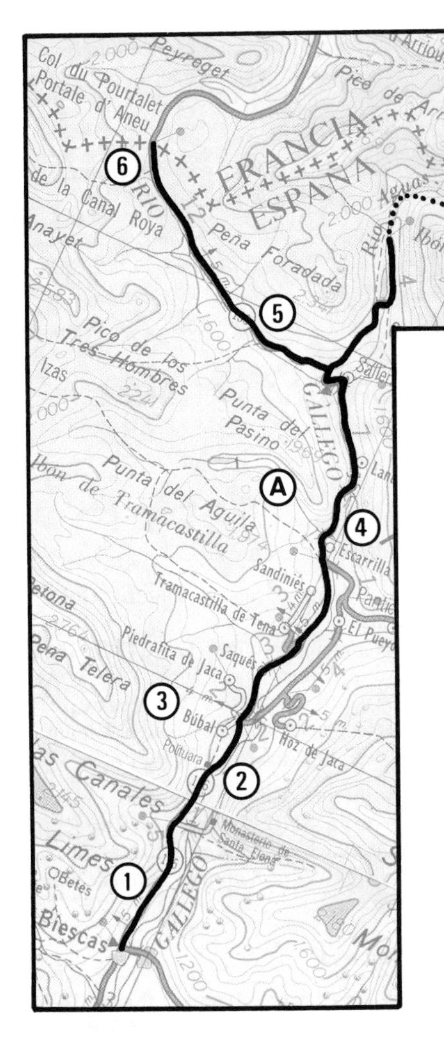

AR.6 PANTICOSA

A high mountain area surrounding the spa town of Panticosa.

Main species

Residents: Bearded Vulture, Golden Eagle, Ptarmigan, Dipper, Alpine Accentor, Wallcreeper, Alpine Chough, Citril Finch, Crossbill.

Summer visitors: Water Pipit, Rock Thrush, Wheatear.

Access

Take the C-136 from Sabiñánigo to Sandinies (28 km), from where you take the minor road to Panticosa and the Balneario or spa (10 km).

Description

The Balneario de Panticosa lies at the foot of Las Argualas, a massif of characteristically glacial origin reaching over 2,800 m in height. The surrounding area is taken up by thinned pine woodland with undergrowth consisting of alpenrose and blaeberry, giving way to mountain pastures at higher levels. There are also many small lakes and some remarkable rock formations.

Accommodation

Tourism in the area is highly developed, meaning that in summer accommodation may be full.

Comments

The best times of year for visiting the area are autumn and spring.

Oscar Díez Sánchez
and Juan Antonio Gil Gallus

Recommended routes

The route proposed consists of an ascent, on foot, from the spa to the lakes at Bachimaña. The walk can be undertaken in roughly 1½ hours. Take the track which starts at the river Caldares and crosses an area of pine woodland where forest-dwelling passerines can be seen. At the Cascada del Fraile, a waterfall, you will reach the top of the treeline; the path then continues up a steep slope to the lakes known as Ibón de Bachimaña Bajo and Ibón de Bachimaña Alto, and subsequently to the Lagos Azules (2,380 m). At this second set of tarns is a mountain refuge from which you can climb up to the Collado del Infierno, a mountain pass at 2,721 m. On the way up you may see Ptarmigan and Wallcreeper.

There are other alternative routes with similar characteristics, also leaving from the Balneario de Panticosa.

Accommodation

Tourism in the surrounding area is well developed, giving rise to a wide range of accommodation. For those on small budgets, the youth hostel in Pueyo de Jaca, the mountain refuge located in Panticosa itself (a stone house) and the Camping Escarra, a campsite in Escarrilla, are all recommended.

Comments

The best times of year for visiting the area are spring and summer.

Oscar Díez Sánchez
and Juan Antonio Gil Gallus

■ AR.7 ORDESA NATIONAL PARK

A high mountain area.

Main species

Residents: Bearded Vulture, Golden Eagle, Ptarmigan, Grey Partridge, Common Sandpiper, Eagle Owl, Black Woodpecker, Water Pipit, Dipper, Alpine Accentor, Wallcreeper, Treecreeper, Alpine Chough, Chough, Snow Finch, Crossbill, Bullfinch.

Summer visitors: Egyptian Vulture, Alpine Swift, Crag Martin, Ring Ouzel, Red-backed Shrike, Citril Finch, Yellowhammer, Ortolan Bunting.

Access

Where the C-140 runs through Torla (27 km from Biescas and 40 km from Sabiñánigo), a minor road takes you to Ordesa, where there is a car park (10 km).

Description

The Ordesa gorge is located at the foot of Tres Sorores, a massif which reaches its maximum height with Monte Perdido (3,355 m). In some places the cliffs forming the walls of the gorge reach more than 300 m, and the lower slopes are covered with a large variety of woodland. The upper parts of the gorge

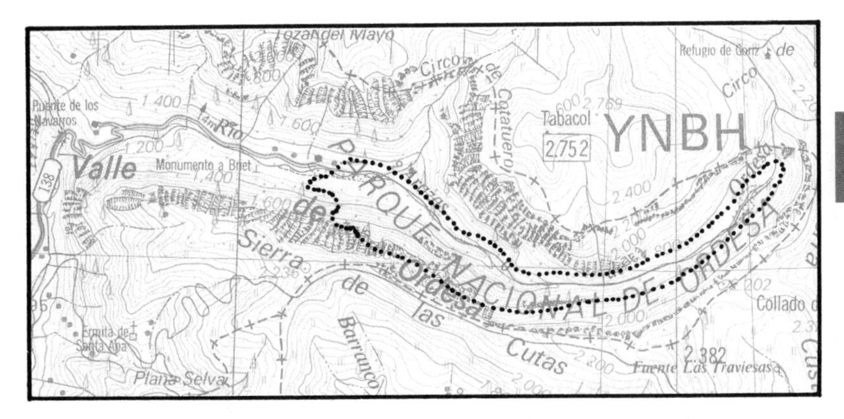

are remarkable for extensive pastures and rocky areas.

The gorge forms the best known and most visited part of the Parque Nacional de Ordesa y Monte Perdido, which in total covers an area of some 15,000 ha. Other areas of this National Park feature in two of the following sections, Añisclo and Pineta.

Recommended routes

The recommended route is a walk of some 17 km, meaning that a full day is needed to complete the itinerary. Leave the car park, following the signs for Senda de los Cazadores, and walk up to the vantage point of Calcilarruego, passing through woods of beech and silver fir where, among other woodland species, you may see Black Woodpecker. From the vantage point, the track continues along Faja de Pelay, running along the side of the valley to the Soaso cirque. In the pine woods you will have sightings of Citril Finch and Crossbill, and on the nearby cliffs you should see Alpine Swift, Crag Martin, Chough and, with luck, Golden Eagle and Bearded Vulture. At Soaso there are extensive alpine meadows where you will see Wheatear, Black Redstart and Water Pipit. Return by the route popular with most visitors to the area, taking you down past the Gradas de Soaso, Bosque de Hayas (a beech wood) and Las Cascadas (waterfalls). This route should only be undertaken during the summer, since in winter it is dangerous to cross the Fajas de Pelay where there may be risk of avalanches.

In addition to this route, you can also go for interesting walks in the Ordesa area, taking you to Cotatuero, La Carriata, etc. Another possible route consists of working your way up the Bujaruelo valley: at the Puente de los Navarros, a bridge 4 km from Torla, you can turn onto a track and drive to the Mesón de San Nicolás, a restaurant, from where it is possible to walk to Ordiso or the banks of the river Otal. The birds you will see on these routes are the same as those in Ordesa itself.

Accommodation

In Torla there is plenty of accommodation, including a campsite.

Comments

Since Ordesa is a National Park, there are strict regulations about visiting which you should keep to at all times. It is better to avoid the months of July and August, when the number of visitors is at its height.

José María Cereza Abadías

AR

AR.8 AINSA – BERGUA

A mountain area.

Main species

Residents: Red Kite, Sparrowhawk, Golden Eagle, Peregrine Falcon, Black Woodpecker, Thekla Lark, Dipper, Blue Rock Thrush, Sardinian Warbler, Chiffchaff, Marsh Tit, Chough, Alpine Chough, Rock Sparrow, Bullfinch.

Summer visitors: Honey Buzzard, Black Kite, Egyptian Vulture, Short-toed Eagle, Booted Eagle, Hobby, Alpine Swift, Wryneck, Tawny Pipit, Orphean Warbler, Spotted Flycatcher, Red-backed Shrike, Ortolan Bunting.

Winter visitors: Wallcreeper.

Access

From the C-138 where it runs through Ainsa (64 km from Barbastro).

Description

A mountain range through which the river Ara runs. The landscape is dramatic with steeply sloping mountainsides and some limestone massifs with interesting cliff formations. Vegetation is very varied in this transitional area, with fields, pastures and woodland consisting of holm oak, Lusitanian oak, beech, pine, etc.

Recommended routes

This route consists of a car journey of some 35 km. Take the C-138 out of Ainsa for Torla, and when you get to Fiscal turn left onto the track for Bergua. The most interesting places are the following:

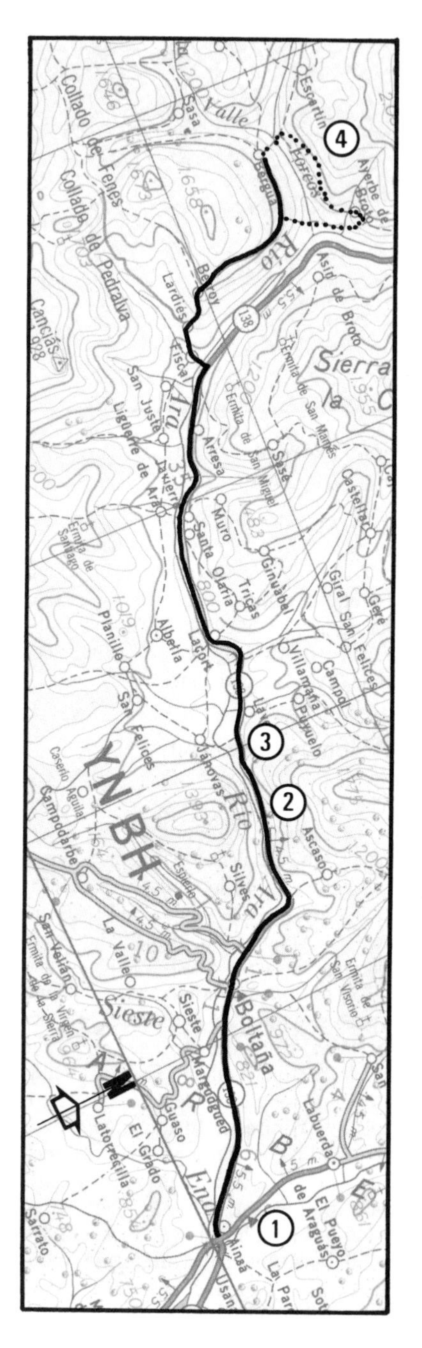

1) Ainsa: an area of fields and grazing land with scattered trees and patches of scrub where you will see various birds of prey, warblers and buntings as well as Bee-eater and Wryneck.

2) Balupor tunnel: a ravine carved by the river Ara where, among other cliff-dwelling birds, you will see Golden Eagle, Egyptian Vulture, Alpine Swift, Chough, etc.

3) Strata at Jánovas: a curious geological formation where, in addition to the birds mentioned for point 2, you will see birds inhabiting waterside habitats such as Dipper and Grey Wagtail.

4) Forcos ravine: from Bergua you can walk along this ravine on a path which leaves the village and works its way up through a large expanse of oak to cross the head of the valley and subsequently descend through an area of beech and pine wood. This walk is interesting in that you can see woodland species such as Black Woodpecker, Marsh Tit and Bullfinch.

Accommodation

Tourism in the area is highly developed, although you may have problems finding accommodation in July and August. Highly recommended are the Hotel Sánchez in Ainsa and the campsites at Boltaña and Fiscal.

Oscar Díez Sánchez and Juan Antonio Gil Gallus

■ AR.9 AÑISCLO CANYON

A mountain area.

Main species

Residents: Bearded Vulture, Goshawk, Golden Eagle, Peregrine Falcon, Ptarmigan, Grey Partridge, Black Woodpecker, Grey Wagtail, Dipper, Alpine Accentor, Goldcrest, Marsh Tit, Alpine Chough, Chough, Bullfinch.

Summer visitors: Egyptian Vulture, Alpine Swift, Crag Martin, Water Pipit, Rock Thrush, Ring Ouzel, Red-backed Shrike, Yellowhammer.

Access

Take the C-138 to Ainsa (64 km from Barbastro), from where you join the minor road for Bielsa. On reaching the village of Escalona (10 km) you will find a clearly marked turning for Ereta

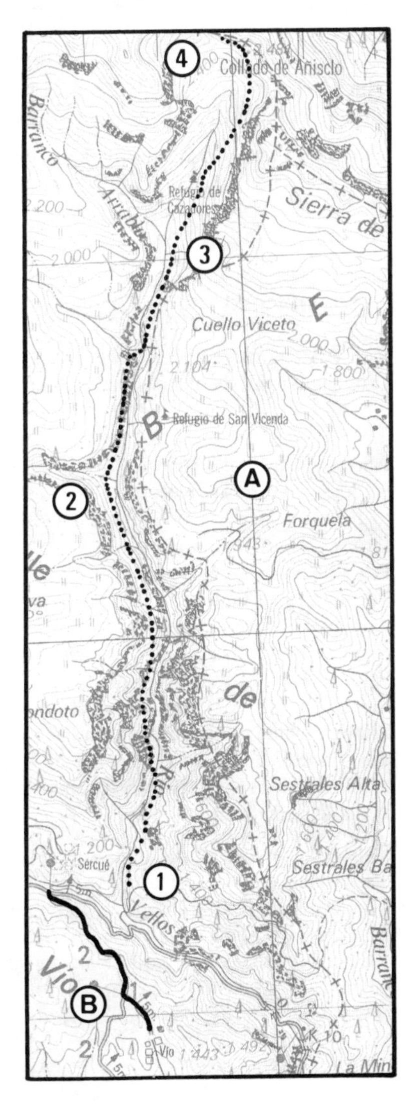

AR

de Bies and the Ermita de San Urbez, a chapel in Añisclo itself (13 km).

Description

The Añisclo gorge, carved by the river Bellos, is one of the best conserved gorges in the Pyrenees. It is remarkable for the spectacular rock walls of Sestrales and Mondoto as well as the dense woodland constituted by beech, pine and silver fir and, dominating the whole, the massif of Tres Sorores which reaches its highest point with Monte Perdido at 3,355 m.

This gorge, along with the valleys of Ordesa, Escuaín and Pineta, forms part of the Parque Nacional de Ordesa y Monte Perdido.

Recommended routes

Route A begins at the car park in San Urbez and consists of a walk along the gorge. You will need a full day, although you can pitch a tent on the Añisclo saddle and return the following day. The most interesting species to be seen in the woodland are Goshawk, Sparrowhawk, Black Woodpecker, Ring Ouzel, Bullfinch, Marsh Tit and Goldcrest. Rocky areas may give opportunities of seeing Golden Eagle, Egyptian Vulture, Peregrine Falcon, Bearded Vulture, Alpine Swift, Rock Thrush, Chough and Alpine Chough, while on the high ground near the Añisclo saddle you may see Ptarmigan, Wallcreeper, Alpine Accentor, Water Pipit and Snow Finch.

Route B consists of a car journey to the village of Vio, where there is a wonderful vantage point commanding the gorge. Between Vio and Buerba the uncultivated land and holm oak and Lusitanian oak woods are the site of Goshawk, Hobby, Wryneck, Red-backed Shrike, Yellowhammer and Dartford Warbler.

Accommodation

Tourism in the area is highly developed, giving rise to numerous hotels and campsites, which may however be full in the months of July and August. We recommend the Hotel Sánchez in Ainsa and the Camping Peña Montañesa, a campsite in Labuerda.

Comments

The best times of year for visiting the area are spring and autumn.

Juan Antonio Gil Gallus
and Oscar Díez Sánchez

■ AR.10 PINETA VALLEY

A high mountain area.

Main species

Residents: Bearded Vulture, Griffon Vulture, Goshawk, Golden Eagle, Peregrine Falcon, Ptarmigan, Capercaillie, Tengmalm's Owl, Black Woodpecker, Alpine Accentor, Dipper, Marsh Tit, Wallcreeper, Treecreeper, Alpine Chough, Chough, Raven, Snow Finch, Bullfinch.

Summer visitors: Nightjar, Alpine Swift, Water Pipit, Rock Thrush, Ring Ouzel, Red-backed Shrike, Siskin.

Access

Take the C-138 to Ainsa, where you then join a minor road to Bielsa (34 km). From Bielsa take another minor road to the Parador Nacional de Monte Perdido, a luxury hotel run by the Spanish government located at the bottom of the Pineta valley (10 km).

Description

The Pineta valley is of glacial origins and runs down from the massif of

Monte Perdido, which reaches over 3,000 m in height. Woods of pine, beech and silver fir abound, while there are also extensive alpine meadows and large rocky areas.

The valley is part of the Ordesa y Monte Perdido National Park.

Recommended routes

Route A is a walk lasting about 4 hours. Start at the chapel of Nuestra Señora de Pineta, close to the Parador, and take the path signed for Valle de Lalarri. The path runs through a magnificent beech wood where you can see various woodland species, and then issues onto some plains which you cross until coming to a waterfall. On this stretch of the route you may see Bearded Vulture, Griffon Vulture, Golden Eagle, Peregrine Falcon, Raven, Chough, Alpine Chough, Alpine Accentor and Water Pipit. Return by the same route until you reach the wood where you take a forestry road westwards, bringing you to the National Park information kiosk, close to the Parador.

Route B is a car journey which takes you along the road from Bielsa to the Parador, turning off for Espierba. From Espierba continue along a forestry road to La Estiva, a spot lying at 2,000 m and providing excellent views of the area. Usually the track is suitable for cars, but if conditions are bad you can complete the route on foot. The itinerary takes about 4 hours and can be prolonged by going for walks. The birds present are the same as those on the previous route with the added possibility of seeing alpine marmot and chamois.

Route C is a high mountain itinerary which requires a certain amount of physical preparation and experience. It starts at the National Park information kiosk and takes you along a forestry

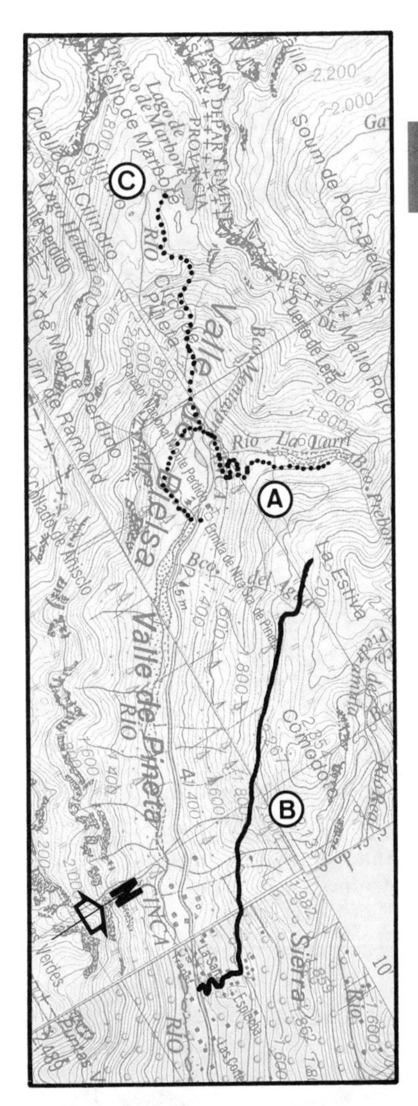

road until you reach the river Cinca. From here there is a marked track which makes the steep climb to the Balcón de Pineta and subsequently to the Lago de Marboré, a tarn. On this stretch of the route you may see Ptarmigan, Snow Finch, Alpine Accentor, Alpine Chough, Citril Finch, Wallcreeper, Golden Eagle, etc. Return by the same route. The whole trip takes about 8 hours. Apart from taking the usual precautions for walking in a high mountain area, you should remember that thunderstorms occur frequently.

Accommodation

In addition to the Parador, there are several hotels, hostels and campsites in Bielsa, among which Hotel Bielsa is to be recommended.

Pepe Sasot Gorgoñón

AR.11 EL TURBÓN

A mountain area.

Main species

Residents: Bearded Vulture, Golden Eagle, Peregrine Falcon, Grey Partridge, Alpine Accentor, Blue Rock Thrush, Wallcreeper, Alpine Chough, Chough, Raven.

Summer visitors: Egyptian Vulture, Alpine Swift, Crag Martin, Rock Thrush, Ring Ouzel.

Access

Make your way to Campo, a village on the C-139, 63 km from Barbastro, and then take the minor road to Vilas de Turbón.

Description

An impressive limestone massif where the bare rock makes for a desolate landscape dotted with ridges, cliffs and pinnacles. The highest part of the area is Castillo de Turbón (2,492 m). Skirting the massif are the rivers Esera and Isábena, which have carved spectacular gorges. Good examples of these are the narrow canyons at Ventamillo and Obarra.

Recommended routes

Route A involves climbing the Turbón massif. To get there, on the road from Campo to Vilas del Turbón, shortly after the village of Serrate, 12-13 km after Campo, you will find a track with restricted access. Walk along this track for 2 hours and you will reach Refugio de La Plana, a mountain refuge. To climb up to the peak, you will find a path leading off to the southeast from the refuge to a place known as Las Pradiellas; once

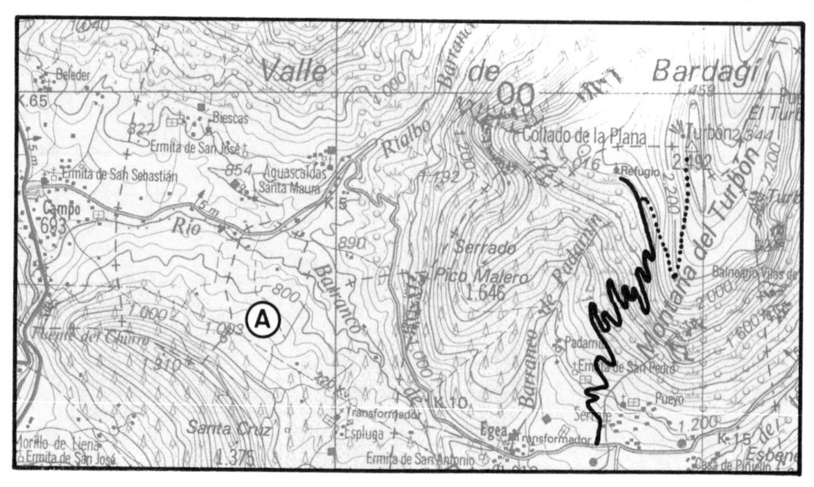

there, continue northwards towards the summit. This part of the route, which can be completed in a couple of hours, will give sightings of various cliff-dwelling species such as Grey Partridge, Rock Thrush, Ring Ouzel, Alpine Accentor, Alpine Chough and, in winter, Ptarmigan.

Route B takes you to Congosto del Ventamillo, a narrow river gorge to be found on the C-139 between the villages of Seira and Castejón de Sos. Park your vehicle shortly after the tunnel (77 km marker post) in one of the few lay-bys on this narrow road. A walk will provide you with a wide range of cliff-dwelling birds of prey as well as Alpine Swift, Wallcreeper, Crag Martin and Chough.

Accommodation

Hostal San Aventín in Campo is recommended, as is Hostal Balneario in Vilas del Turbón. In Serraduy, close to Congosto de Obarra, there is also Hostal Peix.

Luis Lorente Villanueva

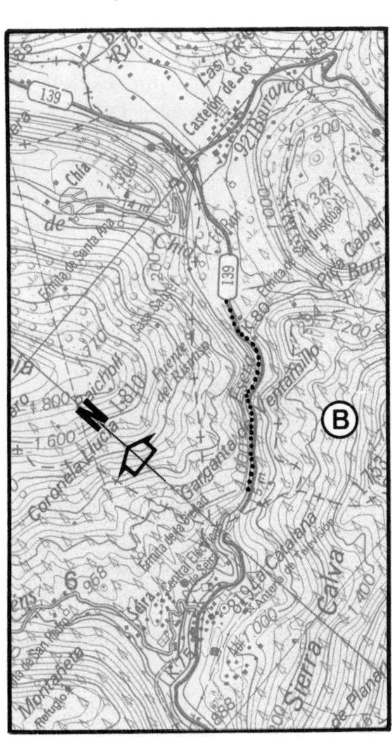

AR.12 BENASQUE VALLEY

A high mountain area.

Main species

Residents: Red Kite, Bearded Vulture, Goshawk, Golden Eagle, Peregrine Falcon, Ptarmigan, Capercaillie, Grey Partridge, Long-eared Owl, Tengmalm's Owl, Black Woodpecker, Dipper, Alpine Accentor, Marsh Tit, Wallcreeper, Alpine Chough, Chough, Raven, Snow Finch, Bullfinch, Yellowhammer.

Summer visitors: Honey Buzzard, Alpine Swift, Whinchat, Rock Thrush, Ring Ouzel, Ortolan Bunting.

Access

Take the C-138 from Barbastro to El Grado, where you then join the C-139 for Benasque (97 km).

Description

The Benasque valley lies between the massifs of Maladeta and Posets, the highest summits in the Pyrenees (Aneto, 3,404 m; Posets, 3,375 m). There is a wide range of habitats, running from hay fields, woods of birch and silver fir to large pine forests growing at an altitude of up to 2,200 m. On reaching the tree line, habitats change, giving way to alpine meadows, rock fields, lakes and some glacial cirques.

Recommended routes

Route A takes you through the valley of Estós. From Benasque take the C-139 and shortly after thc 100 km

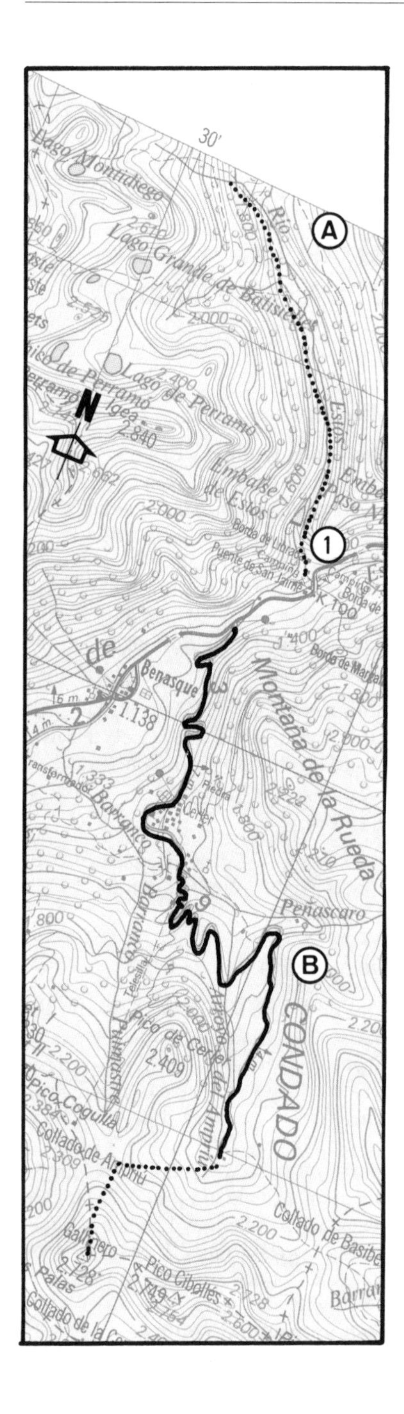

marker post, having crossed the bridge over the river Esera, take the track leading off to the left beside a campsite. A little farther on, you will find a car park. Leave the car here and continue on foot along a track with restricted access, which will bring you to the El Tormo mountain hut in 2 hours. By following the signs from the mountain hut, a track will enable you to walk up to the mountain refuge of Estós in half an hour.

Just before the beginning of the Estós valley, there are some huge rocky cliffs (1), where it is possible to see a wide variety of cliff-dwelling birds of prey. The rest of the route takes you through extensive woodland which is remarkable for the presence of Honey Buzzard, Goshawk, Capercaillie, Tengmalm's Owl, Black Woodpecker, Ring Ouzel, Marsh Tit, Crossbill, etc.

Route B has Benasque as its starting point. From here take the turning for the village of Cerler and continue until Llano del Ampriu, the site of some facilities belonging to the Cerler ski resort. The open spaces in this area may give rise to sightings of Rock Thrush, Whinchat, Quail and Chough. From here, walk up a steep slope to the Collado de Ampriu and subsequently to the summit of El Gallinero (2,728 m), which can be reached in about 2½ hours. On the way up, you may see Grey Partridge, Water Pipit, Alpine Accentor, Alpine Chough and, on the high ground, Ptarmigan and Snow Finch.

Accommodation

The valley offers plenty of accommodation; Fonda Barrabes in Benasque is recommended. There are also several campsites and mountain refuges.

Luis Lorente Villanueva

AR.13 MALLOS DE RIGLOS

A mountain area with large cliffs.

Main species

Residents: Red Kite, Bearded Vulture, Griffon Vulture, Goshawk, Sparrowhawk, Golden Eagle, Bonelli's Eagle, Peregrine Falcon, Grey Partridge, Rock Dove, Eagle Owl, Blue Rock Thrush, Sardinian Warbler, Great Grey Shrike, Chough, Raven.

Summer visitors: Black Kite, Egyptian Vulture, Short-toed Eagle, Montagu's Harrier, Booted Eagle, Hobby, Great Spotted Cuckoo, Nightjar, Pallid Swift, Alpine Swift, Crag Martin, Black Wheatear, Tawny Pipit, Rock Thrush, Spectacled Warbler, Subalpine Warbler, Orphean Warbler, Woodchat Shrike, Red-backed Shrike.

Winter visitors: Hen Harrier, Fieldfare, Wallcreeper, Alpine Accentor, Rook, ducks and other water birds.

Access

The N-240 from Huesca to Pamplona is the main means of gaining access to this area, and from this road many secondary roads will take you to places of interest. From Ayerbe, a town 29 km from Huesca, take the minor road for Sarsamarcuello, Loarre and Aniés. Continuing along the N-240, a right turn will take you to Riglos and, a little farther on, another turn to the left will take you to Agüero. Finally, the Embalse de la Peña lies next to the road and to get to Arguis and Bentué de Rasal (route F) take the C-136 from Huesca towards Sabiñánigo.

Description

Typical pre-Pyrenean ranges on the edge of the Ebro valley. Peaks reach a maximum of roughly 1,600 m. There are some spectacular conglomerate rock formations of vast dimensions, known locally as *mallos*. Vegetation consists of holm oak woods, some pine woods and large areas of scrubland.

There are also 3 reservoirs, including La Peña, where vegetation consists of tamarisk, reedmace and reeds.

Recommended routes

Route A takes you along a track which leaves the village of Riglos in an easterly direction. It runs along the lower part of the *mallos* and cliffs for some 2 km. It is recommended that you walk this stretch. En route you will see birds of prey and other cliff-dwelling species including, in winter, Wallcreeper and Alpine Accentor.

Route B takes you through the area surrounding the village of Agüero along tracks and paths starting from Agüero itself. The main interest of the area lies in the cliff-dwelling species you will see.

Route C starts in Sarsamarcuello, from where you take a track leading you to the vantage point known locally as Safari. Having passed the ruins of the castle, the track surface deteriorates and for this reason it is recommended that you walk this section of the route. The view from the vantage point is spectacular and, apart from the usual cliff-dwelling birds, you may also see Grey Partridge in the area.

Route D will take you to the La Peña reservoir. You will have good views of the open water from the dam, from the village of Triste, and from the N-240 itself, a road which will take you to the far northwestern end of the reservoir. Interest here lies in the observation of water birds.

Route E covers the Loarre area. Every year a group of Alpine Accentor winters in the castle of Loarre, from where

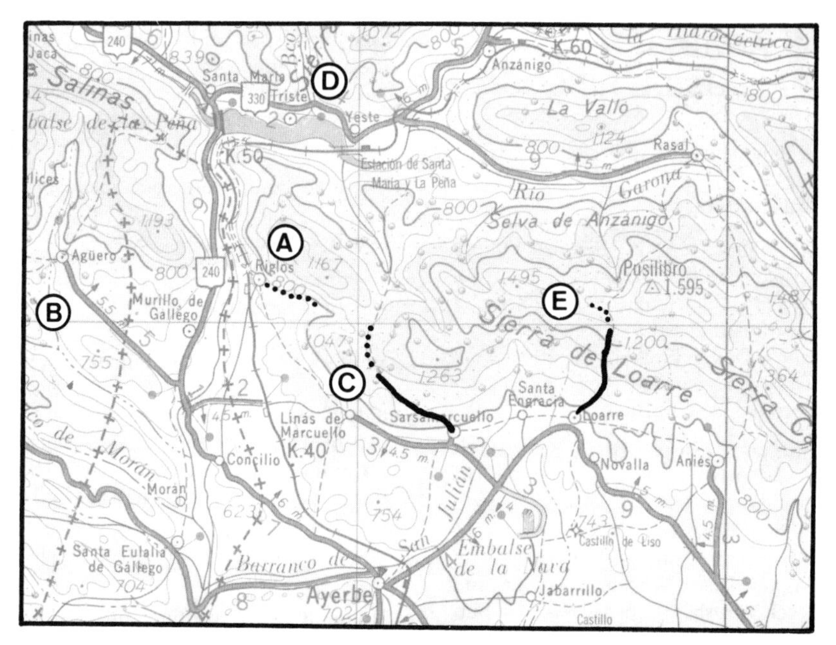

you can take a track up to a telecommunications mast located on top of the range. From here, you can walk through the extensive pine forests and alpine meadows on the high ground.

The starting point of **route F** is the track which starts some 700 m after leaving the village of Arguis on the C-136, on a very sharp bend. This 10 km route will bring you to the village of Bentué de Rasal, and among the species you will see along the way are Red-backed Shrike and Rock Thrush.

Accommodation

You will find accommodation in Huesca, which has a wide range of hotels and hostels.

Comments

Despite the fact that many of the routes described feature tracks which can be driven along, we would entreat you to undertake these routes on foot.

José María Cereza Abadías

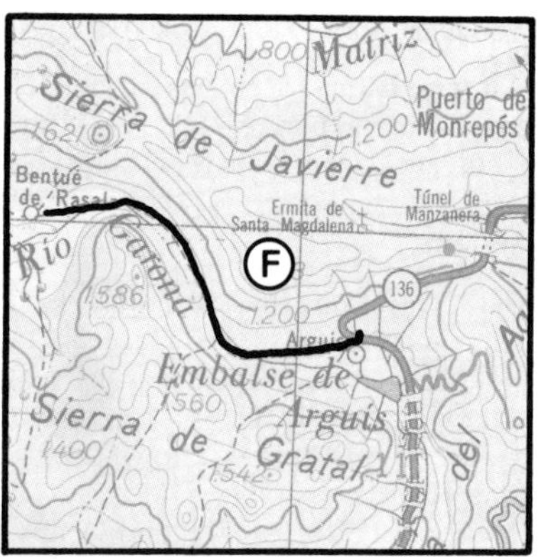

■ AR.14 SALTO DE ROLDÁN – SAN MARTÍN DE LA VAL DE ONSERA

A mountain area.

Main species

Residents: Bearded Vulture, Griffon Vulture, Golden Eagle, Bonelli's

Eagle, Peregrine Falcon, Crag Martin, Blue Rock Thrush, Black Wheatear.

Summer visitors: Egyptian Vulture, Alpine Swift, Rock Thrush.

Winter visitors: Wallcreeper, Alpine Accentor.

Access

Take the N-240 from Huesca towards Barbastro. After 7 km turn left onto the minor road for Loporzano, and from there to Barluenga and San Julián de Banzo. Once in San Julián de Banzo, you will come across a tight bend from which a marked forestry road takes you to the beginning of the path going up to San Martín de la Val de Onsera.

Description

A typical pre-Pyrenean mountain area, with ravines, high rocky cliffs and very steep mountainsides. Peaks vary between 1,000 and 1,500 m, while vegetation, apart from the odd patch of holm oak woodland, is dominated by scrubland consisting of kermes oak and juniper. The ravines, which are gushing torrents in winter, dry up in summer.

Recommended routes

Route A consists of a walk which can be undertaken in 2½ hours. It begins at the end of the above-mentioned track, from where you take the path up to the San Martín ravine. Once there, the path climbs La Viñeta and subsequently drops to the bottom of the ravine, where you will find the waterfall and chapel of San Martín.

For **route B**, when you see the first sign for San Martín, take the track to the right which leads to some farms. From this point a path takes you to the ravine and, once there, another crosses some stock enclosures bringing you to the edge of the Aguila ravine. Subsequently the path climbs up to Peña

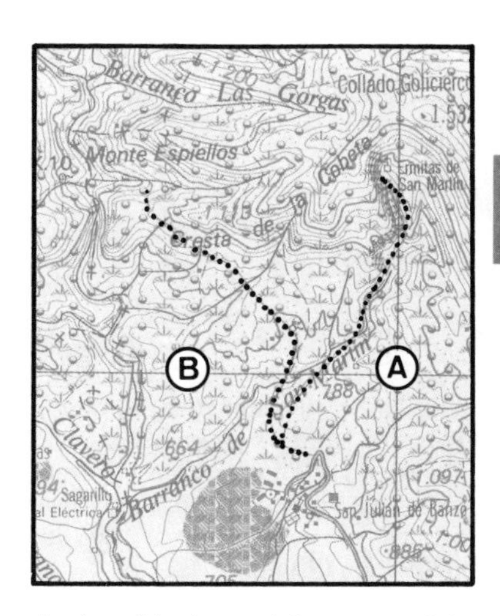

Amán, with views of the course of the river Flumen and Peña de San Miguel, another peak. The route takes a couple of hours.

Accommodation

Huesca is convenient because it is close to the area and offers abundant accommodation.

Comments

Another way of getting to Salto de Roldán is along a forestry road which takes you to the base of Peña de San Miguel. In Huesca, take the minor road to Apies and Santa Eulalia de la Peña and, having gone through Apies, you will find a track leading off to the right.

David Gómez Samitier
and Lourdes Mairal Aranz

■ AR.15 VADIELLO RESERVOIR

A mountain area.

Main species

Residents: Bearded Vulture, Griffon Vulture, Golden Eagle, Bonelli's

Eagle, Peregrine Falcon, Crag Martin, Blue Rock Thrush.

Summer visitors: Egyptian Vulture, Short-toed Eagle, Alpine Swift, Wryneck, Rock Thrush.

Winter visitors: Wallcreeper, Bullfinch.

Access

Take the N-240 out of Huesca towards Barbastro. After 7 km turn left onto the minor road for Loporzano and from there to Sasa del Abadiado, Castilsabas and finally to the Embalse de Vadiello, a reservoir (17 km).

Description

Steep pre-Pyrenean mountain ranges with many cliffs (see AR.13 and AR.14).

Recommended routes

The recommended routes are walks, and their most interesting feature is the observation of cliff-dwelling species.

Route A has its starting point on the dam of the Vadiello reservoir, from where you take the forestry track leading to the San Cosme chapel. From the chapel a path goes through an area of holm oak and kermes oak, climbing towards the Huevo de San Cosme, a distinctive rocky outcrop. The route takes a couple of hours to complete.

Route B starts at the last road tunnel, where you take the path to Nocito. The route crosses the Barranco del Diablo, a ravine, and runs along the left bank of the lake to its far end. You can walk the route in 1 hour.

Accommodation

Huesca is conveniently close and offers a wide range of accommodation. You can also stay at the Peña Guara mountain refuge, located on the Vadiel-

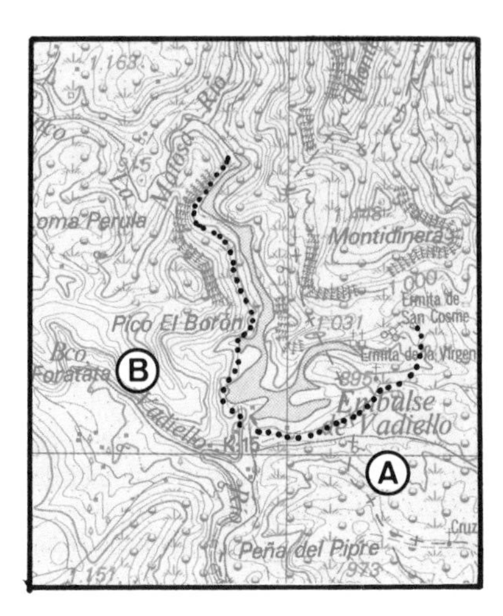

lo road. If you wish to stay in the refuge, ask for the key at the Peña Guara social club in Huesca.

David Gómez Samitier
and Lourdes Mairal Aranz

AR.16 ALCANADRE AND GORGES AT MASCÚN

River gorges.

Main species

Residents: Bearded Vulture, Griffon Vulture, Sparrowhawk, Golden Eagle, Stock Dove, Eagle Owl, Crag Martin, Dipper, Raven.

Summer visitors: Egyptian Vulture, Short-toed Eagle, Booted Eagle, Alpine Swift, Woodchat Shrike.

Winter visitors: Wallcreeper.

Access

From Huesca take the N-240 towards Barbastro. After 29 km, just after the bridge over the river Alcanadre, turn left on to a minor road taking you to Abiego, Bierge and Rodellar. In Rodel-

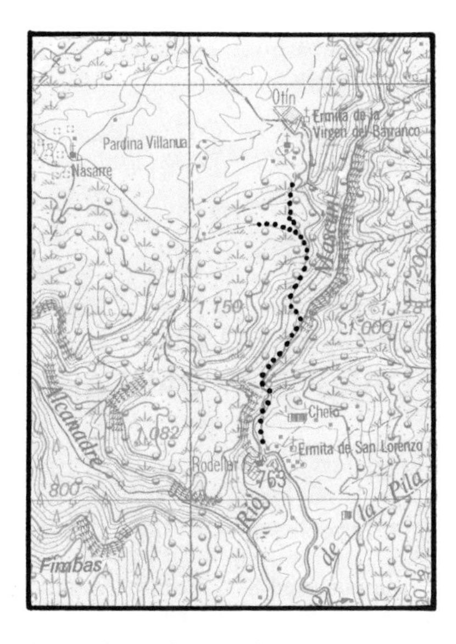

lar, information and maps etc. are available at Bar Florentino or Camping Mascún, the local campsite.

Description

The Alcanadre and Mascún ravines are among the steepest and least accessible in the pre-Pyrenean ranges (see also AR.1, AR.2 and AR.3).

Recommended routes

The only route proposed here begins in Rodellar, where you take a well-trodden path to the head of the Mascún ravine. Once there, you can climb up to the source of the river Mascún, the departure point for a series of paths covering the area. Any of these paths will provide you with a general view of the area and the opportunity to see the most interesting species, particularly cliff-dwellers.

Accommodation

There are 3 campsites in Rodellar and, in Bierge, a bar with rooms. Huesca and Barbastro are also recommended for their wide range of hotel accommodation.

David Gómez Samitier
and Lourdes Mairal Aranz

AR.17 SEVIL RANGE AND GORGES AT BALCÉS

A mountain area.

Main species

Residents: Bearded Vulture, Griffon Vulture, Golden Eagle, Bonelli's Eagle, Peregrine Falcon, Woodcock, Black Woodpecker, Crag Martin, Chough, Raven.

Summer visitors: Honey Buzzard, Egyptian Vulture, Short-toed Eagle, Alpine Swift, Rock Thrush.

Winter visitors: Wallcreeper, Citril Finch, Bullfinch.

Access

In Barbastro take the minor road towards Alquézar and, once through the village of Huerta de Vero, turn left for Adahuesca. In this village take the road to Radiquero and, once there, the forestry road to San Pelegrín.

Description

A typical pre-Pyrenean mountain area with complex landforms and contours, featuring the spectacular Barranco de Balcés, a river gorge with escarpments reaching various heights which are covered by woodland consisting of holm oak, Lusitanian oak, beech, yew, etc. (see also AR.1, AR.2, AR.3 and AR.4).

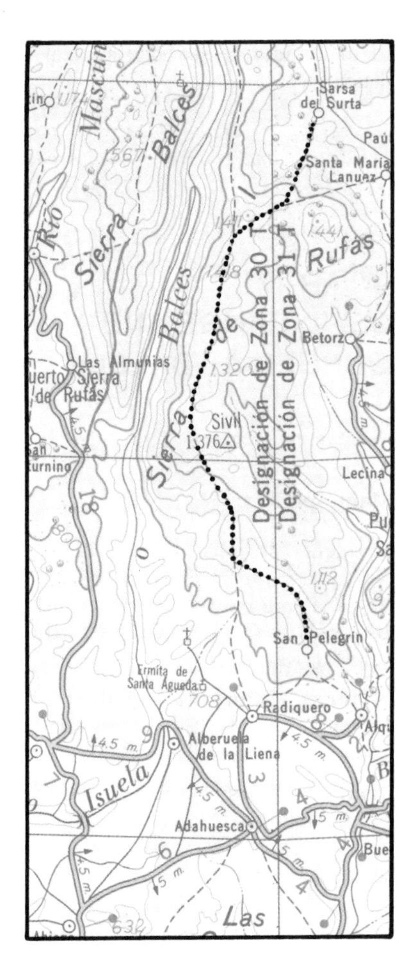

Recommended routes

From San Pelegrín walk or drive in a four wheel drive vehicle along the poorly-marked track which leads up to the high point of Mesón de Sivil (1,273 m). From here the track runs for about 8 km along the Balcés ravine. It is worthwhile making stops to look over the edge of the ravine. The track comes to an end in Sarsa de Surta.

Accommodation

You can stay at Bar Labata in Adahuesca. There are also *fondas* and a campsite in nearby Alquézar. Alternatively, Barbastro offers several hotels and hostels.

David Gómez Samitier
and Lourdes Mairal Aranz

AR.18 RIVER VERO AND FORESTS AT BARCABO

River gorge and woodland.

Main species

Residents: Red Kite, Bearded Vulture, Griffon Vulture, Goshawk, Sparrowhawk, Golden Eagle, Bonelli's Eagle, Peregrine Falcon, Woodcock, Eagle Owl, Long-eared Owl, Crag Martin, Blue Rock Thrush, Chough, Raven, Hawfinch.

Summer visitors: Honey Buzzard, Black Kite, Egyptian Vulture, Short-toed Eagle, Hobby, Alpine Swift.

Winter visitors: Redwing, Wallcreeper, Citril Finch, Crossbill, Bullfinch.

Access

Take the minor road out of Barbastro for Castillazuelo, and from there continue to Alquézar (23 km).

To reach other routes, 3 km before Alquézar take the road to Colungo, Lecina and Barcabo (45 km).

Description

Part of the pre-Pyrenean area which is remarkable for the spectacular qualities of the gorge of the river Vero. The woodland in the area, consisting of holm oak, Lusitanian oak and pine, is also of great interest.

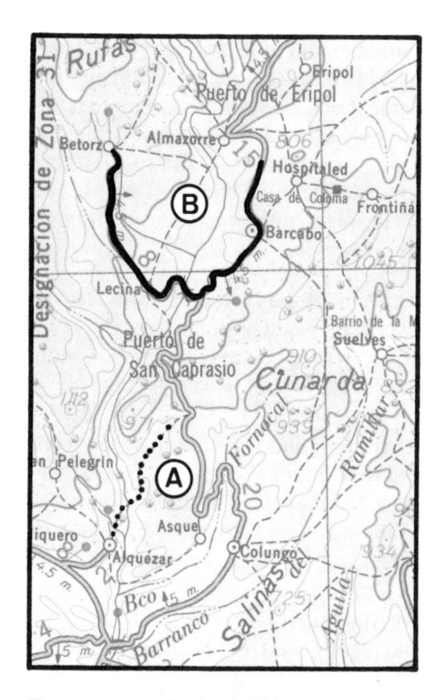

Recommended routes

Route A runs along the base of the Vero gorge. It consists of a walk along the paths which start from the square in the village of Alquézar. These paths run for about 3 km, allowing you to see the main cliff-dwelling species in the area.

You can see another part of the gorge from the road running from Colungo to Lecina.

Route B is a car journey taking you through the forest areas near Lecina, Betorz and Barcabo. It is worth using the network of tracks in the zone in order to take a series of walks, allowing you to see the most interesting woodland species.

Accommodation

In Alquézar there is Fonda Narbona and the Camping Río Vero, a campsite. There is another campsite in Lecina, and Barbastro offers further possibilities.

David Gómez Samitier
and Lourdes Mairal Aranz

■ AR.19 LA SOTONERA RESERVOIR AND SASOS DE GURREA

Rerservoir and steppe area occupied by cereal crops.

Main species

Residents: Marsh Harrier, Little Bustard, Great Bustard, Stone Curlew, Black-bellied Sandgrouse, Pin-tailed Sandgrouse, Calandra Lark, Fan-tailed Warbler.

Summer visitors: Great Spotted Cuckoo.

Winter visitors: ducks (2,500 individuals in January 1990).

On passage: herons, Red-crested Pochard, Crane (7,000 birds in March 1990), waders.

Access

From Huesca, take the N-123 towards Zaragoza and in Almudévar turn right onto the minor road for Tormos (35 km). Stay on this road, which circles the lake bringing you to Montmesa, where the road is no longer surfaced.

To reach Sasos de Gurrea continue along the N-123 and 9 km after Almudévar turn right onto a local road taking you to the plains occurring just before Gurrea de Gállego.

Description

The La Sotonera reservoir, also known as Tormos, dams the waters of the river Gállego. Its main features are its large size, the dramatic changes in water level and the existence of numerous jetties on its irregular shores. In recent years, increasing human presence in the form of hunters and fishermen has somewhat spoiled the reservoir.

The cereal fields at Gurrea make for a small but interesting habitat where you can see steppe-dwelling birds.

Recommended routes

Route A takes in the *embalse* of La Sotonera. From Montmesa take the wide track running through the cereal fields at a short distance from the reservoir, working your way towards a small hill covered with holm oak. This will take you to the Alberca de Alboré, an old reservoir, and by following the same track, of which some stretches are not suitable for cars, you will come to the mouth of the Ardisa canal, where you take the road back to Tormos. The most interesting points are the following:

1) Dam of La Sotonera: provides an excellent vantage point over the open water, where you may see grebes, gulls and ducks.

2) Eastern shores: from the road leading to Montmesa a series of tracks lead down to the shore of the reservoir, facilitating the observation of groups of ducks.

3) Alberca de Alboré: this is the most interesting part of the reservoir, with shallow water and plentiful vegetation. This is the site of ducks, waders, crakes and, in the first half of March, thousands of Crane.

4) Mouth of the Ardisa canal: this is a good spot for watching herons and gulls. The road taking you back to the dam will provide a good view of the centre of the reservoir.

Route B takes you along the farm tracks around Los Sasos de Gurrea. Among other steppe-dwelling birds, you may see Great Bustard.

Accommodation

Almudévar has plenty of facilities, and the city of Huesca is close by.

Alberto Bueno Mir
(Asociación Naturalista Altoaragonesa)

AR.20 HUESCA AND AROUND

Small wetland areas and riverside woodland.

Main species

Residents: Marsh Harrier, Collared Dove, Cetti's Warbler, Fan-tailed Warbler, Penduline Tit, Cirl Bunting.

Summer visitors: Great Spotted Cuckoo, Scops Owl, Subalpine Warbler.

Winter visitors: ducks (2,000 individuals in January 1990), Red Kite (800 in December 1989), Marsh Harrier (40-50 individuals).

On passage: herons, waders.

Access

To reach Alberca de Cortés and the woodland on the river Isuela, take the N-240 out of Huesca towards Pamplona. After 5 km turn right for the village of Chimillas, from where a track suitable for cars will bring you to the area after 1 km.

To get to Alberca de Loreto, take the N-123 out of Huesca towards Zaragoza and when you see the pyramid-shaped building of the Centro de Enseñanzas Integradas, an educational centre, turn right for Cuarte. The reservoir lies beside some farms, about 800 m from the junction.

From Huesca railway station take the minor road to Grañén and, after crossing the Cinca canal (6 km), turn right onto a surfaced road running parallel to the canal and taking you to the Embalse de Valdabra reservoir. Back on the road, continue to the village of Tabernas de Isuela, very close to the confluence of the rivers Isuela and Flumen. The same road will take you to the reedbeds at Sangarrén, 1 km before the village of the same name.

Description

Alberca de Cortés and Alberca de Loreto are two small irrigation reservoirs with abundant marsh vegetation. The Embalse de Valdabra, a reservoir of middling size, was constructed in 1982 to serve as the overflow channel for the Cinca canal. The small area of flooded reedbeds in Sangarrén is an important roosting place for wintering passerines. Finally, the riverside woodland around Alberca de Cortés and on the stretch of the river Isuela between Pompenillo and Tabernas are some of the best conserved patches of riverside woodland in the area immediately around the town of Huesca.

Recommended routes

Since these places are all close together, it is possible to visit them in a single day from Huesca.

1) Alberca de Cortés: you can walk round the reservoir, which is a good place for seeing marsh-dwelling passerines, waders and, during the migration period, Purple Heron.

2) Soto de Cortés: one of the wildest stretches of the river Isuela, where you will see many different species of birds during the migration periods.

3) Alberca de Loreto: the small size of this reservoir makes it an excellent spot for seeing various kinds of wintering ducks.

4) Embalse de Valdabra: the best observation point is the far end of the reservoir, which can be reached by a good track running around the reservoir. In winter large groups of Mallard congregate here, and during the migration periods you will see waders and other water birds.

5) Soto de Tabernas: this is a good place for spotting passerines, including Penduline Tit and Cetti's Warbler.

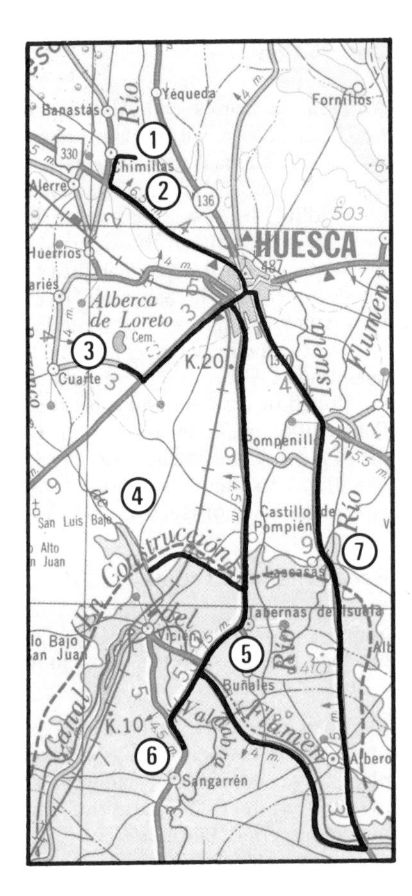

6) Reedbeds at Sangarrén: in summer you will see crakes and Water Rail, and in winter this becomes a huge roosting place for buntings, linnets, starlings, etc.

7) You can return to Huesca via the village of Lascasas. Near the village there is a controlled feeding ground where birds of prey and corvids can be seen.

Accommodation

Huesca has a wide range of hotels as well as a campsite. Restaurante Casa Paco is recommended. In Castilsabás, 15 km away, there is a country house providing full board and lodging and organized bird-watching trips (Casa Scheltus-Secorún).

Alberto Bueno Mir
(Asociación Naturalista Altoaragonesa)

AR.21 SERRETA DE TRAMACED

A small mountain range with gullies and rocky screes.

Main species

Residents: Peregrine Falcon, Red-legged Partridge, Rock Dove, Eagle Owl, Thekla Lark, Crag Martin, Black Wheatear, Blue Rock Thrush, Dartford Warbler, Sardinian Warbler, Rock Sparrow.

Summer visitors: Egyptian Vulture, Bee-eater, Black-eared Wheatear, Orphean Warbler.

Access

Take the C-1310 from Huesca towards Sariñena. After 24 km turn right on to a minor road for Tramaced (6 km).

Description

The Serreta de Tramaced, a small mountain range on the edge of the Ebro valley, makes for an interesting landscape. Erosion has created a wide variety of forms, with gullies, earth screes and cliffs. The slopes are covered with various species of Mediterranean shrub.

Recommended routes

A road route which can be extended with short walks will be enough to gain a general impression of the area. The high rock walls between Tramaced and Fraella are worth a visit since they are

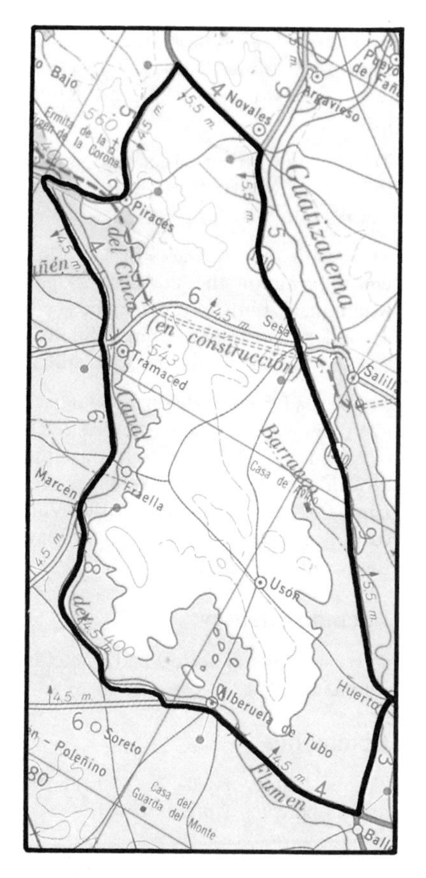

used in winter as a resting place by several dozen Griffon Vulture. The valley of La Sarda, in Piracés, is also of interest.

Accommodation

You will find all the facilities you need in Huesca and the nearby town of Grañén.

Alberto Bueno Mir
(Asociación Naturalista Altoaragonesa)

AR.22 ZUERA–CASTEJÓN FORESTS

Woods consisting of Aleppo pine, and areas of Mediterranean scrubland.

Main species

Residents: Goshawk, Sparrowhawk, Golden Eagle, Peregrine Falcon, Long-eared Owl, Thekla Lark, Sardinian Warbler, Firecrest, Chough, Raven, Rock Sparrow, Crossbill.

Summer visitors: Short-toed Eagle, Booted Eagle, Hobby, Turtle Dove, Great Spotted Cuckoo, Bee-eater, Black-eared Wheatear, Spectacled Warbler, Subalpine Warbler, Orphean Warbler, Bonelli's Warbler, Ortolan Bunting.

Access

Take the N-330 from Zaragoza to Zuera (27 km). From Zuera take the minor road to Las Pedrosas and after 5.6 km turn left onto a track running through the Salado gorge.

Description

The pine woods in Zuera constitute one of the main areas of woodland in this middle section of the Ebro valley. The woods are constituted by indigenous species with Aleppo pine and an undergrowth of kermes oak, box, juniper, etc., alternating with scrubland in various stages of degeneration. On the western edge of these mountains are clay and gypsum cliffs.

Recommended routes

In this area there is a single route, 17 km long, which you can undertake by car, driving along forestry roads in reasonable condition. Work your way along the track running up the Salado

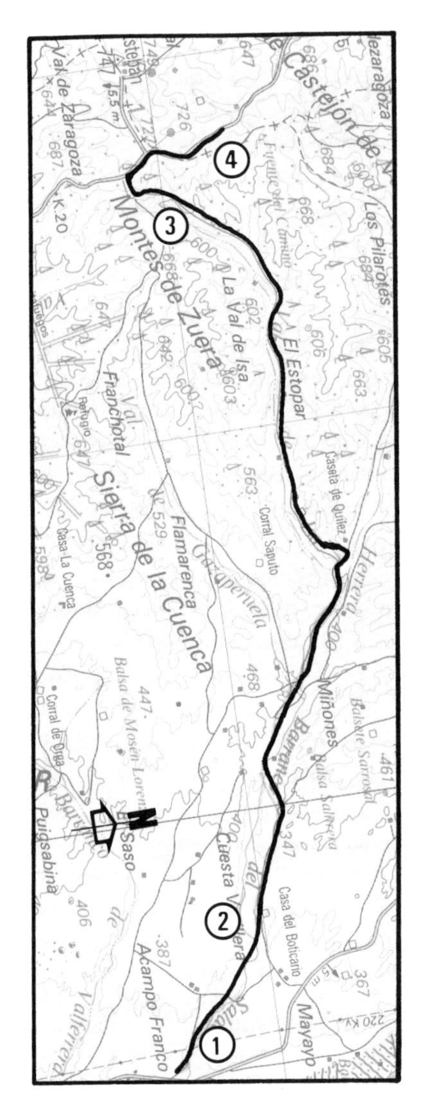

gorge and after 6.5 km you will reach some forestry houses, where you take a left turn which after 7 km comes to the minor road from Castejón de Valdejasa to Villanueva de Gállego. The points of greatest interest are the following:

1) Hillsides covered with scrub at the entrance to the Salado gorge: here you will see various birds of prey as well as Thekla Lark, Subalpine Warbler, Dartford Warbler, Black-eared Wheatear, Ortolan Bunting and Rock Bunting.

2) Reedbed with tamarisks: a good spot for seeing Marsh Harrier, Bee-eater, warblers and Rock Sparrow.

3) Fuente de los Carasoles: a pine wood lying on the northern slopes where many birds of prey can be seen, as well as Turtle Dove, Great Spotted Cuckoo, warblers, tits and Crossbill.

4) The road from Castejón de Valdejasa to Villanueva de Gállego: on the stretch of road lying 21-23 km from Castejón de Valdejasa make several stops to see, among other birds of prey, Griffon Vulture, Egyptian Vulture, Short-toed Eagle, Hobby, etc.

Accommodation

There are several hostels and a hotel in Zuera. Zaragoza is close by.

Comments

The best time of year for visiting the area is between April and July.

Francisco Javier Sampietro Latorre and Enrique Pelayo Zueco

AR.23 ALCUBIERRE RANGE

A mountain range of average height with pine woods and areas of scrubland.

Main species

Residents: Red Kite, Goshawk, Sparrowhawk, Golden Eagle, Peregrine Falcon, Eagle Owl, Long-eared Owl, Thekla Lark, Crag Martin, Black Wheatear, Sardinian Warbler, Firecrest, Chough, Raven, Rock Sparrow, Crossbill.

Summer visitors: Egyptian Vulture, Short-toed Eagle, Booted Eagle, Hobby, Turtle Dove, Red-necked Nightjar, Black-eared Wheatear, Rock Thrush, Subalpine Warbler, Orphean Warbler, Bonelli's Warbler.

Access

Take the N-II out of Zaragoza to Santa Isabel (4 km), from where you join the C-129 for Alcubierre (42 km). From here a forestry track in reasonable condition takes you up to the *ermita* or chapel of San Caprasio on the top of the range. You can also climb to the summit from the villages of Perdiguera and Leciñena, although this is a much more complicated route.

Description

The Alcubierre range reaches maximum heights of around 800 m and commands views over the Los Monegros plains. Vegetation consists of dense Aleppo pine woodland, particularly well-developed on the northern slopes, and small areas of Lusitanian oak and Phoenician juniper.

Recommended routes

This is a single route consisting of a walk 8 km long, running along the range from the Ermita de San Caprasio to Monte Oscuro. The vantage point below the chapel is an excellent place for watching a large variety of birds of prey and some cliff-dwelling species such as Black Wheatear, Rock Thrush, Rock Sparrow, Chough and Raven. Throughout the rest of the route you will see many woodland and scrubland species including Red-necked Nightjar, Bee-eater, Thekla Lark, Black-eared Wheatear, various warblers, Crossbill, etc.

Accommodation

A wide range of accommodation is available in Zaragoza.

Comments

The best time of year for visiting this area is spring.

Francisco Javier Sampietro Latorre and Enrique Pelayo Zueco

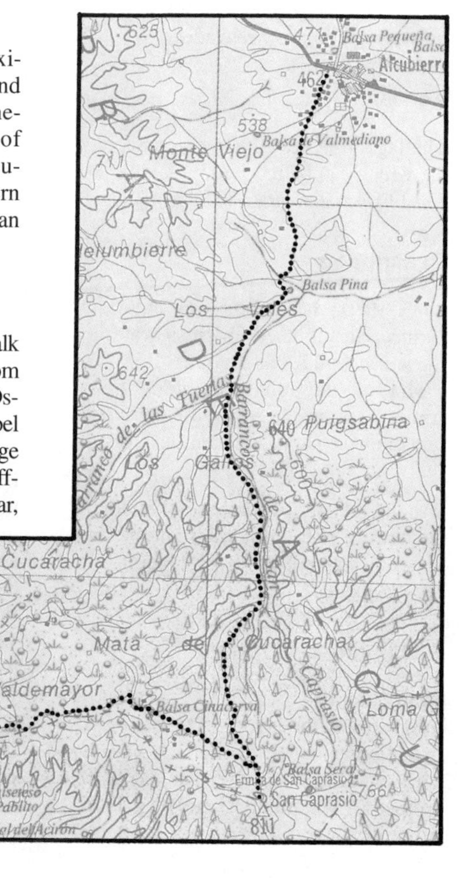

AR.24
SARIÑENA LAGOON

Wetland steppe area.

Main species

Residents: Great Crested Grebe, Cattle Egret, Grey Heron, Marsh Harrier, Lapwing, Black-headed Gull, Kingfisher.

Summer visitors: Little Bittern, Little Egret, Purple Heron, Black-winged Stilt, Little Ringed Plover, Kentish Plover, Redshank, Great Spotted Cuckoo, Roller.

Winter visitors: Cormorant, Greylag Goose, ducks (up to 10,000 individuals), Snipe and other waders.

Access

The lagoon is near the town of Sariñena, which can be reached by taking the C-129 from Zaragoza (71 km).

Description

Until 1980, the lagoon was naturally formed but the need for fresh water in the area called for its draining. It is now a shallow lagoon surrounded by a fringe of marsh vegetation. The water level now remains constant throughout the year.

Around the lagoon are several hundred hectares of rice fields where numerous water birds feed, using the lagoon as a resting place.

Recommended routes

Route A consists of a walk, some 6 km long, around the lagoon. There are two irrigation channels which may be of some hindrance, but they can easily be crossed at the point where they issue from the lagoon.

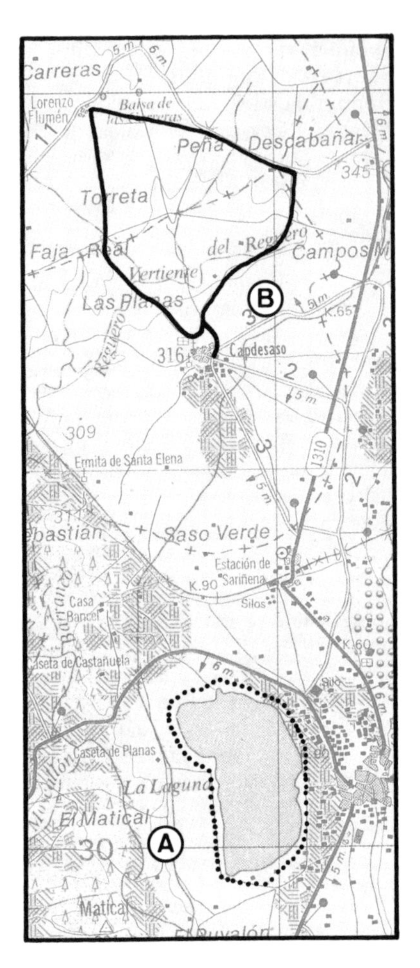

The starting point is in Sariñena, at the crossroads of the roads to Zaragoza and Bujaraloz. In this area you will have no difficulty in seeing, albeit at some distance, grebes, ducks, Coot, Cormorant and herons. Large groups of ducks and gulls congregate in the centre of the lagoon, while the northernmost shores are a good place for watching waders.

Route B consists of a car journey through the rice fields. Start in the village of Capdesaso, where by the village schools you will find a dirt track taking you to San Lorenzo del

Flumen. On arriving at this village, turn left along Calle del Tubo (a named road) and return to Capdesaso along tracks running through the rice fields. En route you will see Redshank, Black-winged Stilt, Lapwing, plovers, Little Egret and Cattle Egret.

Accommodation

There are several pensions in Sariñena, although it is worthwhile making a booking in advance.

Comments

The dirt tracks are easily accessible, but after rain they become extremely slippery.

César Pedrocchi Renault

AR.25 LOWER REACHES OF THE RIVER CINCA

Riverside woodland and steppe area.

Main species

Residents: Grey Heron, Marsh Harrier, Bonelli's Eagle, Stone Curlew, Black-bellied Sandgrouse, Pin-tailed Sandgrouse, Collared Dove, Eagle Owl, Kingfisher, Dupont's Lark, Calandra Lark, Lesser Short-toed Lark, Thekla Lark, Crag Martin, Black Wheatear, Blue Rock Thrush, Dartford Warbler, Sardinian Warbler, Chough, Rock Sparrow, Cirl Bunting.

Summer visitors: Little Bittern, Night Heron, Cattle Egret, Little Egret, White Stork, Egyptian Vulture, Short-toed Eagle, Black-winged Stilt, Short-toed Lark, Great Spotted Cuckoo, Bee-eater, Black-eared Wheatear, Spectacled Warbler.

Access

The town of Monzón is the ideal centre from which to visit this region.

Description

Throughout the lower reaches of the river Cinca there are patches of riverside woodland, reedbeds, areas of gravel, abandoned meanders and riverside cliffs. The area has been spoiled in recent years as a result of the spread of black poplar plantations, the construction of dams and water pollution.

On the right bank of the river Cinca are some interesting steppe areas. Generally, cereal fields dominate the area but in some places, whether as a consequence of the saline nature of the soil or of excessively steep slopes, natural steppes survive.

Recommended routes

Route A runs along the banks of the river Cinca. Between the towns of Monzón and Fraga, several roads run along the course of the Cinca and from these roads you can reach the river in several places. The most interesting points are the following:

1) Sotos de Monzón: this is an area of riverside woodland which can be reached by leaving Monzón in the direction of Huesca. At the turn for Conchel you will find a track leading down to the woods by the river.

2) Isla de Alfántega: having passed the village of Alfántega, the road crosses a small ravine. From the bridge over the ravine a track starts; leave your car here and continue on foot.

3) Galacho de Ripol: from the village of Ripol a track leads to the river. Park your vehicle by the river and continue on foot.

4) In the area surrounding Alcolea de Cinca and Ballobar, at the point where

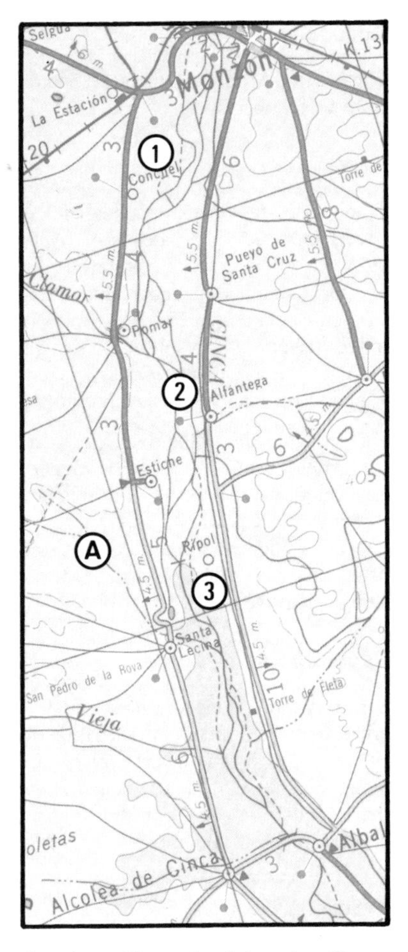

the river Alcanadre joins the Cinca, there are several interesting riverside cliffs.

Route B will acquaint you with the steppe in the lower reaches of the river Cinca. Start from Alcolea del Cinca, a town 24 km from Monzón, and take the road to Ontiñena. After 2 km, at the top of a climb through a series of hairpin bends, a track leads off to the left,

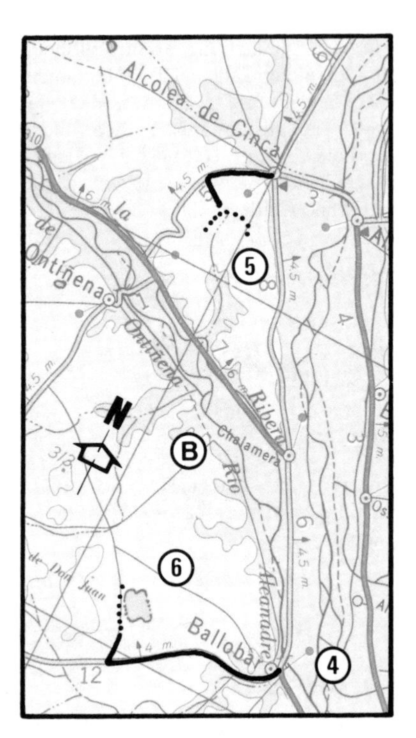

bringing you after some 500 m to the bottom of a hollow (5). Leave the car here and go for a walk to see steppe-dwelling species present in the area.

Another interesting place can be reached from Ballobar. In Ballobar take the minor road to Candasnos and after 5 km, on a long straight stretch of road opposite a public weighbridge, turn right onto a track which will take you to the area of El Basal (6).

Accommodation

There is a wide range of accommodation available in Monzón. The food provided by the Mesón Meler is highly recommended.

ANSAR "VALLE DEL CINCA"

■ AR.26 GALACHO DE JUSLIBOL AND GALACHO DE LA ALFRANCA

Wetland area: abandoned river meanders and riverside woodland.

Main species

Residents: Marsh Harrier, Coot, Water Rail, Kingfisher, Sardinian Warbler, Penduline Tit.

Summer visitors: Little Bittern, Night Heron, Little Egret, Purple Heron, White Stork, Black Kite, Egyptian Vulture, Bee-eater, Wryneck, Sand Martin, Golden Oriole.

Winter visitors: Cormorant, Grey Heron, ducks, Lapwing, Water Pipit, Reed Bunting.

Access

Juslibol is a suburb of the city of Zaragoza. It can be reached via roads leading out of the city or alternatively from the Polígono Santiago, an industrial estate in Barrio del Actur (a suburb). Another option is to reach Juslibol from the exit on the N-123. Once in the area, drive or walk along a track taking you down to the meander.

To reach La Alfranca, leave Zaragoza on the N-II going towards Barcelona. On reaching Puebla de Alfindén (11 km), turn right onto a dirt track leading you to the site.

Description

These meanders, known locally as *galachos*, dried up when the original course of the river became blocked. They are typical of the middle reaches of the river Ebro, and present abundant stands of reeds and reedmace, while

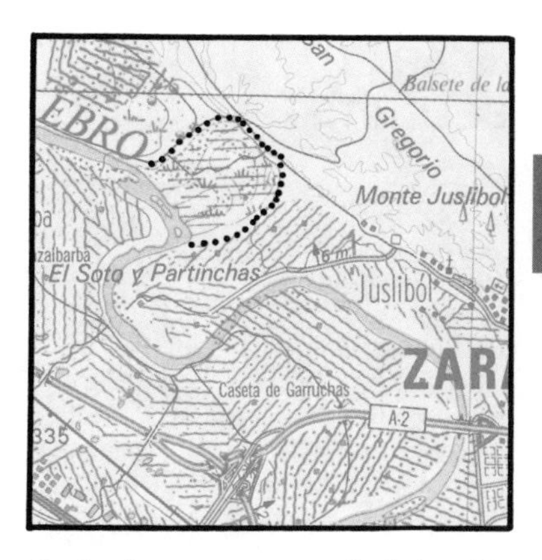

the banks support unspoiled riverside woodland constituted largely by white poplar, black poplar, willow and elm.

Recommended routes

Both meanders are very small, meaning that visitors can choose any route they wish. It is worthwhile extending your visit by going to the main course of the river Ebro if you wish to see more species.

In the case of the meander at Juslibol, the neighbouring gullies and clay and gypsum cliffs will give you sightings of steppe-dwelling and cliff-dwelling birds. You should remember that access to the nearby military zone of San Gregorio (Campo de Maniobras Militares) is forbidden.

Accommodation

Zaragoza is conveniently close and provides all the necessary facilities.

Comments

The meander at La Alfranca has an information centre. There is a project for the installation of walkways and hides in order to make your visit easier. An information centre is also planned for the Juslibol meander.

Francisco Javier Sampietro Latorre

AR.27 BELCHITE

A steppe area.

Main species

Residents: Golden Eagle, Peregrine Falcon, Little Bustard, Stone Curlew, Black-bellied Sandgrouse, Pin-tailed Sandgrouse, Dupont's Lark, Calandra Lark, Lesser Short-toed Lark, Black Wheatear, Sardinian Warbler.

Summer visitors: Egyptian Vulture, Short-toed Lark, Black-eared Wheatear, Spectacled Warbler, Subalpine Warbler, Orphean Warbler, Woodchat Shrike.

On passage: Dotterel.

Access

Take the N-232 out of Zaragoza and after 20 km turn right onto the C-222 for Belchite (29 km). Alternatively, from the N-II through La Almunia de Doña Godina take the C-220 and then the C-221 (44 km).

Description

A part of the Ebro valley where steppe areas alternate with cereal fields and irrigated areas. There are a few high points with stands of pines, and occasional gullies and rockfaces carved out by the river network.

Recommended routes

Route A consists of a visit to the Reserva La Lomaza, a reserve created in 1987 and managed by the Spanish Ornithological Society. Permission to visit the area should be sought in writing from: COMENA (Edificio Pignatelli, Pº María Agustín s/n, 50071 Zaragoza). The reserve can be reached by taking the turn at the 11 km marker post on the C-222. The main species to be seen are Stone Curlew, Pin-tailed Sandgrouse, Dupont's Lark, Short-toed Lark and Lesser Short-toed Lark.

To undertake **route B**, leave Belchite on the minor road for Codo and Quinto. Between these two villages, turn left onto a track taking you to the Balsa de Planerón, a reservoir visible from the road. A little farther on is a bird reserve

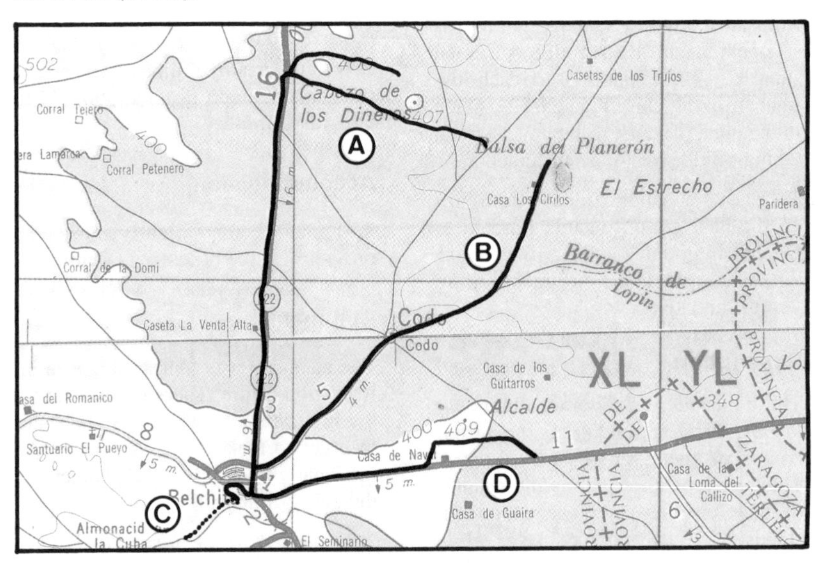

belonging to the Spanish Ornithological Society where you will have no difficulty in seeing Dupont's Lark and other steppe-dwelling birds and, on summer mornings at about 10.00, groups of Black-bellied and Pin-tailed Sandgrouse which go to drink at the reservoir.

Route C consists of a walk along El Tercón, a relatively deep ravine carved out by the river Aguasvivas. It can be reached from Belchite on a track which leaves from the near the flour mill and joins up with an old railway line cutting. The most interesting part of this walk is the observation of cliff-dwelling birds, including some birds of prey. In addition, in the orchards of the area you may see Sardinian Warbler, Melodious Warbler, Golden Oriole and Woodchat Shrike.

Route D consists of a visit to El Saso, a steppe area lying on either side of the road running from Belchite to Azaila. From the road you should see Short-toed Lark, Calandra Lark and Black-bellied Sandgrouse, although the most interesting feature is the guaranteed presence, from late August to late October, of Dotterel, particularly in the fields surrounding the stock enclosures known as Corral de Monís, which lies between the marker posts for km 49 and km 51 on the road.

Accommodation

There is a small hostel next to the petrol station in Belchite.

Comments

In Belchite there is a small information centre about the steppes, run by the Spanish Ornithological Society (SEO), where you can obtain additional information (in Zaragoza, telephone: 976-37 33 08). The centre organizes guided visits to the bird reserves.

Adolfo Aragüés Sancho

■ AR.28 LOS MONEGROS

Steppe area.

Main species

Residents: Golden Eagle, Peregrine Falcon, Little Bustard, Great Bustard, Stone Curlew, Black-bellied Sandgrouse, Pin-tailed Sandgrouse, Dupont's Lark, Calandra Lark, Lesser Short-toed Lark, Crested Lark, Thekla Lark.

Summer visitors: Egyptian Vulture, Lesser Kestrel, Short-toed Lark, Tawny Pipit, Black-eared Wheatear.

Winter visitors: Shelduck, Widgeon and other ducks, Red-crested Pochard, Fieldfare, Redwing.

On passage: Greylag Goose, Dotterel and other waders.

Access

Take the N-II towards Lérida (Lleida), and at Bujaraloz (67 km from Zaragoza), turn onto the minor road for the village of Sástago (28 km).

Description

Los Monegros is an area occupying the most central and driest part of the Ebro valley. It consists of a mosaic of plains taken up by grain fields and hillsides covered with sparse shrub vegetation. In addition to the considerable remaining areas of steppe, Los Monegros is also remarkable for surviving woodland consisting of Spanish juniper (*Juniperus thurifera*) and pine (*Pinus halepensis*), and the so-called *saladas*, seasonal brackish lagoons containing extremely saline water.

Recommended routes

Route A has its starting point in the village of Sástago where, before crossing the bridge over the Ebro, a track takes you to La Sardeta (1). The large rock face which the river has carved out should give sightings of Griffon Vulture, Egyptian Vulture, Peregrine Falcon, Raven and Crag Martin, while in the woodland on the banks of the river and its islands Penduline Tit, Cetti's Warbler and Melodious Warbler abound. Returning to Sástago, take the road leading to Alborge and before crossing the river (2), stop to look out for Black Wheatear.

In Alborge take the road to Bujaraloz and on reaching the plains turn left onto an unsurfaced track. The track is not marked, but is easily recognizable because it is large and heavily used. Keep to this track until you reach the El Camarón brackish lagoon. En route (3) you may have sightings of Lesser Kestrel, Tawny Pipit, Black-eared Wheatear, larks and, with a little luck, Great Bustard, Little Bustard, Black-bellied Sandgrouse and Pin-tailed Sandgrouse. Around the El Camarón lagoon (4), Lesser Short-toed Lark can frequently be seen. If the lagoon is full of water, ducks and waders may also be present.

At the end of the track you will see, on the far side of the road, the La Playa lagoon (5), easily recognizable by the ruins of an old barracks. Take any of the tracks down to the shores of the lagoon to watch birds.

Route B consists of a walk through an area of Spanish juniper and pine, one of the few remaining examples of this kind of woodland. The route starts at Hostal del Ciervo, a hostel at the 381 km marker post on the N-II a little before Bujaraloz. Although you can take any of the tracks in the area, it is recommended that you continue towards Bujaraloz and take a track running off to the right from the road itself. At the first fork you come to keep to the left and after a few kilometres you will

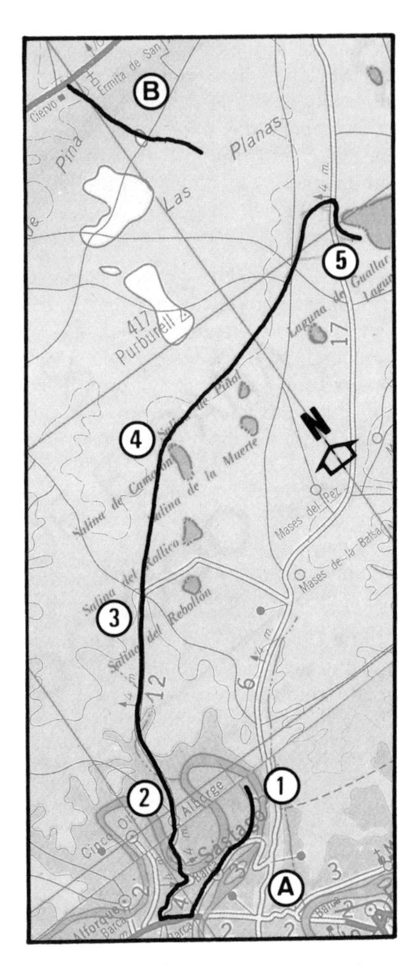

reach a building and subsequently a reservoir, the turning point of the walk. En route you will cross areas of dry-farming land and woodland areas where, apart from a large variety of birds of prey, you will also see Stone Curlew, Thekla Lark, Black-eared Wheatear, Dartford Warbler, Calandra Lark and Tawny Pipit.

Accommodation

There is plenty of accommodation available in Bujaraloz and Sástago. You can also stay at Hostal del Ciervo on the N-II.

Comments

Early spring and the winter months are the best times for visiting the area. It is better to avoid the summer season and days when people are hunting.

Javier Francisco Blasco Zumeta

AR.29 CHIPRANA LAGOONS

Natural lagoons.

Main species

Residents: Little Grebe, Black-necked Grebe, Mallard, Shoveler, Red-crested Pochard, Marsh Harrier, Water Rail, Black-headed Gull, Sardinian Warbler.

Summer visitors: Little Bittern, Purple Heron, Shelduck (nesting), Black Kite, Spotted Crake, Black-winged Stilt, Avocet, Little Ringed Plover, Kentish Plover, Great Spotted Cuckoo, Bee-eater, Golden Oriole, Black-eared Wheatear, Reed Warbler, Great Reed Warbler, Woodchat Shrike.

On passage: Little Crake, Ringed Plover, Little Stint, Dunlin, Ruff, Redshank, Greenshank, Common Sandpiper, Whiskered Tern, Black Tern.

Access

From Caspe, take the C-221 to Chiprana (12 km).

Description

A group of three natural lagoons with varying degrees of salinity. The shores are covered with reeds and reedmace, and the surrounding area is taken up by cereal fields, irrigated crops and olive groves.

Recommended routes

All of the lagoons are small in size and, for this reason, detail will only be given for access to each of the lagoons.

La Estanca can be reached from the road running from Chiprana to the railway station. After some 3 km, turn left onto a track leading to some houses. Go up to the houses, find somebody and ask them if you are allowed to vist the lagoon.

To reach La Salada, take the C-221 towards Escatrón and at the 113 km marker post, with the lagoon in sight, turn left onto a track. The shoreline has lots of inlets, facilitating observation of birds. You are reminded that it is forbidden to cross over to the islets, an undertaking which may also be dangerous since there are deep trenches in the bed of the lagoon.

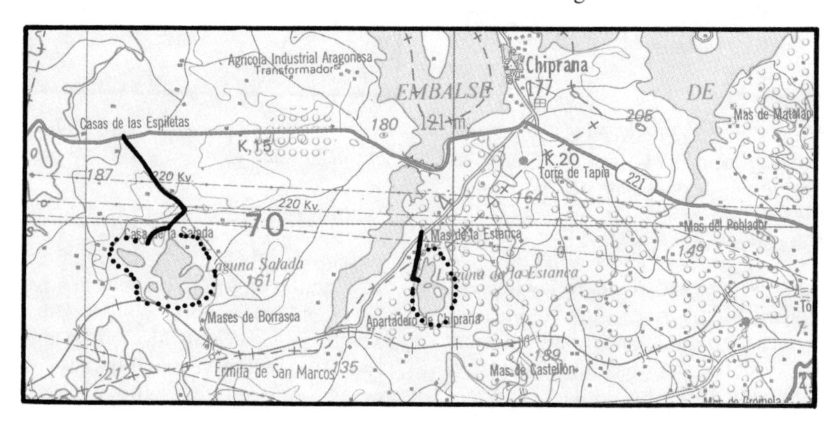

Before reaching Casa de la Salada (a hunters' refuge), a track leads off to the right taking you to Salitrosa, the third lagoon. This lagoon is supplied by water from its neighbour, La Salada.

Accommodation

There are several *fondas* and restaurants in Caspe.

Adolfo Aragüés Sancho

AR.30 GORGES OF THE RIO MARTÍN

River gorges with rocky areas and a reservoir.

Main species

Residents: Great Crested Grebe, Griffon Vulture, Sparrowhawk, Golden Eagle, Bonelli's Eagle, Peregrine Falcon, Eagle Owl, Blue Rock Thrush, Dartford Warbler, Great Grey Shrike, Chough, Rock Sparrow.

Summer visitors: Night Heron, Black Kite, Egyptian Vulture, Short-toed Eagle, Hobby, Alpine Swift, Bee-eater, Black Wheatear, Golden Oriole, Woodchat Shrike.

Winter visitors: Cormorant, Grey Heron, ducks, Wallcreeper (rare).

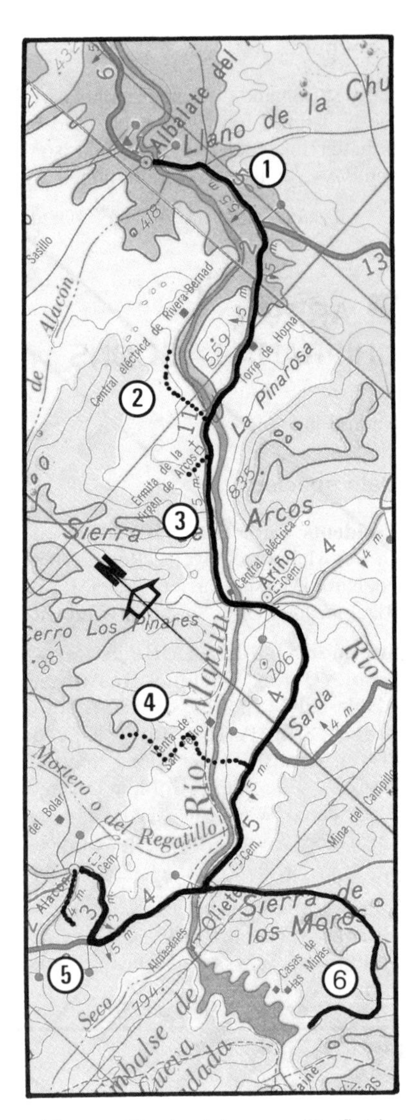

Access

From the N-232 between Zaragoza and Alcañiz, near the village of Hijar, take the turning for Albalate del Arzobispo.

Description

This is a varied route following the course of the river Martín. Various habitats are represented, ranging from rocky cliffs, the breeding ground for 100 pairs of Griffon Vulture, to riverside woodland, plateaux with fields, scrubland, pine woods, a reservoir, etc.

Recommended routes

Starting in Albalate and travelling in the direction of Ariño, make your first stop after 4 km (point 1) to observe the rock faces located to the left of the road. You will have no difficulty in seeing large numbers of vultures,

Egyptian Vulture, Chough and Raven. You may also see Black Kite, attracted by a nearby rubbish dump.

To continue, take the next right turn; after 11 km you will cross a small bridge from where a short stretch of track will bring you to a poplar grove located beside the river. From here, walk for about 2 km until you reach a hydroelectric power station (2); en route you may see vultures, choughs, Hobby, Alpine Swift, rock thrushes, shrikes, warblers, doves and Golden Oriole. With luck you will also see Golden Eagle, Bonelli's Eagle and Short-toed Eagle.

Return to the road and continue to the Ermita de la Virgen de Arcos (a chapel) which has a water supply and car park. This place makes for an excellent vantage point over the Sierra de Arcos (3).

After 10 km, having passed through Ariño and the entrance to some mines, you will come to a crossroads. 100 m after the crossroads turn right onto a track leading to La Sima de San Pedro (point 4): this is an enormous shaft, 100 m deep, inhabited by a large number of Alpine Swift, Rock Dove, martins, starlings, Chough and Rock Sparrow.

Continue along the road until you reach Oliete, from where you can visit the old rubbish dump at Alacón, now fenced off and turned into a feeding ground for vultures (5). Alternatively, you can go to the end of the Cueva Foradada reservoir (6), although to do this you have to travel along dirt tracks which are not always in good condition. In addition, the large number of crossroads may lead to confusion. It is a good idea to follow the route marked on the map, making your way along the most frequented tracks for about 11 km. En route you will see larks and Black Wheatear; on the reservoir itself, during the summer months you will see grebes, Moorhen and ducks, while in winter you should also have sightings of Cormorant, Grey Heron, Coot and a wider variety of ducks.

Accommodation

There are *fondas* and restaurants in Albalate. You can also eat in Oliete, and in Alacón you will find good traditional food and excellent wine at the Bar-Fonda El Castillo.

José Luis Lagares Latorre

AR.31 PONDS AT ALCAÑIZ

Natural brackish ponds, surrounded by steppe, and an irrigation reservoir.

Main species

Residents: Little Bustard, Great Bustard, Black-bellied Sandgrouse, Dupont's Lark, Calandra Lark, Lesser Short-toed Lark, Skylark.

Summer visitors: Little Grebe, Mallard, Montagu's Harrier, Stone Curlew, Pin-tailed Sandgrouse, Short-toed Lark, Tawny Pipit, Spectacled Warbler.

Winter visitors: Great Crested Grebe, Cormorant, Grey Heron, Hen Harrier, Short-eared Owl, ducks.

On passage: Greylag Goose, ducks, Osprey, Crane, waders.

Access

The ponds, known as Las Saladas and La Estanca, lie a short distance from the town of Alcañiz.

Description

Las Saladas is a series of seasonal brackish ponds surrounded by halophytic vegetation. They are in the middle of a steppe area with extensive cereal fields.

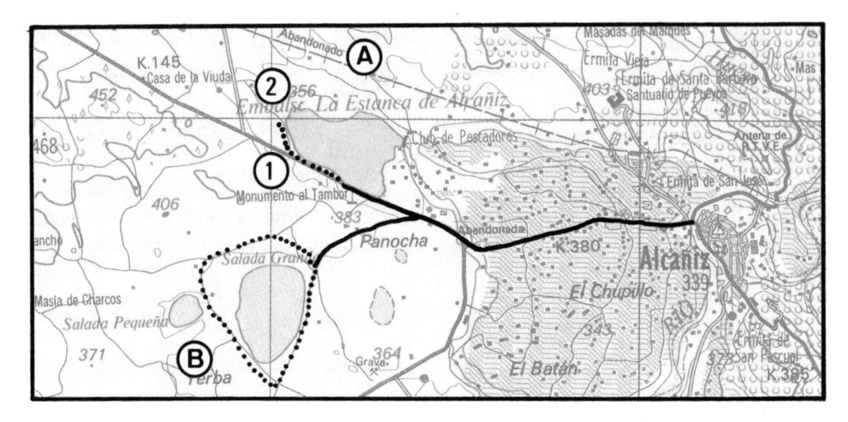

La Estanca was another of these ponds, but has now been turned into a permanent irrigation reservoir where water levels regularly rise and fall. It is surrounded by pine plantations, and the many tracks surrounding the reservoir encourage a steady stream of human visitors. Even so, this is the most important wetland area in the province of Teruel.

Recommended routes

Route A consists of a visit to La Estanca de Alcañiz, 5 km from the town of Alcañiz. From the monument known as the Monumento al Tambor, on the N-232, you will gain a general impression of the reservoir. From the monument (point 1), work your way westward along the reservoir shore (2) where you will see, above all during the autumn passage, many water birds.

Route B takes you to Las Saladas. Leave Alcañiz on the N-232 towards Zaragoza and after 4 km turn left onto a track. Leave your vehicle by a canal under construction and start the walk, which is about 6 km long. In winter you will see many groups of larks and pipits. You may also see Short-eared Owl, Little Bustard, Black-bellied Sandgrouse and, with luck, Golden Eagle and Peregrine Falcon. During the migration periods you may see Greylag Goose, Crane, Marsh Harrier, waders and various ducks, including Shelduck.

If you visit the area in spring you will see, among other larks, Dupont's Lark as well as Stone Curlew, Tawny Pipit and Spectacled Warbler. If you are lucky, you will have sightings of Pin-tailed Sandgrouse, Montagu's Harrier and Great Bustard.

Accommodation

There are plenty of hotels, hostels and *fondas* in Alcañiz, as well as a Parador Nacional.

José Luis Lagares Latorre

■ AR.32 NORTH FACE OF THE MONCAYO MASSIF

A mountain area with various kinds of woodland.

Main species

Residents: Goshawk, Sparrowhawk, Golden Eagle, Grey Partridge, Woodcock, Long-eared Owl, Grey Wagtail, Dipper, Dunnock, Blue Rock Thrush, Song Thrush, Chiffchaff, Firecrest, Goldcrest, Nuthatch, Raven, Rock Sparrow, Citril Finch, Crossbill.

Summer visitors: Honey Buzzard, Short-toed Eagle, Booted Eagle, Nightjar, Tree Pipit, Water Pipit, Crag Martin, Red-backed Shrike, Rock Thrush, Subalpine Warbler, Orphean Warbler, Bonelli's Warbler.

Winter visitors: Alpine Accentor, Redwing.

On passage: Ring Ouzel.

Access

Take the N-232 or the A-68 motorway, and at the Gallur junction (45 km from Zaragoza) turn onto the N-122 for Soria. After 24 km, turn left onto the minor road for Vera de Moncayo (3 km). When you reach Vera de Moncayo, there are two options:

a) Continue in the direction of Tarazona, passing through Trasmoz, until you reach San Martín de Moncayo and then Agramonte, where there are car parks and an information centre.

b) Drive in the direction of Añón until you reach the monastery of Veruela, from where a surfaced track will take you to Agramonte.

Description

El Moncayo, a mountain reaching 2,135 m in height, is the highest peak in the Iberian System within Aragon. Its location, at the point where the Ebro basin meets the Castilian meseta, combined with considerable differences in heights, explain the existence of very abundant and wide-ranging vegetation. There is woodland consisting of holm oak, oak, beech and pine, as well as scrubland and alpine pastures.

Part of the area is a Natural Park, the Parque Natural de la Dehesa del Moncayo, with an area of 1,389 ha.

Recommended routes

Route A consists of a 26 km journey by road, starting at the monastery of Veruela and finishing at the Santuario de la Virgen del Moncayo, a sanctuary. It passes through Agramonte. The points of greatest interest are the following:

1) Maderuela: holm oak and kermes oak woods where Short-toed Eagle, Turtle Dove, Nightjar, Bee-eater, Subalpine Warbler and Dartford Warbler

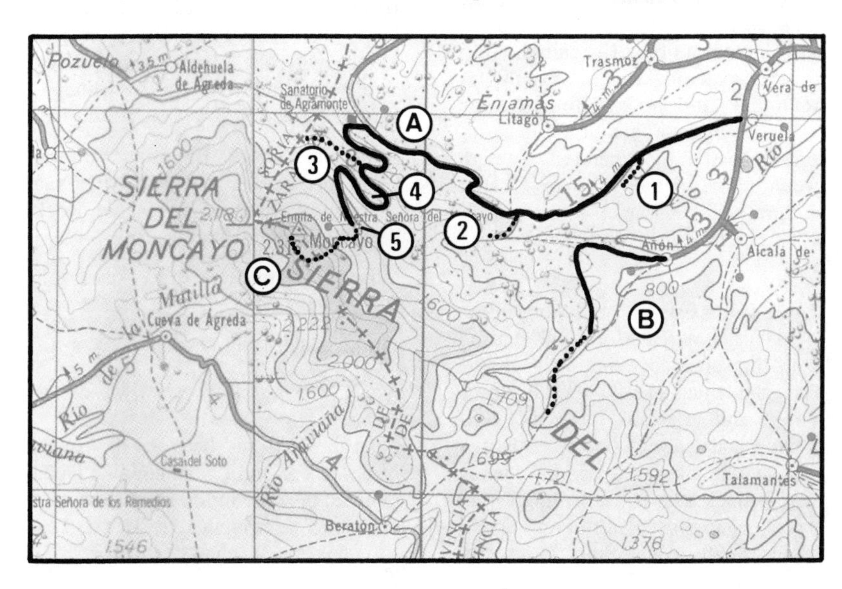

may be seen. At this point in the road a track leads off to the left, allowing you to walk through the holm oak wood along the course of the river Maderuela.

2) La Mata forest: Pyrenean oak woods where Honey Buzzard, Tree Pipit and Bonelli's Warbler can be seen.

3) Castilla ravine: a ravine with beech woods where you will have sightings of woodland-dwelling birds of prey and Woodcock. From this point, you can also walk along the forestry road which works its way up the ravine.

4) Prado de Santa Lucía: pine woods in which, among other species, you may see Crossbill.

5) Santuario de la Virgen del Moncayo: a natural vantage point rising above wooded slopes where you should have sightings of Griffon Vulture, Crag Martin, Citril Finch and Raven.

The starting point for **route B** is Añón, where you take the track leading to the Morana electricity generating station (6.5 km). From the generating station walk along a path leading along the gorge to the point where it opens out into another gorge, Horcajuelo (2.5 km). En route, make stops in the Pyrenean oak and pine woods to see woodland birds, although the most interesting part of the itinerary is the high ground, where you will see Griffon Vulture, Golden Eagle, Alpine Swift, Rock Thrush, Blue Rock Thrush, Rock Sparrow, etc.

Route C consists of a two-hour climb to the peak of El Moncayo, starting from the sanctuary mentioned above. The path, which takes you through pine woods and areas of scree, is well-marked and easy to follow, although you should take care on days when there is thick fog. The most interesting species you will see on the way up are Alpine Swift, Water Pipit, Goldcrest, Citril Finch and, in winter or during the migration periods, Ring Ouzel and Alpine Accentor.

Accommodation

There are several hostels in Borja, Tarazona and Agreda, as well as a hotel in Tarazona. In addition, there is a hospice at the Santuario de la Virgen del Moncayo, although this is only open in the months of July and August. There is also a mountain refuge on the road leading up to the monastery.

Enrique Pelayo Zueco

AR.33 SOUTH FACE OF THE MONCAYO MASSIF AND UPPER REACHES OF THE RIVER ISUELA

A mountain area with many cliffs.

Main species

Residents: Griffon Vulture, Golden Eagle, Peregrine Falcon, Rock Dove, Eagle Owl, Thekla Lark, Dipper, Black Wheatear, Blue Rock Thrush, Chough, Raven, Rock Sparrow, Rock Bunting.

Summer visitors: Egyptian Vulture, Short-toed Eagle, Alpine Swift, Crag Martin, Black-eared Wheatear, Rock Thrush, Ortolan Bunting.

Winter visitors: Alpine Accentor, Wallcreeper.

On passage: Ring Ouzel.

Access

Take the N-II and between the towns of Calatayud and La Almunia de Doña Godina, take the minor road to Morata de Jalón, and from there to Tierga, Trasobares and Calcena (43 km).

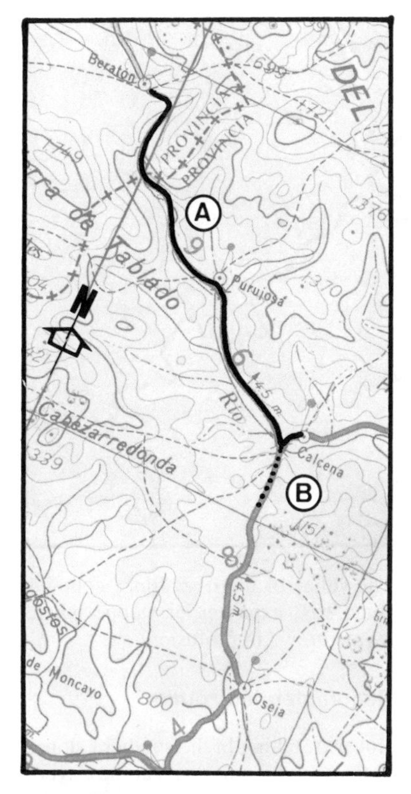

Description

A mountain area around the source of the river Isuela, on the southern slopes of the Sierra del Moncayo. A very rugged landscape with deep gorges and spectacular limestone outcrops and crags. Flora is represented by woods of scrubby holm oak, pine plantations and scrubland.

Recommended routes

The routes recommended for this area take you along roads crossing the zone, enabling you to see the most interesting species without causing disturbance.

Route A lies between Calcena and Beratón. It consists of a 14 km drive along an extremely narrow road with many bends and frequent rockfalls. Make several stops along the route to watch cliff-dwelling birds of prey, Alpine Swift, Black Wheatear, Rock Thrush, Blue Rock Thrush, Rock Sparrow, Chough, Raven and, with luck, Red-rumped Swallow.

Route B is a short walk from Calcena to Peñas del Cabo, running along the road joining Peñas del Cabo with Oseja. The route will provide you with a different impression of the area, but the birds which you may see are virtually the same as for the previous route.

Accommodation

There is a small *fonda* in Tierga, and in La Almunia, Agreda, Borja and Brea de Aragón further accommodation is available.

Enrique Pelayo Zueco

AR.34 CALATAYUD AND AROUND

Mountain ranges and steppe area.

Main species

Residents: Griffon Vulture, Goshawk, Sparrowhawk, Golden Eagle, Black-bellied Sandgrouse, Dupont's Lark, Thekla Lark, Sardinian Warbler.

Summer visitors: Stone Curlew, Short-toed Lark, Black-eared Wheatear, Spectacled Warbler, Orphean Warbler.

Access

The city of Calatayud, on the N-II, is the logical base from which to visit the region.

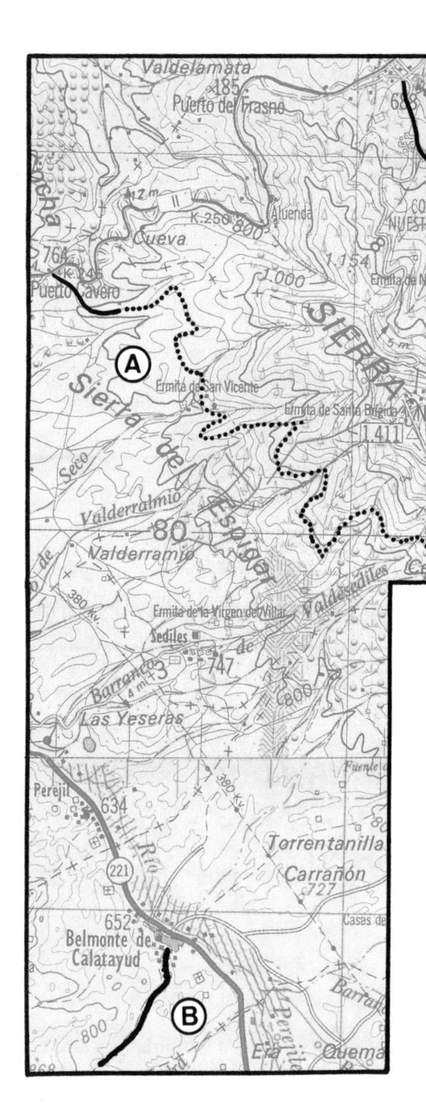

Description

The mountain ranges of Vicort and El Espigar, which reach heights of 1,400 m, are the foothills of the Iberian System which run down to the Ebro basin. Vegetation consists largely of conifer plantations, although there are also substantial areas of holm oak woodland and some stands of Lusitanian oak and juniper.

The valley of the river Jiloca contains some vast expanses of steppe where thyme grows in profusion.

Recommended routes

Route A, taking in the southern slopes of the Vicort range, starts at the Cavero pass, at the 245 km marker post on the N-II. From the pass take a track, indicated with a sign saying *Camino Forestal de la Sierra de Vicort* (Sierra de Vicort forest path), and continue until you reach a forestry hut. From here you can only continue on foot or in a four wheel drive vehicle until, after 4 or 5 km, you will come to the foot of Cerro Castillejo. You will pass through holm oak woodland where you will see up to 4 species of warbler and, in the pine woods, you may see Goshawk, Sparrowhawk and Crossbill. The high ground of the range is covered by scrubland with scattered trees where you may see Tree Pipit, Rock Thrush and the occasional Griffon Vulture or Golden Eagle.

Another alternative is to visit the northern slopes of the range via the minor road running from El Frasno to Santa

Cruz de Grio. Generally speaking, the woodland on this side of the range is more highly developed, although the birds which can be seen are the same.

Route B takes you to the steppe area known as El Campo-La Torrecilla. To reach the area, leave Calatayud on the N-II and after 3 km turn right onto the C-221 for Belmonte de Calatayud. As soon as you have passed through this village, take a track which skirts the upper part of the village and takes you to the plains. En route you will see Thekla Lark, Black-eared Wheatear, Spectacled Warbler and Dartford Warbler, while on the flat land occupied by thyme bushes, Dupont's Lark, Tawny Pipit and Short-toed Lark abound. You will also have rarer sightings of Stone Curlew and Black-bellied Sandgrouse.

Accommodation

Calatayud is a large town offering a wide range of facilities.

Comments

The best time of year for visiting the area is early spring.

Francisco Javier Sampietro Latorre

■ AR.35 MONASTERIO DE PIEDRA – NUÉVALOS

River gorge and reservoir.

Main species

Residents: Little Grebe, Great Crested Grebe, Griffon Vulture, Golden Eagle, Bonelli's Eagle, Peregrine Falcon, Water Rail, Black Wheatear, Blue Rock Thrush, Chough, Rock Sparrow.

Summer visitors: Egyptian Vulture, Alpine Swift, Bee-eater.

Winter visitors: Cormorant, Grey Heron, ducks.

Access

From Calatayud take the C-202 to Nuévalos (25 km).

Description

Limestone gorges worked by the river Piedra, with cliffs of varying height. The banks of the river support riverside woodland consisting of poplar, ash, walnut, etc. Near the village of Nuévalos, where the valley opens out, a reservoir known as La Tranquera has been created. Here there is a large reedbed.

Recommended routes

Route A consists of a 3 km walk along the gorges of the river Piedra. Leave Nuévalos on the minor road to Ibdes and park your car in the large layby at

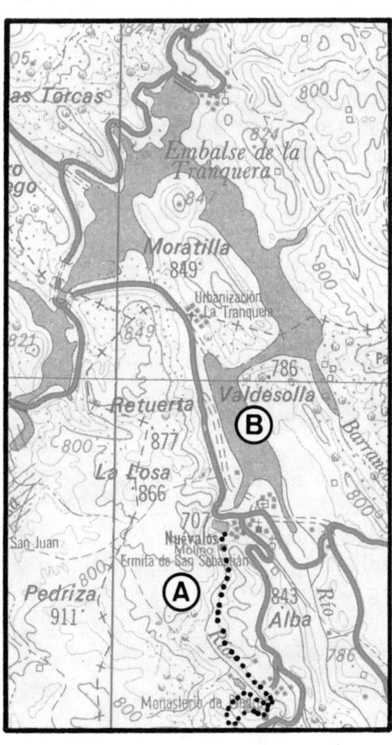

the gorge entrance. The route will give you sightings of various cliff-dwelling birds of prey, Alpine Swift, Black Wheatear, Chough, Blue Rock Thrush and Crag Martin. The route ends at the Monasterio de Piedra, a monastery set in a landscape of great beauty in dense, mature woodland where you should be able to see a wide range of forest birds.

Route B enables you to visit various spots on the shore of La Tranquera, a reservoir. The best site is near the village of Nuévalos, from where you can command a view over an extensive reedbed. In winter, you will see Cormorant, Grey Heron, Great Crested Grebe, Little Grebe, Coot and various ducks.

Accommodation

There is plenty of hotel accommodation available in Nuévalos, as well as a first-class campsite.

Comments

The best time of year for visiting the area is spring. If you are going to visit the Monasterio de Piedra, where you are required to pay an entrance fee, it is worthwhile avoiding weekends in spring and summer since they bring a large influx of visitors.

Francisco Javier Sampietro Latorre

■ AR.36 GALLOCANTA LAKE

A large natural lake of great significance for wintering ducks and Coot (over 200,000 individuals), as well as migrating and wintering Crane (54,000 in November 1989).

Main species

Residents: Little Grebe, Marsh Harrier, Shelduck, Mallard, Gadwall, Red-crested Pochard, Pochard, Coot, Great Bustard, Stone Curlew, Lapwing, Black-headed Gull, Black-bellied Sandgrouse, Dupont's Lark, Calandra Lark.

Summer visitors: Black-necked Grebe, Montagu's Harrier, Little Bustard, Black-winged Stilt, Avocet, Little Ringed Plover, Kentish Plover, Gull-billed Tern, Whiskered Tern, Short-toed Lark, Tawny Pipit, Yellow Wagtail, Wheatear, Reed Warbler, Great Reed Warbler.

Winter visitors: Teal, Pintail, Shoveler, Tufted Duck, Crane.

On passage: Greylag Goose, Crane, waders, marsh terns.

Access

From Daroca take the C-211 towards Cillas. Turn onto the minor road taking you to the village of Gallocanta (22 km).

Description

The Gallocanta lake, considered to be the largest lake in the Iberian Peninsula, is fed by rainwater, giving rise to dramatic changes in water level from year to year, inevitably conditioning the birdlife present both in winter and during the breeding season. In wet years, the lake reaches a maximum size of 7.7 km x 2.5 km, while in other years the lake dries out completely over the summer. The waters of the lake are saline, but fresh water springs allow for localized patches of reeds and reedmace. It should also be pointed out that underwater vegetation is considerable.

The surrounding fields are characteristic of a steppe area.

The altitude of the lake, at some 1,000 m above sea level, gives rise to a climate which is extremely continental in

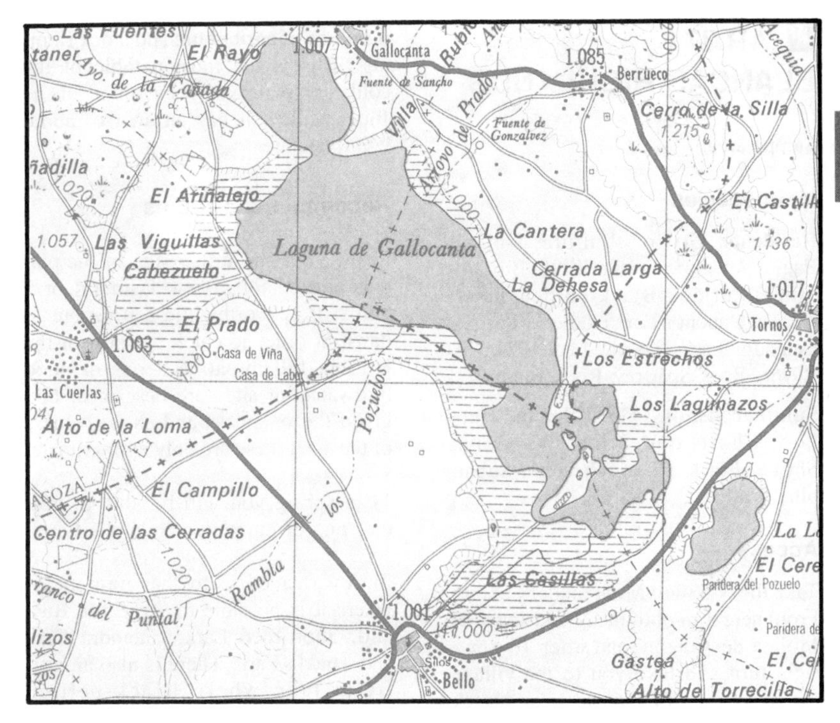

nature, with very low temperatures being reached in winter.

The area is a National Game Refuge (6,720 hectares).

Recommended routes

The main part of the lake lies to the northwest and can be commanded extremely well from the *ermita* or chapel of El Buen Acuerdo, which can be reached from the village of Las Cuerlas. If you want to see Crane coming in to roost at dusk, it is probably better to go to the southern and eastern shores between Las Cuerlas, Bello and Tornos. In spring, the most interesting part of the lake is that lying between Bello and Tornos, where the so-called *lagunazos* (flooded areas) provide an interesting series of ponds, islets, rush beds and areas of halophytic vegetation.

Accommodation

Although there is a small *fonda* in Tornos, it is worthwhile going to the nearby villages of Daroca or Calamocha, where a wider range of accommodation is available.

Comments

Since this a National Game Refuge, it is worth asking for permission to visit the lake of Gallocanta in advance. This can be obtained by contacting the Servicio Provincial de Agricultura, Ganadería y Montes; Sección de Conservación del Medio Natural, c/ Vázquez de Mella, 10; 50009 Zaragoza.

The best time of year for visiting the area is between November and March. Take warm clothing.

Bernardo Arroyo

AR.37 BLANCAS HIGHLANDS

Steppe area.

Main species

Residents: Griffon Vulture, Golden Eagle, Peregrine Falcon, Little Bustard, Stone Curlew, Black-bellied Sandgrouse, Dupont's Lark (some 400 pairs), Calandra Lark, Thekla Lark, Chough, Raven, Rock Sparrow, Rock Bunting.

Summer visitors: Great Spotted Cuckoo, Short-toed Lark, Woodchat Shrike, Black-eared Wheatear, Subalpine Warbler.

Access

Take the N-330 to Monreal del Campo. From here turn onto the N-211 towards Molina de Aragón, and after 10 km a right turn will take you to the village of Blancas. From Blancas take a track leading northwards through an area of hay ricks and subsequently past a dumping ground.

Description

This high plateau forms part of the Iberian System. It was deforested for the purposes of agriculture and stock farming. This is the most notable of the cold, dry plateaux to be found in the Jiloca valley. It has an area of about 2,500 hectares.

Recommended routes

Leave your car at the edge of the plateau and go for a walk lasting 4 or 5 hours. It is worthwhile setting out at dawn in order to catch the best of the larks in full throat. A series of good birdwatching sites are described, but, given the openness and extensiveness of the area, these are only approximate:

1) In spring you will be able to hear the song of numerous Dupont's Lark.

2) An area close to the grain fields where it is possible to see Little Bustard, Short-toed Lark, Calandra Lark and Thekla Lark. There is also an artificial lake where Black-bellied Sandgrouse come down to drink in the heat of the day.

3) Lookout point at Alto del Campanar: from here you will see Griffon Vulture, Golden Eagle and Black-eared Wheatear, and the odd ancient example of Spanish juniper.

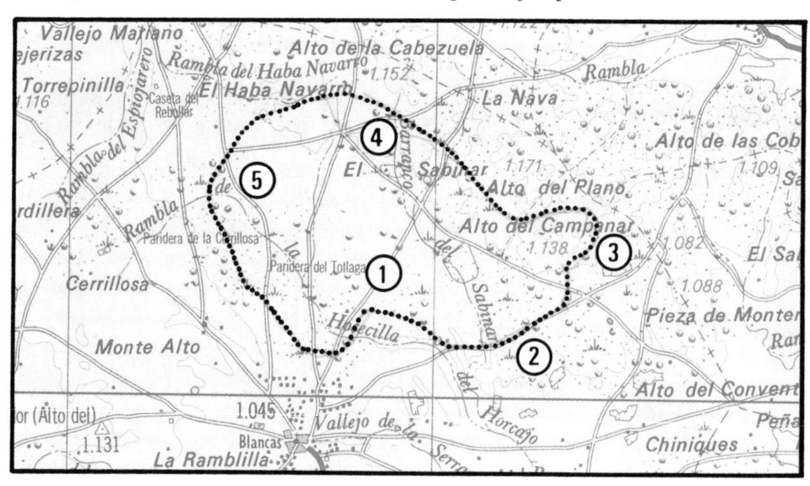

4) As you come down the hill you will see Peregrine Falcon, Black-bellied Sandgrouse, Stone Curlew and, around the stock enclosures, Chough. There is an area of degenerate holm oak woodland near which you may also see Rock Bunting, Woodchat Shrike and Subalpine Warbler.

5) During the migration periods and over the winter you will see flights of Crane making for the nearby Gallocanta lake.

Accommodation

In the villages around Monreal del Campo and Calamocha there are several hotels, hostels and *fondas*.

Comments

To avoid having the sun in your eyes, it is worth walking around the plateau in an anticlockwise direction.

In winter it is extremely cold, so it is a good idea to take plenty of warm clothing.

Chabier de Jaime

■ AR.38 SANT JUST HIGHLANDS

High-altitude plateaux of great interest during the autumn migration period.

Main species

Residents: Griffon Vulture, Golden Eagle, Peregrine Falcon, Chough.

Summer visitors: Egyptian Vulture, Short-toed Eagle, Hobby, Nightjar, Tawny Pipit, Dunnock, Black Redstart, Wheatear, Rock Thrush.

Winter visitors: Alpine Accentor.

On passage: Honey Buzzard, Black Kite, Red Kite, Marsh Harrier, Hen Harrier, Buzzard, Osprey, Crane, Alpine Swift, Bee-eater, swallows and martins, Mistle Thrush.

Access

From Teruel, take the N-420 towards Alcañiz and 5 km after Mezquita de Jarque (53 km from Teruel), turn right onto a track leading you up to the plateau (the track is marked with posts painted red and white).

Description

This is an enormous, rolling plateau lying at a height of 1,500 m. There is practically no soil and bare rock is present everywhere. The slopes are battered by constant, strong winds, intense heat in summer and extremely low winter temperatures. Vegetation consists of low-growing juniper, thorny scrub, short-cropped pastureland and, on the northern slopes, hawthorn, blackthorn and bearberry. Part of the arca has been ploughed and planted with pines.

Recommended routes

Once you have reached the top of the plateau, 3 km from the road, continue along the surfaced road until you reach the telephone exchange, from where the walks begin (point 1). Although the duration and length of the walks is your decision, it is worthwhile making them as long as possible. Many of the species mentioned above are easier to see on the northern edge of the plateau, overlooking the Escucha valley. The track to the survey point at Sant Just (1,522 m) will allow you to see a curious geological phenomenon: some enormous cracks, 1.5 km long and an average of 5 m deep, with widths varying between 15 cm and 3 m.

From here you can continue walking to reach the hill of Trinidad (2), or alternatively, take the track up to the forest

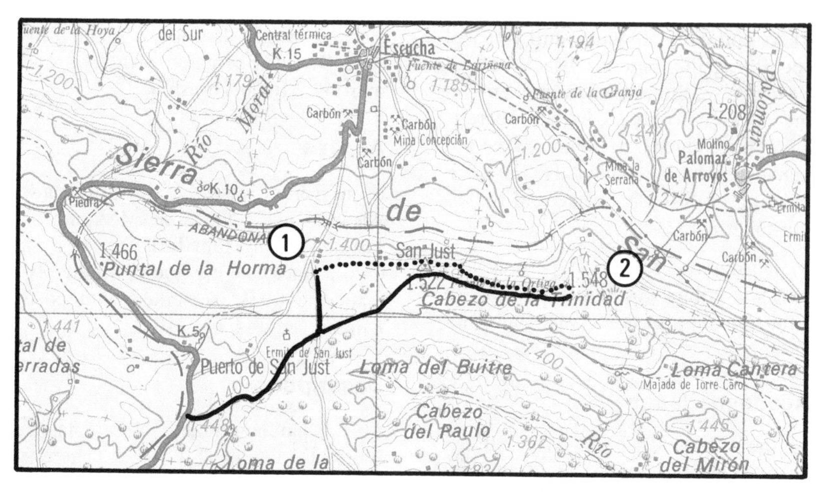

fire lookout point. Migration is intense from mid-August to late September, with remarkably large numbers of Bee-eater, Swallow, martins and swifts. There are also many Black Kite, Honey Buzzard and harriers, while other migratory birds of prey are a little less common. Finally, the groups of Crane and Mistle Thrush present are also remarkable.

Accommodation

There are *fondas* and restaurants in Escucha and Utrillas, respectively 10 and 15 km away.

Comments

It is worth taking several days over your visit in order to see the most interesting species on migration. Take warm, waterproof clothing, even in high summer. Beware of thunderstorms which are frequent and accompanied by lots of lightning and hail. Occasionally fogs come down and do not lift for days.

José Luis Lagares Latorre

AR.39
SOURCE OF THE RIVER PITARQUE

Head of a mountain river with large cliffs.

Main species

Residents: Griffon Vulture, Sparrowhawk, Golden Eagle, Bonelli's Eagle, Peregrine Falcon, Rock Dove, Eagle Owl, Kingfisher, Dipper, Blue Rock Thrush, Mistle Thrush, Chough, Cirl Bunting, Rock Bunting.

Summer visitors: Egyptian Vulture, Short-toed Eagle, Hobby, Alpine Swift, Bee-eater, Rock Thrush, Golden Oriole.

Winter visitors: Alpine Accentor, Wallcreeper.

Access

From Montalbán, take the N-420 towards Alcañiz. At Venta de la Pintada (28 km), turn off for Ejulve. In Ejulve take the road to Villarluengo, and before reaching this village turn right for Pitarque.

Description

This is one of the most beautiful and least spoiled parts of the province of Teruel, with large rocky cliff faces and a torrent of crystal-clear water. Vegetation consists of Lusitanian oak, pine, holm oak and varied Mediterranean scrub. Vegetation becomes more diversified around the river source with the presence of hazel, elm, maple, walnut, yew, etc. Groups of Spanish ibex frequent the rocky mountainsides.

Recommended routes

This route, consisting of a walk beginning from the village of Pitarque, takes you along a well-marked path. It is 5 km long and can be done in about 3 hours. The walk will bring you to the *nacimiento* (river source), located in an angle of the narrow limestone gorge from which a jet of water gushes out with considerable force, straight from the depths of the rock. The most interesting birds of the area can easily be seen along the way.

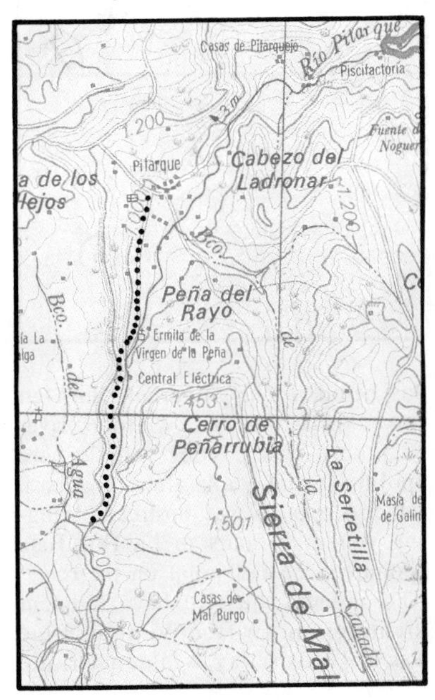

Accommodation

Villarluengo has a *fonda* which also provides meals. There is a hostel next to the fish farm which provides excellent, but rather expensive, traditional food. You can also camp close to Pitarque (Pitarquejo).

Comments

The road running from Ejulve to Pitarque is narrow and has many bends, so be careful when driving.

You can also reach Villarluengo from Cantavieja or Mora de Rubielos, along minor roads crossing the heart of the Maestrazgo area lying within the province of Teruel.

José Luis Lagares Latorre

■ AR.40 GORGES OF THE RIVER GUADALOPE

A limestone mountain range traversed by a river gorge.

Main species

Residents: Griffon Vulture, Golden Eagle, Bonelli's Eagle, Peregrine Falcon, Rock Dove, Long-eared Owl, Eagle Owl, Kingfisher, Dipper, Blue Rock Thrush, Chough.

Summer visitors: Egyptian Vulture, Short-toed Eagle, Hobby, Stock Dove, Alpine Swift, Bee-eater, Black Wheatear, Golden Oriole.

Winter visitors: Cormorant, Grey Heron, ducks.

Access

From Alcañiz, take the N-420 to Calanda (17 km) and from there turn onto the road for Mas de las Matas and Castellote (27 km).

From Teruel, take the N-420 to Venta de la Pintada (115 km), where you turn off for Molinos-Castellote along a road still under construction.

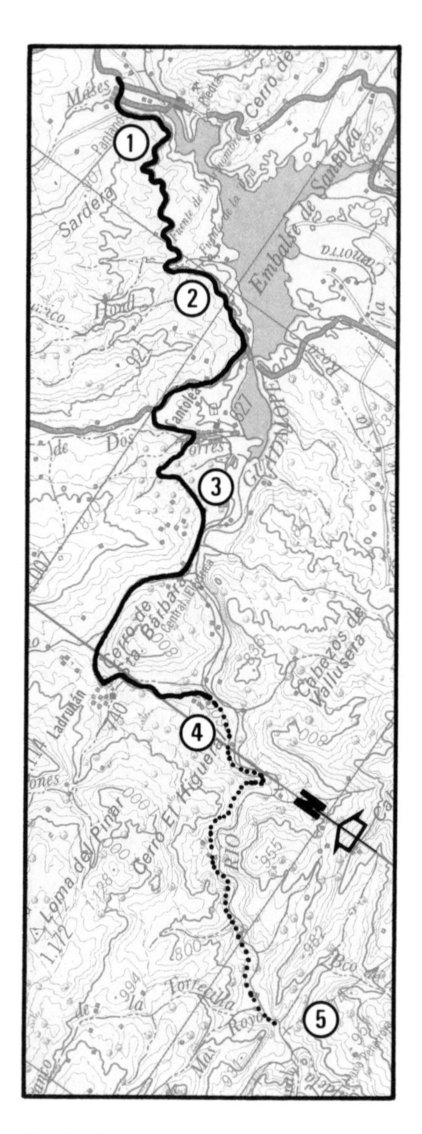

Description

The river Guadalope runs along a steep valley surrounded by high rocky cliffs. Dense Aleppo pine woodland and areas of Mediterranean scrubland cover the crests and valley sides throughout the route. There is riverside woodland on both banks of the river, as well as a reservoir where waterbirds can be seen. The landscape is very beautiful and relatively unspoiled. Groups of Spanish ibex can be seen on the cliffs.

Recommended routes

In Castellote, take the road for the Embalse de Santolea (a reservoir) and after 4.5 km turn right onto the road for Dos Torres-Las Cuevas. After 1 km, you will come to the reservoir where you can make several stops (points 1 and 2) to watch grebes and ducks on the open water. In winter, there are also Grey Heron and Cormorant and, during the migration periods, Osprey. Throughout you will see Stock Dove, Black Wheatear, Chough and, with luck, Egyptian Vulture and Golden Eagle.

Continue and turn left at the next crossroads towards Ladruñán, passing through the abandoned village of Santolea where large numbers of swallows and Spotless Starling frequent the ruins, as well as Kestrel and Barn Owl. 2 km farther on you will come to a layby next to the road (point 3), from where you can see large rockfaces occupied by Griffon Vulture, Egyptian Vulture, Peregrine Falcon, Bonelli's Eagle, Alpine Swift and other cliff-dwelling species. This is also a good spot for watching Hobby and Bee-eater.

Just before reaching Ladruñán, turn left onto a track running down to the river (2.5 km). Leave your vehicle here (point 4) and walk along the path which works its way upstream, bringing you in 2 hours to La Hoz Baja (point 5), the last point on the route. Throughout, you will have frequent sightings of Griffon Vulture, Blue Rock Thrush, Jay, Golden Oriole,

Chough, Rock Dove, Dipper and Kingfisher. You should not have any difficulty in seeing Golden Eagle and Short-toed Eagle and, with luck, Eagle Owl and Long-eared Owl.

Accommodation

For good value for money, try Hostal Castellote in the village of the same name or Fonda Aznar in Ladruñán. The former also serves excellent traditional food.

Comments

The road from the reservoir to Ladruñán is narrow, full of bends and in bad condition, so it is advisable to drive with care. The area is designated as being at high risk from forest fires and, for this reason, camping and the lighting of fires are forbidden.

José Luis Lagares Latorre

ASTURIAS

Wallcreeper
Tichodroma muraria

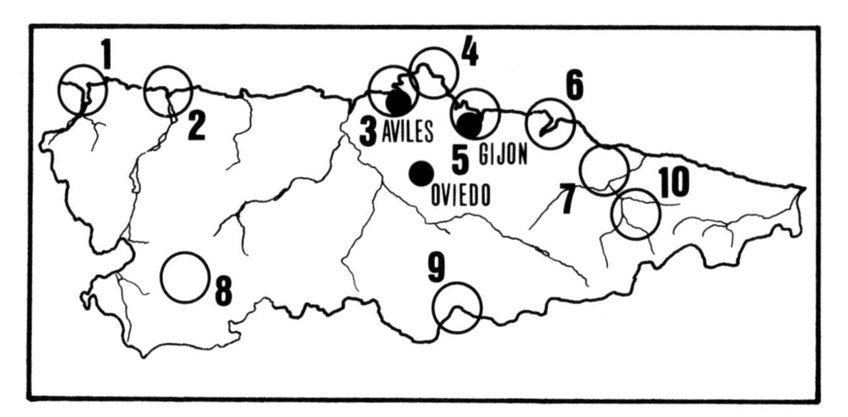

There is no doubt that Asturias is an absolute gem in terms of wildlife. The province covers most of the northern central side of the Cantabrian range, where the mountains are at their highest. High altitudes and abundant rainfall, a consequence of the proximity of the Atlantic, combine to create a steep, green landscape with extensive woodland. By contrast, low-lying flat areas are highly populated and greatly changed; large plantations of eucalyptus to a large extent spoil the original landscape and are of little interest to the birdwatcher. However this is compensated for by the coastline, which is extensive and in most places consists of cliffs.

For various reasons we have selected 3 sites in the mountains of Asturias. The Puerto de Pajares or Payares (AS.9) is an easy option; accommodation is available and ski lifts make this mountain pass more accessible. It has the added bonus of being a picturesque landscape very typical of this area. Muniellos (AS.8) is probably the largest and most unspoiled area of woodland in the whole Cantabrian range. Finally the well-known Picos de Europa (AS.10) provide an impressive high mountain scene with their soaring limestone peaks. There are also many other points of interest throughout the mountains, and the passes of Leitariegos, Somiedo, San Isidro and Tarna make good starting points for interesting alternative trips. The most significant woodland species include Honey Buzzard, Goshawk, Capercaillie, Woodcock, Black Woodpecker, Middle Spotted Woodpecker, Lesser Spotted Woodpecker, Treecreeper, Willow Warbler, Goldcrest, Marsh Tit and Citril Finch. When in open country or near cliffs you may see Golden Eagle, Short-toed Eagle, Griffon Vulture, Grey Partridge, Alpine Swift, Tawny Pipit, Water Pipit, Bluethroat, Rock Thrush, Ring Ouzel, Alpine Chough and Chough; and at higher altitudes Alpine Accentor, Wallcreeper and Snow Finch.

As has already been remarked upon, the open countryside has to a large extent been spoiled by forestry plantations, but nonetheless there are areas with meadows, hedgerows and scrubland consisting of whin and heather which are the habitat of numerous species. These species are decidedly Euro-Siberian, represented by Hen Harrier, Tree Pipit, Red-backed Shrike, Grasshopper Warbler, Bullfinch and Yellowhammer. There are some particularly interesting spots in the small coastal range of mountains known as El Sueve (AS.7).

On the coast there are small estuaries. They include those of the rivers Eo (AS.1), Navia (AS.2), Avilés (AS.3) and Villaviciosa (AS.6), which in terms of birdlife are similar to the estuaries of Galicia. In general terms, the estuaries are interesting for the waders they shelter during migration periods. Also, as is the case all along the Cantabrian coast, winter visitors are scarce although you may see some species, particularly divers, sea ducks and gulls, which are seldom seen at other sites on the Spanish coasts. The many fishing ports, among them Gijón or Xixón (AS.5), may yield some pleasant surprises in winter, particularly when there are cold spells in Europe or in the wake of heavy storms out to sea. As is the case in Galicia, areas with sea cliffs are best known for the autumn passage of sea birds; this takes place between late August and November. These include Manx, Yelkouan, Cory's, Great and Sooty Shearwaters, Gannet, Common Scoter, Grey Phalarope, Common Tern, Sandwich Tern, Arctic Skua, Lesser Black-backed Gull, Kittiwake, Razorbill, Guillemot and Puffin, which can sometimes be seen in spectacularly large numbers. The best promontories for watching the autumn passage are Las Romanelas point (AS.2) cape Busto, cape Vidio and, above all, cape Peñas and the nearby La Vaca point (AS.4).

It should also be said that the flat fields or *rasas* surrounding these promontories are a good place for watching the arrival of passerines on autumn migration (larks, pipits, wagtails, chaffinches etc.) and other coast-dwelling species of interest including Shag, Peregrine Falcon, Oystercatcher (nests in the area), Purple Sandpiper and Snow Bunting, although the last two species are only present in autumn and winter.

■ AS.1
EO RIVER ESTUARY

A medium-sized estuary constituting the most important wetland area in the region.

Main species

Residents: Mallard, Water Rail, Moorhen, Yellow-legged Gull, Oystercatcher, Curlew.

Summer visitors: Little Bittern, warblers.

Winter visitors: Great Northern Diver, Cormorant, Grey Heron, Greylag Goose, duck (about 5,000, including Widgeon, Pintail, Shoveler, Mallard and Teal), Tufted Duck, Red-breasted Merganser, Merlin, Coot, Lapwing, Golden Plover, Redshank, Snipe, Common Gull, Great Black-backed Gull, Razorbill, Fieldfare, Snow Bunting.

On passage: herons, ducks, waders, gulls, terns, aquatic passerines.

Access

The most important town in the area is Ribadeo on the N-634.

Description

The Eo estuary features large mudflats and sand banks as well as open water. It also has rush and reedbeds and flooded fields. Despite high population density and some industry in the surrounding area, the estuary is well conserved.

Recommended routes

We do not recommend routes so much as a series of points which can be reached by car and from where you can see the main areas inhabited by birds.

1) As Figueiras. From the harbour wall you can see the sand banks in the middle of the estuary. These provide a resting place for large numbers of Cormorant, gulls including Great Black-backed Gull, and some waders. With luck you will see sea ducks or the occasional Great Northern Diver on the open water.

2) Castropol. The road leading to the port runs alongside the estuary, giving you a view of the long inlet reaching back to As Figueiras. At low tide this is a feeding ground for large numbers of waders, and the banks and channels are frequented by Mallard, Widgeon and Pintail as well as Grey Heron and Little Egret. Occasionally Greylag Goose and Whooper Swan can be seen.

3) El Tarrón (Vilavedelle). A small inlet with rush beds occupying its shores. The road runs along the inlet. Here you will have sightings of Water Pipit, Great Grey Shrike, Reed Bunting, warblers and, with luck, Water Rail or the occasional crake.

4) From Porto to Reme. From this stretch of road you can see the main resting and feeding grounds for ducks and waders. On some winter days there may be as many as 5,000 ducks on the shore, largely surface feeders with the occasional presence of species seldom seen in Spain. The rush beds and sea walls of the upper part of the inlet are a resting place at high tide for many waders, particularly Curlew, with a scattering of Grey Heron and Cormorant.

5) Ponte dos Santos. From this bridge you can see most of the estuary, although you will need powerful optical equipment to be able to identify the various species on the sand banks or in the creeks. There are many gulls, waders, cormorants, herons and ducks, and, in bad weather, sea birds take shelter in the river mouth.

6) Punta da Cruz, Punta Espiela and the Arnao inlet. The mouth of the es-

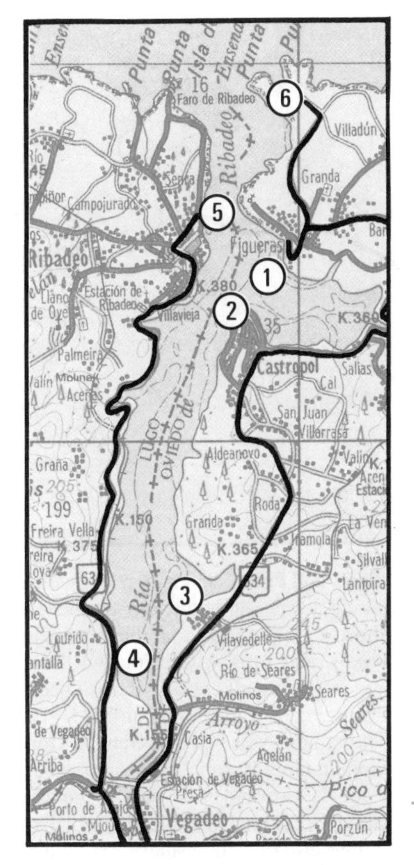

tuary is closed off to the east by Punta da Cruz and Punta Espiela, promontories which can be reached via a well-preserved dirt track. Both promontories provide excellent conditions for watching the passage of sea birds. In winter, the surrounding open country is occupied by numerous Golden Plover and various passerines including Snow Bunting. The Arnao inlet, lying between Punta da Cruz and Ponte dos Santos, is a good place for watching Great Northern Diver, Razorbill and Oystercatcher.

Accommodation

Plenty of accommodation is available, with hotels and hostels in Ribadeo, A Veiga, Castropol and Tapia, although there may not be any vacancies in summer. There are also several campsites, but these only operate over the summer season.

Comments

The best time of year for visiting the area is autumn and winter, although birdlife is present all year round.

One of the attractions of the area is that it can be covered in very little time, which may be of interest to people visiting the Cantabrian coast.

Manuel Quintana Becerra
(Coordinadora Ornitolóxica d'Asturies)

AS.2 RÍA OF NAVIA AND LAS ROMANELAS POINT

A small estuary and a coastal promontory.

Main species

Residents: Shag, Oystercatcher, Yellow-legged Gull.

Winter visitors: Cormorant, Grey Heron, Little Egret, Common Scoter, Curlew, Purple Sandpiper, Great Skua, Common Gull, Herring Gull, Great Black-backed Gull, auks, Kingfisher.

On passage: Shearwaters (including Cory's and Sooty), Gannet, Common Scoter, Skuas (including Pomarine), terns (including Arctic).

Access

The N-632 out of Navia runs alongside the estuary.

To reach Las Romanelas point, drive eastwards out of Navia and after 10 km

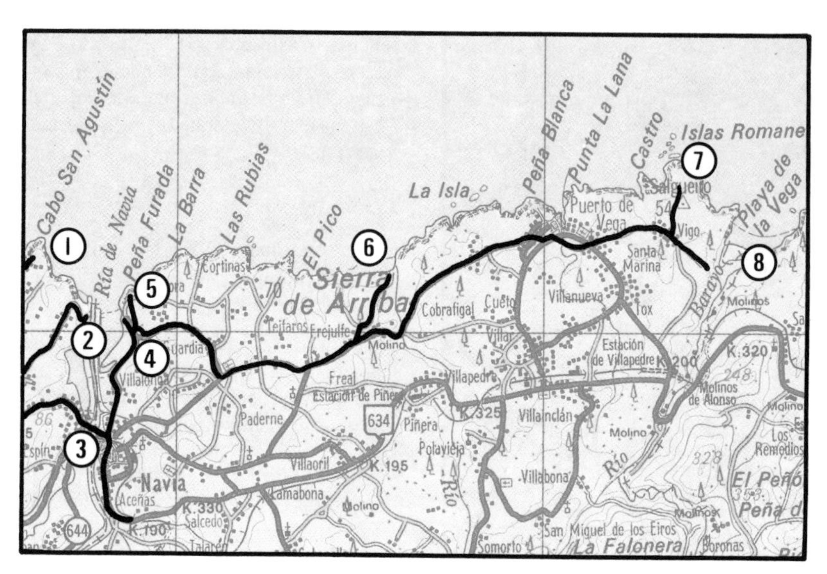

turn onto the local road to Vigu. From here, a track takes you straight up to the promontory.

Description

The Navia estuary is on a rocky coast consisting of sea cliffs. It is surrounded by open countryside and small settlements. The only area of open water is the main channel and surrounding this are mud flats, stands of rushes and flooded fields. At the mouth of the estuary is a small beach. On the right bank, near the village of Navia, a paper factory has been built which pollutes the water with its waste products.

La Punta de las Romanelas is a rocky promontory which, while otherwise unremarkable, makes a wonderful spot for watching sea birds. Nearby are the beaches of Frexulfe and Barayu, the latter with extensive reedbeds. This is a Game Refuge.

Recommended routes

All the way along the central channel of the Navia estuary you will see Cormorant, Kingfisher and, with luck, divers and Purple Sandpiper. It is worth taking a walk along the jetty on the left shore (2), reached via the beach at Foxos, and from where you will have a view of a small creek with rush beds, deeper channels and mud flats. Throughout you will see Gannet, Cormorant, Grey Heron, Little Egret, auks, waders, various gulls and the occasional Red-breasted Merganser. The bridge crossing the estuary (3) is also a good vantage point, while on the right bank the most interesting part is the last stretch (4), where there is a pond (La Poza) and a small beach frequently used by waders, herons, cormorants, gulls and ducks. A small promontory to the east of the beach (5) and the nearby San Agustín cape (1) are good places to watch sea birds (in winter Gannet, Great Skua and auks, and Shag all year round).

By positioning yourself on the eastern, seaward side of Las Romanelas point (7) you will see, often at close range, a stream of migrating shearwaters, scoters, terns, skuas, Gannet, auks and gulls. At low tide in winter, small groups of Purple Sandpiper can be seen among the rocks as well as the occasional Oystercatcher. The islets are a habitual resting place for Cormorant. Many passerines inhabit the surrounding open country, including Fan-tailed Warbler, Tree Pipit and Cirl Bunting, with large groups of pipits, larks and finches in winter as well as mixed groups of Black-headed and Common Gull.

Visit the beaches at Frexulfe (6) and Barayu (8) to see gulls, waders, herons and rails, although their presence is very much conditioned by whether or not there are people around.

Accommodation

There are several hotels and hostels providing accommodation in Navia and nearby villages.

Elías García Sánchez
and Manuel Quintana Becerra
(Coordinadora Ornitolóxica d'Asturies)

AS.3 RÍA OF AVILÉS AND LA GRANDA RESERVOIR

A small, badly deteriorated estuary and a dammed stretch of river.

Main species

Residents: Little Grebe, Yellow-legged Gull, Fan-tailed Warbler.

Summer visitors: Tree Pipit, Red-backed Shrike.

Winter visitors: Cormorant, Grey Heron, Common Pochard, Tufted Duck, Water Rail, Snipe.

On passage: Little Egret, Teal, Oystercatcher, Black-winged Stilt, Great Ringed Plover, Grey Plover, Dunlin, Ruff, godwits, Curlew, Greenshank, Redshank, Spotted Redshank, sandpipers, Turnstone, terns.

Access

Take the road out of Avilés for Luanco (Lluanco) and after 1 km take the turning for cape Peñas (Cabu Peñes). Continue along the road running parallel to the Avilés estuary and as you come into the village of Zeluán leave your car by the beach.

To get to the La Granda reservoir come off the motorway at Avilés and take the N-632 for Tabaza. After 3 km you will come to a petrol station and just afterwards there is a turning to La Granda on the left. As you enter ENSIDESA property you will go through a police check point (there is no need to stop). Continue over several railway lines and, having crossed the last one, turn right. Keep going straight for roughly 1 km and take the first left, leading up a hill and finally to the reservoir.

Description

The Avilés estuary is a highly industrialized area and today the only remaining part of the old coastal marshland is the Llodero inlet near the village of Zeluán; at low tide, mudflats measuring some 25 ha are exposed. Very close by, in the village itself, there is a small saltwater pond surrounded by rushes and reedmace where a hide has been installed.

La Granda is a reservoir measuring 50 ha which was built for industrial purposes. On its shores are a few buildings, stands of willow, large meadows and eucalyptus plantations. At one end of the reservoir is an islet topped with pine trees.

Recommended routes

In Zeluán the first thing to do is visit the pond. From the hide (1) Fan-tailed Warbler, Cirl Bunting, Water Rail,

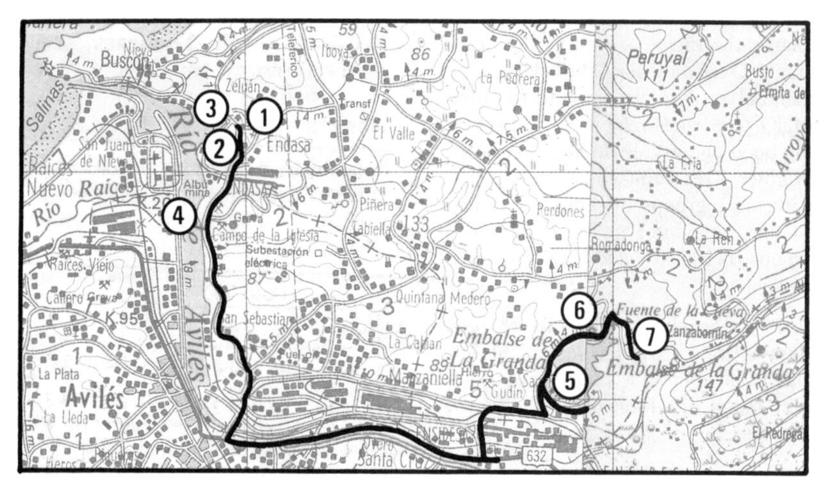

waders and occasional ducks can be seen. Continue by walking along the nearby inlet until you reach point 2, a quarry known as La Llera which is a good spot for watching Cormorant, herons and waders, particularly at high tide. The tidal mudflats in the inlet (3) are a good place for the water birds which abound during the migration periods, particularly waders and gulls.

Midway between Avilés and Zeluan there are mudflats (4). To see them, leave your car by the overflow channels of the estuary. This area is frequented by Cormorant, Yellow-legged Gull and some waders. Nearby are some tall, dry eucalyptus trees used as a roost by several hundred Carrion Crow.

It is worth taking a first look at La Granda reservoir from the dam itself (5); subsequently continue along the western and northern shores via a road running parallel to the water's edge. Opposite the islet (6) with its stand of pines, site of a heron roost, and at the end of the lake (7) you can see Little Grebe, Coot and various ducks including Garganey and Gadwall. With luck, you will also see Purple Heron, Osprey, Marsh Harrier and Goldeneye.

Accommodation

Avilés offers a wide range of accommodation. The Hotel Luzana, beside the Ayuntamiento or town hall, is recommended. There is also a campsite in Bañugues, 17 km from Avilés.

Comments

The keys to the hide in Zeluán are kept at the Servicio de Lucha contra la Contaminación (an organization fighting against pollution) in Calle Galliana, a street in Avilés. In addition there is a guide to the birds of the Avilés area which includes listings of birds seen at Zeluán.

A bus service runs from Avilés to Zeluán and to the La Granda area.

César Manuel Alvarez Laó
(Coordinadora Ornitolóxica d'Asturies)

AS.4 CAPE PEÑAS (PEÑES) AND LA VACA POINT

A coastal area with sea cliffs.

Main species

Residents: Shag, Peregrine Falcon, Yellow-legged Gull, Raven.

Summer visitors: Tree Pipit, Red-backed Shrike.

Winter visitors: Cormorant, auks, Snow Bunting.

On passage: shearwaters, Gannet, Common Scoter, skuas, terns, auks, Tawny Pipit, Whinchat.

Access

In Avilés take the road to Luanco (Lluanco) and after 1 km take the turn for cape Peñas (Cabu Peñes), which is reached via a series of well-signposted local roads (15 km). You can leave your car at the end of the short track skirting the lighthouse to the right.

If you want to go to nearby La Vaca point, it is better to continue as far as Luanco. A steep road leads from the harbour at Luanco through a housing development and then peters out into a dirt track, deteriorated in places, which leads up to the promontory itself.

Description

Cape Peñas is the northernmost coastal promontory in the province of Asturias. Three islets lie off the promontory. The coastline is abrupt, with steep cliffs falling some 100 m down to the sea. The surrounding countryside is quite flat and consists of grazing land and scrubland of heather and whin.

La Vaca point is a smaller promontory with appreciably lower cliffs.

Recommended routes

A walk starting at the lighthouse and taking you along the coast will enable you to see the various islets and cliffs. El Sabín (1) is the breeding ground of Yellow-legged Gull, where the gull chicks can easily be seen, and La Herbosa (2) is a nesting site for Shag. Other birds present are Peregrine Falcon, Cormorant, Raven and, in the nearby fields, Hen Harrier, Tawny Pipit and Red-backed Shrike. From the car park you can take a path which circles the promontory and runs down to its far end, which is a good place for watching sea birds. However, it is very rocky underfoot and not suitable for large numbers of people.

La Vaca point is an even better spot for watching sea birds on migration. By going to the far end of the promontory in summer and autumn, you will see shearwaters, skuas, terns, auks, ducks and waders. Neither is it difficult to spot Peregrine Falcon, which sometimes uses the outcrops as a resting place.

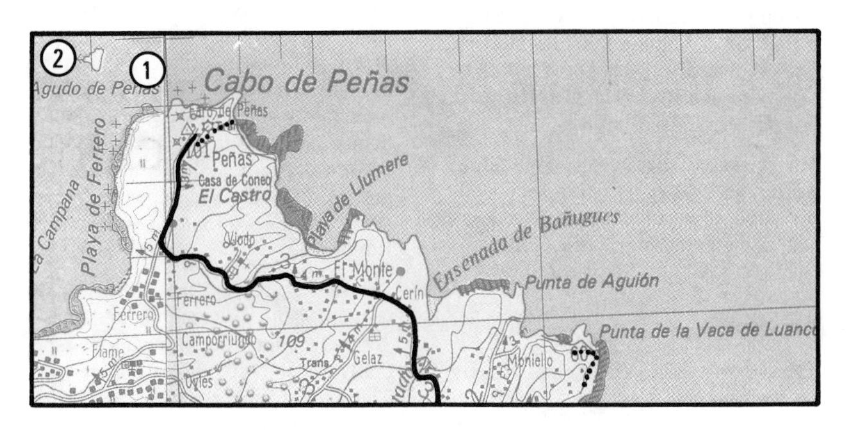

Accommodation

There are some hostels in Luanco and several campsites in the area (Bañugues, Antromero). In Avilés accommodation is also available. Hotel Luzana, beside the Ayuntamiento or town hall, is recommended.

Comments

Buses run between Avilés and Luanco and between other villages and cape Peñas, although the nearest stop is 2 km from the promontory, in El Ferreru.

César Manuel Alvarez Laó
(Coordinadora Ornitolóxica d'Asturies)

■ AS.5 BAY OF GIJÓN (XIXÓN)

A bay largely taken up by port facilities.

Main species

Residents: Shag, Yellow-legged Gull, Collared Dove.

Summer visitors: Red-throated Diver, Black-throated Diver, Great Northern Diver, Red-necked Grebe, Black-necked Grebe, Tufted Duck, Eider, Common Scoter, Velvet Scoter, Purple Sandpiper, Mediterranean Gull, Ring-billed Gull, Common Gull, Herring Gull, Great Black-backed Gull, Kittiwake, Razorbill, Guillemot, Kingfisher, Snow Bunting.

On passage: shearwaters (including Sooty and Cory's), Gannet, Red-breasted Merganser, waders, skuas (including Pomarine), Little Gull, terns (including Arctic), Short-eared Owl.

Access

The city of Gijón (Xixón) lies directly on the bay.

Description

The bay of Gijón takes in the whole shoreline of the city and consists of various wharves, beaches, cliffs, rocks, secluded inlets and fresh water ponds. There is a lot of human presence in the area and a high level of pollution, particularly that caused by industry.

Recommended routes

Virtually the whole bay is readily accessible on foot or by car. The most interesting places are the following:

1) End of the outer wall of the El Musel harbour: a good place for watching sea birds, occasionally at very close quarters. It is a perfect spot for watching the autumn migration. On certain days the number of birds passing over is spectacular, the sea wall and surrounding area being a good site for seeing Snow Bunting in winter and Short-eared Owl in autumn.

2) El Rendiellu or La Rula: if you visit this wharf in winter you will see at least seven kinds of gull, and will have no difficulty in spotting diving birds and terns.

3) Fishing wharf: in winter this is a good place for watching divers, Red-necked Grebes, Black-necked Grebes, Cormorant, Shag and auks.

4) La Osa: this wharf commands a small cove where in winter you will often see divers, Eider, Common Scoter, Cormorant, Shag and auks: more rarely you will see grebes, Velvet Scoter and Long-tailed Duck. From the breakwater you will be able to see groups of Purple Sandpiper and Turnstone at close quarters. Some Snow Bunting also winter here.

5) Arbeyal beach: although this beach is small and very contaminated, it is a good place for watching waders, especially during the migration periods. Throughout the year there are groups

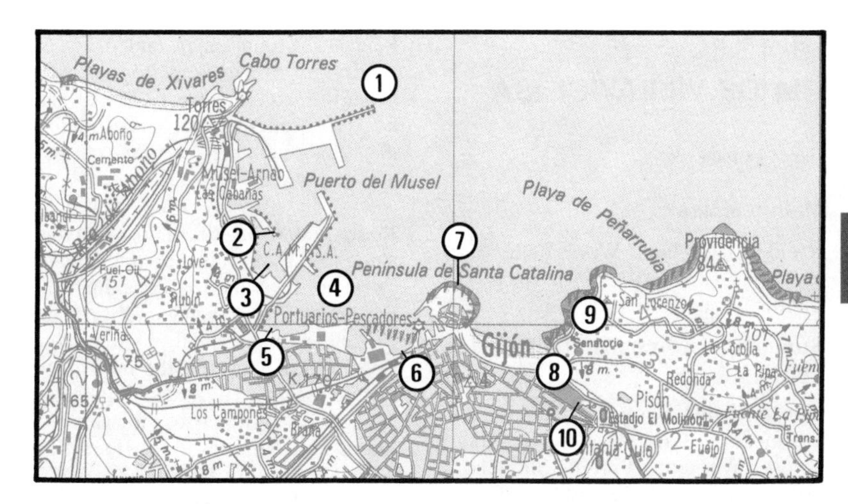

of gulls, almost always including rare types such as Glaucous Gull.

6) Pando cove: it is worthwhile visiting this inlet at low tide when the rocks are uncovered. In winter there are groups of several species of gull including Mediterranean Gull, which in winter are present in larger numbers than anywhere else on the Cantabrian coast. Cormorants, auks, divers, Eider, waders and terns can also be seen (although you can see quite a lot from the sea wall of the local harbour, the only way of seeing some species clearly is to move towards the rocks).

7) La Talaya or Santa Catalina point: this promontory commands both sides of the bay, making it a good place (if you have a telescope) for watching groups of birds resting on the water. It is also a good site for pipits, wagtails, finches and the occasional Snow Bunting.

8) Mouth of the river Piles: a popular resting place for gulls, including Common and Mediterranean Gull, and for waders on passage.

9) El Rinconín promenade: this is the best place for watching Purple Sandpiper and Turnstone at close quarters, particularly at high tide. You can also see sea ducks in the San Lorenzo (San Llorienzu) inlet, the best place for Velvet Scoter, and, in autumn, large groups of Widgeon and Shoveler.

10) Isabel la Católica park: the main lake in this park is a perfect spot for watching water birds at very close quarters since hundreds of Pochard and Tufted Duck winter here along with the odd Pintail, Widgeon or Shoveler. Wintering gulls always include Common and Mediterranean Gull and, in recent years, Ring-billed Gull (which can be attracted by offering them food).

Accommodation

Plenty of accommodation is available in Gijón. There are also a few campsites.

Comments

El Musel is a free port, meaning that you should take the precaution of declaring your optical equipment to customs.

Access to some wharves may be temporarily restricted due to building work.

Elías García Sánchez
(Coordinadora Ornitolóxica d'Asturies)

AS.6
RÍA OF VILLAVICIOSA

River estuary.

Main species

Residents: Mallard, Water Rail, Curlew, Common Sandpiper, Yellow-legged Gull.

Summer visitors: Little Ringed Plover.

Winter visitors: Great Northern Diver, Cormorant, Grey Heron, Greylag Goose, Widgeon, Pintail, Shoveler, Oystercatcher, Golden Plover, Grey Plover, Dunlin, Bar-tailed Godwit, Redshank, Herring Gull, Great Black-backed Gull.

On passage: Little Egret, Teal, Garganey, Ringed Plover, Knot, Sanderling, Curlew Sandpiper, Dunlin, Ruff, Black-tailed Godwit, Whimbrel, Spotted Redshank, Redshank, Greenshank, Green Sandpiper, Turnstone, Sandwich Tern, Common Tern.

Access

From Gijón (Xixón) take the N-632 towards Santander and turn off at Villaviciosa (30 km).

Description

The estuary at Villaviciosa stretches for 9 km from the town of the same name down to the sea. Surrounding the estuary are low hills not rising over 200 m. The main habitats are constituted by intertidal zones, fields known as *porreos*, land reclaimed from the sea by the construction of stone dykes and finally the remains of dunes, today somewhat degenerated.

Recommended routes

Route A takes you along the left bank of the estuary via the local road to El Puntal. The route can be undertaken on foot or by car, making stops at will. From the jetties of the El Puntal harbour you can see the channel joining the estuary with the sea; in the channel you may see divers, auks etc.

Route B starts in Villaviciosa and runs along the right shore of the estuary. There are several different options, the recommended one being to drive to the end of the estuary and then retrace your steps, making stops at the most interesting places. To do this, take the N-632 out of Villaviciosa towards Colunga and Ribadesella (Ribesella). After 5.6 km turn left onto the VV-6, which will take you to the beach at Rodiles. Continue along the beach until you reach some beach cafes at the far end. This is point 1, which commands a view of a large area of dunes, channels and intertidal zones where gulls, herons and waders abound.

Point 2 is the bridge over L'Espinal inlet. From there make your way along a track and a path down to the widest point of the estuary. This is a good spot for seeing waders and ducks. Point 3 is reached via the village of Villaverde. Follow the course of an artificial irrigation channel emptying into the estuary. From here it is possible to watch ducks, waders, herons, gulls and Cormorant on the mudflats; inland, in the nearby fields, ponds and reedbeds you will find rails, ducks, waders and herons. Point 4 is next to the El Gaitero factory, where a small layby gives views onto the head of the estuary. The estuary is still very narrow here, and is frequented by waders, herons and gulls. On the far side of the factory, you can reach the estuary by following a stone wall. Once by the water you can walk along the bank for about 2 km. In and around the central channel you will see waders, herons and ducks, and in the nearby *porreos* (areas of reclaimed farmland) there are geese, herons, ducks, waders and rails.

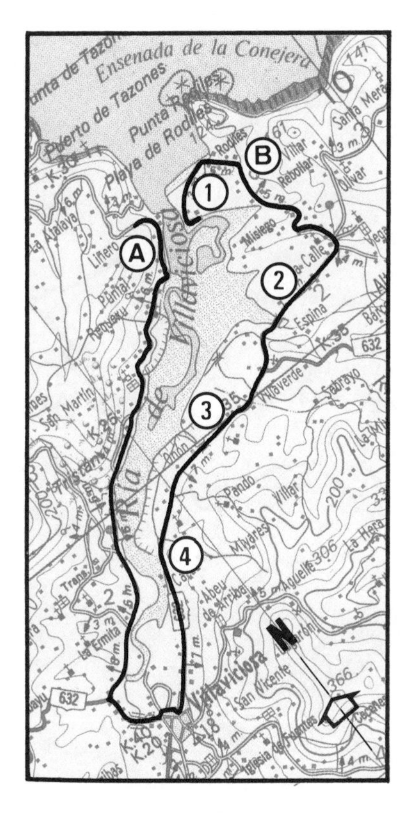

Accommodation

Villaviciosa has several hotels and hostels. There is also a hotel in Villaverde. There are three campsites in and around Rodiles and El Misiegu.

José Angel Diego García
(Coordinadora Ornitolóxica d'Asturies)

AS.7 EL SUEVE

Low mountains and farmland area.

Main species

Residents: Sparrowhawk, Buzzard, Kestrel, Water Pipit, Dipper, Marsh Tit, Bullfinch.

Summer visitors: Hen Harrier, Wryneck, Tree Pipit, Grasshopper Warbler, Golden Oriole, Red-backed Shrike, Woodchat Shrike, Yellowhammer.

Winter visitors: Woodcock, Alpine Accentor, Fieldfare, Siskin.

Access

The biggest villages near the Sierra del Sueve are Arriondas (Les Arriondes) and Colunga. The former is on the N-634, 65 km from Oviedo (Uviéu) and Colunga is on the N-632, 41 km from Gijón (Xixón). The AS-260 joins Arriondas and Colunga, which are 23 km apart. The starting point for Route C (Altu la Llama) can be reached from the 168 km marker post on the N-634, near the village of Infiesto (L'Infiestu), or alternatively from Colunga via the AS-258.

Description

The Sierra del Sueve is a coastal range of mountains. The foothills come to within 2 km of the coast and the highest peak, Picu Pienzu (1,159 m), is only 5 km from the sea. This range is a 7 km-long limestone outcrop, and its orientation means that the fauna growing on its northern and southern slopes is quite differentiated. Apart from pine and eucalyptus plantations, there are also patches of woodland consisting of chestnut, oak, beech, etc. as well as areas of pastureland.

Recommended routes

Route A starts at El Fitu, near the 10 km marker post on the road between Colunga and Arriondas. A path leads off from the road and gradually takes you up through the stock enclosures and meadows of Bustacu, Llavancu and Merguyines until you reach a narrow valley bringing you to the base of Picu Pienzu. This last stretch is quite hard going, but once you reach

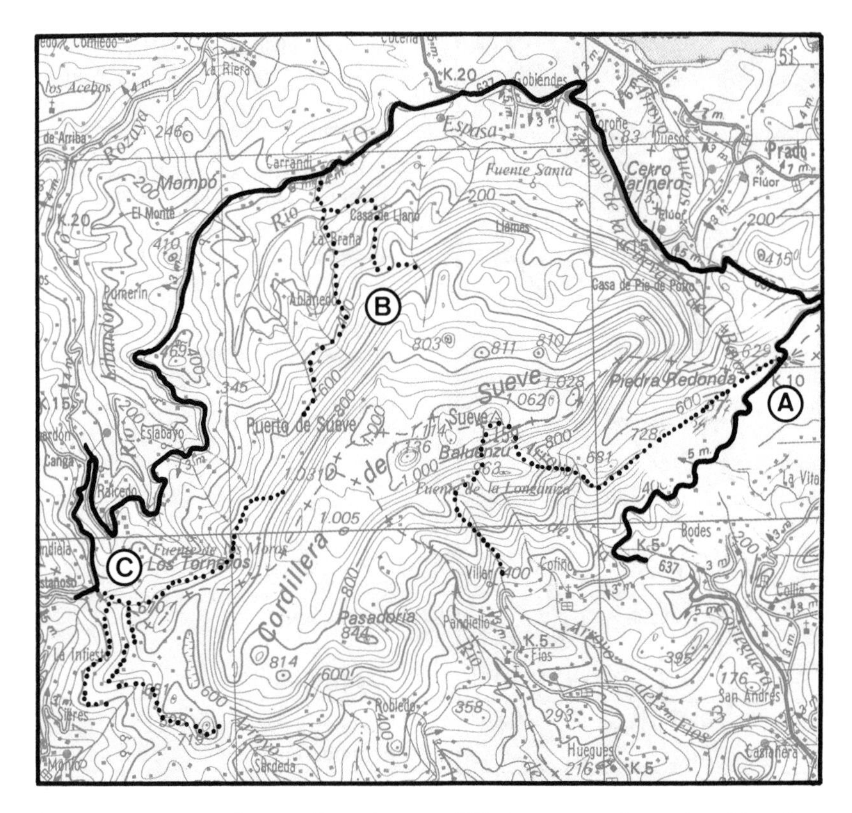

the top you can make small sorties into the woodland on the northern slopes.

To undertake **Route B**, leave Colunga on the road to Ribadesella (Ribesella) and after 2 km turn right for El Fitu. After another 2 km take a right turn to the village of Carrandi, where you can leave your car. Continue on foot along a track leading towards the mountains taking you past streams, woods and pastures. Depending on how energetic you are feeling you can either remain in the area by the stock enclosures encountered on the way or climb up towards the passes over rough terrain dotted with stands of trees.

Route C starts at Altu La Llama and takes you along a series of paths leading to the southern part of the range. This is very rough terrain with quite a lot of trees and small meadows.

Accommodation

Arriondas and Colunga both offer accommodation.

José Angel Diego García
(Coordinadora Ornitolóxica d'Asturies)

■ AS.8 MUNIELLOS (MUNIETCHOS) FOREST

A mountainous area with extensive deciduous woodland.

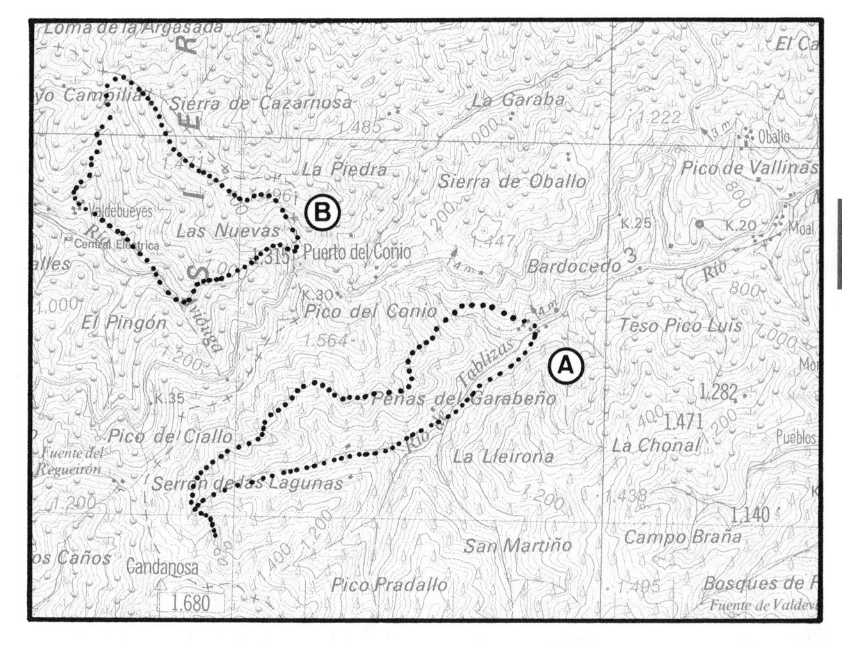

Main species

Residents: Goshawk, Sparrowhawk, Buzzard, Kestrel, Grey Partridge, Capercaillie, Woodcock, Eagle Owl, Tawny Owl, Black Woodpecker, Lesser Spotted Woodpecker, Middle Spotted Woodpecker, Water Pipit, Dipper, Firecrest, Goldcrest, tits, Treecreeper, Raven, Bullfinch.

Summer visitors: Honey Buzzard, Short-toed Eagle, Bonelli's Eagle, Booted Eagle, Hen Harrier, Hobby, Nightjar, Hoopoe, Whinchat, Pied Flycatcher.

Winter visitors: Redwing, Brambling.

Access

Take the N-634 out of Oviedo (Uviéu) to La Espina (60 km), from where you take the C-630 to El Crucero (8 km) and then the C-631 to Cangas del Narcea (33 km). From Cangas take the local road leading to Degaña. When you reach Ventanueva (17 km) turn right for Moal (2 km). From here an unsurfaced track takes you 5 km to the forest rangers' house at Tablizas where there is a car park and a visitors' centre.

Description

Muniellos (Munietchos) forms part of the Cantabrian range, and has one of the largest oak woods in the Iberian Peninsula. Within the area there are also large areas of beech, birch, holly and yew as well as riverside woodland in the valley bottom. It is a National Biological Reserve measuring some 5,600 ha.

Recommended routes

Route A is an 18 km walk which can easily be done in about 6 hours. The starting point is next to the forest rangers' house in Tablizas. An old logging track runs up the Degollada (Degotchada) valley for 10 km through oak woods and quartzite screes, bringing you out by some lakes. Return by following the course of the river Muniellos or the La Candanosa valley.

The whole walk is good for spotting woodland birds, especially the Fonculebrera area which abounds with Capercaillie in summer. The Degollada valley is a good place for seeing Black Woodpecker.

Route B is a 13.5 km walk taking about 6 hours. It starts at the Couñu pass where you leave your car and take a path which runs above the oak woods, passing through patches of broom and stony areas. From here you have a wonderful view of the northern slopes of Valdebois, another mountain in the range. It is also a good spot for watching birds of prey and other birds inhabiting the upper edge of the woodland. There is a lot of heather on the pass overlooking the village of Valdebois, meaning that it is easy to flush Red-legged and Grey Partridge. Go down to Valdebois village and from there follow the river upstream. This will take you back up to the pass through riverside woodland and then oak woodland which has been somewhat damaged by fire.

Accommodation

Cangas del Narcea offers the best options in terms of accommodation, although there are also pensions in San Antolín (Pensión Ibias) and Zarreu (Pensión Degaña). In Moal it is possible to find a room and a meal in a private house —Casa Abel is recommended. There are no campsites in the area.

Comments

Each day, a maximum of 20 people are allowed to visit the park. Each visitor should carry authorization to visit the area. To make a visit you should apply in writing, giving notice of at least 1 week and at the most 3 months. When applying you should include the full names and identity card or passport numbers of yourself and all persons accompanying you. Send your application to: Agencia de Medio Ambiente del Principado de Asturias, Plaza General Ordoñez 1, planta 5, 33007 Oviedo. Visiting hours are 08.00 to 21.00. It is absolutely forbidden to spend the night in the area.

Regulations are different for school groups. In this case, groups of up to 50 people are allowed and are accompanied by a guide. For more information call: 98-5242612 or 98-5242700.

Luis Aurelio Alvarez Usategui
(Coordinadora Ornitolóxica d'Asturies)

■ AS.9 PAJARES (PAYARES) PASS AND VALGRANDE FOREST

A mountain area with extensive beech woodland.

Main species

Residents: Griffon Vulture, Peregrine Falcon, Capercaillie, Grey Partridge, Black Woodpecker, Water Pipit, Blue Rock Thrush, Song Thrush, Marsh Tit, Raven, Snow Finch, Citril Finch, Bullfinch, Yellowhammer, Rock Bunting.

Summer visitors: Honey Buzzard, Egyptian Vulture, Hen Harrier, Booted Eagle, Crag Martin, Tawny Pipit, Tree Pipit, Whinchat, Garden Warbler, Red-backed Shrike.

Winter visitors: Siskin.

Access

Direct access to the Pajares mountain pass (Puertu Payares) is from the N-630 between Oviedo (Uviéu) and León. On the side nearest León, at about 800 m, there is a clearly marked turn leading to the tourist complex of

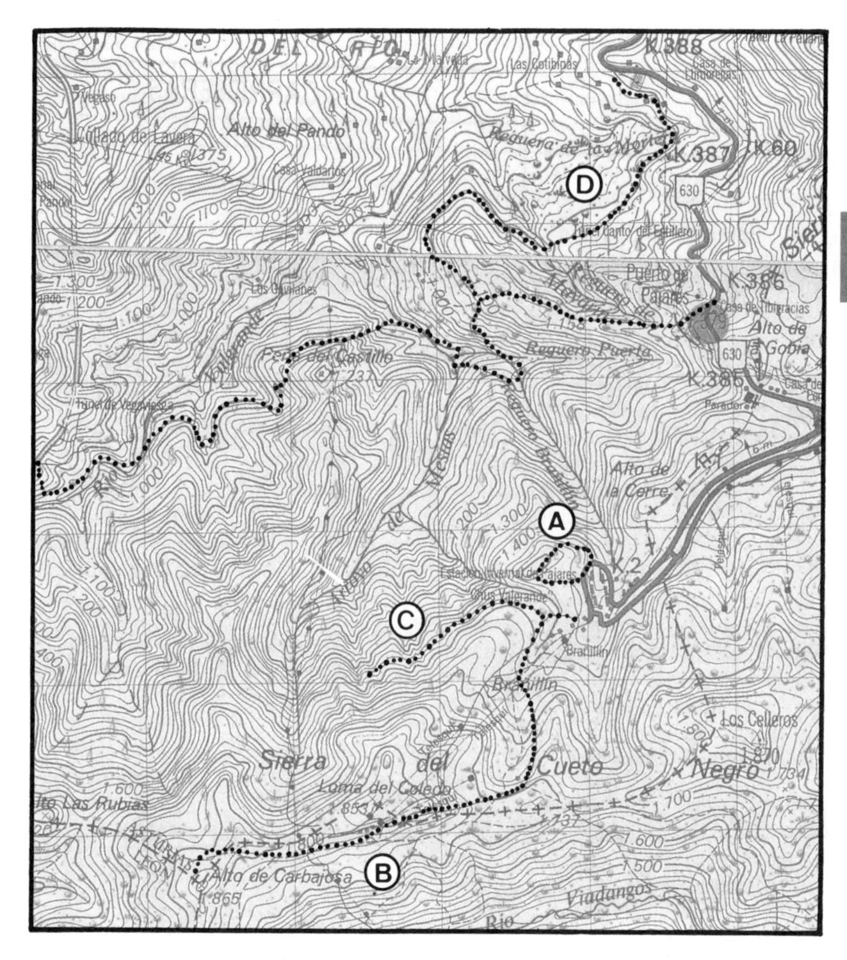

El Brañillín (El Branitchín) which constitutes a good starting point for various trips.

Description

The Puerto de Pajares is a mountain pass traditionally constituting the main means of communication between Asturias and the Meseta of central Spain. For this reason the area is much frequented by people. Today a motorway, a main road and a railway pass through the area in addition to several lines of electricity pylons. There are also tourist facilities and mining operations which have considerably affected the landscape.

Despite this, much of the deciduous woodland around Pajares and Valgrande has survived. The lower and middle regions are dominated by beech trees, while slopes getting more sun are mostly covered with oak. The upper regions are taken up by birch, and the high ground above the treeline is dominated by heath and broom.

Recommended routes

Route A is a 20 minute walk along a cross country skiing route. It starts at the El Brañillín ski resort, rounds a small hill and comes back to the starting point across flat terrain, making for easy walking. In the lower altitude areas near El Brañillín you will be able to see Whinchat, Yellowhammer and Rock Bunting, while open ground will give sightings of Griffon Vulture, Egyptian Vulture, Red Kite, Black Kite, Honey Buzzard, Grey Partridge, Water Pipit, Citril Finch and other rarer birds such as Snow Finch.

Route B takes you up the peak of Cuitu Nigru (1,853 m). In order to make the climb it is worthwhile taking the chair lift from El Brañillín, which is open all year round. From the top you will obtain a good view of the area. It is easy to reach Alto de la Carbayosa and the foot of the cliffs of Peña Ortegal and Peña Esquina. You can make your descent by walking along a path running across heath, isolated stands of birch, meadows and rock screes where you may see Skylark, Wheatear, Water Pipit and, with luck, Citril Finch, Tawny Pipit and Snow Finch.

Route C runs along a narrow path starting near the lift up to Cuitu Nigru. It takes you to the pastures at Mayéu Pedro Cano in the middle of the Valgrande woods. The path also runs through well conserved birch woodland and subsequently enters the beech wood. There and back, the whole walk takes 1½ hours. Birdlife present is typical of deciduous woodland, and includes Capercaillie and Black Woodpecker.

Route D takes you along the track running through Valgrande. It starts at the 388 km marker post on the N-630 and takes you for 10 km along the lower part of the woodland. You can see birds of prey —Egyptian Vulture, Buzzard, Sparrowhawk, Honey Buzzard, Booted Eagle and Peregrine Falcon— as well as passerines —tits, Bullfinch, thrushes, pipits and Siskin. On the lower ground, where beech wood gives way to pastures and scrubland, you will see Yellowhammer, Rock Bunting and Red-backed Shrike.

Accommodation

At the pass itself is the Parador Nacional Puerto de Pajares, a luxury hotel. The resort of El Brañillín has two mountain refuges which are open all year round. These are particularly good value for money, and therefore highly recommended.

Comments

Leaflets containing information about the area are available at El Brañillín ski resort and at the Parador. You are urged to avoid using vehicles on the Valgrande track.

Bruno Barragán Fernández and Fernando Alvarez-Balbuena García (Coordinadora Ornitolóxica d'Asturies)

■ AS.10 PICOS DE EUROPA

A mountain region.

Main species

Residents: Mallard, Goshawk, Sparrowhawk, Buzzard, Bonelli's Eagle, Golden Eagle, Griffon Vulture, Peregrine Falcon, Kestrel, Coot, Woodcock, Tawny Owl, Black Woodpecker, Crag Martin, Water Pipit, Goldcrest, Dipper, tits, Nuthatch, Wallcreeper, Rock Bunting, Citril Finch, Snow Finch, Chough, Alpine Chough.

Summer visitors: Honey Buzzard, Egyptian Vulture, Short-toed Eagle, Rock Thrush.

Winter visitors: Little Grebe, Teal, Redwing.

On passage: Booted Eagle, Redshank, Green Sandpiper, Common Sandpiper, Ring Ouzel.

Access

To get to the lakes at Covadonga (Cuadonga) go to Cangas de Onís (Cangues d'Onís). Take the 6312 and at Soto de Cangas (Sotu Cangues) take the turning for the Covadonga sanctuary and the lakes of Enol and La Ercina (L'Arcina).

To reach the Cares gorge take the road out of Arenas de Cabrales to Poncebos. The road comes to an end where it meets the end of the gorge. You can also reach the area from León; to do this take the C-637 and at the Puerto del Pontón (a mountain pass) turn off for Posada de Valdeón (Posada de Valdión). From here a track goes to Caín, a village at the foot of the gorge.

Description

The Picos de Europa (Picos d'Europa) is a limestone massif reaching the highest altitudes in the Cantabrian range (Torre Cerréu, 2,648 m). The landscape is spectacular with huge rocky outcrops and many steep cliffs of varying sizes. The river Cares has cut out an impressive gorge in the middle of the massif. It is 12 km long and in places the sides rise up to 1,000 m. There are also some glacial lakes, of which the most important are those at Covadonga.

Because of the high altitude, vegetation is very varied; beech woods dominate the lower slopes, giving way to pastures and alpine meadows at higher levels.

Recommended routes

Route A is a walk taking you from the Covadonga lakes to the Vega de Ario (Vega d'Ariu) in 2½ hours. Start at the lake of La Ercina and take the path leading off to the south east through an area of limestone outcrops and rocky areas. The lake will give sightings of Mallard, Coot and, in the breeding season, Little Grebe, Teal, Pochard and Redshank. The rest of the route will enable you to see mountain and cliff-dwelling birds such as Griffon Vulture, Golden Eagle, Egyptian Vulture, Crag Martin, Water Pipit, Rock Thrush, Wallcreeper, Snow Finch, Citril Finch and Alpine Chough.

Route B runs along the Cares gorge between Posada de Valdeón and Poncebos. The walk is 19 km long and can be done in about 7 or 8 hours. With the exception of the stretch between Posada de Valdeón and Caín (7 km), the route lies along a path carved out of the rock. On the first section you may see Goshawk, Sparrowhawk,

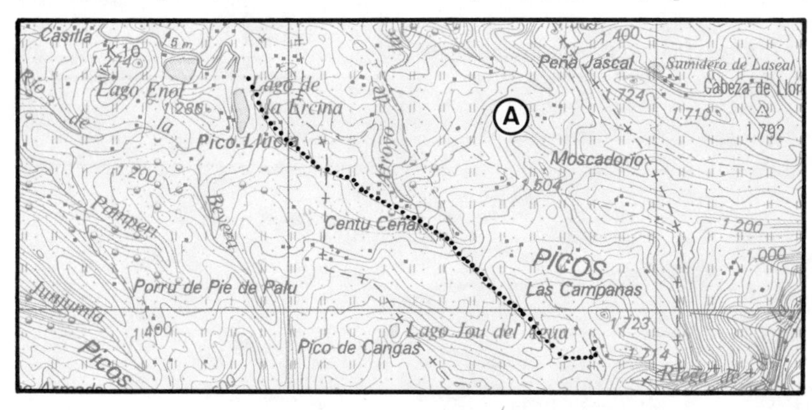

Great Spotted Woodpecker, Woodpigeon, Short-toed Treecreeper, Nuthatch, etc. In the gorge itself there are Griffon Vulture, Egyptian Vulture, Peregrine Falcon, Kestrel and other birds of prey. Outside the breeding season you may also see Snow Finch and Wallcreeper.

Accommodation

There are several hotels and pensions in Cangas de Onís. Posada de Valdeón also has hotels, but in smaller numbers, and in July and August accommodation is not always available. There are 2 campsites near the Covadonga lakes but you are limited to a 3-day stay in either campsite. There is a mountain refuge at Vega de Ario which provides meals, and at Vegarredonda there is a refuge accommodating larger numbers of people.

Comments

The two routes described lie within the Parque Nacional de Covadonga (Covadonga National Park). Although you do not need permission to enter the area, you should first inform yourself of regulations applying to visitors at the ICONA offices in Cangas de Onís or Posada de Valdeón, or at the forest rangers' office.

José Antonio García Fernández
(Coordinadora Ornitolóxica d'Asturies)

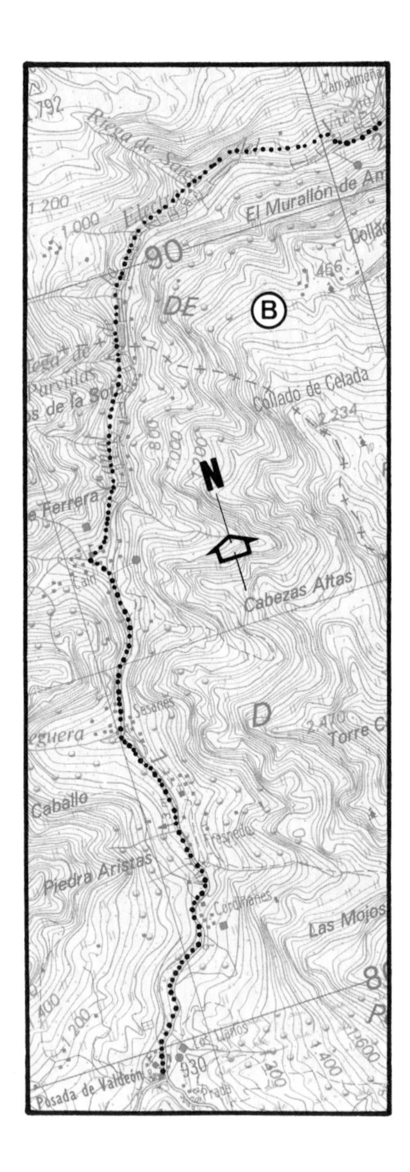

CANTABRIA

Spoonbill
Platalea leucorodia

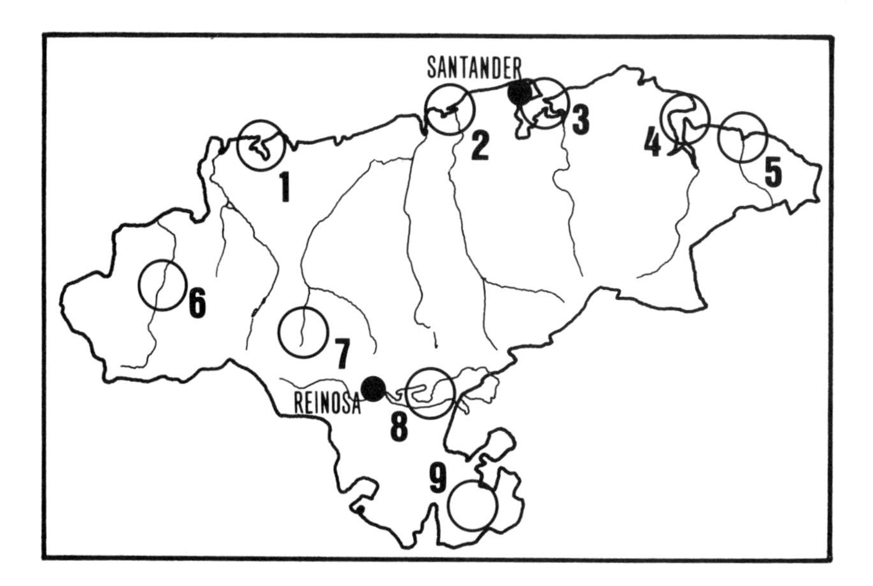

In Cantabria, a small province which has so far remained well preserved, the geographical conditions and species of birds present are generally speaking identical to those found in neighbouring Asturias. Like Asturias, Cantabria also lies on the northern slopes of the Cantabrian Range and has a long coastline. Interesting sites for the ornithologist are limited to the same coastline and mountains.

On the coast are a number of estuaries suitable for birdwatching; of outstanding interest are the estuaries which converge in Santoña to form the largest and most interesting marshland area on the northern coast of Spain (CN.4). In addition to numerous waders and ducks, in particularly large numbers in autumn and winter, many of the Spoonbills which nest in Holland use Santoña as a stopping point on their migratory journeys. Not far away is Monte Candina (CN.5), a small limestone massif where a colony of Griffon Vulture can be seen; this is the only colony in Spain which is located actually on the coast.

Although housing development, industry and rubbish tips have badly affected the broad bay of Santander (CN.3), there are still some places which are worth visiting, particularly the marshes at Parayas. Among other small estuaries we will include those of Oyambre-San Vicente de la Barquera (CN.1) and Liencres (CN.2) which coincide with dune areas of great value in terms of landscape and plant life. Finally, we should mention that on the Cantabrian coastline, as with the coastlines of Galicia and Asturias, it is also possible to watch sea birds on autumn migration, although not in such large numbers as at Peñas and Estaca de Bares capes. A good spot for seeing the autumn passage is Mayor cape, a headland falling within the boundaries of the city of Santander itself (CN.3).

As for the mountains, the first point to be taken into consideration is that the highest altitudes lie in the west of the province where it borders with Asturias, León and Palencia. This area is crossed via the San Glorio and Piedrasluengas passes. It is in the valleys of La Liébana (CN.6), Nansa and Saja (CN.7) that the most important habitats for birds are to be found. The central and eastern valleys of the province (Besaya, Pas, Miera and Asón), while still being of interest, are much less steep. They have been extensively deforested and generally population density is higher. By contrast, in the valleys of La Liébana and Saja, isolated areas of mature deciduous woodland exist where birdlife typical of Cantabrian woodland is perfectly represented. Capercaillie, Woodcock, Middle Spotted Woodpecker, Treecreeper, etc. are present. In La Liébana you can climb up to the Aliva pass and without difficulty see the high mountain birds inhabiting the harsh Picos de Europa (AS.9). These include Alpine Accentor, Wallcreeper, Snow Finch and Alpine Chough.

The list of sites in Cantabria is rounded off by the Ebro reservoir (CN.8) and the Valderredible valley (CN.9). The first, lying next to the Escudo pass, is a large reservoir worth visiting even though its importance as a site for water birds has diminished in recent years. The rough terrain of Valderredible, on the south side of the range, not only displays an interesting biogeographical transition between Atlantic and Mediterranean habitats, but is also the site of the limestone gorges of the upper reaches of the river Ebro. These continue and extend into the neighbouring region of La Lora (CL.7) in the province of Burgos. These gorges have a large and varied population of birds of prey.

CN.1 OYAMBRE AND MARSHLAND AT SAN VICENTE DE LA BARQUERA

A stretch of coast line consisting of marshes, beaches, dunes and sea cliffs.

Main species

Residents: Shag, Mallard, Peregrine Falcon, Kingfisher.

Summer visitors: Egyptian Vulture, Short-toed Eagle, Booted Eagle, Black Kite.

Winter visitors: Great Northern Diver, Cormorant, Little Egret, Greylag Goose, Widgeon, Teal, Shoveler, Oystercatcher, Golden Plover, Grey Plover, Knot, Whimbrel, Guillemot, Razorbill.

On passage: waders, terns.

Access

San Vicente de la Barquera is on the N-634 running from Bilbao to Oviedo. To go to Oyambre, first go to La Revilla, 4 km from San Vicente, and from there join the C-6316.

Description

This area comprises the San Vicente and Rabia estuaries, both notable for their marshland areas. Likewise, the beaches, dunes and sea cliffs running between the two estuaries are of great interest.

Conservationists fought —and won— a tough battle to declare this area a 9,000 ha Natural Park, but the negative influence which the tourist industry continues to have on the area is unavoidable.

Recommended routes

Route A begins at the Cabo de Oyambre, which can be reached via the C-6316. This headland is a good spot

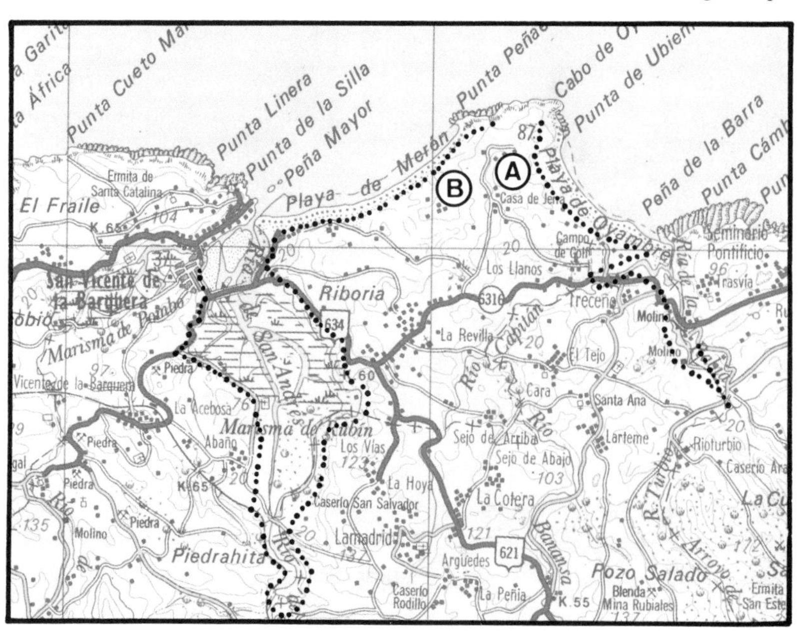

for watching sea birds. From the headland go down to the Oyambre beach, stopping occasionally in the dunes before reaching the mouths of the Capitán and Rabia estuaries. You can walk along the left shores of either of these estuaries and watch ducks and waders. This route, some 10 km in length, can be done in two sections using the C-6316 as a starting point.

Route B also begins at the Oyambre headland, running along the Merón beach and then beside the San Vicente estuary as far as the village of the same name. The route gives you views over the marshes of the rivers Escudo and Gandarillas. Since this route is long, it is advisable to undertake it in several sections, taking advantage of access points provided by the local road network.

Accommodation

There is plenty of accommodation in the surrounding villages and towns, particularly San Vicente de la Barquera and Comillas, as well as several campsites. In summer, the massive influx of visitors should be borne in mind since it makes accommodation harder to find.

Manuel Bahillo

CN.2. LIENCRES DUNES

A system of dunes with a pine plantation, located at the mouth of a small estuary.

Main species

Residents: Shag, Peregrine Falcon, Common Sandpiper, Kingfisher.

Summer visitors: Hen Harrier, Little Ringed Plover, Red-backed Shrike, Whinchat.

Winter visitors: divers, Cormorant, Eider, Common Scoter, Velvet Scoter, Red-breasted Merganser, Grey Plover, Golden Plover, Curlew, Razorbill, Snow Bunting.

On passage: shearwaters, Gannet, Greylag Goose, Knot, Sanderling, Dunlin, Whimbrel, Turnstone, Grey Phalarope, auks, Short-eared Owl.

Access

Take the motorway A-67 out of Santander towards Torrelavega and come off at Boo. There is also a local road which takes you directly from Santander to Liencres (12 km).

Next to the beach at Valdearenas is a large car park which is a good starting point for any trip in the area.

Description

A stretch of dunes which, because of its size and state of preservation, is one of the most important dune areas on the Cantabrian coast. Roughly 75% of the area is covered by pine woods planted to stabilize the dunes. The Dunas de Liencres are now a Natural Park.

Recommended routes

First of all climb Picota, a hill rising up 233 m, by taking a track leaving the car park at the entrance to the Park area. From the top of the hill, you will get a good view of the area and will see some birds of prey. Come down through the moors and heath surrounding the hill and enter the pine wood where various tits, woodland passerines can be seen. Finally, you will come out onto the dunes and the beach, good spots for watching ducks, waders and sea birds.

Accommodation

There is one hostel in the village of Liencres, but nearby Santander offers a wide range of accommodation.

Comments

The best time of year to visit the site is between September and January.

Adolfo Rucabado

■ CN.3 BAY OF SANTANDER

A broad estuary formed by the convergence of the mouths of the rivers Cubas, San Salvador and Bóo.

Main species

Residents: Shag, Mallard, Peregrine Falcon, Yellow-legged Gull, Collared Dove, Kingfisher.

Summer visitors: Garganey, Oystercatcher, Little Ringed Plover, Common Tern.

Winter visitors: Cormorant, Grey Heron, Greylag Goose, Grey Plover,

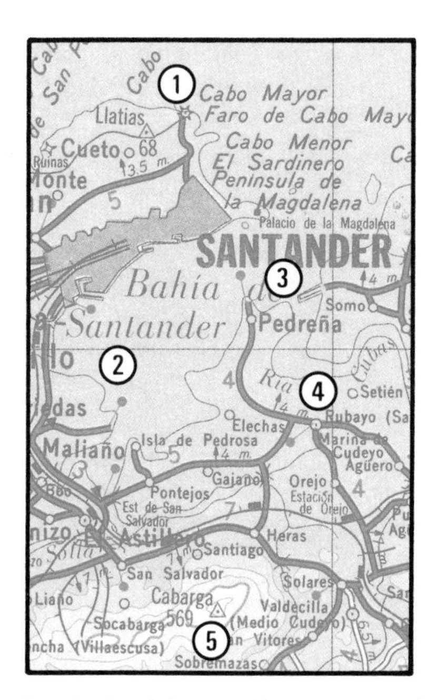

Purple Sandpiper, Whimbrel, Razorbill.

On passage: Great Northern Diver, Manx Shearwater, Gannet, Spoonbill, Shoveler, Red-breasted Merganser, Marsh Harrier, waders, passerines.

Access

The city of Santander, which dominates the bay, is the ideal point from which to undertake the routes proposed.

Description

The bay of Santander, located between the headlands of Ajo and Mayor, has extensive areas of mudflats at low tide and some marshland and intertidal zones on the Cubas estuary. A breakwater known as El Puntal closes off the entrance to the bay. At the entrance of the bay is the island of Mouro. Generally speaking, the bay of Santander is somewhat degenerate and does not have many interesting sites.

Recommended routes

The Cabo Mayor light house (1), which can be reached directly from Santander, is an excellent spot for watching sea birds. From September to November you can also watch large numbers of passerines coming in from across the sea.

To reach point 2, take the dual carriageway running from Santander to Bilbao and after 1 km turn off for the yachting marina known as Marina del Cantábrico. Before reaching the marina you will see a marshland area called Charca de Parayas; this lies within the boundaries of Santander airport and is closed off by a fence. Leave your car on the hard shoulder and watch various ducks, waders and herons.

Back on the dual carriageway, continue as far as El Astillero, where you take the coast road signed for Somo. Once there, a short walk will take you across the dunes to the end of El Puntal (3), from where it is possible to see a large number of waders as well as a smaller number of sea birds such as auks, skuas, scoters and cormorants.

Coming back, make a short stop in Rubayo near the Cubas estuary (4). The marshes and open land here abound with various passerines and some birds of prey.

Finally, it is worth climbing up to the high ground of Peña Cabarga (5), from where you can see the whole of the bay of Santander, as well as watch rock thrushes, Egyptian Vulture, Short-toed Eagle, etc.

Accommodation

The surrounding area caters extensively for tourists, resulting in plenty of hotels and campsites.

Comments

The best time of year to visit this location is from September to January.

Manuel Bahillo

■ CN.4 SANTOÑA MARSHES

CN

An area of coastal marshland, important in terms of both size and ornithological interest.

Main species

Residents: Mallard, Yellow-legged Gull, Coot.

Winter visitors: Red-throated Diver, Black-throated Diver, Great Northern Diver, Black-necked Grebe, Little Egret, Grey Heron, Widgeon, Eider, Common Scoter, Velvet Scoter, Red-breasted Merganser, Oystercatcher, Dunlin, Snipe, Curlew, Black-headed Gull, Lesser Black-backed Gull, Great Black-backed Gull, Razorbill, Guillemot.

On passage: Spoonbill, Avocet, Knot, Sanderling, Curlew Sandpiper, Black-tailed Godwit, Bar-tailed Godwit, Whimbrel, Spotted Redshank, Redshank, Greenshank, Turnstone.

Access

To get to Santoña, take the N-634 from Santander or Bilbao, turning off at Gama or Bárcena de Cicero (50 km from Santander and 73 km from Bilbao).

Description

The Santoña marshes, with an area of about 3,500 ha, are located in the confluence of the estuaries of the rivers Limpias, Rada, Escalante and Argoños. There are a lot of mudflats, sand bars and marshes. Human presence and

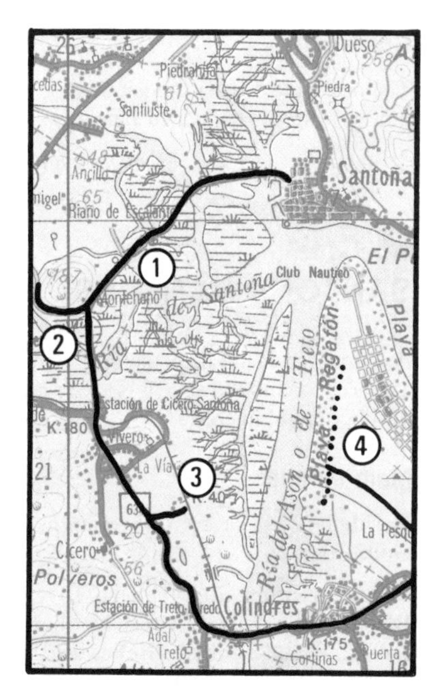

various plans for industrial development and road building seriously threaten this area, which has been declared a Reserva Natural (Nature Reserve).

Recommended routes

To reach point 1, take the road leading out of Santoña to Cicero. Stop at the Monasterio de Montehano, a monastery, from where you can walk to the edge of the marshes. This area, known as El Barco, is a resting place at high tide for Spoonbill, herons, waders and cormorants.

Drive on towards the village of Escalante, stopping in the Montehano quarry from where you can see the polder at Cicero and the Escalante marshes (2), a habitual resting place and refuge for Greylag Goose, Curlew, Lapwing and Snipe.

Point 3, on the Cicero beach, can be reached from the village of the same name. From here, you can see ducks, herons and waders.

Returning to the N-634, continue to Colindres and turn off for the beach at Regatón (4), a good spot for watching waders and sea ducks.

Accommodation

The towns surrounding the marsh area offer a wide variety of hotel accommodation and campsites. This applies especially to Laredo and Santoña.

Comments

The best time to visit Santoña is between September and March.

Adolfo Rucabado

■ CN.5 MONTE CANDINA

A limestone promontory on the coast, rising 470 m above sea level.

Main species

Residents: Shag, Griffon Vulture, Peregrine Falcon, Yellow-legged Gull, Blue Rock Thrush, Chough.

Summer visitors: Honey Buzzard, Black Kite, Egyptian Vulture, Short-toed Eagle, Eagle Owl, Rock Thrush.

Winter visitors: Cormorant, Alpine Accentor, Wallcreeper, Alpine Chough.

Access

Take the N-634 out of Santander or Bilbao and turn off for Oriñón, from where you can reach Sonabia either on foot or by car (55 km from Santander and 50 km from Bilbao).

Description

This rocky karstic outcrop, located on the coast between the Oriñón estuary and the Liendo valley, is the site of the only coastal colony of Griffon Vulture in Spain. It is forested with holm oak

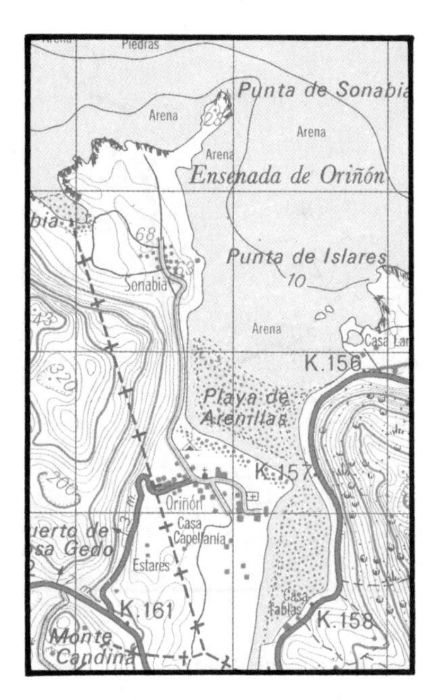

and some oak, beech and chestnut. There is also a small area of yew. On the beach at Sonabia there is a fossil dune of some 100 m in height.

Recommended routes

A walk will provide you with a general impression of the area, which is small and has very clearly defined limits. A few minutes' walk will take you to the Cebollero headland, a good point from which to watch sea birds on migration.

Accommodation

Oriñón has a hostel and a campsite, but both Laredo and Castro Urdiales offer plenty of accommodation.

Adolfo Rucabado

CN.6 LA LIÉBANA VALLEY

A large valley in the Cantabrian range, at the foot of the Picos de Europa mountains.

Main species

Residents: Griffon Vulture, Golden Eagle, Sparrowhawk, Peregrine Falcon, Grey Partridge, Capercaillie, Middle Spotted Woodpecker, Black Woodpecker, Crag Martin, Chough, Alpine Chough, Dipper, Alpine Accentor, Goldcrest, Wallcreeper, Treecreeper.

Summer visitors: Honey Buzzard, Egyptian Vulture, Booted Eagle, Short-toed Eagle, Nightjar, Alpine Swift, Water Pipit, Rock Thrush.

Access

The N-261 runs all the way along the valley to Potes (43 km) and the San Glorio pass.

Description

This is a mountainous area with heights varying between 400 m and 2,600 m. It supports a considerable variety of woodland; holm oak and cork oak in the valley bottom giving way to oak, beech and birch as height is gained. The high ground, impressive for its beauty and enormous rock faces, is dominated by mountain scrubland and alpine pastures.

Another important feature of the landscape which is worth mentioning is the La Hermida gorge, a deep gorge cut by the waters of the river Deva.

Recommended routes

The best way of getting to know the La Liébana valley is to drive along the

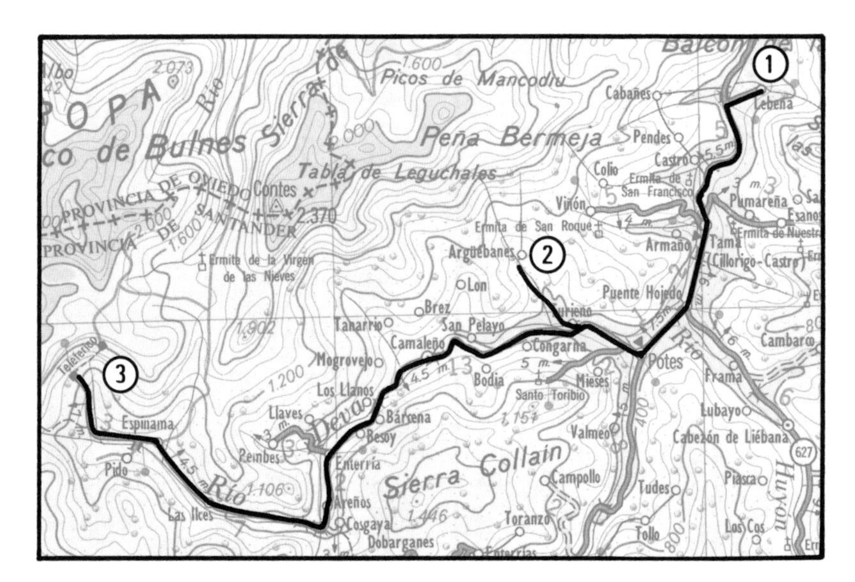

various roads in the area as well as the extensive network of forestry tracks.

Interesting points include the village of Lebeña (1), from where the La Hermida gorge can be seen. Here you will have sightings of Golden Eagle, Griffon Vulture, Short-toed Eagle and Alpine Swift.

Another option is to take the road running from Potes to Fuente Dé, turning off in Turieno to go to Argüébanes (2), from where you can pass through various kinds of woodland to reach the foot of the peak of Sagrado Corazón.

If you wish to go for a walk, at Espinama (3), take the path going up to the Aliva mountain passes from where you can reach the alpine pastures and, on the track to Vueltona, see the rock fields and cliffs typical of the Picos de Europa. For even more convenience, these high places can be reached by cable car from Fuente Dé.

Accommodation

There is plenty of accommodation available throughout the area. There are also campsites, the one in Fuente Dé being recommended. For good food try Restaurante Martín in Ojedo and Restaurante La Cántabra in Potes.

Manuel Bahillo and Isidoro Fombellida

CN.7 SAJA VALLEY AND ALTO CAMPÓO

Mountain areas with substantial deciduous forests.

Main species

Residents: Griffon Vulture, Golden Eagle, Sparrowhawk, Grey Partridge, Middle Spotted Woodpecker, Black Woodpecker, Crag Martin, Chough, Alpine Chough, Dipper, Alpine Accentor, Goldcrest, Treecreeper.

Summer visitors: Honey Buzzard, Egyptian Vulture, Short-toed Eagle, Water Pipit.

Access

Take the N-634 to Cabezón de la Sal, where you turn onto the C-625 which runs the length of the valley of the river Saja up to the Palombera pass. By taking the same road in the opposite direction, you will come to Reinosa on the N-611.

Description

A large area on the northern side of the Cantabrian range, crowned by the Peña Labra massif where heights reach over 2,000 m. A long, steep-sided valley where substantial areas of oak and beech woodland survive, giving over to birch, scrubland and pastures at higher levels. There are still large areas of heath and whin.

This is a National Game Reserve and, in most parts, also a Natural Park.

Recommended routes

Route A (Saja valley) consists of taking the C-625 from Cabezón de la Sal to the Palombera pass. The recommended stops and diversions are perfect starting points for long walks:

1) Turn off for the village of Ucieda, go through the village and continue until you reach a campsite in the woodland. From here, you can walk through oak and beech woods on an extensive network of tracks and paths.

2) Turn off for the village of Bárcena Mayor, which has a car park and a campsite. This is a good starting point for walks through areas of beech and oak woodland.

3) Cambillas, actually on the C-625, has a car park where you can leave your vehicle and walk through the beech woods.

4) At the highest part of the Palombera pass you can see Chough, Alpine Chough, Griffon Vulture, Golden Eagle, Short-toed Eagle, etc. as well as a considerable number of birds on autumn passage.

Route B (Alto Campóo). Coming down from the Palombera pass in the direction of Reinosa you will come to Espinilla, where you take the C-628 to the Braña Vieja ski resort. The following are good starting points for walks:

5) From the village of La Lomba you can follow the course of the river Hijar along paths and tracks taking you through beech and birch woods.

6) From the ski resort you can go up to the peaks of Tresmares (2,175 m) and Peña Labra (2,006 m), a sub-alpine area with cliffs, scrubland and pastures.

A good complement to these routes is a trip to the Nansa valley which runs

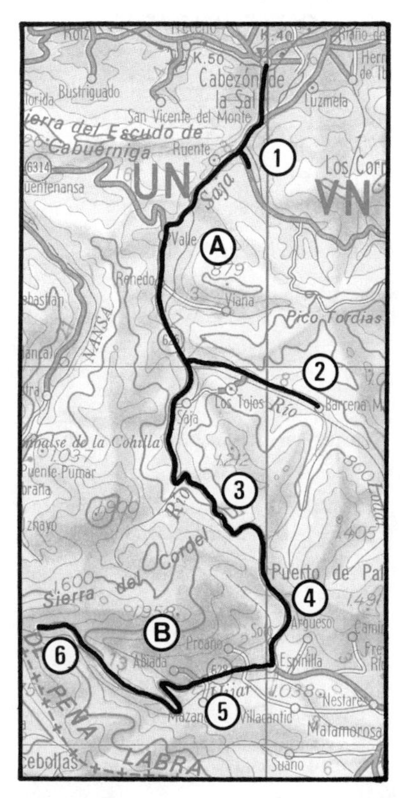

parallel to and immediately west of the Saja valley. At the head of the valley (Valle de Polaciones) there is well-conserved beech and oak woodland, and a good network of tracks and paths climbing the slopes of Peña Labra and Peña Sagra.

Accommodation

A limited number of rooms are available in hotels and hostels in Renedo de Cabuérniga, Bárcena Mayor and Braña Vieja ski resort. Reinosa and Cabezón de la Sal provide a larger amount of accommodation. There are campsites in Ucieda, Bárcena Mayor and Saja.

Isidoro Fombellida Díez

■ CN.8 EBRO RESERVOIR

A large reservoir located on a plain at 800 m, lying between ranges of mountains.

Main species

Residents: Great Crested Grebe, Gadwall.

Summer visitors: White Stork, Red-crested Pochard, Egyptian Vulture, Short-toed Eagle, Black Kite, Hobby, Yellow Wagtail.

Winter visitors: Grey Heron, ducks, Coot.

On passage: Spoonbill, Greylag Goose, Marsh Harrier, waders.

Access

Take the N-611 to Reinosa, a town located at one end of the reservoir, or alternatively the N-623 which runs at a tangent to the eastern shore of the reservoir on the boundary with the province of Burgos.

Description

The Embalse del Ebro, located in the Cantabrian range close to the source of the river Ebro, has a surface area of roughly 500 km^2 and a perimeter of 90 km. On the whole the reservoir is not deep, allowing for abundant growth of underwater vegetation. The shores are largely deserted, being gently sloping and occupied by pasture land, moors with heath and whin and some stands of trees.

Recommended routes

The best means of visiting the Ebro reservoir is to drive along the roads surrounding it, making the stops mentioned below.

Leave Reinosa via the C-6318. The first stop is Orzales (point 1). From the shore you can see ducks, grebes, waders, storks and kites. A little farther on, in Monegro (2), there is an inlet where more birdlife can be observed. After La Costana (3) you have another opportunity in the form of a large inlet with the village of La Riva at its end. Between La Población and Corconte (4), there is a pine plantation where you can camp (with water supply). The shoreline near this part of the road is a very good spot for watching birds.

At the crossroads where this road ends, turn right on to the N-623 and continue to Cabañas de Virtus, from where you go down to the shore of the reservoir on a track built to facilitate sand extraction operations. At this point (5) the banks are high, enabling you to watch birds without having to approach the reservoir.

Continue for a couple of kilometres and then turn right onto a local road which skirts the southern shore of the reservoir and, between Arija and Horna (6 and 7), provides several interesting vantage points, particularly in winter,

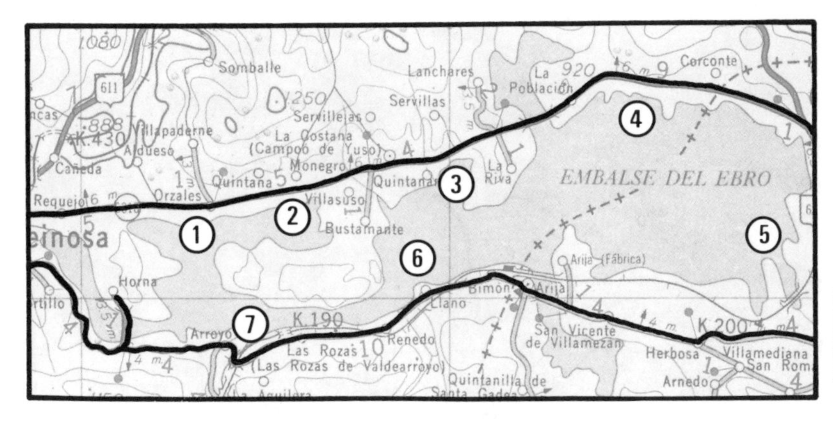

for diving ducks including mergansers and grebes.

Accommodation

Accommodation, albeit scarce, can be found in Reinosa, Corconte and Cabaña de Virtus.

Comments

The water level in the reservoir underwent a dramatic change during the early 1980s, causing a reduction in the number of both nesting and wintering water birds. Previously, the water level was at its highest in spring, slowly subsiding during the course of the summer to reach its lowest in early winter. But after several years of severe drought and winters without snow, the reservoir remains at the same extremely low level throughout the year.

*Isidoro Fombellida Díez
and Manuel Bahillo*

■ CN.9 VALDERREDIBLE VALLEY

Section of the upper Ebro valley located in the transitional area between the Cantabrian range and the Northern Meseta.

Main species

Residents: Griffon Vulture, Golden Eagle, Goshawk, Peregrine Falcon, Crag Martin, Dipper, Chough.

Summer visitors: White Stork, Honey Buzzard, Egyptian Vulture, Short-toed Eagle, Hen Harrier, Montagu's Harrier.

Access

The N-611 and N-623 run around Valderredible, an area lying in the south of the province of Santander, about 100 km from the city of Santander. From these roads you can take a series of minor roads to the sites of greatest interest.

Description

The river Ebro, after the dam of the Embalse del Ebro, runs between hills forested with oak alternating with moors and pastureland. Subsequently, the river course suddenly changes direction and runs across a broad river plain located between the Cantabrian ranges and the spurs of the plateaux of the Meseta, which give rise to many rocky areas and small stands of beech and oak.

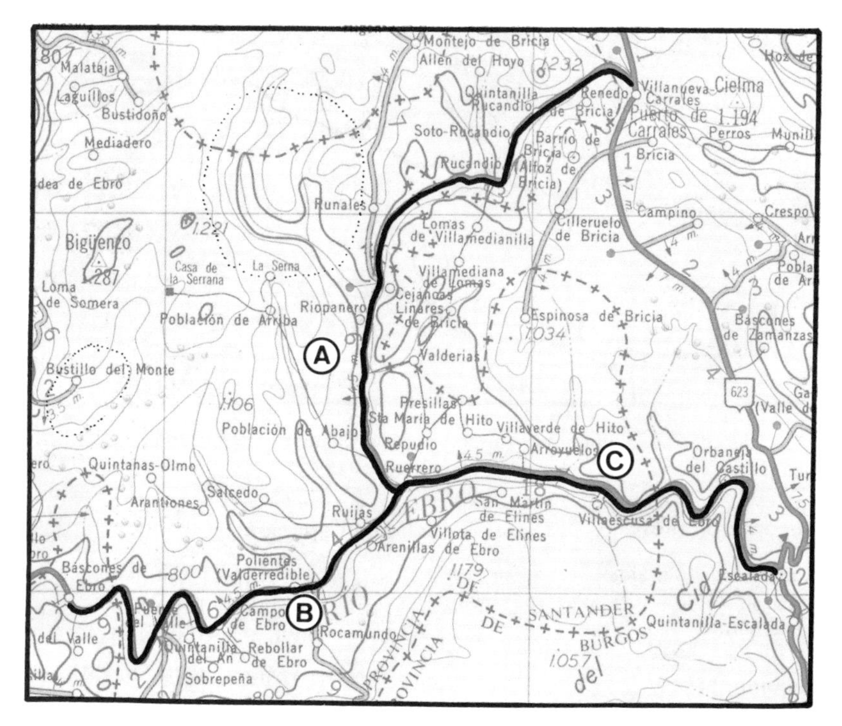

At the boundary with the province of Burgos, the Ebro runs through an interesting limestone gorge where the sides are covered with holm oak and oak woodland (CL.7).

Recommended routes

Route A, which takes you to the oak woods of Monte Hijedo, can be reached from the N-623. At Villanueva Carrales take the minor road for Riopanero and Ruerrero. Between these two villages is a series of paths and tracks which you can take and walk through the woodland, where you will probably see tits, treecreepers, Long-tailed Tit and woodpeckers as well as Short-toed Eagle, Booted Eagle, Goshawk, Honey Buzzard, etc.

Route B consists of driving along the road from Quintanilla de las Torres (off the N-611) to Bascones de Ebro and Polientes. This trip, which can be extended by using dirt tracks, skirts the La Lora plateau and provides lots of opportunities for seeing birds of prey.

Route C, in fact an extension of the previous route, takes you along the Ebro gorge via the local road linking Polientes to Escalada, a village on the N-623. On this route, various cliff-dwelling birds of prey can be seen such as Golden Eagle, Egyptian Vulture, Griffon Vulture and Peregrine Falcon, as well as Crag Martin, Chough, etc.

Accommodation

Villages in the Valderredible area are small and sparsely populated, and thus offer hardly any accommodation. It is therefore advisable to go to Villarcayo, Reinosa or Aguilar de Campóo, where there are several hotels.

Isidoro Fombellida Díez

CASTILE - LA MANCHA

Black-bellied Sandgrouse
Pterocles orientalis

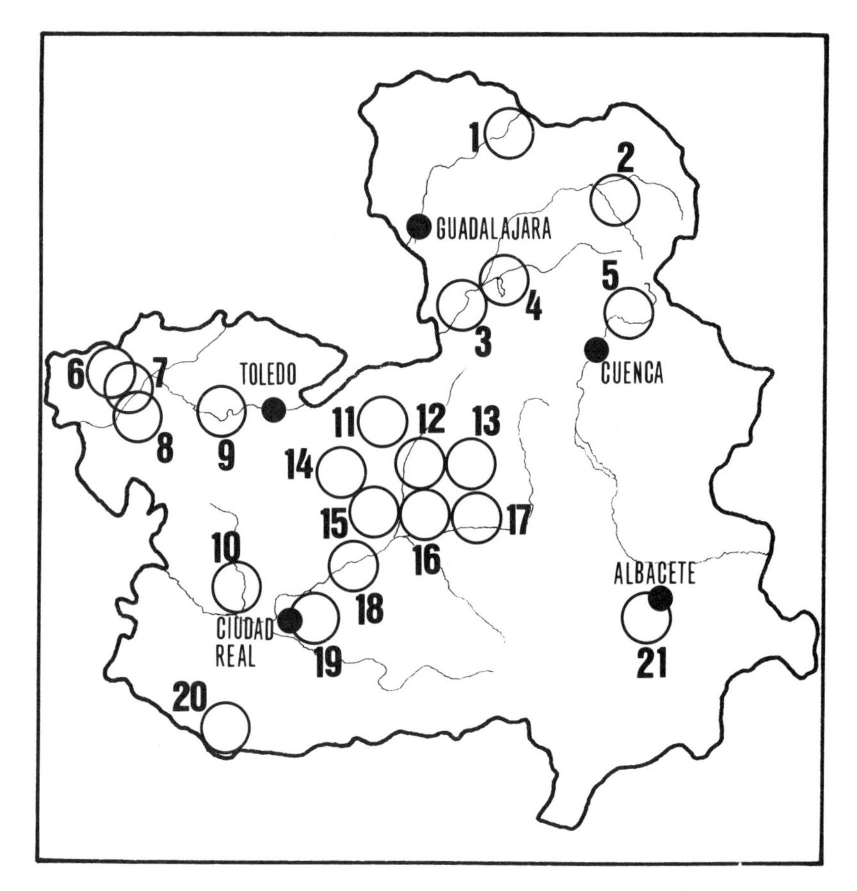

In general terms the boundaries of the Autonomous Region of Castile-La Mancha follow those of the southern Meseta, with the exception of the province of Madrid. As happens in the northern sub-meseta area, this is a very large region, mostly flat and virtually completely surrounded by a ring of mountains, limestone in the east and siliceous in the west. However, there are significant differences between both the flat areas and the mountains of the two Castiles. Whilst in the mountains, of average height and falling fully within the Mediterranean area, the birdlife is relatively scarce, the plains, well endowed with marsh areas, offer considerable attractions to the birdwatcher.

The central region, La Mancha, is the largest flat area in the Iberian Peninsula. Surrounding it is a series of predominantly flat regions which meet the mountains bordering the areas to the east (Campiña del Henares, La Alcarria, La Manchuela, El Corredor de Almansa, El Campo de Hellín and El Campo de Montiel) and west (La Sagra, Oropesa, La Sisla, Campo de Calatrava). All of these go to make up an extensive and somewhat monotonous plain lying at an average height of 700 m with a markedly dry inland climate, which is largely used for dry farming. Apart from the extensive grain fields, similar to those in Castilla la Vieja (Old Castile), there are also huge expanses of vines and a considerable number of olive groves. The few common birds to be found in this area include Kestrel, Red-legged Partridge, Quail, Little Bustard, Stone Curlew, Pin-tailed Sandgrouse, Little Owl, Bee-eater, Hoopoe, Short-toed Lark, Crested Lark, Black-eared Wheatear, Fan-tailed Warbler, Great Grey Shrike, Starling, Magpie, Tree Sparrow, Goldfinch, Linnet and Corn Bunting. In areas where cereal crops predominate you will have no difficulty in seeing Montagu's Harrier, Great Bustard, Black-bellied Sandgrouse and Calandra Lark. In the remaining woods of scrubby holm oak, areas of dry grazing land, small stands of pine, elm which has not been consumed by Dutch elm disease or riverside woodland by rivers and in river beds, you can also expect to see Buzzard, Hobby, Great Spotted Cuckoo, Woodpigeon, Turtle Dove, Scops Owl, Long-eared Owl, Red-necked Nightjar, Roller, Woodlark, Nightingale, Blackbird, Mistle Thrush, Cetti's Warbler, Melodious Warbler, Sardinian Warbler, Subalpine Warbler, Orphean Warbler, Long-tailed Tit, Blue Tit, Great Tit, Short-toed Treecreeper, Golden Oriole, Woodchat Shrike, Azure-winged Magpie, Carrion Crow, Chaffinch, Serin, Greenfinch and Cirl Bunting. Finally, villages and hamlets will bring sightings of Lesser Kestrel, Barn Owl, Swift, Swallow, House Martin, Spotless Starling and Jackdaw. To summarize, the birdlife present is relatively uncomplicated and can be found in many of the inland and southern areas of the Iberian Peninsula.

However, as mentioned above, these regions also have substantial wetland areas. These consist largely of natural lagoons (including Lillo, CM.11; Quero, CM.12; Miguel Esteban, CM.13; Villafranca, CM.14; Alcázar de San Juan, CM.15; Pedro Muñoz, CM.16; Manjavacas, CM.17; Pozuelo, CM.19; Pétrola, Salobralejo and Ontalafia, CM.21), but, in addition, there are stretches of slow-flowing river such as the renowned Tablas de Daimiel (CM.18): reservoirs, sometimes of considerable size and significance (Almoguera, CM.3; Entrepeñas and Buendía, CM.4; Rosarita and Navalcán, CM.6; Azután, CM.8; Castrejón, CM.9). It has to be said that the so-called *La Mancha Húmeda* has lost much of the ornithological importance it had fifty years ago, owing to deliberate draining and excessive exploitation of underground water supplies. It was this that caused the disappearance of Bittern, and is the reason for the minimal numbers of previously common birds such as Purple Heron, Collared Pratincole and Little Tern. However, it is still possible to find interesting waterbirds during the breeding season such as Black-necked Grebe, Shelduck, Red-crested Pochard, White-headed Duck, Marsh Harrier, Avocet, Kentish Plover, Redshank, Whiskered Tern, Gull-billed Tern, Savi's Warbler, Moustached Warbler and Bearded Tit. The list of nesting species includes Little Grebe, Great Crested Grebe, Little Bittern, Night Heron, Cattle Egret, Little Egret, Gadwall, Mallard, Pochard, Water Rail, Moorhen, Coot, Black-winged Stilt, Lapwing, Little Ringed Plover, Black-headed Gull, Yellow Wagtail, Penduline Tit, Reed Warbler and Great Reed Warbler. In winter, Grey Heron, Cormorant and various species of duck are present, while during the migration periods, particularly during the autumn passage, there are many waders on the shallow water and muddy beaches such as those existing at Lillo, Alcázar, Pedro Muñoz, Manjavacas and Pozuelo de Calatrava.

On leaving the central flat areas, you will have no difficulty in encountering rocky hillsides and cliffs where you can look for Egyptian Vulture, Golden

Eagle, Bonelli's Eagle, Eagle Owl, Thekla Lark, Crag Martin, Black Redstart, Stonechat, Black Wheatear, Blue Rock Thrush, Spectacled Warbler, Dartford Warbler, Chough, Raven, Rock Sparrow and Rock Bunting. Hills covered with woods of holm oak, Lusitanian oak and pine become more frequent, the habitat of common forest-dwelling species including Short-toed Eagle, Goshawk, Sparrowhawk, Booted Eagle, Tawny Owl, Nightjar, Great Spotted Woodpecker, Wren, Robin, Blackcap, Bonelli's Warbler, Chiffchaff, Pied Flycatcher, Firecrest, Coal Tit, Nuthatch and Jay. Faster-running rivers will give sightings of Common Sandpiper, Grey Wagtail and Dipper, although this will of course depend on the direction in which you are travelling.

The more hilly regions located to the west and southwest of the area, in the provinces of Toledo and Ciudad Real, belong to the Hercynian plinth of central Spain, being low and having a siliceous substrate. These hills are largely taken up by holm oak woodland, dry grazing lands and pastures, with abundant areas of quartzite screes and rocky areas with stony spurs and river beds filled with *Securinega tinetoria* and oleander (*Nerium oleander*), reminding us repeatedly of the proximity of Extremadura. This is also true of the birdlife in the desert regions of La Jara, Los Montes de Toledo and Ciudad Real, the Alcudia valley and the northern slopes of the Sierra Morena —from Almadén to Villamanrique— which includes remarkably large numbers of birds of prey including Black-shouldered Kite, Red Kite, Black Kite, Black Vulture and Spanish Imperial Eagle. Birds typical of the southwest of the Iberian Peninsula are also present, such as White Stork, Black Stork, Red-rumped Swallow, Azure-winged Magpie and Spanish Sparrow. Of the many possible sites, we have selected two truly remarkable ones, Cabañeros Natural Park (CM.10) and the area around Fuencaliente and the Valle de Alcudia (CM.20).

It would be virtually impossible to see the species mentioned above if one moved from the centre of La Mancha towards the east or northeast. By contrast, this area has high plateaux, deep gorges and isolated ranges of hills covered with pine woodland, making for good opportunities of seeing Griffon Vulture, Peregrine Falcon, Alpine Swift, Skylark, Dupont's Lark, Tawny Pipit, Wheatear, Rock Thrush, Whitethroat, Goldcrest, Crested Tit, Ortolan Bunting, Crossbill and Citril Finch. Good places for these species are river Dulce (CM.1), Alto Tajo (CM.2), Altomira range (CM.4) and Uña-Tragacete in the Serranía de Cuenca mountains (CM.5). All of these sites belong to the Sistema Ibérico, but it should not be forgotten that outcrops of the Sistema Central and the Sierras Subbéticas also lie within the boundaries of Castile-La Mancha, completing this western rim of mountains to the northwest with the province of Guadalajara (ranges of Somosierra, Ayllón, Alto Rey and Pela) and to the south within Albacete (ranges of Alcaraz, Segura and Calar del Mundo). These are isolated, rugged places with birdlife similar to that mentioned above, which are well worth a visit.

CM.1
RIVER DULCE

River gorge.

Main species

Residents: Griffon Vulture, Goshawk, Buzzard, Golden Eagle, Peregrine Falcon, Kingfisher, Grey Wagtail, Dipper, Blue Rock Thrush, Great Grey Shrike, Chough, Rock Sparrow, Cirl Bunting, Rock Bunting.

Summer visitors: Egyptian Vulture, Alpine Swift, Crag Martin, Black-eared Wheatear, Woodchat Shrike, Golden Oriole.

Access

Leave Guadalajara on the N-II towards Zaragoza and after 47 km turn left onto the C-204 for Sigüenza (25 km).

Description

A tributary of the Henares, the river Dulce forms a small valley. Some parts of it are constituted by calcareous cliffs of varying heights. The valley sides and screes are covered with patches of holm oak and Lusitanian oak interspersed with some Spanish juniper. The valley bottom is taken up by fields and irrigated land in the wider areas, while in other places there are small areas of well-developed riverside woodland.

Recommended routes

The best way of getting to know this area is to visit the villages of Pelegrina, La Cabrera and Aragosa, located in the valley of the river Dulce. They can be reached by various turns off the C-204. From each of these small villages, tracks radiate out and run along the valley bottom, making for pleasant walks. Upstream from Pelegrina, between La Cabrera and Aragosa, cliffs predominate, making it possible to see Griffon

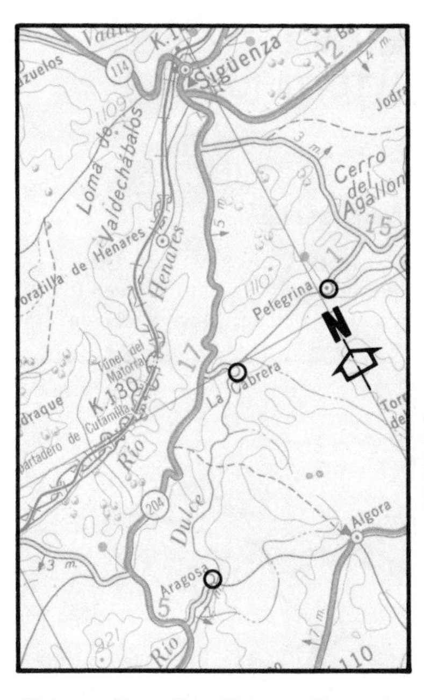

Vulture, Egyptian Vulture, Peregrine Falcon, Alpine Swift, Crag Martin, Blue Rock Thrush, Rock Sparrow, Chough and, with luck, Golden Eagle. Riverside woodland and wooded areas will give rise to sightings of Goshawk, Buzzard, Cuckoo, Golden Oriole, Cirl Bunting, Jay, tits, treecreepers, etc. Along the river itself you will see Kingfisher, Grey Wagtail and Dipper. In addition, in the fields and plateaux surrounding the head of the gorge there are many larks, Black-eared Wheatear, Woodchat Shrike, Great Grey Shrike, Rock Bunting, Red-legged Partridge and Quail.

Accommodation

The town of Sigüenza has several hostels as well as a Parador Nacional. It is worthwhile strolling through the streets of the town to see the many historic buildings.

Comments

Late spring and summer are the best times of year for visiting the area.

Bernardo Arroyo

■ CM.2 ALTO TAJO

River gorge.

Main species

Residents: Griffon Vulture, Goshawk, Sparrowhawk, Buzzard, Golden Eagle, Peregrine Falcon, Chough, Raven.

Summer visitors: Egyptian Vulture, Crag Martin.

Access

The town of Molina de Aragón is the best place from which to visit the area. To reach Molina de Aragón, take the N-211 which joins the N-II at Alcolea del Pinar, 62 km away.

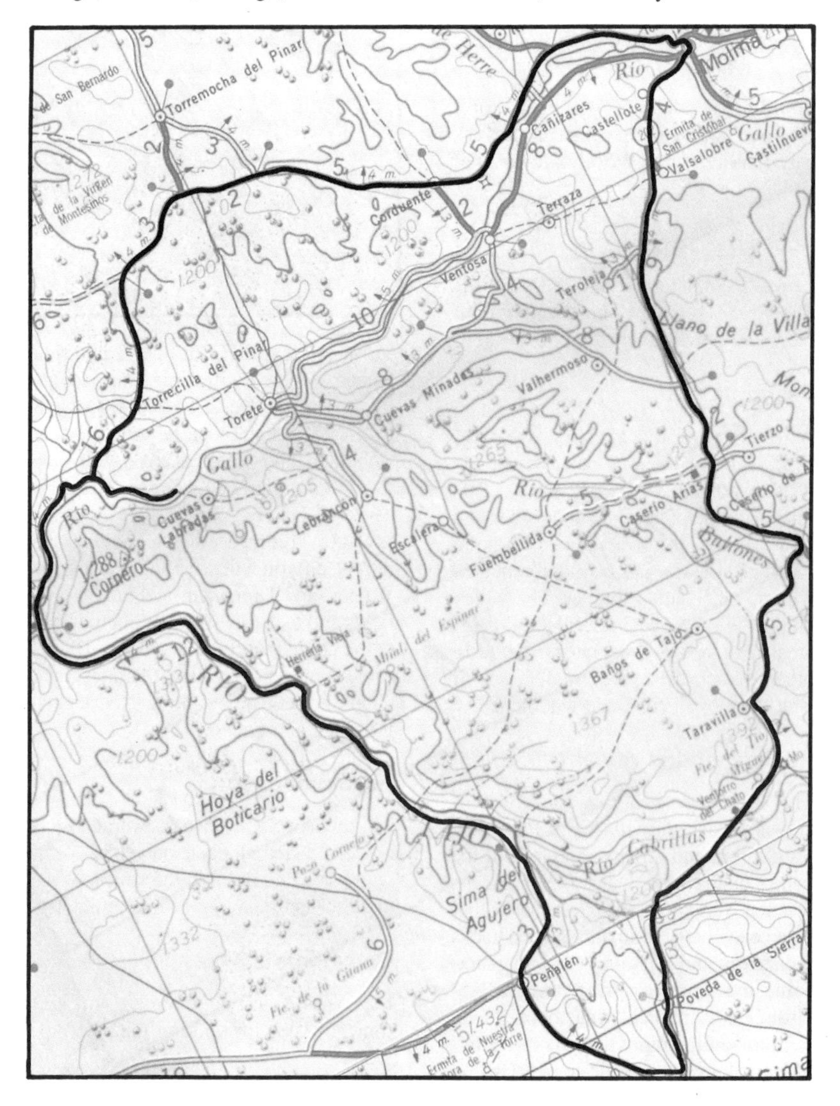

Description

A deep gorge carved by the waters of the river Tagus (Tajo). The gorge is formed by high and virtually uninterrupted cliffs, some of which reach great heights. The sides of the gorge are taken up by abundant pine woods interspersed with isolated stands of Lusitanian oak and holm oak. There is virtually no riverside woodland, although there are stretches of rapids of great beauty.

Recommended routes

For this area a single route is recommended. It consists of a full day's drive through the area of about 80 km. Leave Molina de Aragón on the C-202 going towards Peralejos de las Truchas and Beteta. Between the villages of Salinas de Armalla and Terzaga, turn right onto a minor road for Taravilla and Poveda de la Sierra. Between these two villages, the road first crosses the river Cabrillas and subsequently the Tajo. At the bridge over the Tajo a track leads off to the right and follows the left bank of the river for some 20 km, coming to an end on a road; on reaching this road, turn right for Molina de Aragón.

The track is suitable for any kind of vehicle and en route you can make as many stops as you wish. The pine woods are full of forest-dwelling species, ranging from tits, treecreepers, Chaffinch, Blackbird and Jay to Goshawk, Sparrowhawk and Buzzard. Cliff-dwelling birds are represented by Griffon Vulture, Egyptian Vulture, Golden Eagle, Peregrine Falcon, Chough, Raven, Crag Martin, etc. The best place for seeing cliff-dwellers is the bridge of San Pedro, 1 km before coming to the end of the track and returning to Molina de Aragón.

Accommodation

There are several hotels and hostels in Molina de Aragón.

Comments

The best times of year for visiting the area are spring and summer. Please drive with care during the months of July and August, since the track may be much frequented by other vehicles.

Bernardo Arroyo

■ CM.3 ALMOGUERA RESERVOIR

Reservoir.

Main species

Residents: Red-crested Pochard, Marsh Harrier, Coot, Stone Curlew, Kingfisher.

Summer visitors: Little Bittern, Purple Heron, Bee-eater, Moustached Warbler.

Winter visitors: several species of ducks.

On passage: Osprey, Crane, Black Tern, swallows.

Access

In Guadalajara, take the N-320 towards Cuenca and after 22 km turn onto the C-200. Continue along the C-200 until you reach the turning for Almoguera (31 km), and 2 km before reaching Almoguera there is a turning for the reservoir on the left.

If you are coming from Madrid, the best route is to take the N-III (Madrid-Valencia) and turn off for Tielmes, Carabaña, Mondéjar and Almoguera.

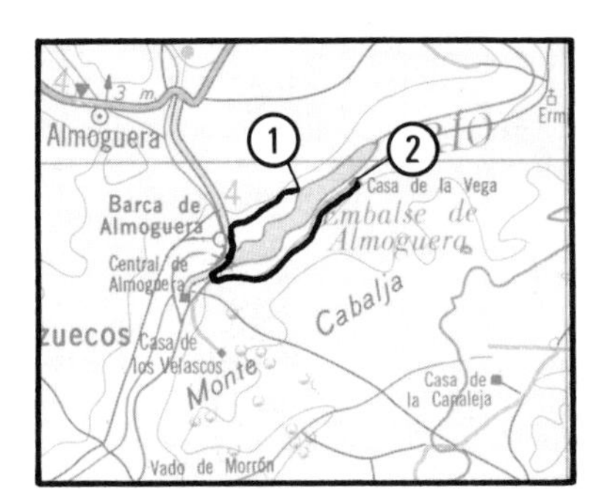

Description

A reservoir located on the middle reaches of the river Tajo (Tagus). The reservoir is 3.5 km long and reaches a maximum width of 450 m. It is surrounded by a thick belt of marsh vegetation consisting mainly of reeds and reedmace. The area around the reservoir is taken up by fields, kermes oak woodland and small stands of holm oak.

Recommended routes

A series of tracks lead off from the dam and circle the reservoir, enabling you to get close to the shore at various points. The path on the right shore ends at a group of houses and a landing stage from where you can hire a boat. It is also a good place for commanding a view of much of the reservoir and for watching ducks (1). The track running along the left shore climbs the nearby hills, not only giving you a general view of the reservoir but also making for sightings of various warblers, buntings, Great Spotted Cuckoo, Thekla Lark, etc. in the kermes oak and holm oak woodland in the area.

This path also terminates at a landing stage (2). Another good observation post is the dam itself, which gives views over an extensive reedbed where you may see Purple Heron, Little Bittern, Marsh Harrier, etc.

Accommodation

There are several hostels and *fondas* or inns in the nearby villages. Pastrana is an interesting place to stay.

Juan A. Malo de Molina
and Guillermo Blanco
(Grupo ALCOR)

■ CM.4 ALTOMIRA RANGE – ENTREPEÑAS AND BUENDÍA RESERVOIRS

Mountains of average height and reservoirs.

Main species

Residents: Marsh Harrier, Golden Eagle, Bonelli's Eagle, Peregrine Falcon, Thekla Lark, Crag Martin, Blue Rock Thrush, Chough, Rock Sparrow, Rock Bunting.

Summer visitors: Alpine Swift, Bee-eater, Black-eared Wheatear, Subalpine Warbler, Orphean Warbler, Woodchat Shrike.

Winter visitors: Cormorant, Grey Heron, ducks, Alpine Accentor, Wallcreeper (occasional).

On passage: Crane.

Access

In Guadalajara, take the N-320 towards Cuenca and turn off at Sacedón (60 km).

Description

A narrow mountain range with many rocky outcrops and dense areas of pine woodland and Mediterranean scrub. The countryside surrounding the ranges are typical of the region of La Alcarria, featuring plateaux given over

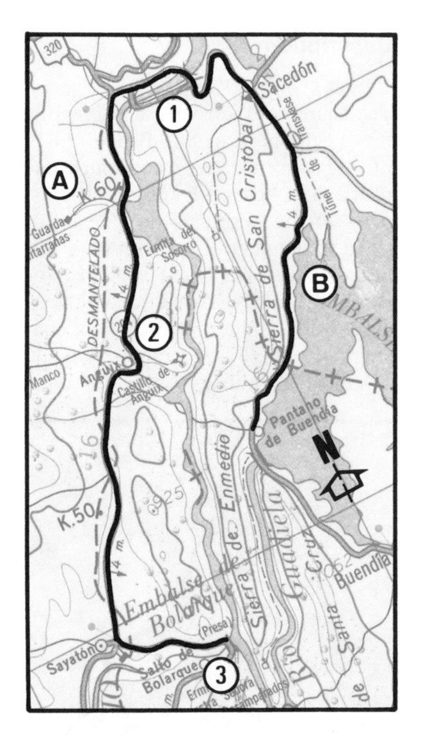

to cereal crops which alternate with slopes covered with degenerate vegetation and valley bottoms with the occasional area of riverside woodland made up of black poplar and elm.

The Entrepeñas reservoir and the surrounding area has to a large extent been spoilt by housing developments, tourism and water sports, although on the river Tajo there are still places of interest located between the Entrepeñas reservoir and the Bolarque reservoir, which have likewise been affected by tourism.

Recommended routes

Route A consists of a car journey. Leave Sacedón on the N-320 in the direction of Guadalajara and after 6 km turn onto the C-204 for Sayatón and the Bolarque dam (*presa de Bolarque*) (30 km). The first stop is at the Entrepeñas dam (1), from where you can command a view of part of the reservoir and the Paso del Infierno, a short gorge where you may see Alpine Swift, Crag Martin, Chough, Blue Rock Thrush, Rock Sparrow and, in season, Alpine Accentor. From point 2 you can see a stretch of the river Tajo, bordered by beds of reeds and rushes. Water birds, while not numerous, are certainly very varied, including Cormorant, Grey Heron, ducks, Marsh Harrier, Coot and waders. Point 3, near the Bolarque dam, is a good place for seeing cliff-dwelling birds of prey such as Egyptian Vulture, Golden Eagle, Bonelli's Eagle and Peregrine Falcon, although this requires a certain degree of patience.

Route B consists of a car journey starting in Sacedón and taking you along the road to Buendía to the dam of the Buendía reservoir. The trip is some 15 km long and runs between the foothills of the Sierra de Altomira and the waters of the reservoir. Make a stop along the way to take a short walk through the scrubland at the foot of the hills to see various warblers, Black-eared Wheatear, Woodchat Shrike and Thekla Lark. Another interesting site is the Buendía dam, which gives a good view of the reservoir and the mountains. Water birds are few and far between on this large body of water, but conversely, there are plenty of cliff-dwelling species. With luck you should see Griffon Vulture, Egyptian Vulture, Golden Eagle or Peregrine Falcon. Sightings of Alpine Swift, Crag Martin, Chough or Blue Rock Thrush are guaranteed.

Accommodation

Limited accommodation is available in Sacedón. There are also some hostels in the villages on the road running from Guadalajara to Cuenca.

Comments

The best time of year for visiting the area is spring, since in summer there is a huge influx of visitors.

Bernardo Arroyo

CM.5 UÑA – TRAGACETE

River gorge and extensive pine woodland.

Main species

Residents: Little Grebe, Mallard, Griffon Vulture, Golden Eagle, Bonelli's Eagle, Water Rail, Moorhen, Coot, Great Spotted Woodpecker, Crested Tit, Goldcrest, Nuthatch, Chough, Raven, Rock Sparrow, Citril Finch, Crossbill.

Summer visitors: Egyptian Vulture, Alpine Swift, Crag Martin, Wheatear, Rock Thrush, Bonelli's Warbler.

Winter visitors: Little Egret, Grey Heron, Penduline Tit, Reed Bunting.

Access

From Cuenca, take the minor road via Villalba de la Sierra, Uña and Huélamo to Tragacete (75 km). Throughout, the road runs along the valley of the river Júcar.

Description

The source of the river Júcar is at the foot of the peak of San Felipe (1,839 m). Its upper reaches run through one of the most beautiful and least spoiled parts of the Serranías de Cuenca or Cuenca mountain range. Between Villalba de la Sierra and the turn for Beamud, the river runs through a deep gorge with uninterrupted cliffs of considerable height. Although riverside woodland is virtually absent, the valley

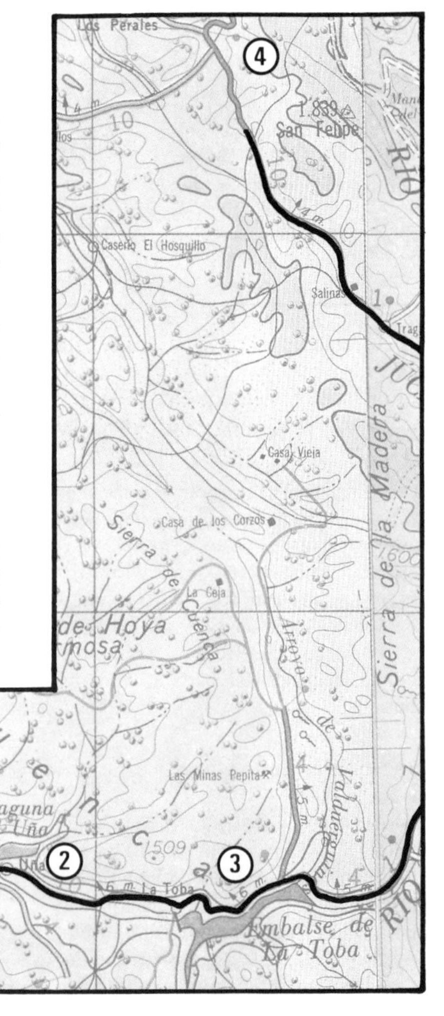

sides and areas of high ground are covered with extensive, mature pine woodland.

Recommended routes

The route recommended is a car journey taking you from Cuenca to Tragacete. The greatest points of interest are the following:

1) Salto del Infierno. A vantage point lying beside the road and giving a panoramic view of the Júcar gorge.

2) Uña. A small lake located near the village of Uña which will enable you to see a wide variety of water birds.

3) La Toba reservoir. From this point you can command a good view of the high rock walls of the gorge. You will have sightings of Griffon Vulture, Egyptian Vulture, Golden Eagle, Bonelli's Eagle, Peregrine Falcon, Alpine Swift, Crag Martin, Raven and Chough. The nearby bridge will enable you to cross the river Júcar and take a walk in the nearby pine woods if you wish to see a wide variety of forest-dwelling species.

4) Source (*nacimiento*) of the river Cuervo. An area of great beauty, although a highly popular tourist attraction. The site is about 15 km from Tragacete.

Accommodation

Plenty of accommodation is available in Cuenca, with a couple of hostels in Uña and a few more in Tragacete.

Comments

Late spring and summer are the best times of year for visiting the area.

Bernardo Arroyo and Ernesto Ferreiro

CM.6 ROSARITO AND NAVALCÁN RESERVOIRS

Reservoirs surrounded by wooded grazing lands.

Main species

Residents: Great Crested Grebe, Cattle Egret, Grey Heron, Black-shouldered Kite, Red Kite, Griffon Vulture, Black Vulture, Spanish Imperial Eagle, Little Bustard, Stone Curlew, Eagle Owl, Crag Martin, Azure-winged Magpie, Spanish Sparrow.

Summer visitors: Little Egret, Night Heron, White Stork, Black Stork, Honey Buzzard, Black Kite, Egyptian Vulture, Short-toed Eagle, Booted Eagle, Hobby, Baillon's Crake, Black-winged Stilt, Great Spotted Cuckoo, Red-necked Nightjar, Bee-eater, Roller.

Winter visitors: Cormorant, Grey Heron, ducks, Crane, Lesser Black-backed Gull, waders.

On passage: Spoonbill, Osprey, Black Tern.

Access

Near Oropesa, at the 148 km marker post on the N-V, take the road running northwards which immediately divides into two minor roads leading respectively to Madrigal de la Vera (Embalse de Rosarito), and Candeleda. 1.5 km after Candeleda turn right to reach the village and reservoir of Navalcán.

Description

Plains located to the south of the Sierra de Gredos consisting of fertile valleys which were flooded when the reservoirs were constructed. The Rosarito reservoir, holding the waters of the river Tiétar, is used to irrigate the fields of La Vera (province of Cáceres), while the Navalcán reservoir lies on the river Guadyerbas and supplies drinking water for the area.

The surrounding land supports unspoiled holm oak woodland which is grazed by large quantities of livestock. The most serious threat to this area is a project for constructing a new reservoir, Monteagudo, between the two existing reservoirs. This would destroy one of the best examples of plain-growing holm oak woodland in the Iberian Peninsula.

Recommended routes

It is worth pointing out that the inadequate network of tracks in the area around the reservoirs considerably limits options in terms of vantage points.

Route A is 8 km long and lasts 2½ hours. Its starting point is the dam of the Rosarito reservoir (point 1), from where you will have sightings of Cormorant, Grey Heron, Great Crested Grebe, Lesser Black-backed Gull and Crag Martin. Continuing along the road towards Oropesa you will see Cattle Egret, White Stork, Crane, Little Bustard and Stone Curlew. When you reach a campsite (8.5 km marker post), park your car at the campsite entrance and continue along a track until you reach the dam wall. From here, work your way around the reservoir to the higher ground, giving you a high observation point (2). The surrounding area will give sightings of various birds of prey, Great Spotted Cuckoo and Azure-winged Magpie. With the help of a telescope, on the reservoir you should see Grey Heron, Spoonbill, Black Stork, Cormorant, Osprey, up to 12 species of ducks, gulls, and waders. In the evening, you will also see Crane coming down to roost.

A variation on this route, which will give a different view of the reservoir, consists of the following; 300 m from the dam in the direction of Candeleda, take the small track which leads off to the right, bringing you to the shore (3).

Route B consists of a 30 km car journey taking you from the Rosarito reservoir to the Navalcán reservoir via Candeleda. The greatest points of interest are the following:

4) Pine woodland. Before reaching the C-501 you will go through an area of pine woodland where you will have sightings of Red Kite, Black Kite, Booted Eagle, Short-toed Eagle, Hobby, White Stork, Red-necked Nightjar and Azure-winged Magpie.

5) Centro de la Naturaleza. A couple of kilometres before Candeleda you will come across a surfaced track leading off to the right. A signpost indicates the way to Centro de la Naturaleza (a wildlife information centre); this road will take you to the Centro de la Naturaleza El Vado de los Fresnos (Fundación José María Blanc). A visit to the centre is optional but recommended, since it will enable you to see a series of species typical of the Sierra de Gredos and the Tiétar valley in an exceptional setting. The visit will consist of a walk of 2 hours. A small fee is payable on entrance.

6) Candeleda. A walk through the streets of this village will allow you to see numerous nests belonging to Crag Martin, Swallow and House Martin.

7) River Tiétar. From Candeleda take the minor road to Oropesa. On crossing the bridge over the Tiétar you can expect to see, among other species, Spanish Imperial Eagle, Short-toed Eagle, Booted Eagle, Eagle Owl, Black Vulture, Griffon Vulture, Egyptian Vulture and Black Stork.

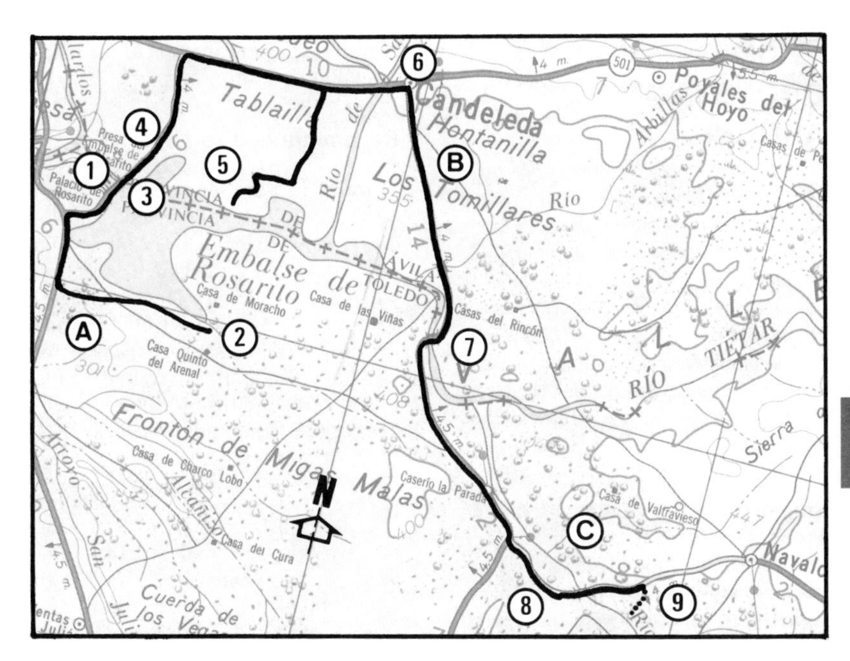

The road continues through one of the best examples of plain-growing holm oak woodland in Spain, which is threatened by a project for a dam. When you reach the junction with the road to Navalcán turn left and you will come to the reservoir.

The starting point of **Route C** is the dam of the Navalcán reservoir (8), from where you will have sightings of Cormorant, Great Crested Grebe and many species of duck. There are no access roads on the right shore, meaning that you can only cover the shore on foot if you wish to see waders. Continuing along the road towards Navalcán, after a couple of kilometres you will come to a right turn onto a track running through holm oak woodland where you may see feeding Crane. Eventually the track brings you out on the shore (9). From here you will command a good view of the reservoir and should see Cattle Egret, Grey Heron, Greylag Goose, ducks, Coot and, with luck, Osprey.

Accommodation

A reasonable amount of accommodation is available in the surrounding villages, particularly Candeleda. There are also some campsites, of which we recommend that at Madrigal de la Vera.

Comments

The best time of year for visiting the area is winter, although the migration periods are also worthwhile. In summer, the large number of human visitors makes it hardly worth visiting the Rosarito reservoir, where birdlife is disturbed by the increasing presence of motorboats.

It is worthwhile taking a telescope. It should be pointed out that the farmland surrounding the lakes is private, so you should keep to the paths.

Rodrigo Muñoz-Pulido

■ CM.7 OROPESA AND AROUND

Grassland, cereal crops, holm oak woodland.

Main species

Residents: Cattle Egret, White Stork, Black-shouldered Kite, Black Vulture, Griffon Vulture, Little Bustard, Great Bustard, Stone Curlew, Black-bellied Sandgrouse, Pin-tailed Sandgrouse, Raven, Spanish Sparrow.

Summer visitors: Egyptian Vulture, Montagu's Harrier, Lesser Kestrel, Hobby, Great Spotted Cuckoo, Red-necked Nightjar, Bee-eater, Roller, Red-rumped Swallow, Black-eared Wheatear.

Winter visitors: Red Kite, Merlin, Golden Plover, Short-eared Owl.

Access

Oropesa is located on the N-V between Talavera de la Reina and Navalmoral de la Mata.

Description

A flat, treeless area in the west of the province of Toledo between the rivers Tiétar and Tajo (Tagus). The area is largely given over to grain fields and pasturelands which are extensively grazed. In winter there are frequently flooded areas. Nearby is a large area of holm oak woodland growing in many places on dry grazing lands; this constitutes one of the largest areas of plain-growing woodland in Spain.

The main threat to the area is posed by an extensive network of electricity pylons and a possible change from traditional farming methods to irrigated farmland, a consequence of the project for the construction of the Monteagudo reservoir.

Recommended routes

Route A is 7 km long and runs along the road joining Oropesa and Candeleda. It runs through grasslands and cereal fields. At the 2.3 km marker post you will find a dump (1) where household rubbish and waste from abattoirs are deposited. This is a good site for watching Cattle Egret, White Stork, Black Vulture, Griffon Vulture, Egyptian Vulture, kites and corvids.

At the 4.5 km marker post you will come across a eucalyptus plantation (2), site of a large roost of Red Kite. Nearby two seasonal streams converge; during winter they give rise to a small flooded area where you will be able to see Golden Plover and other waders.

The finishing point of the route is the village of La Corchuela, on the edge of the holm oak woodland. By the bridge over the Alcañizo stream (3) you may see Hobby, Roller, Bee-eater, Great Spotted Cuckoo, Red-rumped Swallow and Spanish Sparrow.

Route B takes you for 14 km along the road from Oropesa to Madrigal de la Vera. Near the 27 km marker post (point 4) you may be lucky to see Black-shouldered Kite as well as Montagu's Harrier, Bee-eater and Black-eared Wheatear. A couple of kilometres farther on you will come across a telephone exchange; turn left onto a track which runs through the area where holm oak woodland gives way to pasturelands (5) where you may see Black Kite, Spanish Imperial Eagle and other birds of prey. Near the Landrinos stream, a track runs southwards towards La Calzada de Oropesa, crossing a flat area of pasture and cereal fields (6) where Great Bustard, Little Bustard, Stone Curlew, Black-bellied

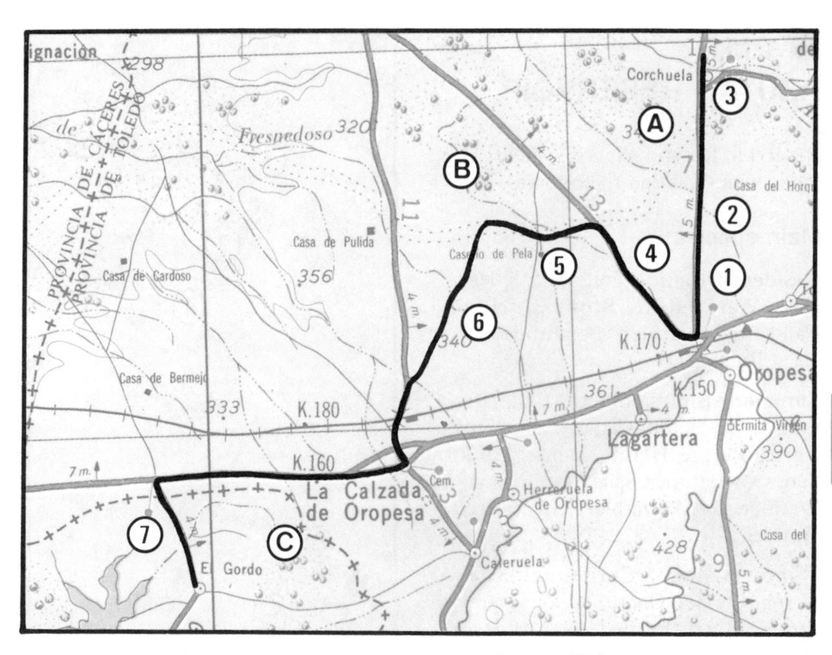

Sandgrouse, Pin-tailed Sandgrouse and harriers are present. The route comes to an end when you reach the road from Ventas de San Julián to La Calzada de Oropesa.

The purpose of **Route C** is to visit the old quarters of the towns of Oropesa, La Calzada de Oropesa and El Gordo, sites of substantial colonies of White Stork and Lesser Kestrel. Particularly interesting is the point where the minor road to El Gordo joins the N-V (7); from here, among other steppe-dwellers, you may see Great Bustard and Little Bustard. It is also a good place for spotting Greylag Goose and Montagu's Harrier. In addition, you will see flights of Crane and Cormorant making for the nearby lake of Valdecañas.

It should be noted that at any point on these three routes you may well see Black Stork, Spanish Imperial Eagle, Black-shouldered Kite and Montagu's Harrier.

Accommodation

There is a Parador Nacional in Oropesa. Other accommodation is available at roadside establishments. Further accommodation is available in the towns of Talavera de la Reina and Navalmoral de la Mata.

Comments

There is a lot of privately-owned farmland in the area and you should respect boundary lines and signs. It is perfectly possible to make interesting sightings from the road or from the tracks indicated above.

It is also worth pointing out that in winter the condition of some tracks deteriorates. Use of a telescope is recommended in some cases.

Rodrigo Muñoz-Pulido,
Alfredo Ortega Sirvent
and Francisco Márquez Sánchez.

CM.8 AZUTÁN RESERVOIR

Reservoir featuring marshy areas, islands with trees and river gorges.

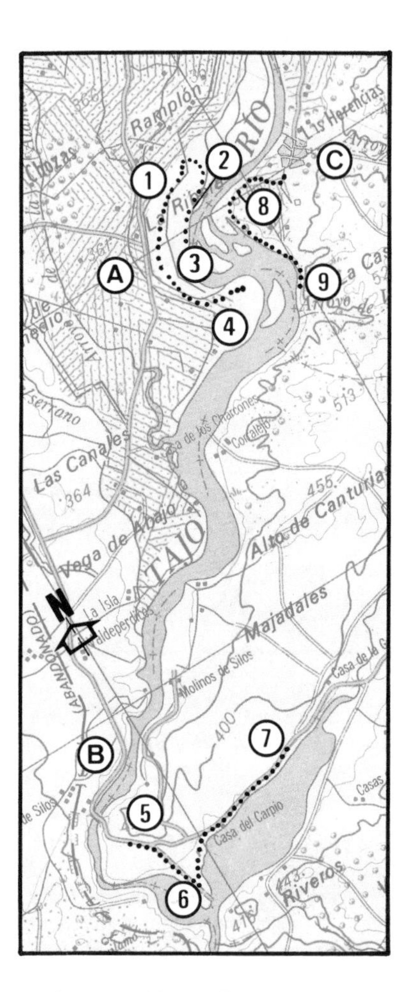

Main species

Residents: Cattle Egret, Marsh Harrier, Water Rail, Stone Curlew, Fan-tailed Warbler, Penduline Tit, Reed Bunting.

Summer visitors: Bittern, Little Bittern, Night Heron, Cattle Egret, Little Egret, Purple Heron, White Stork, Scops Owl, Roller, Sand Martin, Savi's Warbler, Reed Warbler, Great Reed Warbler.

Winter visitors: Cormorant, Grey Heron, Greylag Goose, ducks, Osprey, Snipe, Black-headed Gull, Lesser Black-backed Gull, Meadow Pipit.

On passage: Crane, waders.

Access

In Talavera de la Reina, take the local road for Calera and Chozas and continue until reaching the village of Alberche del Caudillo (9 km). From the main square in Alberche del Caudillo take the Camino General no. 4 (surfaced) which will take you to the starting points of routes A and B.

To reach the starting point of route C, leave Talavera de la Reina on the N-502 in the direction of Alcaudete de la Jara. After 10 km you will come to a right turn for Las Herencias.

Description

The Azután reservoir is on the river Tajo (Tagus). It takes up some 1,600 ha and was built in 1969, flooding large areas of farmland lying on the floodplain of the river. Today the area has an abundant and wide range of marsh vegetation consisting mainly of reedmace and beds of reeds and rushes. There are also some patches of relict riverside woodland, constituted by poplar and tamarisks.

Recommended routes

Route A is a 5 km walk taking 4 hours. Leave your car at the 5 km marker post on the Camino General no. 4 (point 1). From here you will command a view of the beds of reedmace and reeds which are frequented by Marsh Harrier, Purple Heron, Great Crested Grebe, Little Grebe, ducks and Coot. Keep to the left along a road running beside the river until you reach a metal gate, usually closed. Climb over the gate and follow the path through a flooded area with rush beds where you should be able to see Fan-tailed Warbler, Reed Bunting, Water Rail, Reed Warbler and Great Reed Warbler. A little farther on, you will come to the beginning of an abandoned drainage channel (point 2) near a stand of willow where you may see Penduline Tit, Roller, Scops Owl, Golden Oriole and Bittern. In winter the willows are the site of an enormous roost of some 10,000 Jackdaw and Starling. The track continues through pastureland and comes to a large dry eucalyptus tree (point 3) which in winter is the site of large numbers of Cormorant. To reach point 4, return to the surfaced road and continue downstream for some 700 m until encountering a path running off to the left along the river. As you walk along the path, you will see a large number of ducks; if you are lucky you will also see Osprey, which winter in the area.

Route B takes you along the surfaced track to the minor road running from Calera and Chozas to Alcaudete de la Jara. Turn left onto this road; cross the Tajo via the Puente de Silos, a bridge, and after 1.4 km you will come to the old road to Aldeanueva. Walk along the road and, if you wish, go down to the shore of the reservoir to see ducks, Cormorant, gulls and waders (points 5, 6 and 7).

The starting point for **Route C** is Las Herencias, where you can park your car and walk to the entrance of the Villa Aurora, a farm on the road leading to the station (Calle de la Estación). Ask permission at the farm to go to point 8, on the riverbank, from where you can command a good view of the colonies of Cattle Egret, Night Heron and Little Egret. Continuing along the riverbank you will come to the base of some impressive clay cliffs. You can climb the cliffs via well-trodden paths and from the top (9) enjoy a panoramic view of the reservoir.

Accommodation

Talavera de la Reina avails of an abundant and wide range of accommodation.

José Luis de la Cruz,
Fernando Cámara
and Miguel A. de la Cruz

■ CM.9 CASTREJÓN RESERVOIR

Reservoir and deep river gorges.

Main species

Residents: Cattle Egret, Marsh Harrier, Golden Eagle, Bonelli's Eagle, Peregrine Falcon, Little Bustard, Stone Curlew, Black-bellied Sandgrouse, Eagle Owl, Calandra Lark, Blue Rock Thrush, Bearded Tit, Penduline Tit, Raven.

Summer visitors: Night Heron, Purple Heron, Montagu's Harrier, Short-toed Eagle, Booted Eagle, Lesser Kestrel, Great Spotted Cuckoo, Bee-eater, Roller, Red-rumped Swallow.

Winter visitors: Cormorant, Little Egret, Grey Heron, White Stork, Greylag Goose, ducks (over 10,000 in 1989), Lesser Black-backed Gull.

On passage: Black-winged Stilt, Avocet, Osprey, passerines.

Access

From Toledo take the C-502 towards La Puebla de Montalbán. At the 166 km marker post turn left onto a dirt track taking you to the Las Barrancas area. A little farther on, 28 km from Toledo, turn left onto the road for

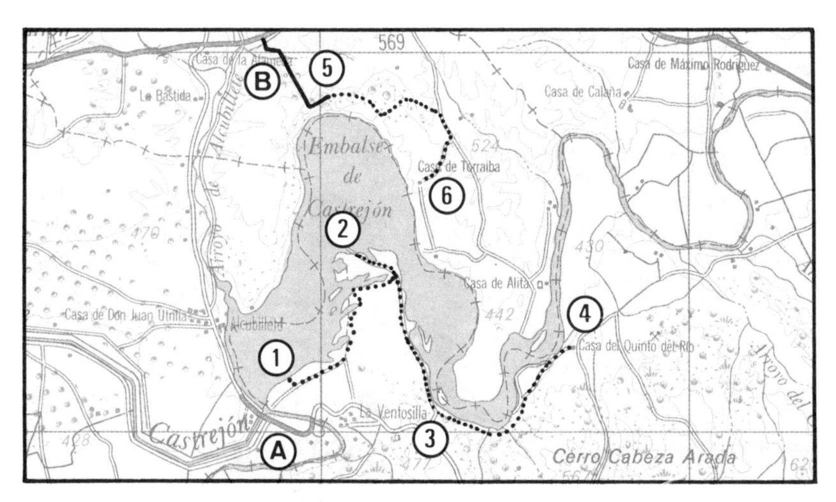

Polán, which runs across the dam of the reservoir. At the 16.2 km marker post on this road, a track closed to traffic leads out to the jetty and, at the 21.7 km marker post, another track runs off to Quinto del Río, an abandoned farm.

It is also possible to reach La Puebla de Montalbán from Maqueda, on the N-V, via the N-403 and the C-403.

Description

The reservoir at Castrejón, extending for some 750 ha, is located on the middle reaches of the Tajo (Tagus), on a stretch of river with a series of sweeping bends. There are many small islets and the banks are taken up by marsh vegetation and, in some places, riverside woodland.

The surrounding land is largely put to agricultural purposes. On the left bank is an area of dry grazing land with holm oak woods, and on the right bank some high clay cliffs known as Las Barrancas.

Recommended routes

Route A is a 6 km walk running along the left shore of the reservoir. Start at the jetty and cover the following points of interest:

1) Jetty. A good place for watching gulls, Cormorant, herons and some ducks.

2) Soto de Batanejo. An area of abundant marsh vegetation with shallow ponds and substantial stands of holm oak. Outside the breeding season, it is worthwhile trying to get as close to the shore as possible to watch Cormorant, Little Egret, Cattle Egret, Grey Heron, Purple Heron, White Stork, ducks, Marsh Harrier, Bearded Tit and Penduline Tit.

3) Cárcava del Palomar. This point can also be reached directly on foot via a dirt track leading off from the 18 km marker post on the Polán road at the junction with the C-502. This site consists of a small cliff from which you can see a wide range of species with great ease.

4) Quinto del Río. A good spot for watching herons, including Night Heron. You can also see Golden Eagle, Bonelli's Eagle, Marsh Harrier and Red-rumped Swallow.

The starting point of **Route B** is the track taking you to Las Barrancas. It is worthwhile undertaking the first stretch of the route by car, passing through an area of cereal fields, olive groves and uncultivated land where you will have opportunities of seeing Montagu's Harrier, Black-bellied Sandgrouse, Little Bustard, Calandra Lark and, with luck, Great Bustard and Stone Curlew. On reaching the cliffs (5), it is better to continue on foot, following the river up to the big house at Torralba (6), 3 km upstream. The route will give rise to sightings of all the water birds as well as Golden Eagle, Bonelli's Eagle, Peregrine Falcon, Lesser Kestrel, Eagle Owl, Bee-eater, Raven, Blue Rock Thrush and wheatears.

Accommodation

Although accommodation is available in Polán (Hostal Luna), Toledo offers a much wider range of possibilities.

Comments

Route A runs entirely across private land. For this reason it is worthwhile asking permission from the rangers at the farm of La Ventosilla de Doña Sol. The last part of route B also runs across private farmland, although this does not usually cause any problems.

It is worthwhile taking a telescope.

Susana Casado Campos
and Alfredo Ortega Sirvent

■ CM.10 CABAÑEROS NATURAL PARK

A Mediterranean range of hills with woodland and scrubland.

Main species

Residents: Black-shouldered Kite, Red Kite, Griffon Vulture, Black Vulture, Goshawk, Sparrowhawk, Buzzard, Golden Eagle, Spanish Imperial Eagle, Kestrel, Little Bustard, Great Bustard, Eagle Owl, Blue Rock Thrush, Dartford Warbler, Sardinian Warbler, Azure-winged Magpie.

Summer visitors: White Stork, Black Kite, Egyptian Vulture, Short-toed Eagle, Montagu's Harrier, Hobby, Great Spotted Cuckoo, Bee-eater, Roller, Black-eared Wheatear.

Winter visitors: Hen Harrier, Merlin.

On passage: Crane.

Access

Leave Ciudad Real on the N-430 and at Piedrabuena (24 km) turn right onto the C-403 for Pueblonuevo de Bullaque (37 km). In this village there is an Information Centre for the Parque Natural de Cabañeros. From the Centre a minor road leads to Santa Quiteria and midway between the two villages you will find the Park entrance.

Description

Cabañeros consists of a large plain of detrital material known locally as *raña* and two ranges of hills which run more or less parallel, surrounding the plain. These hills rise to a height of some 1,000 m. The *raña* is largely given over to pastureland and open land, dotted in some areas with holm oak and Lusitanian oak, while in the hills woodland alternates with patches of scrub. The hills are the home of large numbers of deer and wild boar.

Recommended routes

Since this is a Natural Park, the routes which can be undertaken in Cabañeros are two scheduled trips made in the company of a ranger. Both routes cover the areas of greatest interest and provide a good general impression of the whole, guaranteeing sightings of the most representative species. Of particular interest is the large population of Black Vulture and the plentiful and wide range of other

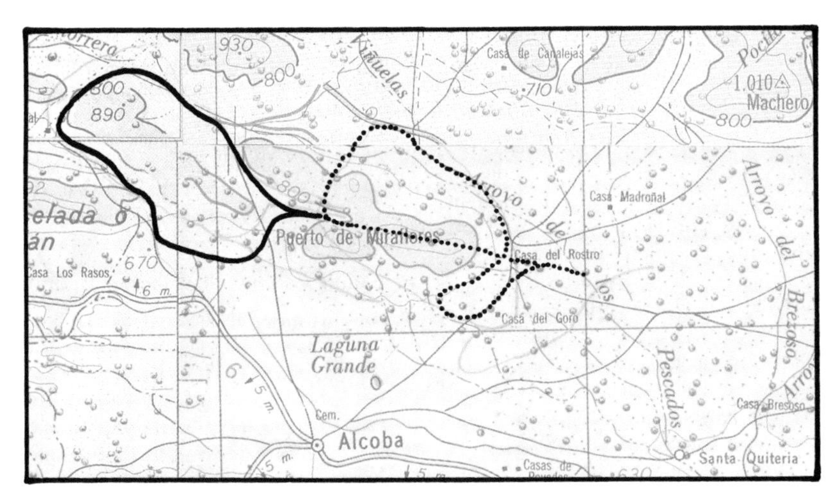

birds of prey, including Griffon Vulture, Golden Eagle, Spanish Imperial Eagle, Short-toed Eagle, Booted Eagle, Montagu's Harrier and, according to season, Black-shouldered Kite. It is also possible to see Great Bustard, Little Bustard, Crane, Black Stork and —of course— large numbers of passerines.

Accommodation

Tourism in the area has not been developed. You can eat and sleep at Casa Paco in Horcajo de los Montes. In Pueblonuevo de Bullaque there are bars which offer accommodation.

Comments

You must ask for permission before making a visit to the area. The address is: Parque Natural de Cabañeros; Calle Alarcos, 21, Planta 3; Ciudad Real.

José Jiménez García-Herrera

■ CM.11 LONGAR (LILLO) LAGOON

Seasonal natural lagoon in a steppe habitat.

Main species

Residents: Little Bustard, Great Bustard, Stone Curlew, Pin-tailed Sandgrouse, Dupont's Lark, Calandra Lark, Thekla Lark, Rock Sparrow.

Summer visitors: Black-winged Stilt, Avocet, Kentish Plover, Redshank, Gull-billed Tern, Bee-eater, Short-toed Lark, Tawny Pipit, Yellow Wagtail, Fan-tailed Warbler, Black-eared Wheatear.

On passage: Black-necked Grebe, Crane, waders.

Access

From Tembleque on the N-IV, take the C-302 to Lillo (24 km). In Lillo take the minor road to Villacañas and after 1.5 km turn right onto a dirt track leading to the lagoon.

Description

The lake of Longar, measuring some 90 ha, is a wetland area surrounded by halophytic, nitrophilous vegetation. Waste water from the village of Lillo has caused this lagoon to become permanent.

The area around the lagoon has changed a lot and is subject to intense human presence, although a sizeable

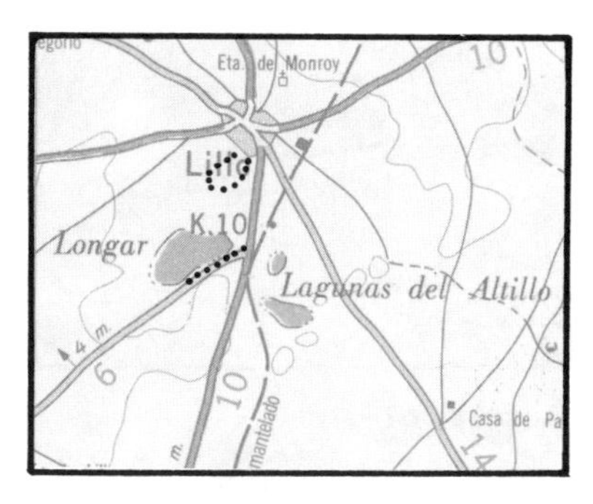

area of scrubland constituted by albardine (*Lygeum spartum*) still remains between the lagoon and the village.

Recommended routes

Since the lagoon is small in size, a walk around the shores will be enough to see the most representative species: Kentish Plover, Black-winged Stilt, Avocet, Redshank and Gull-billed Tern during the breeding season, and during the migration periods Black-necked Grebe and various waders. The surrounding countryside will give sightings of Great Bustard, Stone Curlew, Pin-tailed Sandgrouse, Tawny Pipit, Black-eared Wheatear and Rock Sparrow.

It is also worthwhile covering the albardine area to increase the number of species seen with Little Bustard, Dupont's Lark, Short-toed Lark and Calandra Lark.

It may also be worthwhile going to the nearby lagoons at Altillo.

Accommodation

Accommodation in the area is scarce, although there is a hotel in Villacañas.

Javier Grijalbo, Pedro Molina, Jaime Ollero, Iván A. Sánchez and Tomás Velasco

■ CM.12 QUERO LAGOON

Natural lagoon.

Main species

Summer visitors: Black-winged Stilt, Avocet, Little Ringed Plover, Kentish Plover, Redshank, Gull-billed Tern.

Winter visitors: Shelduck, Teal, Shoveler, Pochard, Avocet, Common Sandpiper, Black-headed Gull.

On passage: ducks, waders.

Access

Take the N-IV from Madridejos to Villafranca de los Caballeros (16 km). In the latter village, take the minor road to Quero (14 km), the site of the lagoon.

Description

This is a medium-sized, brackish lagoon. Water levels vary considerably. There is no marsh vegetation, but there are plenty of dykes and islets where various waders nest. On the north shore, near the village, there are salt works with many salt pans.

Recommended routes

From the road leading to Quero you can see virtually the whole of the lagoon.

Accommodation

Accommodation is available in the nearby towns of Alcázar de San Juan and Quintanar de la Orden, as well as along the N-IV.

Comments

Madrid is close to the lagoons in this part of La Mancha, enabling you to visit several lagoons in one day. A good route would be Madrid – Madridejos (120 km) – Villafranca de los Caballeros(CM.14) – Quero (CM.12) – Alcázar de San Juan (CM.15) – Pedro Muñoz (CM.16) – Mota del Cuervo (Laguna de Manjavacas, CM.17) – Madrid.

Ramón Martí Montes
and Carlos Martín-Novella

CM.13 POZO DE LA PUERTA (MIGUEL ESTEBAN) LAGOON

Natural lagoon.

Main species

Residents: Black-necked Grebe, Little Bustard, Black-bellied Sandgrouse, Pin-tailed Sandgrouse, Cetti's Warbler.

Summer visitors: Shelduck, Red-crested Pochard, Black-winged Stilt, Avocet, Collared Pratincole, Kentish Plover, Redshank, Gull-billed Tern, Whiskered Tern, Bee-eater, Short-toed Lark, Yellow Wagtail.

Winter visitors: ducks, Lesser Short-toed Lark, Calandra Lark.

On passage: ducks, waders.

Access

From Quintanar de la Orden, take the local road to Miguel Esteban. To reach the lagoon drive for a couple of kilometres along the road to El Toboso and near a chapel located beside the road turn off onto a dirt track leading down to the shore. Since there is nowhere to leave your car, it is a good idea to park beside the sewage works.

Description

The lagoon of El Pozo de la Puerta has been partially converted into a series of ponds contained by earth walls. These are used as an outflow for the waste water of the village of Miguel Esteban. Next to these lagoons is an area which remains flooded in winter and spring. This is a SEO Ornithological Reserve.

Recommended routes

From the place where you leave your vehicle, a track leads off to circle the lagoons and enables you to see Black-necked Grebe, Red-crested Pochard, Avocet, Black-winged Stilt, Kentish Plover and Whiskered Tern.

A general impression of the flooded area can be gained from the track or, even better, from the top of one of the walls. When the area is flooded you will see ducks, waders, Gull-billed Tern, Lesser Short-toed Lark and Yellow Wagtail; when it is dry, Little Bustard, Collared Pratincole, Black-bellied Sandgrouse, Calandra Lark and Short-toed Lark.

Accommodation

There is a wide variety of accommodation available in nearby Quintanar de la Orden.

Javier Grijalbo, Jaime Ollero, Iván A. Sánchez and Tomás Velasco

CM.14 VILLAFRANCA LAGOONS

Natural lagoons.

Main species

Residents: Little Grebe, Great Crested Grebe, Marsh Harrier, Mallard, Red-crested Pochard, Little Bustard, Pin-tailed Sandgrouse.

Summer visitors: Purple Heron, Gull-billed Tern.

Winter visitors: Shoveler, Teal, Pochard.

On passage: Garganey, Whiskered Tern.

Access

From Madridejos on the N-IV, take the local road to Villafranca de los Caballeros (16 km). In Villafranca, take the minor road to Quero and after 2.5 km you will come across a signed turn to the left for the lagoons.

Description

Natural lagoons fed by rivers, causing water levels to remain relatively constant and favouring the growth of abundant marsh vegetation. The main lagoon, known as Laguna Grande, has relatively deep, clean water but is subject to a lot of human presence (fishermen, swimmers, walkers, etc.) and extensive sections of its shores

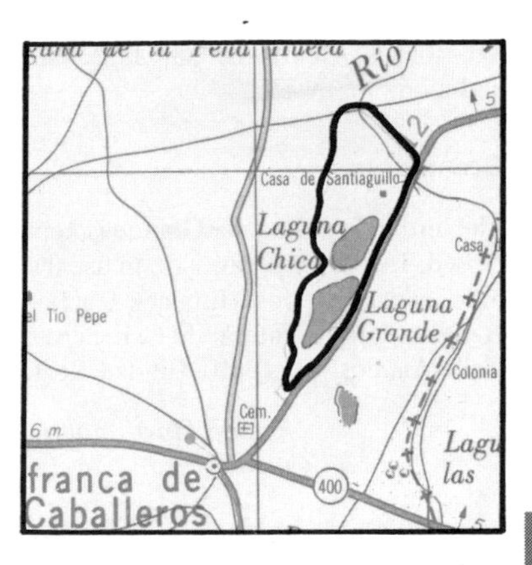

have been the site of building development.

Laguna Chica is a smaller lagoon surrounded by a well-developed belt of reeds.

Recommended routes

A series of tracks, passable by car except when there is heavy rainfall, surround the lagoons and enable you to approach them at various points. Firstly work your way clockwise around Laguna Grande, where the number of birds is usually very low. Pass a small pine wood to reach Laguna Chica and, if you continue along the track, you will cross the Vega de Mazón, an extensive area of *Cladium mariscus* and reeds frequented by Marsh Harrier. Subsequently, the track runs through an area of grazing land and fields where you may see Little Bustard, Pin-tailed Sandgrouse and other steppe-dwelling birds. You will come out at the 7 km marker post on the road from Villafranca to Quero. If, on the other hand, you move in an anticlockwise direction around Laguna Grande the track will bring you to a hide commanding an undisturbed area where water birds congregate.

Accommodation

There is a variety of accommodation in the main towns of the neighbourhood:

Villafranca, Alcázar de San Juan, etc. and along the N-IV.

Comments

The bird hide at Laguna Grande is kept closed. To ask for permission to use the hide, contact D. José Jiménez García-Herrera; Parque Natural de Cabañeros; Calle Alarcos, 21; 13001 Ciudad Real.

Ramón Martí Montes
and Carlos Martín-Novella

■ CM.15 ALCÁZAR DE SAN JUAN LAGOONS

Natural lagoons.

Main species

Residents: Black-necked Grebe, Little Grebe, Shelduck, Mallard, Gadwall, Kentish Plover, Redshank, Black-headed Gull.

Summer visitors: Black-winged Stilt, Avocet, Gull-billed Tern, Whiskered Tern, Black Tern.

Winter visitors: ducks, Coot, Common Sandpiper.

On passage: Pintail, Garganey, Grey Plover, Dunlin, Ruff, Black-tailed Godwit.

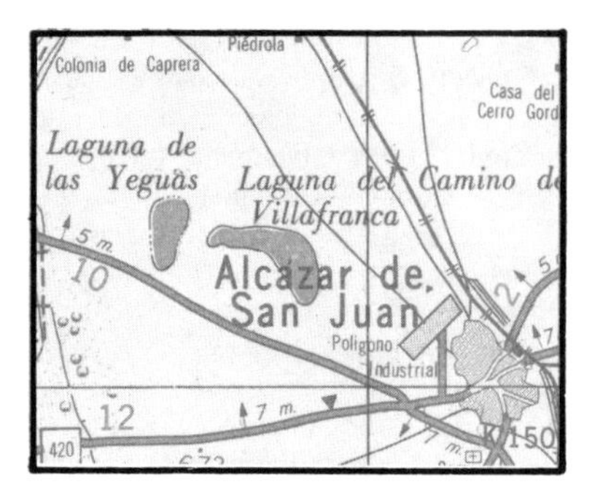

Access

From Alcázar de San Juan, take the C-400 towards Madridejos. At about 600 m from the 91 km marker post on this road, to the left of the road near two white farm cottages, a track runs around the southern shores of both lagoons.

Description

The natural lagoon of Las Yeguas is saline, shallow and subject to drastic changes in water level. The shores are muddy and devoid of marsh vegetation. The salinity of the water means that the lagoon is not popular with water birds, although in winter Shelduck are present and there is a large roost of Black-headed Gull.

The Camino de Villafranca lagoon, linked to the previous lagoon by a channel, is large and shallow. It is also subject to dramatic seasonal changes in water level and its saline water has been badly contaminated by urban and industrial waste. The shores are devoid of vegetation but there is an island where a large colony of terns and waders is present.

Recommended routes

The size of the lagoon and the absence of marsh vegetation or other natural obstacles, make observation of water birds on these lagoons possible from the access road. There are two hides on the Camino de Villafranca lagoon, one of which is near an island constituting the breeding ground for Gull-billed Tern, Black-winged Stilt and Avocet.

Accommodation

Accommodation is available in Alcázar de San Juan, Manzanares and Quintanar de la Orden. There are also plenty of hotels and hostels strung along the N-IV. Madrid is some 135 km away, making it possible to organize trips from the capital.

Comments

The hides are kept locked, so you should ask for permission beforehand to use them. Contact D. José Jiménez García-Herrera; Parque Natural de Cabañeros; Calle Alarcos, 21; 13001 Ciudad Real.

Ramón Martí Montes
and Carlos Martín-Novella

CM.16 PEDRO MUÑOZ LAGOON

Saline lagoon.

Main species

Residents: Gadwall, Red-crested Pochard, White-headed Duck, Bearded Tit.

Summer visitors: Black-necked Grebe, Black-winged Stilt, Whiskered Tern.

Winter visitors: Marsh Harrier, ducks.

On passage: Osprey, Pintail, Garganey, Ferruginous Duck, Knot, Dunlin, Ruff, Black-tailed Godwit, Spotted Redshank, Redshank, Greenshank, Black Tern.

Access

From Quintanar de la Orden on the N-IV, take the minor road to El Toboso and subsequently to Pedro Muñoz (17 km). The lagoon is located next to Pedro Muñoz on the road leading to El Toboso.

Description

This is a semi-permanent saline lagoon in which changes in water level are attenuated by the addition of waste water. Rubbish has been thrown into the lagoon, causing the area of the whole to be reduced to its present 38 ha. The lagoon was acquired by the local government of Castile-La Mancha and various restoration projects have taken place.

There is a hide on the west shore which is open to the public.

Recommended routes

It is worthwhile using the observatory, although the glass in the windows may make it difficult to use a telescope. Birds can be seen at very close range. There is also a track running around the perimeter of the lagoon which is worthwhile walking along to see waders and the occasional heron. A small nearby hill provides an excellent vantage point over the entire lagoon.

Accommodation

Villages in the area avail of accommodation. Hostal La Parada in Pedro Muñoz is recommended; this estab-

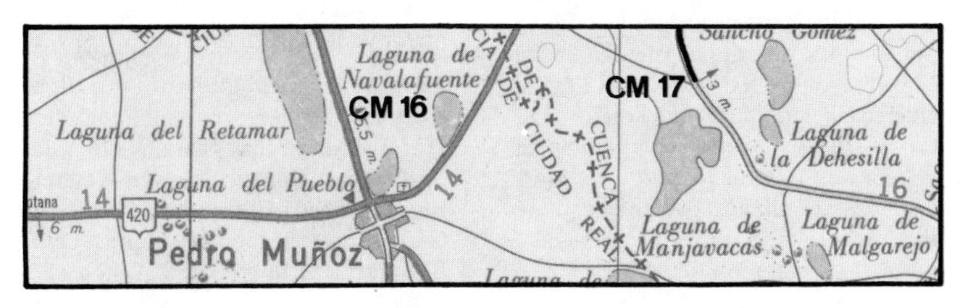

CM

lishment also provides typical Manchegan food at a reasonable price.

José Jiménez García-Herrera

CM.17 MANJAVACAS LAGOON

Natural lagoon in a steppe habitat.

Main species

Residents: Black-necked Grebe, Little Grebe, Mallard, Gadwall, Red-crested Pochard, Pochard, Coot, Black-headed Gull.

Summer visitors: Black-winged Stilt, Avocet, Kentish Plover, Gull-billed Tern, Whiskered Tern, Black Tern.

Winter visitors: Shelduck, Teal, Shoveler, Pochard.

On passage: Garganey, Dunlin, Ruff, Black-tailed Godwit and other waders.

Access

Access is from Mota del Cuervo on the N-301. From this village, take the N-420 towards Alcázar de San Juan and just as you are leaving the centre of Mota, turn onto the minor road for Las Mesas. After 3 km you will reach the chapel of Manjavacas, from where you will gain a good view of the lagoon.

Description

A natural lagoon of some 200 ha. This is one of the few permanent lagoons in the complex of lagoons of western La Mancha, but it is subject to drastic changes in water level, causing its area to vary greatly. Well-developed marsh vegetation, extensive muddy shores and areas of shallow water constitute the site of large numbers of waders during the migration periods.

Recommended routes

A track, passable except after heavy rain, leads off from the chapel at Manjavacas. The track runs around the lagoon and enables you to approach the shores at various points. From the road to Las Mesas, other tracks lead off enabling you to reach other parts of the lagoon.

Accommodation

Accommodation is available in the nearby towns of Mota del Cuervo, Alcázar de San Juan and Quintanar de la Orden. Since Madrid is close by, it is possible to organize trips from the capital.

Ramón Martí Montes
and Carlos Martín-Novella

CM.18 TABLAS DE DAIMIEL

Extensive wetland area lying in the confluence of two rivers.

Main species

Residents: Little Grebe, Great Crested Grebe, Black-necked Grebe, Gadwall, Mallard, Red-crested Pochard, Pochard, Marsh Harrier, Water Rail, Moorhen, Coot, Little Bustard, Stone Curlew, Lapwing, Redshank, Black-headed Gull, Pin-tailed Sandgrouse, Cetti's Warbler, Fan-tailed Warbler, Moustached Warbler, Bearded Tit, Penduline Tit, Great Grey Shrike, Spanish Sparrow, Reed Bunting.

Summer visitors: Little Bittern, Night Heron, Cattle Egret, Little Egret, Purple Heron, White Stork, Black Kite, Montagu's Harrier, Lesser Kestrel, Black-winged Stilt, Whiskered Tern, Great Spotted Cuckoo, Scops Owl, Bee-eater, Black-eared Wheatear,

Savi's Warbler, Reed Warbler, Great Reed Warbler.

Winter visitors: Cormorant, Grey Heron, Widgeon, Teal, Pintail, Shoveler, Tufted Duck, Hen Harrier, Golden Plover, Snipe, Short-eared Owl, Meadow Pipit, Starling.

On passage: Black Stork, Greylag Goose, Garganey, Crane, Avocet, Collared Pratincole, Dunlin, Ruff, Black-tailed Godwit, Sand Martin, Bluethroat.

Access

Daimiel is on the N-430 between Ciudad Real (29 km) and Manzanares (23 km). If you are coming from Madrid, take the N-420 from Puerto Lápice. Once in Daimiel, signs will take you directly to the visitors' centre of the Parque Natural (Natural Park) (11 km).

Description

Located at the confluence of the rivers Guadiana and Cigüela, the Tablas de Daimiel is a large-scale marsh area with extensive areas of *Cladium mariscus*, open water forming a labyrinth of canals and *tablas* (marshy islets) and shores covered with reeds, reedmace and stands of tamarisk. The surrounding countryside is flat and virtually entirely taken up by fields, formerly cereal crops and vineyards but now largely irrigated maize fields. It was precisely this extraction of underground water for irrigation which caused the virtual drying out of the *tablas*. The area now survives thanks to a water supply from the canal linking the river Tajo (Tagus) with the river Segura.

The area is a National Park measuring 5,410 ha.

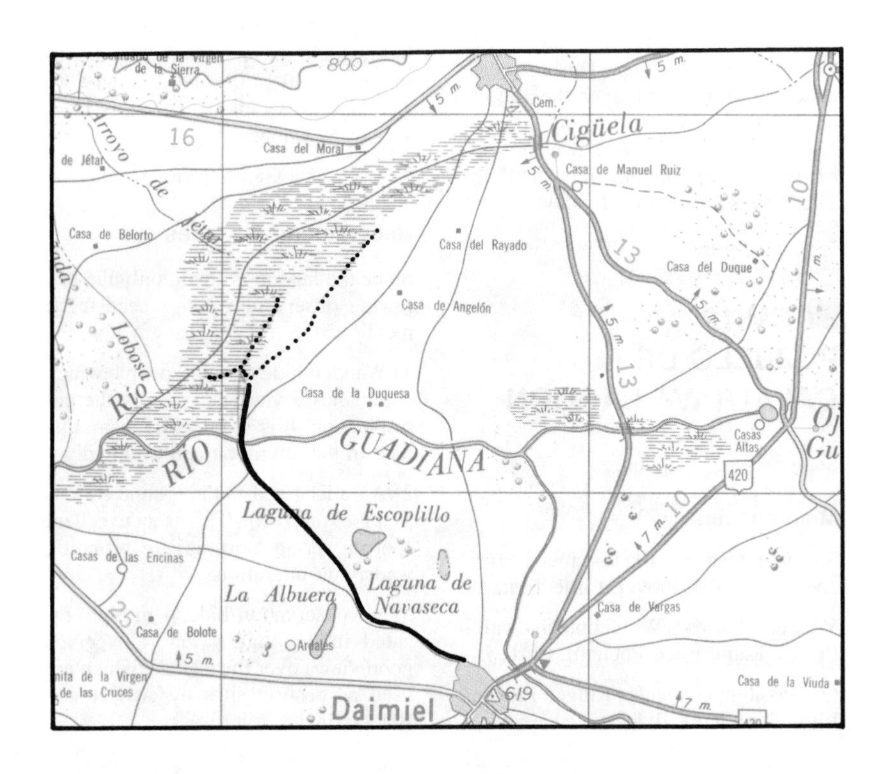

Recommended routes

From the visitors' centre of the Park, a series of paths lead off to hides (Isla del Pan, Torreta de Prado Ancho, Isla de Algeciras), giving you a good general impression of the area and sightings of the most representative species. A network of farm tracks enables you to reach other parts of the area. In addition, next to the visitors' centre there is a small collection of captive birds (*Laguna de aclimatación*, an area for rehabilitation and recovery).

Accommodation

There are some hostels in Daimiel, and also in Puerto Lápice, Manzanares and Ciudad Real.

Comments

You can obtain maps and leaflets at the visitors' centre of the National Park. It is open 09:00-21:00 in summer and 10:00-18:00 in winter. During weekends in spring and over the Easter holiday the number of visitors may be restricted, so it is worthwhile enquiring beforehand (telephone: 926-852058). The Park is closed on Mondays.

Eduardo de Juana Aranzana

■ CM.19 POZUELO DE CALATRAVA LAGOON

Seasonal saline lagoon.

Main species

Summer visitors: Black-winged Stilt, Avocet, Kentish Plover, Little Tern.

Winter visitors: Widgeon, Gadwall, Pintail, Red-crested Pochard, Curlew.

On passage: Garganey, Ringed Plover, Little Stint, Ruff, Black-tailed Godwit, Spotted Redshank, Greenshank, Black Tern.

Access

From Ciudad Real, take the C-415 towards Murcia until reaching the town of Pozuelo de Calatrava (12 km). You can reach the lagoon, located beside Pozuelo de Calatrava, via a dirt track leading off from beside the petrol station.

Description

A seasonal saline lagoon. The waters are shallow and the dumping of rubbish has reduced the lagoon to an area of 54 ha. Although several restoration projects have been undertaken, rubbish continues to be dumped in the lagoon. It is also worth mentioning the existence of underwater vegetation of great botanical interest.

The lagoon has two hides and a raised hide which are open from Monday to Friday, 09:00-14:00 and 16:00-19:00. The lagoon is closed to visitors from July to November.

The area is a Game Refuge.

Recommended routes

Since the lagoon is small, only the following observation points need to be mentioned:

1) Wooden hide taking 8 people which commands a view of virtually the entire lagoon. It is worthwhile using this hide in the afternoon and evening.

2) A trailer fixed to the ground for use as a lookout point. This is an excellent spot on spring mornings for watching waders on migration.

3) An observation hide, 4 m high, located in the pine wood. This gives good views over the islands, which are used as nesting sites by Avocet and Black-winged Stilt.

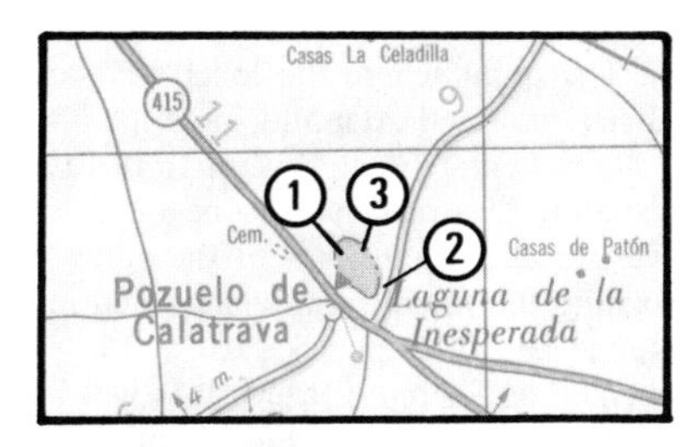

Accommodation

Although Pozuelo de Calatrava does not cater for visitors, accommodation can be found in Almagro and Ciudad Real.

Comments

There is currently a move to expropriate the section of the lagoon, which is private property, in order to proceed with restoration work.

José Jiménez García-Herrera

■ CM.20 FUENCALIENTE – VALLE DE ALCUDIA

Mountains with cliffs and Mediterranean woodland; a broad valley occupied by pastures and holm oak parkland.

Main species

Residents: Black-shouldered Kite, Red Kite, Griffon Vulture, Black Vulture, Goshawk, Spanish Imperial Eagle, Golden Eagle, Bonelli's Eagle, Peregrine Falcon, Eagle Owl, Little Bustard, Stone Curlew, Great Spotted Woodpecker, Crag Martin, Calandra Lark, Thekla Lark, Woodlark, Wren, Robin, Black Wheatear, Blue Rock Thrush, Mistle Thrush, Dartford Warbler, Sardinian Warbler, Blackcap, Long-tailed Tit, Nuthatch, Great Grey Shrike, Jay, Azure-winged Magpie, Chough, Raven, Rock Sparrow, Hawfinch, Rock Bunting.

Summer visitors: White Stork, Black Stork, Egyptian Vulture, Short-toed Eagle, Booted Eagle, Red-necked Nightjar, Bee-eater, Roller, Short-toed Lark, Red-rumped Swallow, Redstart, Black-eared Wheatear, Melodious Warbler, Subalpine Warbler, Orphean Warbler, Bonelli's Warbler, Chiffchaff, Golden Oriole, Woodchat Shrike.

Winter visitors: Merlin, Crane, Lapwing, passerines.

CM

Access

From Puertollano, take the N-420 towards Córdoba until reaching Brazatortas (16 km). Having crossed the small pass of Pulido, the road traverses the Alcudia valley and enters the Sierra Morena. Fuencaliente is 41 km from Brazatortas.

Alternatively, you can reach Fuencaliente from the south via the N-IV (42 km from Villa del Río).

Description

Fuencaliente is at the heart of the Sierra Morena, at the point where the province of Ciudad Real meets those of Córdoba and Jaén. Vegetation is relatively well-conserved with stands of holm oak, cork oak, Lusitanian oak and frequent examples of Pyrenean oak. These trees grow tall and dense in some places on the northern slopes; there are also patches of low mountain vegetation (strawberry tree, *Phillyrea* spp., heather, etc.), areas of scrubland and pine plantations. These mountains have quartzite crests rising to some height.

The Valle de Alcudia is a large depression located just to the north of the main ranges. It is taken up by pastures and, to a lesser extent, dry grazing lands with holm oak woods (*dehesa*). The

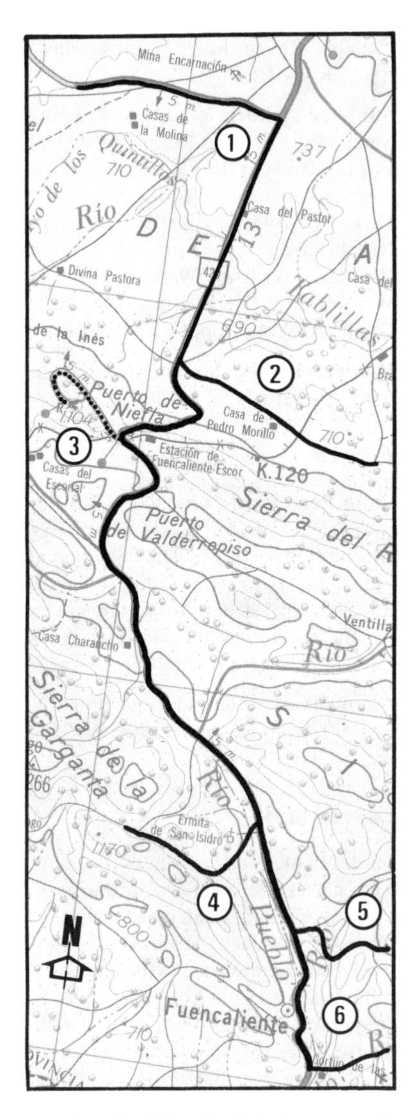

area is a traditional wintering ground for nomadic herds of sheep.

Recommended routes

The N-420 runs through the area from north to south, allowing for easy access to the various habitats present. The most interesting points are the following:

1) The point where the local road to Bienvenida and Alamillo joins the N-420, the latter being 44 km from the junction. The road enables one to travel westwards through part of the valley, visiting the broad pasturelands rich in steppe-dwelling species such as Little Bustard and Stone Curlew. It is worth visiting the ruins of the abandoned mines, some of which lie close to the junction, which are the nesting ground for White Stork, Kestrel, Chough and other species.

2) Just before starting the climb to the Niefla pass, an unsurfaced track leads off to the east, crossing excellent examples of *dehesa* lying at the foot of the Sierra del Rey. Continue along this track as far as you wish, making sure that you close the gates after you. It is worthwhile casting an eye over the rock faces of the nearby mountains.

3) By the pass is a surfaced track, closed to traffic with a chain and a sign designating the area as a *zona militar* or military zone, which you can walk along. A couple of hours' walk will enable you to visit the high ground located to the southwest (Chorreras, 1,095 m), crossing large areas of strawberry tree and a small rocky area. Apart from providing wonderful views over the Alcudia valley, the walk will enable you to see numerous mountain-dwelling passerines (Robin, Blackcap, Chiffchaff, Nuthatch) and birds of prey (kites, vultures, Booted Eagle, Golden Eagle).

4) On the road itself, next to a chapel on the banks of a stream, there is a stand of mature Lusitanian oaks inhabited by numerous forest-dwelling passerines. Near the chapel, a track leads off westwards along the northern slopes of Puerto Viejo, crossing interesting areas of Pyrenean oak woodland.

5) Peña Escrita, a cave with prehistoric paintings lying at the foot of some cliffs. The short stretch of surfaced road taking you to the cave runs through various habitats and provides starting points for walks.

6) A couple of kilometres south of Fuencaliente a track runs along the river Navalmanzano towards the mountain range of the same name and the Sierra de Quintana. Both of these ranges approach heights of 1,300 m and present cliffs inhabited by birds of prey.

Accommodation

Accommodation is available in Puertollano, Brazatortas and Fuencaliente (for example, in Fuencaliente you will find Hotel Peña Escrita and Hotel Los Azores).

Comments

The best times of year for visiting the area are spring and winter.

Eduardo de Juana Aranzana

CM.21 PÉTROLA, SALOBRALEJO AND ONTALAFIA LAGOONS

A system of natural lagoons in a steppe habitat.

Main species

Residents: Marsh Harrier, Red-crested Pochard, Little Bustard, Great Bustard, Stone Curlew, Black-bellied Sandgrouse, Pin-tailed Sandgrouse, Calandra Lark, Thekla Lark, Fan-tailed Warbler, Dartford Warbler, Bearded Tit, Rock Sparrow.

Summer visitors: Black-necked Grebe, Little Bittern, Black-winged Stilt, Avocet, Kentish Plover, Gull-billed Tern, Whiskered Tern, Short-toed Lark, Black-eared Wheatear, Spectacled Warbler, Subalpine Warbler.

Winter visitors: Shelduck, Gadwall, Pintail, Tufted Duck, Little Stint, Dunlin, Ruff.

On passage: Little Egret, Greater Flamingo, Garganey, Spotted Redshank, Greenshank, Green Sandpiper, Wood Sandpiper, Black Tern.

Access

The city of Albacete, main town of the province of the same name, is located on the N-301. It is the starting point for the routes recommended here.

Description

High ground lying at 800-900 m on the edge of the Southern Meseta. The little developed natural drainage network allows for the existence of closed depressions in the ground which are the site of up to 24 lagoons, mostly of small dimensions and high salinity, which dry up during the summer and are full in winter. The area surrounding the lagoons is taken up by fields, scrub-by holm oak woodland and areas of esparto grass.

Recommended routes

Route A takes you to the lagoons of Salobralejo and Pétrola, a journey of some 100 km. Leave Albacete on the N-430 in the direction of Almansa and, after 37 km, turn right onto the local road for Pétrola (10 km). To reach the lagoon at Salobralejo, continue for 1 km more along the N-430 and turn left for Higueruela. 1 km after crossing the bridge over the railway line, a track leads off to the right down to the lagoon. The main points of interest are the following:

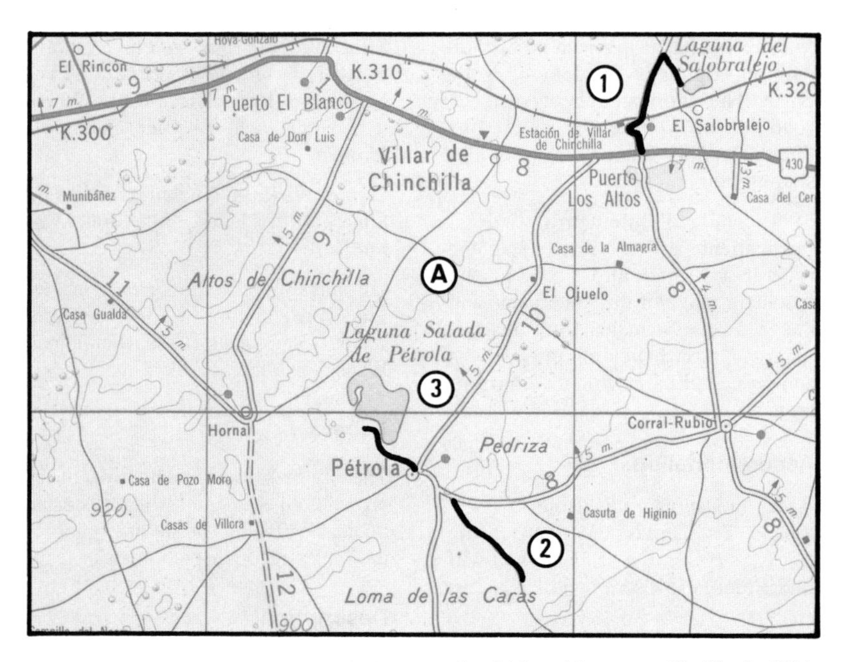

1) Salobralejo lagoon (also known as Salobrejo). From the road you can see the whole lagoon, where Black-necked Grebe are present in summer and, in winter, numerous water birds including Gadwall, Pintail, Red-crested Pochard and Tufted Duck.

2) Steppe at Pétrola. This area can be reached from a track running off the road to Fuente-Alamo just after the junction with the road to Corral Rubio. By travelling for a couple of kilometres along this track, you will have sightings of Little Bustard, Great Bustard, Stone Curlew, Pin-tailed Sandgrouse, Black-bellied Sandgrouse, Calandra Lark, Short-toed Lark and Black-eared Wheatear.

3) Pétrola lagoon. From the village of Pétrola, a track runs around the lagoon, giving good sightings of Black-winged Stilt, Avocet, Kentish Plover, Redshank, Greenshank, sandpipers, etc. A little farther on, to the right, you can climb a small hill overlooking the lagoon. With the help of a telescope you should be able to see Shelduck, Widgeon, Gadwall, Pintail, Shoveler, Red-crested Pochard, Gull-billed Tern, etc.

Route B takes you to the lagoon at Ontalafia. The route, some 80 km long, is best undertaken in the afternoon and evening. Take the N-301 towards Murcia and at Pozo Cañada (24 km) take the

minor road to Pozohondo. After 6 km turn left for Abuzaderas. Just after Abuzaderas, the road forks; take the left fork for Ontalafia (6 km). The northwest shore of the lagoon is the best place for watching ducks, grebes, Marsh Harrier, Whiskered Tern and, with luck, Little Bittern and Bearded Tit.

Accommodation

The virtually complete absence of accommodation in the nearby villages makes it worthwhile going to Albacete where a wide range of accommodation is available. Good value for money can be had at Hotel-Residencia Castilla in Albacete (Paseo de la Cuba, 3).

Comments

Access roads to the lagoons are usually in bad condition, particularly after periods of rainfall.

Juan Picazo Talavera

CASTILE - LEÓN

Great Bustard
Otis tarda

The nine provinces of Castile-León make up the largest of the Autonomous Regions of Spain, occupying nearly 20% of the surface area of the Iberian Peninsula. Broadly speaking Castile-León coincides with the northern part of the Meseta, although it also includes a substantial part of the virtually unbroken cordon of mountains circling the Meseta. These mountains are formed by the Cantabrian range to the north, the Iberian System to the east and the Sistema Central to the south. While in geographical and biological terms the Meseta gives the area its essential characteristics, the peripheral landforms create transition areas giving rise to a more extended range of flora and fauna.

As is well known, the centre of the Meseta is dominated by plains. This is the result of a recent basin of Tertiary sediment where the soft material remained unfolded, to be eroded by the Duero river system into a characteristic series of plateaux and plains of considerable dimensions. Dry-land cereal growing and extensive sheep farming are the traditional (and still predominant) activities in the area, and these combined with low mean precipitation have resulted in a landscape with the characteristics of a steppe. Although the recent agricultural intensification has caused a lot of destruction, there are still parts of this area which are worth a visit to see large groups of Great Bustard. This is the case in the areas surrounding Villafáfila (CL.18), the Tierra de Campos (CL.19, CL.20 and CL.21), the Campiña de Villalar (CL.24), the Campo de Medina (CL.26) and La Moraña (CL.27). Other interesting species to be seen in these areas are Montagu's Harrier, Peregrine Falcon, Lesser Kestrel, Little Bustard, Black-bellied Sandgrouse, Pin-tailed Sandgrouse (localized), Calandra Lark, Short-toed Lark, Tawny Pipit, Wheatear and, in winter, along with numerous larks, pipits, chaffinches and other small birds, the ubiquitous Red Kite, Hen Harrier, Merlin, Rook and, in the province of Zamora, the now very rare Bean Goose.

Other steppe formations occur on the eastern edges of the Duero river basin, on the plateaux of Burgos, Soria and some places in Segovia. These are low-growing, open pastures and scrubland with frequent outcrops of limestone. Bird communities in these areas are dominated by Skylark and Wheatear — species which elsewhere are mountain-dwelling birds— followed by Dupont's Lark, Short-toed Lark, Tawny Pipit and Black-bellied Sandgrouse, among others. Such habitats occur at places such as Páramo de Masa (CL.8), Calatañazor (CL.16), the gorges of the river Riaza (CL.28) and the gorges of the river Duratón (CL.30), although the largest area with these characteristics is that near Barahona, to the south of Almazán (CL.17).

However, Castilla la Vieja (Old Castile) does not consist entirely of steppe. In many places, particularly on the pla-

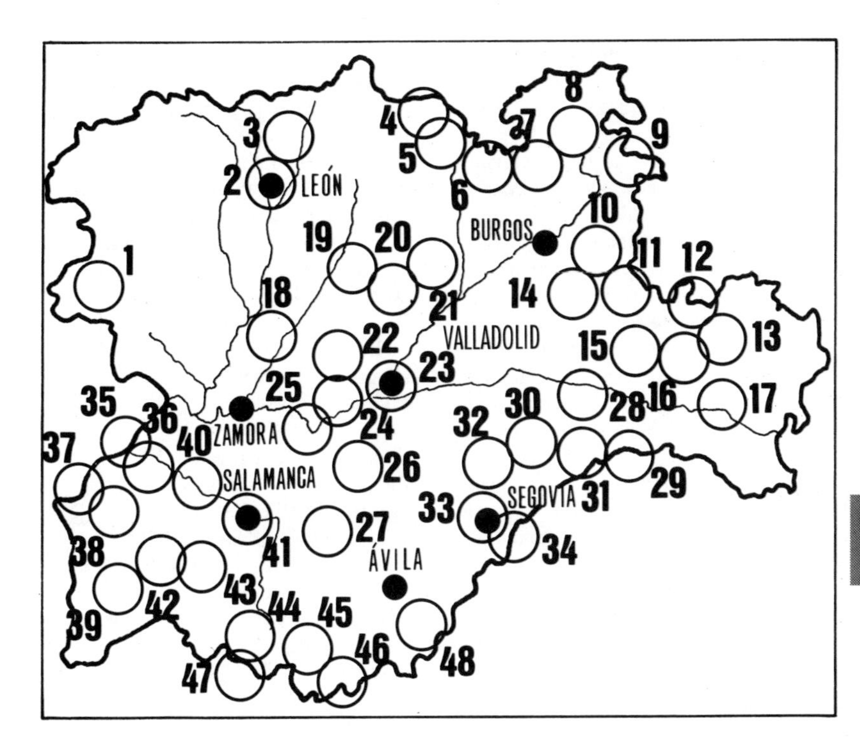

teaux, there are hills covered with Spanish juniper (*Juniperus thurifera*), holm oak (*Quercus rotundifolia*), Lusitanian oak (*Quercus faginea*) or Pyrenean oak (*Quercus pyrenaica*), usually in shrub form. There are also extensive areas of pine woodland, usually maritime pine (*Pinus pinaster*), although there are few mature trees and virtually no undergrowth. Broad-leaved and pine woods would seem to shelter a very small variety of woodland dwelling wildlife, but nonetheless Red-necked Nightjar, Bonelli's Warbler, Subalpine Warbler, Orphean Warbler, Woodchat Shrike and Azure-winged Magpie as well as other southern species can still be found. Birds of prey are also present, such as Black Kite, Goshawk, Buzzard, Booted Eagle, Hobby and Long-eared Owl; they sometimes congregate in stands of trees which, like islands, rise out of the extensive plains. Examples of these semi-wooded areas can be found at Montes Torozos (CL.22) and at many of the other selected sites, including the areas around León (CL.2), Soria (CL.13), Almazán (CL.17), Valladolid (CL.23), Cantalejo (CL.32) and Segovia (CL.33).

To the west of the sedimentary basin is the siliceous plinth of the Iberian Peninsula. Although the land is largely flat, soils are acidic and thin, meaning that the land is used largely for stock farming, resulting in better conserved tree cover. Thus, to the south of Zamora and around Salamanca extensive areas of wooded grazing land (*dehesa*) predominate, in fact the continuation of those of Extremadura. The same birdlife is also present, with Black Stork, Black-shouldered Kite, Red-rumped Swallow and Spanish Sparrow among other representative species. Good examples of this kind of terrain can be found at Ciudad Rodrigo (CL.39), Ledesma (CL.40) and the area around Salamanca (CL.41).

All of these flat areas feature a certain number of small lakes or ponds. Many of these bodies of water were dried out, including a large lake known as La Nava or Mar de Campos (CL.21), where a partial recovery has now been achieved. Other interesting lakes are at Villafáfila (CL.18) —with a large wintering population of Greylag Goose— La Moraña (CL.27), Cantalejo (CL.32), and the peneplains around Salamanca, with the small lakes of El Cristo and La Cervera (CL.42). Some reservoirs, the best example being the one at San José del Duero or Castronuño (CL.25), and certain stretches of the larger rivers help to some degree to alleviate the general lack of wetland areas in this region. There are few water birds, such as Night Heron, Grey Heron or Marsh Harrier, whose populations in this region constitute a substantial part of the totals for Spain. There is very little remaining riverside woodland, and in many places it has been substituted by rather boring poplar plantations. However these plantations are nonetheless worth visiting, particularly during the hottest hours of the day, when areas of open land are apparently devoid of wildlife. It is perhaps at this time of day that the importance of the role played by the poplar plantations in terms of providing shelter for many species becomes more evident. Species include Black Kite, Scops Owl, Green Woodpecker, Blackcap, Long-tailed Tit, Penduline Tit, Golden Oriole, Rook (only around León) and Cirl Bunting. There are interesting areas of riverside woodland on the following rivers; the Bernesga in León (CL.2), the Duero in Almazán (CL.17), the Carrión near Palencia (CL.20), the Agueda in Ciudad Rodrigo (CL.39), and the Tormes in Ledesma and Salamanca (CL.40 and CL.41).

As you draw away from the centre of the Duero river basin in any direction and approach rougher terrain, cliffs become more frequent and cliff-dwelling species make their appearance. These include Egyptian Vulture, Griffon Vulture, Golden Eagle, Bonelli's Eagle, Peregrine Falcon, Eagle Owl, Alpine Swift, Crag Martin, Black Redstart, Blue Rock Thrush, Chough and Rock Sparrow. This is particularly true of the eastern edge of the basin, consisting of mesozoic limestone rocks giving rise to fascinating sites such as Peña Amaya (CL.6), the gorges of the river Rudrón and the Alto Ebro (CL.7), the Montes Obarenes at Pancorbo (CL.9), the Frentes range near Soria (CL.13), the Arlanza valley (CL.14), the river Lobos (CL.15), Calatañazor (CL.16), the gorges of the river Riaza (CL.28), the ruins at Tiermes (CL.29) and the gorge of the river Duratón (CL.30).

But in the far south-west, the river Duero has also carved impressive gorges through granite rock such as those in Los Arribes del Duero (CL.35, CL.36, CL.37 and CL.38). This wonderful region, very Mediterranean in appearance, will give rise to sightings of the species mentioned above as well as Black Stork, Rock Dove, Red-rumped Swallow and Black Wheatear.

Finally there are the surrounding high mountains. Each massif has its individual characteristics, but all of the ranges have more water and woodland than the surrounding plains. For brevity, the reader is asked to look for more information in the pages devoted to the other Autonomous Regions through which these ranges run in addition to Castile-León, that is to say; Asturias and Cantabria in the case of the Cantabrian range; La Rioja in the case of the Northern Iberian System; and Extremadura and Madrid in the Sistema Central. For now, it will suffice to point out, in the form of a brief reminder, that the Cantabrian range (CL.1, Sanabria; CL.3, valley of the river Curueño; CL.4, Fuentes Carrionas; CL.5, Aguilar de Campóo reservoir), comprises the only sites in the region where Capercaillie, Black Woodpecker, Middle Spotted Woodpecker, Wallcreeper, Alpine Chough and Snow Finch are present; that the Iberian System (CL.10, La Demanda range; CL.11, Neila range, and CL.12, Picos de Urbión) have some species in common with the Cantabrian range which do not appear farther to the south in Spain. These include Hen Harrier, Grey Partridge, Woodcock, Marsh Tit, Red-backed Shrike and Yellowhammer. In addition the Sistema Central (CL.31, Riaza; CL.34, San Ildefonso and Valsaín; CL.43, Peña de Francia; CL.44, Béjar and Candelario ranges; CL.45 to CL.48, Gredos range), while offering less variety of species, allows for sightings of Bluethroat (also nesting at certain points in the Cantabrian range), Black Vulture and Spanish Imperial Eagle.

■ CL.1 SANABRIA

A mountain area with the largest glacial lake in the Iberian Peninsula.

Main species

Residents: Golden Eagle, Hen Harrier, Goshawk, Sparrowhawk, Grey Partridge, Common Sandpiper, Tawny Owl, Kingfisher, Crag Martin, Water Pipit, Dipper, Bullfinch.

Summer visitors: Short-toed Eagle, Montagu's Harrier, Hobby, Bluethroat, Rock Thrush, Red-backed Shrike.

Access

Take the N-525 to Puebla de Sanabria. To reach the Sanabria lake, before entering Sanabria turn right onto a well-marked road (14 km).

Description

A mountainous area covered with Pyrenean oak interspersed with scrubland. High ground is dominated by heath and broom alternating with mountain pastures.

The focus and greatest attraction of the area is constituted by the lake of Sanabria, of glacial origin and fed by the rivers Tera, Cárdena and Segundera. These rivers run through steep ravines coming down from the high ground, which reaches its highest with Peña Trevinca at 2,049 m. The glacial nature of the area is of great interest, and the presence of wolves is also remarkable. Much of the area is a Natural Park.

Recommended routes

Route A takes you to the small lake or Laguna de los Peces (1,707 m) via the gorge of the river Forcadura. The journey there and back takes some 6 hours. From the lake of Sanabria, drive to the nearby village of Vigo de Sanabria and from there walk along a track, well-marked except for the last stretch, which runs up the gorge taking you above the tree line and into the area of broom and alpine pastures where you can see Grey Partridge, Water Pipit, Bluethroat and Dipper. The route can be prolonged by visiting the high ground, which is more easily accessible. You can also reach the lake by car along a surfaced road from the village of San Martín de Castaneda.

Route B climbs up to the Cárdena lake by the gorge of the same name. The trip lasts for a total of about 4 hours. Leave your vehicle in Ribadelago Viejo and there, just before the turning for the hydroelectric power station, a

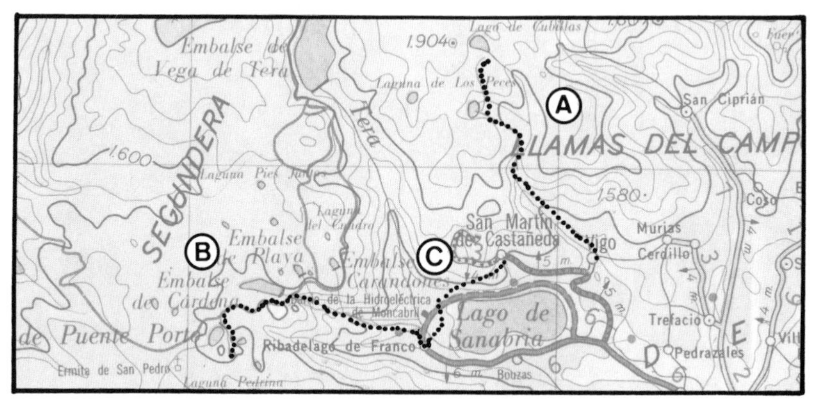

track leads off to the lake. Ask for directions in the village, since at some points the path is not well-marked. The most interesting species to be seen on this route are the same as those for route A.

Route C takes you along the left shore of the lake of Sanabria from San Martín de Castaneda to Ribadelago Viejo, along a paved track of medieval origin known as the *Senda de los Monjes* or monks' causeway. You will have sightings of Short-toed Eagle, Goshawk, Sparrowhawk, Hobby, Red-backed Shrike, Bullfinch as well as Mallard and Common Sandpiper.

Accommodation

There is a Parador Nacional in Puebla de Sanabria as well as a wide range of other accommodation and restaurants. Camping near the lake is prohibited, but there are 3 campsites, one of which is open year round.

Comments

The best times of year for visiting the area are the months of June and September; at high summer the area attracts large numbers of visitors.

When the area was declared a Natural Park an information centre was set up in the monastery of San Martín de Castaneda (XII century). The monastery was restored for this purpose, and the centre will provide any information you may require.

Nicolás González Sánchez
and Salvador J. Peris Alvarez

■ CL.2 LEÓN AND AROUND

A medium-sized city surrounded by fields and some woodland.

Main species

Residents: Hen Harrier, Red-legged Partridge, Stock Dove, Collared Dove, Long-eared Owl, Kingfisher, Cetti's Warbler, Fan-tailed Warbler, Dartford Warbler, Penduline Tit, Rook, Rock Sparrow, Cirl Bunting, Rock Bunting.

Summer visitors: Little Bittern, Night Heron, White Stork, Montagu's Harrier, Booted Eagle, Hobby, Black-winged Stilt, Stone Curlew, Little Ringed Plover, Turtle Dove, Great Spotted Cuckoo, Scops Owl, Bee-eater, Wryneck, Short-toed Lark, Tree Pipit, Tawny Pipit, Nightingale, Reed Warbler, Great Reed Warbler, Melodious Warbler, Subalpine Warbler, Bonelli's Warbler, Red-backed Shrike, Woodchat Shrike.

Winter visitors: Grey Heron, Red Kite, Merlin, Lapwing, Green Sandpiper, Black-headed Gull, Water Pipit, Firecrest, Hawfinch, Yellowhammer.

On passage: waders, gulls, terns and marsh terns.

Access

In the section on recommended routes details of access to the various places around the city of León are given. In all cases, you can leave your vehicle at the starting point of the route.

Description

Urban parks with sparse shrub and tree cover and an excess of paved areas. On the bank of the river Bernesga, near the black poplar plantations, there is a partially preserved area of original riverside woodland consisting of willow and white poplar.

The area around León features a mosaic of cereal crops, meadows, hedgerows and scrubland. There are also some stands of oak, holm oak and a pine plantation which has remained unexploited for many years.

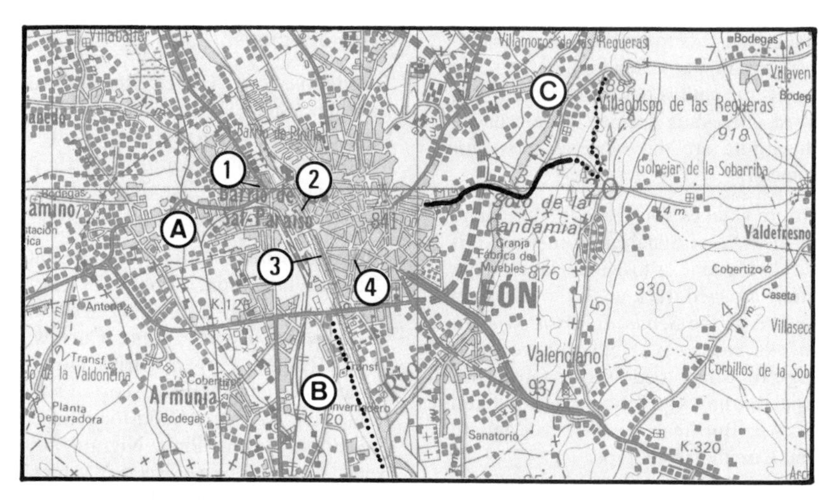

Recommended routes

Route A is predominantly urban, taking you to the parks of Quevedo (1), Condesa (2), Papalaguinda (3) and San Francisco (4). The order in which you visit the parks depends on where you are staying, although the small size of the city of León will allow you to cover the 4 parks in a single morning. Despite the fact that the area inevitably does not present a very wide range of birdlife, it is possible to see interesting species, particularly in winter in the gardens lying beside the river Bernesga; Common Tern, Kingfisher, Water Pipit, Firecrest, Dipper, Hawfinch, Spotless Starling and Rook.

The starting point for **route B** is beside the bull ring in León, on the bridge over the river Bernesga. From here, follow a walkway which runs parallel and above the riverbed to its end, 2 km farther on. En route you will see Penduline Tit, Cetti's Warbler, Nightingale, warblers, buntings, Golden Oriole, Little Ringed Plover and, although more rarely, Little Bittern, Black-winged Stilt, Bee-eater and Kingfisher. In summer, groups of White Stork and Night Heron congregate on the bank, with groups of Black-headed Gull, Grey Heron, Lapwing, Green Sandpiper, etc. in winter. The hedgerows and black poplar plantations located to the right of the walkway will give sightings of Turtle Dove, Melodious Warbler, Rook and, less frequently, Collared Dove.

Route C takes you along a forestry track leading into a pine plantation known locally as La Candamia. It is easily accessible by car; leave your car at the entrance of the pine plantation and continue on foot for 1½ hours along the forestry track. En route you will see Bonelli's Warbler, Tree Pipit, Nightingale, Melodious Warbler, warblers in general, Cirl Bunting and, very occasionally, Booted Eagle. In winter you will see large groups of tits, Goldcrest, Firecrest, Short-toed Treecreeper, etc. as well as Sparrowhawk and groups of Long-eared Owl.

Accommodation

Plenty of accommodation is available in the city of León.

Comments

If you have time, it is worth going to the area known as La Sobarriba, bordering the pine plantation, which can be reached by the local road (surfaced) from Villavente, or alternatively from the pine plantation itself. Here you will see Red-legged Partridge, Stock Dove, Great Spotted Cuckoo, Black-eared Wheatear, Subalpine Warbler and, less frequently, Orphean Warbler and Spectacled Warbler.

Angel Hernández and Joaquín Alegre

■ CL.3 VALLEY OF THE RIVER CURUEÑO

Mountain area.

Main species

Residents: Griffon Vulture (not breeding), Hen Harrier, Golden Eagle, Red-legged Partridge, Grey Partridge, Water Pipit, Dipper, Alpine Accentor (rare), Dartford Warbler, Marsh Tit, Wallcreeper, Penduline Tit, Alpine Chough, Chough, Raven, Rock Sparrow, Bullfinch, Hawfinch, Yellowhammer, Cirl Bunting, Rock Bunting.

Summer visitors: White Stork, Honey Buzzard, Short-toed Eagle, Booted Eagle, Lapwing, Scops Owl, Bee-eater, Wryneck, Crag Martin, Tawny Pipit, Bluethroat, Whinchat, Rock Thrush, Blue Rock Thrush, Melodious Warbler, Subalpine Warbler, Bonelli's Warbler, Red-backed Shrike, Ortolan Bunting.

Access

From León, take the N.621 towards Santander. After 25 km you will come to Barrio de Nuestra Señora (some road maps confuse this village with Ambasaguas de Curueño). From Barrio de Nuestra Señora, a minor road which is narrow but in good condition climbs the valley to the mountain pass of Vegarada.

Description

A narrow valley some 56 km long, located on the southern side of the Cantabrian range. The head of the valley, at the *puerto* or pass of Vegarada, has been badly degraded as a consequence of the intensive grazing which takes place there. The area is largely dominated by heath with extensive pastureland and scattered stands of beech, birch and holly. In this area chamois, stoat and wolves are present.

The middle reaches of the valley are largely taken up by oak woodland and associated vegetation. The vegetation here is less degenerate, giving rise to holm oak woodland and remains of original riverside vegetation. Mankind has created poplar and conifer plantations and meadows and fields on the valley floor.

Recommended routes

The single route for this area consists of a car journey from Barrio de Nuestra Señora to the Vegarada pass. On the way, make the following stops and go for walks:

1) From the village itself you can reach the right bank of the river. Walk upstream for some 600 m and come back through fields and hedgerows. You will see White Stork, Goshawk, Scops Owl, Bee-eater, Kingfisher, Dipper, Sand Martin, Penduline Tit and Melodious Warbler.

2) Between the villages of Pardesivil and Sopeña de Curueño, 1 km apart, you may have sightings of Booted Eagle, Short-toed Eagle, Hen Harrier, Melodious Warbler, various other warblers, Bonelli's Warbler, Bullfinch, Hawfinch and various buntings.

3) A 1 km route taking you along the Valdeteja gorge. At the turning for La Braña and Arintero there is an area where you can leave your car. Here

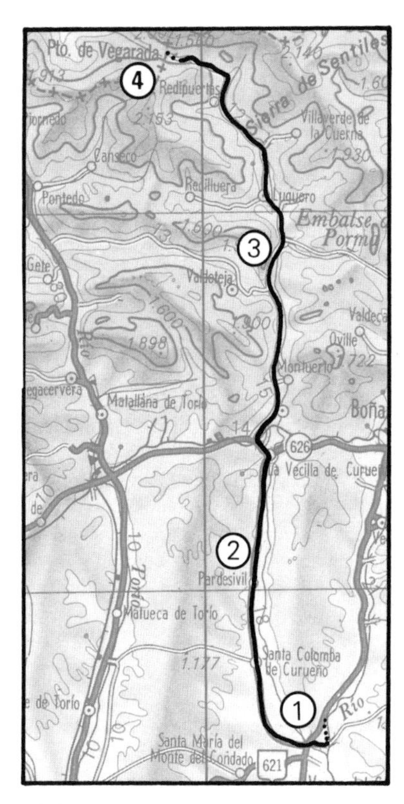

cliff-dwelling species dominate, including Egyptian Vulture, Griffon Vulture, Peregrine Falcon, Crag Martin, Chough, Alpine Chough, Rock Thrush, Blue Rock Thrush, Wallcreeper and Rock Sparrow.

4) At the Vegarada pass you will find a restaurant. From here walk to the boundary line with the province of Asturias. This will take you past pastures, heath and limestone outcrops. You may see Grey Partridge, Water Pipit, Red-backed Shrike, Raven, Whinchat, Bluethroat and the occasional Golden Eagle, Alpine Accentor and Snow Finch.

Accommodation

Fondas and restaurants are available in Barrio de Nuestra Señora and La Vecilla. The restaurant at the Vegarada pass is only open in summer.

Comments

A newly constructed road joins the Vegarada pass with the San Isidro ski resort.

Joaquín Alegre
and Angel Hernández

CL.4 FUENTES CARRIONAS

Mountain area with deciduous woodland.

Main species

Residents: Griffon Vulture, Golden Eagle, Peregrine Falcon, Grey Partridge, Black Woodpecker, Middle Spotted Woodpecker, Alpine Accentor, Wallcreeper, Snow Finch.

Summer visitors: Honey Buzzard, Black Kite, Egyptian Vulture, Short-toed Eagle, Booted Eagle, Hobby, Nightjar, Bluethroat, Rock Thrush.

Access

From Palencia, take the N-611 towards Santander, turning off at Herrera de Pisuerga (72 km) onto the C-627 for Cervera de Pisuerga (40 km). Cervera de Pisuerga is the starting point for the routes, which take you along narrow, winding roads.

Description

Fuentes Carrionas, located in the Cordillera Cantábrica or Cantabrian range, is a huge National Game Reserve occupying the northwestern half of the province of Palencia.

The geography of the area, dominated by the peaks of Curavacas (2,520 m) and Espigüete (2,450 m), is particularly steep, with deep valleys and large rockfaces. The mountain sides are covered with oak and beech woodland interspersed with areas of heath and broom. The high ground features scrubland and pastureland in addition to many rocky outcrops.

There are four reservoirs in the area, which is one of the last redoubts of the brown bear. There are also quite a few wolves in the area.

Recommended routes

The routes recommended provide a general impression of the area. Both routes are to be undertaken by car. Below is a list of the most interesting points.

Route A leaves Cervera de Pisuerga in the direction of Guardo (57 km) along a minor road passing the Ruesga, Camporredondo and Compuerto reservoirs. The best observation posts are the following:

1) The Parador Nacional at Fuentes Carrionas. The oak woodland surrounding the Parador will give sightings of Middle Spotted Woodpecker, Honey Buzzard, Goshawk, Sparrowhawk and Booted Eagle. At the Ruesga reservoir, located in the valley bottom, you will see various water birds.

2) Santibáñez de Resoba. The peaks looming above the village are frequented by Golden Eagle, Griffon Vulture, Egyptian Vulture, Peregrine Falcon and Chough.

3) Cardaño de Abajo and Cardaño de Arriba. From these two villages, located below the Espigüete peak, you can climb up to the high ground where Snow Finch, Wallcreeper, Alpine Accentor and Alpine Chough have their nesting sites at over 1,800 m.

You can return to Cervera de Pisuerga via Guardo on the C-626 (37 km). This

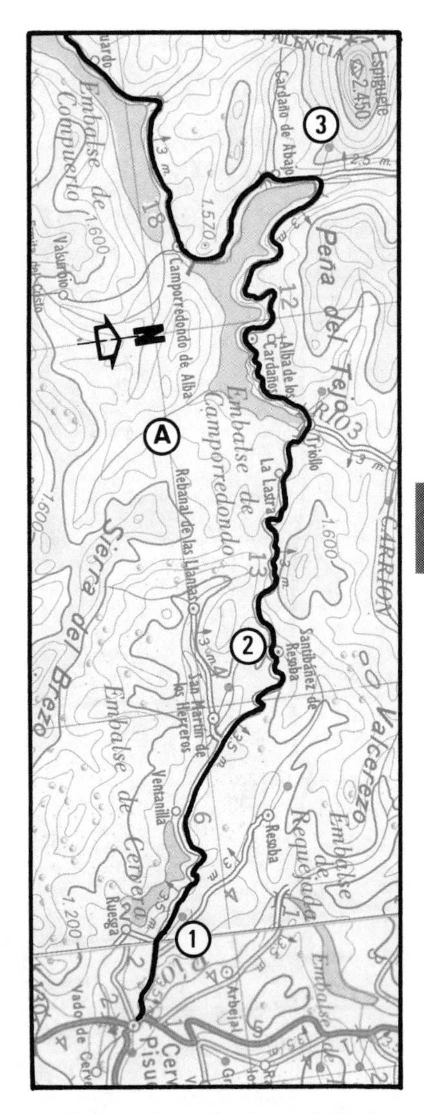

road runs along the foot of the impressive Sierra del Brezo, another mountain range.

The starting point of **route B** is Cervera de Pisuerga, from where you take the C-627 in the direction of Potes. On reaching the village of Camasobres (23 km), leave your car and make your way on foot to the following sights:

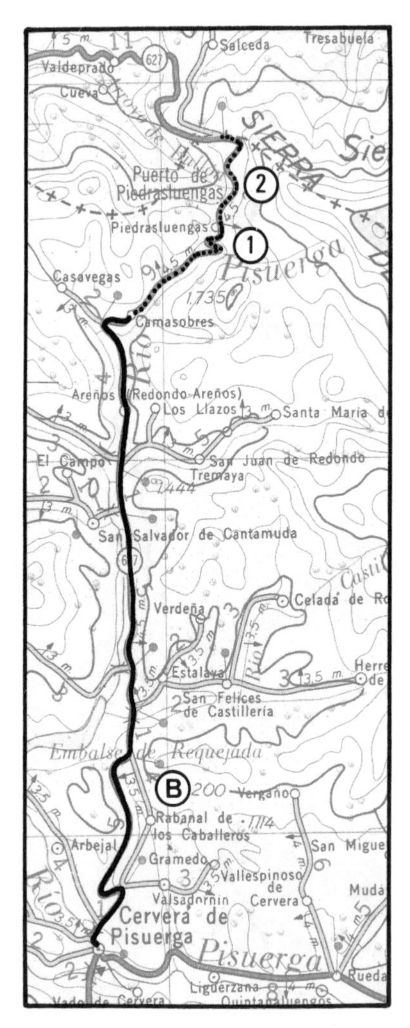

1) Las Hoces. A limestone gorge where you will have sightings of Golden Eagle, Peregrine Falcon and Chough. In October and November this is also a good spot for watching the passage of Crane, Greylag Goose and ducks.

2) The beech wood located to the west of the road is a good place for seeing Black Woodpecker, Treecreeper, Nuthatch and forest-dwelling birds of prey. On the heaths located on the high ground you may see Hen Harrier and Grey Partridge.

Accommodation

There are plenty of hostels and restaurants in Guardo and Cervera de Pisuerga.

Comments

For walking in the mountains it is advisable to use boots which support your ankles and, in winter and spring, to wear protective clothing. Take care when you are in the woods, since it is very easy to get lost.

Fernando Jubete

■ CL.5 AGUILAR DE CAMPÓO RESERVOIR

Artificial lake.

Main species

Residents: Little Grebe, Great Crested Grebe, Gadwall.

Winter visitors: Cormorant, Grey Heron, ducks.

On passage: waders.

Access

From Aguilar de Campóo, the minor road to Salinas de Pisuerga will take you all the way around the reservoir.

Description

The Aguilar de Campóo reservoir, the largest in the province of Palencia, has a series of shallow inlets, giving rise to sandy beaches and abundant underwater vegetation.

The area surrounding the reservoir is taken up by immature oak woodland and pine plantations.

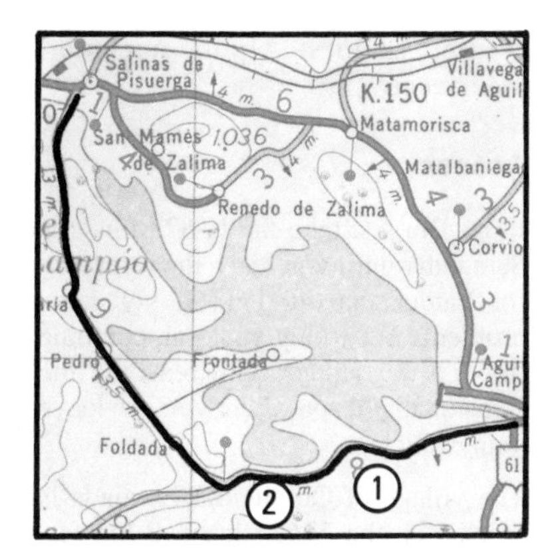

Recommended routes

This is a single route consisting of a car journey around the perimeter of the reservoir. Virtually any point along the route is good for watching water birds, but the following are particularly recommended.

1) Playa de Aguilar de Campóo. A stretch of beach much frequented by man, but during the migration periods there are many waders and gulls.

2) Quintanilla de la Berzosa. This is the largest inlet of the reservoir and one of the places most frequented by wintering ducks as a resting ground. Going down to the water's edge will give you sightings of Cormorant, diving ducks and gulls.

In the woods surrounding the reservoir you may have sightings of Nightjar, Wryneck, Bonelli's Warbler and buntings as well as Black Kite, Griffon Vulture and Egyptian Vulture.

Accommodation

There is a wide range of accommodation available in Aguilar de Campóo.

Comments

In winter, snow and frosts are frequent, so you should be particularly careful when using the roads.

Fernando Jubete

■ CL.6 PEÑA AMAYA

A mountain range with cliff faces.

Main species

Residents: Griffon Vulture, Hen Harrier, Golden Eagle, Bonelli's Eagle, Peregrine Falcon, Stone Curlew, Eagle Owl.

Summer visitors: Egyptian Vulture, Montagu's Harrier, Alpine Swift, Water Pipit, Rock Thrush.

Winter visitors: Alpine Accentor, Wallcreeper.

Access

From Burgos, take the N-120 towards León and turn off at Villanueva de Argaño (21 km) onto the C-627 for Villadiego and Sotresgudo (35 km). In Sotresgudo take the minor road for Amaya, 7 km away.

Description

A limestone massif broken up by small valleys and featuring some impressive rock faces. The slopes have been deforested and are now covered with scrub, while in lower areas cereal crops alternate with woodland consisting of Pyrenean oak, Lusitanian oak, holm oak and, in some areas, pine plantations.

Recommended routes

This is a single route consisting of a walk, lasting a total of some 3 hours, from Amaya to Villamartín de Villadiego. The route takes you along a newly constructed minor road, allowing one to observe the cliffs from some distance but at a good angle. Throughout you will be able to see all the cliff-dwelling birds present in the area.

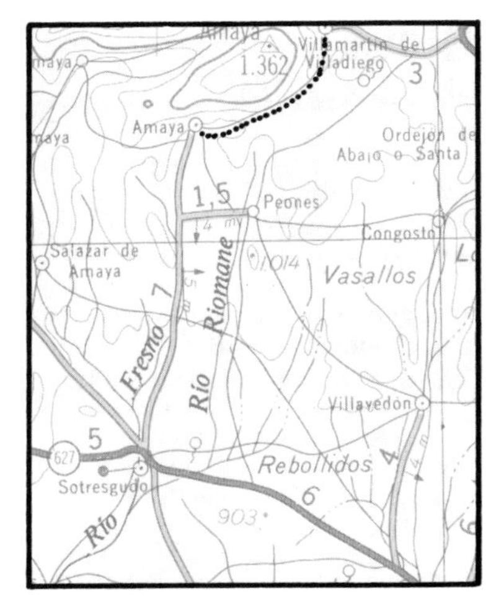

Accommodation

It is worth returning to the city of Burgos where a wide range of accommodation is available.

Comments

The best time of year for visiting the area is between the months of March and July.

Luis Miguel Ansola

■ CL.7 GORGES OF THE UPPER EBRO AND THE RIVER RUDRÓN

River gorges.

Main species

Residents: Griffon Vulture, Hen Harrier, Goshawk, Sparrowhawk, Golden Eagle, Bonelli's Eagle, Peregrine Falcon, Kingfisher, Grey Wagtail, Dipper, Chough, Alpine Chough.

Summer visitors: Black Kite, Egyptian Vulture, Nightjar, Alpine Swift, Redstart.

Winter visitors: Alpine Accentor, Wallcreeper.

Access

From Burgos, take the N-623 towards Santander until you reach the right turn for Valdelateja (46 km). If you have problems in parking your car, continue through the village until reaching the ruins of an old spa where you can leave your vehicle.

The village of Quintanilla Escalada is located on the N-623 itself, 3 km farther on. You can leave your car near the petrol station.

Description

The gorges of the rivers Ebro and Rudrón were formed by the erosive action of the rivers on the limestone rock of the range of La Lora in the transitional area between the northern Meseta and the Cantabrian range or *cordillera*. The valleys are narrow, deep and winding, flanked by vertical rock walls and steep slopes.

The valley bottoms contain riverside woodland and small areas of cereal crops, while the valley sides are covered with very degenerate woodland consisting of beech, Lusitanian oak and holm oak.

Recommended routes

The starting point of **route A** is Valdelateja, either in the village or at the spas. It takes you up the left bank of the river Rudrón. After the spa, a rudimentary stone bridge enables you to cross to the far bank, where a narrow path runs along the bottom of the valley side to Barrio de Nápoles (San Felices). Shortly after the fishermen's refuge, a bridge similar to the first one will allow you to cross the river again. The route, 3.5 km long, can be undertaken in 1½ hours. To return, retrace

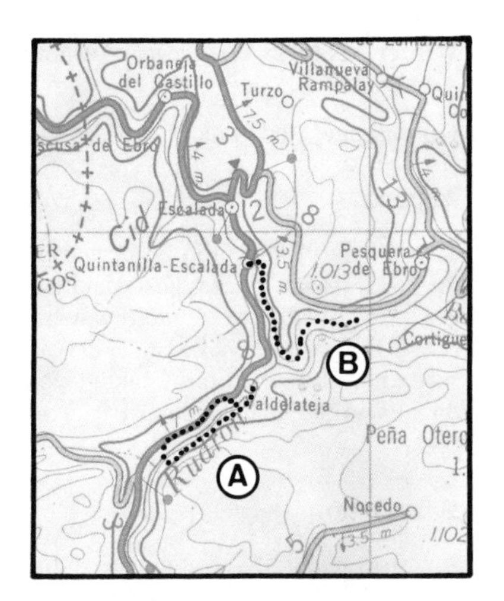

your steps along the same track or walk along the road.

Route B begins in Quintanilla Escalada and runs along the left bank of the river Ebro as far as an electricity generating station. There and back, the route totals 12 km. It starts from the bridge and can be undertaken on foot or by car.

Both routes provide the opportunity of seeing a wide variety of cliff-dwelling birds as well as species frequenting rivers such as Dipper or Grey Wagtail.

Accommodation

Since there is very little accommodation available in the nearby villages, it is worth returning to the city of Burgos where there are many hotels.

Comments

The best time of year for visiting the area is between the months of March and July.

Luis Miguel Ansola

CL.8 MASA MOOR

Steppe.

Main species

Residents: Hen Harrier, Little Bustard, Stone Curlew, Little Owl, Long-eared Owl, Calandra Lark.

Summer visitors: Montagu's Harrier, Short-toed Lark, Tawny Pipit, Whinchat, Rock Thrush, Spectacled Warbler, Orphean Warbler.

Access

From Burgos, take the N-623 towards Santander and shortly after Sotopalacios turn right onto the C-629 (11 km). Continue along this road until you reach the junction with the minor road for Masa and Poza de la Sal (24 km). Here there is plenty of space for parking your car.

Description

Masa moor is a flat and relatively uniform limestone plateau reaching heights of between 1,000 and 1,100 m. Vegetation is constituted by pastures and small patches of scrubland alternating with areas of dry farming. There are also small stands of holm oak, Lusitanian oak and oak as well as pine plantations.

Recommended routes

Route A consists of a walk around the plateau, starting from the point where you park your car and finishing at the Pozo Rubio stock pens, 3 km to the northwest.

The starting point for **route B** is at the 5 km marker post on the road to Poza de la Sal. From here you can walk towards Los Cabezuelos, located 4 km to the northwest.

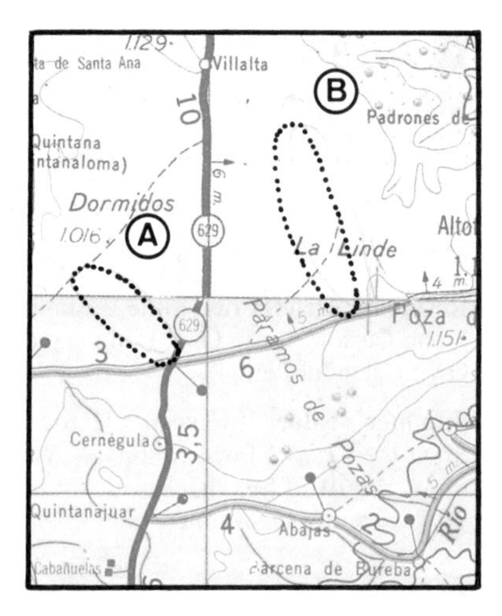

Both routes take you through flat areas. Take any of the paths you encounter.

Accommodation

Since there is very little accommodation available in the nearby villages, it is worth returning to the city of Burgos where there are plenty of hotels.

Comments

The best time of year for visiting the area is from April to July.

Luis Miguel Ansola

CL.9 PANCORBO

A mountain range and a gorge with high cliffs.

Main species

Residents: Griffon Vulture, Peregrine Falcon, Crag Martin, Black Redstart, Chough, Raven, Yellowhammer, Rock Bunting.

Summer visitors: Egyptian Vulture, Rock Thrush.

Winter visitors: Wallcreeper, Alpine Accentor.

On passage: Red Kite.

Access

The village of Pancorbo is located on the N-I (303 km marker post), and can also be reached from the motorway between Burgos and Málzaga. There are several well-marked turns taking you directly to the main square of Pancorbo.

Description

A narrow, naturally-created pass in the Montes Obarenes, with high limestone cliffs rising over the village. These cliffs are the home of a small colony of Griffon Vulture and a range of other cliff-dwelling species. The area is also good for watching migrants particularly Red Kite on autumn migration.

Recommended routes

Leave your car in the main square and go up a steep alleyway until you reach the ruins of the castle dominating the village. This will take about 15 minutes. From here you will see the vultures' nests, located on the high rocks to the north. Those who are feeling energetic can continue to climb across the cliff face to Las Cuevas (1,000 m), from where you can enjoy a beautiful view over the region of La Bureba and the nearby mountain ra

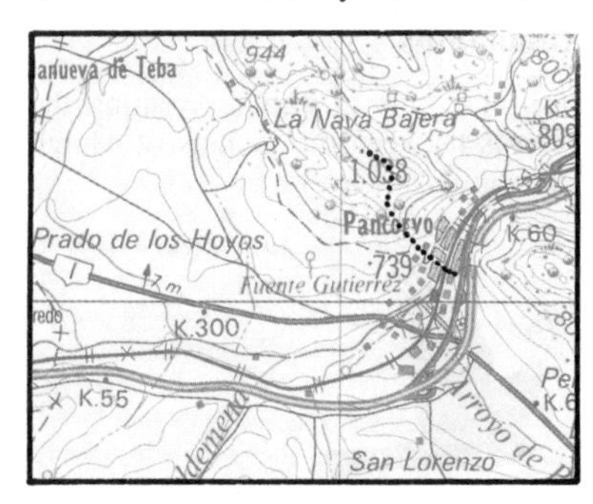

of Sierra de la Demanda. Going at a good pace, this ascent will take you a little over half an hour.

Accommodation

It is possible to stay at Hostal Pancorbo in the village.

Fernando de Juana Aranzana

■ CL.10 LA DEMANDA RANGE

A mountain area with considerable areas of woodland.

Main species

Residents: Grey Partridge, Woodcock, Lesser Spotted Woodpecker, Water Pipit, Goldcrest, Marsh Tit, Nuthatch, Treecreeper, Citril Finch, Bullfinch.

Summer visitors: Honey Buzzard, Short-toed Eagle, Booted Eagle, Redstart, Wheatear, Rock Thrush, Pied Flycatcher.

Access

From Burgos take the N-120 towards Logroño and turn off for Ibeas de Juarros (14 km). As you leave Ibeas de Juarros you will see a right turn onto a minor road for Pradoluengo. Take this minor road and continue for 18 km until reaching the village of Alarcia.

Description

The Sierra de la Demanda, part of the Iberian System, reaches its highest point with the peak of San Millán (2,131 m), lying in the province of Burgos. The topography of the area, evidencing remains of Quaternary glacial formations, is characterized by deep gorges worked by the network of rivers.

On the high ground, vegetation consists of extensive areas of pastureland and scrubland, while the valley sides and lower ground feature ancient beech woodland. In some places, scrubland has been substituted by pine plantations.

Recommended routes

This is a single route consisting of a car journey to the peak of Trigaza (2,033 m). 1.5 km after the village of Alarcia, before the road starts to drop abruptly downwards, you will see a surfaced forestry road, closed by a metal gate, leading off to the right. You are allowed to use this track, but always remember to close the gate behind you.

The first part of the climb takes you through areas of pine plantations and, 5 km later, after a sharp bend with a freshwater spring and picnic area, you will reach a pass. Leave the car here and walk along the track running off to the left, taking you into the beech wood and allowing for sightings of forest-dwelling species typical of the area including Treecreeper and Marsh Tit.

Once the road reaches an altitude of over 1,700 m it is no longer surfaced, although it is nonetheless in good con-

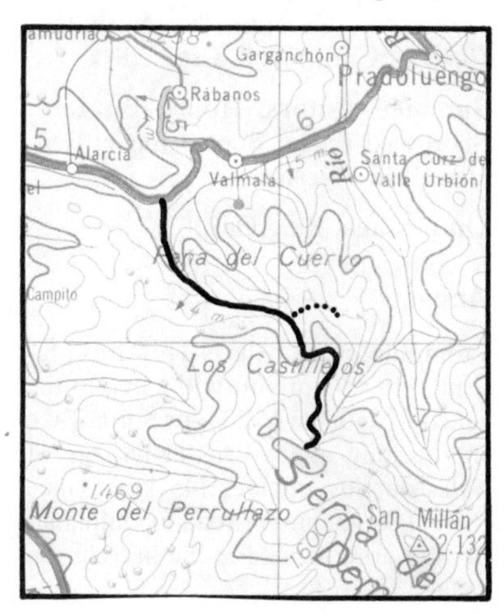

dition up to the point where it reaches the peak. Here woodland has disappeared, giving way to meadows and scrubland where you may see Grey Partridge, Rock Thrush, Citril Finch, etc.

Accommodation

Although there are several *fondas* in Pradoluengo it is worthwhile returning to Burgos, where a wide range of accommodation is available.

Comments

The best time of year for visiting the area is during the summer months.

Fernando Román Sancho and Carlos Palma Barcenilla

■ CL.11 NEILA RANGE

A mountain area with extensive pine woods.

Main species

Residents: Golden Eagle, Grey Partridge, Rock Pipit, Alpine Accentor, Goldcrest, Crested Tit, Nuthatch, Chough, Citril Finch, Crossbill.

Summer visitors: Honey Buzzard, Short-toed Eagle, Booted Eagle, Redstart, Pied Flycatcher.

On passage: Ring Ouzel.

Access

From Burgos, take the N-I towards Madrid. After 9 km you will come to the junction with the N-234 for Soria. Take this turning and go to the village of Salas de Los Infantes (45 km). Once there, take the minor road to Quintanar de la Sierra, located at the base of the range (24 km).

Description

Located at the edge of the Iberian System, the Sierra de Neila rises to just over 2,000 m in height. Vegetation is dominated by extensive pine woods which give way on high ground to scrubland and pastureland. Valley bottoms are taken up by areas of dry grazing land featuring oak, beech, pine and holly.

From the summit of La Campiña, at 2,049 m, you can make out small glacial cirques now covered by a series of small lakes.

Recommended routes

The route recommended takes you through pine woodland and areas of high ground. As you leave Quintanar de la Sierra in the direction of Neila, before leaving the village you will come across a well-marked road up to the Laguna Negra. This lake is at 1,900 m, and it is possible to drive up and park your car.

The 14 km climb takes you through uninterrupted pine woodland; although anywhere is a good place for spotting Wryneck, Citril Finch and other forest-dwelling species, it is worth climbing up to the high ground as well. Once you reach the lakes you will be rewarded by walking around them, passing through alpine pastures, scrubland and rocky areas, giving rise to sightings of species typical of high mountain areas.

Accommodation

Accommodation is available in Neila and Quintanar de la Sierra. There is a wider range of possibilities in Salas de Los Infantes.

Comments

The best time of year for visiting the area are the summer months. In winter,

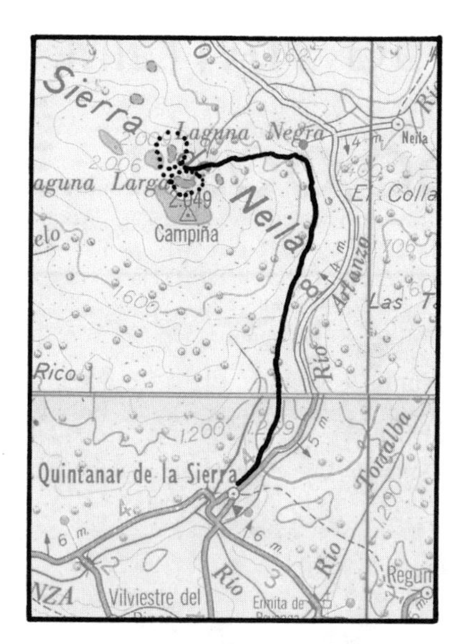

access may be difficult because of snow or ice.

Carlos Palma Barcenilla and Jacinto Román Sancho

CL.12 PICOS DE URBIÓN

A mountain area with extensive pine woods.

Main species

Residents: Griffon Vulture, Great Spotted Woodpecker, Water Pipit, Dunnock, Alpine Accentor, Goldcrest, Marsh Tit, Citril Finch.

Summer visitors: White Stork, Short-toed Eagle, Booted Eagle, Bee-eater.

Access

From Soria, take the N-234 towards Burgos and drive as far as Cidones (14 km). Here, take the minor road to Vinuesa and Santa Inés mountain pass (30 km).

Description

The Picos de Urbión, which reach a maximum height of over 2,200 m, are part of the Iberian System. The high ground is steep and features many rocky outcrops, alpine meadows and heaths, while the lower slopes are covered with extensive mature pine woodland and some stands of oak.

Recommended routes

Before reaching Vinuesa it is worth making a stop at the reservoir of La Cuerda del Pozo where you will be able to see some water birds. Greater numbers are present during the migratory season.

Route A takes you to the Laguna Negra. You can reach the area surrounding the lake by car from the road from Vinuesa to Puerto de Santa Inés. At any point on the ascent or around the lake itself it is worth taking a short walk in the pine woods to see, among other forest species, Marsh Tit, Citril Finch and, with luck, Woodcock. Skirt the lake and continue along a well-marked but steep track to reach the Pico de Urbión (2,228 m). The climb, taking two hours, will give rise to sightings of Water Pipit, Alpine Accentor and other birds inhabiting areas of high ground.

The starting point of **route B** is the Santa Inés pass where you can leave your car and continue on foot along the path leading off to the left. The pine woods will give sightings of Crossbill, and on the surrounding heathland you may see Grey Partridge. The whole area is occupied by shooting butts for hunting Woodpigeon. During the migration periods you will also see geese, Crane, birds of prey on passage etc.

Accommodation

There are hostels in Vinuesa, Covaleda and other nearby villages. There is a

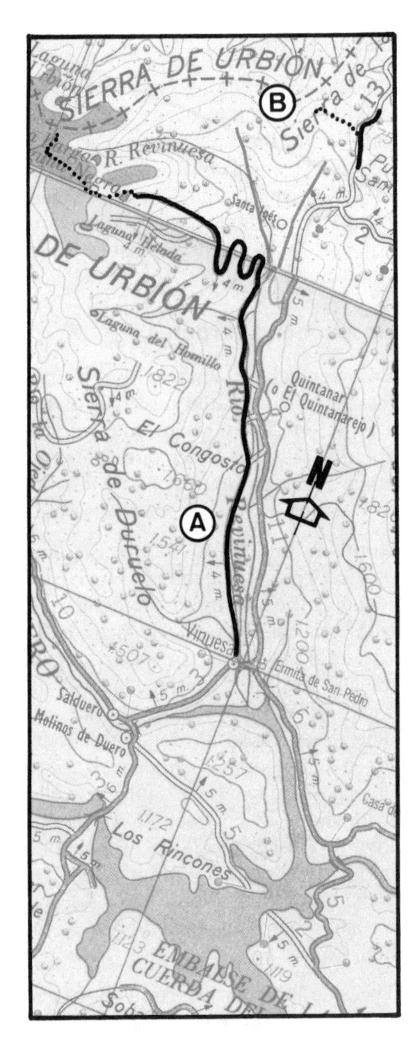

campsite next to the reservoir (Playa Pita) and wild camping is allowed in certain places.

Alvaro Camiña

■ CL.13 VALONSADERO – FUENTETOBA

Wooded dry grazing land.

Main species

Residents: Red Kite, Goshawk, Sparrowhawk, Buzzard, Common Sandpiper, Tawny Owl, Green Woodpecker, Great Spotted Woodpecker, Lesser Spotted Woodpecker, Woodlark, Grey Wagtail, Mistle Thrush, Firecrest, Nuthatch, Great Grey Shrike, Jay, Azure-winged Magpie, Chough, Raven, Rock Bunting.

Summer visitors: Black Kite, Short-toed Eagle, Booted Eagle, Hobby, Turtle Dove, Cuckoo, Scops Owl, Nightjar, Bee-eater, Hoopoe, Wryneck, Rock Thrush, Pied Flycatcher, Golden Oriole, Woodchat Shrike.

Access

From Soria, take the N-234 towards Burgos. The area lies 6 km from the city of Soria.

Description

Hills of dry grazing land covered with oak and pine. Small river courses run through the area with scattered stands of black poplar. There are also pastures with sandstone outcrops where White Stork congregate before migration.

3 km farther on is Fuentetoba, a rocky area where the river Golmayo has it source. This is an interesting and picturesque spot which is well worth a visit.

Recommended routes

One recommended route consists of a two-hour walk through the pinewood along the course of the river Cubillo. It begins at the 353 km marker post on the N-234, where there is space to leave your car. This is also the starting point for an athletes' training circuit. Throughout the route you will be able to see the birds listed above.

Another possibility is to continue to the 355 km marker post and turn right onto

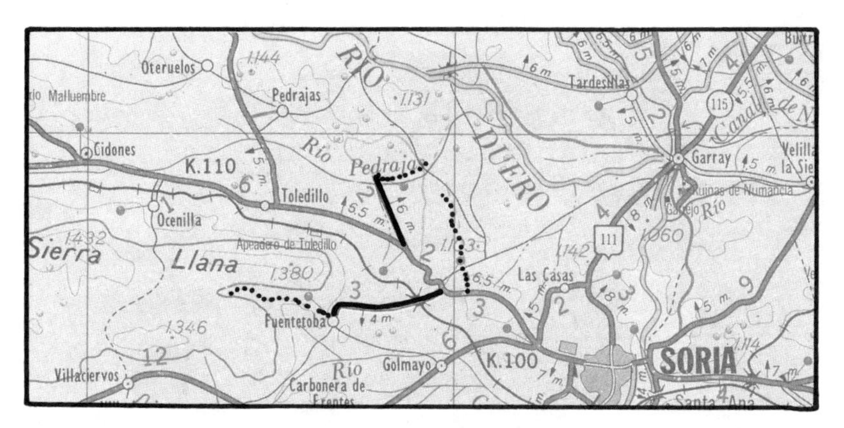

a track leading to a forest ranger's hut. From here you can walk for some 2.5 km along the Pedrajas river course.

The Fuentetoba area can be reached via a marked turning. It is worthwhile walking up the river Golmayo to its source. This route will take you through an area of cliffs where you will be able to see Rock Thrush and other cliff-dwelling species.

Accommodation

Soria has a Parador Nacional and various other hotels.

Comments

The best time of year for visiting the area is spring.

Fernando Chaguaceda Tomás and José Beltrán

■ CL.14 PEÑAS DE CERVERA – ARLANZA VALLEY

An area of cliffs and woodland consisting of Spanish juniper.

Main species

Residents: Griffon Vulture, Golden Eagle, Peregrine Falcon, Thekla Lark, Blue Rock Thrush, Dartford Warbler, Crested Tit, Azure-winged Magpie, Chough, Rock Sparrow, Rock Bunting.

Summer visitors: Egyptian Vulture, Alpine Swift, Redstart, Subalpine Warbler, Orphean Warbler, Bonelli's Warbler, Woodchat Shrike, Ortolan Bunting.

Winter visitors: Alpine Accentor, Wallcreeper.

Access

From Burgos, take the N-I towards Madrid. After 9 km turn left onto the N-234 towards Soria. This will take you to the village of Hortigüela (32 km), departure point for the recommended routes.

Description

The rugged geography of this area consists of a series of ranges of average height with cliff faces of very variable altitude. The main river is the Arlanza, which runs along a narrow, winding valley and features interesting riverside woodland made up mainly of alder and black poplar. The surrounding river network drains into the Arlanza, including the river Mataviejas which

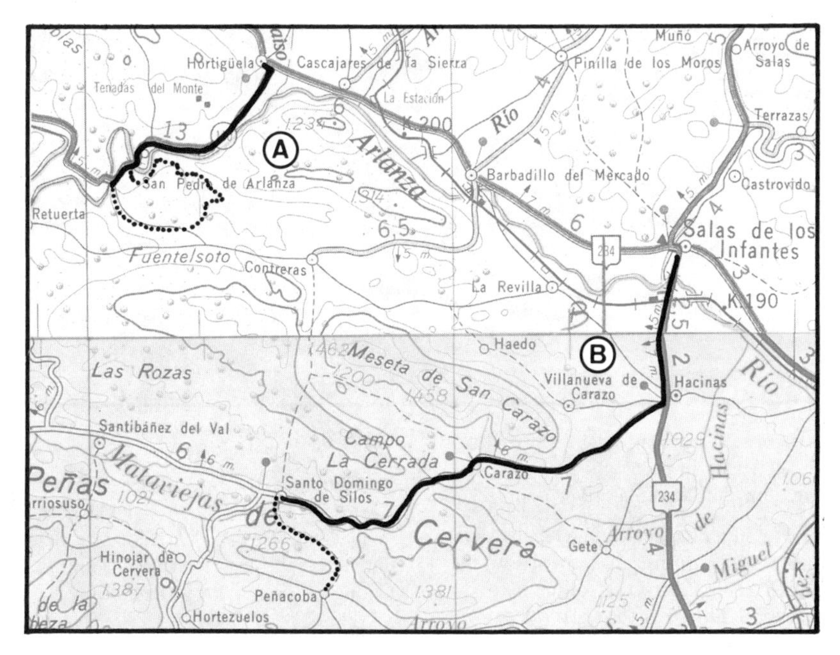

runs along a ravine several kilometers long. Woodland consists of Spanish juniper and holm oak interrupted only by small fields and some stands of oak.

Recommended routes

Route A consists of a 12 km walk running through wooded areas, rock faces and river. From Hortigüela take the C-110 towards Covarrubias and, having passed the ruins of the monastery of San Pedro de Arlanza (7 km), you will come to two bridges over the river Arlanza. These bridges lie 1 km apart; the second of these bridges is the departure point for this route, and you can leave your car beside the bridge. The track leads off about 10 m before the bridge and runs parallel to the river along its left bank. After 500 m the track climbs up a small valley bringing you after 4 km to some sheep folds. En route you will see Azure-winged Magpie, Orphean Warbler, Subalpine Warbler, Dartford Warbler, Bonelli's Warbler, Ortolan Bunting, etc.

After the sheep folds, the track climbs for a short distance to then immediately drop down into a broader valley of dry grazing land dotted with Spanish juniper. After 1 km, just after an abandoned gravel pit, the path converges with another. Turn left onto this path and work your way down the valley towards some reddish cliffs where you will be able to see a wide range of cliff-dwelling species. At this point the path runs out, so make your way along a small gorge to the river Arlanza. Continue for a couple of kilometers downstream, and you will reach the first of the bridges and the road, along which you can continue to return to your departure point.

Route B is a 33 km car journey covering various areas of rockfaces. Any point along the way is excellent for watching various cliff-dwelling species. Leave Hortigüela on the N-234 towards Salas de los Infantes and Hacinas. In Hacinas take the minor road to Santo Domingo de Silos. As you leave Santo Domingo, you will see a signed turning for the Yecla gorge. At this point, leave your car and walk along the track. On a far side you will find a picnic area and a swimming pool which provide an excellent observation point over the cliff faces and the birds associated with them.

Accommodation

There is a *fonda* in Hortigüela, and a series of *fondas*, pensions and hotels in Salas de los Infantes and Santo Domingo de Silos.

Comments

The best time of year for visiting the area is during the summer months, although it is better to avoid undertaking the routes during the middle of the day. You will find a telescope extremely useful.

Jacinto Román Sancho
and Fernando Román Sancho

■ CL.15 RÍO LOBOS

River gorge.

Main species

Residents: Griffon Vulture, Golden Eagle, Peregrine Falcon, Eagle Owl, Kingfisher, Dipper, Black Redstart, Black Wheatear, Azure-winged Magpie, Chough, Rock Sparrow, Citril Finch, Rock Bunting.

Summer visitors: Egyptian Vulture, Short-toed Eagle, Scops Owl, Alpine Swift, Black-eared Wheatear, Subalpine Warbler, Ortolan Bunting.

Winter visitors: Merlin, Redwing, Fieldfare, Goldcrest, Wallcreeper.

Access

From Soria take the N-122 towards Valladolid and in El Burgo de Osma (58 km) turn right onto the minor road for Ucero. Continue for 2 km after Ucero along a winding road and you will come across a well-marked forestry road running off to the left and taking you into the river gorge.

Another way of reaching the gorge is to take the N-234 out of Soria towards Burgos. When you reach San Leonardo de Yagüe (53 km), turn left onto the minor road for Santa María de las Hoyas and after 5 km you will come to a bridge where you can leave your car.

Description

The gorge of the river Lobos, 18 km long, is a river gorge typical of Castile. It is very irregular and features large limestone cliffs. At some points riverside woodland is present, made up largely of black poplar and willow, while the mountain sides are covered with Spanish juniper and pine.

Recommended routes

Route A takes you along the lower part of the river gorge, starting at the village of Ucero. Drive the first 3 km until reaching a chapel where you can leave your car. From the chapel a track runs off parallel to the river. This track is easy to walk along and you can follow it as far as you wish.

Route B takes you along the gorge itself, but starting from the road bridge of Santa María de las Hoyas. As with the previous route, you can walk as far as you want. We felt it advisable to separate the route along the gorge into two sections, since it is perhaps too long to be able to walk there and back in a single trip.

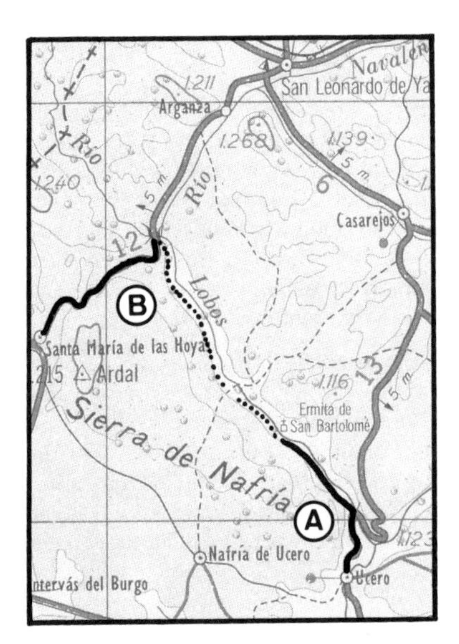

Both routes will allow for sightings of the main cliff-dwelling species present in the area as well as other species more typical of woodland and scrubland areas.

However, at weekends and times of year when there are likely to be large numbers of people present, it is more worthwhile undertaking route B which is on the whole less popular with visitors.

Accommodation

Some accommodation is available in Burgo de Osma, with a wider variety on offer in the nearby city of Soria. Camping is only allowed at the beginning of the gorge, in the area lying beside the bar.

Comments

Please go with care and do not stray far off the path during the vulture breeding season, since the path runs along the rockfaces where the vultures nest.

Guillermo Doval
and Félix Martínez

CL.16 CALATAÑAZOR – MURIEL

Woodland consisting of Spanish juniper with small river gorges.

Main species

Residents: Griffon Vulture, Golden Eagle, Peregrine Falcon, Eagle Owl, Kingfisher, Dupont's Lark, Dipper, Chough, Rock Sparrow.

Summer visitors: Egyptian Vulture, Short-toed Lark, Crag Martin, Tawny Pipit, Black-eared Wheatear, Subalpine Warbler, Bonelli's Warbler, Ortolan Bunting.

Winter visitors: Merlin, Redwing, Goldcrest, Citril Finch.

Access

From Soria, take the N-122 towards Valladolid and turn right for Catalañazor (31 km). The village is 1 km after the junction, and Muriel de la Fuente 5 km farther along the same minor road.

Description

The geography of this area is relatively uneventful and its main characteristic is the extensive areas of Spanish juniper which grow there. There are also areas of holm oak, Lusitanian oak and pine, as well as scrubland and fields. The landscape also features a network of small rivers which have carved out a series of small gorges. The river source known as Fuentona de Muriel is remarkable for its beauty.

Recommended routes

Route A is about 8 km long and can be undertaken in 3 or 4 hours. In Calatañazor, take the path running along the right bank of the river Abión until

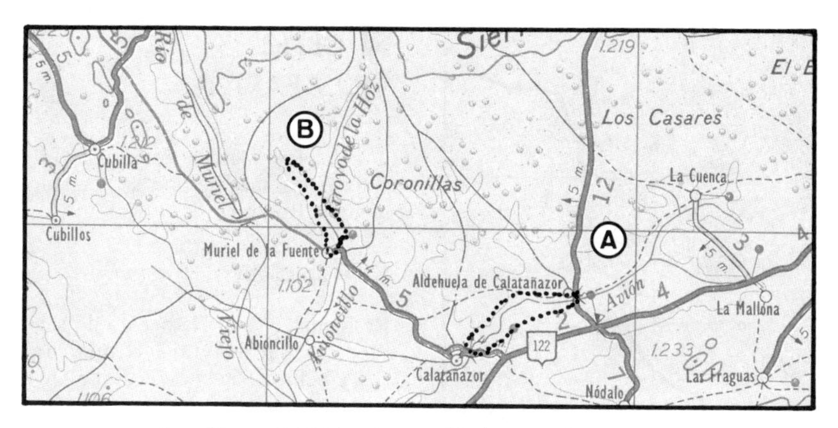

you come to the village of Aldehuela de Calatañazor. Here, cross the river by the road bridge and work your way back along the other bank, following a track which climbs up through the area of Spanish juniper and brings you back to Calatañazor. The route runs through a wide range of habitats and will give you the opportunity of seeing the most interesting species in the area.

Route B is a 4 km walk which takes you up the river Abioncillo from the village of Muriel de la Fuente. The route enables you to walk along either bank of the river, bringing you out a little farther upstream from La Fuentona; it will give you sightings of cliff-dwelling species such as Griffon Vulture and Golden Eagle.

Accommodation

Burgo de Osma and the city of Soria are the best places for seeking accommodation.

Félix Martínez Olivas,
Guillermo Doval
and Belén Pacheco

■ CL.17 ALMAZÁN

Riverside woodland.

Main species

Residents: Little Grebe, Grey Heron, Red Kite, Sparrowhawk, Kingfisher, Great Spotted Woodpecker, Grey Wagtail, Cetti's Warbler, Firecrest, Nuthatch, Azure-winged Magpie, Raven, Cirl Bunting.

Summer visitors: Little Bittern, Black Kite, Short-toed Eagle, Booted Eagle, Hobby, Turtle Dove, Cuckoo, Scops Owl, Nightjar, Bee-eater, Wryneck, Sand Martin, Great Reed Warbler, Bonelli's Warbler, Penduline Tit, Woodchat Shrike.

Access

Almazán is the main town of the region.

Description

Almazán is located at the point where the steppes of the Meseta, taken up by cereal crops, meet the extensive pine woods occupying the foothills of the Iberian System. Between the plains and the foothills runs the river Duero, on the banks of which are areas of riverside woodland constituted by willow, birch and ash.

Recommended routes

Before beginning the route, it is worthwhile climbing the Cerro del Cinto (1),

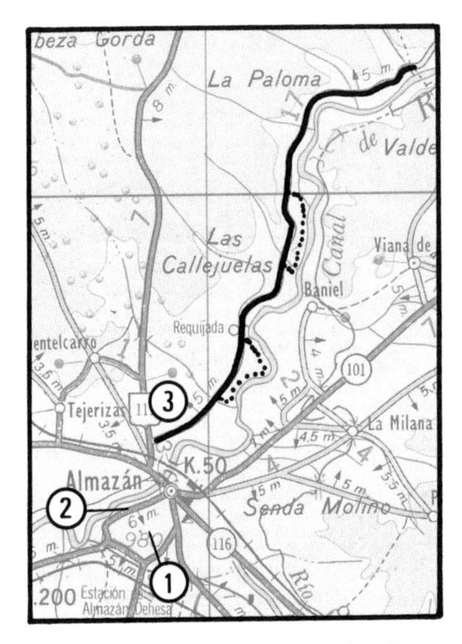

a hill located above Almazán, from which you will gain an overall view of the area. It is also worth walking through the Parque de la Arboleda (2) via a path running along the right bank of the river Duero.

The route itself is a car journey. 1 km out of Almazán (3) take the road to Cubo de la Solana. This road runs parallel to the river Duero, and a series of tracks leads down from the road to the river bank. By alternating driving with walking, you will be able to see the birds most typical of the area.

Accommodation

There is some accommodation available in Almazán, but possibilities are greater in the nearby city of Soria.

Comments

The best time of year for visiting the area is spring.

Fernando Chaguaceda Tomás

CL.18 VILLAFÁFILA

System of natural lakes surrounded by grain fields, the site of a large colony of Great Bustard.

Main species

Residents: Marsh Harrier, Little Bustard, Great Bustard, Lapwing, Black-bellied Sandgrouse, Little Owl, Calandra Lark.

Summer visitors: Montagu's Harrier, Lesser Kestrel, Black-winged Stilt, Short-toed Lark.

Winter visitors: Hobby, Greylag Goose (16,000 individuals in January 1990), ducks, Curlew.

On passage: Spoonbill, Crane, Ruff.

Access

From Zamora take the N-630 towards Benavente. After 40 km you will come to a crossroads; turn right onto the minor road for Villafáfila (10 km).

You can also reach the area on various minor roads from Villalpando or San Esteban del Molar, villages located on the N-VI (running from Madrid to La Coruña).

Description

La Salina Grande (194 ha), La Salina de Barrillos (118 ha) and La Salina de Villarrín (80 ha) are the largest lakes of the system and virtually the only remaining lakes belonging to the landlocked Salado river basin, which in the 1900s included up to 22 small lakes. The three remaining lakes contain saline water reaching a maximum depth of about 1 m. In recent years they have been subject to a process of severe silting.

The area around the lakes is gently rolling and completely devoid of trees. It is used for intensive cereal crop growing. The dovecots around the villages, typical of this area of Spain, are interesting because of the species which take shelter in them.

Recommended routes

Route A is a car journey starting from Villafáfila and running around the Salina Grande lake. The following stopping points are recommended:

1) 1 km outside the village, beside a farm, you will gain a general impression of the lake, which is the perfect place for watching geese and surface-feeding ducks.

2) Take the first left turn for the village of Otero de Sariegos, where you may see Lesser Kestrel, White Stork and Little Owl.

3) Walk from the village towards the lake and you will reach an area of high ground beside some dovecots from where you will be able to see Greylag Goose, Widgeon, Pintail, Teal, Shoveler, Marsh Harrier, Coot, etc. With luck you will also see accidental species such as Barnacle Goose, White-fronted Goose and Bar-headed Goose.

4) Walk around the lake on a broad, well-surfaced track until you reach, on the edge of Villafáfila, an old Roman bridge which is a perfect spot for watching Snipe, Avocet, Dunlin, Ruff, Black-winged Stilt, Redshank and Fan-tailed Warbler.

Route B is highly recommended if you want to see steppe-dwelling birds. To reach the area indicated on the map, take any of the tracks leading off from the village of Otero de Sariegos. It is impossible to specify a fixed route since the existing tracks are highly complex and extremely numerous. Work your way around the area until you find an area of higher ground which will give you a good general view. Among other species, you will see Great Bustard, Little Bustard, Crested Lark, Short-toed Lark, Montagu's Harrier, Merlin, etc.

Route C takes you along a track skirting the southern end of the lake of Salina de Barrillos. It is worth making this route a walk, lasting about 3 hours. En route you will see various ducks and waders. By casting an eye over the surrounding cereal fields you may also see Black-bellied Sandgrouse, Stone Curlew and Calandra Lark.

Accommodation

Benavente or Zamora are the best places for looking for accommodation.

Comments

It is worth taking a telescope. You are reminded that during the winter months it is better not to stray off the

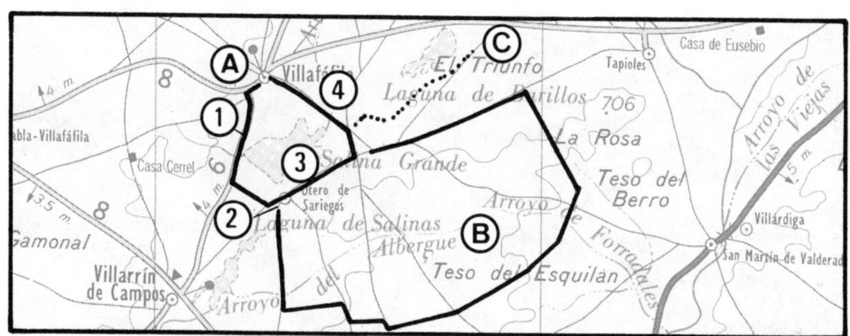

main track, since your vehicle may be in danger of being bogged down in the mud.

At the Ayuntamiento or Town Hall in Villafáfila you can obtain maps and information on the area.

Jacinto Román
and Fernando Jubete

CL.19 TIERRA DE CAMPOS

Cereal fields.

Main species

Residents: Marsh Harrier, Great Bustard, Stone Curlew, Black-bellied Sandgrouse, Calandra Lark.

Summer visitors: Montagu's Harrier, Lesser Kestrel, Little Bustard, Short-toed Lark, Tawny Pipit.

Winter visitors: Hen Harrier, Merlin, Lapwing, Short-eared Owl.

Access

From Palencia, take the N-610 towards Villalón de Campos and at Villarramiel (33 km) turn right onto the minor road for Guaza de Campos (9 km). For route B, take the N-620 out of Palencia towards Valladolid and at Dueñas (18 km) turn right onto the minor road for Ampudia.

Description

This area is a huge cereal growing plain lying at an average height of 800 m. Its only irregularity consists of small hillocks which cause the land to be slightly rolling. Alternating with fields of barley and wheat are other fields of leguminous crops. Stands of holm oak and Lusitanian oak exist only on the edges of the area.

Recommended routes

Route A is a circular walk along farm tracks in the area of Guaza de Campos and Frechilla. The walk will last about 4 hours. Any area of higher ground is a good place for watching Great Bustard (some 80 individuals in the area), Montagu's Harrier, Marsh Harrier, Calandra Lark and Short-toed Lark, while the alfalfa crops and fallow land are good places for seeing Black-bellied Sandgrouse, Little Bustard and Red-legged Partridge. It is also worth visiting the church at Frechilla, a breeding ground for White Stork, Lesser Kestrel, Rock Sparrow and Black Redstart.

Route B takes you across a plateau with woodland consisting of holm oak and Lusitanian oak. From Dueñas, travel along the road to Ampudia for about 6 km until you see a telecommunications mast. From here walk for a couple of kilometers along the left side of the road to give you sightings of Booted Eagle, Great Spotted Cuc-

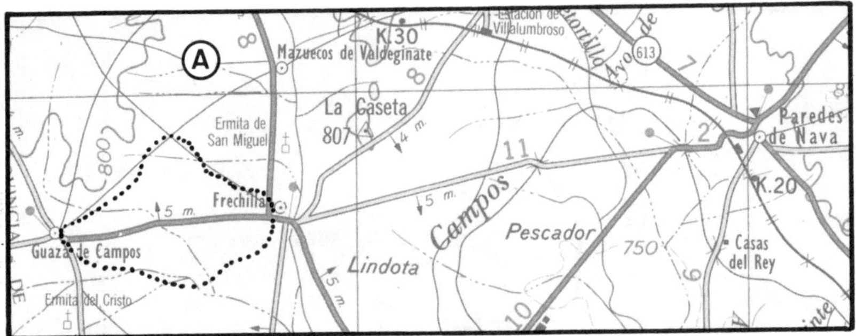

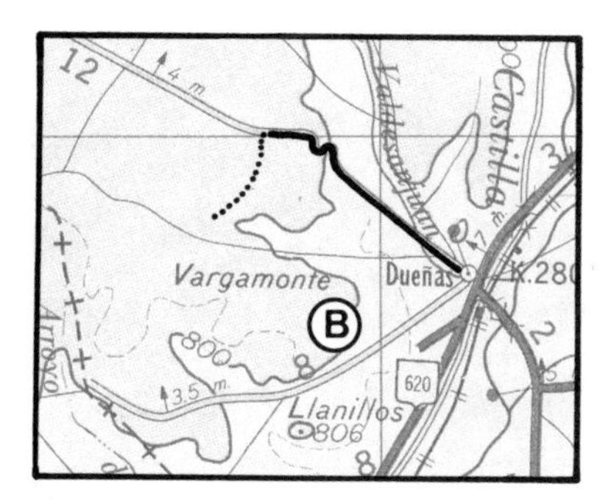

koo, Thekla Lark, Orphean Warbler, Spectacled Warbler, Subalpine Warbler, Black-eared Wheatear, Cirl Bunting, etc.

Accommodation

Some accommodation is available in Villarramiel and Dueñas, although possibilities are far greater in the city of Palencia.

Comments

It is not worth undertaking route A between the months of April and June since the cereal crops will be high, making observation of steppe-dwellers extremely difficult.

Fernando Jubete

■ CL.20 RIVERSIDE WOODLAND ON THE RIVER CARRIÓN

Riverside woodland and small lakes.

Main species

Residents: Little Grebe, Great Crested Grebe, Marsh Harrier, Coot, Lapwing, Water Rail, Calandra Lark, Cetti's Warbler, Fan-tailed Warbler, Penduline Tit.

Summer visitors: Little Bittern, Night Heron, Purple Heron, White Stork, Gadwall, Black Kite, Bee-eater, Great Reed Warbler, Melodious Warbler, Golden Oriole.

Winter visitors: Grey Heron, ducks, Long-eared Owl.

On passage: Greylag Goose, Red-crested Pochard, waders.

Access

From Palencia, take the N-611 towards Santander and turn off onto the minor road for Ribas de Campos and San Cebrián de Campos (14 km). Continue along this road until you reach the Canal de Castilla, a canal, where you can leave your car.

Description

On the bank of the river Carrión and to a lesser extent on the bank of the Canal de Castilla, there are areas of dense riverside woodland made up largely of poplar, alder and elm. These woods are the site of a large colony of Night Heron (over 200 pairs in 1989). Along the canal is a series of small flooded areas whose existence depends on leakage from the canal.

The areas around the river are given over to cereal crops and irrigated farmland.

Recommended routes

Route A is a walk lasting some 4 hours. From the place where you have left your car (beside the canal), take a farm track running parallel to the right bank of the Canal de Castilla and continue for some 5 or 6 km. The points of greatest interest are the following:

1) Charca de la Toja. A pond surrounded by reeds where you should have sightings of Marsh Harrier, Lapwing, Purple Heron, Night Heron and, in winter, various species of ducks.

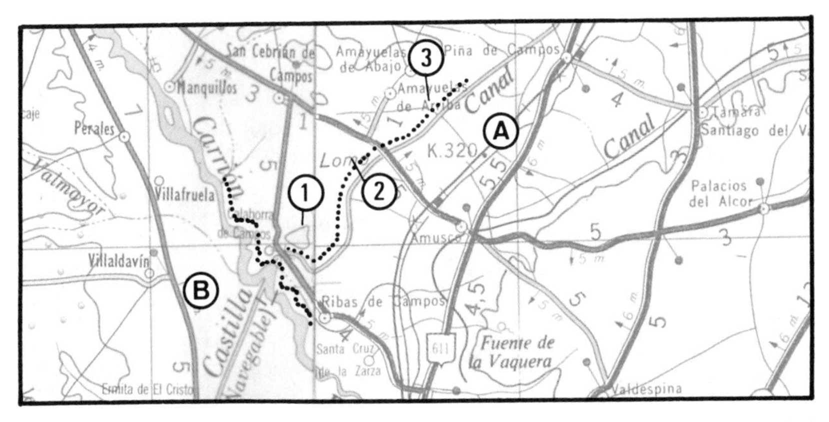

2) Charca de Amayuelas. A good spot for seeing Gadwall, Little Grebe, Coot, Water Rail and Great Reed Warbler.

Throughout the route, leave the canal to see typical steppe-dwellers such as Great Bustard, Little Bustard, Short-toed Lark and Calandra Lark (3).

The starting point for **route B** is the same as that for route A. This route takes you through the woodland on the river Carrión, either upstream or downstream as you prefer. You can make this route as long as you wish, although at some points you may find vegetation blocking your way. It is possible that you will see Golden Oriole, Cetti's Warbler, Bee-eater, Black Kite, Penduline Tit and also Night Heron, which uses this stretch of river as a fishing ground.

Accommodation

There is plenty of accommodation available in Palencia.

Comments

Engineering works, mills, bridges and factories, were built along the Canal de Castilla during the 19th and 20th centuries and are now of special cultural interest. This applies especially to the Calahorra de Campos sluice, located at the starting point of both recommended routes.

Fernando Jubete

■ CL.21 LA NAVA DE FUENTES

Landlocked wetland area.

Main species

Residents: Mallard, Marsh Harrier, Peregrine Falcon, Water Rail, Lapwing, Fan-tailed Warbler, Cetti's Warbler.

Summer visitors: White Stork (during the post-mating season as many as 500 individuals), Garganey, Shoveler, Black-tailed Godwit (has bred in the area).

Winter visitors: Grey Heron, ducks.

On passage: Spoonbill, waders.

Access

From Palencia, take the N-610 towards Villalón de Campos, and at Mazariegos (17 km) turn onto the minor road for Fuentes de Nava. Some 4 km before Fuentes de Nava you will find signs for the wetland area, which lies to the right of the road.

Description

The marsh, which was recuperated in April 1990, is but a small part of the original Laguna de la Nava. The original lake, with an area of 5,000 ha, was one of the most important wetland areas in northern Spain. The lake was drained about 50 years ago.

Today, it has a surface of some 65 ha and reaches a maximum depth of 50 cm. It is surrounded by flooded fields and small reedbeds. The recovery project was undertaken jointly by Habitat, a nature conservancy group, and the European Nature Heritage Fund. The project aims to extend the wetland area in the very near future.

Recommended routes

A walk from the road to the marsh and along its western shore will enable you to see the most important birds of the area. It is worth going to Casa de Don Marcelo, a house located on the shore, and the dam where the water enters the lake, soon to be the site of a raised hide. In addition, cast an eye over the flooded meadows in the area.

Accommodation

In Fuentes de Nava there are two bars which will provide food and accommodation. You should give them a few hours' warning.

Comments

Leaflets containing information about the site can be obtained from the Ayuntamiento or Town Hall in Fuentes de Nava.

Fernando Jubete

■ CL.22 MONTES TOROZOS

Holm oak woodland surrounded by cereal fields.

Main species

Residents: Rock Dove, Stock Dove, Calandra Lark, Thekla Lark, Dartford Warbler, Penduline Tit, Rock Sparrow.

Summer visitors: Great Spotted Cuckoo, Red-necked Nightjar, Bee-eater, Black-eared Wheatear, Olivaceous Warbler, Melodious Warbler, Subalpine Warbler, Bonelli's Warbler.

Winter visitors: Hen Harrier, Short-eared Owl, Redwing.

Access

From Valladolid take the N-601 to La Mudarra, where you turn right onto the minor road for Castromonte. From Castromonte follow signs for the monastery of Santa Espina and after 6 km, just after the road crosses a riverbed, leave your car on the sandy track leading off to the right (38 km).

Description

The Montes Torozos are plateaux typical of Castile, left dry by the river network. Patches of holm oak woodland are surrounded by cereal fields. Tree cover, including Lusitanian oak and juniper, is relatively well con-

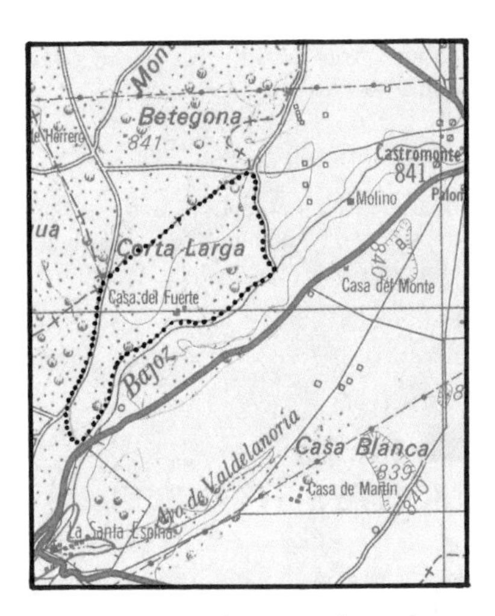

served, although in some places dense scrubland has taken over. The habitat is completed by stands of willow and black poplar lining the riverbeds. There are wolves in the area.

Recommended routes

In the area where you leave your car, tracks take you into the holm oak woodland and provide opportunities for longer or shorter walks, depending on the time you have available. A couple of hours will be enough to locate the most important species. It is worthwhile working your way along the Molino stream, which runs parallel to the road. A small reservoir has been constructed on this stream, which is the site of various ducks and grebes. The surrounding irrigated land and riverside woodland are also interesting, giving rise to sightings of Penduline Tit. The sandy screes are the home of colonies of Bee-eater and Sand Martin.

Accommodation

There is a good hotel in La Mudarra. Alternatively, both Valladolid and Medina de Rioseco avail of plenty of hotel accommodation.

Alejandro Onrubia Baticón

■ CL.23 VALLADOLID AND AROUND

Woodland consisting of pine and scrubby holm oak.

Main species

Residents: Black-shouldered Kite, Long-eared Owl, Woodlark, Thekla Lark, Dartford Warbler, Great Grey Shrike, Azure-winged Magpie, Rock Sparrow, Hawfinch.

Summer visitors: Black Kite, Booted Eagle, Hobby, Little Ringed Plover, Scops Owl, Nightjar, Red-necked Nightjar, Bee-eater, Roller, Sand Martin, Melodious Warbler, Subalpine Warbler, Orphean Warbler, Woodchat Shrike.

Winter visitors: Red Kite, Redwing.

On passage: herons, ducks, waders, passerines.

Access

From Valladolid take the C-610 and continue for 7 km until you reach the artillery barracks of Teniente Galiana (not to be confused with another barracks, located 1 km beforehand). Between the barrack walls and the fence around a parking lot, turn left onto a surfaced track and continue for about 2 km. Leave your car by the third crossroads, distinguished by a firebreak and a chain running across the track and blocking it to vehicles.

To reach the Esparragal pine wood, continue along the C-610 until reaching the village of Puente Duero (11 km). Immediately after crossing the river, turn right onto a track running through an area of houses where you can leave your vehicle.

Description

The pine woods of Antequera, Laguna and Esparragal consist of mature umbrella pines (*Pinus pinea*), in places combined with maritime pines (*Pinus pinaster*). These are old plantations abounding in large trees. The clearings produced by fellings are the site of dense scrubland.

The proximity of the city of Valladolid makes itself felt in terms of human presence in these areas, which have been used for recreational and leisure facilities.

Recommended routes

Route A takes you through the Antequera and Laguna pine woods. The route is about 7 km long and can be done in 3 hours. Start at the firebreak and turn right to reach an irrigation channel bordered by black poplar. Follow the irrigation channel until you reach a partially flooded gravel pit. The walls of the gravel pit are the home of colonies of Bee-eater and Sand Martin. In winter and during the migration periods you may see some waders. Continue along the canal, crossing the railway line, until you reach another firebreak. Walk along this firebreak and then turn into a second running at right angles to the first, bringing you full circle back to your car. The route will allow for sightings of forest species and those characteristic of the scrubland areas present in the area.

Route B takes you through the Esparragal pine wood and has the added attraction of running near the river Duero, allowing for sightings of numerous water birds. This route can be done on foot or by car, making use of the tracks and paths in the area.

Accommodation

There is plenty of accommodation available in Valladolid.

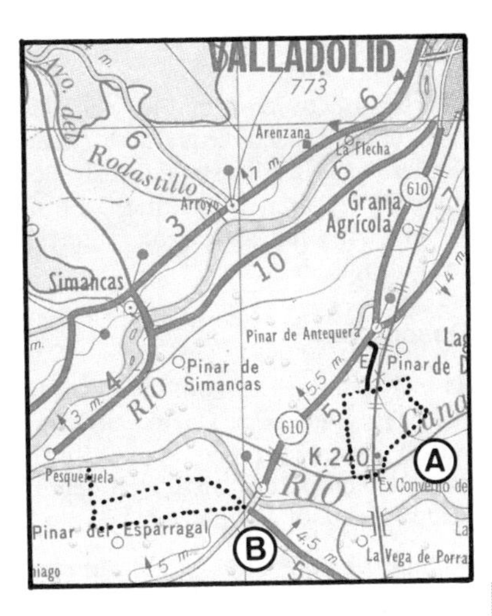

Comments

The recommended routes run through the least spoilt areas of pine wood where there is relatively little human interference. The large quantity of tracks and paths provide many possibilities, although it is quite easy to become lost.

Alejandro Onrubia Baticón

■ CL.24 CAMPIÑA DE VILLALAR

A cereal-growing plain.

Main species

Residents: Red Kite, Buzzard, Kestrel, Red-legged Partridge, Little Bustard, Great Bustard, Stone Curlew, Black-bellied Sandgrouse, Calandra Lark, Azure-winged Magpie, Rock Sparrow.

Summer visitors: Montagu's Harrier, Booted Eagle, Hobby, Great Spotted Cuckoo, Bee-eater, Black-eared Wheatear.

Winter visitors: Hen Harrier.

Access

The N-VI between Mota del Marqués and Tordesillas and the N-122 between Tordesillas and Villaester de Arriba demarcate the area in question. From either of the roads mentioned, tracks lead off into the fields.

Description

This region, lying on the middle reaches of the river Duero, is dominated by cereal crops, although irrigated crops are also well represented (beetroot and potatoes).

Another feature of this area are the small stands of umbrella pine which, being located in the middle of the plain, offer shelter for many birds of prey.

Recommended routes

The route recommended consists of a car journey with stops at the points of greatest interest. Leave Tordesillas on the N-122 and after about 7-8 km you will come across some pine woods where you will see various birds of prey, as well as Great Spotted Cuckoo and Azure-winged Magpie. A little farther on, 10 km from Tordesillas, turn right onto a track which will give sightings of Montagu's Harrier, Great Bustard, Little Bustard, Black-bellied Sandgrouse and Calandra Lark. The track comes out on a road; turn left and you will come to the village of Villalar de los Comuneros, from where you take the road to Marzales. After 4 km turn left onto a track bringing you to an interesting point for watching steppe-dwelling species. Continue towards Marzales and you will come to the N-VI. Make for Tordesillas and at the 190 km marker post, you will across other small stands of pine frequented by numerous birds of prey.

It is also worth visiting the nearby banks of the river Duero in the area around the village of Torrecilla de la Abadesa (8 km from Tordesillas), where there is well-developed riverside woodland sheltering abundant birdlife.

Accommodation

There is plenty of accommodation available in Tordesillas, including a Parador Nacional.

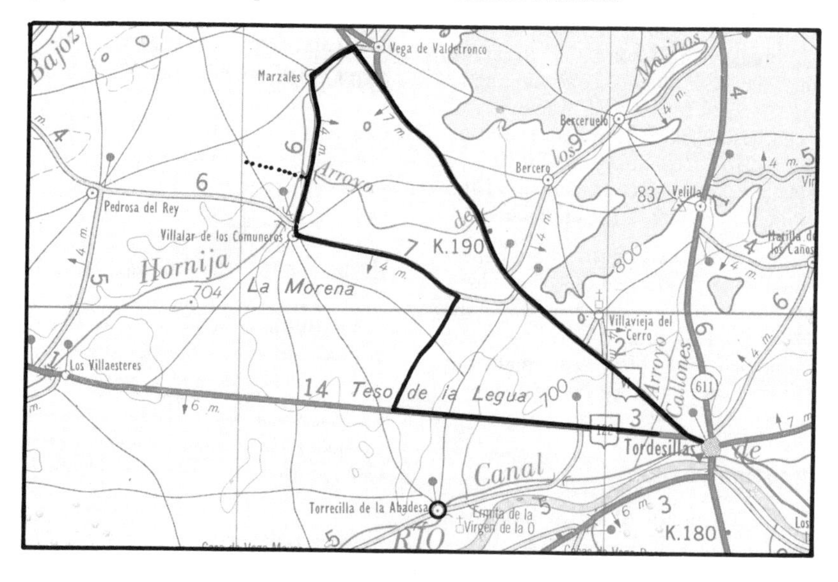

Comments

During rainy periods, some tracks may become impassable for ordinary cars.

Carlos Palacín Moya

■ CL.25
SAN JOSÉ DEL DUERO RESERVOIR

An artificial lake and a stretch of river with stands of trees.

Main species

Residents: Great Crested Grebe, Black-necked Grebe, Grey Heron, Marsh Harrier, Peregrine Falcon, Long-eared Owl, Tawny Owl, Stone Curlew, Kingfisher, Azure-winged Magpie.

Summer visitors: Purple Heron, White Stork, Hobby, Pin-tailed Sand-grouse, Great Spotted Cuckoo, Roller, Bee-eater, Penduline Tit.

Winter visitors: Cormorant, Greylag Goose, ducks, Avocet, Golden Plover, Bluethroat, Fan-tailed Warbler, Rook.

Access

From Tordesillas, which is on the N-VI, take the N-620 towards Salamanca. After 5 km turn right onto the minor road for Pollos and Castronuño.

Description

The San José artificial reservoir dams the waters of the river Duero as it passes through Castronuño. The banks support dense reedbeds and the re-mains of areas of riverside woodland. There are also extensive plantations of black poplar in addition to an area of privately owned, well-conserved holm oak woodland.

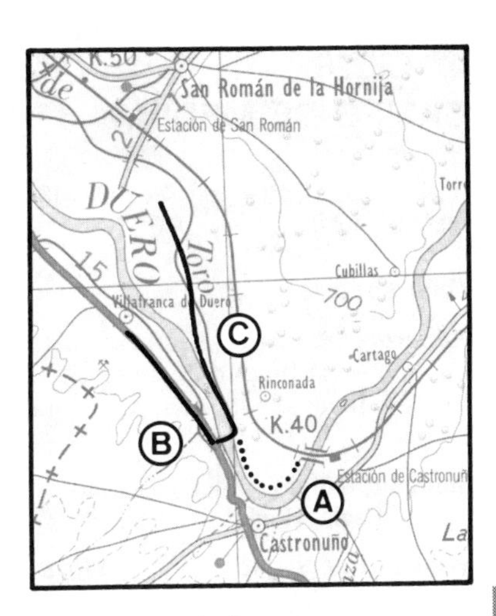

Recommended routes

Route A consists of a walk along the right bank of the reservoir, taking you from the dam to the railway bridge. The route, some 3 km long, will give rise to sightings of virtually all the water birds present in the area.

Route B takes you along the road to-wards Toro. If you continue for some 3-5 km you will have opportunities of seeing Stone Curlew, Pin-tailed Sand-grouse and Rook.

Route C runs along the minor road to San Román de Hornija. In the nearby pine woods and holm oak woods you will see birds of prey as well as Roller and Azure-winged Magpie. In addition, at Prado de la Requijada, a flooded area straddling the road 5 km from the dam, you can see various species of wader.

Accommodation

Plenty of accommodation is available in Toro and Tordesillas.

Francisco Campos Sánchez-Bordona

■ CL.26
CAMPO DE MEDINA

A plain taken up by cereal crops with seasonal ponds.

Main species

Residents: Buzzard, Kestrel, Little Bustard, Great Bustard, Stone Curlew, Black-bellied Sandgrouse, Calandra Lark.

Summer visitors: Montagu's Harrier, Booted Eagle, Hobby, Wheatear.

Winter visitors: ducks, Golden Plover and other waders.

On passage: waders.

Access

From Ataquines on the N-VI, take the minor road for Fuente del Sol and Cervillejo de la Cruz (13 km).

Description

The extensive plains in this area are virtually exclusively given over to cereal crops. In certain places it is still possible to find *lavajos*, shallow seasonal ponds used by ducks and waders when on migration and for wintering. Today most of these ponds have disappeared and only a few of them reappear after a season of heavy rain.

Recommended routes

The best means of getting to know the area is by driving along the road joining the villages of Cervillejo de la Cruz and Castrejón. The best points for observing steppe-dwellers is on the stretch of road between Cervillejo and Bobadilla del Campo and at the area around the survey point on Cuesta del Lomo, to the right of the road some 4 km before Castrejón.

From Carpio, a track takes you to the pond known as Lavajo de las Lavanderas. From the pond, a track continues to the survey point mentioned above, passing close to Lavajo de la Nava, another pond. It is possible to see ducks and waders on both of these ponds.

Also of interest is the village of Nava del Rey, 12 km from Castrejón. The church in Nava del Rey houses a substantial colony of Lesser Kestrel.

Carlos Palacín Moya

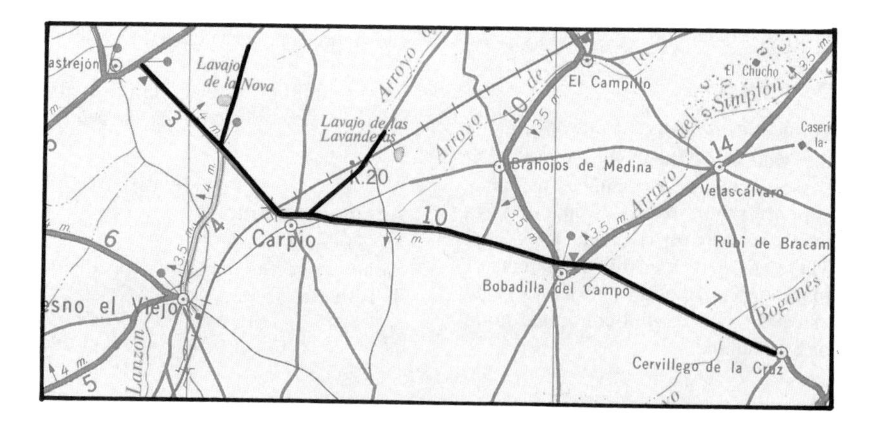

CL.27
LA MORAÑA

Steppe taken up by cereal crops with stands of pine and small seasonal ponds.

Main species

Residents: Red Kite, Buzzard, Kestrel, Great Bustard, Black-bellied Sandgrouse, Pin-tailed Sandgrouse, Long-eared Owl, Calandra Lark, Azure-winged Magpie.

Summer visitors: White Stork, Black Kite, Montagu's Harrier, Booted Eagle, Lesser Kestrel, Hobby, Quail, Little Bustard, Stone Curlew, Nightjar, Roller, Short-toed Lark, Tawny Pipit, Wheatear.

Winter visitors: Greylag Goose, ducks, Hen Harrier, Merlin, Peregrine Falcon, Crane, Stock Dove, Rook.

Access

You can reach this area from various points on the N-501 from Avila to Salamanca, between the villages of San Pedro del Arroyo and Peñaranda de Bracamonte. The area is also readily accessible from Arévalo on the N-VI.

Description

An extensive plain with cereal crops located in the Duero river basin, between the north of the province of Avila and the northeast of the province of Salamanca. There are areas where irrigated agriculture has supplanted cereal crops, this process becoming more marked near the larger centres of population. Changes in land use and the proliferation of electricity pylons associated with this change pose a serious threat to the area. Irrigated farmland predominates the eastern part of the area. There also pine plantations. The western areas retain large expanses of dry-land cereal crops. There are also some scattered dew ponds (which become flooded with rain) and grazing land.

Recommended routes

The area located between Cantalapiedra, Peñaranda de Bracamonte and Arévalo can be covered via a multitude of minor roads and farm tracks, giving rise to some interesting observations. The route recommended here is for guidance only, but guarantees sightings of the main steppe-dwelling species, as well as taking you to isolated stands of pine and seasonal ponds. Some of the most interesting points are the following:

1) Outside Castellanos de Zapardiel is a roost of Red Kite in the black poplars beside the river. A little farther on, on the road to Madrigal, there is an area frequented by Great Bustard.

2) Laguna de los Lavajares. In this area, you may at any time of year see Great Bustard, Black-bellied Sandgrouse and Pin-tailed Sandgrouse, particularly at dawn. In summer you will see Stone Curlew and in winter, if the lake contains water, various species of duck. If this is the case, do not go too close since you will frighten them.

3) Slightly to the south of San Cristóbal de Trabancos is a place where you may see Great Bustard. You will be able to see them from the road itself. You will disturb them if you try to move any closer.

4) This area is of special interest during the winter months.

Accommodation

Accommodation is available in the most important towns of the area; Arévalo, Madrigal de las Altas Torres and Peñaranda de Bracamonte. Food in the area is excellent, and we especially rec-

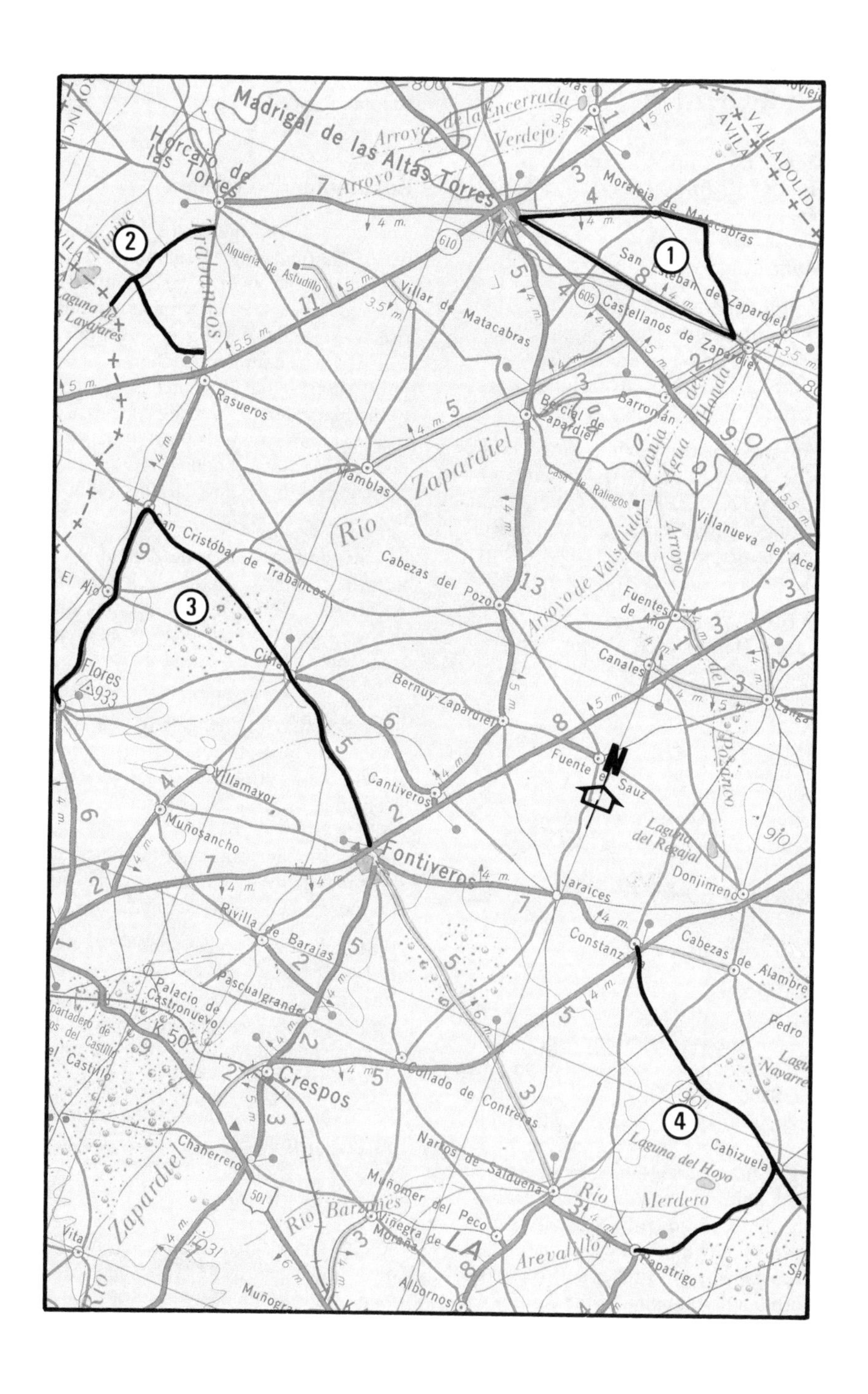
Madrigal de las Altas Torres
Horcajo de las Torres
Moraleja de Matacabras
San Esteban de Zapardiel
Castellanos de Zapardiel
Villar de Matacabras
Alquería de Astudillo
Laguna de las Lavajares
Rasueros
Bercial de Zapardiel
Barromán
Mamblas
Río Zapardiel
Casa de Raliegos
Villanueva del Aceral
San Cristóbal de Trabancos
Cabezas del Pozo
El Ajo
Fuentes de Año
Canales
Flores
Bernuy-Zapardiel
Langa
Fuente el Sauz
Cantiveros
Villamayor
Muñosancho
Laguna del Regajal
Fontiveros
Donjimeno
Jaraices
Rivilla de Barajas
Constanzana
Cabezas de Alambre
Pascualgrande
Palacio de Castronuevo
Crespos
Collado de Contreras
Chaherrero
Narros de Saldueña
Laguna del Hoyo
Cabizuela
Muñomer del Peco
Río Merdero
Viñegra de Moraña
Río Arevalillo
Rapatrigo
Albornos
Río Zapardiel
1
2
3
4

ommend the roast suckling pig available in Arévalo.

Comments

Be particularly careful from January to May not to disturb Great Bustard. Use a telescope and do not stray from the tracks and roads.

César San Segundo,
Luis José Martín, Ignacio Martín,
Lorenz Corrales and Gabriel Sierra.

■ CL.28
GORGES OF THE RIVER RIAZA

A river gorge with large numbers of birds of prey.

Main species

Residents: Griffon Vulture, Golden Eagle, Peregrine Falcon, Eagle Owl, Kingfisher, Dupont's Lark, Thekla Lark, Black Wheatear, Azure-winged Magpie, Chough, Rock Sparrow.

Summer visitors: Egyptian Vulture, Alpine Swift, Bee-eater, Wryneck, Crag Martin, Tawny Pipit, Black-eared Wheatear, Rock Thrush, Spectacled Warbler, Subalpine Warbler, Bonelli's Warbler.

Winter visitors: Hen Harrier, Merlin, Alpine Accentor, Redwing, Goldcrest.

Access

At the 134 km marker post on the N-I, turn right onto the minor road for Montejo de la Vega de la Serrezuela (10 km).

Description

The river Riaza has carved a deep gorge through the limestone rock of this area, where woodland consisting of holm oak and Spanish juniper is interspersed with cereal crops and scrubland. The most important feature of this area are the large populations of Griffon Vulture and Egyptian Vulture, as well as a wide range of other cliff dwellers. Much of the area is a Game Refuge which is jointly managed by ADENA, the Spanish Wildlife Association, and the Confederación Hidrográfica del Duero, the River Duero Hydrographical Confederation. There is a plan to declare this area a Natural Park in the near future.

Recommended routes

CL

Route A runs upstream along the left-hand side of the Riaza river gorge. The route starts in the village of Montejo de la Vega and is 9 km long. To return, retrace your steps. Throughout the route you will see Griffon Vulture, Egyptian Vulture, Chough and Peregrine Falcon as well as a variety of birds typical of farmland and riverside woodland.

To undertake **route B**, in Montejo de la Vega take the road to Fuentelcésped and from there, the C-144 towards Ayllón. After some 10 km turn right for the dam of the Linares reservoir marked with a sign saying "ADENA-CHD, Refugio de Rapaces". Continue until reaching an old quarry where you can leave your car; you cannot get beyond the quarry by car. The route continues along the gorge until coming to the chapel of El Casuar, 10 km from the dam. However, you can turn back when you wish, since return is by the same route. The route will give you sightings of a wide variety of birds inhabiting the stands of Spanish juniper and holm oak, as well as abundant vultures and other cliff-dwelling species. It is also worth making your way down to the reservoir via the steps from the dam, where you can see even more species such as ducks, gulls and grebes

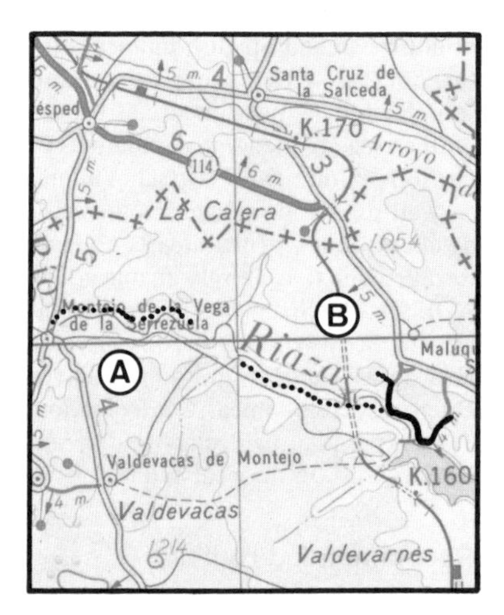

(in winter). Another interesting option is to climb to the top of the plateau where you will be able to hear larks, including Dupont's Lark.

Accommodation

There are *casas rurales* (farm stays) in Montejo de la Vega. To obtain information about this option, phone the Cooperativa Hoces del Riaza; telephone: 911-543046. Alternatively, there are several hotels in Aranda de Duero.

Félix Martínez Olivas,
Jesús Cobo Anula and
Fidel José Fernández y
Fernández-Arroyo.

■ CL.29 RUINS AT TIERMES

Rock faces.

Main species

Residents: Griffon Vulture, Golden Eagle, Peregrine Falcon, Eagle Owl, Raven, Chough.

Summer visitors: Egyptian Vulture.

Access

From the N-I, take the N-110 towards Soria. In Cerezo de Abajo, 3 km after Ayllón, turn onto the minor road for Retortillo de Soria. After the village of Torresuso and before Carrascosa de Abajo, turn right for the ruins at Tiermes. After 2 km you will come to the chapel of Nuestra Señora de Tiermes, where you can leave your car. Roads in the area are in bad condition.

Description

The ruins of the pre-Roman city of Tiermes are located on the high Meseta of Castile, at a height of some 1,200 m. They lie close to the boundary between the provinces of Soria and Guadalajara. The landscape, heavily influenced by the way it has been used for arable and stock farming, is remarkable for the presence of a series of reddish rock walls made up of sandstone and Triassic conglomerate rock. Although these cliffs do not reach any great height, they are the home of a substantial colony of Griffon Vulture. It is also easy to see other cliff-dwelling species.

Recommended routes

The vulture colony can easily be seen from the place where you have left your vehicle. Please do not stray far

from the car park so as to avoid disturbing the birds unnecessarily.

Accommodation

Since this area is rather remote, there is no accommodation available in the surrounding villages. This also applies to restaurants and petrol stations. The closest places providing these facilities are Ayllón, San Esteban de Gormaz, Burgo de Osma and Berlanga de Duero.

Fernando de Juana Aranzana

■ CL.30 HOCES DEL DURATÓN

River gorge.

Main species

Residents: Griffon Vulture, Peregrine Falcon, Eagle Owl, Tawny Owl, Long-eared Owl, Azure-winged Magpie, Chough, Thekla Lark.

Summer visitors: Egyptian Vulture, Common Sandpiper, Great Spotted Cuckoo, Roller, Dupont's Lark, Crag Martin, Black-eared Wheatear, Blue Rock Thrush, Spectacled Warbler.

Access

From Segovia take the N-601 towards Valladolid. Turn onto the C-603 after 7 km for Cantalejo (42 km), from where you then take the minor road to Sepúlveda (19 km), the village located at the head of the gorge of the river Duratón. You can also reach this point from the N-I by taking the turning for Boceguillas.

Description

The Duratón gorge, some 25 km long, runs from Sepúlveda to the dam of the Burgomillodo reservoir. For the first two thirds of its course the river runs along the valley bottom, passing through abundant riverside vegetation. For the last third, the dammed water is in direct contact with the rock walls, some of which reach 100 m in height. This part is the most spectacular section of the gorge, with bends going through 270°. The plateaux rise sheer from the water.

Recommended routes

This area was recently declared a Natural Park with a series of reserve areas. Entry to these areas is restricted or forbidden, depending on circumstances and susceptibility to change. The vulture breeding colonies lie within the reserve areas. If you wish to enter these areas between January and July, you must ask for permission. Visiting hours are also restricted, as are group sizes, etc. Until work on the future Information Centre is completed (located in Sepúlveda), if you wish to visit the park, the best thing is to write to the

CL

Servicio Territorial de Medio Ambiente y Ordenación del Territorio (Parque Natural Hoces del Río Duratón), Junta de Castilla y León, c/ Santa Catalina, 15; 40003 Segovia, or alternatively call 911–417244 to request the relevant permit and receive complementary information.

Recommended observation points are the road from Sepúlveda to Villar de Sobrepeña, lying to the south of the gorge, and the chapel of San Frutos located on top of the cliffs. To reach the chapel, take the track out of the village of Villaseca which crosses the plateau (you may see Dupont's Lark).

Accommodation

Although accommodation is relatively difficult to find, you can stay in the villages of Boceguillas, Cantalejo, Sepúlveda, Cabezuela and Turégano.

Comments

It is worth taking food and drink when you undertake any of these routes, since there is nowhere where you can buy provisions.

Javier F. Sánchez Vaquero and Francisco Sánchez Aguado

CL.31 RIAZA

A mountain area with woodland and scrubland.

Main species

Residents: Goshawk, Sparrowhawk, Buzzard, Tawny Owl, Great Spotted Woodpecker, Woodlark, Black Redstart, Goldcrest, Dartford Warbler, Great Grey Shrike, Raven, Rock Bunting.

Summer visitors: Booted Eagle, Nightjar, Water Pipit, Whinchat, Wheatear, Rock Thrush, Mistle Thrush, Garden Warbler, Whitethroat, Bonelli's Warbler, Pied Flycatcher, Golden Oriole, Woodchat Shrike.

Winter visitors: Woodcock, Siskin.

On passage: Greylag Goose, Crane, Woodpigeon, thrushes and other passerines.

Access

Take the N-I to Cerezo de Abajo and from there the N-110 towards Soria. After 12 km you will come to the town of Riaza.

Description

The northern side of the Sierra de Ayllón (Sistema Central), where maximum heights reach over 2,200 m. On the peaks, heath and broom are interspersed with alpine meadows, while the mountainsides are covered with Pyrenean oak at lower levels and beech at higher levels. This is the southernmost area where beech is present in Spain.

The valley bottoms, around the centres of population, are taken up by areas of intensive farming interspersed with oak wood, scrubland and pasture.

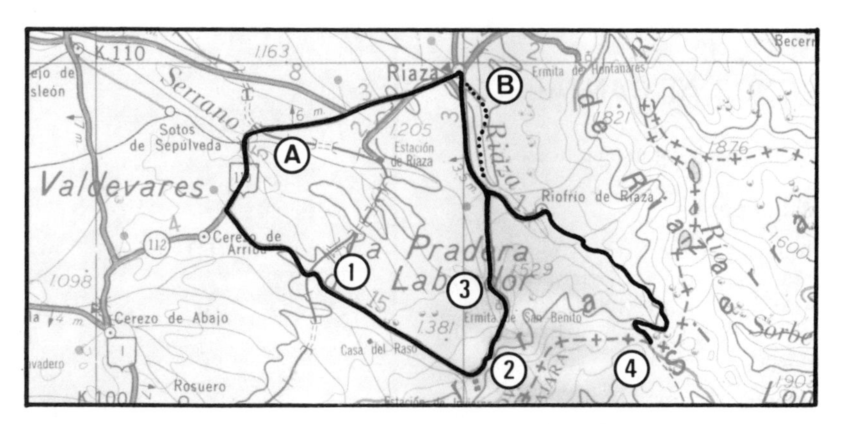

Recommended routes

Route A consists of a car journey giving you a general impression of the area. Leave Riaza on the N-110 in the direction of Segovia and, after 8 km, turn left for La Pinilla ski resort and from there continue to Puerto de la Quesera, a mountain pass. The main points of interest along the route are the following:

1) Pastureland with patches of scrub and small stands of oak; the most characteristic birds of this area are Woodlark, Whitethroat, Whinchat, Cuckoo, Hoopoe and Great Grey Shrike.

2) La Pinilla. Extensive pine plantations in which you will see various tits, Goldcrest, Crossbill, etc. From the ski resort itself you can climb up to the peak of El Lobo (2,273 m). This route will take you through extensive areas of scrubland where you may see Dunnock, Dartford Warbler, Linnet and Wheatear. With luck you will also see Golden Eagle and Bluethroat.

3) Ermita de San Benito. The extensive ash and oak woodland surrounding this chapel are the site of a varied range of forest-dwelling species, similar to those inhabiting the oak woodland you will find a little farther on.

4) Puerto de la Quesera. The road running up to the mountain pass crosses an area of beech woodland. When you reach the high ground, take a short walk through the alpine meadows and heathland to see accentors, warblers, wheatears, rock thrushes, etc.

Route B consists of a walk starting from Riaza along a path running down to the river. Once at the river, cross by means of a narrow bridge beside a mill and continue along a path running beside the riverbed and taking you to the village of Riofrío de Riaza (4 km). Return by the road. The route takes you through dense riverside woodland where you will be able to see Nightingale, Whitethroat, Cuckoo, Cetti's Warbler, Wren and Golden Oriole.

Accommodation

Accommodation is scarce in the area, although there are hostels in Riaza and it is possible to find accommodation in La Pinilla during the winter skiing season.

Comments

It is worth visiting the area in late spring and summer since winter conditions are somewhat harsh.

Fernando Barrio Fuentenebro
and Manuel Toro Velasco

CL.32 PONDS AT CANTALEJO

Small lakes lying in pine forests.

Main species

Residents: Little Grebe, Grey Heron, Red Kite, Marsh Harrier, Buzzard, Water Rail, Lapwing, Redshank, Common Sandpiper, Azure-winged Magpie.

Summer visitors: White Stork, Black Stork, Black Kite, Booted Eagle, Hobby, Roller.

Winter visitors: Greylag Goose, Teal, Pochard.

Access

To reach Cantalejo, take the N-I to Cerezo de Abajo, where you turn onto the C-112. From Cantalejo, reach the ponds by continuing along the C-112 towards Cuéllar. After 7 km turn left onto an unmarked track. You will recognize it by a large heap of earth and rubble which has been dumped at the point where it joins the road.

Description

The ponds of Cantalejo lie in the sand beds of the Duero basin in extensive pine woods which are exploited for resin. The ponds are surrounded by water meadows subjected to intense grazing.

The whole consists of a baker's dozen of small lakes, some of which are seasonal and some permanent, although the latter experience dramatic drops in water level during dry years.

Recommended routes

The recommended routes in this case should be undertaken on foot or with a four-wheel drive vehicle since the extent and depth of the sand beds which

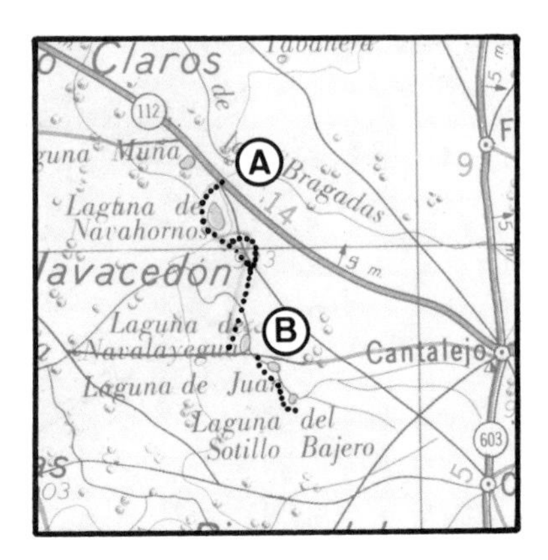

have to be crossed make driving in an ordinary car extremely difficult. It should also be pointed out that the large quantity of tracks, none of which are much used, and the absence of signposting make it relatively easy to become lost.

Route A takes a total of about 5 hours there and back, and begins at the point indicated above on the road from Cantalejo to Cuéllar. From here, a track leads off and skirts the western shore of the Navahornos pond, subsequently running along the edge of the pine wood. Keep to this path, not always very obvious, and you will come in turn to the ponds of La Cerrada, Navalagrulla and Navalayegua, which lies on the minor road from Cantalejo to Lastras de Cuéllar. The ponds will give you sightings of Little Grebe, waders, ducks, Marsh Harrier, Water Rail, Black-headed Gull, Grey Heron, White Stork and Black Stork, while the surrounding pine woods may give you sightings of Booted Eagle, kites, Hobby, Azure-winged Magpie and Roller.

The starting point of **route B** is to the left of the Cantalejo–Lastras de Cuéllar road, about 700 m before coming to the pond of Navalayegua, the only pond which can be seen from the road, about 7 km from Cantalejo. To enter the pond area, go to a clearing in the pine wood which is flooded at certain times of the year. To the right of a fence surrounding a field, a path runs off parallel to the fence. Stay on this path and you will come to the pond of Navacornales (named Juan on the map) and subsequently Sotillo Bajero, a favourite wintering spot for geese and ducks. This pond is also frequently the site of large groups of Grey Heron. In the fields lying between the two ponds you may see groups of storks, and in the surrounding pine woods, Azure-winged Magpie and Roller. The route can be easily done in a couple of hours.

Accommodation

The scant accommodation available in the area is in Cantalejo, where we recommend the Hostal-Restaurante El Polvorín. Some accommodation is also available in Sepúlveda, Turégano and Cuéllar.

Francisco J. Sánchez-Aguado

■ CL.33 SEGOVIA AND AROUND

A medium-sized historical city surrounded by cereal crops and holm oak woods growing on dry grazing lands.

Main species

Residents: Red Kite, Griffon Vulture, Black Vulture, Spanish Imperial Eagle, Buzzard, Peregrine Falcon, Barn Owl, Stone Curlew, Kingfisher, Thekla Lark, Woodlark, Calandra Lark, Black Redstart, Great Grey Shrike, Chough, Raven, Cirl Bunting.

Summer visitors: White Stork, Black Kite, Short-toed Eagle, Booted Eagle, Lesser Kestrel, Scops Owl, Bee-eater, Wheatear, Black-eared Wheatear, Woodchat Shrike.

Access

The most interesting sites around Segovia can easily be reached in car. Access is described for each of the routes in the relevant section.

Description

The city of Segovia, lying in a bend of the river Eresma, is located at the foot of the Sierra de Guadarrama. The city is remarkable for its old quarter, which is walled and contains important monuments —the Roman aqueduct, the Alcázar or fortress, the cathedral and numerous churches and convents.

The area surrounding the city is given over to cereal crops, uninterrupted except for the courses of the rivers Eresma and Tejadilla, lying in small gorges.

The Monte de Riofrío, woodland consisting of holm oak with a few small areas of oak and Spanish juniper, was originally a royal hunting ground. Most of the area is now dry grazing land, and shelters a large population of fallow deer.

Recommended routes

Route A is a largely urban route taking you to the most interesting points in the city.

1) Roman aqueduct. From the vantage point located beside the city walls, you will see 8 nests of White Stork as well as the comings and goings of a large colony of Swift which inhabit the stone blocks of the aqueduct.

2) Plaza Mayor–cathedral. Around the cathedral big groups of Chough congregate and, during the month of July, large numbers of White Stork roost there, making for one of the traditional sights of the city.

3) Alcázar. From this natural lookout point you will see Jackdaw and

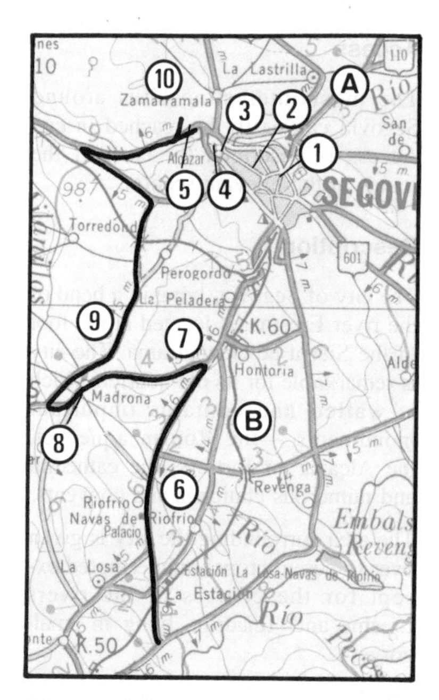

Chough. This is also a good spot for watching vultures, kites and other birds of prey.

4) River Eresma. The dense, mature riverside woodland located beside the Eresma is a good spot for seeing Kingfisher, Green Woodpecker, Golden Oriole, Nightingale, etc.

5) Santuario de la Fuencisla. This chapel lies at the foot of a small cliff which is the breeding ground for Jackdaw, Black Redstart, Rock Dove and other species.

Route B consists of a car journey leaving Segovia on the N-603. After 15 km turn right for Palacio and Monte de Riofrío (6) (royal hunting lodge and grounds). The road runs through grazing lands with holm oak woods frequented by Griffon Vulture, Black Vulture, Booted Eagle, Black Kite and Red Kite. Since it is forbidden to leave your car within the area, as you leave the park climb the hill located just to the left of the north gate which makes for an excellent observation post. If you wish, you can then continue on foot for some distance following the stone wall surrounding the park. Return to your car and after 1 km in the direction of Segovia, turn left for the valley of Matamujeres. As you enter the valley, stop to see a scattered colony of Bee-eater. On the nearby cliffs you may also see Raven, Barn Owl and Black Redstart (point 7).

The next stop is the village of Madrona, where the church is the annual site of White Stork, Lesser Kestrel, Swift and Chough (8). Continuing along the N-110 towards Segovia, you will cross an area of cereal fields (9) where you can stop to see various larks, wheatears, Corn Bunting and Stone Curlew. The next point is the Segovia rubbish dump (10) which can be reached from a turning near the Santuario de la Fuencisla. In late July, the dump is the site of several hundreds of White Stork and numerous kites, as well as Jackdaw, starlings, wagtails, etc. In winter, large numbers of Red Kite are present.

It may also be worth visiting the riverside woodland at Revenga, 6 km from Segovia on the N-603 towards Madrid. Near the Ermita de Santa María, a chapel, there is a colony of White Stork and other interesting birds associated with this riverside habitat.

Accommodation

Segovia offers plenty of hotel accommodation. There is also a campsite.

Comments

It is worth visiting the city in the month of July when the number of city-dwelling birds is at its height.

At Riofrío, you can buy a ticket to enter the Monte or a combined ticket for your car and to visit the Palacio or royal hunting lodge, which has an interesting Hunting Museum. You are not allowed to stop on the road or get out of your vehicle except in the area near the Palacio. For this reason, you are advised to drive slowly and to keep a sharp lookout.

Manuel Toro Velasco
and Fernando Barrio Fuentenebro

CL.34 SAN ILDEFONSO (LA GRANJA) AND VALSAÍN

A mountain area with extensive woodland.

Main species

Residents: Red Kite, Griffon Vulture, Black Vulture, Goshawk, Sparrowhawk, Spanish Imperial Eagle, Golden Eagle, Stock Dove, Long-eared Owl, Tawny Owl, Woodlark, Dipper, Black Redstart, Crested Tit, Nuthatch, Raven, Citril Finch, Crossbill, Rock Bunting.

Summer visitors: White Stork, Black Kite, Short-toed Eagle, Booted Eagle, Hobby, Cuckoo, Bee-eater, Short-toed Lark, Crag Martin, Water Pipit, Tawny Pipit, Dunnock, Alpine Accentor, Bluethroat, Rock Thrush, Goldcrest, Firecrest, Bonelli's Warbler, Chiffchaff, Garden Warbler, Whitethroat, Pied Flycatcher, Ortolan Bunting.

Access

From Segovia take the N-601 to San Ildefonso or La Granja (11 km).

Description

The Sierra de Guadarrama, forming part of the Sistema Central, reaches its greatest heights in this area (Peñalara, 2,430 m). The mountainsides are covered by extensive, well-developed pine woods which give way on lower ground to woods of Pyrenean oak. The high ground is dominated by pastures and broom with frequent rocky outcrops.

The Reales Jardines (Crown parkland) in La Granja should be mentioned since they are extensive, full of plant life and present a wide range of habitats.

Recommended routes

Route A is a walk through the Reales Jardines; check for visiting hours. It is worth taking in the avenues and walks of the lower as well as the upper part, which is more wooded and wild. Spend a full morning in the park to see all the forest-dwelling species of the area.

Route B is a walk taking you up to the mountain pass of El Reventón via Peña Buitrera, a peak. It runs along paths and then across country over steep slopes and rocky passes. The distance up to the mountain pass is 8 km but climbing to the pass and then descending again will take a full day. The most interesting species you will see on this route are those related to an alpine habitat, such as Bluethroat, Ortolan Bunting, Alpine Accentor, Water Pipit and others such as Golden Eagle and Griffon Vulture.

Accommodation

You will find a varied and plentiful range of hotel accommodation in the nearby city of Segovia, although you

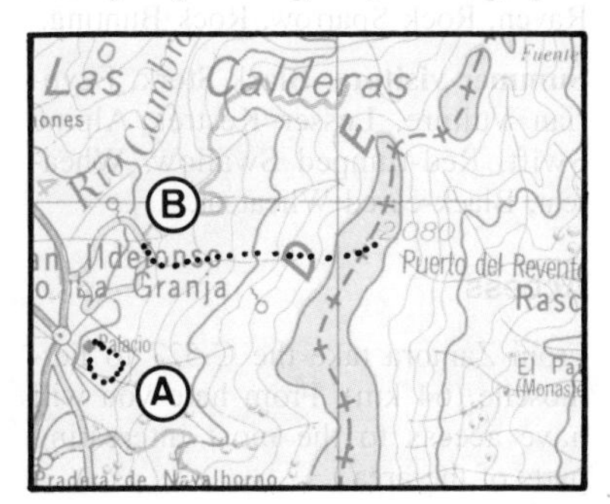

can also stay in La Granja (Hotel Roma) and at the Navacerrada mountain pass. There is a campsite between San Ildefonso and Segovia (Camping El Lago).

Comments

In Valsaín, 3 km from La Granja, you will find the Centro Nacional de Educación Ambiental (National Centre for Environmental Education). The Centre is open to the public and is worth visiting to see exhibitions on the fauna, flora and geography of the area.

This route can easily be combined with that taking you to the passes of Navacerrada and Cotos (M.1).

Francisco Bernis

■ CL.35 ARRIBES DEL DUERO (PROVINCE OF ZAMORA)

A rocky riverside area with high cliffs of granite and slate.

Main species

Residents: Griffon Vulture, Golden Eagle, Bonelli's Eagle, Peregrine Falcon, Rock Dove, Stock Dove, Eagle Owl, Woodlark, Crag Martin, Black Redstart, Blue Rock Thrush, Chough, Raven, Rock Sparrow, Rock Bunting.

Summer visitors: Black Stork, Egyptian Vulture, Lesser Kestrel, Alpine Swift, Red-rumped Swallow, Wheatear, Black-eared Wheatear.

Access

From Zamora take the C-527 to Fermoselle (64 km). From here you will have access to the most interesting parts of the area.

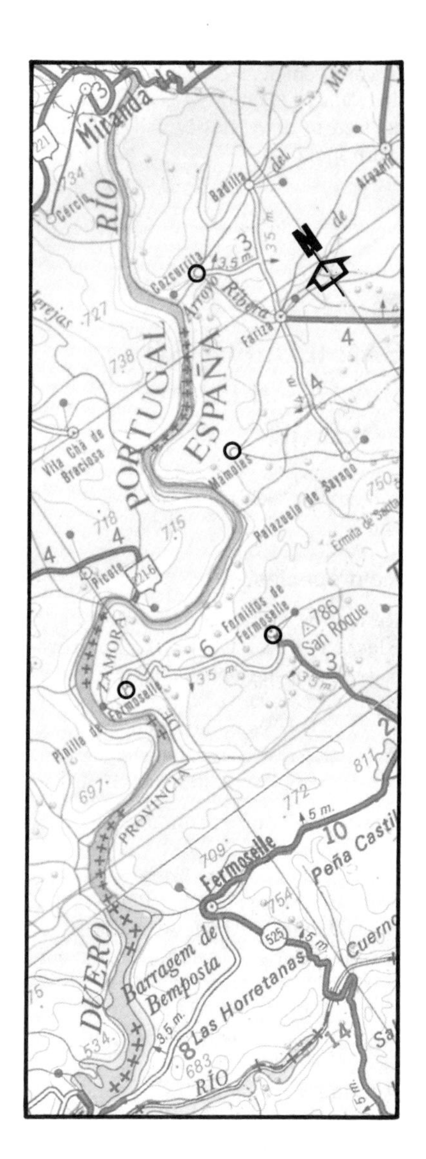

Description

15 km from the city of Zamora, the river Duero runs increasingly more between cliffs of granite and slate which occasionally reach heights of over 200 m. The way the river is enclosed makes for the existence of warm microclimates, and it is thanks to this that vegetation unique in the whole of the

Northern Meseta area is able to develop. The hills and plains surrounding the gorge, at an average height of 700 m, are covered with scrubland consisting of cistus, broom and red lavender as well as oak and holm oak woodland.

The riverside escarpment of the Duero, which is prolonged by the final stretches of its tributaries the rivers Tormes, Huebra and Agueda, has a length of some 200 km.

Recommended routes

From the C-527 you can take any one of a series of minor roads, some of which take you to villages and others to the edge of the cliffs. In the former case, paths and tracks lead down to the cliffs. Recommended places are Torregamones, Cozcurrita, Fariza, Mámoles, Fornillos and Pinilla de Fermoselle. From Fermoselle a minor road leads off to the dam of Bemposta, on the border with Portugal.

Accommodation

Facilities for tourists in the area are minimal and are mostly based in Fermoselle.

Comments

During the breeding season, please take the utmost care not to unnecessarily disturb the most sensitive birds (birds of prey and Black Stork).

Carlos M. Martín Jiménez and Carlos Sánchez Alonso

CL.36 ARRIBES DEL TORMES

A very narrow river course with large rock faces.

Main species

Residents: Griffon Vulture, Golden Eagle, Peregrine Falcon, Rock Dove, Stock Dove, Eagle Owl, Woodlark, Crag Martin, Black Redstart, Blue Rock Thrush, Chough, Raven, Rock Sparrow, Rock Bunting.

Summer visitors: Black Stork, Egyptian Vulture, Lesser Kestrel, Alpine Swift, Red-rumped Swallow, Wheatear, Black-eared Wheatear.

Access

From Zamora, take the C-527 in the direction of Fermoselle and turn off for Cibanal (53 km). In Cibanal, turn left onto a minor road leading to the Almendra dam (6 km), the starting point of Arribes.

Another option is to continue along the C-527 until you reach the bridge of San Lorenzo, 5 km after Fermoselle.

Description

The erosion caused by the river Tormes has carved a deep gorge with granite and slate cliffs which at times reach heights of over 100 m. This gorge, several kilometres long, joins with that formed by the river Duero (see CL.35).

The area is relatively undisturbed, giving rise to a wide and plentiful variety of cliff-dwelling species.

Recommended routes

Route A, starting at the Almendra dam, consists of walking downstream for some 3 or 4 km along the left bank of the river Tormes.

Route B provides the alternative of making your way along the right bank of the river Tormes from the San Lorenzo bridge to the Almendra dam. However, this route is more difficult since the terrain is somewhat rough.

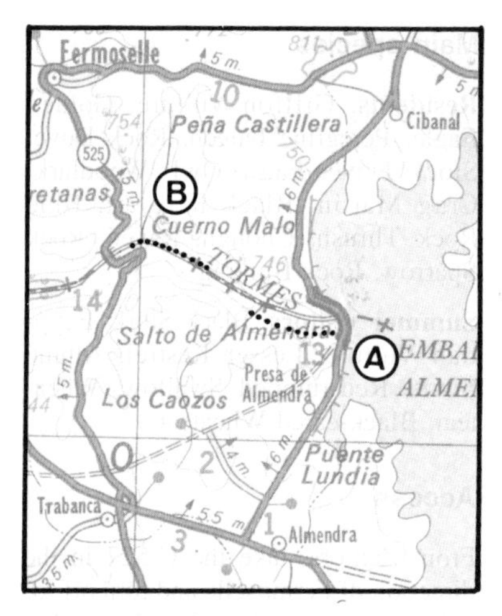

Accommodation

Accommodation is available in Fermoselle, but for those whose requirements are more demanding, it is worth going to Zamora where a wider variety of accommodation is available.

Comments

Please remember that during the breeding season, birds of prey and Black Stork are easily disturbed, so please go with great care.

Carlos M. Martín Jiménez and Carlos Sánchez Alonso

■ CL.37 ARRIBES DEL DUERO (PROVINCE OF SALAMANCA)

Granite river gorge.

Main species

Residents: Griffon Vulture, Golden Eagle, Bonelli's Eagle, Kestrel, Peregrine Falcon, Eagle Owl, Kingfisher, Crag Martin, Dipper, Blue Rock Thrush, Azure-winged Magpie, Chough, Rock Bunting.

Summer visitors: Black Stork, Egyptian Vulture, Short-toed Eagle, Great Spotted Cuckoo, Alpine Swift, Bee-eater, Red-rumped Swallow, Sardinian Warbler, Orphean Warbler, Golden Oriole.

Access

From Salamanca, take the C-517 to Lumbrales (95 km). From Lumbrales you can reach various points on local roads; details for access are given in the section on recommended routes.

Description

The main axis of the Los Arribes region is constituted by the river Duero, which runs along a deep gorge carved through granite rock, making for an extremely spectacular landscape. The area also contains valleys of some of the tributaries of the Duero; these valleys have a similar morphology, with those of the rivers Tormes, Huebra and Agueda being the best examples (see CL.35 and CL.36).

The areas surrounding the gorge are covered with holm oak woodland interspersed with various kinds of scrub. The temperate nature of the climate at the bottom of the gorges, caused by the sudden drop in altitude, makes it possible to cultivate olive trees, vines and orange trees.

It should also be pointed out that the rivers in the area have been used to create hydroelectric energy; the resulting large dams have modified the natural flow of the water.

Recommended routes

Route A consists of a car journey along minor roads. It leaves Lumbrales and takes you through Saucelle, Vilvestre, La Zarza de Pumareda, Aldeadávila de

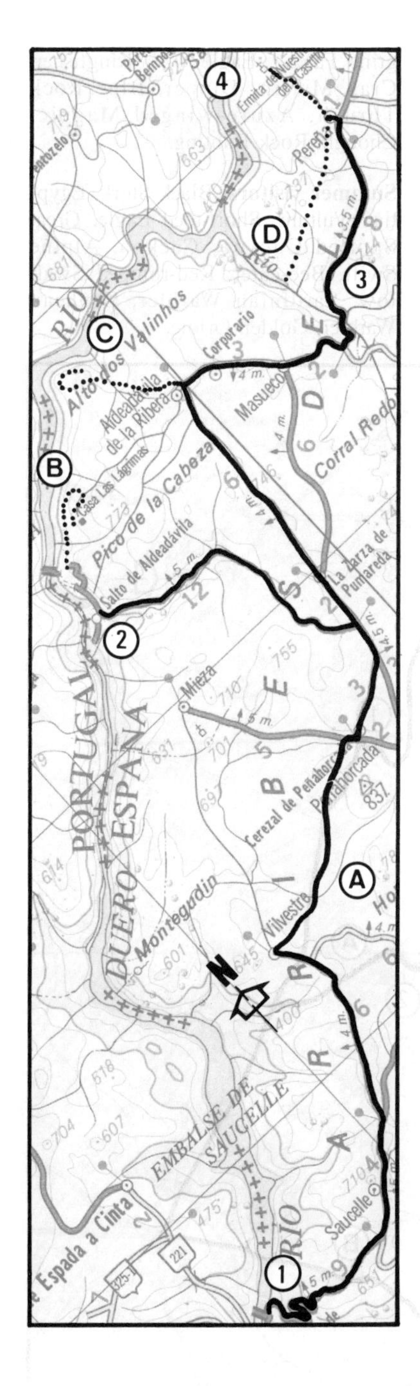

la Ribera and Pereña. Make stops or detours at the following points:

1) The climb from the Saucelle dam up to the village.

2) Dam at Aldeadávila.

3) Bridge over the river Uces.

4) Ermita de Nuestra Señora del Castillo, a chapel.

Route B is a walk starting at the Aldeadávila dam (point 2 for route A). Walk upstream along the left bank of the river Duero for some 3 km (this is a cross country route, there are no marked paths). There and back, the route will take about 1½ hours.

Route C is a walk starting from the village of Aldeadávila and taking you along farm tracks to the place known as La Fragua-Retornos. The walk there and back will take about 3 hours.

The starting point for **route D** is the village of Pereña and consists of walking along farm tracks until you reach the Pozo de los Humos, a waterfall known by this name (literally, the smoking well) because of the mist formed by the water as it falls. There and back this walk takes about 4 hours.

All these routes are exceptional for their great beauty in terms of landscape, as well as good opportunities of seeing the main cliff-dwelling species present.

Accommodation

Reasonably priced accommodation and food can be found in Lumbrales and Vitigudino. The Hostal Los Arribes in Saucelle also offers good value for money.

Nicolás González Sánchez
and Salvador J. Peris Alvarez

■ CL.38 ARRIBES DEL HUEBRA

A river valley which for its last stretches runs between granite cliffs.

Main species

Residents: Griffon Vulture, Golden Eagle, Bonelli's Eagle, Kestrel, Peregrine Falcon, Eagle Owl, Kingfisher, Crag Martin, Dipper, Blue Rock Thrush, Azure-winged Magpie, Chough, Rock Bunting.

Summer visitors: Black Stork, Egyptian Vulture, Short-toed Eagle, Great Spotted Cuckoo, Cuckoo, Alpine Swift, Bee-eater, Red-rumped Swallow, Sardinian Warbler, Orphean Warbler, Golden Oriole.

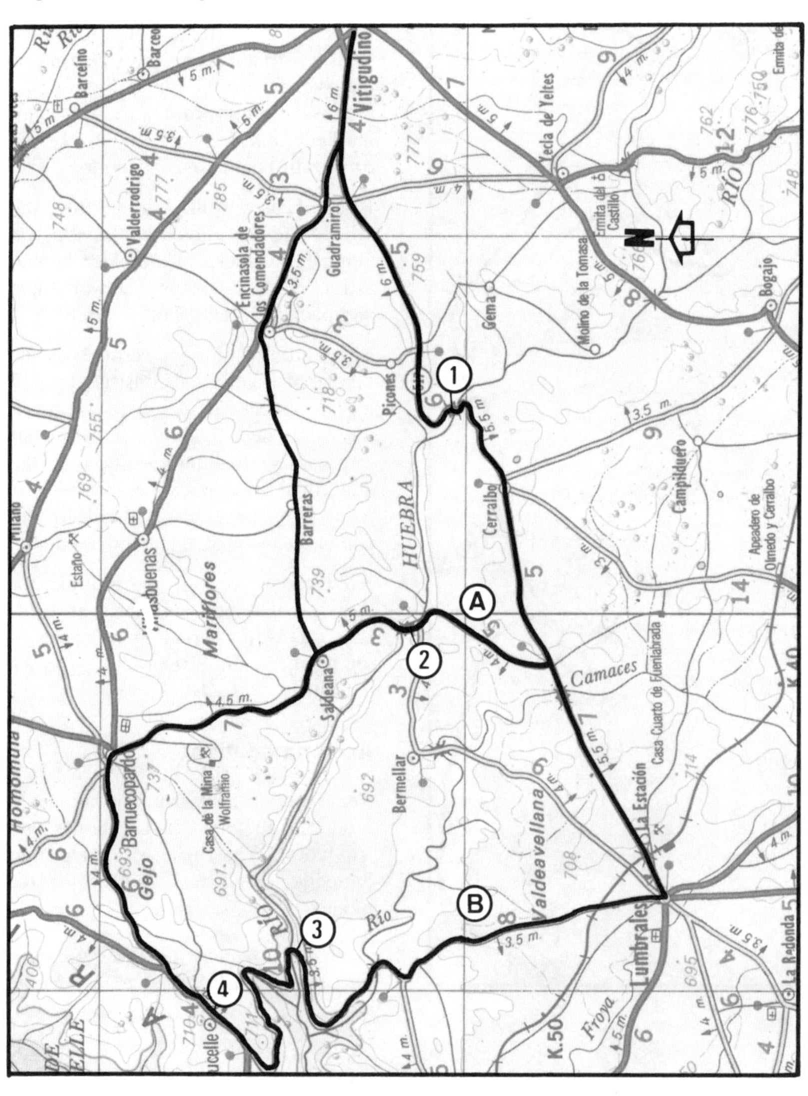

Access

From Salamanca, take the C-517 to Lumbrales (95 km). At the 80 km marker post on the C-517 you will cross the river Huebra for the first time, a little before reaching the village of Cerralbo. To have access to the area you have two options; turn off at the 88 km marker post onto the minor road for Saldeana, or alternatively continue to Lumbrales, and from there to Saucelle.

Description

The valley of the river Huebra falls within the region generally known as Arribes del Duero. The last stretch of the river runs through a narrow valley between granite cliffs, which rise up almost vertically to 250 m (see CL.35, CL.36 and CL.37).

Recommended routes

Route A (Vitigudino–Cerralbo–Saldeana–Encinasola de los Comendadores–Vitigudino) is a car journey with stops at the points indicated below where you can walk down to the river and make your way along its banks. If you follow the tracks made by grazing animals, it will make movement in this area easier since there are many obstacles to be overcome. An indication of this is that a 4 km walk may well take you 1½ hours.

1) Puente de Cerralbo. When you reach this bridge, walk downstream along the right bank of the river.

2) Bridge on the road to Saldeana. Here, we recommend that you walk upstream along the right bank of the river.

Route B is a car journey taking you from Lumbrales to Saucelle, Berruecopardo, Saldeana and Vitigudino. Along the way, make the following stops:

3) Bridge over the river Huebra.

4) The climb up to Saucelle.

It is worthwhile spending about an hour in each of these places in order to be able to see most of the cliff-dwelling species typical of the area: Black Stork, Golden Eagle, Bonelli's Eagle, Griffon Vulture, Egyptian Vulture, Peregrine Falcon, Alpine Swift. The best time of day to visit these places is at midmorning (10:00-12:00).

It is also worth visiting the rubbish dumps in Vitigudino and Lumbrales, sites of a large number of birds of prey and corvids.

Accommodation

Cheap accommodation is easy to find in Lumbrales and Vitigudino. The Hostal Los Arribes in Saucelle also provides good value for money. You can camp wild anywhere in the area.

Comments

The best times of year for visiting the area are spring and autumn. In summer, heat is excessive, and in winter the range of birds is smaller.

The projected declaration of the region as a protected area may change the conditions for visiting, which are currently completely unrestricted.

Nicolás González Sánchez
and Salvador J. Peris Alvarez

■ CL.39 CIUDAD RODRIGO

Dry grazing woodlands (*dehesas*) and riverside woodland.

Main species

Residents: Little Grebe, Red Kite, Griffon Vulture, Calandra Lark, Fantailed Warbler, Dartford Warbler, Penduline Tit, Azure-winged Magpie, Hawfinch.

Summer visitors: White Stork, Black Stork, Black-shouldered Kite, Black Kite, Egyptian Vulture, Short-toed Eagle, Booted Eagle, Lesser Kestrel, Hobby, Little Bustard, Redshank, Great Spotted Cuckoo, Bee-eater, Roller, Red-rumped Swallow, Black-eared Wheatear, Moustached Warbler, Subalpine Warbler, Ortolan Bunting.

Access

From Salamanca, take the N-620 for Sancti-Spiritus (71 km) and then Ciudad Rodrigo, 17 km farther on.

Description

Extensive area of *dehesa* with holm oak, Lusitanian oak and the occasional stand of Pyrenean oak which are given over to cattle breeding. The only area with scrubland is the Sierra de Camaces, a gently rolling range of hills reaching 700-900 m in height. However, the area around the village of Castillejos has extensive cistus scrubland which provides shelter for wild boar and the occasional pair of wolves.

The banks of the river Agueda downstream from Ciudad Rodrigo are taken up by riverside woodland consisting of ash, alder and elm, with the occasional cultivated area.

Recommended routes

Route A consists of a car journey through the *dehesas*. Just after the village of Sancti-Spiritus turn right onto a track located on a bend next to the bridge over the river Gavilanes. This track, surfaced only for a few metres, will take you to the Finca Paradinas, a farm; 400 m before reaching the houses stop at the first iron gate you see on the left. Pass through the gate (closing it behind you) and continue along the

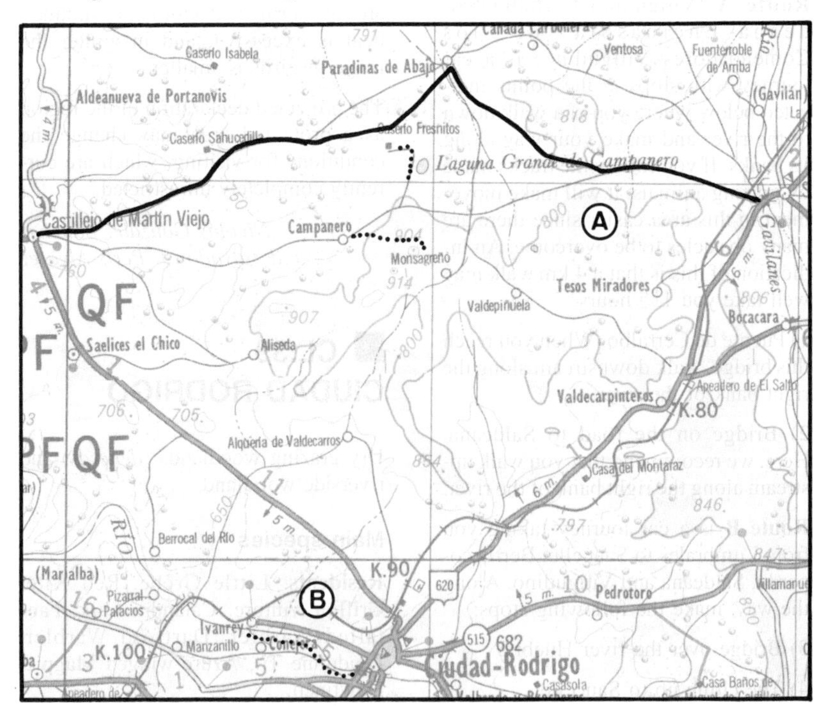

track until you reach the Campanero farm, keeping the pond of the same name to your right. When you reach the farmhouses, take the track for the village of Castillejo de Martín Viejo, from where you can return to Ciudad Rodrigo via a minor road.

Drive this route very slowly so that you will be able to see most of the species mentioned. It is also worth going to the Campanero pond, a major breeding ground for Little Grebe and Great Reed Warbler. From the houses at Campanero various tracks lead to other similar *dehesa* areas (you will have a greater chance of finding Black Stork in those lying to the north), although you should only take to these tracks if you have a detailed map or if you ask people in the area for directions beforehand, since it is easy to become lost.

Another alternative is to leave your car and walk to the Sierra de Camaces, which will take about an hour. If you have time, take the well-marked track from Castillejo down to the river Agueda. You will come across a well-conserved stretch of river where you will be able to see Dipper, Grey Wagtail, Azure-winged Magpie, etc.

Route B is a walk along the banks of the river Agueda, downstream from Ciudad Rodrigo. This spot can be reached from the city itself and although you can work you way along both banks via well-marked tracks, we recommend that you walk along the right bank until you reach the mill at Carbonero (3 km).

Accommodation

In Ciudad Rodrigo there is a Parador Nacional as well as various hotels and hostels. If you are looking for value for money, we recommend the Hotel Conde Don Rodrigo in the city centre.

Comments

Do not hesitate to ask the few locals who you will come across while you are on the *dehesas* for directions, since some of the tracks and paths could become modified with time. All tracks cross areas with livestock, meaning that land is often fenced off. Although you are free to pass through these areas, you must remember to close the gates after you, preventing stock from escaping (watch out for the fighting bulls).

Salvador J. Peris Alvarez
and Nicolás González Sánchez

■ CL.40 LEDESMA

Dry grazing woodlands (*dehesas*) and riverside woodland.

Main species

Residents: Little Grebe, Bonelli's Eagle, Stone Curlew, Azure-winged Magpie.

Summer visitors: Great Crested Grebe, Little Bittern, Night Heron, Black Stork (very rare), White Stork, Black-shouldered Kite (rare), Black Kite, Egyptian Vulture, Booted Eagle, Great Spotted Cuckoo, Red-necked Nightjar, Red-rumped Swallow.

Winter visitors: Cormorant, Grey Heron, Red Kite.

Access

From Salamanca, take the minor road to Ledesma (37 km).

Description

The first stretch of the river Tormes downstream from Ledesma runs through riverside woodland consisting of willow and ash but, after 1 km, at

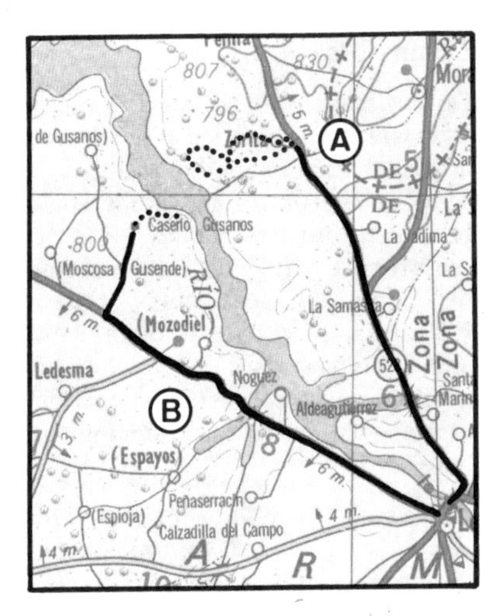

the end of the Almendra reservoir, it runs through an area of rocks. The surrounding land is taken up by dry grazing woodlands with holm oak. Holm oak woodland on the right bank is denser and more closely packed.

Recommended routes

Route A takes you along the right bank of the river Tormes. In Ledesma, take the C-528 towards Zamora and after 6 km, turn left onto the minor road for Pelilla. From Pelilla, work your way down to the river at Finca Zorita, a farm, via a track leading off to the left from the 55.5 km marker post. On reaching the farm, ask the local people to find out which of the two routes down to the river is the more passable. Once by the river, go for a short walk through the area.

Route B allows you to go down to the same stretch of the river, but on the left bank. In Ledesma, take the minor road to Villaseco de los Reyes; just after the 46 km marker post, turn right onto the track leading to Finca Gusanos (a farm); having gone past the houses, the track runs down to the river.

Either of these routes will allow you sightings of the species mentioned above.

Accommodation

We recommend the Hostal Venancia in Ledesma. In addition, just before the village you will come across the spa of Baños de Ledesma which has a more luxurious hotel. Should you wish to prolong your journey and take in Los Arribes del Duero, you could seek accommodation in Vitigudino.

Comments

The routes proposed here are just two examples of the various similar options you can choose from.

You should bear in mind that since you are crossing private land, you should go to the houses to ask permission. Permission is always given, but it is polite to ask in the first place. Likewise, gates should be closed as soon as you go through them (and not just on the way back) so that stock does not escape.

Salvador J. Peris Alvarez and Nicolás González Sánchez

CL.41 SALAMANCA AND AROUND

A medium-sized city surrounded by holm oak woodland and fields.

Main species

Residents: Little Grebe, Great Crested Grebe, Red Kite, Coot, Little Bustard, Great Bustard, Common Sandpiper, Kingfisher, Cetti's Warbler, Penduline Tit.

Summer visitors: Night Heron, Little Bittern, White Stork, Black Kite, Stone Curlew, Bee-eater, Short-toed Lark, Sand Martin, Reed Warbler, Great Reed Warbler, Subalpine Warbler.

Winter visitors: Cormorant, Grey Heron, Widgeon, Gadwall, Shoveler, Pochard, Tufted Duck, Black-headed Gull.

Access

Access to the points of greatest interest are given in the section on recommended routes.

Description

The centre of Salamanca consists of two clearly delineated areas, the old town and the new town. The old part of the city, abounding with monumental buildings, is the most interesting part from the ornithological point of view.

The course of the river Tormes passes to the south of the city and presents riverside woodland consisting of poplar, ash and alder, as well as extensive reedbeds and floating vegetation. Away from the river, holm oak woodland alternates with cereal crops, irrigated areas and alfalfa fields.

Recommended routes

Route A takes you through the old part of the city, enabling you to see the monuments and enjoy urban birdlife: White Stork, Spotless Starling, Jackdaw, House Martin, Swift, etc. You can extend the route by walking down to the river to see water birds and riverside birds.

Route B will enable you to visit part of the riverside woodland lying beside the river Tormes. Leave the town in the direction of Ciudad Rodrigo and Portugal (via Tejares) and before reaching the N-620, turn right for Santibáñez del Río, skirting the area of the old powder magazine. In Santibáñez del Río, 7 km from Salamanca, walk for some 2 km along the river course via a well-marked track until you reach a small dam. This area is rich in birdlife and is remarkable for high numbers of Penduline Tit. In winter, this is a place where ducks congregate.

If you continue along the road and take the first turn to the right, you will cross the river and come to a gravel pit where will have sightings of Sand Martin, Bee-eater, Grey Heron and, occasionally, Purple Heron, Kingfisher, ducks, etc.

Route C will take you to the cereal fields around Salamanca. Leave Salamanca by the C-125 towards Aldeatejada (5 km). From this latter village walk along the farm tracks to see Great Bustard, Little Bustard, Stone Curlew and also Quail, Red-legged Partridge, Crested Lark, Skylark, Calandra Lark and Short-toed Lark.

CL

Accommodation

There is a wide range of accommodation available in Salamanca. There are also two campsites.

Nicolás González Sánchez
and Salvador J. Peris Alvarez

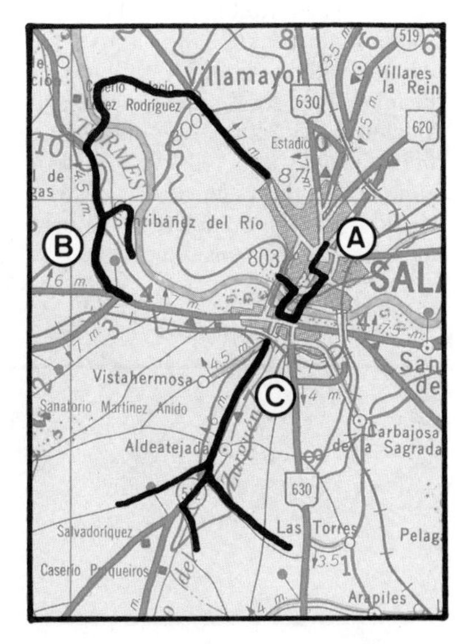

CL.42
EL CRISTO AND LAGUNA LA CERVERA PONDS

Small natural lakes surrounded by dry grazing woodlands (*dehesas*).

Main species

Residents: Little Grebe, Coot, Common Sandpiper.

Summer visitors: Great Crested Grebe, White Stork, Black Kite, Little Ringed Plover, Whiskered Tern, Bonelli's Warbler.

Winter visitors: Black-necked Grebe, Grey Heron, Widgeon, Shoveler, Teal, Tufted Duck, Golden Plover, Redshank, Green Sandpiper, Snipe, Black-headed Gull.

On passage: Black Stork, Spoonbill, Gadwall, Crane.

Access

From Salamanca, take the N-620 towards Ciudad Rodrigo and Portugal. Continue for 54 km and just after the junction with the C-525, turn left onto the minor road for Campo Cerrado and Aldehuela de Yeltes. Continue along this road and after 10 km you will come across the Laguna del Cristo, a small lake lying to the left of the road opposite a house typical of the area.

The Cervera pond is 3 km from the latter small lake, just after the village of Aldehuela de Yeltes and at the point where the roads for Morasverdes and Alba de Yeltes meet.

Return to Salamanca via Tamames, passing through slightly more rolling dry grazing lands than those you passed through on the outward journey. You may see various birds of prey in this area.

Description

The Laguna del Cristo, the main semi-natural body of water in the province, has an average size of 800 x 500 m and a depth of 3 m. Located in an area of grazing woodlands and surrounded by stone walls, there is a plantation of reed mace and rushes on its left bank which offers suitable shelter for water birds. The lake was dug out and made deeper during the 1970s so as to prevent it drying out in summer, and to facilitate its use as a watering hole for livestock.

The Cervera pond, 300 x 300 m with an average depth of 1.5 m, houses a smaller number of species, although they can be seen with greater ease.

Recommended routes

Before leaving the N-620, it is well worth going to the rubbish tip at La Fuente de San Esteban, where in winter about 100 Rook, over 150 Raven and up to 240 Red Kite congregate. The abundance of voles in the nearby alfalfa fields makes for the presence, in autumn and winter, of up to 4 Black-shouldered Kite. In any case, throughout the route you will be able to

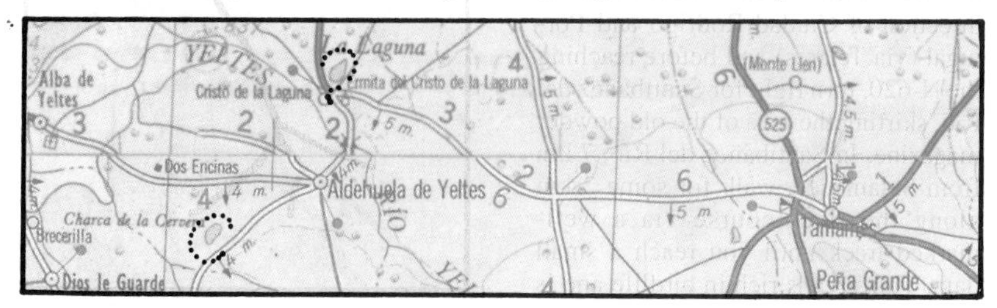

see, particularly in winter, large numbers of Red Kite, Buzzard and Kestrel.

Once you reach the El Cristo pond, park your car by the chapel and walk around the right shore of the pond, where you will be hidden by the stone wall. During the breeding season, it is possible to see several pairs of Great Crested Grebe, Mallard, Coot and Little Grebe.

The Cervera pond is easy to visit and does not need any directions. Please avoid approaching the nesting grounds at both ponds.

If you have time, visit the reservoir of La Zarza, a wintering ground for Black-necked Grebe, ducks, sandpipers and Redshank. Reach this reservoir by taking the road to Boada and Villavieja from La Fuente de San Esteban.

4 km from Tamames on the road to La Alberca, there is another small lake which you can visit; in summer, this lake hosts storks and surface-feeding ducks, while in winter it is the site of Golden Plover.

Accommodation

There is a hostel in La Fuente de San Esteban, and it is also possible to camp near Cervera pond. If you are planning to continue to La Peña de Francia, you can stay in La Alberca (see CL.43).

Comments

You do not need permission to visit the ponds but, since you are on private land, please close the gates after you and take care not to damage the stone walling. If you wish for information about the El Cristo lake, ask at the farm for Agustín and/or his son, who work as shepherds in the area and know the wildlife well.

Salvador J. Peris Alvarez and Nicolás González Sánchez

CL.43 PEÑA DE FRANCIA – LAS BATUECAS

A mountain area with extensive woodland and areas of scrub.

Main species

Residents: Griffon Vulture, Black Vulture (rare), Golden Eagle, Peregrine Falcon, Lesser Spotted Woodpecker, Thekla Lark, Grey Wagtail, Dipper, Black Wheatear, Dartford Warbler, Chough.

Summer visitors: Black Kite, Egyptian Vulture, Short-toed Eagle, Lesser Kestrel, Great Spotted Cuckoo, Alpine Swift, Bee-eater, Crag Martin, Red-rumped Swallow, Black-eared Wheatear, Rock Thrush, Blue Rock Thrush.

Access

From Salamanca, take the C-512 to Vecinos, and from there the minor road to Tamames, from where you continue to La Alberca (75 km). Before reaching La Alberca, take a marked turn climbing up to the Peña de Francia (in winter you may have difficulties because of ice or snow). Another option is to take the track to Monsagro, which you will find midway along this road.

From La Alberca you can make your way down to the Batuecas valley via the extremely winding road for Las Mestas (province of Cáceres).

Description

Peña de Francia (1,723 m) is the highest point of the Sierra de Francia, a range of mountains lying at the far western end of the Sistema Central. The monastery at the peak is the best point for looking out over the surrounding countryside: oak and

chestnut occupy the northern slopes, while shrubby holm oak woodland takes up the southern slopes. Most of the area falls within the Batuecas National Game Reserve (Spanish ibex and wild boar).

Recommended routes

First of all, climb the Peña de Francia, from where you will not only be able to see the differences in vegetation on the northern and southern slopes, but also the Gabriel y Galán reservoir to the south and the city of Salamanca to the northeast. From the peak you will also be able to see Griffon Vulture and Blue Rock Thrush. On the way down to La Alberca, you will pass through oak woods where you may see Lesser Spotted Woodpecker. Having visited the village of La Alberca, take the road towards Las Mestas and on reaching the monastery of Las Batuecas, park your car and take a 3-hour walk along the paths climbing up the valley. Some of these paths lead to an area with cave paintings and the high ground, where you will be able to see Griffon Vulture, Golden Eagle, Black Wheatear and Chough. From the monastery, continue to Las Mestas or alternatively return to La Alberca.

Accommodation

There are half a dozen hotels and hostels in La Alberca, of which we recommend the Hotel Las Batuecas. You can also sleep at the Peña de Francia monastery, although this is only possible in summer.

Comments

There is a scheme for the creation of an Information Centre in La Alberca.

Salvador J. Peris Alvarez
and Nicolás González Sánchez

■ CL.44 BÉJAR AND CANDELARIO RANGES

A mountain area with oak and pine woodland.

Main species

Residents: Red Kite, Griffon Vulture, Woodlark, Skylark, Water Pipit, Dunnock, Chough, Raven, Citril Finch, Crossbill, Rock Bunting.

Summer visitors: Booted Eagle, Tawny Pipit, Bluethroat, Wheatear, Whitethroat, Ortolan Bunting.

Access

From Salamanca, take the N-630 to Béjar (70 km). Candelario is 4 km from Béjar along a minor road, and from there you can climb up the range via a road reaching an altitude of 1,850 m.

Description

The Béjar and Candelario ranges constitute the westernmost sector of the Sierra de Gredos (Sistema Central), reaching a maximum height of 2,430 m. The mountainsides are covered with oak and chestnut woods and pine plantations, while the high ground is taken over by broom, alpine pastures and rocky outcrops. Along the rivers and streams is woodland consisting of alder, ash and willow.

Recommended routes

Route A has its starting point in Candelario, from where you drive to the end of the road climbing the range. En route, make stops in the pine plantations where, in addition to Chaffinch and tits, you may see the occasional Crossbill and Citril Finch. From the point where you leave your car, you will be able to climb to the top of the range in a couple hours via a path marked with stone markers. En route you may see Griffon Vulture, Bluethroat, Wheatear, Chough and Raven.

Route B consists of driving from Béjar along the N-630 towards Salamanca until you reach the junction with the C-500. Turn onto the C-500 and continue until reaching the village of La Hoya. From there a 9 km track takes you to La Covatilla; this track is in bad conditions, particularly when it reaches the high ground, for which reason it is worthwhile undertaking this route in a four-wheel drive vehicle. The track climbs up to 1,900 m and, en route, in addition to the species mentioned above, you may have sightings of Booted Eagle, Red Kite, Buzzard and Kestrel.

To undertake **route C**, leave Candelario on the minor road for La Garganta. After 4 km you will cross a bridge over the river Cuerpo de Hombre, from where a forestry road leads off which is closed with a metal gate to prevent entry of cars. This place, known as the Dehesa de Candelario, is an unspoiled

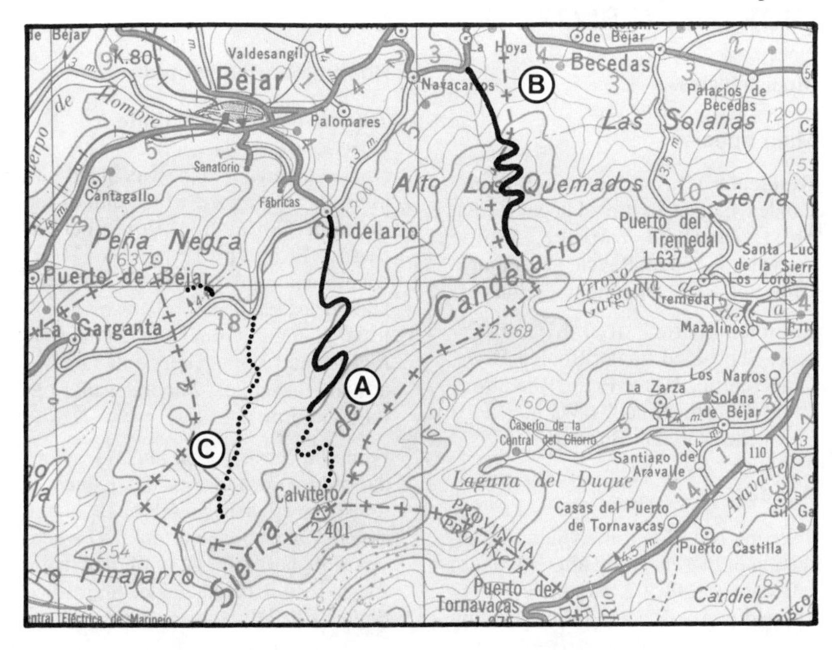

CL

area of woodland consisting of oak with pines on the high ground. It is a good spot for taking a walk and seeing a wide range of forest-dwelling species.

Another option is to continue along the road for some 800 m until you come to another road, this time closed with a chain. A 10-minute walk will bring you to the Béjar reservoir (also known as Navanuño), which you can walk around on a track, increasing the number of species seen.

Accommodation

Accommodation is available in both Béjar and Candelario. On the road climbing up the mountain range, at 1,650 m (La Plataforma), you will find a hotel-restaurant.

Raúl Bueno

■ CL.45 GREDOS RANGE (NORTHERN SLOPES)

Mountain area.

Main species

Residents: Griffon Vulture, Buzzard, Golden Eagle, Kestrel, Dipper, Goldcrest, Dartford Warbler, Alpine Accentor, Chough, Raven, Citril Finch, Crossbill, Rock Bunting.

Summer visitors: Red Kite, Black Kite, Short-toed Eagle, Booted Eagle, Crag Martin, Water Pipit, Bluethroat, Rock Thrush, Bonelli's Warbler, Pied Flycatcher, Ortolan Bunting.

Access

Take the N-110 out of Avila in the direction of Plasencia and after 4 km turn left onto the C-502. Continue for 47 km and you will come to the junction with the C-500. Here, turn right for the village of Hoyos del Espino (18 km). From this village, a road leads to the heart of the Gredos range.

Description

The Sierra de Gredos (Sistema Central) is a large granite massif presenting plenty of evidence of Quaternary glacial influence. Its maximum height is reached with the summit of Almanzor (2,592 m). Most of the northern slopes have been deforested and are now covered with dense scrubland consisting of broom, although there are some stands of pine and oak in the Tormes valley. It is worth pointing out that there is also a substantial population of Spanish ibex.

Despite various proposals for housing developments and skiing facilities, the Gredos area was declared a regional park by the Junta de Castilla-León (regional government body). Currently, the main threat to the area is posed by the large influx of visitors during the summer months.

Recommended routes

The starting point for **route A** is Navarredonda de la Sierra. The route crosses an area of pine woodland and joins up with a road which climbs the Sierra de Gredos from Hoyos del Espino. This road, in excellent conditions, will take you to the place known as La Plataforma, where you leave your car. From here, continue on foot to the Laguna Grande de Gredos, a small glacial lake 2 hours' walk from La Plataforma.

From the petrol station in Navarredonda, 5 km from Hoyos del Espino, a forestry road takes you through a large area of pine woodland (point 1) where you will have sightings of Red Kite, Black Kite, Booted Eagle, Short-toed Eagle, Citril Finch and Crossbill, as well as a wide variety of forest-dwelling species. The track continues through the interior of the pine wood, following the right bank of the river Tormes (2) where you will have no difficulty in seeing Dipper. It is worthwhile making the occasional stop on the road running up to La Plataforma (3) in order to see species typical of the broom covered slopes: Dunnock, Whitethroat, Dartford Warbler, Rock Bunting, Ortolan Bunting, etc.

To make the climb on foot, a track, paved to begin with, climbs up to Prado de las Pozas (4), an extensive area of meadows where Water Pipit abounds. After the meadows, you will cross a ravine by means of a bridge and begin the climb, through broom and rock fields, to Los Barrerones (5). En route you will see Bluethroat although you will have to keep a sharp lookout. Los Barrerones (2,150 m), some outcrops to the right, will provide an improvised vantage point allowing you to see the whole of the cirque and the Garganta de Gredos, a gorge. From here you will have no difficulty in seeing Golden Eagle, Griffon Vulture, Raven, Chough and Rock Thrush.

As you drop down to the Laguna Grande, watch out for Alpine Accentor which frequents the high parts of the cirque and the area surrounding the mountain refuge by the lake (6).

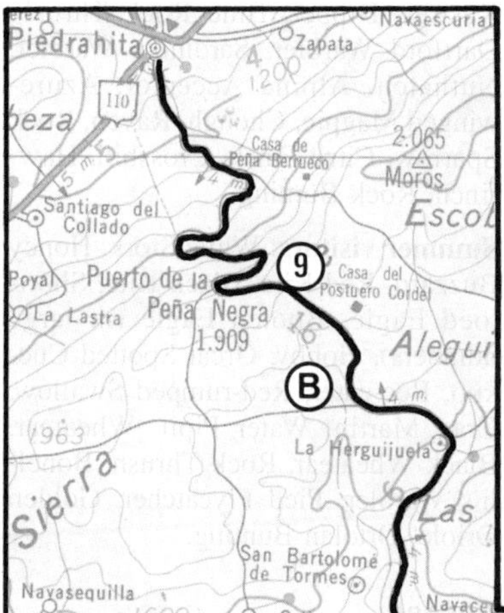

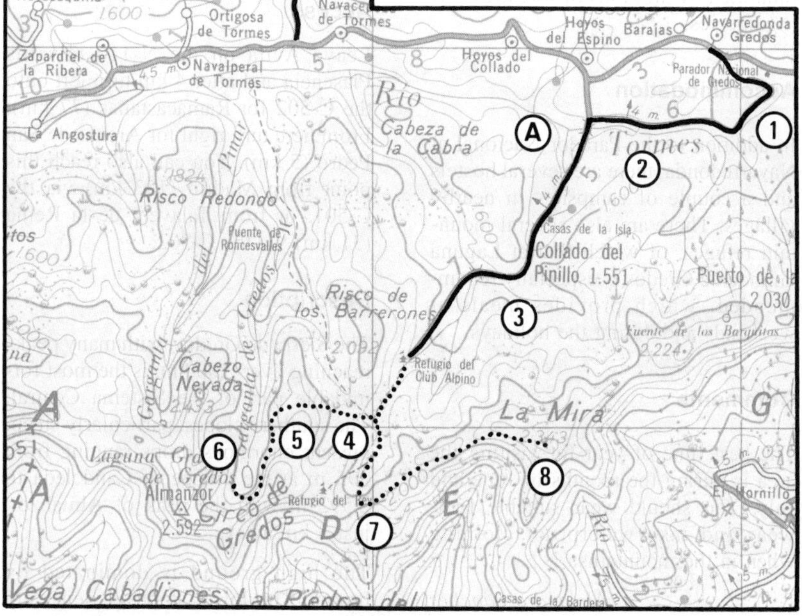

For those who are staying longer in the area, it is worth climbing the peak of Almanzor or alternatively going to the Cinco Lagunas cirque; both of these routes will take about 3 hours. An alternative route from La Plataforma is to go to the Candeleda pass (7) and from there up to the summit of La Mira (2,343 m) (8). The track is very easy and gives wonderful views over both sides of the range. Although excellent for seeing birds of prey, the route is longer (4 hours on the outward-bound journey) and you will have less chance of seeing Alpine Accentor.

Route B takes you up to the Peña Negra mountain pass (9) via the road joining Piedrahita with Navacepeda on the C-500, 8 km from Hoyos del Espino. At the top of the pass (1,909 m) expanses of broom are interspersed with alpine meadows where you may see Bluethroat, Rock Thrush and Water Pipit. The descent to Piedrahita takes you through dense woodland consisting of Pyrenean oak inhabited by all kinds of forest-dwelling species.

Accommodation

In addition to the Parador Nacional at Navarredonda, there are several hostels and a couple of campsites in nearby villages. There are also several mountain refuges, of which that at Laguna Grande de Gredos is especially recommended, which provides meals at weekends and during the holidays.

Comments

The best time of year for visiting the area is during the months of June and July. You should wear suitable footwear and take waterproof clothing when in the mountains.

Alejandro Sánchez

■ CL.46 GREDOS RANGE (SOUTHERN SLOPES)

Mountain area.

Main species

Residents: Griffon Vulture, Goshawk, Sparrowhawk, Buzzard, Golden Eagle, Kestrel, Dipper, Blue Rock Thrush, Dartford Warbler, Sardinian Warbler, Nuthatch, Alpine Accentor, Azure-winged Magpie, Chough, Raven, Rock Sparrow, Citril Finch, Crossbill, Hawfinch, Rock Bunting.

Summer visitors: White Stork, Honey Buzzard, Red Kite, Black Kite, Short-toed Eagle, Booted Eagle (in large numbers), Hobby, Great Spotted Cuckoo, Bee-eater, Red-rumped Swallow, Crag Martin, Water Pipit, Wheatear, Black Wheatear, Rock Thrush, Bonelli's Warbler, Pied Flycatcher, Golden Oriole, Ortolan Bunting.

Access

Leave Avila on the N-110 towards Plasencia and after 4 km turn left onto the C-502 for Ramacastañas (77 km). From here turn right for Arenas de San Pedro (5 km). You can also reach this point from Madrid (153 km) via the C-501, or from Talavera de la Reina (31 km) via the C-502.

Description

The Sierra de Gredos, with many peaks reaching over 2,000 m, is the most formidable part of the Sistema Central. The southern slopes, particularly steep, present enormous drops ranging from 395 m at the village of Candeleda to 2,592 m with the peak of Almanzor, just 3 km away.

The high ground is dominated by broom. The lower slopes, extensively deforested on the western half of this section of the range, are elsewhere covered with dense pine woodland.

Much of the area is a Regional Park.

Recommended routes

Route A consists of a drive up to the El Pico pass (1,352 m). Leave Arenas de San Pedro and drive to Ramacastañas, from where you take the road towards Avila. As you approach the village of Mombeltrán, you will see terracing where olive trees, vines, cherry trees and chestnut trees are cultivated and you may see Hawfinch, Azure-winged Magpie, Jay, Nuthatch, etc. Just after the village of Cuevas del Valle, on a very sharp bend, a surfaced track leads off to the left for El Arenal and El Hornillo. This track leads through a substantial area of pine woodland where a walk will enable you to see numerous forest-dwelling passerines, as well as Booted Eagle, Short-toed Eagle, Hobby, Goshawk, Sparrowhawk and Buzzard.

Back on the main road, continue to the Pico pass where you can leave your car and go for a walk through the meadows and broom covered slopes of the area. You may see Rock Thrush, Rock Bunting, Ortolan Bunting, Bluethroat, Wheatear and Dartford Warbler. The eastern side of the pass, much steeper, is a good place for spotting Spanish ibex.

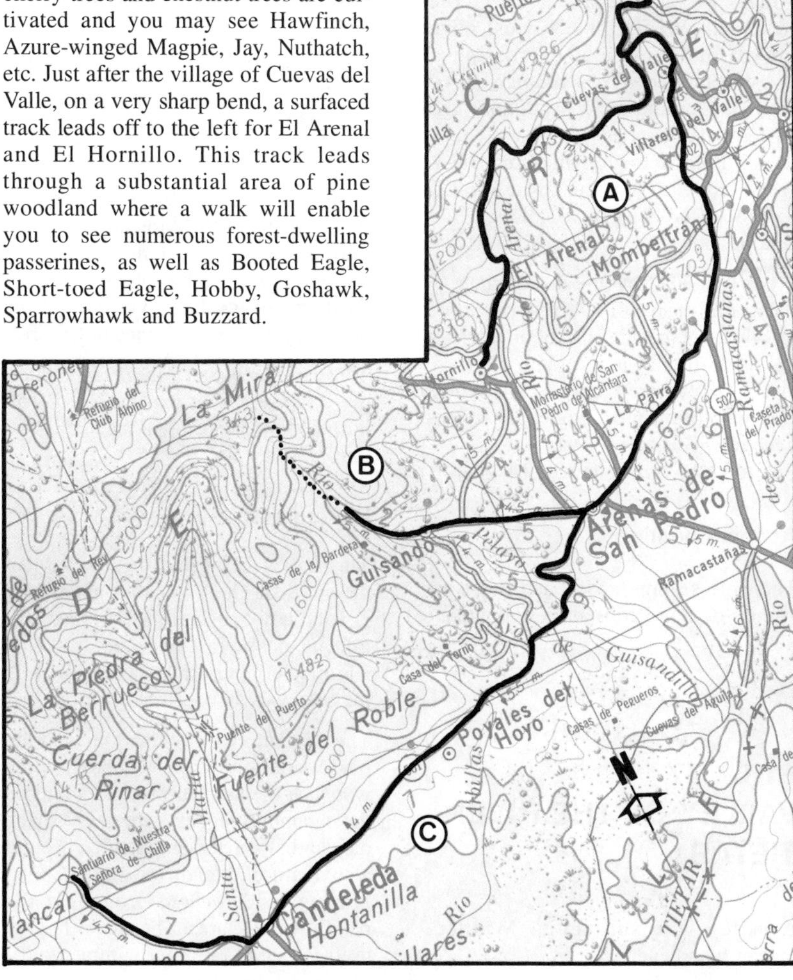

CL

Route B starts in Arenas de San Pedro and climbs up, via the village of Guisando, to El Nogal del Barranco, a large roundabout where you can leave your car. From here a path takes you into the mountains towards Los Galayos. Go as far along this path as you wish, bearing in mind that to return you will be retracing your steps. The high ground is a good place for spotting Golden Eagle, Griffon Vulture, Rock Thrush, Blue Rock Thrush and Alpine Accentor.

Route C consists of a car journey from Arenas to Candeleda (30 Km). The road runs through pine woods, olive groves and fields, also crossing a couple of river gorges running down from the mountain. Throughout the route, make a series of optional stops to see Booted Eagle, Buzzard, Black Kite, Red Kite, Hoopoe, Great Spotted Cuckoo, Red-rumped Swallow, Crag Martin and Azure-winged Magpie.

From Candeleda you can continue to the nearby chapel of La Virgen de Chilla, where there is a substantial patch of oak woodland surrounded by hayfields. Here you may see Honey Buzzard, Short-toed Eagle, Pied Flycatcher, Bonelli's Warbler, Rock Sparrow and Azure-winged Magpie.

Accommodation

There are several hostels and hotels in Arenas de San Pedro and Candeleda.

Angel Gómez Manzaneque

■ CL.47 VALLEY OF THE RIVER TIÉTAR

A valley with substantial Mediterranean woodland.

Main species

Residents: Cattle Egret, Grey Heron, Black Stork, Black-shouldered Kite, Griffon Vulture, Black Vulture, Spanish Imperial Eagle, Golden Eagle, Peregrine Falcon, Stone Curlew, Eagle Owl, Azure-winged Magpie, Spanish Sparrow.

Summer visitors: Little Egret, White Stork, Honey Buzzard, Black Kite, Egyptian Vulture, Short-toed Eagle, Montagu's Harrier, Booted Eagle, Hobby, Great Spotted Cuckoo, Red-necked Nightjar, Bee-eater, Roller, Black-eared Wheatear.

Winter visitors: Cormorant, Red Kite, Crane.

Access

From San Martín de Valdeiglesias, take the C-501 to Santa María del Tiétar (15 km), the first village in the valley. This road runs for 85 km along the right hand side of the Tiétar valley until the boundary with the province of Cáceres.

You can reach San Martín de Valdeiglesias from Avila via the N-403 (59 km) or from Madrid, via the C-501 (68 km).

Description

This valley is located to the south of the Sierra de Gredos, and its geography is relatively uneventful. The most significant peaks rise to some 1,200 m, while other landforms, largely isolated massifs, vary between 500 and 700 m.

The predominant vegetation is holm oak woodland with extensive pine woods at the head of the valley and on the mountain slopes, where Pyrenean oak and, to a lesser extent, chestnut also feature. Meadows and wooded grazing land (*dehesa*) complete the plant life in the area. The area is largely used for stock farming, with a significant proportion of income coming from forestry.

Fires, increasingly more frequent, pose the largest threat to the area. Another threat is the project for the construction of a new road from Ramacastañas to Candeleda, which would cut cross an unspoiled area of great importance for birds and other vertebrates.

Recommended routes

Route A is a car journey 17 km long, lasting about 2 hours. It begins in the village of La Adrada, where you take the minor road for La Iglesuela; it runs through an area of pine wood and brings you to the river Tiétar (point 1), where you will have sightings of Egyptian Vulture, Black Kite, Griffon Vulture, Black Vulture, Hobby, Dipper and Kingfisher. Continuing along the road, the pine woodland progressively gives way to holm oak woodland (2) where you may see Booted Eagle, Short-toed Eagle, Bee-eater and Azure-winged Magpie. At the crossroads take the turning for Casavieja and continue until you cross the river Tiétar again, the end of the route. At this point (3) you should have sightings of White Stork, Black Stork, Grey Heron and, at the right time of year, the pre-breeding migration of Greylag Goose and Crane.

Route B is 18 km long and takes 2½ hours. The starting point is the village of Casavieja, where the church and town hall are the sites of various storks' nests. From here, take the minor road for Mijares and Gavilanes, which runs through the pine woodland on the skirts of the range and takes you through numerous gorges and riverbeds. Make stops at will to see many forest-dwelling species as well as Golden Eagle, vultures, Peregrine Falcon, Short-toed Eagle and the occasional Honey Buzzard. Back on the main road (4), you will have sightings of Cattle Egret, Booted Eagle, Great Spotted Cuckoo and Azure-winged Magpie.

The starting point for **route C** is the village of Ramacastañas, from where a track leads off to Las Cuevas del Aguila, passing through an area of holm oak woodland where you will see numerous birds of prey including Spanish Imperial Eagle, Black Kite, Booted Eagle and Short-toed Eagle. You may also see Roller, Bee-eater, Great Spotted Cuckoo, Red-necked Nightjar and Azure-winged Magpie. At Las Cuevas del Aguila, caves which you

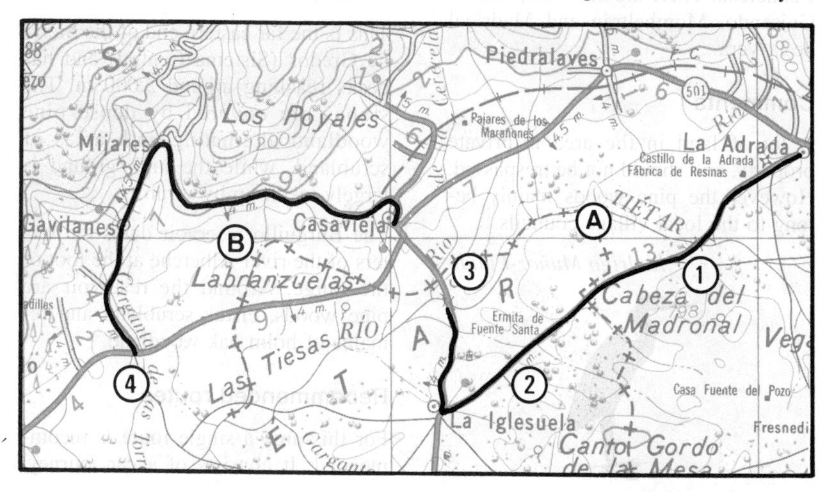

CL

can visit if you wish, park your vehicle and walk down to the river Tiétar, where you may have sightings of Black Stork, Little Egret, Grey Heron, Cattle Egret, Cormorant and Red-rumped Swallow. The route is about 7 km long and will take 1½ hours to complete, without including a visit to the caves (Cuevas del Aguila).

Accommodation

Although in general terms accommodation is scarce, the considerable number of villages in the valley makes up for this lack. Look in the larger villages such as Arenas de San Pedro, Piedralaves, Sotillo de la Adrada and Candeleda. There are also campsites in Guisando, Mombeltrán and Madrigal de la Vera.

Comments

A lot of land in the area is private property, and should not be trespassed. However the pine woods mainly belong to the local village councils.

Rodrigo Muñoz-Pulido

CL.48 EL TIEMBLO

A mountain area with dense pine woods and reservoir.

Main species

Residents: Red Kite, Black Vulture, Stock Dove, Dipper, Black Wheatear, Dartford Warbler, Azure-winged Magpie, Spanish Sparrow, Rock Sparrow, Cirl Bunting, Rock Bunting.

Summer visitors: Honey Buzzard, Black Kite, Short-toed Eagle, Booted Eagle, Red-rumped Swallow, Black-eared Wheatear, Rock Thrush, Melodious Warbler, Subalpine Warbler, Orphean Warbler, Whitethroat, Bonelli's Warbler.

On passage: Greylag Goose, Crane, Woodpigeon.

Access

From Avila, take the N-403 towards Toledo and turn off at El Tiemblo (46 km). The village can also be reached from Madrid via San Martín de Valdeiglesias (C-501 and C-500).

Description

This is the far eastern end of the Sierra de Gredos (Sistema Central) and has peaks reaching around 2,000 m. The slopes are covered by dense pine woodland alternating with areas of scrubland, while the high ground is largely taken up by scrub.

The Burguillo reservoir dams the waters of the river Alberche at the foot of the range. Around the reservoir are pine woods, cistus scrubland and remains of holm oak woodland.

Recommended routes

For this area a single route is recommended. It consists of a car journey,

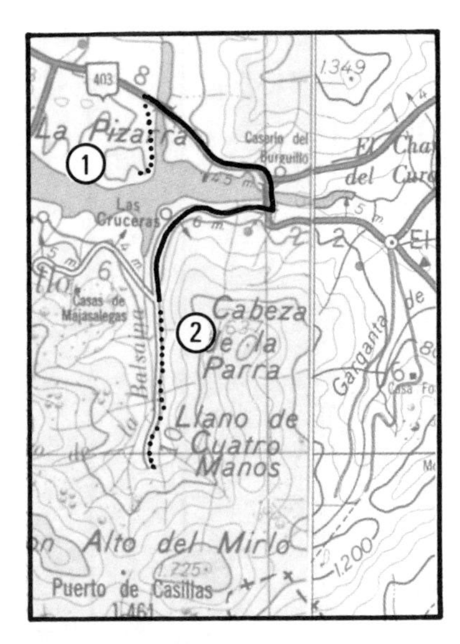

and the main points of interest are the following:

1) Burguillo reservoir. As soon as the N-403 starts to run around the artificial lake, find a place to park your car and walk down to the shore. You will see various warblers and Black Wheatear in the surrounding shrubs and granite outcrops.

2) Iruelas valley. Just on the other side of the dam a road runs off to the right, taking you to the forestry house of Las Cruceras. Leave your car at the house and walk along a road, which subsequently becomes a track, taking you to the Casillas mountain pass. You can make this walk as long as you wish. The track runs for its length through pine woods where you will see Black Vulture and other birds of prey, as well as a wide range of forest-dwelling species.

Accommodation

There are several hotels in El Tiemblo and San Martín de Valdeiglesias. There is also an area in the Iruelas valley where camping is permitted.

Comments

You are requested not to stray off the track in the Iruelas valley.

It is also worthwhile visiting the nearby area of Toros de Guisando, close to San Martín de Valdeiglesias, which is a site of historic interest. Near Toros there is also an area of riverside vegetation.

César San Segundo Ontín

CATALONIA

Audouin's Gull
Larus audouinii

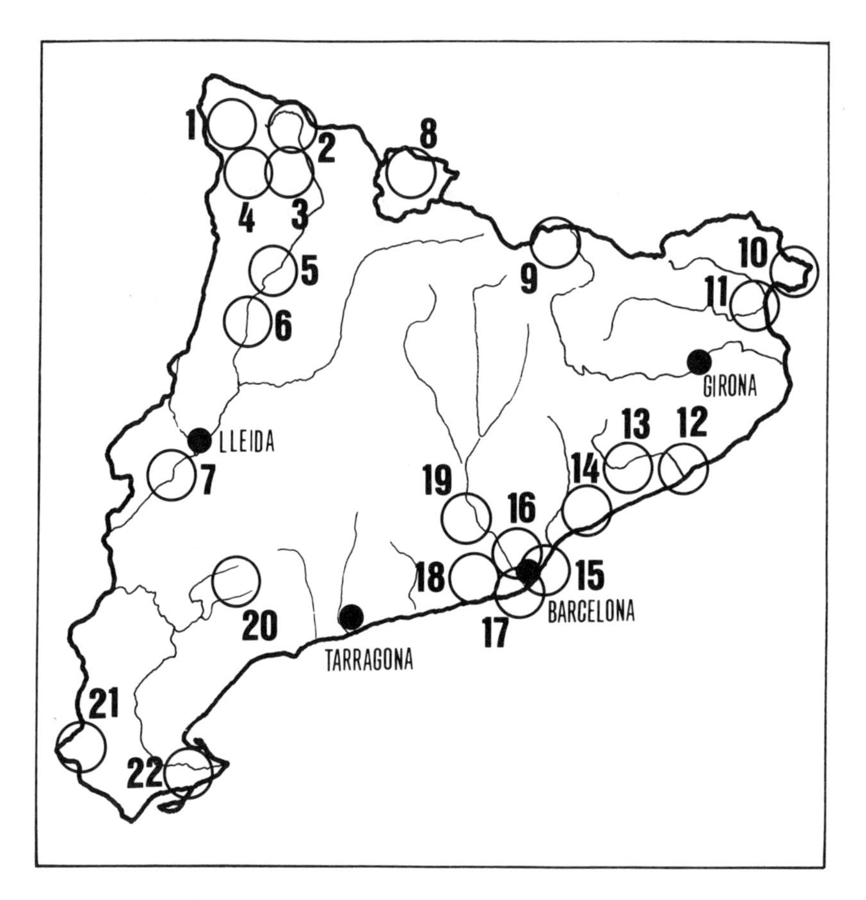

The relatively small area occupied by Catalonia offers the naturalist a remarkable variety of habitats with corresponding birdlife. In addition to the interesting transition between the Central European and Mediterranean climates habitual in northern Spain, we also find, in close proximity, high Pyrenean mountain areas, coastal areas, steppe areas and wetland areas, including in this latter category an area of exceptional size and wealth, the delta of the river Ebro. All of this gives rise to a remarkably large quantity of nesting species, unequalled in any other area of Spain. Geographical and ecological conditions are also very favourable in terms of migration and wintering. However, it should be pointed out that human presence in Catalonia is very marked, as is industrial activity. A lot of hunting takes place, and mass tourism swamps the beaches and mountains during the summer months, a factor which, while making for good accommodation and road networks, is frequently troublesome. However Catalonia does not lack isolated places and rugged landscapes and, taken as a whole, there is no doubt that this part of the Iberian Peninsula gets full recommendations as an ornithological site.

In the Catalan Pyrenees all the high mountain birdlife present in the

Aragonese Pyrenees can also be seen, including Ptarmigan, Wallcreeper, Alpine Accentor, Alpine Chough and Snow Finch among other unusual alpine species, and Capercaillie, Tengmalm's Owl, Black Woodpecker, Ring Ouzel, Goldcrest, Citril Finch and Siskin are the main attractions of the subalpine pine woods. Highest altitudes occur on the boundary with the region of Aragon. In this area the sites offering the best possibilities are the following; Aran valley (CA.1), Puerto de La Bonaigua mountain pass (CA.2) and the Aigüestortes and Sant Maurici National Park (CA.3 and CA.4). Slightly to the east is the principality of Andorra (CA.8), the Cadí mountain range and the Freser valley (CA.9), which are also very interesting and, in addition, may be more accessible to the traveller.

At various altitudes in the Pyrenees nearly all of the species typical of northern Spain can be found; Honey Buzzard, Grey Partridge, Woodcock, Tree Pipit, Whinchat, Marsh Tit, Treecreeper, Red-backed Shrike, Bullfinch, Yellowhammer. In the woodland of the Aran valley you may also see Lesser and Middle Spotted Woodpecker. These species are usually also to be found in the foothills of the Pyrenees, where they overlap with many Mediterranean species such as Bee-eater, Thekla Lark, Blue Rock Thrush, Subalpine Warbler and Sardinian Warbler. The foothills of the Pyrenees falling within the province of Lleida present impressive ravines and cliff faces (Boumort, CA.5; Montsec, CA.6), making for sightings of cliff-dwelling species seldom seen in Catalonia as a whole, such as Bearded Vulture, Egyptian Vulture, Griffon Vulture and Chough.

To the south of these mountains is a broad section of the Ebro basin, lying around the city of Lleida (Lérida). The area is semi-arid, although the plentiful waters of the river Segre have allowed for the development of extensive irrigation systems where you can see much of the birdlife also present in central Aragon such as White Stork, Black Kite, Roller and Penduline Tit among other representative birds. In the villages, it is interesting to see how Starling and Spotless Starling, both new arrivals in this area of Spain, breed side by side. This area is also the only site in Catalonia of a habitat very characteristic of the Iberian Peninsula as a whole, the large plains occupied by dry-farming cereal crops and the typical steppe-dwelling birdlife associated with such a habitat: Montagu's Harrier, Little Bustard, Stone Curlew, Pin-tailed Sandgrouse, Dupont's Lark, Calandra Lark, etc. (Lleida, CA.7). Modern-day intensification of agricultural activity has caused the interest held by this area to diminish considerably, making it perhaps more worthwhile to visit the nearby steppe near the river Cinca (AR.25) or Los Monegros (AR.28), in the neighbouring region of Aragon. However, you may nonetheless come across the rare Lesser Grey Shrike.

Moving on to the coastal area of Catalonia, in the far northeast of the Empordà (Ampurdán) region (province of Girona) you will have the last opportunity of seeing Lesser Grey Shrike in the Iberian Peninsula and a second chance in Catalonia to see species inhabiting open spaces such as Montagu's Harrier, Stone Curlew, Roller, Short-toed Lark and Spectacled Warbler (CA.10 and CA.11). Other coastal regions of Catalonia generally present more rugged terrain and greater tree cover consisting largely of pine woods and occasionally of holm oak and cork oak woodland. This gives rise to large numbers of forest-dwelling birds of prey such as Buzzard, Goshawk, Sparrowhawk and Tawny Owl. Wryneck and Redstart are also present, both of which require a habitat with mature woodland. Near Barcelona, the city's parks (CA.15), the Marina range (CA.13), the Collserola suburban park (CA.16) and the Montserrat mountain range (CA.19) allow for sightings of these species and others belonging to Mediterranean woodland areas such as Great Spotted Cuckoo, Red-necked Nightjar, Woodlark, Melodious Warbler, Subalpine Warbler, Orphean Warbler, Bonelli's Warbler, Woodchat Shrike or Cirl Bunting. Also close to Barcelona is the massif of El Garraf (CA.18), a good example of coastal limestone mountains which are drier, more bare and abounding in ravines and cliffs, making them suitable for species such as Bonelli's Eagle, Eagle Owl, Thekla Lark, Crag Martin, Tawny Pipit, Black Wheatear, Rock Thrush, Blue Rock Thrush, Dartford Warbler, Great Grey Shrike, Rock Sparrow and Ortolan Bunting. Similar species are present in the many ranges of hills and mountains in the province of Tarragona including Montsant moutain range (CA.20) and Tortosa–Besceit (CA.21), these latter being spurs of the Maestrazgo mountains.

Logically enough, the coastline gives rise to sightings of sea birds. On the Costa Brava and other areas with cliffs you will be able to see many Yellow-legged Gull and, in specific places, Shag, which breed on the cliffs in the company of Pallid Swift, Blue Rock Thrush and Raven. Wintering and migratory species, many of which are present year round, include Black-throated Diver, Red-throated Diver, Cory's Shearwater, Yelkouan Shearwater, Storm Petrel, Gannet, Cormorant, Eider, Common Scoter, Velvet Scoter, Arctic Skua, Mediterranean Gull, Little Gull, Audouin's Gull, Lesser Black-backed Gull, Sandwich Tern, Razorbill and Puffin, some of which use the open waters of the Golfo de León as an important over-wintering site. The capes of Creus and Norfeu (CA.10), the l'Estartit headland off which the Medes islands lie, the breakwaters of the harbours at Arenys de Mar (CA.14) and Barcelona (CA.15), and the outermost points of the deltas of the rivers Llobregat (CA.17) and Ebro (CA.22) are all highly recommended sites.

The four wetland areas selected all have different characteristics. The Utxesa reservoir (CA.7) is the only inland area and has extensive reedbeds. The delta of the river Llobregat (CA.17) is interesting because of its close proximity to the city of Barcelona. At the Aiguamolls de l'Empordà (CA.11), an intelligent scheme for the recovery of the habitat and the establishing of several hides has optimized a series of small coastal lakes and marshes where some of the most interesting species include Bittern, Glossy Ibis (in winter), Garganey (nesting), Purple Gallinule (reintroduced) and Moustached Warbler. Finally, the Delta del Ebro (CA.22) is one of the largest and best wetland areas in the Mediterranean, competing in terms of interest with the delta of the river Danube, the Camargue or the Marismas del Guadalquivir (Coto Doñana). During the breeding season the number and variety of herons present in the Ebro delta is remarkable (no less than eight nesting species including Bittern and Squacco Heron); there are also ducks (Shelduck, Gadwall, Red-crested Pochard), waders (Oystercatcher, Black-winged Stilt, Avocet, Collared Pratincole, Kentish Plover, Redshank) and above all gulls and terns, with a dozen species including Slender-billed Gull, Audouin's Gull (the largest colony in the world), Lesser Black-backed Gull (only colony in the Mediterranean) and Sandwich Tern (only nesting population in the Iberian Peninsula). Interesting passerines include Lesser Short-toed Lark, Savi's Warbler, Moustached Warbler, Bearded Tit and Reed Bunting. In winter the number of water birds present is remarkable (Cormorant, grebes, herons, ducks, Coot, gulls, stints, plovers, godwits...), reaching over 200,000 individuals at times. During the spring and autumn migrations a huge variety of species can be seen, particularly waders.

A last word on Catalonia in general terms: its location in the far northeast of Spain makes it more likely than in other areas of Spain that you will see migrating species of a more eastern distribution such as Glossy Ibis, Great White Egret, Red-footed Falcon, Marsh Sandpiper, White-winged Black Tern and Red-throated Pipit.

CA.1 BARICAUBA – ARTIGA DE LIN (ARAN VALLEY)

A mountain area with substantial forests.

Main species

Residents: Golden Eagle, Capercaillie, Black Woodpecker, Goldcrest, Marsh Tit, Treecreeper.

Summer visitors: Bearded Vulture, Griffon Vulture.

Access

Vielha (Viella), the village lying at the head of the Aran valley, is the departure point for visiting this area.

Description

The Aran valley is broad and the only valley in the Spanish Pyrenees lying on the northern slopes of the range. The climate is Atlantic, giving rise to woods of beech and silver fir, of which the wood at Baricauba is a good example.

Recommended routes

The route recommended here is a car journey. Leave Vielha in the direction of Gausac, where a surfaced track crosses the Baricauba silver fir woods. When you reach the track taking you to es Bòrdes, keep to the bank of the river Joeu until you reach the era Artiga de Lin mountain refuge, the finishing point of the route.

You can make stops anywhere along the way to take a walk and see Black Woodpecker, Goldcrest, Treecreeper and other forest-dwelling species.

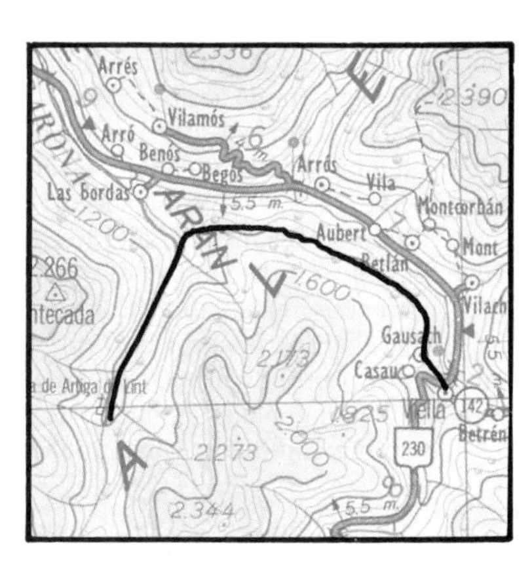

Accommodation

There is plenty of accommodation available in the form of hotels and campsites in Vielha and other nearby villages.

Comments

The best time of year for visiting the area is from late May to October.

Jordi Canut and Diego García

CA.2 BERET – BONAIGUA

High mountain area.

Main species

Residents: Bearded Vulture, Golden Eagle, Capercaillie, Black Woodpecker, Water Pipit, Goldcrest, Treecreeper, Alpine Accentor.

Summer visitors: Griffon Vulture.

Access

From Tremp, take the C-147 towards Vielha and stop in Esterri d'Aneu (78 km).

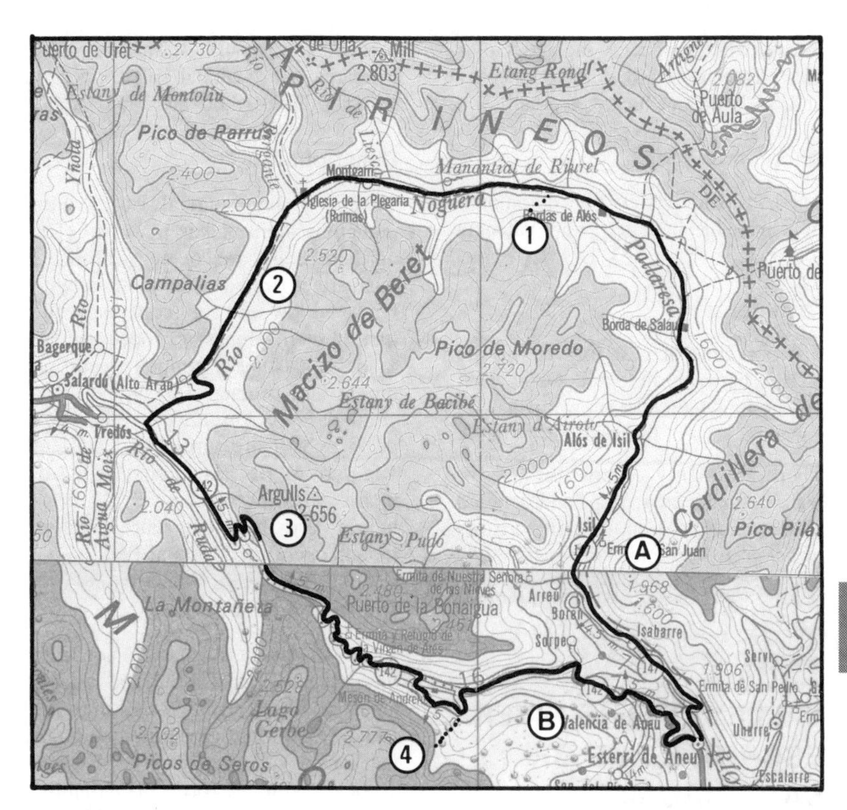

Description

The Beret-Bonaigua area is a part of the spine of the Pyrenees, constituting the dividing line between the Mediterranean slopes and the Atlantic slopes, in parts reaching 2,700-2,800 m. The main habitats consist of subalpine woodland with silver fir and pine and, on the high ground, alpine meadows.

Recommended routes

Route A is a trip for which a four-wheel drive vehicle is required. Begin in Esterri d'Aneu, where you take the minor road to Borén, Isil and Alós d'Isil, from where you continue along a forestry road climbing up to the source of the river Noguera Pallaresa. Having passed a cluster of houses (on the edge of Isil), the track crosses the river and ascends through woodland consisting of silver fir and mountain pine (1). By walking in this area you may see Black Woodpecker and even Capercaillie. The climb brings you out by Plan de Beret (2), where the track joins the road for Vaquèira (Baqueira). In Vaquèira join the C-147 taking you to the mountain pass of Bonaigua (3). These last two points make for good sightings of Griffon Vulture, Water Pipit and Alpine Accentor.

Route B takes you along the C-147 from Esterri d'Aneu to the Bonaigua mountain pass. After passing the Hotel Los Abetos, the road crosses a bridge and passes into the wood known as La Mata de València. Leave your car on the first bend to the right (4) and walk into the middle of this wonderful area of silver fir where you should see forest-dwelling species such as Goldcrest, Treecreeper, Black Woodpecker and, with a lot of luck, Capercaillie.

Accommodation

There is a wide variety of accommodation available in Esterri and València d'Aneu.

Comments

The best time of year for visiting the area is between June and October. If you go in winter, take snow chains and check the state of the roads beforehand.

There are plenty of possibilities for walking in the area. Maps and detailed guides can be obtained in various places in Esterri and Sort.

Jordi Canut and Diego García

■ CA.3 VALLEY OF THE RIVER ESCRITA (LAKE OF SANT MAURICI)

A high mountain area.

Main species

Residents: Bearded Vulture, Golden Eagle, Ptarmigan, Capercaillie, Black Woodpecker, Dipper, Goldcrest, Firecrest, Alpine Chough, Chough, Raven, Citril Finch, Siskin, Crossbill.

Summer visitors: Griffon Vulture, Woodcock, Crag Martin, Water Pipit, Grey Wagtail, Dunnock, Alpine Accentor, Ring Ouzel, Marsh Tit, Wallcreeper, Bullfinch, Rock Bunting.

Access

Take the C-147 to Llavorsí and the reservoir of La Guingueta from where, beside the dam, a road runs up to Espot. As you enter the village of Espot you will see a small information centre (the area is a National Park), open in summer 09:00-13:00 and 16:00-20:00.

Description

This is a steep glacial valley with numerous alpine lakes (*estanys*). The northern slopes are covered with Scots pine, silver fir and mountain pine with birch, willow and service trees, while the southern slopes are occupied by moors consisting of juniper, alpenrose, broom and heather. The alpine areas abound in rock screes, needles and peaks which are virtually devoid of vegetation. Els Encantats, two immense outcrops reaching 2,747 m in height, are the most representative mountains of the National Park.

Recommended routes

The route consists of an excursion from the village of Espot. From the village, a surfaced road takes you 8 km to the lake of Sant Maurici via the bottom of the glacial valley of the river Escrita. To begin with, the road runs along the valley sides, which are covered with Scots pine, beside the river and through meadows bordered with shrubs and birch where you may see Yellowhammer and Whinchat. After 3 km you will enter a lush wood of silver fir just before the entrance to the National Park. Apart from many forest-dwelling passerines, you may also see Black Woodpecker. The upper areas of woodland are occupied by Capercaillie, Woodcock and Tengmalm's Owl, species as interesting as they are difficult to see.

The Estany de Sant Maurici, a lake, is a popular place in summer, but in the early morning or at dusk it is a good spot for watching birds. The Pui Pla mountain range, lying to the north of the lake, is one of the best places for watching Bearded Vulture, Golden Eagle and Griffon Vulture. From the

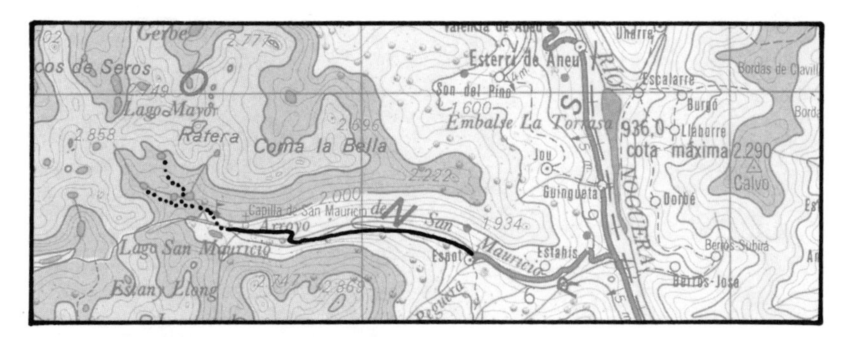

lake continue along a forest track to the *estanys* of Ratera and Amitges. On the way, you will have no difficulty in seeing Crested Tit, Citril Finch, Crossbill and the occasional Siskin. You will come across an old barracks belonging to the Guardia Civil, after which the woodland opens out. At a height of 2,100 m, the track crosses a mountain stream and shortly after this you will come to the Ratera lake, where you should not fail to take the time to watch birds typical of subalpine woodland, including Capercaillie. The surrounding peaks are frequented by Chough, Alpine Chough, and large birds of prey.

Continue along the path to reach Las Basses de Ratera, a former lake which has now silted up; near this lake you may see Ring Ouzel. A turning for Estany la Munyidera, another lake, is on the left, but continue up a steep slope to reach the lakes at Amitges, in the middle of a completely alpine landscape. There is a mountain refuge at Amitges where you can sleep. Near the refuge you will see chamois as well as Water Pipit, Alpine Accentor and Ptarmigan.

Accommodation

There are plenty of hostels in Espot, as well as some private houses which rent rooms. Meals can be had at Casa Palmira, Restaurant Juquim, Hostal Saurat, Hostal Sant Maurici and Hostal Roya. Once within the park area, you can only camp at selected mountain refuges (Ernest Mallafré, Sant Maurici and Amitges). However, there are 2 campsites in Espot and others in La Guingueta and Esterri.

Comments

The best time of year for watching birds in this area is mid May to early July. In summer it is worthwhile keeping away from popular places and starting out on your trips early in the morning. In winter, the road to Sant Maurici is blocked by snow, making for an interesting walk along the road. However, you should take adequate clothing and equipment for walking in snow.

The address of the park is: Parc Nacional d'Aigüestortes i Estany de Sant Maurici; Camp de Mart, 35; 25004 Lleida.

Oriol Alamany

■ CA.4 SANT NICOLAU VALLEY (AIGÜESTORTES)

High mountain area.

Main species

Residents: Bearded Vulture, Golden Eagle, Black Woodpecker, Goldcrest,

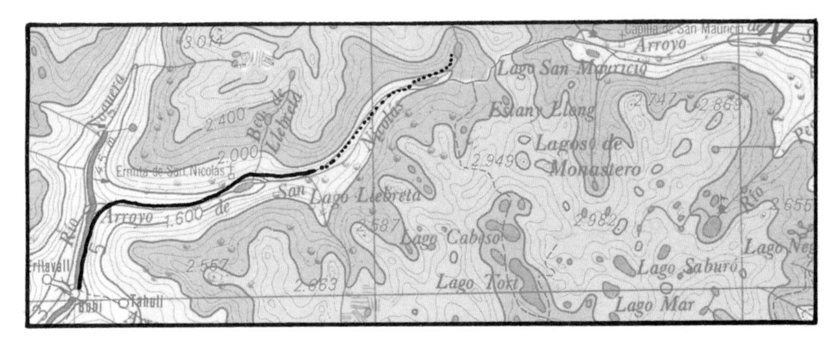

Crested Tit, Dipper, Alpine Chough, Chough, Raven, Citril Finch, Siskin, Crossbill.

Summer visitors: Griffon Vulture, Woodcock, Crag Martin, Dunnock, Whinchat, Black Redstart, Ring Ouzel, Nuthatch, Red-backed Shrike, Bullfinch, Rock Bunting.

Access

From Pont de Suert on the N-230, head in the direction of the Aran valley and after 3 km turn right for Caldes de Boí. Less than 1 km from the turning for Erill-la-vall a road leads off to the right for Boí, the departure point for the route. There is a small information centre (belonging to the National Park) in the village square where you can obtain maps and guides.

Description

A high mountain valley lying on the spine of the Pyrenees. The valley is completely unspoiled and presents glacial features with abundant mountain streams, alpine lakes and peat bogs. The lower part of the valley is taken up by hay fields and small stands of deciduous woodland. The middle part is taken up by subalpine woodland consisting of Scots pine, beech, birch, silver fir and mountain pine with undergrowth of alpenrose and blaeberry, replaced on the southern slopes by moors consisting of juniper, bearberry, alpenrose and broom. The high ground is dominated by alpine meadows, rock screes and peaks. Portarró de Espot, a pass at 2,423 m, links the head of this valley to that of the Escrita or Sant Maurici valley (CA.3).

Recommended routes

The starting point of the route is a couple of kilometres north of Boí, from where a forestry track ascends to the National Park (5 km). The climb up the valley of Sant Nicolau runs through meadows and stands of trees where, among other species, you will see Garden Warbler, Golden Oriole, Red-backed Shrike and Yellowhammer. Just as you come into the park, at 1,600 m, you will see the *estany* or lake of la Llebreta, surrounded by flooded meadows. The shore farthest from the road is occupied by mixed woodland consisting of beech, aspen, birch, silver fir and mountain pine (Bosc de Llacs). The road snakes up to the *Pla* of Aigüestortes, a former lake which silted up and turned into a small plain. The river runs across this plain via a series of channels, leaving islands where silver fir and mountain pine grow. Among the many forest species present are Goshawk, Black Woodpecker, Mistle Thrush, Chiffchaff, Goldcrest, Marsh Tit, Crested Tit, Nuthatch and Citril Finch. The river will give rise to sightings of Dipper and, on the rugged slopes and cliffs rising up to the left of the road, you will see Bearded Vulture, Griffon Vulture, Golden Eagle, Kestrel and Raven, as well as the occasional chamois.

If you have time, continue along the forestry road until you reach the *Pla* of Aigües d'Ací, the site of another silted lake. Here you will see species typical of subalpine woodland, including Ring Ouzel. On the far side of the plain the climb up to the *estany* or lake of Llong begins; this takes you through an area of mountain pine to a height of 1,980 m.

Accommodation

There are plenty of hostels and restaurants in the Boí valley, particularly in Boí and Erill-la-vall, although you may have difficulty in finding vacancies in summer. It is forbidden to camp inside the park, but there is a campsite at Barruera (Camping Boneta) and, next to the Llong lake, a mountain refuge.

Comments

The best time of year for visiting the area is from late May to early July. In summer, the presence of thousands of visitors makes it difficult to spot birds, making it advisable to set out early in the morning and stay away from the most frequented routes. It is recommended that you wear walking boots and take waterproof clothing. There are frequent summer thunderstorms.

The address of the park is: Parc Nacional d'Aigüestortes i Estany de Sant Maurici; Camp de Mart, 35; 25004 Lleida.

Oriol Alamany

■ CA.5 BOUMORT

Mountain area.

Main species

Residents: Bearded Vulture, Griffon Vulture, Golden Eagle, Peregrine Falcon.

Summer visitors: Egyptian Vulture, Short-toed Eagle, Bee-eater.

Access

From Tremp, take the C-147 to la Pobla de Segur (14 km). From there take the minor road to Hortoneda, Aramunt, Sant Martí de Canals and Pessonada (9 km).

Description

The Boumort mountain range is a limestone massif forming part of the area known as the Prepirineo, the foothills of the Pyrenees. The terrain is extremely rugged, abounding in rocky cliffs. There is a dramatic drop in altitudes between the valley bottoms and the peaks, making for differences of over 1,500 m. This feature, in combination with the fact that the slopes face in several different directions, gives rise to a wide variety of both Mediterranean and Central European habitats.

Recommended routes

You can walk from the village of Pessonada to the boundary fence of the

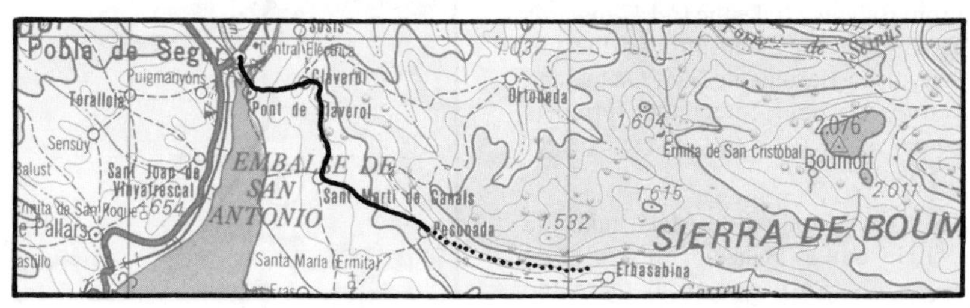

Restricted Hunting Area (Zona de Caza Controlada) in some 2½ hours; although this route can be undertaken in a four-wheel drive vehicle it is preferable to do it on foot. The route runs for its length along the lower edge of a large rockface where you will have sightings of Griffon Vulture, Bearded Vulture, Egyptian Vulture, Golden Eagle, Peregrine Falcon and other cliff-dwelling species.

Accommodation

There are several hostels, *fondas* and a campsite in Tremp and la Pobla de Segur.

Comments

Camping is forbidden within the Restricted Hunting Area (Zona de Caza Controlada).

Jordi Canut and Diego García

■ CA.6 MONTSEC

Mountain area.

Main species

Residents: Bearded Vulture, Griffon Vulture, Golden Eagle, Peregrine Falcon.

Summer visitors: Egyptian Vulture, Short-toed Eagle, Bee-eater.

Access

From Balaguer, take the C-147 towards Tremp. Having gone through the village of La Baronia de Sant Oïsme and before the road enters the Terradets gorge, turn left for the village of Ager (35 km).

To reach Vilanova de Meià, take the C-1313 out of Balaguer to Artesa de Segre (24 km), and from there the C-131 towards Tremp. After 8 km turn left onto the road for Alentorn, Gàrzola and Vilanova de Meià (12 km).

Description

A limestone massif lying in the Prepirineo area, the foothills of the Pyrenees. The massif reaches its maximum height with Puig Mirapallars (1,684 m). The rivers Noguera Pallaresa and Noguera Ribagorçana cross the range, cutting deep gorges and separating the three mountains making up the range.

The terrain is generally very rugged with drops varying between 800 and 1,000 m. The southern side of the range forms a virtually uninterrupted cliff, while the northern side presents relatively gentle slopes. Although small areas of beech and oak woodland are present, vegetation is predominantly Mediterranean.

Recommended routes

Route A has its starting point in Ager, where you take the path for Santa Lis and coll d'Ares. Leave your car at coll d'Ares and walk westwards along the crest of the range. This walk, lasting 1½ hours, will give you a fantastic view of the Pyrenees as well as sightings of cliff-dwelling birds of prey.

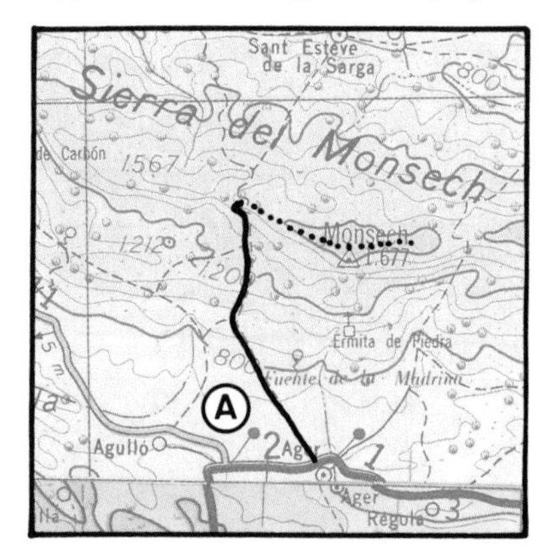

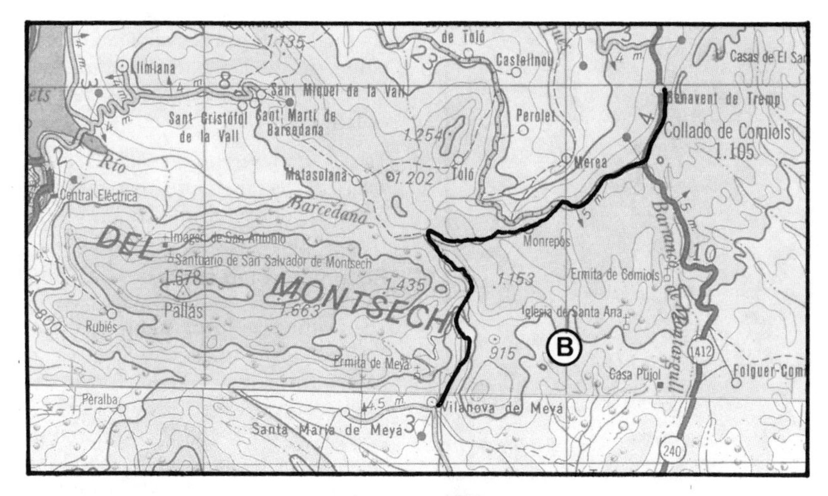

The starting point for **route B** is Vilanova de Meià, and for preference should be undertaken in a four-wheel drive vehicle. Take the road for the Pas Nou and before entering the gorge stop to watch the cliff-dwelling birds present. The road joins a dirt track; take the track and continue, taking the first right turn to bring you to the road for Sant Salvador de Toló, from where you can continue to the Comiols mountain pass and subsequently to Benavent. From the village itself you will be able to see cliff-dwelling species such as Griffon Vulture, Egyptian Vulture, Peregrine Falcon and, with luck, Golden Eagle and Bearded Vulture.

In addition to these two routes, it is worthwhile visiting the awe-inspiring gorge of Terradets.

Accommodation

There are several hostels and *fondas* in Ager, Vilanova de Meià and Artesa de Segre. There is also a campsite in Ager.

Comments

The best time of year for visiting the area is between April and July.

Jordi Canut and Diego García

CA.7 DRY FARMING AREAS OF LLEIDA AND UTXESA RESERVOIR

Steppe area and reservoir.

Main species

Residents: Marsh Harrier, Black-bellied Sandgrouse, Pin-tailed Sandgrouse, Little Owl, Long-eared Owl, Calandra Lark, Lesser Short-toed Lark, Thekla Lark, Cetti's Warbler, Sardinian Warbler, Penduline Tit, Great Grey Shrike, Raven, Starling, Rock Sparrow, Cirl Bunting.

Summer visitors: Purple Heron, White Stork, Short-toed Eagle, Hobby, Little Bustard, Stone Curlew, Great Spotted Cuckoo, Scops Owl, Red-necked Nightjar, Bee-eater, Roller, Short-toed Lark, Black-eared Wheatear, Reed Warbler, Great Reed Warbler, Spectacled Warbler, Subalpine Warbler, Lesser Grey Shrike, Woodchat Shrike.

Access

From Lleida (Lérida) take the N-230 to Albatàrrec, from where you join the

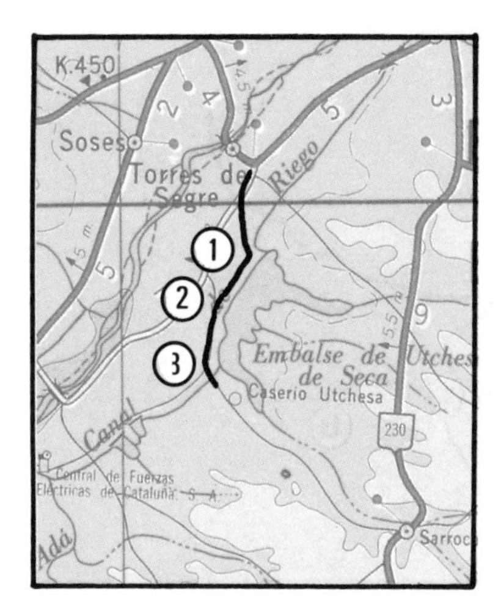

minor road to Alfés (15 km). To reach the Utxesa reservoir, continue along the N-230 and after 3 km turn right for Sudanell and Torres de Segre (15 km).

Description

As yet, these fields do not have an irrigation system and, since they lie within an area of major agricultural importance, they are considered marginal. For this reason they are frequently used as dumping grounds, for conifer plantations, and for building farms and industrial warehouses. In the *secans* or dry-farming areas lying to the south, where land is alternately sown and left fallow, there are a few areas of pastureland and small patches of natural vegetation, while the northern areas are taken up by barley and smaller areas of fallow ground.

The Utxesa reservoir is small and characterized by an impressive reedbed, perhaps the largest in Catalonia.

Recommended routes

The starting point of **Route A** is the junction of the road from Sudanell to Aitona with the road to Torres del Segre. As you leave Torres del Segre a track leads off to the left, surfaced to begin with, taking you to the Serós canal and subsequently skirting the Utxesa reservoir. In winter, it is worthwhile undertaking this route at dusk to watch Starling returning to their roosts, in some years numbering over 1,000,000. Once you reach the locks of the Serós canal, you can continue either by car or on foot. The most interesting points are the following:

1) Earth dam closing off the Secà valley. Here a small area of open water has been formed where large numbers of ducks and herons congregate. A little farther on is another place with similar characteristics.

2) A hillock from which you can command a view of the entire reedbed, allowing for sightings of Marsh Har-

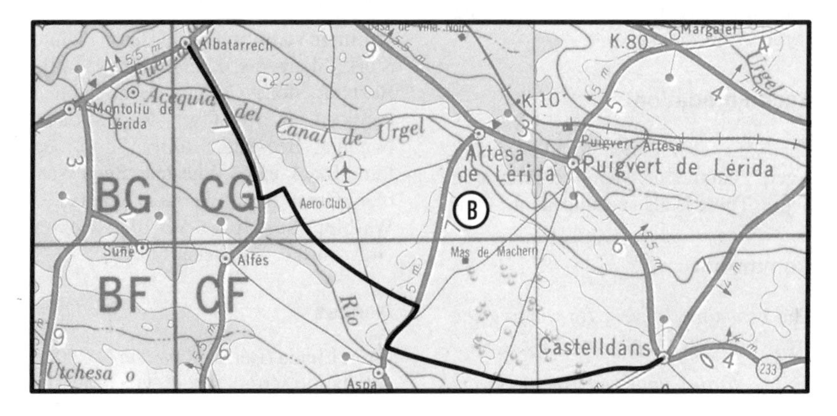

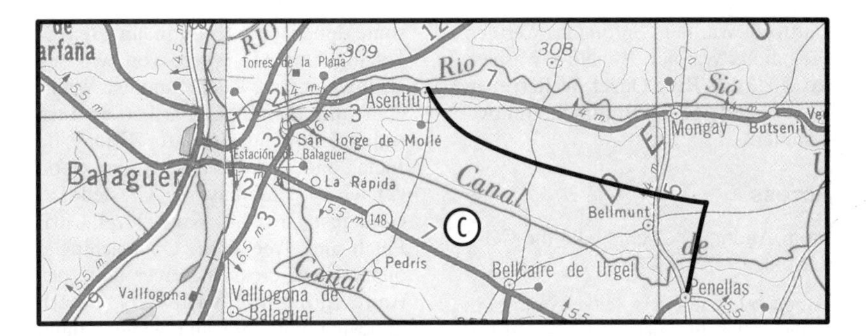

rier, ducks and herons. In winter this is the best place for watching starlings coming in as well as Merlin and Hen Harrier.

3) Bridge over the Serós canal. From here you can spot small marsh-dwelling passerines and ducks.

Route B starts in Albatàrrec and takes you along the road to Alfés. To begin with, the road runs through fruit orchards but soon passes to steppe-like dry land where it is easy to see Bee-eater and Roller resting on overhead wires. 1 km after passing beneath the A-2 motorway bridge turn left onto a track running beside a small reservoir lying parallel to the road. Shortly afterwards you will come to a junction; turn right and after some 5 km you will come to the road from Artesa de Lleida to Aspa. This stretch of the route will give sightings of Pin-tailed Sandgrouse, Stone Curlew, Calandra Lark, Short-toed Lark, Lesser Short-toed Lark and, in winter, Merlin and Hen Harrier. There is a small population of Dupont's Lark in the neighbourhood. In the almond groves you may see, in addition to Great Grey Shrike and Woodchat Shrike, the rare Lesser Grey Shrike, this area being one of the few locations for this species in Spain. The route continues along the track linking Aspa to Castelldans, passing through a more rugged area of scrubland where birds of prey abound, including juvenile Golden Eagle and Bonelli's Eagle.

The main attraction of **route C** is sighting Little Bustard in the months of April and May. The starting point for the route is the village of Penelles which can be reached from the C-148 between Balaguer and Tàrrega. Walk through the fields lying between the villages of Penelles, Bellmunt, Mongai and La Sentiu to have sightings of Montagu's Harrier, Hobby, Stone Curlew, Red-necked Nightjar, various larks and Black-eared Wheatear.

Accommodation

There is a wide variety of accommodation available in the city of Lleida.

Joan Estrada i Bonell

CA.8 ANDORRA

High mountain area.

Main species

Residents: Bearded Vulture, Golden Eagle, Ptarmigan, Capercaillie, Grey Partridge, Black Woodpecker, Alpine Accentor, Goldcrest, Treecreeper, Alpine Chough, Chough, Rock Sparrow, Snow Finch, Citril Finch, Siskin.

Summer visitors: Griffon Vulture, Crag Martin, Water Pipit, Whinchat,

Dartford Warbler, Sardinian Warbler, Melodious Warbler, Bonelli's Warbler, Rock Thrush, Ring Ouzel, Wallcreeper, Red-backed Shrike, Bullfinch, Yellowhammer.

Access

From Andorra la Vella, take the CG-2 to Soldeu (18 km).

To reach Os de Civís, leave Andorra la Vella in the direction of La Seu d'Urgell and on reaching the village of Aixovall turn right.

Description

Andorra, in the heart of the Pyrenees, is an extremely mountainous country with peaks reaching almost 3,000 m. The lower ground is taken up by holm oak woodland, giving way to woods of pine and silver fir at higher levels. The high ground features alpine meadows and many rocky outcrops.

The extensive development of commerce and tourism has had an adverse effect on the wildlife and landscapes of Andorra, although the area is still of considerable interest.

Recommended routes

Route A consists of a walk, taking half a day, along the Incles valley. Leave your vehicle at the start of the valley, 1 km from Soldeu, from where you take the dirt track leading along the valley bottom. The first stretch of the route takes you through an area of grazing land (1) where you will see Yellowhammer, Rock Bunting, Whinchat and Dunnock. Farther on turn right, following signs for Estany de Juclar, and you will enter a pine wood (2) where you may see Crested Tit, Goldcrest, Crossbill, Ring Ouzel, Citril Finch and Tree Pipit. On reaching a picnic area, cross the river and continue along the valley by a path indicated with red and white-painted markings. Point 3 will give you sightings of Golden Eagle, Grey Partridge, Alpine Accentor, Wallcreeper, Chough and Alpine Chough. Finally you will reach the *estanys* (lakes) of Juclar, from where you can continue up to the mountain passes of Juclar and Alba, increasing your chances of seeing Ptarmigan. Return by the same route.

Route B starts in Os de Civís, where you follow the road until reaching the Hostal Borda la Plana. Continuing along the dirt track for 1 km, you will come to a right turn where you can leave your vehicle and continue on foot. The surrounding meadows (4) will give rise to sightings of Tree Pipit, Yellowhammer and Red-backed Shrike; subsequently the track enters a pine wood (5) where you may see Black Woodpecker, Crossbill, Bullfinch, Siskin and on the far side of the valley, which is more barren, Golden Eagle. The track comes to an end at the river and if you wish you can climb the path to the Conflent mountain pass (6)

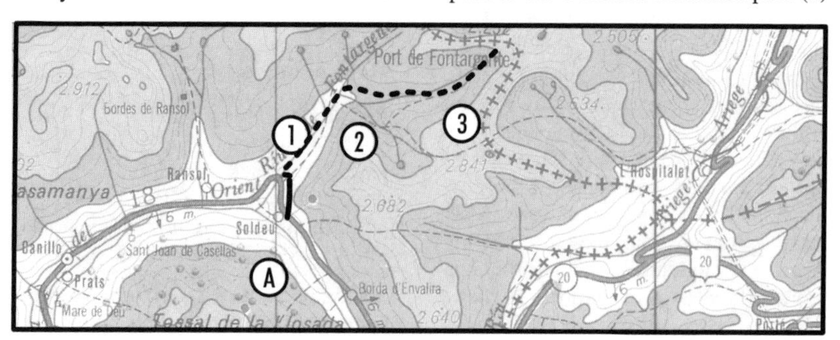

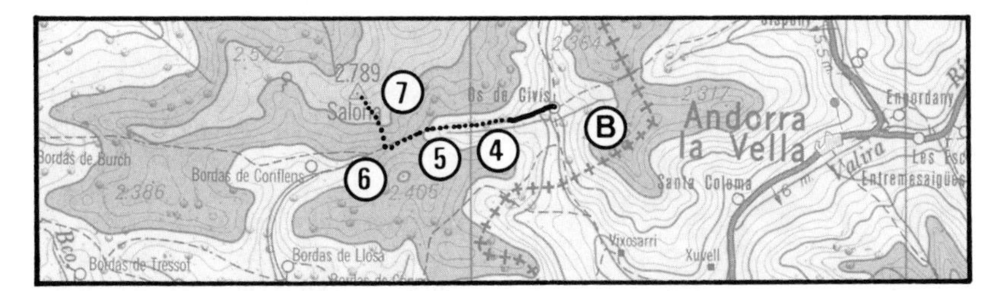

where you will see Citril Finch, Water Pipit, Grey Partridge, Chough and Alpine Chough. From here, a taxing climb will take you to the peak of Salòria (2,789 m) where you may see Ptarmigan. The head of the valley (7) is a good place for watching Griffon Vulture and Bearded Vulture. The route may take less than 2 hours, although by choosing the longer option it may take a whole day.

Accommodation

Andorra offers a wide range of accommodation to suit all requirements.

Comments

If you are going to undertake route A or the long version of route B, you should be physically fit and equipped with suitable walking boots and protective clothing, since the weather may change suddenly. The best time of year for visiting the area is late spring and summer, although summer finds Andorra full of visitors.

Anna Motis and Jaume Orta

■ CA.9 NÚRIA – UPPER REACHES OF THE FRESER VALLEY

High mountain area.

Main species

Residents: Bearded Vulture, Golden Eagle, Ptarmigan, Dipper, Goldcrest, Crested Tit, Alpine Chough, Chough, Raven, Crossbill, Snow Finch.

Summer visitors: Crag Martin, Tree Pipit, Water Pipit, Alpine Accentor, Rock Thrush, Ring Ouzel, Song Thrush, Chiffchaff, Wallcreeper, Red-backed Shrike, Citril Finch, Bullfinch, Yellowhammer, Rock Bunting.

Access

Take the N-152 to Ribes de Freser (15 km from Ripoll). From Ribes, climb up to the little village of Queralbs, at 1,236 m the last centre of population in the valley. From here you can take the rack railway (known locally as *El Carrilet*), which climbs up to the sanctuary at Núria.

Description

This is the last high mountain area of the eastern Catalan Pyrenees. From this point on altitudes drop considerably. The heads of the rivers Freser and Ter largely coincide with Freser-Setcases National Game Reserve. The geography of the area is rugged and mountainous. It is glacial and reaches its highest point with Puigmal at 2,913 m. The northern slopes are covered with extensive areas of Scots pine and mountain pine, while the lower levels are taken up by deciduous woodland consisting of beech, oak, ash, black poplar, hazel and alder. There are also

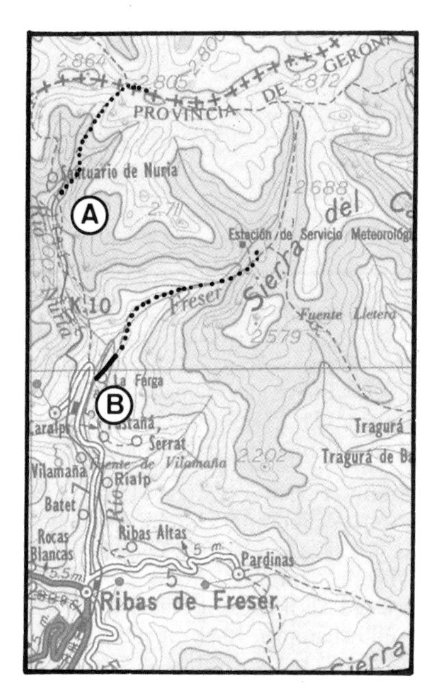

moors, peat bogs, alpine meadows, cliffs, rock screes and river gorges.

Núria is a sanctuary dedicated to Our Lady of Núria. Located at 2,000 m, there is also a ski resort, a hotel and a mountain refuge.

Recommended routes

To undertake **route A**, leave your car in Queralbs and take the rack railway up to Núria. The route takes you from 1,200 to 2,000 m via an impressive ravine, running through different levels of vegetation. Once you arrive at the top, many trips are possible. We recommend taking the track which leads from the train station, following the Mulleres stream towards La Coma de Nou Creus. The first stretch of the route skirts the Bosc de la Verge, a wood where it is possible to see Sparrowhawk, Ring Ouzel, Crossbill, Citril Finch, Siskin and other forest species.

After 1 km, cross the stream and head for the Noufonts valley leading off to the left. Climb up to the pass of the same name at 2,260 m. As you make the steep climb you will see chamois as well as Skylark, Water Pipit, Wheatear, Black Redstart, Dunnock and, if you are lucky, Rock Thrush, Alpine Accentor and Ptarmigan. Once at the crest, continue eastwards along the range for 1 km, increasing your chances of seeing alpine birds and enabling you to enjoy the spectacular view over the valley of Carançà, which lies in France and is the only valley in the area with alpine lakes. Subsequently, retrace your steps to the Nou Creus pass and descend to the sanctuary.

The starting point of **route B** is on the road from Ribes de Freser to Queralbs, 1 km before Queralbs. At the Pont del Molí, a bridge beside the school known as La Farga, a partially surfaced track leads off to the right to the electricity generating station of El Daió. Once you reach the generating station take a narrow path to the right which runs along the river Freser, climbing up the narrow valley to the distant mountain refuge of Coma de Vaca. The path takes you along the bases of high cliffs and through small areas of deciduous woodland and scrubland. After 1 km you will come to the El Grill waterfall lying between high cliff faces inhabited by Wallcreeper. Some 250 m farther on, the path takes a sharp left turn, giving a beautiful view of the head of the valley. To the left is the Sierra de Torreneules (2,731 m), much frequented by Chough and birds of prey —including the occasional Bearded Vulture. To the right of the river are pine woods where, among other forest species, Black Woodpecker and Capercaillie (rare) are present. At 1,700 m, the track crosses the river (Las Marrades bridge). Here the landscape becomes much more open with meadows and rocks where, among other species, you may see Golden Eagle, Chough, Alpine

Chough, Ring Ouzel, Crossbill and Citril Finch.

Accommodation

Queralbs has several hostels and excellent restaurants, but in Núria there is only one hotel and the mountain refuge.

Comments

The alpine areas of Núria are extremely dangerous from late autumn until early spring, and each year serious accidents occur because of the cold, fog, avalanches and carelessness on the part of visitors. The best time of year to visit the area is mid June to early August. To undertake the routes described it is vital that you have walking boots, protective clothing (even in summer), a map and food supply.

Oriol Alamany

CA.10 CAP DE CREUS PENÍNSULA

A coastal massif running down to the sea. It is the easternmost point of the Iberian Peninsula.

Main species

Residents: Yelkouan Shearwater, Cory's Shearwater, Bonelli's Eagle, Peregrine Falcon, Thekla Lark, Black Wheatear, Blue Rock Thrush, Dartford Warbler, Rock Sparrow.

Summer visitors: Pallid Swift, Red-rumped Swallow, Tawny Pipit, Black-eared Wheatear, Rock Thrush, Subalpine Warbler, Spectacled Warbler, Orphean Warbler, Woodchat Shrike, Ortolan Bunting.

Winter visitors: Gannet, Great Skua, Razorbill, Alpine Accentor, Wallcreeper.

On passage: Arctic Skua, Little Gull, Kittiwake, Short-eared Owl.

Access

From the A-7 motorway or the N-II (both running from Barcelona to La Jonquera), take the Figueres exit and continue along the C-260 towards Roses. About 2 km before Roses turn left for Cadaqués.

Description

The peninsula formed by the cape of Creus consists of ranges of hills, gorges and hillsides running down to the sea and projecting some 10 km beyond the rest of the coastline. This gives the area the feeling of an island which, combined with the strong *tramuntana* (local name for the North wind), the rocky soils and the deforestation which has occurred over the course of centuries, makes for a bleak landscape largely composed of scrubland and shrubs.

Other habitats are also present, such as rocky coastal areas, sea cliffs, inland cliffs, small woodland areas consisting of pine plantations, holm oak and cork oak, river beds, ponds and fields taken up largely by vines and olive trees.

Recommended routes

The starting point for **route A** is Cadaqués. From here, a surfaced road takes you to the Cap de Creus (9 km). For the first few kilometres, the landscape features olive groves with scrubland areas and some pines. Look out for Red-legged Partridge and Thekla Lark along the way.

5.5 km out of Cadaqués, a track leads off to the left to Mas Rabassers de Baix, a restored farmhouse. Leave your

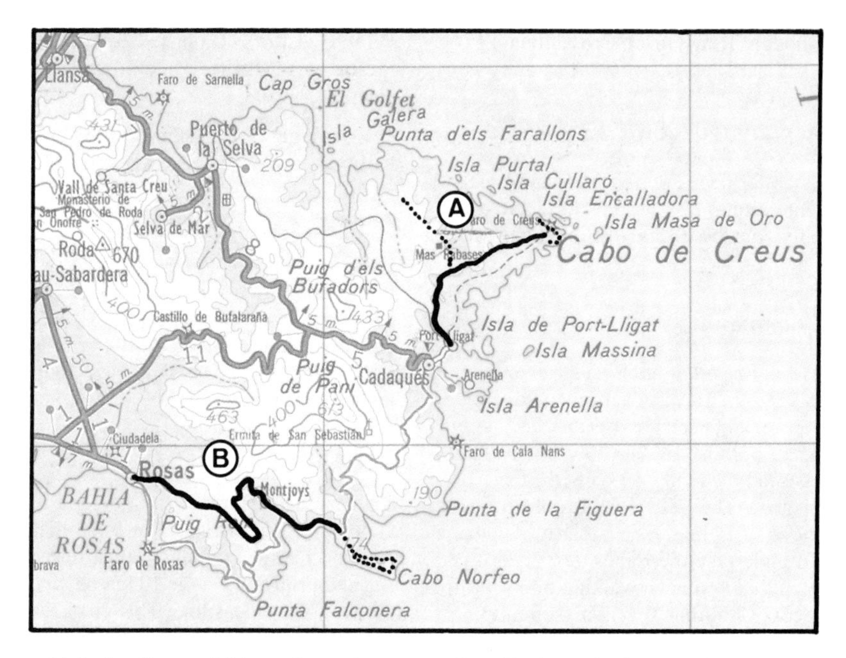

vehicle by the roadside and continue on foot along the track. This area is particularly rewarding during the migration periods: eight species of *Sylvia* warblers, Melodious Warbler, Ortolan Bunting, Wheatear and Black-eared Wheatear can be seen at this time. At other times of year the area is interesting for spotting resident birds such as Blue Rock Thrush or Black Wheatear. Return by the same route.

Continue by driving along the road until you reach the lighthouse or *faro* of Cap de Creus. From here you can walk to the end of the headland. Follow the red and white markings of the long distance footpath (Grandes Routes) GR11. From here you will be able to see large numbers of sea birds and birds of prey as well as waders and passerines on migration. The best months are March and April. Throughout the year it is worth going to the tip of the headland at about 16.00 on weekdays, when fishing boats returning to Roses are followed by a multitude of gulls, shearwaters and skuas.

A walk through the area between the lighthouse and the tip of the headland will enable you to see Black Wheatear, Rock Thrush, Dartford Warbler and in winter, if you are lucky, Wallcreeper.

Route B begins in Roses, which you must drive through to get to the road for Cala Jóncols. Of the 10 km separating Roses from cape Norfeu, about 7 km are surfaced. However the road is narrow and full of bends, so you should drive with care.

The landscape you will see en route consists of large areas of terracing. In some places olive groves survive, but many of the other terraces have been taken over by scrub. There are also stands of pine and some meadows.

On reaching the headland, leave the car at the start of a track leading off to the right and continue on foot. There are many paths; it is worth working your way around the perimeter of the area, beginning on the north side and coming back on the south side. Calculate on taking 4 or 5 hours.

The predominantly shrubby vegetation is the home of Red-legged Partridge, Thekla Lark, Woodchat Shrike, Tawny Pipit, Black-eared Wheatear and Subalpine Warbler, among others.

From the tip of the headland it is possible to see some of the birds which use the cliffs as a feeding or breeding ground. These include Shag, Pallid Swift, Alpine Swift, Blue Rock Thrush, Raven, Peregrine Falcon and Kestrel. Unfortunately it is no longer possible to see Lesser Kestrel, which died out in this area during the mid 1980s.

Accommodation

There are plenty of hotels and campsites both in Cadaqués and Rosas, although it may be difficult to find accommodation in summer and during the Easter week.

Jordi Sargatal and Deli Saavedra

■ CA.11 AIGUAMOLLS DE L'EMPORDÀ

A coastal wetland area, the second most important in Catalonia after the Ebro Delta.

Main species

Residents: Bittern, Cattle Egret, Little Egret, Grey Heron, Marsh Harrier, Purple Gallinule, Stone Curlew, Collared Dove, Kingfisher, Moustached Warbler, Penduline Tit.

Summer visitors: Little Bittern, Purple Heron, Garganey, Short-toed Eagle, Black-winged Stilt, Kentish Plover, Great Spotted Cuckoo, Beeeater, Roller, Lesser Grey Shrike.

Winter visitors: Black-throated Diver, Cormorant, Glossy Ibis, ducks (17,000 individuals in January 1993), Golden Plover, Curlew, Razorbill.

On passage: Greater Flamingo, waders, terns.

Access

Access to this area is easy. From the A-7 or the N-II, both running from Barcelona to La Jonquera, take the Figueres exit. Continue along the Figueres bypass and then take the C-260 to Roses. 11 km from Figueres, between Castelló d'Empúries and Sant Pere Pescador, shortly after a petrol station, turn left onto a signed road which after 1 km will bring you to the information centre of a Natural Park.

At the information centre, known as El Cortalet, there are maps and leaflets in various languages. During the summer months, the Park organizes guided visits.

Timetable: open in the mornings all year round 09:30–14:00; the park is open at the following times in the afternoon; October to March, 15:30–18:00; April to September, 16:30–19:00.

Description

The Aiguamolls are the remains of the formerly extensive coastal marshlands of the Empordà area. They are located in the bay of Roses, around the mouths of the rivers Muga and Fluvià. Over the course of time, the wetlands were largely substituted by fields, grazing land or the building of tourist resorts. The remaining area was saved after a long campaign which culminated in 1983 with the creation of a Natural Park. The main habitats encountered are saline coastal lagoons, freshwater lagoons, coastal sandy areas, meadows subject to periodic flooding (known as *closes*), riverside woodland, rice fields and other crops.

Recommended routes

Route A starts at the information centre and takes you round Integral Reserve 2, enabling you to see freshwater lagoons, saline lagoons, *closes*, reedbeds and coastal sandy areas. The route consists of a walk taking 5 or 6 hours. The points of greatest interest are the following:

1) El Cortalet, a freshwater lagoon. 3 hides facilitate the observation of ducks, Coot and Black-winged Stilt, among other species. This is a good place for photographing birds.

2) Raised hide known as El Pallejà, from where you can command a view of a substantial part of the coastal lagoon system. This is a wonderful place for watching ducks in winter and autumn, and Marsh Harrier all year round.

3) Flooded areas at El Matà. Former rice fields now taken over by water-loving vegetation kept down by herbivores, mainly Camargue horses. This area is very interesting in spring with large congregations of waders and Garganey. In winter it is easy to see Glossy Ibis, and Purple Gallinule all year round.

4) Bridge over the channel draining the westernmost of the lagoons (La Massona). Surrounded by an extensive reedbed, this is a good place for watching marsh-dwelling passerines including Moustached Warbler and, with luck, Little Bittern and Bittern.

5) During winter you can see interesting seabirds from the beach such as Black-throated Diver, Common Scoter, Velvet Scoter, Eider and Razorbill. When there are storms out to sea Gannet, Yelkouan Shearwater, and Cory's Shearwater can be added to the list.

6) All the way along the beach you will see waders (Avocet, Oystercatcher, Whimbrel) and passerines (Short-toed

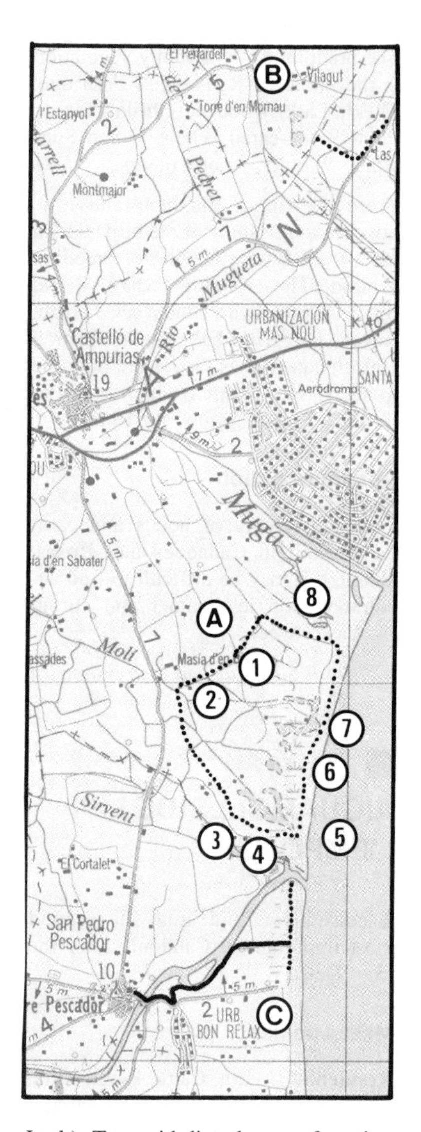

Lark). To avoid disturbance of nesting birds, this area is closed from the April 1 to June 15.

7) Laguna de la Rogera, the most saline lagoon in the system. In winter you will see numerous duck, with Greater Flamingo, waders and terns during the migration periods. This area is also out of bounds for the dates mentioned above.

8) Areas of salicornia and halophytic vegetation where it is possible to see Lesser Grey Shrike. During the migration periods, look out for Dotterel.

Route B covers Integral Reserve 1, coinciding almost exactly with the former lagoon of Castelló d'Empúries. The area is now divided into a series of small freshwater ponds (*estanys*) with extensive reedbeds. These ponds are easily reached from the road linking the villages of Castelló d'Empúries and Palau-saverdera. The pond of Vilaüt is especially recommended. To reach Vilaüt, leave your car at the Restaurant Aiguamolls and walk for some 800 m along the road until finding a marked track leading off to the right. Follow the track for another 800 m and you will come to a hide from where you may have sightings of Purple Heron, Bittern, Little Bittern, Marsh Harrier, Purple Gallinule, Water Rail and Moustached Warbler. The riverside woodland, woodland and fields in the surrounding area are also worth covering, since they are home to interesting species such as Roller, Great Spotted Cuckoo, Penduline Tit and Lesser Grey Shrike.

Finally, **Route C** runs along the right bank of the river Fluvià from Sant Pere Pescador to the beach, allowing you to see the island of Caramany (the third Integral Reserve of the Park, to which access is strictly forbidden). In winter this is the site of an impressive roost of herons, corvids, Woodpigeon and Stock Dove. The end of the route, at the mouth of the river Fluvià, is a good spot for watching wintering sea birds such as divers, scoters and Razorbill.

Accommodation

Tourism in the area is highly developed, with numerous hotels, hostels and campsites which may be full during the months of July and August. It is worth staying in Castelló d'Empúries (hotels All i Oli, Canet, Ca l'Anton) or Sant Pere Pescador (hotels Coll Verd, El Pescador).

Josep del Hoyo, Jordi Sargatal

CA.12 MOUTH OF THE RIVER TORDERA

Coastal river area.

Main species

Residents: Yelkouan Shearwater, Shag, Cetti's Warbler, Fan-tailed Warbler.

Summer visitors: Cory's Shearwater, Little Ringed Plover, Kentish Plover, Great Spotted Cuckoo, Scops Owl, Bee-eater, Short-toed Lark, Yellow Wagtail, Reed Warbler, Melodious Warbler.

Winter visitors: Great Crested Grebe, Gannet, Eider, Mediterranean Gull, Razorbill, Penduline Tit, Reed Bunting.

On passage: Cormorant, Night Heron, Cattle Egret, Little Egret, Grey Heron, Purple Heron, Garganey and ducks in general, Spotted Crake, Black-winged Stilt, Avocet, Ringed Plover, Grey Plover, Knot, Sanderling, Little Stint, Curlew Sandpiper, Dunlin, Ruff, Black-tailed Godwit, Whimbrel, Spotted Redshank, Greenshank, Green Sandpiper, Wood Sandpiper, Arctic Skua, Little Gull, Audouin's Gull, Gull-billed Tern, Little Tern, Whiskered Tern, Black Tern.

Access

Take the N-II and turn off near Malgrat for Blanes. Continue for a little more than 4 km, when you will come to a bridge over the river Tordera. Just before the bridge two tracks lead off, one going downstream to the La Tordera campsite and the second running upstream.

Description

The mouth of the river Tordera is the remains of an old delta where lagoons have been substituted by irrigated farmland and tree plantations. Much of the water in the river is used for irrigation and human consumption, causing the water level to be low at all times; it usually dries out completely in summer. This factor, combined with the narrowness of the riverbed, makes for easy observation of the waders and other birds present.

Generally speaking the area has been quite spoiled, but it is nevertheless of some significance as a resting place for birds on passage.

Recommended routes

The recommended route is 1.5 km long and runs along the track leading to the La Tordera campsite on the right bank of the river. Make your way down to the riverside. Make stops at various points, particularly on the stretch nearest the river mouth. The most interesting feature is the presence of waders, although herons, ducks, rails, etc. can also be seen. The river mouth, which can be reached by going through the campsite, is a good place for watching terns, marsh terns, gulls and various sea birds such as Gannet, Shag, Razorbill, shearwaters and skuas.

If you are visiting the area in spring or summer, when the river mouth is frequented by large numbers of people, it is worth taking the track which leads upstream since many waders resort to this part of the river as a place where they are relatively undisturbed. In winter and early spring, it is worth extending the walk for some 3 km along the beach until you come to the railway

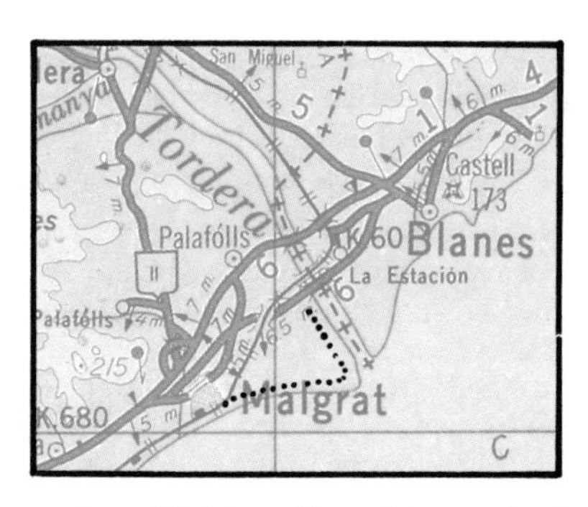

station at Malgrat. Along this stretch of the route you may see Black-throated Diver, grebes and sea ducks. It is also worth checking the concrete platform lying in the sea off Malgrat, which is used as a perch by Shag and the occasional Cormorant.

Accommodation

Plenty of accommodation is available in all towns in the area.

Comments

The best time of year for visiting the area is spring, during the pre-breeding migration.

Enric Badosa i Malagelada,
José M. Arcos Pros
and Jordi Pou Oliver.

■ CA.13 MARINA RANGE

A range of hills lying on the coast, covered with Mediterranean woodland.

Main species

Residents: Dartford Warbler, Sardinian Warbler, Cirl Bunting, Rock Bunting.

Summer visitors: Great Spotted Cuckoo, Scops Owl, Nightjar, Red-necked Nightjar, Alpine Swift, Bee-eater, Short-toed Lark, Sand Martin, Black-eared Wheatear, Melodious Warbler, Subalpine Warbler.

On passage: Short-toed Eagle, Booted Eagle.

Access

The motorways A-19 (Barcelona to Mataró) and A-7 (Barcelona to La Jonquera) and the N-II from Barcelona to Blanes all run along the coast, giving access to this range of hills.

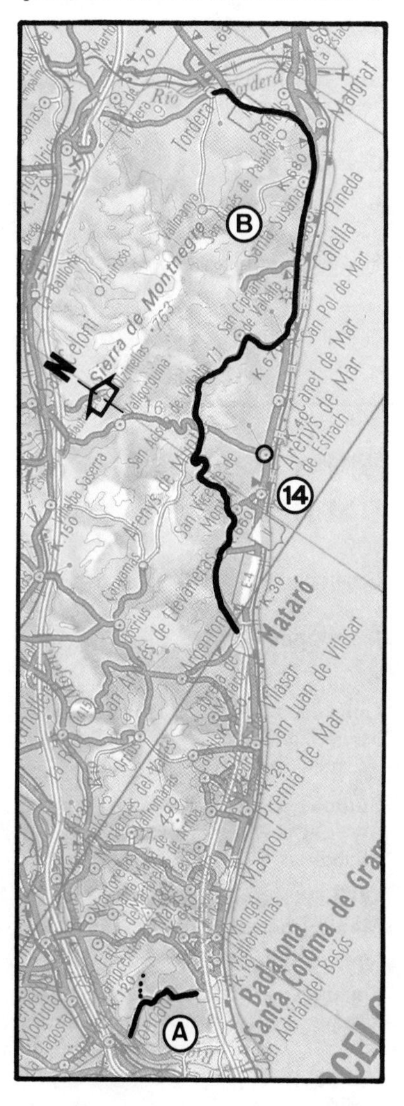

Description

The Serra de Marina runs from north to south along the Catalan coastline between the rivers Tordera and Besós. On the whole this region is densely populated, owing both to the proximity of the city of Barcelona and to the nearby major tourist centres located in the coastal region of El Maresme, giving rise to the existence of numerous housing developments.

The hills are relatively steep, with heights reaching some 700 m. In addition to cultivated areas, there are also extensive pine woods and, more locally, patches of holm oak, oak and cork oak.

Recommended routes

Route A consists of a trip along the road joining Badalona and Montcada. You can make a stop at the Vallesana pass, from where a track leads off to the right. Take a walk if you wish to see warblers, wheatears, Blue Rock Thrush, Nightjar, Red-necked Nightjar and, during the migration periods, various birds of prey.

Route B takes you along the minor road from Mataró to Arenys de Munt, and subsequently to Sant Cebrià de Vallalta and Tordera. You can make stops at will; especially recommended is the pass of Can Benet, lying between the latter two villages.

Accommodation

Since tourism in this area is highly developed, it is possible to find accommodation in virtually any town in the area.

Guillem Chacón
and Jaume Campderròs

CA.14
ARENYS DE MAR

A fishing port located on a stretch of sandy coastline.

Main species

Residents: Yelkouan Shearwater, Black-headed Gull, Yellow-legged Gull, Sandwich Tern.

Summer visitors: Cory's Shearwater.

Winter visitors: Gannet, Eider, Great Skua, Mediterranean Gull, Lesser Black-backed Gull, Kittiwake, Razorbill.

On passage: Storm Petrel, Arctic Skua, Little Gull, Audouin's Gull, Gull-billed Tern, Caspian Tern, Common Tern, Little Tern, Black Tern.

Access

Take the N-II out of Barcelona and after the traffic lights for Arenys de Mar take the first right down to the port. Once there, park your vehicle in front of the Restaurant Portiñol, from where you can reach the Dic de Llevant (harbour wall) and the Punta Vella lighthouse.

Description

Arenys de Mar is a fishing port and marina, one of the most important on the coast around Barcelona. One of the harbour walls, known as Dic de Llevant, runs out to sea for some 300 m. Go to the breakwater between 16:00 and 18:00 to watch the fishing boats coming in with the birds accompanying them.

Recommended routes

The far end of the harbour wall is the best place for watching sea birds. In spring and autumn you will see the migration of large numbers of terns, shearwaters, Gannet, Razorbill, petrels and gulls. In winter these are joined by Mediterranean Gull, Kittiwake and, with luck, Common Gull. At this time of year you may also see Yelkouan Shearwater, Arctic Skua, Great Skua, Razorbill and the occasional sea duck.

Accommodation

Tourism is highly developed in the area, giving rise to a wide range of possibilities. The Pensió Premsa in Arenys de Mar is recommended as being a cheap option.

Comments

Pay particular attention to the wake of the fishing boats. It is also worth having powerful optical equipment.

Enric Badosa i Malagelada,
José M. Arcos Pros
and Jordi Pou Oliver.

CA.15
BARCELONA

Urban parks and harbour areas.

Main species

Residents: Grey Heron, Yellow-legged Gull, Sandwich Tern, Collared Dove, Monk Parakeet, Wryneck, Sardinian Warbler, Short-toed Treecreeper.

Summer visitors: Scops Owl, Alpine Swift, Bee-eater, Hoopoe, Redstart, Melodious Warbler, Bonelli's Warbler.

Winter visitors: Great Crested Grebe, Mediterranean Gull, Lesser Black-backed Gull, Razorbill.

On passage: Cory's Shearwater, Yelkouan Shearwater, Gannet, ducks, waders, Arctic Skua, Little Gull and other gulls, passerines.

Access

The places of greatest ornithological interest in the city of Barcelona are the parks located in the city centre, which can easily be reached by using public transport.

To reach the harbour breakwater you can take the *golondrinas*, small boats which leave from the area near the monument to Christopher Columbus (*Colón*).

Description

A large city remarkable for its parks and gardens, some of which contain abundant natural vegetation. Thus it is possible to see interesting species within the city such as Alpine Swift.

Recommended routes

Route A consists of a trip to the far end of the harbour breakwater. This takes you several kilometres out to sea, allowing for observations of strictly marine species. It is worth spending some 3 hours on the breakwater, providing sightings, in autumn and winter, of Sandwich Tern, Mediterranean Gull, and other less common gulls. In April, migration is intense and you should see Gannet, shearwaters, ducks, Arctic Skua, Little Gull, etc.

Route B takes you to the Ciutadella park, featuring walks, flower beds and dense wooded areas. The Barcelona zoo lies within the park, and it is from the zoo that various species have escaped and become wild. These include Monk Parakeet which is now widely

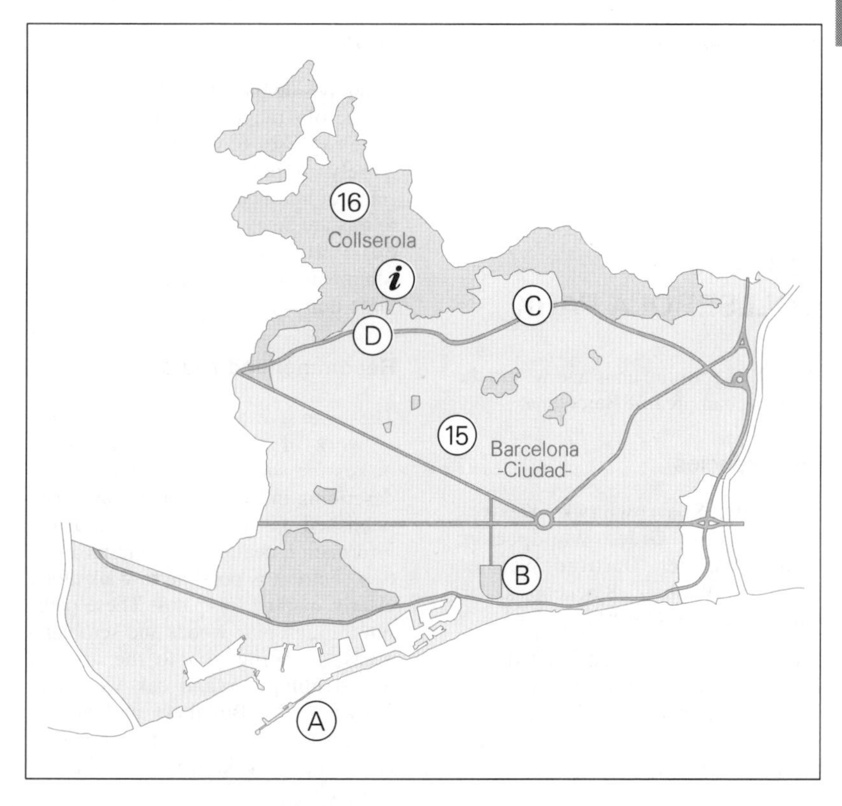

spread throughout Barcelona, making their large nests in palm trees growing in gardens and on the streets. There are also a couple of ponds where you can see water birds.

Route C in the Laberint d'Horta park, offers the same possibilities as the former, but, since there is greater tree cover you may see other species such as Wryneck. The only problem is that more people frequent this park.

Route D takes in the La Oreneta park, located in the up-town part of the city where it joins the range of hills known as Collserola. With the exception of some fruit trees, vestiges of former farmland, most of the area is taken up by natural vegetation. You may see Hoopoe, Golden Oriole, Melodious Warbler, Sardinian Warbler, Subalpine Warbler, Redstart, tits and finches.

Accommodation

Plenty of accommodation is available in Barcelona.

Joan Estrada i Bonell

■ CA.16 COLLSEROLA PARK

Woodland forming an island within the metropolitan area of Barcelona.

Main species

Residents: Sparrowhawk, Kestrel, Woodpigeon, Green Woodpecker, Cetti's Warbler, Dartford Warbler, Sardinian Warbler, Blackcap, Chiffchaff, Firecrest, Great Grey Shrike.

Summer visitors: Great Spotted Cuckoo, Bee-eater, Wryneck, Subalpine Warbler, Orphean Warbler, Bonelli's Warbler, Woodchat Shrike, Golden Oriole.

Winter visitors: Dunnock, Goldcrest, Siskin.

On passage: Honey Buzzard, Marsh Harrier and other predators (particularly during autumn migration), Alpine Swift.

Access

From the A-2 motorway or the N-II go to Molins de Rei and from there take the road to Santa Creu d'Olorda which connects with the road running from Vallvidrera to Sant Cugat. At Vil.la Joana, 4.7 km from Sant Cugat, is the information centre which has a small exhibition on the most interesting topics relating to the area, including fauna. It is also possible to reach Collserola from Barcelona and the towns lying on the edge of the park area.

Description

Lying beside the city of Barcelona, the Collserola range is characterized by large expanses of woodland consisting largely of pine with the occasional stand of holm oak and oak. In addition to this are areas taken up by crops, uncultivated land and scrubland. Mammals present include wild boar (in large numbers), squirrel and genet.

Recommended routes

The extensive and perhaps excessive network of tracks, paths and roads makes for various itineraries. Leaflets describing individual routes have been published and can be obtained at the information centre. From the information centre it is possible to walk along clearly marked footpaths. These paths run through pine woods and scrubland areas, bringing you to the area of mixed holm oak and oak woodland known as La Budallera and nearby streams. It is also worth taking a walk along the track known as El Pas del

Rei linking the road from Horta to Cerdanyola with Font Groga, a spring.

In September and October it is worth climbing to Turó del Maltau or Turó de la Magarola, areas of high ground which are excellent spots for watching birds of prey on passage.

Accommodation

Plenty of accommodation is available in Barcelona and surrounding towns. There are also camping areas within the park, but you should apply in writing for permission to camp from the: Patronat Metropolità Parc de Collserola; Carretera de l'Església 92; 08017 Barcelona.

Comments

Although there are no species of major ornithological interest in the Collserola area, the diversity of habitats and above all location within the Barcelona area, inhabited by 3 million people, make for an extremely interesting and very accessible site.

Francesc Llimona

■ CA.17 DELTA OF THE RIVER LLOBREGAT

Coastal flood plain occupied by fields, pine woods, small ponds and beaches.

Main species

Residents: Little Grebe, Marsh Harrier, Kentish Plover, Sandwich Tern, Monk Parakeet, Cetti's Warbler, Fan-tailed Warbler, Sardinian Warbler, Short-toed Treecreeper.

Summer visitors: Little Bittern, Purple Heron, Black-winged Stilt, Little Ringed Plover, Audouin's Gull, Great Spotted Cuckoo, Scops Owl, Short-toed Lark, Yellow Wagtail.

Winter visitors: Yelkouan Shearwater, Gannet, Cormorant, Cattle Egret, Little Egret, ducks, Golden Plover, Little Gull, Mediterranean Gull, Razorbill, Kingfisher, Moustached Warbler, Penduline Tit.

On passage: shearwaters, herons, predators, waders, skuas, terns, marsh terns, Bee-eater, passerines.

Access

From Barcelona take the dual carriageway to Castelldefels and stop at the bridge over the river Llobregat, starting point of route A, or at the 11 km marker post, starting point of route B. The large number of roads traversing the area may lead to confusion. Route B can be reached by bus (line L-90, Barcelona to Castelldefels). There is also a railway station at el Prat de Llobregat; in summer buses ply between the beach of el Prat and the town centre and L'Hospitalet del Llobregat.

Description

Lying just to the south of the city of Barcelona, the delta of the river Llobregat is densely populated. The entire northern part of the delta has been built up while the southern part is taken up by the airport, industrial estates and service industries. However, there is also a series of marshes, lagoons, pine woods, fields and beaches.

The protection of this natural habitat, which includes two Partial Nature Reserves (288 ha) and an extensive buffer area where hunting is prohibited, was achieved after a long conservation campaign.

Recommended routes

Route A combines a car journey with a walk, beginning at the petrol station

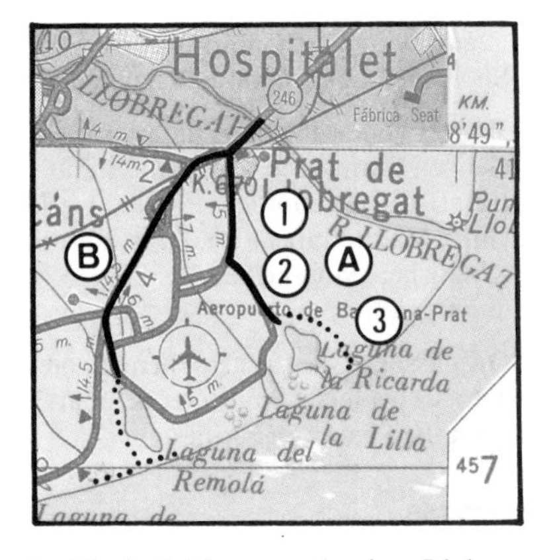

beside the bridge over the river Llobregat. The first point of interest is the pond lying close to the Pryca hypermarket (1) where various herons can be seen and a colony of Monk Parakeet, which inhabits a nearby stand of palm trees. Go in the direction of Barcelona and cross the centre of el Prat del Llobregat, following signs for *Platja* or beach and subsequently *Campo de Golf-Playa* (golf course and beach). The fields near the airport (2) are, at the relevant times of year, the site of Marsh Harrier, Buzzard, Golden Plover and, less frequently, Hen Harrier and Merlin. Leave your vehicle near the beach and take a walk to see Kentish Plover and sea birds such as Audouin's Gull, Mediterranean Gull and Little Gull. Another interesting point (3) is the mouth of the La Ricarda pond.

Route B has its starting point at the 11 km marker post on the dual carriageway to Castelldefels, where you take the turning for the Camping Toro Bravo, a campsite. Immediately after the turning you will come to El Remolar pond (4), where you can leave your car and walk along the right shore of the pond until you reach the beach. En route you may see Little Bittern, Purple Heron, Marsh Harrier, Water Rail, Great Spotted Cuckoo, Fan-tailed Warbler, Moustached Warbler and Penduline Tit. On the beach you will see gulls, including Audouin's Gull, Kentish Plover and other sea birds.

Accommodation

There is plenty of accommodation available in Barcelona and Castelldefels. There are also campsites close to both of the recommended routes.

Comments

It is worth avoiding visiting the area at weekends and on holidays during the summer. You should respect private property and the signs located on the beach to protect areas where Kentish Plover are present.

In el Prat del Llobregat there is the Museu del Delta, a museum of the area with a collection of birds. The address is: Casal de Cultura, Plaza de Pau Casals s/n, and entrance is free.

Contact address: Reserves Naturals Delta del Llobregat; Direcció General del Medi Natural; Còrsega 329, 5º; 08037 Barcelona.

Ricard Gutiérrez

■ CA.18. GARRAF MASSIF

A karstic massif lying on the coast.

Main species

Residents: Bonelli's Eagle, Red-legged Partridge, Eagle Owl, Thekla Lark, Crag Martin, Black Wheatear, Blue Rock Thrush, Dartford Warbler, Sardinian Warbler, Rock Sparrow.

Summer visitors: Nightjar, Pallid Swift, Alpine Swift, Bee-eater, Tawny Pipit, Black-eared Wheatear, Rock Thrush, Spectacled Warbler, Subalpine Warbler, Bonelli's Warbler, Woodchat Shrike, Ortolan Bunting.

Summer visitors: Alpine Accentor, Wallcreeper.

On passage: birds of prey.

Access

From Barcelona, take the dual carriageway to Castelldefels. A few kilometres after the exit for the town centre of Castelldefels turn right, where there is a sign for *Platja* (beach), Port Ginesta and Palau Novella. Continue towards Palau Novella. The road runs through the Rat Penat housing development and takes you to the top of the range.

Description

The Garraf hills are characterized by their karstic nature, where drastic erosion of the limestone rock has given rise to karrens, dolinas, hundreds of potholes and the occasional cave. Hills do not reach great heights and, although the hillsides slope quite gently, there are some steep ravines and, on the coastal side, sea cliffs. Due to fires and the stony nature of the soil, vegetation is scarce. There are some areas of pine woodland but scrubland, featuring mastic tree and kermes oak, predominates. Dwarf fan palm is also present, in addition to considerable expanses of *Ampelodesma mauritanica*, a large-gramineous plant.

Recommended routes

This route combines car journeys with walks and, if it is to be undertaken at leisure, requires half a day. Once through the Rat Penat housing development, the road starts to climb through some very sharp bends. On coming to the second big bend to the left, park your car (1); from here you can command a distant view of the Vallbona gully where you will see various cliff-dwelling birds such as Alpine Swift or Crag Martin. A little farther on a small rocky area located to the right of the road (2) will give rise to sightings of Blue Rock Thrush and Black Wheatear. When you reach a flat area with the ruins of a house (La Pleta), leave your car and go for a walk (3). The abandoned fields and stands of pine in this area will give sightings of Great Grey Shrike, Hoopoe, various tits, warblers and, at night, Nightjar and Eagle Owl. Continue along the road and after 1.5 km you will come to a right turn (4). Leave your car at this point and walk along the track leading off to the right for some 2 hours. The ground is gently rolling and vegetation is low-growing, making it easy for you to see Black-eared Wheatear, Rock Thrush, Great Grey Shrike, Sardinian Warbler, Dartford Warbler, etc. Continue straight on, past the turning for the telecommunications station until reaching Campgràs (5), former fields where Thekla Lark, Ortolan Bunting, Tawny Pipit and Spectacled Warbler are present. From here, you can prolong the walk by climbing up to la Morella (592 m) which is the highest point in the area; alternatively you can return to your vehicle. The last stretch of the route is by car and terminates at Palau Novella. On this last stretch, be on the lookout for species such as Bonelli's Eagle, Blue Rock Thrush or Raven.

Accommodation

There is plenty of accommodation available in Barcelona and the coastal area around Gavà and Castelldefels.

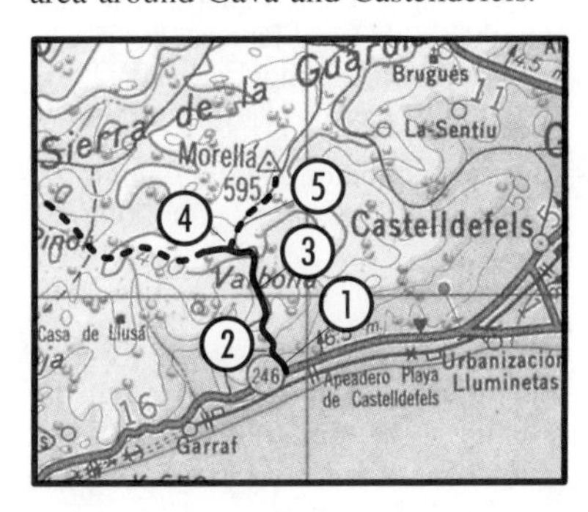

CA

Comments

The Garraf hills can be visited throughout the year, although spring is the best season. Wear suitable shoes, do not stray off the path, and take something to drink since there are no water sources anywhere in the area.

Jaume Orta and Anna Motis

■ CA.19 MONTSERRAT

A massif featuring extraordinary rock formations.

Main species

Residents: Bonelli's Eagle, Peregrine Falcon, Red-legged Partridge, Eagle Owl, Collared Dove, Crag Martin, Blue Rock Thrush, Sardinian Warbler, Dartford Warbler, Rock Sparrow.

Summer visitors: Alpine Swift, Bee-eater, Rock Thrush, Subalpine Warbler, Bonelli's Warbler, Woodchat Shrike, Ortolan Bunting.

Winter visitors: Alpine Accentor, Wallcreeper.

Access

Take the A-7 motorway out of Barcelona in the direction of Tarragona and come off at the Martorell exit. Continue along the N-II towards Lleida and, before coming to Esparraguera, turn right onto the C-1411 to Manresa. On reaching Monistrol, a minor road takes you up to the monastery of Montserrat.

To reach Collbató, continue along the N-II and take the turning for Collbató.

Description

A mountain which rises abruptly over the plains and neighbouring hills, reaching its maximum height with the peak of Sant Jeroni (1,236 m). The erosion of the conglomerate rock constituting Montserrat has given rise to a most unusual appearance, with countless rocky fingers which are the origin of the name of Montserrat —literally, saw-toothed mountain.

Vegetation consists of thick holm oak and pine woodland on the lower slopes. This woodland was severely affected by the terrible fires which desolated much of the mountain in 1986. Today shrubs predominate, although large areas of holm oak lying on high ground were saved.

Recommended routes

The two routes recommended here are circular and are to be undertaken on foot. It is worth spending half a day on each walk.

Route A starts at the monastery of Montserrat, where you can see Alpine Swift and Peregrine Falcon. From the funicular railway stations of Sant Joan and Santa Cova, a well-surfaced, broad track leads off to the campsite and Pla de Sant Miquel (1) where you will find holm oak woodland, untouched by the fire, bordering with the scrubland which has replaced the burned areas of woodland. Here you can see Sardinian Warbler, Subalpine Warbler and Rock Bunting. At Pla de Sant Miquel four paths meet; take the track which climbs up to the left, signed for Sant Joan, which will bring you to the upper station of the funicular railway. Continue along a track marked with yellow paint to reach a vantage point (2), a good spot for watching birds. The path continues to the peak of Sant Jeroni (3) where you can see Black Redstart, Alpine Swift, Peregrine Falcon and, in winter, Alpine Accentor and Wallcreeper. To return, retrace your steps but just before reaching Cap de Mort, a rock resembling a human skull which you will have seen on the way up, take a path leading off to the left down to

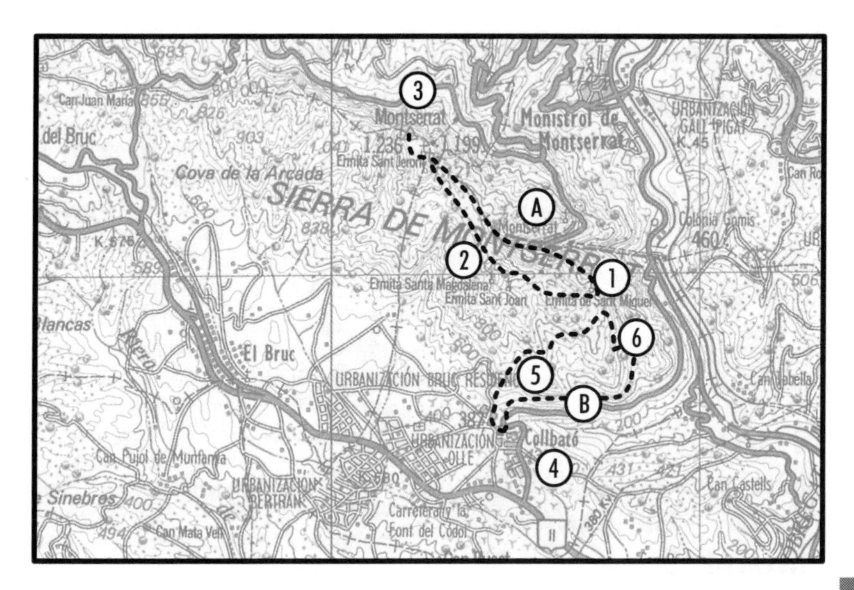

the valley bottom. On reaching Pla de Ocells continue to descend to the monastery, following the yellow, red and white markings.

The starting point of **route B** is Collbató (4) where you will see Collared Dove, Starling, Cirl Bunting and Melodious Warbler. Take the road for the Coves del Salnitre, caves open to the public which are located at the foot of a large cliff. You may well see Rock Sparrow near the caves. A path marked with red, yellow and white markings leads off from the caves, signed with the words *Al monasterio por Santa Cova* (to the monastery via Santa Cova). This area (5) is a good place for seeing Peregrine Falcon, Bee-eater, Crag Martin, Blue Rock Thrush, Sardinian Warbler and, in winter, Alpine Accentor and Wallcreeper. The path turns and climbs along a ravine (6) where you may see Rock Thrush. Subsequently, it climbs up to a pass with an old electricity pylon and comes to a point from where you can see the valley of the river Llobregat. Keep a close lookout for a turn to the left, not easily seen, indicated by the words Sant Miquel painted on a rock. The path, marked with white and yellow paint, climbs up to the Pla de Sant Miquel, where it meets with three other paths. Take the path marked for Collbató. You will gently drop down through the areas which were not affected by the fire. Here you can see numerous forest-dwelling species. Finally, you will come to a flat area occupied by olive groves frequented by Woodchat Shrike and Golden Oriole. Continue along a dirt track with yellow markings which will take you down to Collbató.

Accommodation

In addition to the wide variety of accommodation available in Barcelona and the surrounding area, there is a hotel and a campsite at the monastery of Montserrat.

Comments

The best time of year for visiting the area is spring and early summer. You should bear in mind that both routes require a certain amount of physical effort because of the climbs involved, although this should not present problems for anybody who is minimally used to hill walking. In summer and on public holidays a lot of people visit Montserrat, making it advisable to start route A early in the morning (route B is much less frequented by visitors).

Joan Estrada,
Anna Motis
and Jaume Orta

CA.20 MONTSANT MOUNTAIN RANGE – SIURANA MOUTAINS

Typically Mediterranean mountain ranges; extremely rocky.

Main species

Residents: Golden Eagle, Bonelli's Eagle, Red-legged Partridge, Eagle Owl, Thekla Lark, Crag Martin, Black Wheatear, Blue Rock Thrush, Dartford Warbler, Sardinian Warbler, Rock Sparrow.

Summer visitors: Nightjar, Red-necked Nightjar, Alpine Swift, Bee-eater, Red-rumped Swallow, Tawny Pipit, Black-eared Wheatear, Rock Thrush, Melodious Warbler, Subalpine Warbler, Orphean Warbler, Bonelli's Warbler, Woodchat Shrike.

Winter visitors: Alpine Accentor, Wallcreeper.

On passage: Honey Buzzard, Black Kite and other birds of prey.

Access

From Reus, take the N-420 towards Falset. After 7 km turn right onto the C-242 taking you to Cornudella (22 km).

Description

The mountains of Montsant and Siurana are part of the Cordillera Litoral Catalana. The southern side of Montsant, which reaches its highest point with Roca Corbatera (1,166 m) is covered by shrubs and presents a massive cliff running for 12 km. Small clefts known as *graus* enable you to climb the cliffs and reach the top of the massif.

In contrast, the northern slopes are covered with substantial pine and holm oak woodland. The river Montsant runs along a gorge through the northern side. The area is beautiful and of great ecological value, but is soon to be transformed by the construction of an reservoir.

The Siurana moutain range is slightly lower than that of Montsant, but supports more extensive areas of woodland, largely made up of pine and holm oak.

Recommended routes

Route A starts in Cornudella, where you take the road climbing up to the village of La Morera. Leave your vehicle in La Morera and, in the upper part of the village, take the path marked for Grau de la Grallera. A little farther on take the path for Grau de l'Agnet which climbs the cliff and leads you to the top of the Montsant range. En route you will see various cliff-dwellers such as Peregrine Falcon, Alpine Swift, Blue Rock Thrush, Crag Martin, Raven, Black Wheatear and, in winter, Wallcreeper and Alpine Accentor. The scrublands are interesting for sightings of Black-eared Wheatear, Sardinian Warbler, Dartford Warbler and, on more open land, Tawny Pipit. Follow the spine of the range in the direction indicated by the metal sign for Cabassers, and when you reach another sign for

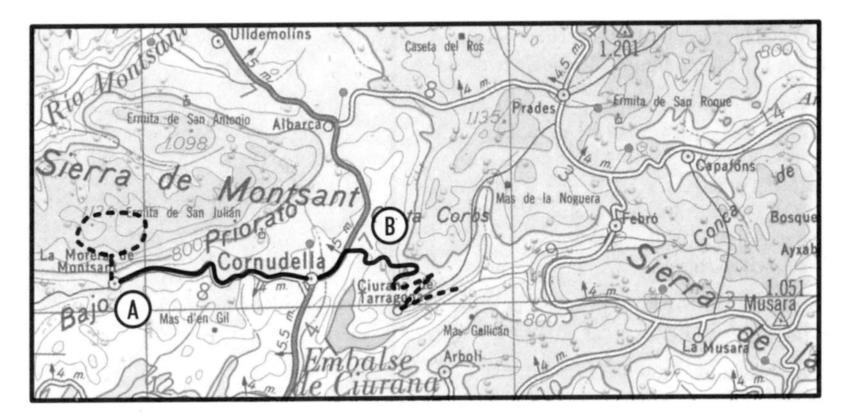

Grallera-La Morera, make your way down to the village again, passing through an area where you may see Rock Thrush.

Route B also starts in Cornudella, but this time leaves the village in the direction of Ulldemolins. Just as you leave Cornudella, turn right onto a track signed for Siurana and after 3 km, on a bend, turn right onto a track which is usually closed with a chain. Leave your vehicle here and continue on foot. When you reach the point where the track divides into three, take the left-hand path which is closed off with a chain to prevent vehicles entering. Look out for a path leading off to the left and climbing up to Siurana, about 500 m before reaching a farm (Mas d'en Candi). On the rock faces you may see Golden Eagle, Bonelli's Eagle, Peregrine Falcon, Blue Rock Thrush and Raven. In the village of Siurana you may see Alpine Swift, Red-rumped Swallow and Crag Martin. Return by the only track leaving the village. When you come to a fork keep to the left; this track is signed for Cornudella and will bring you to your car. From Siurana there is a short cut which will save you for having to walk along a large part of this track.

If you are going at a gentle pace, each of these routes will take half a day.

Accommodation

Plenty of accommodation is available in Tarragona, Reus, and the coastal towns of Salou and Cambrils. There are also *fondas* in the small inland villages of the Montsant area.

Comments

The best time of year for visiting the area is spring, between the months of April and June. For route A, it is worth wearing thick-soled boots with plenty of grip, since the terrain is very rocky. It is also worth taking drinking water. You are recommended not to undertake the route if it is foggy, since it may be difficult to find your way on the high ground.

Jaume Orta and Anna Motis

■ CA.21 PORTS DE TORTOSA

A large, extremely rocky and steep massif.

Main species

Residents: Griffon Vulture, Golden Eagle, Bonelli's Eagle, Red-legged Partridge, Eagle Owl, Thekla Lark, Crag Martin, Black Wheatear, Blue

Rock Thrush, Dartford Warbler, Sardinian Warbler, Chough, Rock Sparrow.

Summer visitors: Nightjar, Red-necked Nightjar, Bee-eater, Tawny Pipit, Black-eared Wheatear, Melodious Warbler, Orphean Warbler, Garden Warbler, Subalpine Warbler, Spectacled Warbler, Bonelli's Warbler, Woodchat Shrike.

Winter visitors: Alpine Accentor, Goldcrest, Wallcreeper, Citril Finch.

On passage: Honey Buzzard, Black Kite and other species.

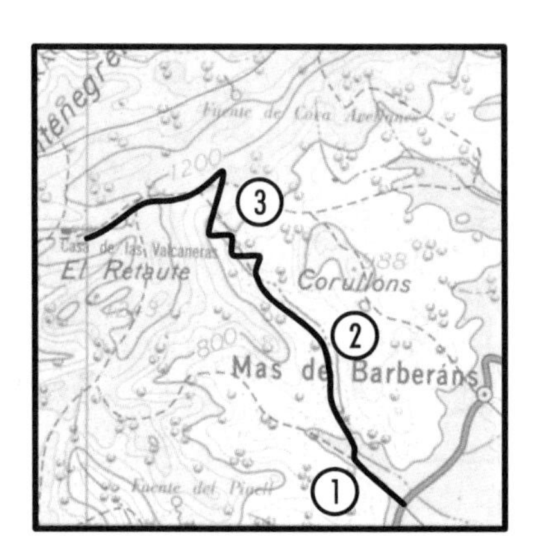

Access

In Tortosa, cross the river Ebro and take the N-230 towards Gandesa. Shortly afterwards turn left for Roquetes, virtually next to Tortosa. From Roquetas a road runs to La Sènia and Mas de Barberans (16 km).

Description

The Ports de Tortosa–Beseit (Beceite) are the easternmost spurs of the ranges of the Maestrazgo (part of the Iberian System). Many of the peaks rise to over 1,000 m. This range lies close to the coast and is characterized by extremely complicated and steep contours combining valleys, gorges, cliffs and rocky pinnacles. Plant life is abundant and varied, with many endemic species. Generally speaking the area is dominated by pine woods, although there are also holm oak woods, other kind of woodland and various shrubland habitats. Small-scale farming has decreased in recent years, cultivated land now being limited to lowland areas and areas near villages. There is a large population of Spanish ibex.

Recommended routes

The recommended route is a car journey starting in Mas de Barberans. You will need at least 4 hours. Having left the village, between the 13 and 14 km marker posts a dirt track runs off to the right, beside a traffic sign for dangerous bends. The track, 17.5 km long, climbs the La Galera gorge and is accessible to any kind of vehicle, although the last stretch of the track is usually in bad condition.

At the beginning of the track, take a walk through the olive groves in the area (1) to see Hoopoe, Turtle Dove, Black-eared Wheatear, Woodchat Shrike, Orphean Warbler, Cirl Bunting, etc. During the migration periods this is a good place for seeing Honey Buzzard, Black Kite and Marsh Harrier on passage. A little farther on, after a small patch of olive trees, you will cross an area dotted with shrubs and pines where you may have sightings of Tawny Pipit. Continue until you come to a fork in the road. Keep to the left and farther on, having crossed a river bed, usually dry, you will come to another crossroads. Turn right here and when you reach the point where the gorge narrows (2) look out for Griffon Vulture, Peregrine Falcon, Alpine Swift, Blue Rock Thrush, etc. You will pass a track leading off to the right, usually closed with a chain; from here the track you are following zig-zags up the hill. In this area (3), stop to watch Griffon Vulture, Golden Eagle, Short-toed Eagle and Peregrine Falcon. The track continues to a place called Casetes Velles where there are a few holiday houses. The track finishes 1.5 km after the houses, and you can branch off on various routes to see more forest and scrubland-dwelling birds.

If you have time, it is worthwhile climbing Mont Caro, the highest point in the range (1,447 m). This can easily be reached on a surfaced road, signed from the village of Roquetes.

Accommodation

There are plenty of hotels and restaurants in Tortosa and neighbouring towns.

Anna Motis and Jaume Orta

■ CA.22 EBRO DELTA

A coastal wetland area; the most important area of its kind in Spain, in conjunction with the Marismas del Guadalquivir (Coto Doñana area).

Main species

Residents: Bittern, Cattle Egret, Little Egret, Greater Flamingo, Shelduck, Red-crested Pochard, Avocet, Kentish Plover, Slender-billed Gull, Sandwich Tern, Whiskered Tern, Lesser Short-toed Lark, Moustached Warbler, Bearded Tit, Reed Bunting.

Summer visitors: Little Bittern, Night Heron, Squacco Heron, Purple Heron, Black-winged Stilt, Collared Pratincole, Audouin's Gull, Gull-billed Tern, Lesser Crested Tern, Little Tern, Black Tern, Bee-eater, Short-toed Lark, Savi's Warbler.

Winter visitors: Great White Egret, herons (up to 18,000), Marsh Harrier, Hen Harrier, Peregrine Falcon, ducks (up to 90,000), waders (up to 28,000), Mediterranean Gull, Short-eared Owl, Bluethroat.

On passage: Glossy Ibis, Osprey, Temminck's Stint, Marsh Sandpiper, Caspian Tern, Transsaharan passerines.

Access

First of all, it is worth visiting one of the two information centres. One is located in Deltebre and can be reached by taking any of the exits to Deltebre from the N-340. The second is beside L'Encanyissada lagoon and can be reached from Amposta along the road to Sant Jaume d'Enveja, following signs for *Refugi-Museu de la Casa de Fusta*.

The Information Centres will provide maps and leaflets containing general information. You should bear in mind that the road network is very complex and lacking in signs, making it vital to have a good map. Both centres are open an year round 10:00-14:00 and 15:00-18:00 on weekdays. On Saturdays they are open 10:00-13:00 and 15:30-18:00. On public holidays they are open 10:00-13:00 (the Casa de Fusta Information Centre is closed on Mondays).

Description

The Delta del Ebro (Ebre) is a flood plain of some 32,000 ha, projecting about 20 km out to sea. Much of the area is cultivated, but in addition to the rice fields, which occupy 20,000 ha and are of major importance as a feeding ground for a multitude of water birds, there are still extensive areas of natural habitat in the Delta, making it one of the biggest wetland areas in the Iberian Peninsula. While it cannot be denied that the most remarkable habitats are those related to coastal environments (beaches, sand bars, bays and tidal marshes), there are also large areas of salt pans and salt marshes, coastal lagoons and unspoiled areas of riverside woodland.

Recommended routes

The starting point for **route A** is the Deltebre Information Centre. It consists of a 15 km car journey which can be undertaken in half a day. The route takes you to the rice fields, El Fangar bay and El Fangar point with their extensive areas of sand flats and dunes. The points of greatest interest are the following:

1) Rice fields between Deltebre and La Marquesa beach. During spring and summer you will see Purple Heron, Little Bittern, Whiskered Tern, terns in general and Gull-billed Tern, the latter favouring greatly the area around the cemetery. From October to March herons, Lapwing and gulls abound, and at the end of the winter it is well worthwhile casting an eye over flooded fields to see groups of waders on passage. It is also worth watching fields where tractors are ploughing the stubble into the ground, since these are the site of vast congregations of birds.

2) El Fangar bay and El Fangar point. During the autumn and winter months this area abounds with Grey Plover, Curlew and other coastal waders, while the bay is frequented by Great Crested Grebe, Black-necked Grebe and Red-breasted Merganser. At the end of El Fangar point you will often see groups of Common Scoter and, depending on the year, Velvet Scoter and Eider. The entire area, but particularly the far point and the areas surrounding the lighthouse, is excellent for seeing Gannet, Yelkouan Shearwater, Great Skua, Arctic Skua, Razorbill and various species of gulls including Mediterranean Gull. In spring and summer you will see gulls and waders on passage, but the greatest point of interest is provided by the large colony of Common Tern and Little Tern which can be seen from the track. This is also the breeding ground for Kentish Plover and a few pairs of Oystercatcher.

Route B starts at the same point as route A, covering the rice fields on the north bank of the Ebro as far as the area around El Garxal, a lagoon which is being created by the formation of sand banks, dunes, salt marshes and areas of extremely shallow water. The route is 15 km long and takes approximately half a day.

3) Rice fields between Deltebre and Riomar. The characteristics of these areas and the species present are identical to those described for route A.

4) El Garxal. This area is interesting during the migration periods when you can see large groups of various species of waders and gulls, such as Audouin's Gull, Mediterranean Gull and Slender-billed Gull. Terns congregate here before the breeding season, and it is a particularly good place for seeing Caspian Tern. April and May will give rise to sightings of large groups of ducks including Garganey and Red-crested Pochard. Finally you will also see various larks and, between the housing development and the beach, Collared Pratincole.

Route C is the most comprehensive of the routes, beginning at the Casa de Fusta Information Centre and taking you to the rice fields, L'Encanyissada and La Tancada lagoons, Els Alfacs bay and La Banya point. This route will take a whole day and covers 25 km.

5) Vantage point over L'Encanyissada lagoon and the El Través road bridge. From these two spots one can command a view of various areas of the L'Encanyissada lagoon, the largest in the Delta. In autumn and winter ducks, cormorants, grebes, gulls, Marsh Harrier, etc. abound. At the end of the winter, when the water level is lower, you will often see Greater Flamingo,

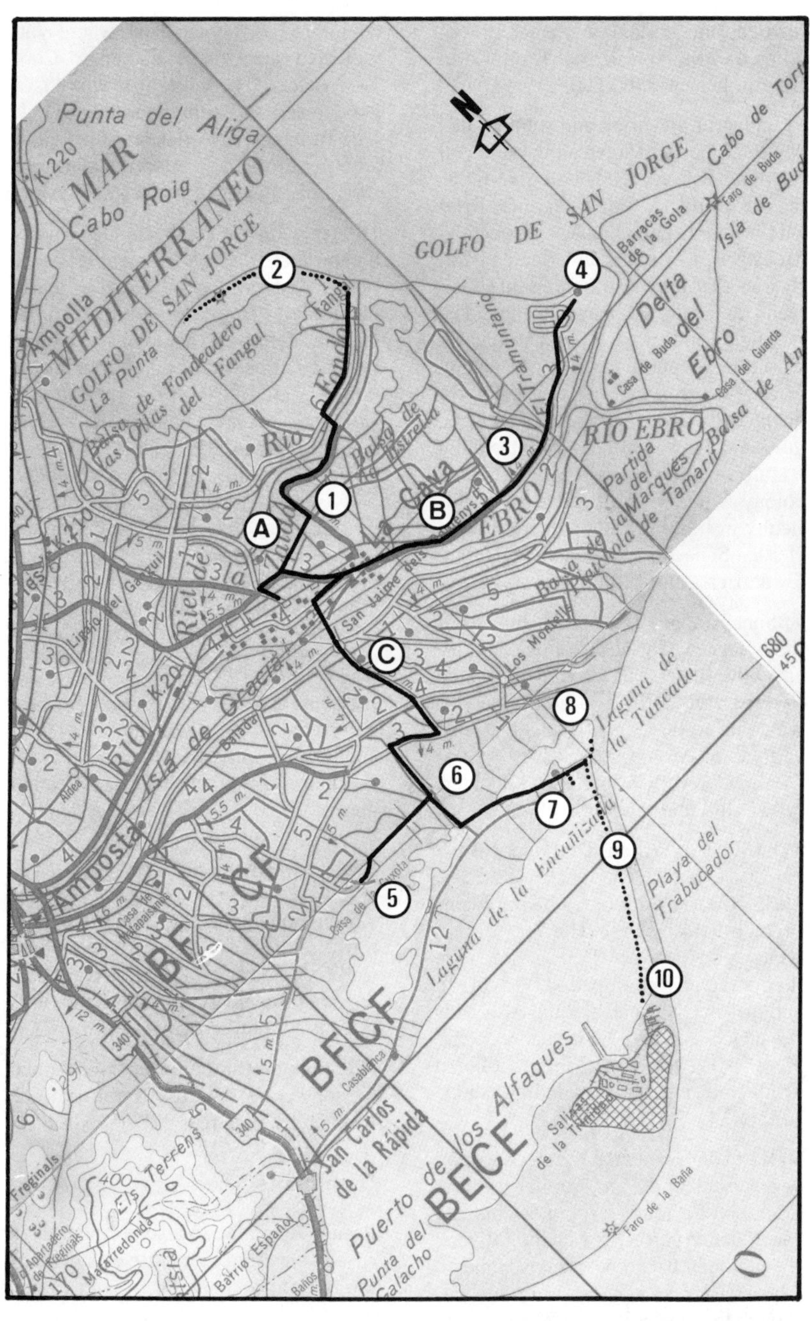

Avocet and Black-tailed Godwit. In spring and summer you will see large quantities of ducks, especially Mallard and Red-crested Pochard. The marshes surrounding the lagoon shelter Black-winged Stilt, Whiskered Tern, Little Bittern, herons and egrets.

6) La Nòria. In spring and summer this is one of the most interesting points on the route. The reedbeds will give sightings of warblers, Savi's Warbler, Reed Bunting and, although less frequently, Moustached Warbler and Bearded Tit; Bearded Tit may also be present in the reedbeds at the El Travès bridge. The rice fields and irrigated land around La Nòria are a good place for watching feeding water birds, and are usually frequented by large numbers of waders, gulls, etc. However the most interesting feature of this area is the large mixed colony of herons. You will have no difficulty in spotting Little Bittern, Purple Heron, Squacco Heron, Night Heron, Cattle Egret and Little Egret.

7) Sant Antoni saltpans. At the end of the winter, when the rice fields are dry and birds have gathered in the scarce flooded areas, this is a good spot for watching waders and herons. It is also a good place for seeing Little Tern, Common Tern, Caspian Tern, Slender-billed Gull and Audouin's Gull.

8) La Tancada lagoon. This lagoon is the best place in the Delta for seeing grebes, ducks, Coot, Cormorant, Greater Flamingo, herons, Marsh Harrier, etc. In winter you may see Hen Harrier and, during the migration period, Osprey. In summer the salt marshes and rush beds beside the lake are a good site for seeing Kentish Plover, Little Tern, Collared Pratincole and larks including Short-toed and Lesser Short-toed Lark.

9) Barra del Trabucador. Els Alfacs bay is a site for birds very similar to those described for route A (point 2), but is a much better place for watching divers; the number of grebes is also higher. Make stops at regular intervals, although the best points are located at the beginning of the sand bar where you will also see Greater Flamingo, Coot and waders. The edge of the bay is a good place for seeing Bar-tailed Godwit, Turnstone and Slender-billed Gull. At other times of year (spring and summer), this area is of much less interest.

10) Hide on La Banya point. This is the perfect place for watching water birds. Waders seen on a regular basis include all the species common to the Iberian Peninsula and the occasional rarity such as Red-necked Phalarope, which can be seen in spring and autumn. The salt pans are the site of Avocet, Greater Flamingo, Slender-billed Gull and, in smaller numbers, herons and Shelduck. In autumn and winter this area is the location of groups of hundreds of Cormorant, thousands of Dunlin and tens of thousands of duck, including large numbers of Mallard, Widgeon, Teal, Shoveler, Gadwall and Pintail.

In spring and summer this is the best part of the Delta to see Audouin's Gull and, more rarely, Mediterranean Gull, Caspian Tern or even Lesser Crested Tern.

Accommodation

Accommodation is available in the main towns of the area such as Amposta, Sant Carles de la Ràpita, Deltebre, etc. There are also several campsites, and it is possible to rent apartments or houses.

Additional information can be obtained by contacting: Centre d'Informació de Deltebre; telephone: 977-489679.

Comments

Routes A and B can also be undertaken by bicycle, although route C is perhaps too long to be undertaken with ease.

Albert Martínez Vilalta

EXTREMADURA

Black-shouldered Kite
Elanus caeruleus

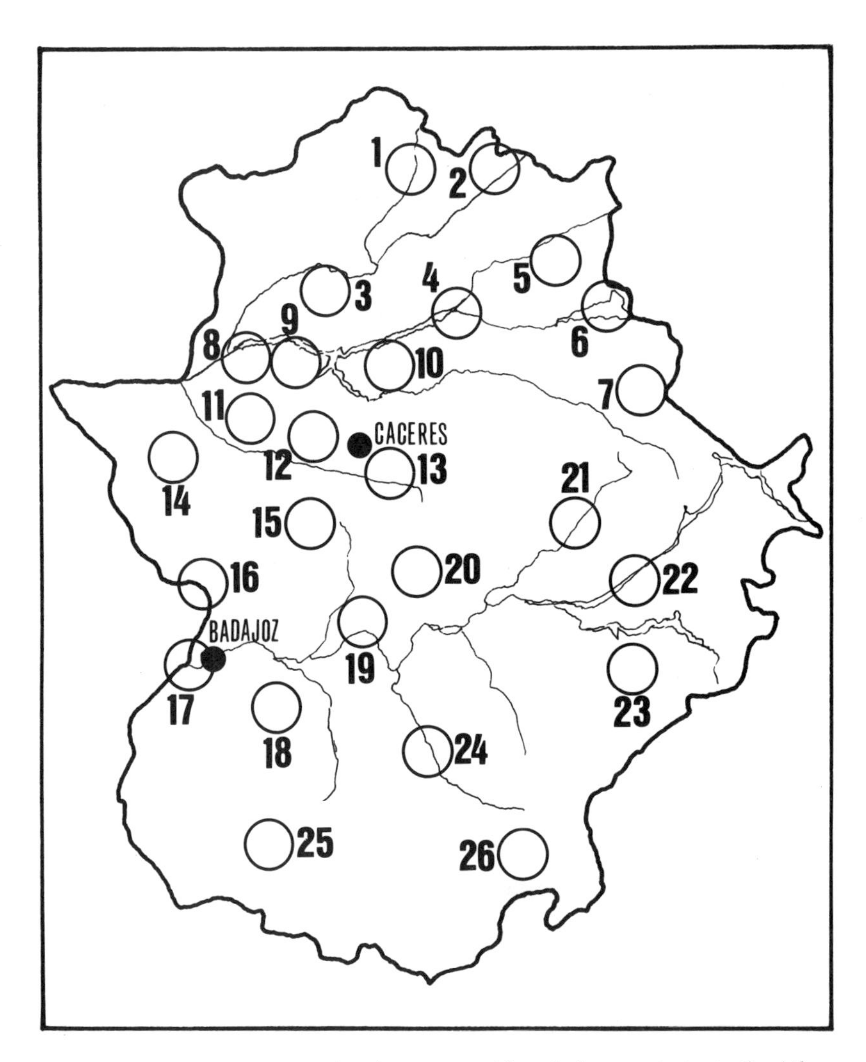

Despite the fact that Extremadura has only two provinces, Cáceres and Badajoz, it is one of the biggest regions of Spain, smaller only in size than Castile-León, Andalusia, Castile-La Mancha and Aragon. It is also indisputably one of the most interesting regions in terms of wildlife and birds.

Geographically speaking, it occupies quite a small part of the western section of the southern Meseta. However, its average altitude, which is quite low, and its relative proximity to the Atlantic make for more temperate, damper winter climates than those characterizing the unforgiving Castilian Meseta. In fact, the winter months in this area enable a very high primary biological production with grazing land, acorns and other fruits typical of Mediterranean woodlands, enabling vast numbers of birds to winter in the region. This is in stark contrast to the summers, which are extremely long, dry, hot and unproductive. The area lies on a core of Palaeozoic origin, and the presence of slate, quartzite and granite makes for shallow, acid soil unsuitable for intensive farming methods. On a very few flood plains Tertiary and Quaternary sediments are present, giving rise to deep soil and the recent development of irrigation systems. For these reasons, much of the region has been predominated for centuries by stock farming, with transhumant herds of sheep making the most of the winter pastures. This traditional activity means that human population has remained low in the area and has ensured that the region retains its remarkably good general state of conservation, even today.

Mediterranean dry grazing woodland (*dehesa*), an archetype for balanced and sustainable land use, still occupies vast areas of Extremadura and the neighbouring regions of Portugal, Castile and Andalusia. It comprises holm oak (*Quercus rotundifolia*) and cork oak (*Quercus suber*), open woods with grazing land and cereal crops, grown on a rotational basis over the course of several years. This does not only give the landscape a very individual appearance, but also allows for the sustaining of notable birdlife which, while perhaps reduced in terms of numbers of species and with very few typical forest-dwellers, includes Black-shouldered Kite, Black Kite, Great Spotted Cuckoo, Red-necked Nightjar, Orphean Warbler, Woodchat Shrike, Great Grey Shrike, Azure-winged Magpie and Spanish Sparrow. The livestock inhabiting the *dehesas* also provide food for the many vultures, kites and Raven which breed in the nearby hills, while in winter acorns provide food for large groups of Crane and Woodpigeon.

While substantial areas of *dehesas* are present virtually everywhere, the same cannot be said of mountains of any size. Only in the northeastern corner, in the regions of La Vera and the valley of the river Jerte (EX.2), do peaks reach over 2,000 m, enabling you to see the high mountain habitat characteristic of the Gredos range and the Sistema Central as a whole, with Skylark, Water Pipit, Dunnock, Alpine Accentor, Bluethroat, Black Redstart, Wheatear, Rock Thrush and Ortolan Bunting being representative species. This is also the main site in Extremadura where Pyrenean oak and chestnut grow, the habitat of forest-dwelling species such as Honey Buzzard, Sparrowhawk, Nightjar, Lesser Spotted Woodpecker, Robin, Redstart, Blackcap, Bonelli's Warbler, Nuthatch and Hawfinch. Finally there are also mountain rivers and streams, often frequented by Common Sandpiper, Grey Wagtail and Dipper.

Some of these species are also present on the massif of Las Villuercas (EX.7), a spur of the Montes de Toledo which reaches a height of 1,600 m; however, it is highly exceptional to see them in other Extremaduran ranges. These are residual land forms which sometimes stand up like islands in the middle of the peneplain. However, it is probably in these small ranges where Extremaduran birdlife is at its best, with sites such as Monfragüe (EX.4), San Pedro range (EX.14 and EX.15), Montánchez range (EX.20), Pela range (EX.22), the area around the García Sola dam or Puerto Peña (EX.22), the hills between Castuera and Cabeza del Buey (EX.23), the small ranges at Oliva de Mérida and Hornachos (EX.24), the foothills of the Sierra Morena lying to the south of Jerez de los Caballeros (EX.25), and those at Llerena and Azuaga (EX.26). In these areas, the screes on the mountain crests and the gorges carved out by rivers —with wonderful examples at Monfragüe—

are the breeding ground of cliff-dwelling species such as Black Stork, Griffon Vulture, Egyptian Vulture, Golden Eagle, Bonelli's Eagle, Peregrine Falcon, Eagle Owl, Alpine Swift, White-rumped Swift (very localized), Red-rumped Swallow, Crag Martin, Black Wheatear, Blue Rock Thrush, Chough, Jackdaw and Raven. The relative lack of good cliff faces makes for large concentrations of birds at the few suitable sites. This means that man-made constructions in Extremadura, such as castles and large bridges, are also well worth a visit.

On the northern slopes of the ranges, patches of temperate woodland still remain, with cork oak, holm oak, wild olive tree (*Olea europea*), wild pear (*Pyrus bourgeana*) and strawberry tree (*Arbutus unedo*). Deer, Spanish lynx and Egyptian mongoose coexist with birds of prey who use the trees as nesting places, such as Black Vulture, Red Kite, Short-toed Eagle, Goshawk, Buzzard, Spanish Imperial Eagle, Booted Eagle and Hobby. The cistus scrubland, mastic trees (*Pistacia lentiscus*), rock fields and small olive groves on the valley sides will give sightings of, among other interesting passerines, Thekla Lark, Woodlark, Rufous Bush Robin, Black-eared Wheatear, Melodious Warbler, Dartford Warbler, Spectacled Warbler, Subalpine Warbler, Sardinian Warbler, Orphean Warbler, Great Grey Shrike, Woodchat Shrike and Rock Bunting.

In some regions there are also deforested plains, which are used for dry cereal growing and sheep grazing. These are the best areas for steppe-dwelling birds in Western Europe. Common species include Montagu's Harrier, Kestrel, Red-legged Partridge, Little Bustard, Great Bustard, Stone Curlew, Black-bellied Sandgrouse, Pin-tailed Sandgrouse, Little Owl, Roller, Calandra Lark, Short-toed Lark, Crested Lark, Thekla Lark, Black-eared Wheatear and Corn Bunting. In winter Hen Harrier, Merlin, Crane, Golden Plover, Lapwing, Skylark, Meadow Pipit and Pied Wagtail are present, among other common species. Examples of interesting steppe areas are: Talaván (EX.10), Brozas (EX.11), the Salor reservoir (EX.13), La Albuera (EX.18), Zorita–Madrigalejo (EX.21), Llerena–Azuaga (EX.26) and particularly La Serena (EX.18), where there are vast areas of grazing land.

Although areas of irrigated land are indisputably very artificial and support a large human population, they are also of interest to the birdwatcher, who should concentrate above all on the irrigation and drainage channels and the flooded rice fields. During the breeding season Cattle Egret, Quail, Water Rail, Moorhen, Black-winged Stilt, Collared Pratincole, Crested Lark, Cetti's Warbler, Fan-tailed Warbler, Great Reed Warbler and Avadavat are present, the latter being a recent but highly successful colonizer of the Vegas del Guadiana area. You may also see waders during the migration periods when Ruff and Black-tailed Godwit are present. But, in winter, the range and above all numbers of birds present are at their highest with Grey Heron, Little Egret, Black-shouldered Kite, Red Kite, Marsh Harrier, Buzzard, Kestrel, Crane, Lapwing, Snipe, Black-headed Gull, Lesser Black-backed Gull, Pied Wagtail, Meadow Pipit, Stonechat, Chiffchaff and Reed Bunting among other common and representative species. There are areas of irrigated land at Campo Arañuelo and Regadíos del Tiétar (EX.5), Badajoz (EX.17), Mérida (EX.19) and Zorita–Madrigalejo (EX.21).

Although Extremadura does not have natural wetland areas of any great significance, the range of water birds present is large thanks to rivers, ponds and reservoirs. The rivers Tajo (Tagus) and Guadiana cross the region, with large tributaries such as the Tiétar, Alagón and Zújar. Reservoirs are numerous and sometimes on a large scale: Gabriel y Galán (EX.1), Jerte (EX.2), Portaje (EX.3), Torrejón (EX.4), Alcántara (EX.4), Arrocampo (EX.5), Valdecañas (EX.6), Garrovillas (EX.9), Talaván (EX.10), Salor (EX.13), Montijo (EX.19), Cornalvo (EX.20), Orellana (EX.22), García Sola (EX.22), Zújar (EX.23), La Serena (EX.23), Los Molinos de Matachel (EX.24), Alange (EX.24), Valuengo (EX.25), Llerena (EX.26)... In addition, tanks or ponds for irrigation, watering livestock and breeding tench occur quite frequently, with examples at Villa del Rey and Mata de Alcántara (EX.8), Brozas (EX.11), Arroyo de la Luz (EX.12), El Zangallón (EX.16), Valverde de Leganés (EX.17), La Albuera (EX.18) and Madrigalejo (EX.21). Because of this, during the breeding season it is possible to see Little Grebe, Great Crested Grebe, Little Bittern, Night Heron, Little Egret, Grey Heron, Mallard, Coot, Little Ringed Plover, Gull-billed Tern, Little Tern, Kingfisher and Sand Martin; in winter, Cormorant, Marsh Harrier, Widgeon, Teal, Shoveler, Pochard, Tufted Duck and Lesser Black-backed Gull; and during the migration period Purple Heron, Spoonbill, Greylag Goose, Garganey, Osprey, Black Tern and Whiskered Tern, among many other species.

Finally, one cannot talk of the birds of Extremadura without making special mention of the town centres which frequently have surprisingly large colonies of White Stork and Lesser Kestrel. With luck, you should also be able to see Pallid Swift among the many swifts, martins and swallows.

■ EX.1 GABRIEL Y GALÁN RESERVOIR

Reservoir

Main species

Residents: Great Crested Grebe, Grey Heron, Little Egret, Black-shouldered Kite, Black Vulture, Goshawk, Dartford Warbler.

Summer visitors: Black Stork, Short-toed Eagle, Booted Eagle.

Winter visitors: Cormorant, Greylag Goose, ducks, Crane.

On passage: Spoonbill, Whiskered Tern, Black Tern.

Access

From Plasencia, take the N-630 towards Béjar. After 28 km turn left onto the C-531 for Zarza de Granadilla (5 km).

Description

The Embalse de Gabriel y Galán, a reservoir formed by damming the waters of the river Alagón, is located in an area of rolling countryside. The surrounding land is taken up by pine plantations, and to the south is a series of holm oak woods growing on grazing lands and areas of irrigated land where wintering Crane feed.

Recommended routes

Route A is 3 km long, taking you from Zarza de Granadilla to Granadilla, an abandoned village which can be reached by a dirt track with a good surface. The route runs through extensive pine woods where you may see Black Vulture, Goshawk, Booted Eagle, Short-toed Eagle and numerous forest-dwelling species. From Granadilla you can command a view of part of the reservoir. This point is good for watching grebes, ducks and Crane.

Route B starts from Zarza de Granadilla and takes you towards the dam wall, which is a good point for watching the daily comings and goings of Crane. From here and from the road linking the villages of Mohedas and La Pesga, you can see some interesting water birds.

Accommodation

There are two hostels in Zarza de Granadilla, and more accommoda-

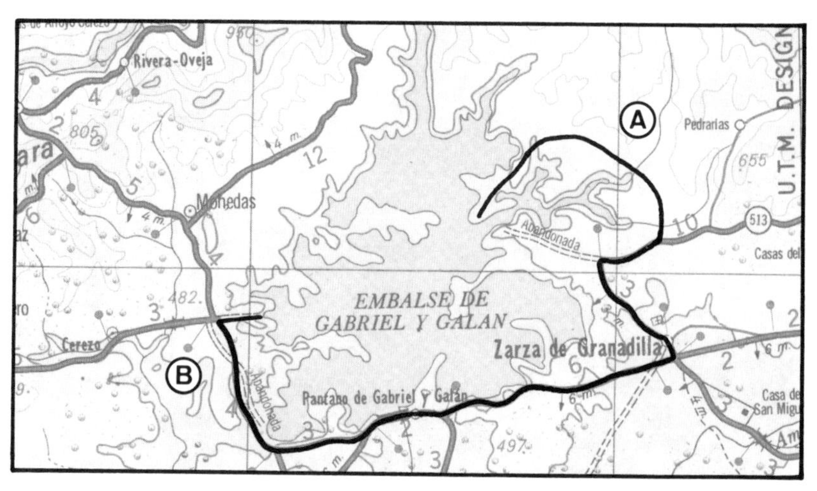

tion is available in the nearby city of Plasencia.

Angel Sánchez García

EX.2 VALLEY OF THE RIVER JERTE

A mountainous area of varying altitudes.

Main species

Residents: Red Kite, Griffon Vulture, Goshawk, Sparrowhawk, Peregrine Falcon, Common Sandpiper, Eagle Owl, Tawny Owl, Great Spotted Woodpecker, Lesser Spotted Woodpecker, Thekla Lark, Crag Martin, Grey Wagtail, Dipper, Dunnock, Alpine Accentor, Robin, Black Redstart, Black Wheatear, Blue Rock Thrush, Mistle Thrush, Dartford Warbler, Sardinian Warbler, Blackcap, Crested Tit, Nuthatch, Chough, Raven, Rock Sparrow, Rock Bunting.

Summer visitors: Black Stork, Honey Buzzard, Egyptian Vulture, Short-toed Eagle, Booted Eagle, Great Spotted Cuckoo, Nightjar, Red-necked Nightjar, Water Pipit, Bluethroat, Redstart, Wheatear, Black-eared Wheatear, Melodious Warbler, Whitethroat, Garden Warbler, Bonelli's Warbler, Ortolan Bunting.

Winter visitors: Woodcock, Siskin, Bullfinch.

Access

The N-110 running from Plasencia to Avila runs over the mountain pass of Tornavacas and all the way along the Jerte valley. Between the villages of Cabezuela del Valle and Jerte, take the N-630 which will take you to Hervás via the Honduras mountain pass. This is a minor road with a bad surface, numerous bends and steep gradients, although it is nonetheless passable for any normal car. Alternatively you can turn off the N-110 for Piornal. Again, the only difficulties you will encounter are bends and steep gradients. This road runs across the range to Garganta la Olla in the La Vera region.

Description

A bird's eye view of the Jerte valley shows a huge gap in the mountains of the Sistema Central. It stretches for over 40 km, separating the Sierra de Gredos and the Sierra de Béjar.

The Trasierra is a spur running westwards along the valley from the peak of Calvitero (2,425 m) to the Sierra de Cabezabellosa. Peaks reach more than 1,800 m and are covered with broom inhabited by interesting communities of passerines. Lying parallel, the Sierra de Tormantos starts with Covacha del Losar (2,399 m) and drops down to the Sierra de San Bernabé near Plasencia.

The valley bottom is intensively farmed, being used mainly for cherry orchards although there are also areas of irrigated land and olive groves. Trees range from holm oak on lower ground to cork oak woodland and, on the higher slopes, Pyrenean oak woodland. There are also extensive areas of chestnut, while above the tree line expanses of broom and mountain pastures predominate.

Recommended routes

Route A consists of a drive along the Valle del Jerte from Plasencia to the Tornavacas mountain pass. You can make as many stops as you wish, although it is worthwhile going to the Jerte reservoir (Figure (1), off the map), 6 km from Plasencia, as well as taking a walk along the Garganta del Infierno, a gorge (2), located to the right of the road between the villages

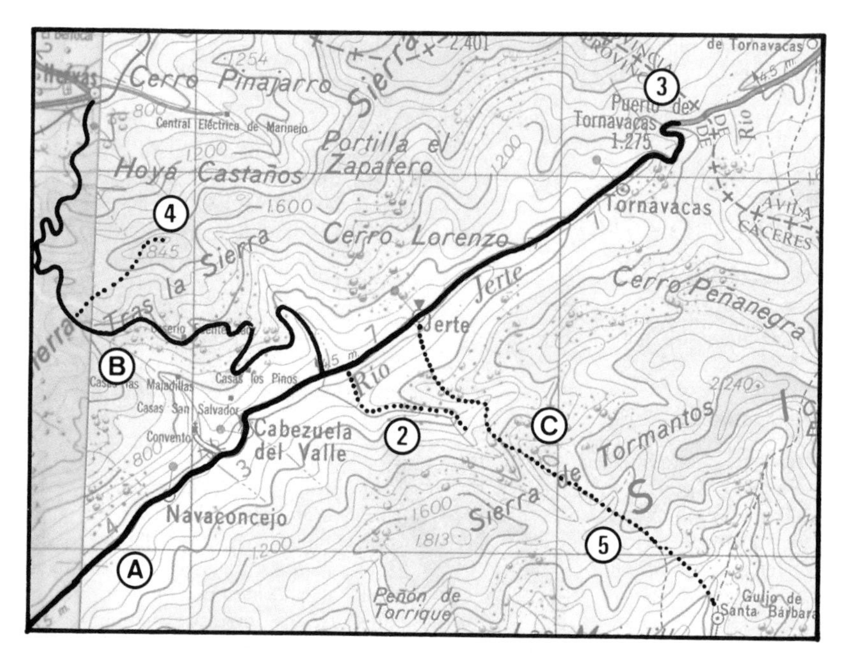

of Cabezuela del Valle and Jerte. It is also worth stopping to walk among the expanses of broom at the Tornavacas pass (3).

Route B takes you from Hervás to Jerte via the Honduras mountain pass. This is also a car journey. It takes you to the head of the river Ambroz, passing through woods of oak and chestnut where you can take short walks. From the top of the pass, you should not miss walking up to the Cerro Valdeamor (1,845 m), reached after 4 km of steep climb (4). In the expanses of broom you will see, among other species, Wheatear, Bluethroat and Rock Thrush.

Route C is a walk from Jerte to Guijo de Santa Bárbara. The route is tough and you should have some experience of mountain walking. The best time of year to undertake the route is in June. From Jerte, tracks climb up the Garganta de los Infiernos to the Collado de las Yeguas (5), a mountain pass with a mountain refuge in which you can spend the night. From here, work your way down to Guijo de Santa Bárbara on the other side of the range and across the western side of the Jaranda gorge. The main attraction of this route is the observation of mountain-dwelling species.

Accommodation

Plenty of hotel accommodation is available in Plasencia, in addition to several hostels and *fondas* in nearby villages. There are also campsites in Valle del Jerte and La Vera.

Juan J. Ferrero, Juan J. Negro and José A. Román

■ EX.3 PORTAJE RESERVOIR

An artificially-created wetland area.

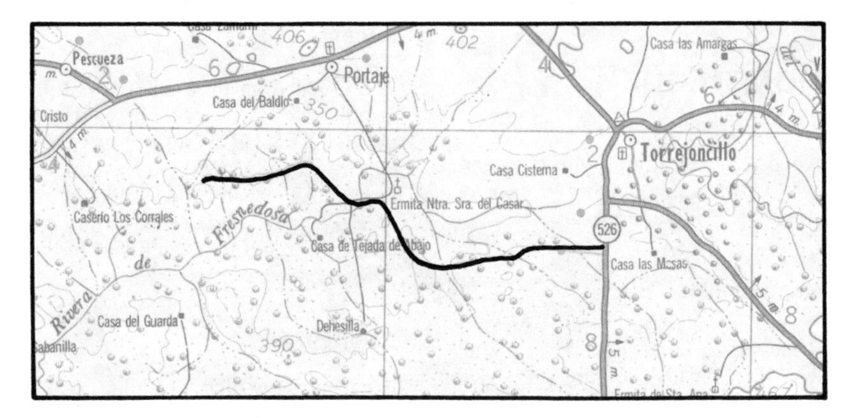

Main species

Residents: Little Grebe, Great Crested Grebe, Grey Heron, Red Kite, Black Vulture, Spanish Imperial Eagle, Coot, Kingfisher.

Summer visitors: Black Stork, Black Kite, Black-shouldered Kite, Egyptian Vulture, Short-toed Eagle, Booted Eagle, Little Ringed Plover.

Winter visitors: Cormorant, Little Egret, Widgeon, Teal, Shoveler, Pochard, Tufted Duck, Crane, Avocet, Golden Plover, Lesser Black-backed Gull.

On passage: Spoonbill, Greylag Goose.

Access

From Coria, take the C-526 in the direction of Cáceres until you reach Torrejoncillo (12 km). Leave this village behind you and, after 2 km, you will see a narrow surfaced track leading off to the right down to the reservoir.

Description

The Portaje reservoir was built to be able to irrigate some 8,000 ha of holm oak woodland, although subsequently initial plans were considerably reduced and mixed irrigated land was created consisting of holm oak woodland interspersed with grazing land. Near one end of the reservoir is a small area which can be flooded with shallow water with the aim of providing a breeding ground for water birds. The areas around the reservoir are covered with dry grazing woodlands, occupied by holm oak and cork oak, and extensive areas of scrubland.

Recommended routes

The access road skirts around half of the reservoir. From this road, you can make a series of stops to watch the most interesting water birds present. It is worth going for a walk in the holm oak woods in the area where, in the company of shrikes, Azure-winged Magpie, Hoopoe and Bee-eater, you can also see vultures, kites, Egyptian Vulture, Spanish Imperial Eagle, Booted Eagle and Black-shouldered Kite.

Accommodation

There are three hotels in Coria, and accommodation is also to be found in Torrejoncillo.

Andrés Rodríguez Rodríguez
and Angel Rodríguez Martín

■ EX.4 MONFRAGÜE

Wooded ranges of hills with river gorges. A remarkable number of birds of prey, above all vultures.

Main species

Residents: Black-shouldered Kite, Red Kite, Griffon Vulture (over 300 pairs), Black Vulture (the largest known colony with over 200 pairs), Goshawk, Sparrowhawk, Spanish Imperial Eagle, Golden Eagle, Bonelli's Eagle, Peregrine Falcon, Eagle Owl, Crag Martin, Thekla Lark, Woodlark, Black Wheatear, Blue Rock Thrush, Sardinian Warbler, Great Grey Shrike, Azure-winged Magpie, Chough, Raven, Rock Bunting.

Summer visitors: Black Stork, Egyptian Vulture, Black Kite, Short-toed Eagle, Booted Eagle, Hobby, White-rumped Swift, Red-rumped Swallow, Rufous Bush Robin, Subalpine Warbler, Orphean Warbler, Golden Oriole, Woodchat Shrike.

Winter visitors: Great Crested Grebe, Cormorant, Grey Heron, Alpine Accentor.

Access

The C-524 from Plasencia (N-630) to Trujillo (N-V) crosses this area. From the N-V it is also possible to reach the area by taking the C-511 in Navalmoral de la Mata in the direction of Plasencia; on arriving at La Bazagona, a turn towards the south will bring you to the Torrejón reservoir.

Description

A series of low ranges of hills crossed by the rivers Tajo (Tagus) and Tiétar, which run along very narrow courses featuring occasional high quartzite cliffs. The rivers have been dammed (tail ends of the Embalse de Alcántara and Embalse de Torrejón). With the exception of a few eucalyptus plantations, vegetation is well-preserved, particularly on the northern slopes where mature cork oak combines with holm oak and Lusitanian oak. There are also large, isolated areas of Mediterranean hillside vegetation (strawberry tree, turpentine tree, mastic tree, briar (*Erica arborea*), laurustinus (*Viburnum tinus), Phillyrea media*,...) On the banks of the rivers and streams, small stands of alder and ash grow, and on northern and southern slopes alike, dry grazing lands cover enormous areas. Mammals in the area are very interesting, including Spanish lynx and Egyptian mongoose.

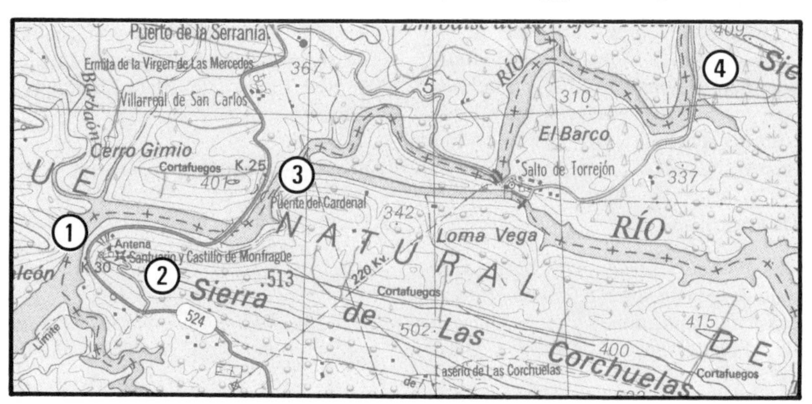

This area is a Natural Park (17,852 ha).

Recommended routes

The small village of Villarreal de San Carlos, on the C-524, lies in the far north-western corner of the Park and makes a good base for trips into the Park. There is a small information centre. The area of the Park open to the public is relatively small but is enough to gain a good idea of the species present. Points of special interest are the following:

1) Salto del Gitano. Leave your car on the roadside; from here you will have views from close quarters of the high Peñafalcón cliffs, lying on the far bank of the river Tajo. The cliffs are the home of a flourishing colony of Griffon Vulture as well as other cliff-dwelling nesting species including Black Stork, Egyptian Vulture, Bonelli's Eagle, Peregrine Falcon and Eagle Owl.

2) Castillo de Monfragüe. The remains of an old castle with a small chapel giving excellent panoramic views and frequent sightings of birds of prey in flight, above all Griffon Vulture, Black Vulture, Black Kite and Booted Eagle. On the rock faces you will see Crag Martin, Black Wheatear, Blue Rock Thrush and, in winter, Alpine Accentor. The climb up the south face can be done partly by car, taking you up through stands of wild olive trees inhabited by large groups of wintering passerines. A long path works its way down the northern side the banks of the river, passing through an interesting area of Mediterranean hillside vegetation.

3) Cardenal bridge lies on a stretch of road which was abandoned after the construction of the Alcántara reservoir. Among martins and swallows, you may also see White-rumped Swift.

4) The road leading from Villarreal de San Carlos to the village beside the Torrejón dam and subsequently along the banks of the river Tiétar. This road passes close to screes which are the breeding ground for Black Stork and subsequently runs through highly representative areas of wooded grazing land in the region known as Campo Arañuelo.

Accommodation

There are a couple of bars which provide food in Villarreal de San Carlos. There are also some restored shepherds' huts which provide basic accommodation (with permission from the Agencia de Medio Ambiente de Extremadura, Calle Enrique Díez Canedo s/n, 06800 Mérida). A wide variety of accommodation as well as a campsite can be found in Plasencia and likewise in Torrejón el Rubio, Trujillo, Jaraicejo and Navalmoral de la Mata.

Comments

The best time of year for visiting the area is spring, from April to June. It is worthwhile taking a telescope.

Eduardo de Juana Aranzana

■ EX.5 CAMPO ARAÑUELO AND IRRIGATED LAND BESIDE THE RIVER TIÉTAR

Grazing lands with holm oak and cork oak woodland.

Main species

Residents: Cattle Egret, Black-shouldered Kite, Red Kite, Griffon Vulture, Black Vulture, Little Bustard, Stone Curlew, Azure-winged Magpie, Spanish Sparrow, Hawfinch.

Summer visitors: Little Egret, White Stork, Black Stork, Black Kite, Egyptian Vulture, Montagu's Harrier, Short-toed

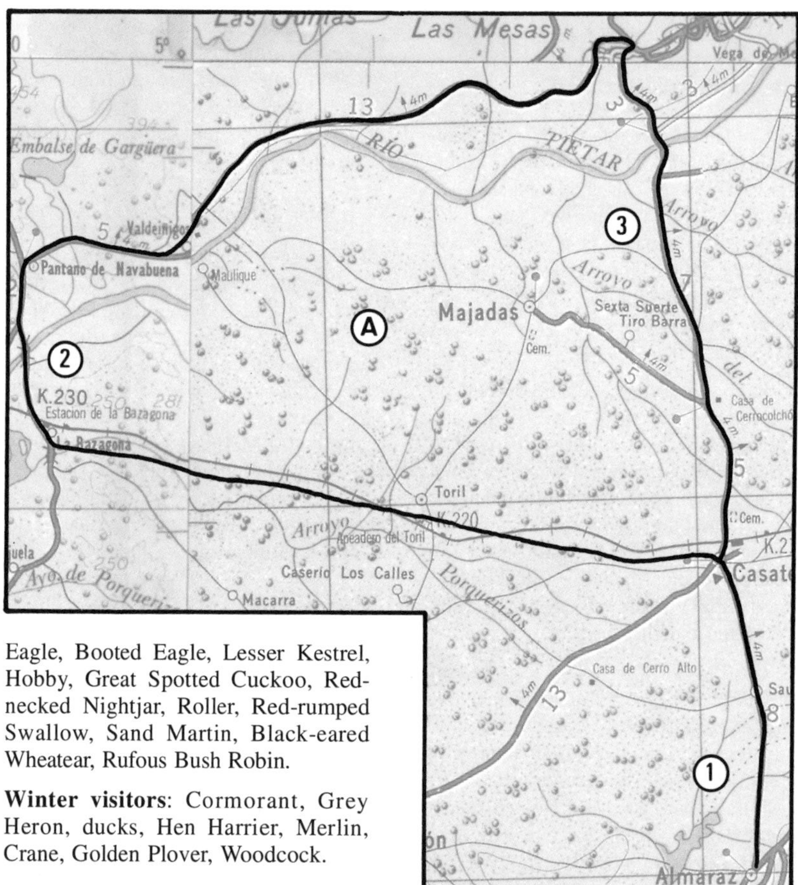

Eagle, Booted Eagle, Lesser Kestrel, Hobby, Great Spotted Cuckoo, Red-necked Nightjar, Roller, Red-rumped Swallow, Sand Martin, Black-eared Wheatear, Rufous Bush Robin.

Winter visitors: Cormorant, Grey Heron, ducks, Hen Harrier, Merlin, Crane, Golden Plover, Woodcock.

Access

The C-511 from Navalmoral de la Mata to Plasencia forms the main axis of the region. The stretch of the N-V between Navalmoral de la Mata and Almaraz is also a good starting point for getting onto minor and local roads in the area.

Description

Campo Arañuelo, located between the rivers Tiétar and Tajo (Tagus), is a plain with large areas of grazing lands taken up by holm oak, cork oak and Pyrenean oak, although this area has been reduced by the progressive development of irrigation systems in the north of the region on the Tiétar river plain. The banks of the river Tiétar are well-preserved and flanked by woods of mountain pine.

Recommended routes

Route A consists of a car journey starting in Almaraz, where you take the road to Casatejada. Before reaching Saucedilla, to the left of the road you will see the body of water of the Arrocampo reservoir (1), where you may see White Stork and, in winter, hundreds of Cormorant, gulls and ducks. Black Vulture from the Parque Natural de Monfragüe often fly over the area.

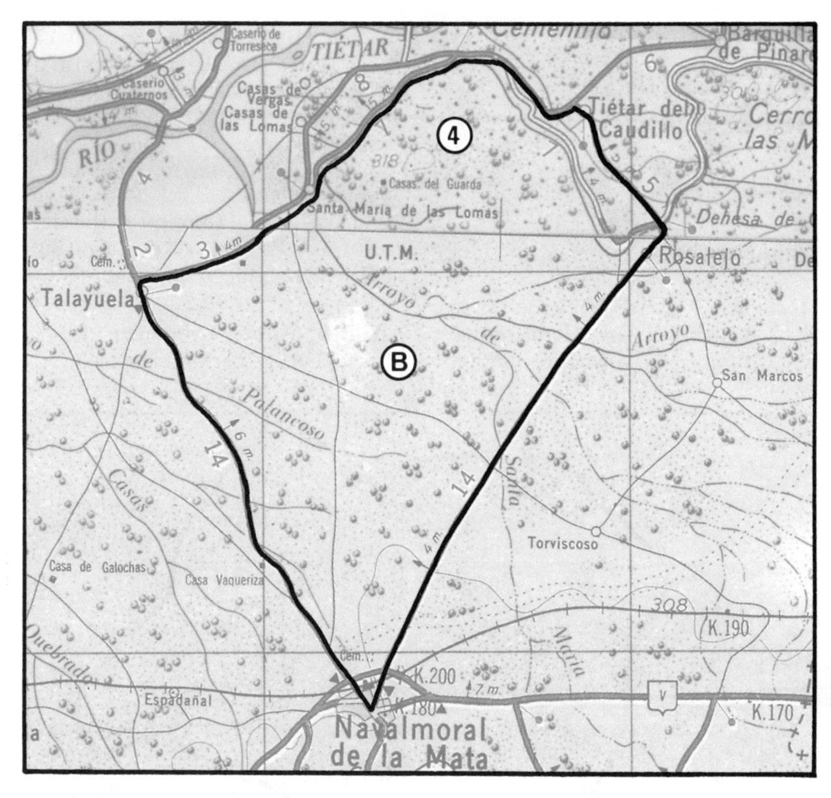

In Casatejada, take the C-511 towards Plasencia and on the stretch before the bridge of La Bazagona, which crosses the river Tiétar, Black-shouldered Kite is almost sure to be present. From this bridge (2), you may be lucky enough to see the occasional Black Stork on the sandy banks of the river.

If you have not seen Crane or Black-shouldered Kite on this part of the route, you can try again on the road leading from Casatejada to Jaraiz de la Vera between the turning for Majadas del Tiétar and the river (3).

Route B consists of a car journey through the dry grazing lands of Campo Arañuelo. Start in Navalmoral de la Mata and continue via Talayuela, Santa María de las Lomas, Tiétar, Rosalejo and back to Navalmoral again. Among many other species, you may see White Stork, Cattle Egret, Black-shouldered Kite and Crane. From the road between Lomas del Saliente and Robledillo de la Vera, it is worth going down to the areas of riverside woodland, consisting of alder and willow, beside the river Tiétar (4) if you wish to see a wider variety of species.

Accommodation

Plenty of hotel accommodation and other facilities are available in Navalmoral de la Mata.

Juan J. Ferrero and José A. Román

EX

■ EX.6 VALDECAÑAS RESERVOIR

Reservoir

Main species

Residents: Great Crested Grebe, Cattle Egret, Little Egret, Grey Heron, White Stork, Black-shouldered Kite, Griffon Vulture, Black Vulture, Spanish Imperial Eagle, Little Bustard, Black-bellied Sandgrouse, Pin-tailed Sandgrouse, Dartford Warbler, Azure-winged Magpie.

Summer visitors: Black Stork, Egyptian Vulture, Montagu's Harrier, Short-toed Eagle, Booted Eagle, Gull-billed Tern, Little Tern, Roller.

Winter visitors: Cormorant, ducks, Crane, Lesser Black-backed Gull.

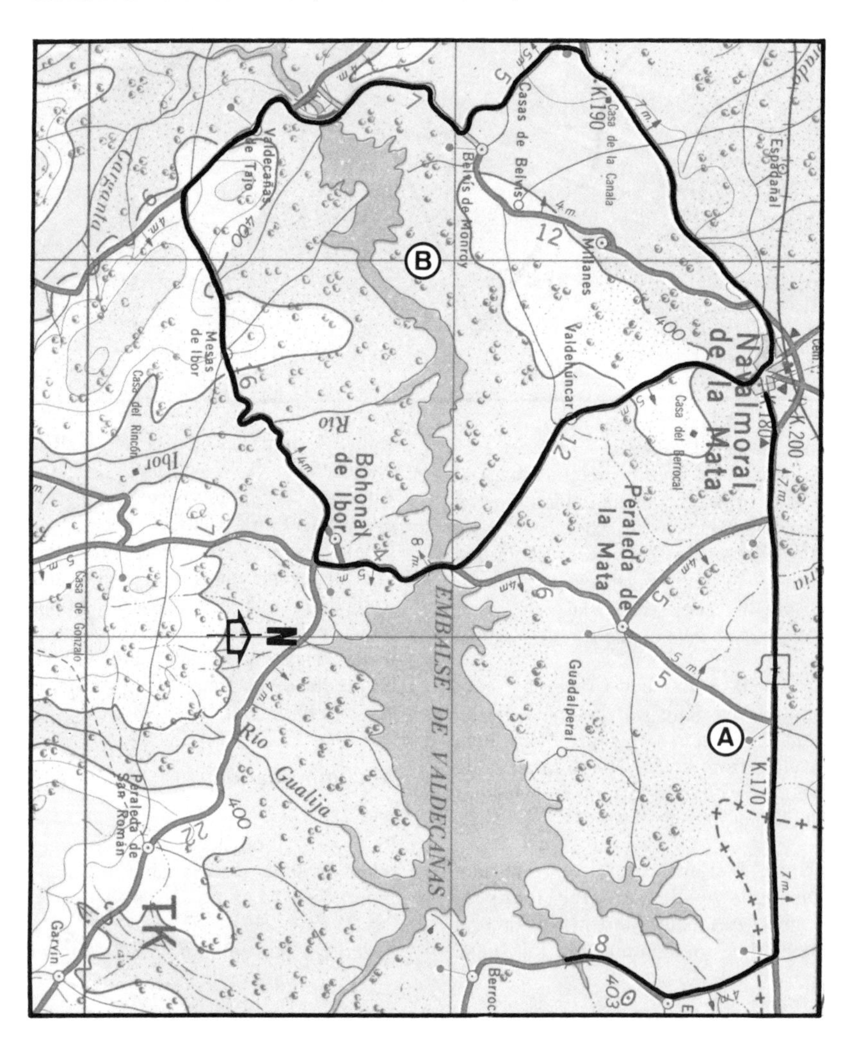

Access

The N-V skirts around the north of the Valdecañas reservoir. From this road, several roads make it easy to get close to the reservoir.

Description

The Valdecañas reservoir, containing the waters of the river Tajo (Tagus), has a surface area of 7,500 ha. The main part of the reservoir lies in the middle of an extensive and extremely flat flood plain, which terminates in relatively steep ranges of hills with frequent granite cliffs.

There are several islands in the middle of the reservoir which are used in spring by gulls and waders as a breeding ground. These islands are used in winter as a roost by Cormorant and Crane. This reservoir is the site of the largest group of wintering Cormorant in Spain, with over 4,000 individuals during the 1989-90 season.

Recommended routes

Route A takes you to the central section of the reservoir starting from the village of El Gordo. In the village itself, there is a substantial colony of White Stork and during July and August up to 400 individuals congregate on the shores of the reservoir. The shores can be reached along a series of tracks and from them, depending on the time of year, you will see Cormorant, Greylag Goose and various ducks, waders and gulls, Crane and, with luck, the occasional Black Stork.

Route B is a 40 km drive along the road which leaves Navalmoral de la Mata in the direction of Valdehúncar, Bohonal de Ibor, Mesas de Ibor and Belvís de Monroy, all of which lie in the foothills of the range of Las Villuercas. The bridge crossing the reservoir gives you a good observation point for watching the comings and goings of water birds; here and in the area immediately beside the dam you will frequently see birds of prey such as Griffon Vulture, Bonelli's Eagle, Spanish Imperial Eagle and Black-shouldered Kite. It is worthwhile walking around the towns of Navalmoral de la Mata and Belvís de Monroy where, in addition to the colonies of White Stork, there are also colonies of Lesser Kestrel.

Accommodation

There are several hotels and hostels in Navalmoral de la Mata; in El Gordo, there is a pension which is perfectly located for watching the storks inhabiting the church tower.

Comments

There is a plan to construct bird hides in and around El Gordo.

Angel Sánchez García

EX.7
LAS VILLUERCAS

A mountain area with Mediterranean woodland and many cliffs.

Main species

Residents: Red Kite, Griffon Vulture, Black Vulture, Goshawk, Sparrowhawk, Golden Eagle, Spanish Imperial Eagle, Bonelli's Eagle, Peregrine Falcon, Eagle Owl, Long-eared Owl, Kingfisher, Great Spotted Woodpecker, Crag Martin, Dipper, Black Wheatear, Blue Rock Thrush, Long-tailed Tit, Crested Tit, Nuthatch, Azure-winged Magpie, Chough, Raven.

Summer visitors: Black Stork, Egyptian Vulture, Short-toed Eagle, Booted Eagle, Hobby, Great Spotted Cuckoo, Red-necked Nightjar, Nightjar, Alpine Swift, Roller, Red-rumped Swallow,

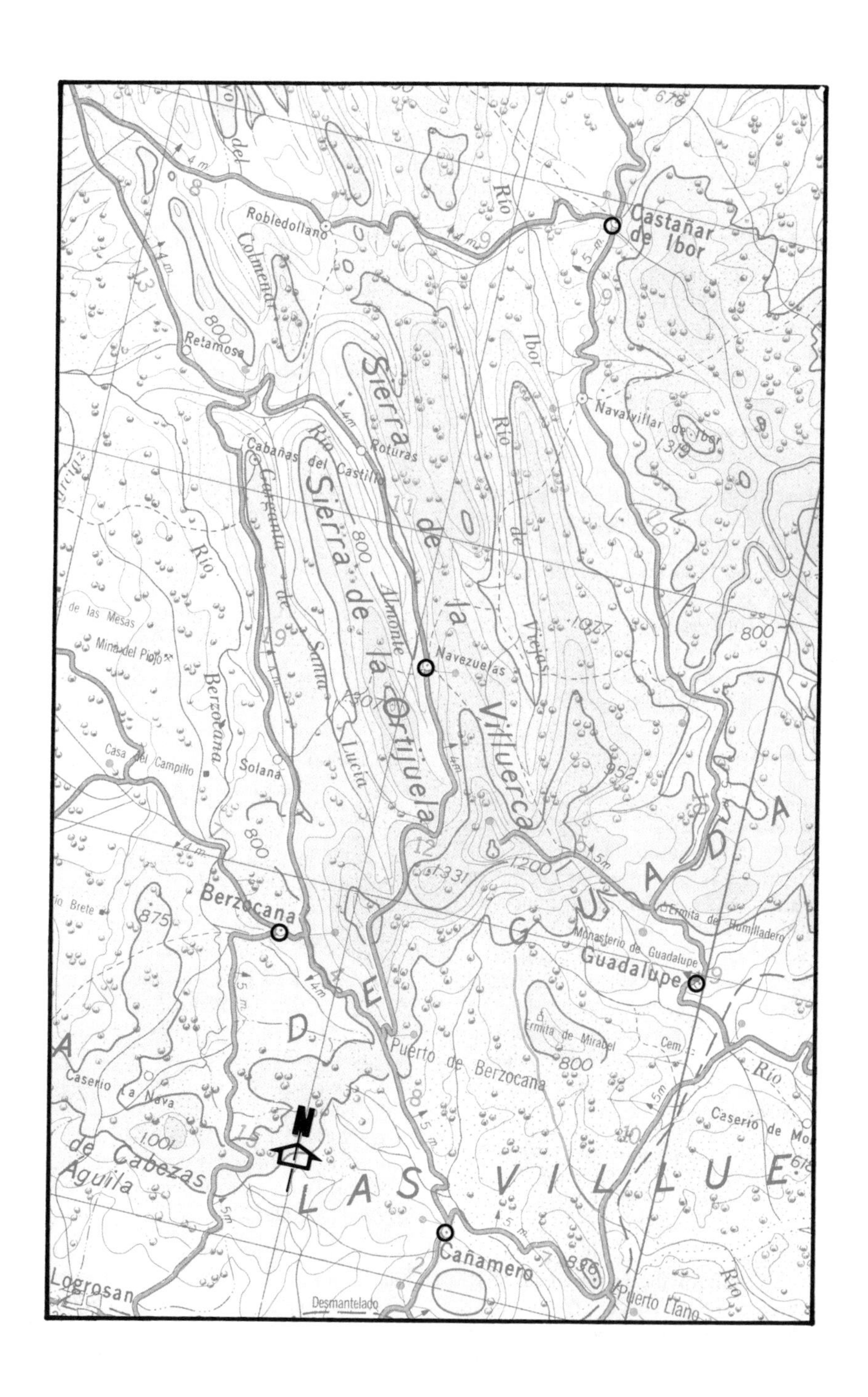
Castañar de Ibor
Robledollano
Colmenar
Retamosa
800
Río Ibor
Navalvillar de Ibor
Sierra de la Villuerca
Sierra de la Ortijuela
Cabañas del Castillo
Roturas
Río Almonte
Navezuelas
Río de Viejas
1027
Santa Lucía
1307
952
de las Mesas
Mina del Piojo
Berzocana
Casa del Campillo
Solana
1331
1200
Berzocana
875
Ermita de Humilladero
Monasterio de Guadalupe
Guadalupe
Ermita de Mirabel
Cem.
Puerto de Berzocana
Caserío La Nava
1001
de Cabezas
Aguila
LAS VILLUE
Cañamero
896
Logrosan
Desmantelado
Puerto Llano

Wheatear, Black-eared Wheatear, Orphean Warbler, Golden Oriole.

Winter visitors: Woodcock, Fieldfare, Song Thrush.

Access

From Navalmoral de la Mata, take the minor road to Guadalupe (75 km). Guadalupe can also be reached from the south via the C-401 between Cañamero and Alía.

Description

The Villuercas massif, part of the Montes de Toledo, is a series of steep ranges reaching a maximum height of 1,601 m. The ranges run parallel to each other and are crowned by formidable quartzite cliffs. The slopes are occupied by irregular but extensive areas of scrubland and woodland consisting of holm oak, Lusitanian oak, Pyrenean oak, chestnut and cork oak.

Recommended routes

Given the extensive nature of the area, it is worth undertaking a trip to gain a general impression along the roads between Deleitosa, Castañar de Ibor, Guadalupe, Cañamero, Berzocana and Navezuelas. The route can be complemented by a series of walks and optional stops at the points you consider to be most suitable. One of the main attractions of this area is the population of birds of prey, with large numbers of cliff-dwelling and forest-dwelling species, although the list of species seen on a regular basis is very long given the number of habitats present.

Accommodation

Guadalupe, a town of artistic and historic interest, provides plenty of accommodation including a Parador Nacional. It is also possible to find accommodation in Castañar de Ibor, Cañamero and Logrosán.

Comments

The best time of year for visiting the area is in spring and early summer.

Magín Murillo Fernández

■ EX.8 WOODED GRAZING LANDS AT VILLA DEL REY AND MATA DE ALCÁNTARA

Wooded grazing lands with interesting wetland areas.

Main species

Residents: Little Grebe, Great Crested Grebe, Cattle Egret, Mallard, Gadwall, Red Kite, Coot, Stone Curlew, Little Ringed Plover, Common Sandpiper, Azure-winged Magpie.

Summer visitors: Black Kite, Egyptian Vulture, Booted Eagle, Little Egret, White Stork, Black-winged Stilt, Great Spotted Cuckoo, Bee-eater, Roller, Red-rumped Swallow, Woodchat Shrike.

Winter visitors: Cormorant, Teal, Widgeon, Shoveler, Pochard, Tufted Duck, Crane, Golden Plover, Lapwing, Snipe, Lesser Black-backed Gull.

Access

From Cáceres, take the N-521 in the direction of Valencia de Alcántara. After 12 km, after Malpartida de Cáceres, turn onto the C-523 for Alcántara and continue to Villa del Rey (40 km).

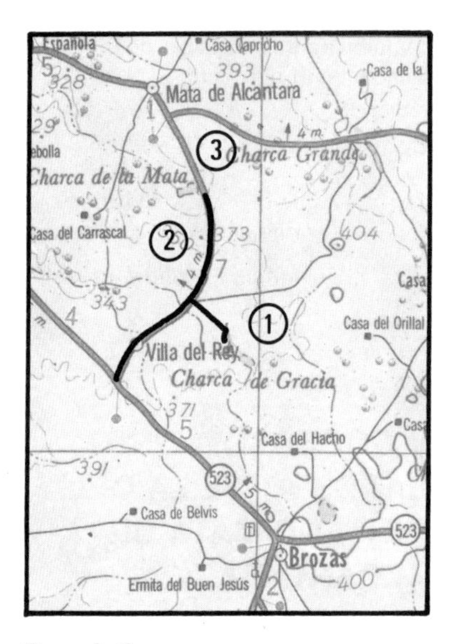

Description

Old areas of wooded grazing land (*dehesas*) traditionally used for agriculture, stock farming and forestry, although today they are used almost exclusively for stock farming. Within the area is a series of interesting ponds.

Recommended routes

The road linking the towns of Villa del Rey and Mata de Alcántara runs for 9 km through the most interesting parts of these dry grazing lands. Points worth noting are the following:

1) The main access point for the *dehesas* of Villa del Rey lies 2.8 km along the road from Villa del Rey to Mata de Alcántara. Having reached this access point, bear right to bring you down to the García pond where you may see ducks, waders, Grey Heron and Black Stork. En route you may see, in addition to birds characteristic of wooded grazing lands, Lapwing and Crane during the winter months. By bearing left at the main access point you will find similar areas of interest.

2) At kms 4.4 and 5.7 paths lead off into the *dehesas* of Mata de Alcántara, where you can go for a walk.

3) After 6 km you will find the Mata de Alcántara pond to the left of the road. On this pond you may see grebes, ducks, Grey Heron, Black Stork and waders.

Accommodation

Some accommodation is available in Brozas and Alcántara.

Inés María Flores Tapia

■ EX.9 PINE WOODS AT GARROVILLAS

Extensive woodland consisting of umbrella pine.

Main species

Residents: Little Grebe, Grey Heron, Buzzard, Coot, Great Bustard, Great Grey Shrike, Azure-winged Magpie.

Summer visitors: White Stork, Black Stork, Black Kite, Booted Eagle, Montagu's Harrier, Turtle Dove, Great Spotted Cuckoo, Bee-eater, Roller, Black-eared Wheatear.

Winter visitors: Cormorant, Mallard, Red Kite, Golden Plover, Lesser Black-backed Gull, Stock Dove.

Access

You can reach the area from Cáceres via the N-630. After 24 km, turn left onto the C-522 for Garrovillas (10 km). To reach the pine woods, continue along the road to Navas del Madroño, or alternatively take the minor road to Alcántara.

Description

Mature woodland consisting of umbrella pine (*Pinus pinea*); it measures 5,000 ha and is the largest of its type in Extremadura. Although the umbrella pine is not indigenous, the sandy soil and climatic conditions present are perfect and ensure that it flourishes. The inaccessibility of the tops of these high

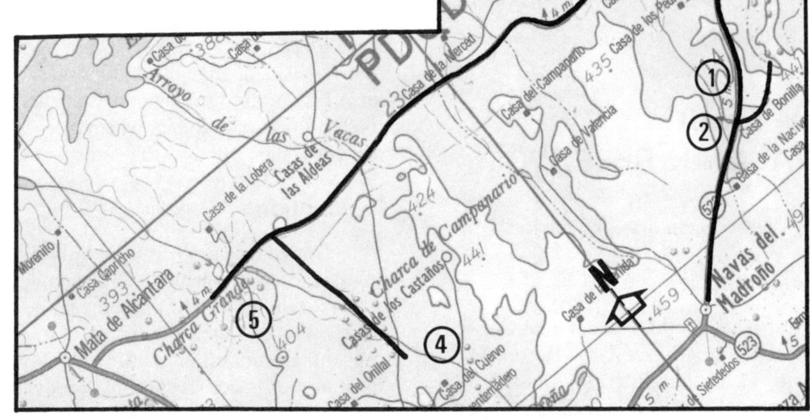

trees makes them good nesting places for interesting species, which make use of the pine woods, wetland areas, steppes and wooded grazing lands in the neighbourhood as feeding grounds. The number of kites, Booted Eagle and Buzzard present is considerable.

Recommended routes

Route A is a car journey along the road from Garrovillas to Navas del Madroño. The points of greatest interest are the following:

1) 16 km from Garrovillas. From here you will gain a good general impression of the pine woods.

2) 17.2 km from Garrovillas. To the left of the road a well-surfaced track runs off; after 800 m it forks. Keep to the left and you will come to the Garrovillas reservoir, where you will be able to watch water birds and, with luck, Black Stork. This is also a good place for watching birds of prey in flight and other forest-dwelling species.

Route B takes you along the road from Garrovillas to Alcántara. The points of greatest interest are the following:

3) 4.4 km from Garrovillas. A campsite. From here you can go for a walk alongside the river Rehana.

4) Perero pine woods. 14.8 km from Garrovillas a well-surfaced track leads off to the left. Continue for 5 km and you will reach the pine wood. To the right of the track you will see a colony of 30 pairs of White Stork.

5) Charca de Cueto. 19.3 km from Garrovillas a track leads off to the left to a small reservoir where you will have interesting sightings of water birds. There is also a substantial area of riverside woodland which will enable you to see a wider range of birds.

Accommodation

There are several pensions in Garrovillas, and accommodation is also available in Brozas and Alcántara.

Comments

It is worth visiting the centre of Garrovillas, where the churches are the breeding ground for many storks.

Sebastián Martín Ruano

■ EX.10 TALAVÁN RESERVOIR

An reservoir in a steppe habitat.

Main species

Residents: Little Grebe, Great Crested Grebe, Cattle Egret, Grey Heron, Mallard, Red Kite, Buzzard, Coot, Little Bustard, Great Bustard, Stone Curlew, Kingfisher, Great Grey Shrike, Raven.

Summer visitors: White Stork, Black Stork, Black Kite, Egyptian Vulture, Short-toed Eagle, Montagu's Harrier, Booted Eagle, Little Ringed Plover, Turtle Dove, Bee-eater, Roller, Short-toed Lark, Rufous Bush Robin, Black-eared Wheatear, Woodchat Shrike.

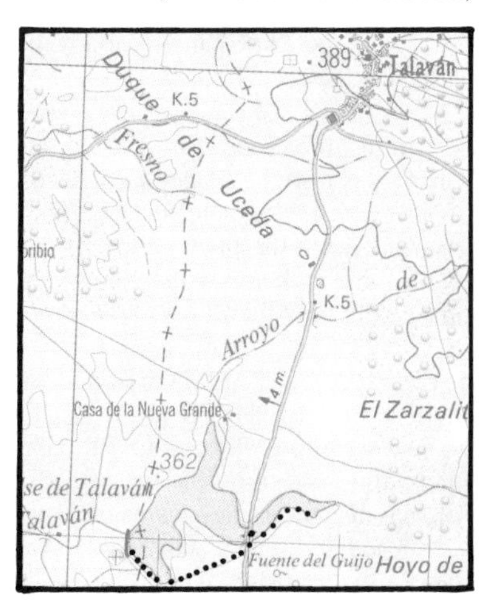

Winter visitors: Cormorant, Little Egret, Widgeon, Teal, Shoveler, Pochard, Tufted Duck, Crane, Avocet, Golden Plover, Lapwing, Lesser Black-backed Gull.

Access

From Cáceres, take the N-630 towards Salamanca. After 29 km, just on the far side of the Alcántara reservoir, turn right onto the road for Hinojal and Talaván (17 km). From Talaván continue along the road to Torrejón el Rubio, which crosses the end of the reservoir after some 6 km.

Description

The Talaván reservoir is relatively small and was constructed to supply water for the village of the same name. Its banks have been deforested, but present abundant vegetation in the form of reed mace, rushes and reeds.

Recommended routes

This route consists of visiting the southern shore of the reservoir, starting from the bridge crossing the reservoir. Walk along to the end of the reservoir and at the mouth of the river which feeds it you will see Widgeon, Black Stork, Cattle Egret, Red Kite, Black Kite, Bee-eater, Roller, etc. Subsequently, continue along the track towards the dam of the reservoir, climbing a hillside which dominates the main body of water and the surrounding plains. From here, at dawn or dusk you will be able to see the comings and goings of Crane and other birds such as Great Bustard, Little Bustard, Montagu's Harrier and Red Kite.

Before reaching the dam, you will go past a creek where you may see gulls, Cormorant, grebes, ducks and waders, while in the surrounding fields you may see Stone Curlew, Little Bustard, Black-eared Wheatear, etc. Near the dam you will see Crane coming down to roost; since this is also the area where the water is at its deepest, there is also a larger number of Cormorant and gulls.

Accommodation

Cáceres has plenty of hotel accommodation, although you may have problems during the Easter period.

Andrés Rodríguez Rodríguez and Angel Rodríguez Martín

EX.11 BROZAS

Dry cereal fields and wetland area.

Main species

Residents: Little Grebe, Great Crested Grebe, Cattle Egret, Grey Heron, Gadwall, Black-shouldered Kite, Griffon Vulture, Black Vulture, Coot, Little Bustard, Great Bustard, Stone Curlew, Black-bellied Sandgrouse, Pin-tailed Sandgrouse, Calandra Lark, Great Grey Shrike, Raven.

Summer visitors: White Stork, Black Stork, Egyptian Vulture, Black Kite, Montagu's Harrier, Booted Eagle, Lesser Kestrel, Black-winged Stilt, Little Tern, Great Spotted Cuckoo, Bee-eater, Roller, Short-toed Lark, Black-eared Wheatear, Woodchat Shrike.

Winter visitors: Cormorant, Little Egret, ducks, Red Kite, Hen Harrier, Crane, Golden Plover and other waders, Lesser Black-backed Gull, Kingfisher.

On passage: Spoonbill, Greylag Goose, waders.

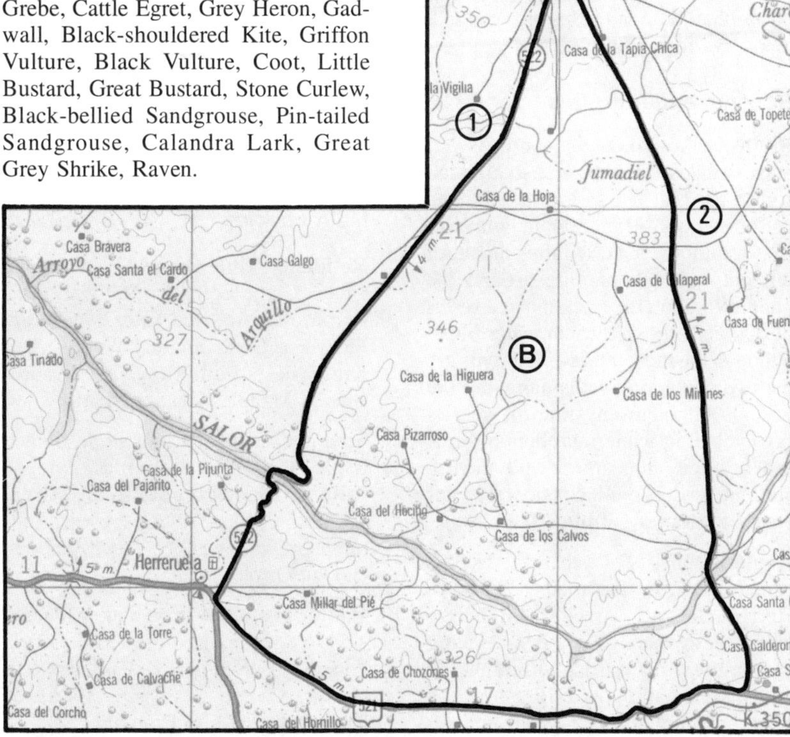

EX

Access

Leave Cáceres on the N-521 in the direction of Valencia de Alcántara; after the village of Malpartida de Cáceres the road joins the C-523 running towards Alcántara. Brozas is 50 km from Cáceres.

Description

Brozas lies at the centre of a large plain given over to cereal fields. The plain is unspoilt; there are no electricity pylons, there are hardly any roads crossing the area, and traditional methods of agriculture are still in use.

Near the village is a pond with a surface area of some 50 ha which continues to be used in the traditional way as a watering hole for stock and for the breeding of tench, a much-prized delicacy in the area. The decline of these activities in recent years has meant that the pond is less frequented, a positive factor for birdlife.

Recommended routes

Route A takes you to the pond. As you leave Brozas, turn onto a small road signed for San Gregorio just after the petrol station. After 800 m you will pass a furniture factory; after this, turn left onto a track running around the pond. While on the track make a series of optional stops to watch water birds, although the most interesting points are the two containing walls damming the waters. Although any time of year is favourable, in winter numbers of birds are at their maximum and during autumn waders will considerably increase the variety of birds seen.

Route B consists of a drive across the cereal fields via the roads leading to Herreruela and Aliseda. Anywhere along these roads is good for seeing steppe-dwelling birds, although the best place of all is the bridge over the river Jumadiel at the 24.8 km marker post on the Herreruela road (1), and the 7.7 km marker post on the road to Aliseda (2). From a hillside located at this latter point, you will be able to see Crane and, in summer, large groups of White Stork and Montagu's Harrier.

It is also worthwhile visiting the village of Brozas, where 44 pairs of White Stork form one of the largest urban populations of stork in Spain. There are also several colonies of Lesser Kestrel, and at the convent of San Francisco you may see Roller.

Accommodation

In Brozas there is a hotel and several pensions.

Sebastián Martín Ruano

■ EX.12 PETIT PONDS (ARROYO DE LA LUZ)

Wetland area: small lakes with riverside woodland and colonies of herons.

Main species

Residents: Little Grebe, Great Crested Grebe, Cattle Egret, Little Egret, Grey Heron, Mallard, Red Kite, Water Rail, Moorhen, Great Spotted Woodpecker, Kingfisher, Penduline Tit, Azure-winged Magpie, Spanish Sparrow.

Summer visitors: White Stork, Booted Eagle, Lesser Kestrel, Black-winged Stilt, Little Ringed Plover, Great Spotted Cuckoo, Scops Owl, Red-rumped Swallow, Great Reed Warbler, Golden Oriole.

Winter visitors: Cormorant, Widgeon, Teal, Shoveler, Red-crested Pochard, Pochard, Tufted Duck, Curlew, Redshank, Green Sandpiper, Lesser Black-backed Gull, Brambling.

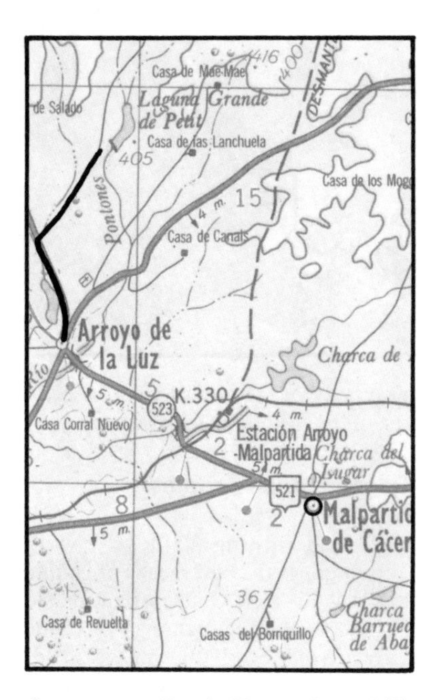

On passage: Purple Heron, Spoonbill, Black Stork, Greylag Goose, waders.

Access

Take the N-521 out of Cáceres in the direction of Valencia de Alcántara. After 12 km you will come to Malpartida de Cáceres, where you join the C-523. 2 km after Arroyo de la Luz, a track leads off to the right down to the ponds. These are easy to spot since an enormous metal grain silo stands beside them.

Description

The small ponds at Petit were constructed during the 14th century for washing wool and irrigating farmland, although today they only fulfil the latter function. They are surrounded by rushes, reeds and riverside woodland consisting of poplar, black poplar, ash and many brambles. Not far off are the remains of Mediterranean woodland, with magnificent examples of cork oak and holm oak.

Recommended routes

A walk along the shores of the ponds will be enough to see the birds most typical of the area. The wall of the upper pond provides an excellent vantage point over both ponds. The numbers of Cattle Egret, Little Egret, Grey Heron and White Stork nesting in large groups in the poplar groves are remarkable, although the list of water birds present increases considerably with grebes, ducks, Spoonbill, Cormorant, gulls, Water Rail, etc. Groves, bramble patches, nearby hilly areas and buildings also contribute to a still wider variety of birds.

It is worth visiting the village of Malpartida de Cáceres where there are 20 White Stork nests in the church. 3 km from the village are Los Barruecos, ponds much frequented by water birds in winter, and a series of large-scale granite blocks used by storks as nesting grounds, making for a spectacular colony.

Accommodation

There is a wide range of accommodation available in Cáceres. In addition, as you come into Arroyo de la Luz you will find Hostal Divino Morales, highly recommended for its food and reasonable prices.

Comments

The ponds are on private property, so you should first ask permission from the owners to visit them.

Adrián Chaves Palacios

■ EX.13 SALOR RESERVOIR

An reservoir surrounded by holm oak woods occupying grazing lands and plains used for cereal growing.

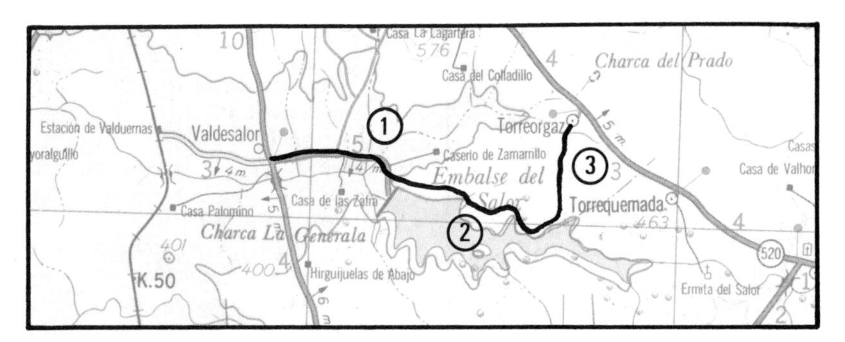

Main species

Residents: Little Grebe, Great Crested Grebe, Grey Heron, Mallard, Black-shouldered Kite, Red Kite, Moorhen, Coot, Little Bustard, Black-bellied Sandgrouse, Great Bustard, Stone Curlew, Little Ringed Plover, Kingfisher, Great Grey Shrike.

Summer visitors: White Stork, Black Stork, Black Kite, Egyptian Vulture, Short-toed Eagle, Montagu's Harrier, Booted Eagle, Lesser Kestrel, Black-winged Stilt, Turtle Dove, Great Spotted Cuckoo, Roller, Woodchat Shrike, Yellow Wagtail.

Winter visitors: Cormorant, Little Egret, Widgeon, Gadwall, Teal, Shoveler, Pochard, Tufted Duck, Crane, Golden Plover, Lapwing, Green Sandpiper, Redshank, Lesser Black-backed Gull.

Access

From Cáceres, take the N-630 towards Mérida. On reaching the hamlet of Valdesalor (11 km), turn left onto a road leading to the dam and continue along the right shore of the reservoir until reaching Torreorgaz, on the C-520.

Description

A reservoir surrounded by holm oak woods growing on dry grazing lands and grain fields. There are also areas of irrigated land and a series of channels for water distribution. The proximity of the city of Cáceres gives rise to intense human presence.

Recommended routes

The road joining Valdesalor with Torreorgaz is the best means of getting to know this area. On the irrigated land (1) you will have sightings of Cattle Egret, White Stork and, in the stands of trees, Buzzard, Red Kite and Black Kite. At the dam there is a fishermen's hut and a car park, from where you can command a view of the reservoir and see a wide variety of water birds. A series of tracks runs off from the road allowing you to approach the reservoir at several points along its shore. The most interesting part is the end of the reservoir (2) where you may see Grey Heron, Black Stork, Avocet, Black-winged Stilt, assorted plovers, grebes, etc. Finally, cross an area of dry grazing land and irrigated land frequented by Black-shouldered Kite and Crane. Continue, and in the cereal fields around Torreorgaz (3) you should have no difficulty in seeing Great Bustard, Little Bustard, Montagu's Harrier, Roller, etc.

Accommodation

A wide variety of accommodation is available in the city of Cáceres.

Andrés Rodríguez Rodríguez
and Angel Rodríguez Martín

EX.14
SAN PEDRO RANGE (WESTERN END)

A low range of hills with excellent Mediterranean woodland and wooded grazing lands.

Main species

Residents: Black-shouldered Kite, Griffon Vulture, Black Vulture, Buzzard, Golden Eagle, Spanish Imperial Eagle, Bonelli's Eagle, Eagle Owl, Long-eared Owl, Kingfisher, Blue Rock Thrush, Great Grey Shrike, Azure-winged Magpie.

Summer visitors: Black Stork, Black Kite, Egyptian Vulture, Short-toed Eagle, Booted Eagle, Turtle Dove, Great Spotted Cuckoo, Scops Owl, Bee-eater, Woodchat Shrike, Golden Oriole.

Winter visitors: Red Kite, Crane, Lapwing, Woodpigeon, Stock Dove.

Access

The main means of reaching this area is via the N-521 between Cáceres and Valencia de Alcántara.

Description

The Sierra de San Pedro, constituting the western spurs of the Montes de Toledo, is a series of gently rolling hills and valleys reaching a maximum altitude of 703 m with Torrico de San Pedro. The range runs for nearly 100 km, straddling the provinces of Cáceres and Badajoz up to the Portuguese border. Vegetation consists of cork oak and holm oak woodland predominating the hills, with wooded grazing lands and extensive areas of scrubland. In some places, eucalyptus plantations have unfortunately made

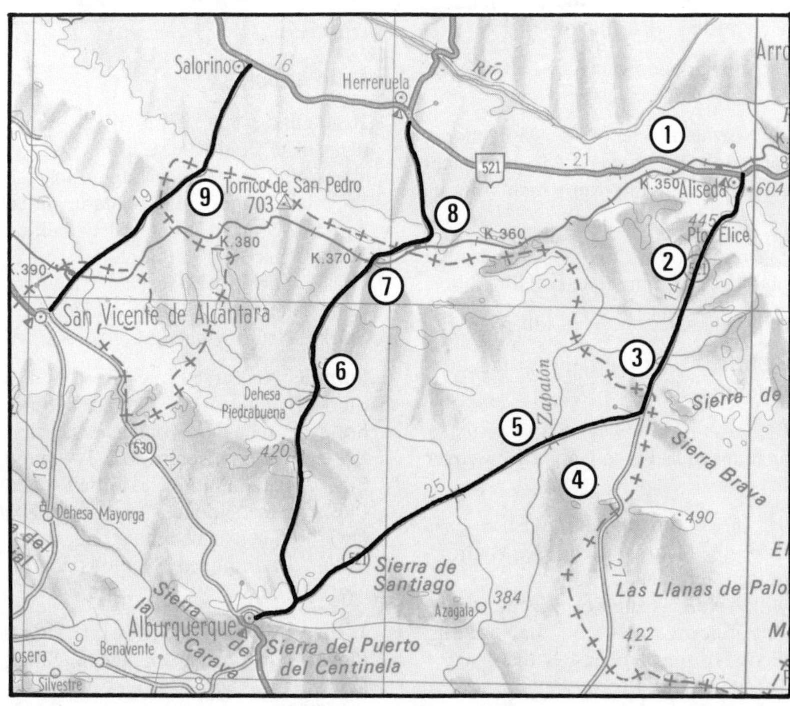

their appearance. Along the river courses there are some areas of extremely interesting riverside woodland.

Recommended routes

The best and most convenient means of seeing the birdlife present in the Sierra de San Pedro is to drive along the roads in the area, making frequent stops. This area is remarkable for the presence of large birds of prey, which can best be seen on the stretches of road between Aliseda and Alburquerque, Herreruela and Alburquerque, and Salorino and San Vicente de Alcántara. The points of interest are the following:

1) From the crossroads with the Brozas road, you can command a view of the Sierra del Aljibe lying to the south.

2) At the 5.7 km marker post, a road runs off to the right to the Ermita del Campo, a chapel. The lay-by close to this point will give you a panoramic view of the hills.

3) Another good vantage point is at the 13.4 km marker post.

4) Northern side of the Mercadores range, a dense area of Mediterranean hillside vegetation over which vultures and eagles fly.

5) Bridge over the river Zapatón, a good place for watching river-dwelling birds.

6) Bridge over the river Albarrajena.

7) Bridge over the railway line from Madrid to Lisbon.

8) Herreruela railway station, virtually abandoned and giving good views over the range.

9) The climb up to the Elice pass through an area of dense Mediterranean scrubland. From the top you will have a magnificent view of the surrounding hills and dry grazing lands. To the southeast is the peak of Torrico de San Pedro.

Accommodation

Although accommodation is hard to come by, it can be found in the main towns of the area: Aliseda, Villar del Rey, Alburquerque, San Vicente de Alcántara and Valencia de Alcántara.

Comments

The extremely well-preserved state of the San Pedro hills is thanks to the extensive big game reserves to which access is strictly forbidden. For this reason you should not stray from the road or enter private property.

Sebastián Martín Ruano

■ EX.15 THE ROAD FROM CÁCERES TO BADAJOZ

Fields, pastures, wooded grazing land and hills.

Main species

Residents: Cattle Egret, Black-shouldered Kite, Red Kite, Griffon Vulture, Black Vulture, Golden Eagle, Spanish Imperial Eagle, Little Bustard, Great Bustard, Stone Curlew, Black-bellied Sandgrouse, Pin-tailed Sandgrouse, Great Spotted Woodpecker, Calandra Lark, Blue Rock Thrush, Great Grey Shrike, Azure-winged Magpie, Raven.

Summer visitors: Little Egret, White Stork, Black Stork, Egyptian Vulture, Short-toed Eagle, Montagu's Harrier, Lesser Kestrel, Hobby, Black-winged Stilt, Collared Pratincole, Little Ringed Plover, Great Spotted Cuckoo, Scops Owl, Red-necked Nightjar, Bee-eater, Roller, Red-rumped Swallow, Woodchat Shrike.

Winter visitors: Crane, Golden Plover, Lapwing, Woodpigeon, Stock Dove.

Access

The N-523 joins the cities of Cáceres and Badajoz (89 km).

Description

This road runs through the main natural habitats of Extremadura and its value lies precisely in the fact that it will give you an overall impression of the area. The road crosses extensive cereal growing plains, pastures, wooded grazing lands (*dehesas*) and the eastern end of the Sierra de San Pedro (see EX.14).

Recommended routes

Before starting off, it is worth walking around the old quarter of Cáceres which is full of monuments housing large populations of White Stork and Lesser Kestrel.

Once you take to the road, the first point of interest (1) is 13 km from Cáceres, from where a dirt track runs off to the right of the road, taking you through wooded grazing lands and plains towards the confluence of the rivers Ayuela and Salor. Here you may see Black-shouldered Kite, Short-toed Eagle, Crane, Great Bustard, Golden Plover, Little Bustard, Black-bellied Sandgrouse and Pin-tailed Sandgrouse. The telegraph poles strung along the road act as perches for Roller, kites, kestrels, etc. A little farther on, from the saddle at Clavín (2), you will be able to enjoy an excellent view over the plains. From this point you will be driving for 20 km through the Sierra de San Pedro. You could make a stop on the boundary between the provinces of Cáceres and Badajoz at the Covacha pass (3), where there is a wonderful cork oak wood which will give interesting sightings of passerines and large birds of prey including Black Vulture and Spanish Imperial Eagle.

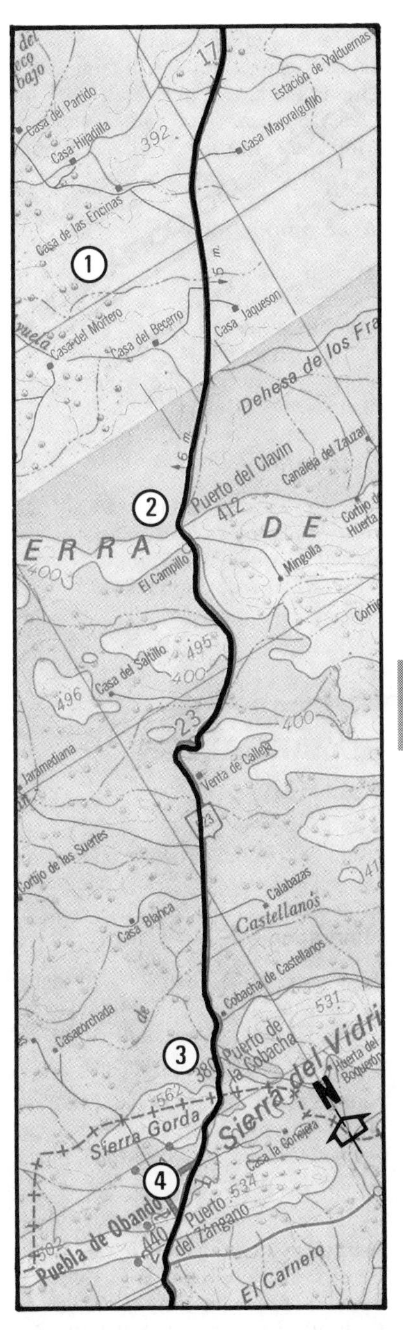

You could make another stop at the Zángano pass (4). The last stretch of the journey, after La Roca de la Sierra, runs across wooded grazing lands and irrigated areas which will increase the variety of birds seen, with Montagu's Harrier, Collared Pratincole, Black-winged Stilt, etc.

Accommodation

Accommodation is plentiful both in Cáceres and Badajoz. About midway along the route, in Puebla de Obando (41 km), there is a good restaurant where you can try the regional specialities.

Comments

You are advised not to stray off the road or the tracks, particularly on the stretches crossing the plains of Cáceres and the Sierra de San Pedro.

Adrián Chaves Palacios

■ EX.16 EL ZANGALLÓN (BÓTOA)

Holm oak woods growing on grazing lands with cereal crops and ponds.

Main species

Residents: Little Grebe, Black-shouldered Kite, Mallard, Little Bustard, Stone Curlew, Black-bellied Sandgrouse, Azure-winged Magpie.

Summer visitors: Montagu's Harrier, Black-winged Stilt, Avocet, Great Spotted Cuckoo, Red-necked Nightjar, Roller, Golden Oriole, Woodchat Shrike.

Winter visitors: Cattle Egret, Little Egret, Grey Heron, Red Kite, Buzzard, Spanish Imperial Eagle, Widgeon, Gadwall, Teal, Pintail, Shoveler, Pochard, Tufted Duck, Crane, Golden Plover, Lapwing, Snipe, Black-tailed

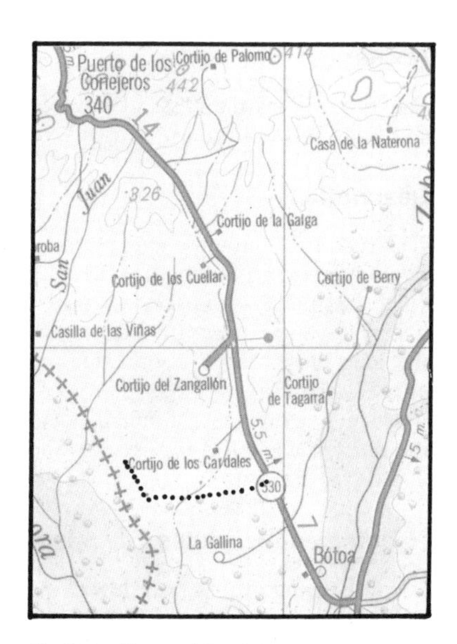

Godwit, Spotted Redshank, Redshank, Lesser Black-backed Gull, Woodpigeon, Fieldfare.

Access

From Badajoz, take the C-530 towards Alburquerque. After 53 km, between the farm of Bótoa and the Conejeros pass, a local road takes you to the old gun emplacement of Aguaszorras.

Description

Well-preserved holm oak woods growing on dry grazing lands in which the most interesting features are the ponds which form in winter, providing a site for large numbers of ducks and waders.

Recommended routes

A walk around the ponds will be enough to see the most interesting species in the area. The ponds lie surrounded by fields to the right of the minor road. To the north of some police barracks is an area popular with Crane as a roosting ground.

Accommodation

There are several hotels in Alburquerque. A much wider range of accommodation is available in Badajoz.

Comments

Since this is private land used for breeding fighting bulls, you should ask for permission before visiting the area.

Carlos de la Cruz
and Florentino de Lope

■ EX.17 BADAJOZ AND AROUND

A city and river course surrounded by cereal crops, holm oak woodland and irrigated land.

Main species

Residents: Cattle Egret, Little Egret, Black-shouldered Kite, Buzzard, Lesser Kestrel, Little Bustard, Great Bustard, Kingfisher, Spotless Starling, Avadavat.

Summer visitors: Little Bittern, White Stork, Lesser Kestrel, Collared Pratincole, Little Ringed Plover, Little Tern, Bee-eater, Alpine Swift, Swift, Sand Martin, House Martin.

Winter visitors: Grey Heron, Glossy Ibis, Spoonbill, Crane, Black-headed Gull, Lesser Black-backed Gull, Black-bellied Sandgrouse, Pied Wagtail, Reed Bunting.

Access

Access to the areas of greatest interest around Badajoz are detailed in the section on recommended routes.

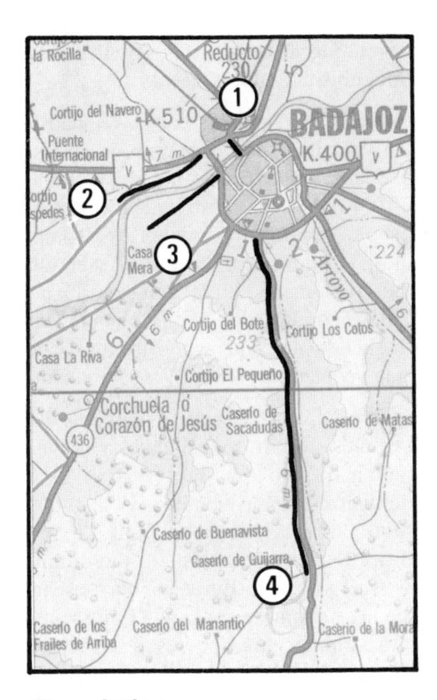

Description

The river Guadiana skirts the city to the north, providing various points of interest, particularly those where abundant marsh vegetation is present. There are also areas of irrigated and wooded grazing lands with holm oak and cork oak.

Recommended routes

The points of most interest are the following:

1) Puente de Palmas. From this bridge you can see a substantial colony of House Martin and, at dusk, Alpine Swift which nest in the crevices of the bridge.

2) Cross the Puente de la Universidad (another bridge) in the direction of Portugal (N-V) and by the petrol station take the road to Rincón de Caya, which leads off towards the river Guadiana. When you reach a greenhouse, you will see a herons' roost where up to 10,000 individuals congregate. The dominant species is Cattle Egret, although there are also many Grey Heron and Little

Egret. Occasionally, Glossy Ibis and Spoonbill are also present.

3) Complejo Deportivo de La Granadilla. Near this sports complex is an old people's home beside the river. Some 300 m downstream from the old people's home is a colony of 2,500 pairs of Sand Martin and some Bee-eater. On the river banks Little Ringed Plover, Little Tern and Collared Pratincole can frequently be seen, while in the riverside vegetation you may see Avadavat.

4) Road from Badajoz to Valverde de Leganés. 10 km from Badajoz you will find a turn to the right leading to a rubbish dump. In winter several thousands of Black-headed and Lesser Black-backed Gull come to the dump, as well as Cattle Egret which roost in the nearby pine woods, while in spring and summer the species present are White Stork and Black Kite. The dump is in the middle of an extensive cork oak wood where finches, tits, Buzzard, kites and nocturnal birds of prey abound. Continue along the road to Valverde de Leganés and 19 km from Badajoz, some 200 m to the right, is a reservoir where you may see ducks, waders and other marsh-dwelling species. The surrounding area also features a Crane roost, and you may see Great Bustard, Black-bellied Sandgrouse, Little Bustard, etc.

Accommodation

Plenty of accommodation is available in Badajoz.

Carlos de la Cruz
and Florentino de Lope

■ EX.18
LA ALBUERA

Wooded grazing lands with cereal crops and natural ponds.

Main species

Residents: Little Grebe, Black-shouldered Kite, Mallard, Moorhen, Coot, Little Bustard, Great Bustard, Stone Curlew.

Summer visitors: Montagu's Harrier, Black-winged Stilt, Avocet, Great Spotted Cuckoo, Red-necked Nightjar, Golden Oriole.

Winter visitors: Cattle Egret, Little Egret, Grey Heron, Red Kite, Buzzard, Widgeon, Gadwall, Teal, Pintail, Shoveler, Red-crested Pochard, Pochard, Tufted Duck, Crane, Lapwing, Golden Plover, Snipe, Black-tailed Godwit, Curlew, Spotted Redshank, Redshank.

Access

Leave Badajoz on the N-432 in the direction of Zafra and stop at La Albuera (26 km). Just after La Albuera, turn left onto minor road for El Entrín. After 1.5 km a track runs off to the left taking you to the ponds. Leave your vehicle near an abandoned house which can be used as a hide.

Continuing along the road to El Entrín, a series of tracks run off to the left to the Valdelagrana farm, in the middle of

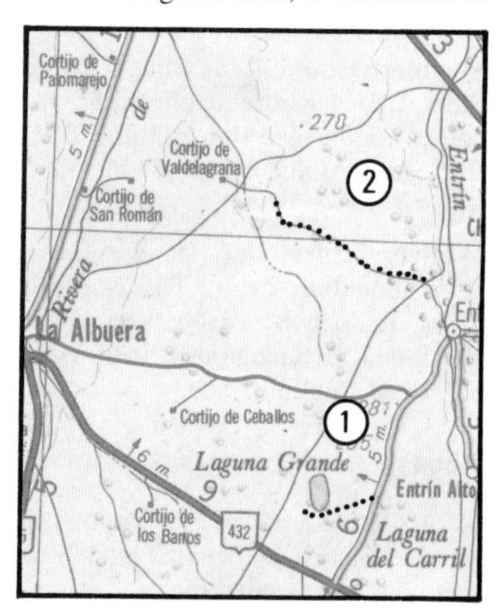

an area of steppe used for growing cereal crops.

Description

A landscape typical of Extremadura, where dry grazing lands with holm oak alternate with dry cereal farming. There is also a series of ponds which are the site of interesting water birds.

Recommended routes

The ponds (1) can be seen from the abandoned house where you leave your vehicle. From here we can approach the ponds for further watching.

In the fields (2), there is no fixed route since the birds move around a lot. The best idea is to take some general walks through the area to see large groups of Great Bustard and other steppe-dwelling species.

Accommodation

Accommodation is available in La Albuera, but options are more plentiful in the city of Badajoz.

Carlos de la Cruz
and Florentino de Lope

■ EX.19 MÉRIDA AND AROUND

Urban habitat, wooded grazing lands, fields and river banks.

Main species

Residents: Little Grebe, Great Crested Grebe, Cattle Egret, Little Egret, Mallard, Black-shouldered Kite, Red Kite, Buzzard, Kestrel, Quail, Water Rail, Moorhen, Coot, Little Bustard, Stone Curlew, Common Sandpiper, Black-bellied Sandgrouse, Long-eared Owl, Kingfisher, Calandra Lark, Woodlark, Crag Martin, Mistle Thrush, Cetti's Warbler, Fan-tailed Warbler, Sardinian Warbler, Long-tailed Tit, Penduline Tit, Great Grey Shrike, Azure-winged Magpie, Raven, Spanish Sparrow, Rock Sparrow, Avadavat, Hawfinch, Cirl Bunting.

Summer visitors: Little Bittern, Night Heron, Purple Heron, White Stork, Black Kite, Montagu's Harrier, Booted Eagle, Lesser Kestrel, Black-winged Stilt, Collared Pratincole, Little Ringed Plover, Gull-billed Tern, Little Tern, Turtle Dove, Cuckoo, Great Spotted Cuckoo, Scops Owl, Red-necked Nightjar, Pallid Swift, Alpine Swift, Bee-eater, Roller, Red-rumped Swallow, Sand Martin, Rufous Bush Robin, Black-eared Wheatear, Great Reed Warbler, Melodious Warbler, Spectacled Warbler, Subalpine Warbler, Orphean Warbler, Spotted Flycatcher, Woodchat Shrike.

Winter visitors: Cormorant, Grey Heron, Greylag Goose, Widgeon, Gadwall, Teal, Pintail, Shoveler, Pochard, Tufted Duck, Marsh Harrier, Hen Harrier, Sparrowhawk, Merlin, Crane, Lapwing, Golden Plover, Snipe, Woodcock, Black-tailed Godwit, Redshank, Greenshank, Green Sandpiper, Lesser Black-backed Gull, Black-headed Gull, Short-eared Owl, Redwing, Starling, Siskin, Bullfinch.

On passage: Spoonbill, Garganey, Osprey, waders, terns, marsh terns.

Access

Mérida lies at the crossroads of the two main roads running through southwestern Spain: the N-V from Madrid to Lisbon and the N-630 (Vía de la Plata).

A regional road joins Mérida with Montijo, running along the right bank of the river Guadiana and passing through the towns of Esparragalejo, La Garrovilla and Torremayor. Thus Montijo is linked with La Roca de la Sierra (on the N-523) and La Nava de Santia-

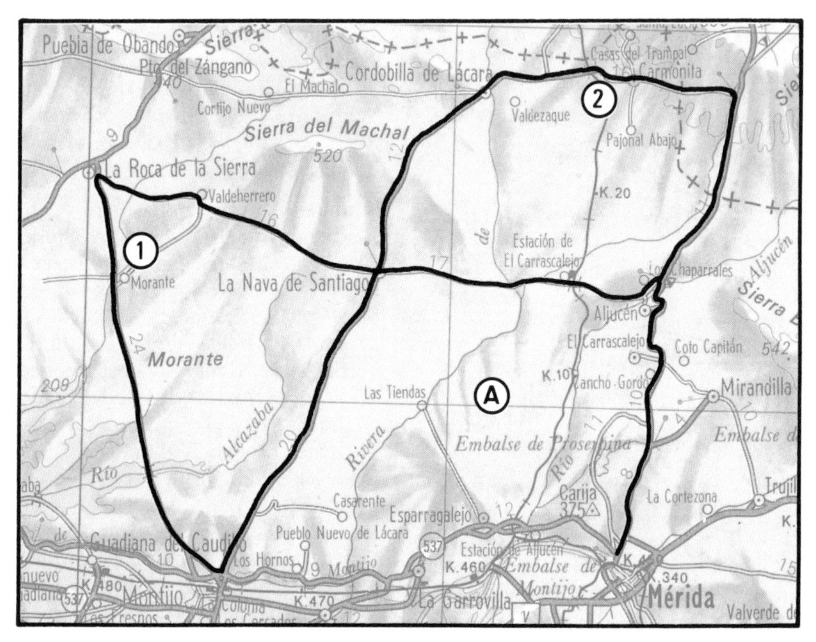

go. Both of these villages are joined by a road ending in Aljucén, 18 km from Mérida.

From the N-630, a little before the mountain pass of Las Herrerías (30 km from Mérida), a road runs off to Carmonita and Cordobilla de Lácara, passing the reservoirs of Horno, Tejero and Boquerón at the head of the river Lácara. Cordobilla and La Nava de Santiago are 11 km apart.

Description

This area is located at the far eastern end of the San Pedro Range and the Vegas Bajas del Guadiana irrigation area, presenting wooded grazing lands, dry farming, irrigated areas, riverside woodland and a series of reservoirs.

Recommended routes

Route A consists of a car journey broken up by a series of stops and walks. Leave Mérida on the N-630 and pass through Aljucén, La Nava de Santiago, La Roca de la Sierra, Montijo, La Nava de Santiago again, Cordobilla de Lácara and Carmonita, returning to Mérida by the road mentioned above. It is worth spending a whole day on this trip, which is best undertaken in spring or winter. It will enable you to visit various kinds of wooded grazing lands, varying from areas of dense woodland to fields with scattered trees where you may see White Stork, Cattle Egret, Booted Eagle, Black Kite, Black-shouldered Kite, Montagu's Harrier, Crane and Roller. The most interesting points are the Morante reservoir (1), between Montijo and La Roca de la Sierra, and the reservoirs of Horno, Tejero and Boquerón, between Cordobilla de Lácara and Carmonita (2).

Route B consists of a 12 km walk along the river Aljucén from its mouth to the village of the same name. This is a pleasant, flat walk running through holm oak woods growing on dry grazing lands and along river banks covered with stands of ash, willow and oleander. You may see White Stork, Cattle Egret, Black-shouldered Kite,

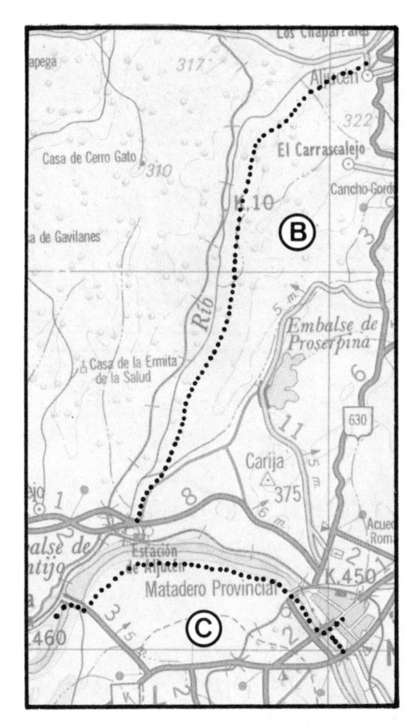

Red Kite, Black Kite, Roller, Azure-winged Magpie and Avadavat.

Route C is a walk around Mérida and the surrounding area which can be undertaken in 3 hours. Start at Plaza de España and from there go to the Puente Romano, a bridge, from which you can make your way down to a spur of land lying between the two main river courses. The bridge itself is a nesting site for Alpine Swift, Swift, Pallid Swift and House Martin. The Puente Nuevo, a new bridge 500 m upstream, is a breeding ground for Crag Martin. This area is a good place for seeing Little Egret, Cattle Egret, Grey Heron, Lesser Kestrel, Little Tern, Black-headed Gull and Lesser Black-backed Gull.

Having crossed the Roman bridge, continue along the left bank of the river Guadiana. Downstream from the railway bridge are the islets at the end of the Montijo reservoir, in an area which has undergone drastic transformations because of the construction of a dual carriageway. Make your way along the road following the riverbank to approach the Montijo dam. On this stretch of the route, you will see breeding colonies of Cattle Egret, Little Egret and Night Heron. Avadavat is also frequent.

Accommodation

Plenty of accommodation is available in Mérida, including a Parador Nacional and a campsite.

Juan J. Ferrero, Juan J. Negro and José A. Román

■ EX.20 CORNALVO RESERVOIR AND MONTÁNCHEZ RANGE

An reservoir dating from Roman times and wooded grazing lands with holm oak and cork oak.

Main species

Residents: Little Grebe, Cattle Egret, Little Egret, Mallard, Black-shouldered Kite, Red Kite, Spanish Imperial Eagle, Water Rail, Coot, Little Bustard, Stone Curlew, Eagle Owl, Tawny Owl, Kingfisher, Thekla Lark, Woodlark, Crag Martin, Black Wheatear, Blue Rock Thrush, Mistle Thrush, Fan-tailed Warbler, Cetti's Warbler, Dartford Warbler, Sardinian Warbler, Crested Tit, Long-tailed Tit, Nuthatch, Great Grey Shrike, Azure-winged Magpie, Raven, Spanish Sparrow, Rock Sparrow, Hawfinch, Cirl Bunting, Rock Bunting.

Summer visitors: White Stork, Black Stork, Honey Buzzard, Egyptian Vulture, Black Kite, Short-toed Eagle, Montagu's Harrier, Booted Eagle, Lesser Kestrel, Little Ringed Plover, Great Spotted Cuckoo, Scops Owl, Red-necked Nightjar, White-rumped Swift, Bee-eater, Roller, Red-rumped Swallow, Rufous Bush Robin, Black-eared Wheatear, Great Reed Warbler, Spectacled Warbler, Subalpine Warbler, Orphean Warbler, Spotted Flycatcher, Golden Oriole, Woodchat Shrike.

Winter visitors: Great Crested Grebe, Cormorant, Grey Heron, Widgeon, Gadwall, Teal, Shoveler, Pochard, Tufted Duck, Hen Harrier, Marsh Harrier, Sparrowhawk, Merlin, Crane, Woodcock, Green Sandpiper, Redwing, Firecrest, Alpine Accentor, Siskin, Bullfinch.

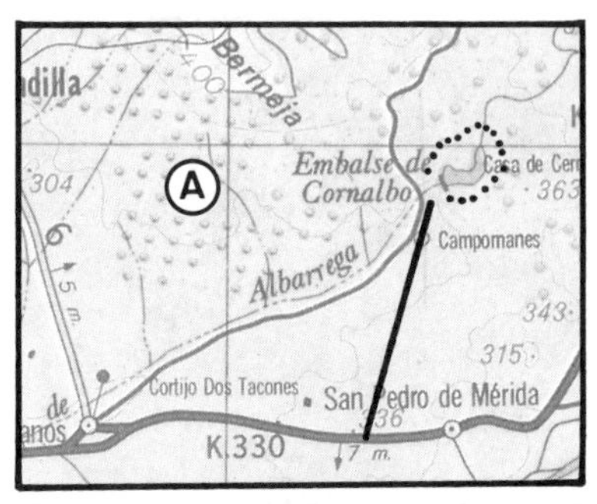

Access

The Cornalvo reservoir and the Natural Park in which it is included can be reached from the N-V between the villages of San Pedro de Mérida and Trujillanos, via the only surfaced track leading into the Natural Park. After 5 km you will come across the dam; the road continues to the spot known as Presa de las Muelas. The Natural Park does not as yet have any facilities for visitors. You can obtain information from AMA (c/ Díaz Canedo s/n; 06800 Mérida) and ADENEX (c/ Cuba, 10; 06800 Mérida).

Montánchez can be reached via Trujillo along a local road passing through Ruanes and Torre de Santa María. There are also other alternatives.

Description

The wooded grazing lands (*dehesas*) at Cornalvo stretch from the flood plains of the river Guadiana to the foot of the Montánchez range. Holm oak and cork oak woodland alternate with small areas of cereal crops. The wetland habitat is represented by the reservoir, built by the Romans, and the small dam of Las Muelas.

The Sierra de Montánchez is a granite batholith where holm oak and cork oak gives way to small areas of Pyrenean oak near the highest point (994 m). The landscape is shaped by traditional hillside agriculture with olive groves, vineyards and meadows.

Recommended routes

Route A consists of a 10 km walk around the perimeter of the Cornalvo reservoir. From the Roman dam it is possible to continue along a road for 6 km to the Las Muelas reservoir. This route takes you through the small pass of Coto Picón, giving extensive views over the area.

The starting point for **route B** is Montánchez, where you take the narrow surfaced track leading up to the television mast on the highest point of the range. From here turn right onto a path leading southwards to the Los Molinos spring and subsequently dropping down along the ravine of the same name. This path comes out in the village of Arroyomolinos de Montánchez, where a colony of storks inhabits the church. This is a pleasant walk on which you will be able to see warblers, wheatears, buntings and other passerines. You may also see White-rumped Swift, which breeds in the nests made by Red-rumped Swallow in the screes.

The route can be completed by a visit to the area around Montánchez. In the village Lesser Kestrel, swifts and martins breed, while the castle is the home of Crag Martin, Blue Rock Thrush, Black Wheatear and, in winter, Alpine Accentor. From the village a series of bridle paths leads southwards into the hills, providing opportunities for seeing a large number of birds.

Accommodation

In Montánchez there is Hostal Montecalabria, although possibilities are greater in Mérida, Alcuéscar and Miajadas. In Miajadas there is also a campsite, at the 301 km marker post on the N-V.

Juan J. Ferrero, José A. Román and Juan J. Negro

■ EX.21 ZORITA–MADRIGALEJO

Wooded grazing lands and fields.

Main species

Residents: Cattle Egret, Black-shouldered Kite, Little Bustard, Great Bustard, Stone Curlew, Black-bellied Sandgrouse, Pin-tailed Sandgrouse, Thekla Lark, Avadavat.

Summer visitors: White Stork, Little Egret, Grey Heron, Marsh Harrier, Montagu's Harrier, Lesser Kestrel, Collared Pratincole, Little Tern, Bee-eater, Roller, Red-rumped Swallow, Tawny Pipit.

Winter visitors: Greylag Goose, ducks, Red Kite, Hen Harrier, Golden Plover, Lapwing, Lesser Black-backed Gull.

On passage: Spoonbill, Avocet, Whiskered Tern, Black Tern.

Access

From Trujillo, take the C-524 to Zorita (28 km), and from there the minor road to Madrigalejo (19 km).

Alternatively, from Miajadas on the N-V, take the C-401.

Description

Most of the area is taken up by extensive cereal fields, although these are interspersed, on poorer soils, with extensive pastures used for stock grazing. The remains of thinned holm oak woodland are also present, although wooded grazing lands abound more on the eastern edge of this region. In addition, around Madrigalejo there are also areas of irrigated land which are used mainly for the cultivation of rice and maize.

Recommended routes

Route A consists of a car journey some 40 km long. Leave Zorita on the C-401 in the direction of Alcollarín and Campolugar, from where you continue until reaching the local road joining Zorita to Madrigalejo. Throughout the route, but particularly on this last stretch, you will have excellent chances of seeing steppe-dwelling birds such as Great

Bustard, Little Bustard and Montagu's Harrier.

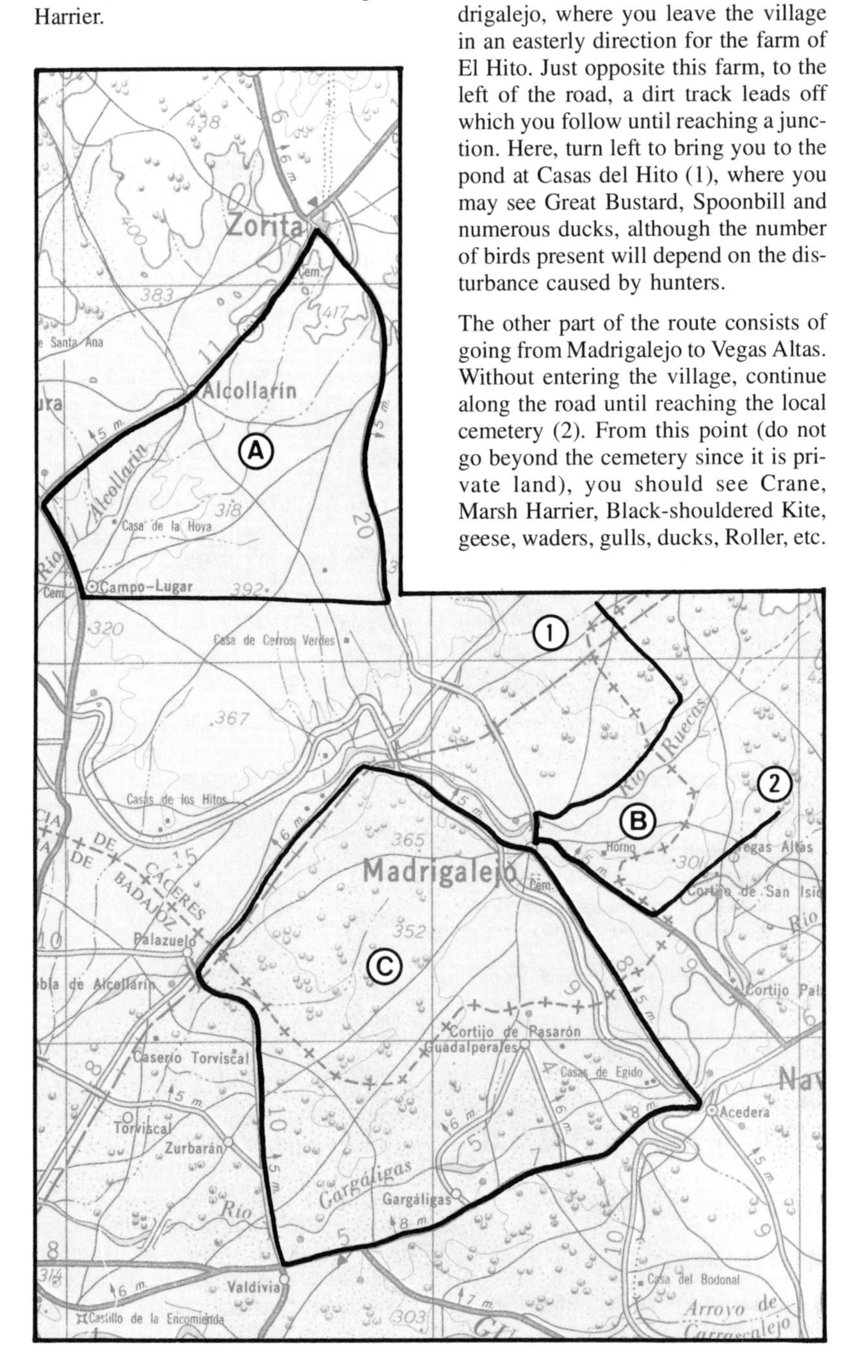

The starting point for **route B** is Madrigalejo, where you leave the village in an easterly direction for the farm of El Hito. Just opposite this farm, to the left of the road, a dirt track leads off which you follow until reaching a junction. Here, turn left to bring you to the pond at Casas del Hito (1), where you may see Great Bustard, Spoonbill and numerous ducks, although the number of birds present will depend on the disturbance caused by hunters.

The other part of the route consists of going from Madrigalejo to Vegas Altas. Without entering the village, continue along the road until reaching the local cemetery (2). From this point (do not go beyond the cemetery since it is private land), you should see Crane, Marsh Harrier, Black-shouldered Kite, geese, waders, gulls, ducks, Roller, etc.

Route C leaves Madrigalejo and takes you westwards along the road running parallel to an irrigation channel to the village of Palazuelo. From Palazuelo, continue to Zurbarán and Valdivia, where you join the N-430 to Acedera. Return to Madrigalejo from Acedera. This route, taking you through the areas of irrigated land, is good for seeing Black-shouldered Kite and other birds linked to these semi-aquatic habitats. In January and February you will see Crane, which at this time of year move from the holm oak woodland to the areas of irrigated land.

Accommodation

You can spend the night in hostels of middling category in Zorita, Madrigalejo and Navalvillar de Pela.

Comments

It must be stressed that you should not approach the area immediately surrounding the lake at Casas del Hito and that you should be content with watching the birds from the track. The same applies to the area around the cemetery at Vegas Altas.

Angel Sánchez García

■ EX.22 ORELLANA RESERVOIR AND PELA RANGE

A reservoir and range of hills of average height.

Main species

Residents: Little Grebe, Great Crested Grebe, Cattle Egret, Little Egret, Mallard, Red-crested Pochard, Red Kite, Griffon Vulture, Golden Eagle, Coot, Stone Curlew, Common Sandpiper, Eagle Owl, Great Spotted Cuckoo, Thekla Lark, Woodlark, Crag Martin, Black Wheatear, Blue Rock Thrush, Mistle Thrush, Dartford Warbler, Sardinian Warbler, Great Grey Shrike, Azure-winged Magpie, Raven, Spanish Sparrow, Rock Sparrow, Rock Bunting.

Summer visitors: Night Heron, Black Stork, Egyptian Vulture, Short-toed Eagle, Booted Eagle, Lesser Kestrel, Black-winged Stilt, Collared Pratincole, Little Ringed Plover, Gull-billed Tern, Little Tern, Great Spotted Cuckoo, Scops Owl, Bee-eater, Roller, Red-rumped Swallow, Rufous Bush Robin, Black-eared Wheatear, Melodious Warbler, Subalpine Warbler, Orphean Warbler, Golden Oriole, Woodchat Shrike.

Winter visitors: Black-necked Grebe, Cormorant, Widgeon, Gadwall, Pintail, Shoveler, Pochard, Tufted Duck, Marsh Harrier, Hen Harrier, Sparrowhawk, Crane, Golden Plover and other waders, Black-headed Gull, Lesser Black-backed Gull, Alpine Accentor.

On passage: Osprey, waders, Whiskered Tern, Black Tern.

Access

The N-430, known as the *carretera de los pantanos* or reservoir road, is the main means of access to the area. This road connects with the N-V via the C-520 from Miajadas to Don Benito.

Description

The area is dominated by the Orellana reservoir on the river Guadiana; the reservoir runs for 35 km from the village of Orellana la Vieja to the García de Sola dam (Puerto Peña). This is a major wintering ground for water birds, with over 20,000 individuals in some years. Some of the islets in the reservoir are the sites of colonies of herons, gulls and waders.

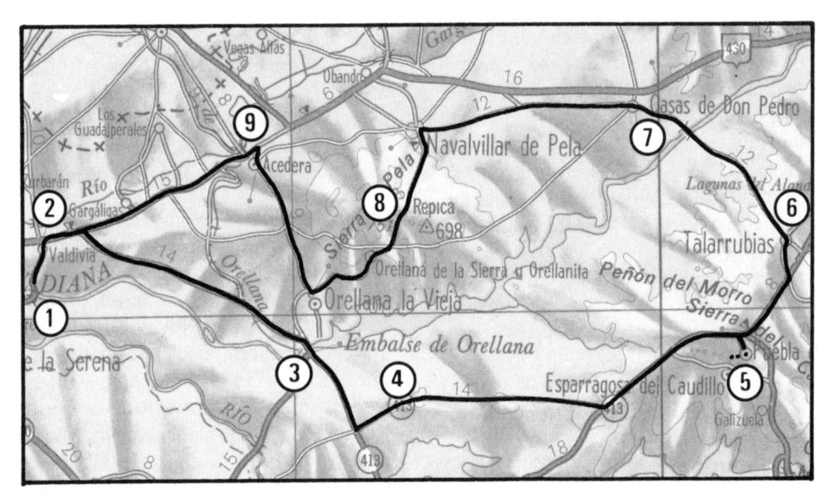

The Sierra de Pela (743 m) rises up on the right shore of the reservoir, dominating the Vegas Altas del Guadiana irrigation area. Below the quartzite cliffs, areas of cork oak woodland survive along with cistus, mastic tree and strawberry tree. There are also olive groves and eucalyptus plantations.

Recommended routes

This route consists of a car journey with discretional stops taking up a whole day. The route leaves Villanueva de la Serena on the N-430 and goes towards Valdivia, the Orellana dam, Puebla de Alcocer, Talarrubias, Casas de Don Pedro, Navalvillar de Pela, Orellanita, Orellana la Vieja and Acedera, returning to Villanueva de la Serena on the N-430. The main points of interest are the following:

1) Bridge over the river Guadiana, 5 km from Villanueva. Here you will see herons, storks, waders, Roller and Alpine Swift.

2) La Jarilla. A good spot for seeing Black-shouldered Kite and Crane. In the rice fields you will also see waders, particularly Black-tailed Godwit, in January and February.

3) Orellana dam. A good place for watching water birds.

4) Road from Orellana to Puebla de Alcocer. A good place for watching Crane and other steppe-dwelling species.

5) Puebla de Alcocer. In the village you will see many Lesser Kestrel and White Stork, and in the castle Blue Rock Thrush, Black-eared Wheatear, Black Wheatear, Roller and Alpine Accentor.

6) Talarrubias. The parish church in Talarrubias has a large colony of White Stork.

7) Bridge at Casas de Don Pedro, over the reservoir.

8) Hoyo de Pela. A good site for watching various birds of prey.

9) Acedera. In the village, Lesser Kestrel and White Stork and, in the surrounding area, Black-shouldered Kite.

Accommodation

In Navalvillar de Pela there is a hostel (El Imprevisto, at the 145 km marker post on the N-430) and another in Puebla de Alcocer (La Codorniz, at the crossroads). There are also some pensions in Orellana la Vieja.

Juan J. Ferrero and José A. Román

EX.23
LA SERENA

Grazing land and cereal fields; one of the largest steppe areas in Spain.

Main species

Residents: Griffon Vulture, Kestrel, Little Bustard, Great Bustard, Stone Curlew, Black-bellied Sandgrouse, Pin-tailed Sandgrouse, Little Owl, Calandra Lark, Thekla Lark, Fan-tailed Warbler, Chough, Great Grey Shrike.

Summer visitors: Egyptian Vulture, Short-toed Eagle, Cattle Egret, White Stork, Montagu's Harrier, Lesser Kestrel, Collared Pratincole, Bee-eater, Roller, Great Spotted Cuckoo, Short-toed Lark, Red-rumped Swallow, Black-eared Wheatear.

Winter visitors: Red Kite, Merlin, Crane, Golden Plover, Lapwing, Skylark, Meadow Pipit.

Access

From Miajadas, on the N-V, go to Don Benito (22 km). Continue to Villanueva de la Serena (6 km) and from there take the C-420 to Castuera (38 km).

Description

La Serena, measuring almost 1,000 km^2, is a rolling and completely treeless peneplain located in the east of the province of Badajoz. Much of the area is covered by grazing land with numerous slate outcrops known as *dientes de perro* or hound's teeth, which make farming difficult and give the landscape a strange appearance.

Traditionally, part of the pastureland is used for cereal crops, leaving the stubble for a year or more. There are a lot of large isolated farms in the area which are dedicated to extensive sheep farming.

Recommended routes

Route A consists of a drive from Castuera to Puebla de Alcocer (42 km). Throughout the route you will see nesting boxes fixed to telegraph posts which are occupied by Kestrel and Roller. The most interesting points are the following:

1) Mines at Miraflores. Old lead and silver mines which are reached via a track running off to the left from the road at the 94 km marker post. You will have sightings of Kestrel, Lesser Kestrel, Little Bustard, Pin-tailed Sandgrouse, Great Spotted Cuckoo, Roller, Bee-eater and Chough.

2) Returning to the road, make another stop 2 km farther along to walk along the banks of the Mejoral stream, where you may see Red-rumped Swallow and some river-dwelling species.

3) Turn left at the 87 km marker post to gain a good view of the area. You may also see Great Bustard and Little Bustard.

4) On the other side of the road, a badly surfaced track leads off to cross the heart of the La Serena area. After 10 km you will come to the abandoned mines of Peñalobosa, from where you will have views of a landscape extremely characteristic of La Serena. Throughout you will see Pin-tailed Sandgrouse, Black-bellied Sandgrouse, Stone Curlew, Little Bustard, Great Bustard, Montagu's Harrier, as well as having frequent sightings of Griffon Vulture and Egyptian Vulture.

5) When you reach the turning for Cabeza del Buey, make for this village. If you are undertaking this itinerary in winter, you will see Crane. When the road ends, turn right again for Castuera. Shortly afterwards you will come to the castle of Almorchón situated on top of a rocky outcrop, a good spot for seeing cliff-dwelling species as well as for

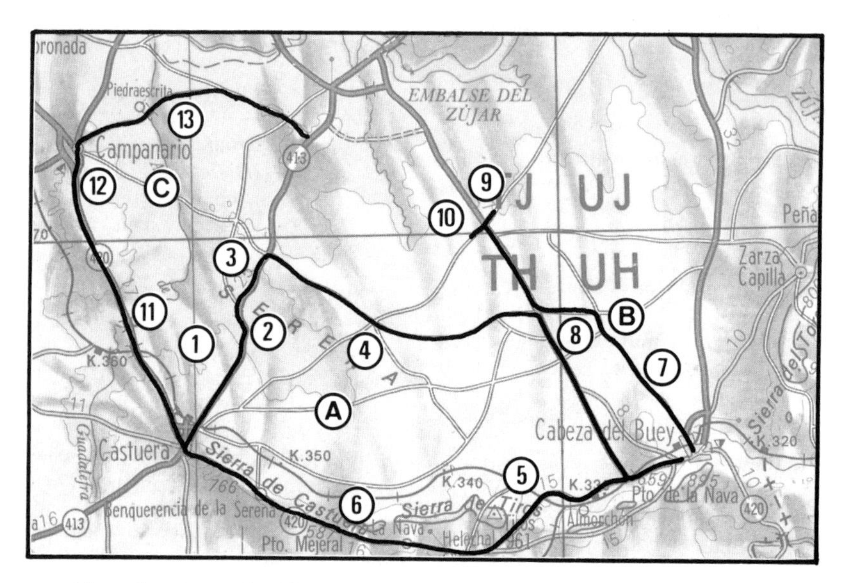

watching Crane moving from their feeding grounds to their roosts.

6) Puerto Mejoral is another wonderful spot for watching large groups of Crane. At dusk they fly from the holm oak woodland lying to the south of the range to the treeless plains north of the range. ADENEX has established a small Bird Observatory here which can accommodate small groups of visitors.

Route B is also a car journey, leaving Cabeza del Buey in the direction of Córdoba. Make your way over a level crossing and continue along the unsurfaced but perfectly passable track leading off from opposite the crossing for some 13 km. In this area grazing land and cereal fields are evenly interspersed. The most interesting points are the following:

7) Over the first 5 km you may often see Stone Curlew, Black-bellied Sandgrouse and Collared Pratincole.

8) On the second section of the trip you will have greater opportunities of seeing Great Bustard, Little Bustard and large groups of White Stork.

9) and 10) On reaching the road from Cabeza del Buey to La Serena reservoir, turn right and after 3 km you will come across an unsurfaced track. In this area it is common to see Great Bustard on both sides of the road.

Route C takes you along surfaced roads. The starting point is Castuera; travel towards Villanueva de la Serena on the C-420. Make stops at the following points:

11) Some 8 km from Castuera, stop to watch groups of Crane feeding in the holm oak woodland.

12) The Campanario rubbish dump, lying to the right of the road just before reaching the village of the same name. Vast numbers of storks, Cattle Egret and kites feed on the rubbish dump. In winter Black-headed Gull and Lesser Black-backed Gull are also present.

13) Ermita de Piedra Escrita, a chapel on the banks of the river Guadalefra; this area is much frequented by Little Bustard and Pin-tailed Sandgrouse.

Accommodation

Accommodation is hard to come by in this area. Hostal Los Naranjos in Castuera is recommended, although it is advisable to make a reservation beforehand.

If you wish to stay at the Bird Observatory (Estación Ornitológica de Puerto Mejoral), you should get in touch with ADENEX; c/ Cuba, 10; 06800 Mérida; telephone: 924-317202.

María de las Nieves de Borbón and Cristina Barros

■ EX.24 HORNACHOS RANGE, LOS MOLINOS AND ALANGE RESERVOIRS

An isolated range of hills and two reservoirs.

Main species

Residents: Little Grebe, Great Crested Grebe, Little Egret, Mallard, Black-shouldered Kite, Red Kite, Griffon Vulture, Golden Eagle, Bonelli's Eagle, Peregrine Falcon, Coot, Little Bustard, Eagle Owl, Kingfisher, Thekla Lark, Woodlark, Crag Martin, Black Wheatear, Blue Rock Thrush, Fan-tailed Warbler, Dartford Warbler, Sardinian Warbler, Great Grey Shrike, Azure-winged Magpie, Chough, Raven, Spanish Sparrow, Rock Sparrow, Hawfinch, Cirl Bunting, Rock Bunting.

Summer visitors: Black Stork, Egyptian Vulture, Short-toed Eagle, Montagu's Harrier, Booted Eagle, Lesser Kestrel, Little Tern, Turtle Dove, Great Spotted Cuckoo, Scops Owl, Red-necked Nightjar, Bee-eater, Red-rumped Swallow, Rufous Bush Robin, Melodious Warbler, Subalpine Warbler, Orphean Warbler, Spotted Flycatcher, Golden Oriole, Woodchat Shrike.

Winter visitors: Cormorant, Grey Heron, Greylag Goose, Widgeon, Gadwall, Teal, Shoveler, Pochard, Tufted Duck, Crane, waders, Lesser Black-backed Gull, Alpine Accentor, Black Redstart, Redwing, Bullfinch.

Access

From Mérida, a minor road passes through Alange, Palomas and Puebla de la Reina, providing interesting views of the Alange reservoir and the ranges of hills in the surrounding area (45 km). The area can be reached from the N-630, being 25 km from this main road either via Villafranca de los Barros and Ribera del Fresno, or via Los Santos de Maimona and Hinojosa del Valle.

Description

The Hornachos range is an isolated range of hills typical of Extremadura, rising up from the midst of extensive plains with sides covered with cork oak and Mediterranean scrubland. On top are extensive rocky areas and large quartzite screes. It reaches its maximum height with Peñón de Marín (951 m).

The dams at Alange and Los Molinos hold back the waters of the river Matachel, the main river of the region. The former is a new reservoir on a large scale, the site of considerable numbers of wintering water birds. The Los Molinos reservoir lies upstream and is smaller but nonetheless interesting. Both are used as roosts by Crane.

Recommended routes

Route A consists of a car journey taking a full day with discretional stops. The starting point is Mérida; the route takes you through Alange, Palomas,

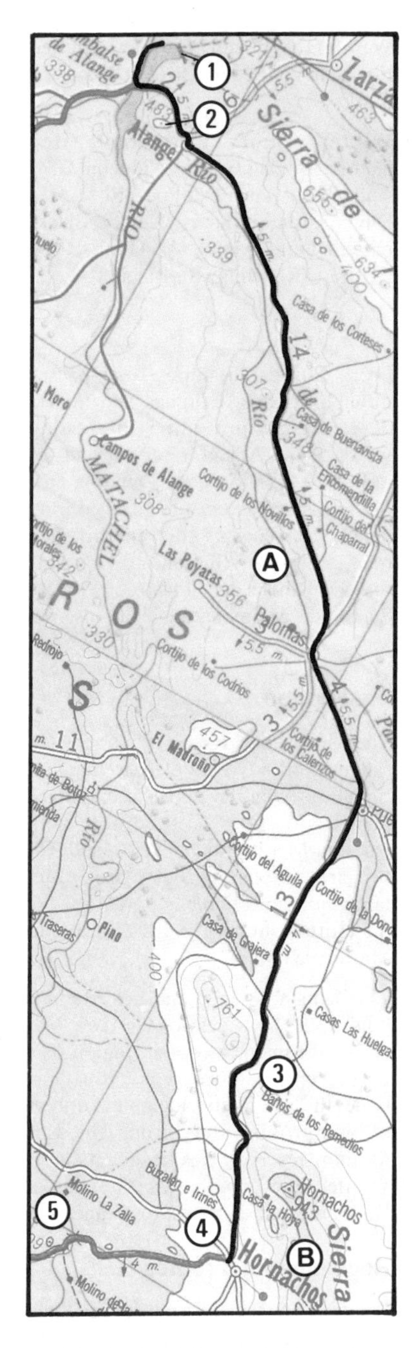

Puebla de la Reina and Hornachos, coming to an end at the reservoir of Los Molinos on the road to Hinojosa del Valle. The main points of interest are the following:

1) Embalse de Alange. The reservoir is a good place for watching water birds.

2) Alange castle. A panoramic view of the reservoir, combined with the opportunity of seeing Blue Rock Thrush, Black Wheatear, Crag Martin and Alpine Accentor.

3) Puerto Llano. This pass gives a good general view of the Hornachos range, looking also over the valley of the river Matachel.

4) Hornachos. Castle on top of a rocky outcrop with cliff-dwelling species.

5) Embalse de Los Molinos. This reservoir is a good place for watching water birds.

Route B (not indicated on the map), consists of a guided tour of the reserve managed by ADENEX in the Sierra de Hornachos.

Accommodation

There is a pension in Hornachos, and ADENEX provides accommodation actually within the reserve. To visit this reserve, you should contact the ADENEX headquarters beforehand; c/ Cuba, 10; 06800 Mérida; telephone: 924-317202.

Further accommodation is available in Alange (which has a spa) and other nearby villages such as Almendralejo and Zafra.

Juan J. Ferrero, Juan J. Negro, José A. Román and Francisc Blanco.

EX.25 JEREZ DE LOS CABALLEROS

Wooded grazing lands with holm oak and cork oak.

Main species

Residents: Cattle Egret, Little Egret, Mallard, Black-shouldered Kite, Griffon Vulture, Black Vulture, Sparrowhawk, Buzzard, Spanish Imperial Eagle, Crested Tit, Azure-winged Magpie.

Summer visitors: White Stork, Black Stork, Egyptian Vulture, Black Kite, Short-toed Eagle, Booted Eagle, Lesser Kestrel, Red-necked Nightjar, Red-rumped Swallow.

Winter visitors: Cormorant, ducks, Red Kite.

Access

Jerez de los Caballeros is the centre of this region. It can be reached on the N-630 via Zafra and Burguillos del Cerro, or alternatively from the N-V via Badajoz.

Description

Extensive wooded grazing lands (*dehesas*) with holm oak and cork oak located on the rolling ground of the last

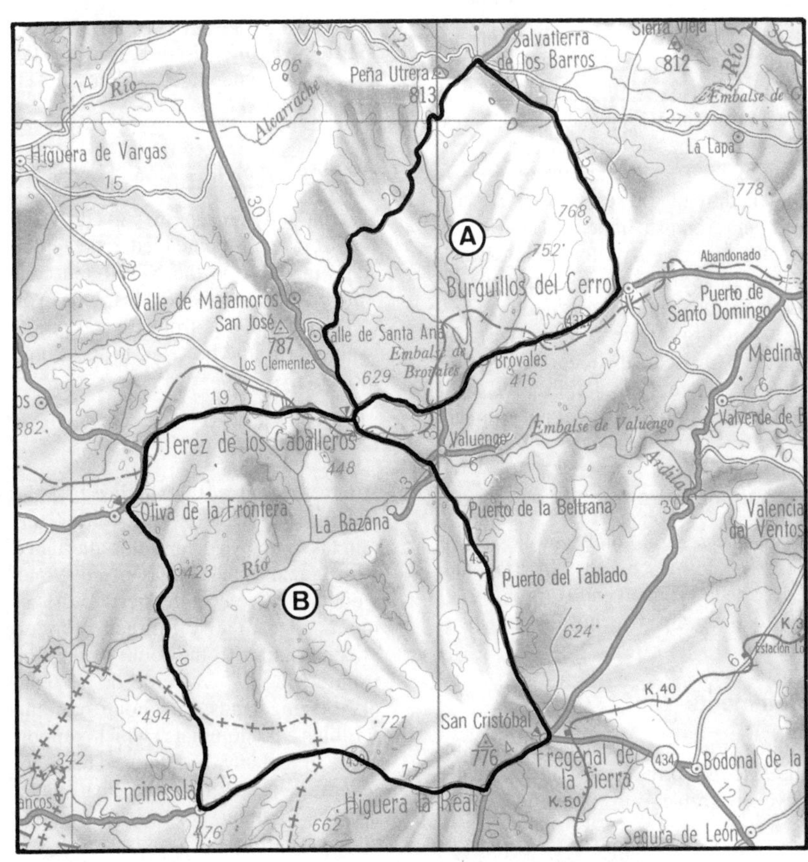

foothills of the Sierra Morena. They are remarkable for their great size and completely unspoiled state. There are also two small reservoirs and some areas of cereal fields and irrigated land.

Recommended routes

Route A consists of a car journey of some 60 km along the roads joining Jerez de los Caballeros, Salvatierra de los Barros and Burguillos del Cerro. In addition to the interesting landscape, you will also see many vultures, which are attracted by the vast amount of livestock present in the region, and other birds of prey. In the area around the Brovales reservoir, you may see Black-shouldered Kite, Grey Heron, Little Egret, Cattle Egret and various ducks.

Route B is also a car journey, starting in Jerez de los Caballeros and running along the roads to Oliva de la Frontera, Encinasola and Fregenal de la Sierra. This route is similar to route A, although the range of birds of prey is widened by the presence of Black Vulture and Spanish Imperial Eagle. This is also a good place for seeing Black Stork. In addition, it is worth walking through the wooded grazing lands to see, among other forest-dwelling species, Crested Tit (in cork oaks) and Azure-winged Magpie. Finally, visit the old quarters of the villages to see, in addition to storks, Lesser Kestrel.

Accommodation

There are several hotels and hostels in Jerez de los Caballeros. In Fregenal, Oliva de la Frontera and Burguillos del Cerro there are also hostels and pensions.

Comments

Although much of the land occupied by the *dehesas* is private, you will not usually have any problems in visiting them.

Angel Sánchez García

■ EX.26 LLERENA – AZUAGA

Cereal fields and holm oak woodland.

Main species

Residents: Black-shouldered Kite, Griffon Vulture, Black Vulture, Montagu's Harrier, Golden Eagle, Spanish Imperial Eagle, Bonelli's Eagle, Little Bustard, Great Bustard, Black-bellied Sandgrouse, Pin-tailed Sandgrouse, Calandra Lark, Chough.

Summer visitors: White Stork, Black Stork, Black Kite, Short-toed Eagle, Booted Eagle, Lesser Kestrel, Short-toed Lark, Tawny Pipit.

Winter visitors: Red Kite, Greylag Goose and other ducks, Hen Harrier, Crane, Skylark.

Access

Llerena and Azuaga are linked by the N-432, a well-maintained road which starts in Zafra on the N-630 and continues eastwards towards Córdoba. You can reach the area from several points to the north, the best and fastest being the C-413.

Description

A large region in the southeast of the province of Badajoz with rolling terrain taken up by cereal fields alternated with grazing land. Areas of holm oak woodland have been reduced to the remains of radically thinned wooded grazing lands. To the south of the line from Azuaga to Valverde de Llerena, dry grazing lands with holm oak and scrubland predominate, which support a lot of grazing livestock. There are several game reserves and small game is very common, giving rise to large numbers of birds of prey.

Recommended routes

Route A consists of a car journey from Llerena to Reina, Ahillones, Berlanga, Maguilla, Casas de Tío Piche and Casas de Pila. This long route takes you past various wintering grounds for Crane, and it is worth making at least one stop at the castle in Reina and another at the Los Conejos reservoir (Llerena) where, in addition to Crane, you will also see geese and ducks. Particularly near Ahillones and throughout the route in general, you may see Montagu's Harrier, Hen Harrier, Great Bustard, Little Bustard, Pin-tailed Sandgrouse and Black-bellied Sandgrouse.

Route B runs along the roads from Azuaga to Granja de Torrehermosa, Peraleda del Zaucejo and Campillo de Llerena. The species which you may see are similar to those described for route A. However, an area of holm oak woodland near the turning for Granja

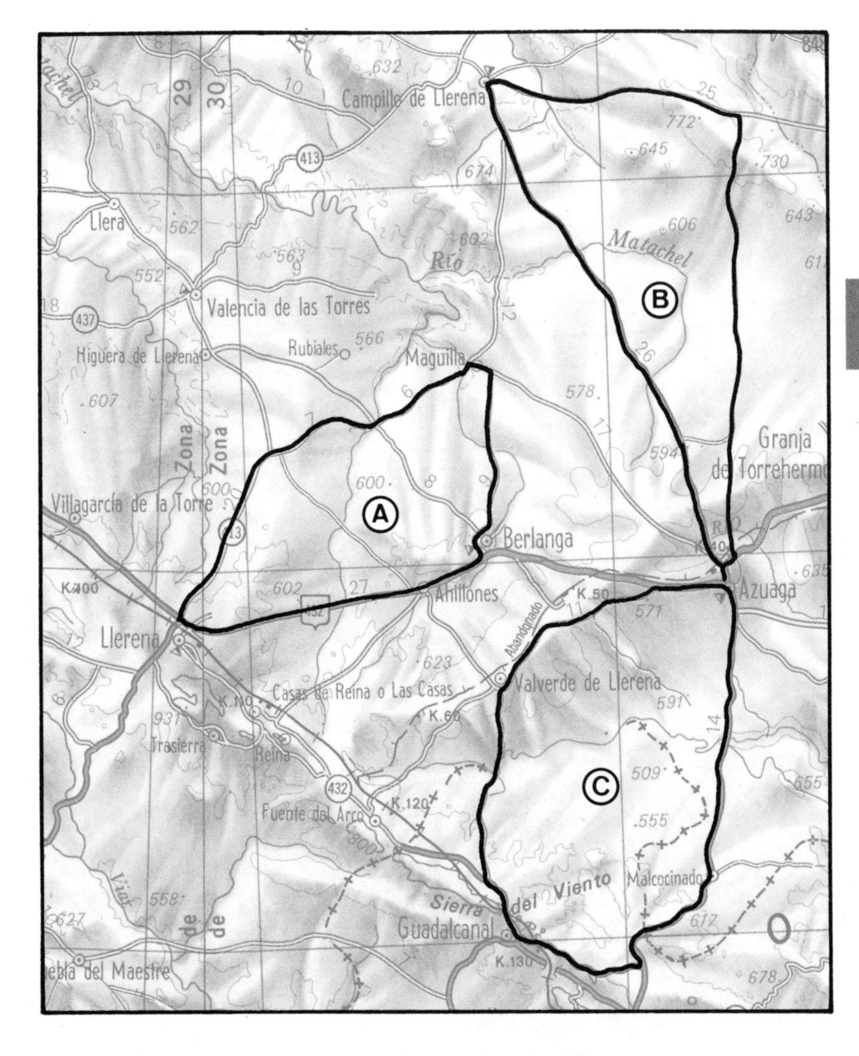

de Torrehermosa on the road from Azuaga to Campillo de Llerena will give you virtually guaranteed sightings of Black-shouldered Kite.

Route C, between Azuaga, Valverde de Llerena, Guadalcanal and Malcocinado, provides opportunities of seeing a wide range of birds of prey including Black Vulture and Spanish Imperial Eagle. If you are very lucky, you may also see Black Stork. It is also well worth walking along the river Sotillo, although the high number of fences will make this route difficult.

Accommodation

The best options are in Llerena and Azuaga; Hotel Las Conchas in Azuaga is recommended. There are hostels and pensions in the small villages.

Angel Sánchez García

GALICIA

Guillemot
Uria aalge

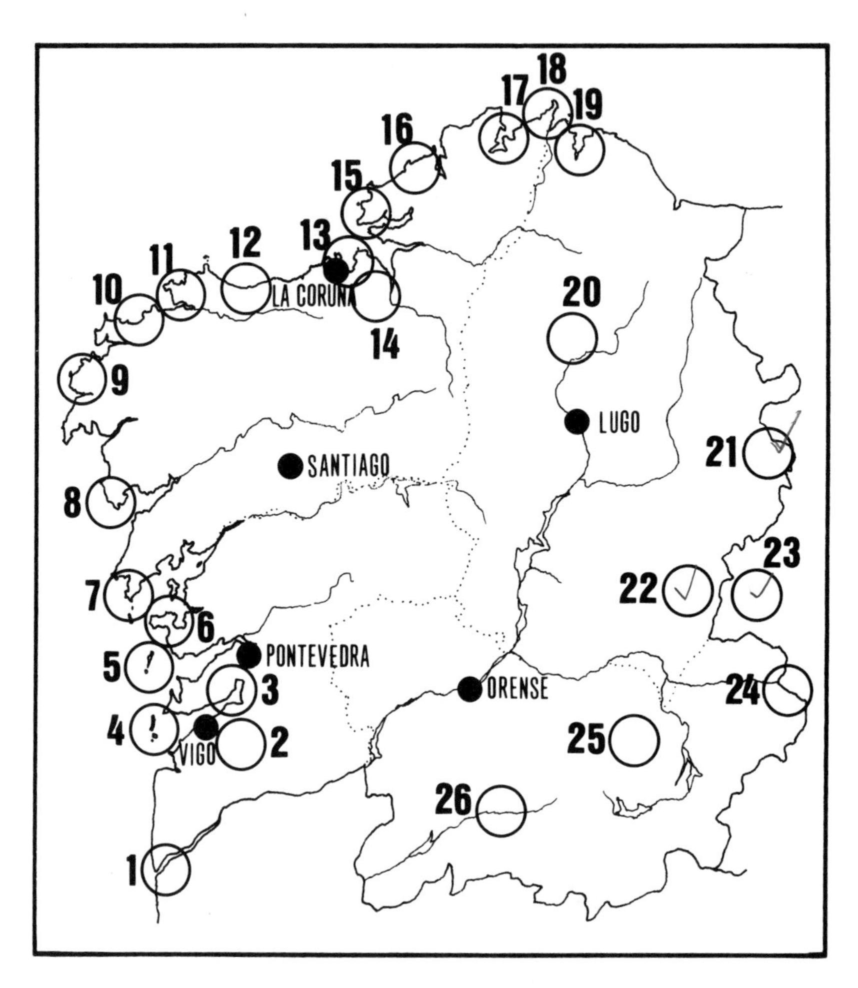

From an ornithological point of view this attractive area in the far northwest of Spain stands out for its sea birds and estuarine birds. For this reason most of the locations we have selected are coastal sites.

Yellow-legged Gull and Shag commonly nest in the area. Whilst Guillemot is now on the edge of extinction here, Lesser Black-backed Gull and Kittiwake have recently begun to colonize this area, although as yet the population is quite small. The islands of Cíes (G.4) and Ons (G.5) and the islets off Cabo Vilán (G.9) are good sites for watching this group of birds, who share the wave-battered cliffs with Peregrine Falcon, Rock Dove, Alpine Swift, Black Redstart, Chough and Raven. Of even greater interest are the numerous promontories along the rocky coastline, which are excellent spots for watching migrating sea birds at close quarters, particularly in autumn. Such promontories include Cabo Silleiro (G.3), Cabo Finisterre or Fisterra, Cabo Touriñán, Cabo Vilán or Villano (G.9), Cabo Roncudo (G.11), Cabo Prior, Cabo Ortegal (G.17) and, above all, the renowned Estaca de Bares (G.18) where the Cantabrian coast joins the Atlantic coast. From September through to November a spectacular stream of Gannet, shearwaters, scoters, terns, skuas and gulls of all different species occurs.

Estuaries in Galicia run along *rías*, fjord-like inlets running in from the sea corresponding to submerged river valleys; interest here is focused on waders, whose presence is remarkable for variety as opposed to quantity. Again the passage periods bring the widest range of species, but in some places the numbers of wintering species reach relatively high levels, as is the case at O Grove (G.6) and Ortigueira (G.18). In winter the coastline of Galicia has the added attraction of being the wintering haunt of fairly regular, small groups of northern species which are rare or exceptional in most of the rest of the Iberian Peninsula. These include Black-throated Diver, Great Northern Diver, Brent Goose, Red-breasted Merganser, Velvet Scoter, Scaup, Eider, Great Black-backed Gull, Common Gull, Glaucous Gull, Purple Sandpiper and Snow Bunting. Galicia seems to see vagrants from North America, particularly gulls and waders, more frequently than other parts of Spain. This occurs mainly in September and October. G.10, G.11 and G.12 are particularly good spots for seeing these vagrants. Unfortunately, birdlife in the estuaries is greatly reduced by the presence of large numbers of people gathering shellfish and, on a local level, of hunters. It is probably because of this that numbers of birds are often low, few water birds nesting here other than common species such as Little Grebe, Mallard, Coot or Moorhen.

Although Galicia is a very mountainous area with virtually no flat areas, mountains are generally low, rolling and gentle. Only in the far southwest are there mountains of any height with the ranges of Ancares (G.21), Caurel (G.22), Peña Trevinca (G.24) and San Memede and Queixa (G.25). Alpine birdlife is noticeably limited to species such as Golden Eagle, Grey Partridge, Water Pipit and Wheatear. However, these mountains are also the site of the surviving areas of deciduous woodland which used to extend throughout Galicia, and these areas are inhabited by some interesting woodland species. This is the case of the Sierra de los Ancares, where Honey Buzzard, Capercaillie, Woodcock, Black Woodpecker, Goldcrest and Marsh Tit are present. Special mention should be made of the unusual character of the Encina da Lastra range (G.23); it borders with the Bierzo region in the province of León, and a pronouncedly Mediterranean climate coupled with limestone cliffs makes for the occasional presence of species such as Egyptian Vulture, Bonelli's Eagle, Red-rumped Swallow, Blue Rock Thrush and Rock Sparrow, which are exceptional elsewhere in Galicia.

The fact that the main massifs (mentioned above) constitute only a very small part of this Autonomous Region, allows Atlantic influence to affect most of Galicia, making for a rainy, green region with predominantly Euro-siberian flora. However, the lack of high mountains which might act as a dividing line also allows Mediterranean influence to enter from the south, continuing the gentle slopes characteristic of Portugal. This gives rise to a curious mixture of northern and Mediterranean species which elsewhere in Spain are usually clearly segregated. For example, some of the commonest birds to be seen in the Galician countryside are Dunnock, Song Thrush and Bullfinch, representing northern species, alongside with Hoopoe, Dartford Warbler, Rock Bunting, Cirl Bunting and Golden Oriole. By contrast species which are relatively common in other areas of northern Spain such as Tree Pipit, Red-backed Shrike or Yellowhammer are relatively rare. In the same way, many Mediterranean or southern species are seldom seen or concentrated very locally, examples being Woodchat Shrike, Subalpine Warbler, Black-eared Wheatear, Nightingale and Corn Bunting. Thus, occasional stops in the Galician countryside, typically a mosaic of close-packed fields, meadows, scrub and pine woods, will bring sightings of a considerable variety of species of birds, especially of small-sized ones. There are rather fewer large birds, perhaps because of the unusual distribution (for Spain) of human population with houses and hamlets scattered all around. For this reason, perhaps, the only commonly seen diurnal raptors are Buzzard, Sparrowhawk, Goshawk and Kestrel.

Another significant gap in Galician birdlife is, logically enough, birds dwelling in flat, open spaces. These are limited almost exclusively to two areas, the Terrachá in the province of Lugo (G.20) and La Limia (G.26) in the province of Orense. These are almost the only places in Galicia where Little Bustard, Lapwing, Stone Curlew and Tawny Pipit are present. Both areas included large lagoons, Cospeito and Antela respectively, which were of great ornithological significance, but unfortunately they were drained.

G.1 ESTUARY OF THE RIVER MIÑO

River estuary.

Main species

Residents: Kingfisher, Fan-tailed Warbler, Sardinian Warbler, Common Waxbill.

Winter visitors: Cormorant, Little Egret, ducks (particularly Red-breasted Merganser and Tufted Duck), Oystercatcher, Turnstone, Sanderling, Great Black-backed Gull, Sandwich Tern.

On passage: waders (mainly Bar-tailed Godwit and Whimbrel), terns.

Access

From Vigo take the C-550 towards Baiona and A Guarda (52 km), or alternatively the N-120 to Porriño from where you take the N-550 to Tui and, before crossing the border with Portugal, take the C-550 to A Guarda (57 km).

Description

This is a broad estuary on the Portuguese border where intertidal zones predominate. The mouth of the river, the largest in Galicia, has beaches and breakwaters. Farther upstream are small mudflats, salt marshes and large islands covered with herbaceous vegetation which alternate with extensive sand banks at low tide. On the banks are patches of riverside woodland and reedbeds. Mankind has had a major influence on the surrounding countryside and on considerable stretches of the shores of the estuary, now taken up by building work, crops, pine and eucalyptus plantations, etc. The eastern, most inland part of the estuary is a Game Refuge measuring 900 ha.

The whole Miño estuary can be seen from Monte Santa Tecla, an area of high ground which is also of archaeological interest.

Recommended routes

Take the C-550 out of A Guarda to Playa de Camposancos, a beach. From here you can walk or drive to the far end of the mouth of the Miño (1). Here you can see Gannet, auks and other sea birds (in larger numbers during the migration period), Oystercatcher, Turnstone and, with luck, Purple Sandpiper. This point also overlooks the route of birds entering and leaving the estuary to rest or feed, such as Cormorant and Sandwich Tern.

Point 2 is the Armona inlet, which can be reached by returning to the C-550. After about 200 m you will come to a blind bend with an unmarked right turn. Take this turn to get down to the water's edge. Here take the dirt track leading off to the left from where, at low tide, you will see Little Egret, ducks, waders and Sandwich Tern. Continue along the track until you reach Pasaxe (3) with its housing development and wharves, from which you can see Cormorant, Red-breasted Merganser, Kingfisher and, if they have been disturbed in other parts of the bay, large numbers of ducks, particularly Tufted Duck. Continue along the road towards A Guarda and about 300 m farther on take the signed right hand turn to the Observatorios Ornitológicos (hides) and the Camping Santa Tecla, a campsite. Points 4 and 5 are the two hides which are good spots when the tide is high or ebbing for large numbers of herons (sometimes Spoonbill as well), ducks (with the occasional Scaup among Tufted Duck), waders and gulls.

From the second hide (point 5, on the far side of the campsite) return on the track running at right angles to the es-

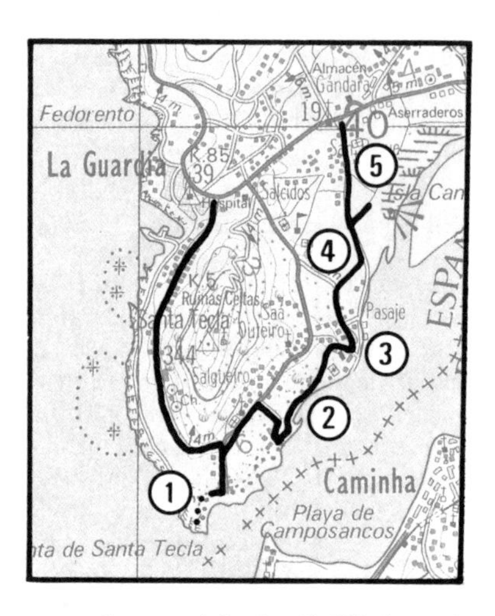

tuary shore to join the C-550 from A Guarda to Tui. En route you will pass through Xunqueira de Salcidos where Water Rail, Great Reed Warbler, Fan-tailed Warbler and other marsh dwellers abound including a new addition, the Common Waxbill.

The route can and should continue along the Portuguese side of the estuary (see Comments). Some stops can be omitted and the route can be done in reverse, at your convenience.

Accommodation

Generally there is plenty of accommodation in Vigo and Baiona, with some in A Guarda. Recommended is Hotel O Muiño on the beach at Camposancos. It is suggested that you avoid the Camping Santa Tecla, a campsite, because of the effect it has had on the marshland.

Comments

Taking the estuary as a whole, birds move between both shores, and for this reason it is well worthwhile going over to Portugal. You can cross the border at Tui or on the ferry running from Goián to Vilanova de Cerveira. Make a halt on the jetty at Seixas where large numbers of waders congregate as the tide turns (Grey Plover, Ringed Plover, Dunlin and Sanderling among others) as well as the occasional Osprey. Farther on, in Caminha and all the way along the shore from the N-13 leading to Viana do Castelo, Cormorant, herons, Red-breasted Merganser and gulls can be seen. Finally it is worth stopping at Mata Nacional do Camarido, a large pine wood with dunes at the mouth of the estuary near the fortress island of A Insua, a major resting place for Cormorant, waders and terns.

It is worth coordinating your stops with the state of the tide. The best time of year for seeing wintering birds is from November to February inclusive. Migration periods in September-October and April-May are also very rewarding with frequent appearances of: unusual birds such as divers, grebes, Shelduck, Marsh Harrier, Avocet, marsh terns, etc.

Over the summer months the presence of large numbers of people and river craft do not make for a worthwhile trip. Also bear in mind that Thursdays, Sundays and public holidays are days for hunting, so on these days you should take the utmost care not to disturb the birds and cause them to move to unprotected areas.

If your base is Vigo, this trip can be combined with G.2 (Gándaras de Budiño) and G.3 (Ría de Vigo, Route B) in a single day, although two days would be preferable.

Jorge Mouriño, Francisco Arcos and Francisco Sierra Abraín

■ G.2 BANK OF THE RIVER LOURO (GÁNDARAS DE BUDIÑO)

A wetland area with lakes, peat bogs and riverside woodland.

Main species

Residents: Grey Heron, Teal (only regular nesting place in the Iberian Peninsula), Water Rail, Cetti's Warbler, Fan-tailed Warbler, Sardinian Warbler.

Summer visitors: Little Bittern, White Stork, Kingfisher, Savi's Warbler (some years).

Winter visitors: ducks.

On passage: Purple Heron, Marsh Harrier, marsh terns, a few waders, Bluethroat.

Access

Take the N-120 out of Vigo towards Porriño (20 km). In Porriño turn onto the N-550 to Tui and the Portuguese border. After about 4 km you will see a right turn signed for the Observatorio Ornitolóxico (hide) and Polígono Industrial Las Gándaras (an industrial estate). At the end of the long straight road crossing the industrial estate, turn right and immediately after a small group of houses turn right again. 150 m along this road you will come to a small car park next to a dirt track taking you to the hides.

Description

A clay river plain with several lakes including the Lagoa de Budiño, site of the hides mentioned above. Flora consists of heath, peat bogs, meadows and riverside woodland which are subject to seasonal flooding.

Virtually the whole area is surrounded by an industrial estate which is responsible for the indiscriminate dumpings of contaminating substances. The expansion of the industrial estate and the tree felling which is taking place reduce the area of this site year by year. What is more, the site is threatened by projects for new communication networks.

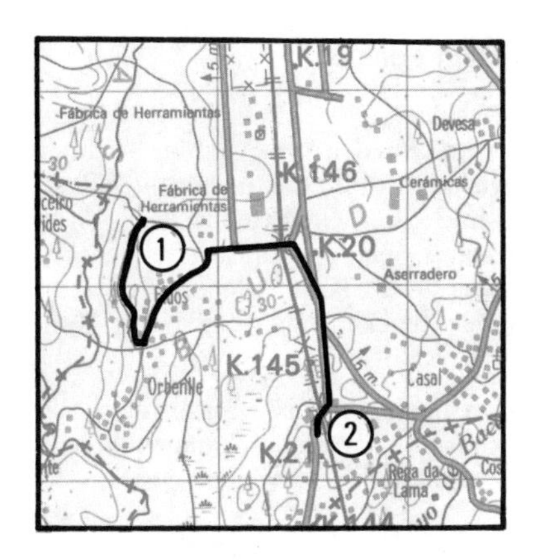

The most interesting areas constitute a 60 ha Game Refuge.

Recommended routes

The hides (point 1) are a perfect spot to see, with time and patience, Little Bittern, Water Rail and the occasional crake on passage. The nearby riverside woodland is home to large numbers of passerines, particularly in winter. These include Chiffchaff, Redwing and various finches.

In 1989 and 1990 a pair of White Stork nested in the area. This is the northwestern most storks' nest in Spain and is located on top of a chimney beside the N-550, about 500 m from the industrial estate (point 2).

Accommodation

There is plenty of accommodation in and around Vigo.

Francisco Arcos, Jorge Mouriño and Francisco Sierra Abraín

■ G.3 RÍA OF VIGO

A typical Galician estuary with a broad, deep mouth running into the sea.

Main species

Residents: Water Rail, Fan-tailed Warbler, Sardinian Warbler. **Winter visitors**: divers, Cormorant, Shag, Little Egret, Grey Heron, ducks (with Scaup occurring quite frequently), Turnstone, Purple Sandpiper, Great Black-backed Gull, Sandwich Tern, Razorbill.

On passage: Cory's Shearwater, Yelkouan Shearwater, Common Scoter, waders, terns, skuas, auks.

Access

Access to all points of interest on the estuary is easy and convenient. The C-550 (between Vilaboa-Hío and Vigo-A Guarda) takes in most of the estuary.

Description

The Vigo estuary, one of the largest in Spain, is a centre of dense human population which is reflected in the river being heavily exploited by tourism, harbour traffic, fishing, etc. Nonetheless some sections have remained relatively unspoiled. This is the case with the Vilaboa inlet, the upper reaches of the San Simón inlet and in some places in the Bahía de Baiona, the bay lying to the southwest of the Vigo estuary. The most interesting habitats are these estuaries, which have intertidal flats and small salt marshes as well as jetties and beaches.

The uppermost part of the estuary (Ensenada de San Simón, an inlet) is a Game Refuge (1,900 ha).

Recommended routes

Route A covers all of the San Simón inlet. The main lookout points, which can easily be reached by car, are the following:

1. San Adrián point.
2. Santa Cristina de Cobres wharf.
3. Os Caralletes landing stage.
4. Vilaboa salt pans.
5. Arcade wharf.
6. Cesantes beach.
7. Cesantes wharf.

From points 1, 2, 6 and 7 the open water in the southern half of the inlet can be seen. From October to February, points 1 and 2 will give you sightings of groups of duck, Cormorant and terns; in the scrubland lying next to the estuary you should see Sardinian Warbler. Point 7 will give you sightings of Little Egret and two interesting resting places for Cormorant and Grey Heron.

Points 3, 4 and 5 command the main intertidal zones in the northern part of the inlet. Point 4 lies at the most up-

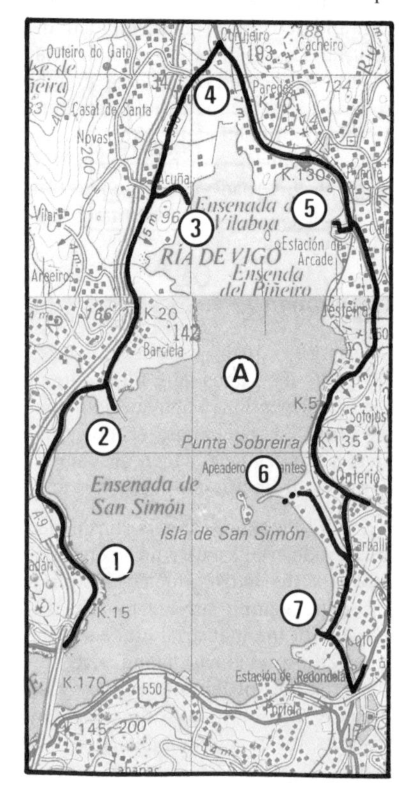

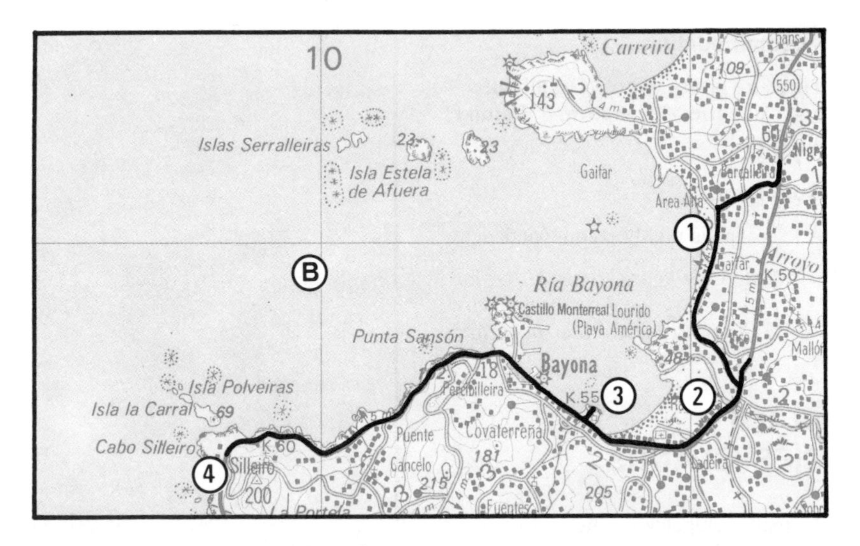

stream part of the estuary where there are 4 former salt pans (of historical interest because they are exceptional in Galicia). The pans are patchily covered with salt and freshwater marshes where you may see Water Rail, Kingfisher and a wide range of passerines. From points 3 and 5 you can see Cormorant, Grey Heron, ducks and smaller numbers of waders and terns.

Route B focuses on the bay of Baiona. The main observation points which can be reached by car are;

1. Playa América, a beach near the village of Panxón.

2. Estuary of the river Miñor by the village of A Ramallosa.

3. Santa Marta do Burgo chapel.

4. Cape Silleiro.

It is only worth going to point 1 if there are not many people about. There are resting places for gulls and terns, and Razorbill and Common Scoter can often be seen, the latter mainly in autumn. In the northwest of the inlet, opposite Panxón, a colony of Yellow-legged Gull inhabits the islets known as the Estelas.

Low tide at point 2 brings Grey Heron, Little Egret, waders and gulls, including Great Black-backed Gull.

Point 3 gives views over the central area of the bay, and from there Cormorant, Common Scoter (particularly in autumn), Razorbill and, less frequently, divers can be seen. With luck you may see sea ducks unusual for Spain such as Eider, Long-tailed Duck, etc. Oystercatcher, Turnstone and Sandwich Tern may be present on the neighbouring beaches at O Burgo and Ladeira.

To reach point 4, turn off the C-550 from Baiona to A Guarda onto a dirt track leading to a rubbish tip on the sea shore. Lying off the promontory are numerous small rocky islands which Cormorant and Shag use as resting places, to be joined, usually at high tide, by small groups of Oystercatcher, Turnstone and Purple Sandpiper. Out at sea, shearwaters, Gannet, scoters, skuas, Kittiwake, terns and auks can be seen on passage, while nearby fields are the site of Fan-tailed Warbler, Sardinian Warbler and Dartford Warbler.

Accommodation

There are plenty of hotels of all different categories in Vigo and Baiona alike.

Comments

A telescope is highly recommended.

José A. de Souza, Jorge Mouriño, Francisco Arcos and Francisco Sierra Abraín

■ G.4 CÍES ISLANDS

A small archipelago lying just off the coast with large colonies of sea birds.

Main species

Residents: Shag (400 pairs), Peregrine Falcon, Yellow-legged Gull, Lesser Black-backed Gull, Guillemot, Rock Dove, Chough, Raven, Sardinian Warbler.

Summer visitors: shearwaters, Nightjar, Alpine Swift.

Winter visitors: divers, Gannet, Cormorant, Great Skua, Sandwich Tern, auks.

On passage: Gannet, scoters, skuas, terns, auks.

Access

Boats providing public transport leave the Estación Marítima de Ría, the docks serving the estuary in Vigo. This is next to the Real Club Naútico (Yacht Club) and the Oficina de Turismo or Tourist Office. Boats only run in summer (15 June to 15 September), over the Easter holiday and on sunny spring weekends.

Access in private craft is permitted all year round, although the number of visitors per group must not exceed 10.

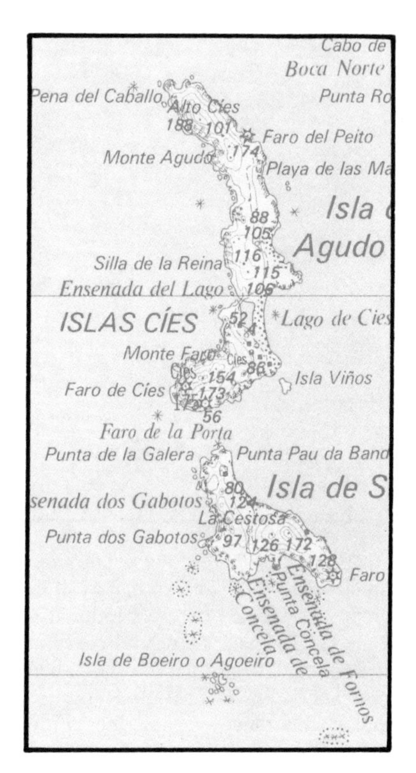

Description

The three islands constituting the archipelago lie at the mouth of the Vigo estuary. They are long and lie very close together. Their eastern sides are sandy and gently sloping with unspoiled beaches and dunes. By contrast the western sides, which face the open sea, are very steep and of great beauty.

Plant life in the dunes and on the cliffs is of great interest to botanists.

Recommended routes

The small size of the archipelago enables you to cover the islands on foot via the network of paths. All of them have paths leading to lighthouses which are perfectly located for birdwatching. There are also two bird observatories.

It should be pointed out that the crossing from Vigo is one of the main features of a birdwatching trip to Las Cíes.

Accommodation

There is a campsite on the islands. The site is open in summer only, and can take 800 people. In and around Vigo there are plenty of hotels of various categories.

Comments

Since the islands have been declared a Natural Park, access is limited in some areas. There is an information service providing leaflets and booklets and, in addition, a 1:10,000 map of the islands has been published, which is highly recommended.

If you wish to cover all aspects in your visit to the islands, it is worthwhile spending a couple of days there. In addition to ornithological interest, it has other natural and cultural attractions.

Francisco Sierra Abraín,
Jorge Mouriño and Francisco Arcos

■ G.5 ONS ISLANDS

A small archipelago just off the coast with large colonies of sea birds.

Main species

Residents: Shag, Yellow-legged Gull, Rock Dove, Chough, Raven, Fan-tailed Warbler.

Summer visitors: Yelkouan Shearwater, Cory's Shearwater (non-breeding), Alpine Swift.

Winter visitors: Gannet, Cormorant, Great Skua, Sandwich Tern, auks.

On passage: Gannet, scoters, skuas, terns, auks and many passerines.

Access

The islands can be reached by boat. There is a public boat service which runs from 15 June to 15 September, leaving from Bueu, Sanxenxo or Portonovo.

Description

The archipelago consists of the islands of Ons (450 hectares) and the much smaller Onza, which you cannot land on, in addition to some islets.

The sea, cliffs together with large areas of hills and some cultivated areas, are the habitats most characteristic of the islands.

Recommended routes

There is a good track which runs right around the island of Ons, providing a series of interesting lookout points.

It should not be forgotten that the boat crossing is one of the features of this

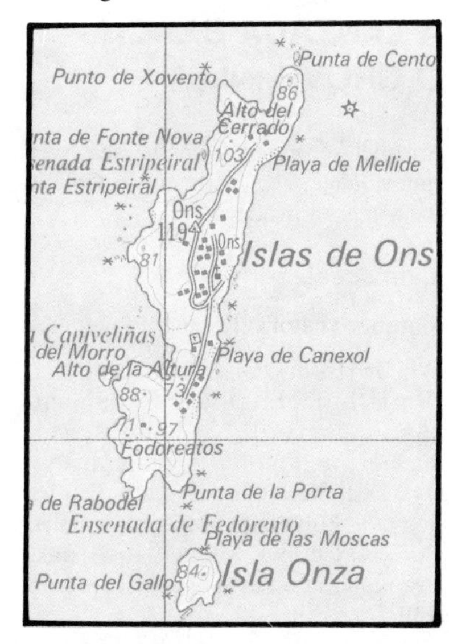

G

trip and will enable you to see some of the birds in the area.

Accommodation

There are a couple of pensions on the island but they are usually reserved or full. There are also two campsites with basic services consisting of water supply, rubbish collection and toilets.

In Bueu, Portonovo and Sanxenxo there are also plenty of hotels and campsites.

Comments

The island of Ons is a Game Refuge and is subject to special legislation, giving rise to some areas where access is restricted. The information service provides explanatory booklets.

It is worthwhile spending a couple of days on Ons to fully appreciate its attractions.

Francisco Sierra Abraín, Jorge Mouriño and Francisco Arcos

G.6 A LANZADA BEACH – O GROVE INLET

An inlet separated from the sea by a spit of sand. The main site in Galicia for wintering waders.

Main species

Summer visitors: Kentish Plover.

Winter visitors: Black-throated Diver, Great Northern Diver, Cormorant, Shag, Spoonbill, Common Scoter, ducks (roughly 1,700 individuals), Oystercatcher, Grey Plover, Dunlin (roughly 4,000 individuals), Bar-tailed Godwit, Curlew, Spotted Redshank, Greenshank, Turnstone, Common Gull, Razorbill.

On passage: shearwaters, Gannet, waders, terns, Razorbill.

Access

Take the C-550 out of Pontevedra to the beach at A Lanzada (30 km). From here you can circle the inlet via O Grove and the island of A Toxa, or by going to Cambados. Alternatively take the N-550 out of Compostela for Vigo, joining the C-550 at Pontecesures signed for Vilagarcía, Cambados and O Grove (75 km).

Description

A sheltered, shallow inlet covering about 1,200 ha. It has extensive intertidal zones of combined mud and sand, areas of salt marsh, numerous islets and one large island (A Toxa). The river Umia empties into the northern end of the inlet, and to the south-west the inlet is closed off by the isthmus of A Lanzada which consists of largely stabilized dunes. The area is subject to intense shellfishing activity, and three roads as well as an old landing strip run along the isthmus.

It is a Game Refuge included in the Ramsar Convention.

Recommended routes

Route A is a car journey beginning at the Our Lady of La Lanzada chapel and runs along the beach at A Lanzada and others located farther north. Near the chapel (1), you can see Cormorant, Shag, Razorbill and the occasional Guillemot. In winter, divers and scoters are frequently seen on the beach at A Lanzada (2) with rarer appearances from grebes, Eider, Long-tailed Duck and, during the migration periods, Manx Shearwater, Gannet and terns. The beaches farther along (points 3 and 4) are good sites for watching the spring passage of Sanderling, Bar-tailed Godwit and Whimbrel.

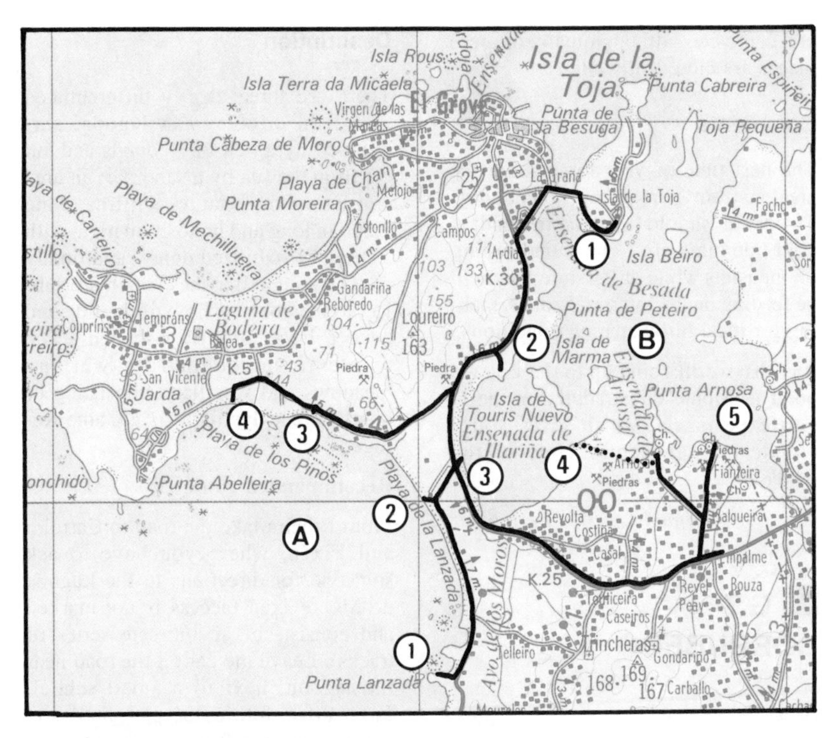

Route B starts on the island of A Toxa and runs round most of the inlet. It can be done by car and on foot (about 2-3 hours), and the most interesting stopping places are the following:

1) The far southwest of the island of A Toxa, from where (in winter) Oystercatcher, Ringed Plover, Grey Plover, Curlew, Turnstone, Common Gull and Great Black-backed Gull can be seen.

2) Punta Surmuiño (a promontory) and around: the main features here are the islets of Tourís and Marma, resting places for Cormorant, Little Egret, Grey Heron, Spoonbill, ducks and waders in winter. At low tide you can see all these birds feeding on the intertidal zone at O Bao, which has large expanses of eelgrass (*Zostera*).

3) All points along the road running beside O Bao are perfect spots for watching large groups of waders, who congregate 2-3 hours before low tide to feed.

4) Leiros: small islets with halophytic vegetation. At high tide this is a resting place for many waders including Grey Plover and Dunlin. To reach this site, go to the petrol station in Vilalonga and from there take the road to Arnosa and Fianteira. Stop by the ceramics factory in Arnosa and walk westwards along the shore for about 800 m.

5) Fianteira: a small landing stage commanding an extensive intertidal zone where ducks and waders such as Black-tailed and Bar-tailed Godwit, Curlew, Spotted Redshank, Redshank and Greenshank are present.

Accommodation

Tourism in the area has been highly developed, meaning that there is a wide range of hotel accommodation and several campsites, although many of these places are closed in winter.

Comments

The best time of year for visiting the area is from November to February. Tide tables should be borne in mind; at high tide birds are to be found resting on the islets while at low tide they will be feeding on the intertidal zones, making for ideal birdwatching conditions.

It is also worth going up to the vantage point at Monte da Siradella on the O Grove peninsula, which gives you a wonderful panoramic view of the whole area.

Miguel Lorenzo Fernández

■ G.7 CORRUBEDO

A coastal wetland area.

Main species

Residents: Kentish Plover, Stone Curlew.

Summer visitors: Great Reed Warbler.

Winter visitors: divers, Gadwall, Shoveler, Tufted Duck, Common Scoter, Oystercatcher, Grey Plover, Curlew, Greenshank, Great Black-backed Gull, Razorbill.

On passage: shearwaters, Gannet, many different species of wader including Sanderling, Bar-tailed Godwit and Whimbrel.

Access

Take the N-550 out of Pontevedra to Padrón, where you then take the C-550 to Santa Eugenia de Ribeira (80 km). Alternatively take the C-543 from Santiago de Compostela to Noia and from there the C-550 to Ribeira (72 km).

Description

There are three clearly differentiated areas; the Montevixán lagoon, surrounded by a belt of reedbeds and cut off from the sea by a sand bar; an area consisting of a large, shifting dune 1,200 m long and up to 20 m high, with a string of stabilized dunes, and finally the O Carregal marshes which are subject to the ebb and flow of the tide and have a large area of rush beds. The whole is surrounded by wetland meadows and woodland consisting of pine and eucalyptus. It is a Game Refuge.

Recommended route

From Ribeira take the road to Carreira and Vixán, where you have to ask someone for directions to the Laguna de Montevixán (access is not marked and consists of an intricate series of tracks). Leave the car on the road near the lagoon, next to a small school. From there, follow the path until you reach a stone wall by the lagoon. It is slightly higher than the lagoon, making for easy birdwatching (point 1). In winter you will see, among other species, Cormorant, Grey Heron, Teal, Gadwall, Shoveler, Pochard, Tufted Duck, Coot and Curlew.

Leave the lagoon and return to Carreira. Turn left there and having passed all the houses (Vilar) turn left again onto a track which passes through a pine forest and takes you to the beach. Leave the car where the sand banks begin and embark on a walk of 3-4 hours.

From the top of the beach you can command a good view of the open sea where you may see divers, Common Scoter, Sandwich Tern and Razorbill (2). Walk northeastwards through the dunes, watching out for Stone Curlew on the way, to reach the southernmost end of the marshes where there is a small intertidal zone frequented by

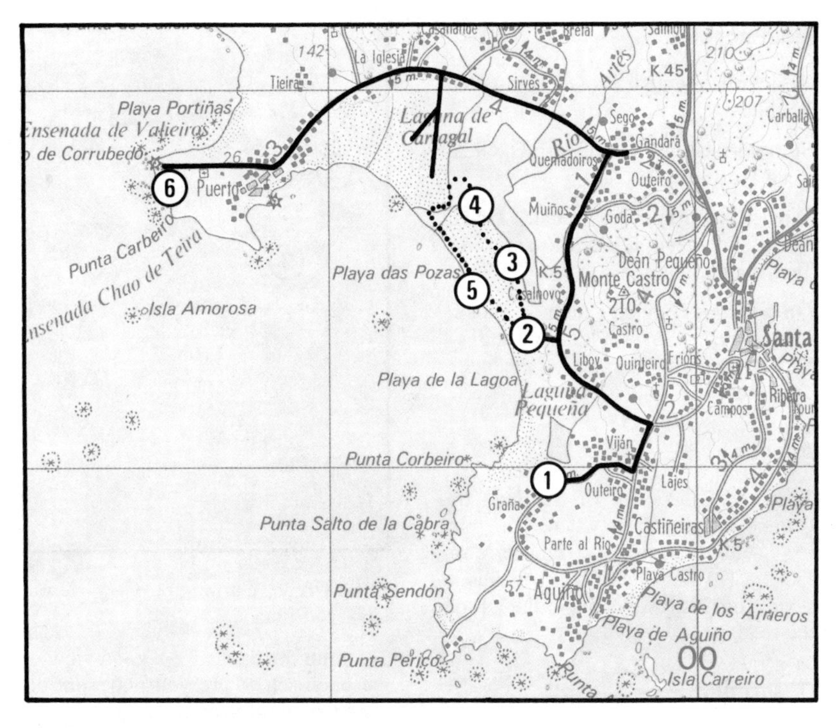

waders including Dunlin, Greenshank and Curlew (3).

There is a large intertidal zone in the drainage channel of the marsh which is a site for Oystercatcher and many other waders (4). At low tide it is worth covering the channels since waders tend to go there in search of food.

You can return to your vehicle through the dunes lying adjacent to the beach, making stops to see Kentish Plover and Sanderling (5).

The mouth of the marshes at O Carregal can also be reached from Olveira. Take the road from Carreira to Corrubedo and turn onto a track leading off to the south which is signed *A las Dunas* (to the dunes).

Point 6 is the lighthouse at Corrubedo, beside the village of the same name. From here you can see sea birds, such as shearwaters, Gannet and auks, on passage.

Accommodation

There are several hostels in Ribeira and several campsites in the villages around Corrubedo. Camping in the dunes is strongly discouraged.

Comments

The best times of year to visit the area are winter and the migration periods, particularly the spring one.

Jesús Domínguez Conde and Antonio Fernández-Cordeiro

■ G.8 LOURO LAGOON

A coastal lagoon.

Main species

Residents: Kentish Plover, Fan-tailed Warbler.

Summer visitors: Reed Warbler, Great Reed Warbler.

Winter visitors: Black-throated Diver, Great Northern Diver, Cormorant, Teal, Tufted Duck.

On passage: Gannet, Common Scoter, many species of waders (including Sanderling and Whimbrel), Sandwich Tern, auks.

Access

Take the C-543 out of Santiago de Compostela to Noia, where you join the C-550 to Muros and Finisterre or Fisterra (75 km). The lagoon is about 5 km from Muros, visible to the left of the road.

Description

A small saltwater lagoon formed by the river Longarelo with the addition of seawater in winter. A string of dunes reaching 16 m in height separates the lagoon from the sea. Although the centre of the lagoon is quite deep there are extensive beds of reeds and rushes around the edges. The lagoon is surrounded by fields and patches of scrubland consisting mainly of whin. It is a Game Refuge.

Recommended routes

A single route consisting of a walk lasting a maximum of 2 hours with the following stops:

1) From the road you have an all-round view of the lagoon and the beach, allowing for an initial observation without the risk of disturbing the birds.

2) Follow a path across the fields and scrubland until you reach the edge of the lagoon, from where you will see

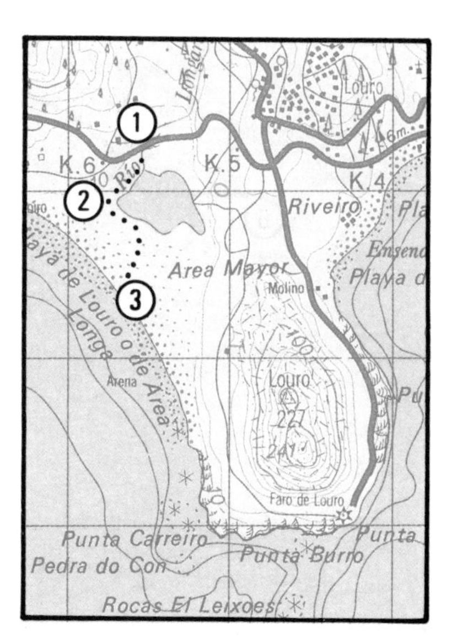

Little Grebe, Cormorant, Grey Heron, Coot and ducks.

3) Climb the dunes for a good view of the open sea where you may spot divers, Common Scoter, Sandwich Tern, Razorbill and, in the breeding season, Kentish Plover. During the migration periods there are waders and terns, and, in the spring one, Gannet is frequently seen.

Return by the same route or alternatively make your way around the lagoon.

If you have no luck in spotting sea birds, particularly divers, try the beach at Carnota, 11 km away in the direction of Fisterra on the same road, where they are also often present.

Between Louro and Noia on the C-550 you could make the following additional stops:

a) Punta de Louro (the promontory immediately next to the lagoon) is a good place for watching Cormorant and Shag.

b) The middle of the Muros and Noia estuary; if you go to the Figueroa jetty or any nearby high vantage point you should see a group of 10-30 Red-breasted Merganser, who winter here every year.

c) The gardens in the village of Noia are the home of numerous Collared Dove. If you go to the jetty at low tide the intertidal zone will give sightings of Great Black-backed Gull and various kinds of wader.

Accommodation

There are several hostels in Louro and Muros. There are also a couple of campsites near the lagoon.

Comments

The best times of year for a visit are during winter and the spring migration, when a wider range of species can be seen.

Antonio Fernández-Cordeiro and Rafael Costas

G.9 ISLETS OFF CAPE VILÁN

Small islets lying off the coast with interesting colonies of seabirds.

Main species

Residents: Shag, Peregrine Falcon, Yellow-legged Gull, Kittiwake, Chough, Black Redstart.

Winter visitors: Cormorant, scoters, gulls, Razorbill, shearwaters.

Access

Take the C-545 out of Santiago de Compostela and at Baio turn onto the C-552 to Vimianzo. From there, take the local road to Camariñas (88 km). Coming from A Coruña, the C-552 will take you to Vimianzo (68 km). In Camariñas go to the harbour, as you leave the village on the right, and you will find a road which takes you to the lighthouse on cape Vilán (4 km).

Description

The islets, known as Vilán de Dentro and Vilán de Fora, are two granite outcrops linked by a narrow isthmus. The nearest islet is about 60 m from the mainland. They are about 30 m high and have almost no vegetation.

Recommended routes

Access to the islets is only possible when the sea is perfectly calm and, although observation from the beach is

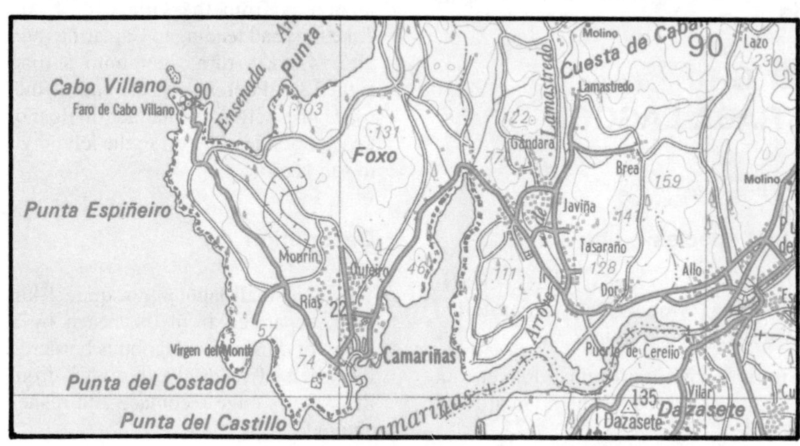

G

somewhat limited, it is nonetheless rewarding. It is worthwhile chosing a spot near the lighthouse. Telescopes are recommended.

Upper levels are occupied by Herring Gull and the cliffs, especially those on the northern side, by Kittiwake. Shag are present in various cavities, while Guillemot (the population of which has dropped dramatically from 30 pairs in 1986 to just 7 in 1989) can be seen on the northern cliffs.

The rock lying to the right of the base of the islets is used by young Shag when learning to fly and fish, and in the breeding season the rock sees continuous movement of the birds. In winter you can watch seabirds moving around, particularly Gannet.

Accommodation

Accommodation is available in Camariñas. In summer it is advisable to book in advance.

Comments

For dirt track enthusiasts there is a wonderful route from Cabo Vilán to Arou which takes you past some of the most spectacular spots on the Galician coast.

Juan Rodríguez Silvar

■ G.10 TRABA LAGOON

A small coastal lagoon.

Main species

Residents: Mallard, Water Rail, Moorhen, Stone Curlew, Fan-tailed Warbler, Reed Bunting.

Summer visitors: Kentish Plover (not every year), Reed Warbler, Great Reed Warbler.

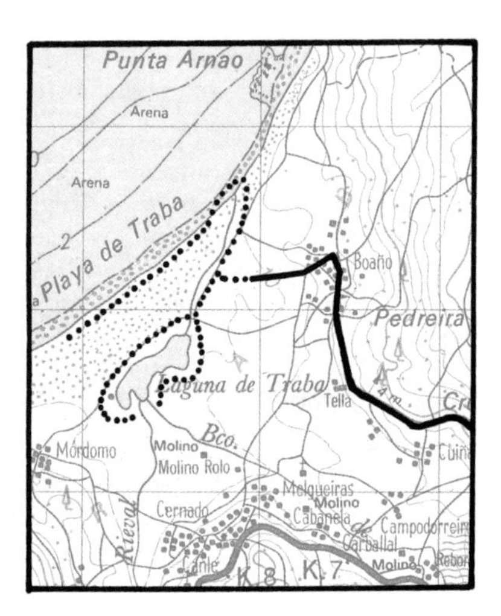

Winter visitors: Curlew, Snipe, Great Black-backed Gull.

On passage: a wide range of species with quite a few vagrants having been registered.

Access

If you are coming from A Coruña, take the C-552 to Carballo and from there take the local roads to Buño, Ponteceso and Laxe (63 km). From Santiago de Compostela take the C-545 to Baio (54 km).

The best way of getting to the Traba lagoon is from the village of Laxe. Take the road leading to Camariñas and after 4.5 km turn right onto a road signed for Pedreña. At the end of this road, just before the hamlet of Boaño, take a track leading off to the left down to the lagoon.

Description

This is a small lagoon, not quite 1 km long, separated from the beach by a string of dunes. The lagoon is bordered by a belt of reeds. Farther back from the water's edge reedmace and rushes abound.

Recommended routes

The main route consists of a simple circuit round the lagoon, starting at the northeastern end, where there is a bridge enabling you to cross the drainage channel. However, should the water outlets in the southwest of the lagoon create obstacles, you may prefer to cover the two shores separately. In either case it is worth taking wellington boots or waders.

A second possibility is to walk along the beach. Follow the outlet channel down to its mouth, where there are usually large groups of gulls and, at low tide, waders.

Accommodation

Accommodation is available in Laxe, Carballo and Vimianzo (on the C-552).

Comments

The best time for a visit is autumn when, particularly if strong winds are blowing from the west, nearctic vagrants may be present.

José Luís Rabuñal Patiño

■ G.11 ESTUARY OF CORME AND LAXE

An estuary typical of the Costa da Morte with an extremely wide mouth and a coastline consisting largely of cliffs. Upstream is the estuary of the river Anllóns (the Insua inlet).

Main species

Residents: Shag, Mallard, Oystercatcher, Kentish Plover, Curlew, Collared Dove, Fan-tailed Warbler, Reed Bunting, Chough, Raven.

Summer visitors: Tree Pipit, Reed Warbler, Garden Warbler.

Winter visitors: divers, ducks, Whimbrel, Ringed Plover, Grey Plover, Turnstone, Dunlin, Little Stint, Greenshank, Redshank, godwits, Great Black-backed Gull, Sandwich Tern, Razorbill.

On passage: a wide range of species including large and varied quantities of sea birds and waders. In autumn, especially when strong winds are blowing from the west, nearctic waders such as Pectoral Sandpiper may be present.

Access

The village of Ponteceso, at the head of the estuary, is the best starting point for any route since roads lead off to Corme and Laxe. To reach Ponteceso, take the C-552 out of A Coruña to Fisterra, turning right in Carballo onto a local road for Ponteceso (50 km).

Description

The Insua inlet is virtually closed off by a peninsula consisting of sand and dunes. At low tide this is the site of mudflats where many waders can be seen. Nearby, on the last stretch of the River Anllóns, there is a marsh area with reedbeds which has been somewhat spoiled by the nearby village of Ponteceso.

Despite the fact that the open part of the estuary is assailed by wind and waves, it is a refuge and wintering place for several species of birds.

Recommended routes

To visit the Insua inlet, leave Ponteceso on the road leading to Corme and 1 km from the village, in Cospindo, turn left onto an unsurfaced track taking you to Currás, from where you have direct access to the end of the inlet. From there it is worthwhile working your way along the shoreline on foot, making for a walk 3 km in length.

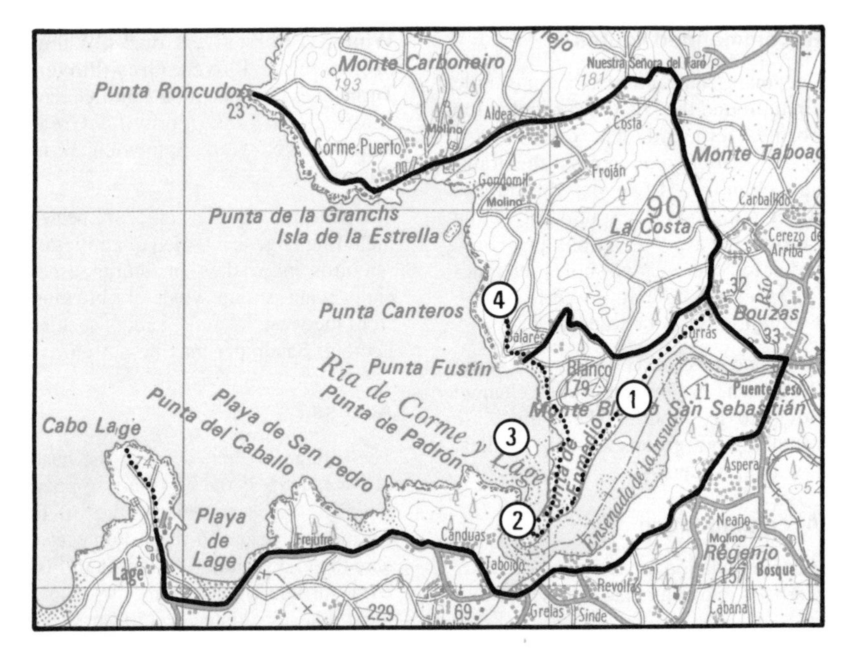

At low tide the mudflats are exposed, which are easily accessible throughout their length (point 1). At high tide, birds congregate on the La Barra promontory (2), allowing for easy and precise counts except on days when hunting occurs, when they take shelter on the islet of Tiñosa (3).

The best location for watching the open part of the estuary is the coastline where the promontories of La Facha, Canteros and El Verdillo (4) are located. These can be reached on foot from the beach at Balarés (the road is signed from Cospindo). Areas near these promontories are usually the site of sea ducks and, on days when hunting occurs, of the surface-feeding ducks which are normally at large in the estuary. You can also see Shag and Chough, which nest on the cliffs. Other observation posts, albeit much more limited, are the harbour walls at Corme and Laxe.

Finally the Roncudo promontory (accessible by car from the harbour at Corme) and the Laxe headland (reached by taking a short walk through the village cemetery) are wonderful places for watching large quantities of different kinds of seabirds on passage.

Accommodation

Although there are no hotels in the strictest sense of the word, accommodation can be found in Ponteceso, Corme and Laxe. Also to be recommended is the Restaurante Zürich in Laxe, which offers top quality fish and shellfish.

José Luis Rabuñal Patiño

G.12 BALDAIO (BALDAYO)

A series of coastal lagoons which, together with Corrubedo, constitutes the largest dune system in Galicia.

Main species

Summer visitors: Kentish Plover.

Winter visitors: Great Northern Diver, Black-throated Diver, waders (particularly Grey Plover, Dunlin, Curlew, Bar-tailed Godwit), Great Black-backed Gull, Short-eared Owl, Snow Bunting.

On passage: many species of wader.

Access

From Carballo take the minor road to Razo (8 km). Once there, leave the car on the headland which rises up beside the beach beyond all the houses.

Another route, running along the coast, consists of leaving the C-552 at Arteixo and taking a minor road towards Caión. Just before starting the descent to the village, take a left turn and after 5 km turn right to drop down to Baldaio (25 km). All turns are well signed for the *Camping Baldaio*, a campsite. These signs are completely reliable.

Description

Baldaio is a complex consisting of a lagoon (covering some 80 ha, currently divided in two), a marshland area, a string of dunes some 5.5 km in length with some dunes reaching 10 m in height, and areas of coastal open land lying between the lagoon and the dunes.

Recommended routes

Route A runs along the string of dunes and can be done in a couple of hours. In the breeding season you will see Kentish Plover, and in the migration period other waders such as Sanderling or Ringed Plover. In winter, divers, Short-eared Owl, Snow Bunting, Chough, etc. can often be seen.

Route B circles the lagoon and can be walked in an hour. It begins at the sluices which give access to the northern lagoon and runs clockwise around the shore. This is the main feeding ground for gulls and waders, giving rise to sightings of Grey Plover, Dunlin, Curlew and Bar-tailed Godwit.

Morro Mortaxa, on the other side of the outlet channel of the lagoon, is a good spot for watching sea birds.

Accommodation

There are two campsites in the area and plenty of hotels in A Coruña.

Ramón F. Ramón

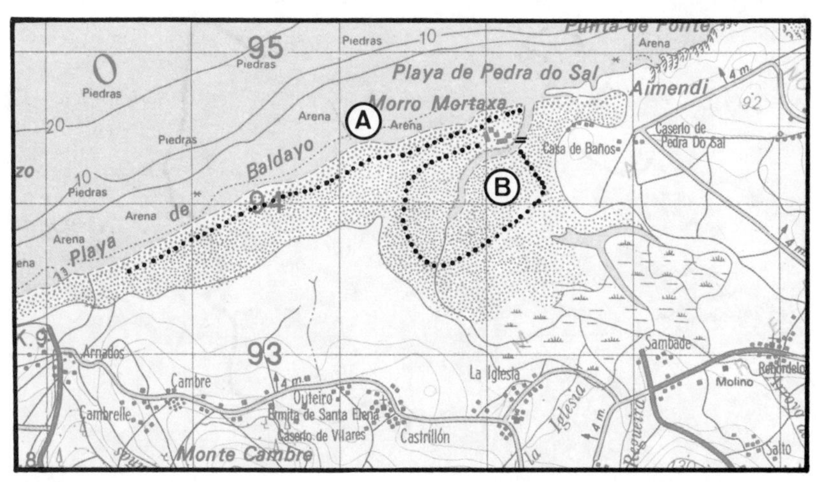

G.13
A CORUÑA ESTUARY AND SABÓN RESERVOIR

An open estuary, remarkable for groups of wintering gulls, and an associated small coastal reservoir.

Main species

Residents: Peregrine Falcon, Yellow-legged Gull, Collared Dove, Sardinian Warbler; on the reservoir; Little Grebe, Mallard, Coot, Moorhen, Water Rail.

Winter visitors: divers, ducks (on the reservoir large numbers of Tufted Duck), Purple Sandpiper, Turnstone, gulls, Razorbill.

On passage: on the reservoir; waders, terns and marsh terns.

Access

The city of A Coruña dominates the estuary of the same name, and the Sabón reservoir can easily be reached via the C-552 going towards Carballo. The lake is to the right of the road, just before reaching the town of Arteixo (12 km).

Description

The A Coruña estuary is open and has the form of a crescent running from north to south. Its beaches are extensive and its mouth is of little ornithological interest. The Sabón reservoir is 12 km from A Coruña. Its shores slope gently and are covered with abundant waterside vegetation.

Both areas are subject to a lot of pressure from human presence. The estuary is the site of a large industrial port, and the reservoir supplies water to a nearby industrial estate.

Recommended routes

Route A runs along the eastern shore of the estuary, enabling you to see most of the sandbanks in the area. When you

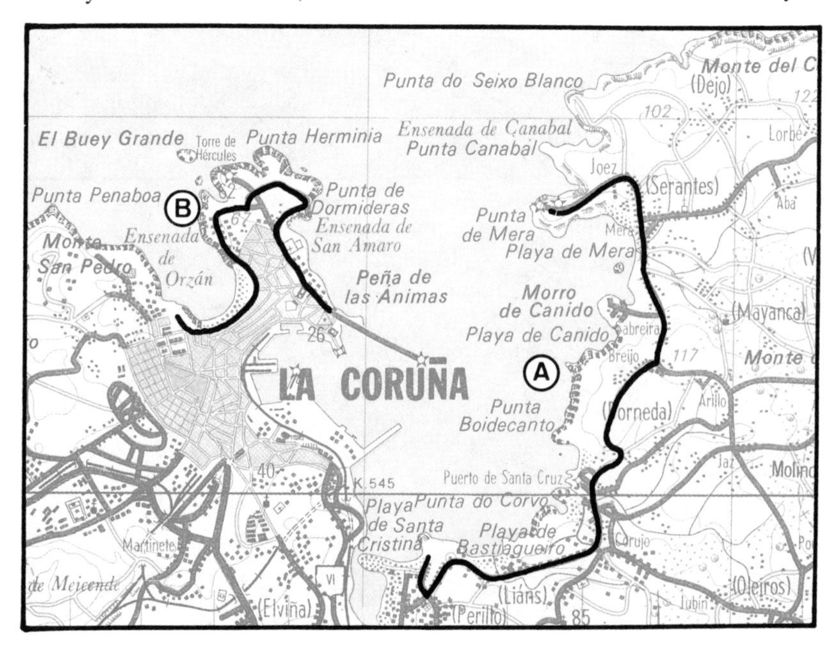

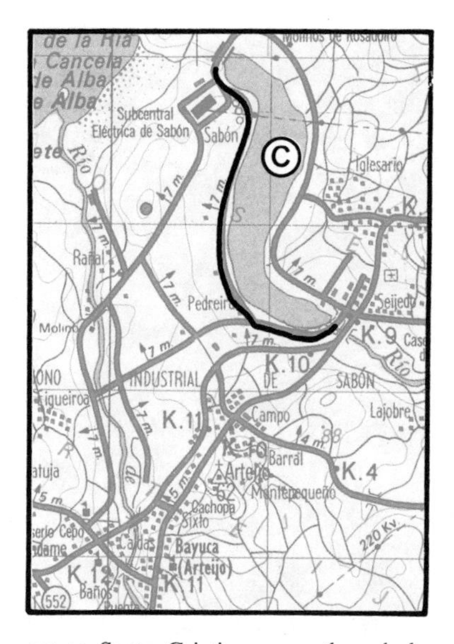

get to Santa Cristina, scan the whole inlet with a telescope since divers, grebes and sea ducks are often present between November and April. When there are big storms out at sea, you will often see pelagic birds such as petrels and skuas, etc.

Route B lies within the city of A Coruña and takes in the westernmost part of the estuary. The breakwaters of Colegio de las Esclavas (by the Riazor roundabout) and the cliffs near the Torre de Hércules are interesting, since you will see Turnstone and with some luck, Purple Sandpiper. If you are in the area during the autumn migration, you may also see some interesting seabirds.

Route C takes you around the Sabón reservoir via either shore. The most interesting part is the end of the reservoir, where most of the birds are to be found. The beach at Alba, next to the power station, is the site of vast numbers of gulls.

Accommodation

There is a wide and varied range of accommodation available in A Coruña. Oleiros, on the east bank of the estuary, has the Hotel Portocobo which is recommended. Between May and September a Cory's Shearwater comes to the hotel every night to roost. Oleiros also has a couple of campsites.

Ramón F. Ramón

■ G.14 CECEBRE RESERVOIR

A small reservoir with interesting waterside woodland.

Main species

Residents: Little Grebe, Mallard, Coot, Moorhen, passerines.

Winter visitors: ducks, especially Tufted Duck.

On passage: ducks and waders.

Access

In A Coruña take the N-VI towards Lugo. On reaching San Pedro de Nos (8 km) turn right immediately after the Sala de Fiestas El Seijal (function rooms). Continue along this road until you come to a blind bend to the left followed by a triple junction. Go straight ahead and pass under the A-9 motorway bridge. Continue until you reach Cecebre and 1 km after passing under the railway bridge you will come across the reservoir (25 km).

Description

The Cecebre reservoir supplies water for the city and region of A Coruña, and is fed by the rivers Mero and Barcés. Its gently sloping shores have allowed for the establishing of abundant waterside vegetation. One of the most important areas of riverside woodland in Galicia is to be found where the river Mero joins the reservoir.

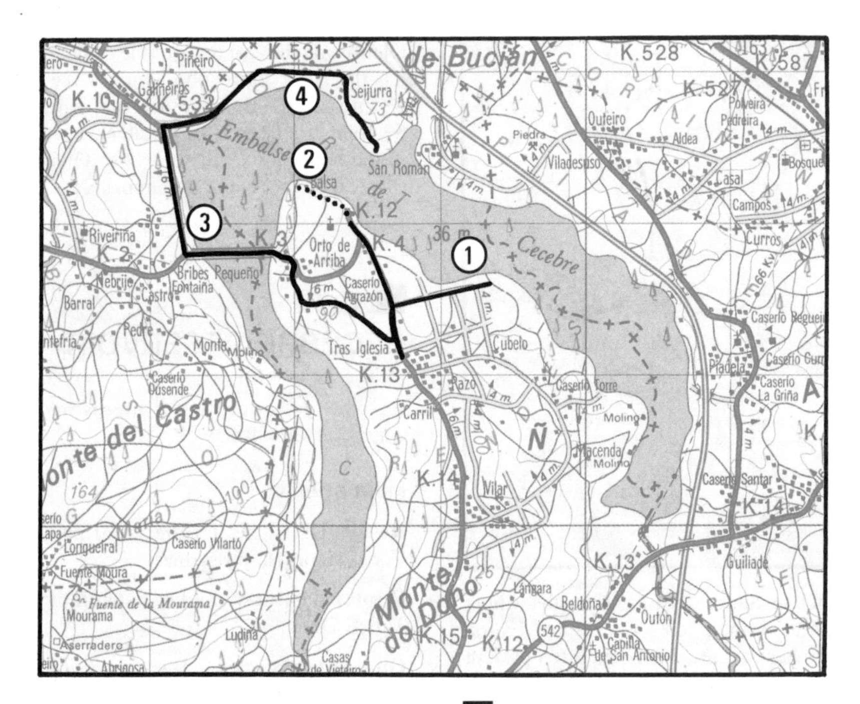

Recommended routes

It is worth visiting the point where the river Mero joins the reservoir at all times of year. In spring and summer most of the nesting birds congregate there; in autumn, when the water level falls, large mudflats are exposed which attract large numbers of waders. The best observation point is from the shore at San Pedro de Crendes (point 1).

In winter most waterbirds congregate on the open water of the reservoir. Any point along the road running round the reservoir is a good place for birdwatching (points 2, 3 and 4).

Accommodation

There is plenty of hotel accommodation available in A Coruña, and a campsite at Santa Marta de Babío (Guísamo).

Ramón F. Ramón

■ G.15 DONIÑOS LAGOON

A small coastal lagoon and the area surrounding it.

Main species

Residents: Little Grebe, Shag, Coot, Moorhen, Yellow-legged Gull, Lesser Black-backed Gull, Fan-tailed Warbler, Chough.

Summer visitors: Marsh Harrier, Hobby, Alpine Swift, Sand Martin, Black-eared Wheatear, Whinchat, Woodchat Shrike.

Winter visitors: Black-necked Grebe, Cormorant, Tufted Duck, Scaup, Curlew, Golden Plover, Lapwing, Curlew, Snow Bunting.

Access

Take the N-VI or the A-6 motorway (Autopista del Atlántico) from Betanzos to Ferrol. From the main square of Ferrol, Plaza de España, take the minor road to Doniños and at the Balón crossroads turn left for Fontá. Follow this road until you reach the Doniños beach at Punta Penencia.

Description

A coastal lagoon closed off from the sea by a sand bar and a line of dunes colonized by halophytic plants. There is a drainage channel at the far north-western end of the lagoon which crosses a military shooting range (go with care!).

The lagoon is quite deep, meaning that marsh vegetation is scarce and limited to a margin of reeds and some water lilies in the northern third of the lagoon. The area is assigned for limited hunting.

Recommended routes

Leave the beach and walk anti-clockwise round the lagoon so as to get a good view of the whole area. From point 1, in the dunes, numerous passerines can be seen; point 2 lies nearest to the reedbeds falling within the shooting range (which cannot be entered) and is where most of the Coot present congregate. Another interesting spot is an oak tree beside the track, which dominates the section of the lagoon frequented by Mallard and Tufted Duck.

Continue by circling the lagoon on the surfaced road leading to Outeiro (points 4 and 5). From here you can go down to the beach at Doniños. Walk along the beach or through the dunes (be aware of **shooting exercises with live ammunition** which occur frequently except in summer, and are indicated by flags).

It is worthwhile visiting the cliffs lying opposite the Gabeiras islands. To get to the cliffs, take the road to Outeiro and 1 km after you have left the beach take a track leading off to the left up

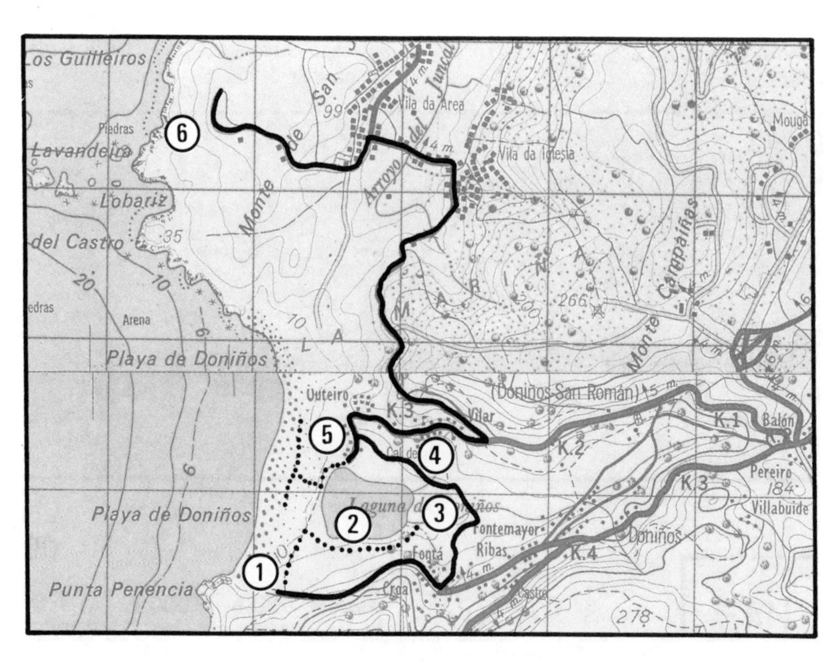

into the hills of Vila da Area. Follow the wheel ruts up to Castro de Lobadiz (an unexcavated archaeological site), from where you will have a good view of the islands. You will be able to see Cormorant and Shag.

Accommodation

Ferrol offers a wide range of accommodation and there is a campsite at Cobas, 3 km from the lagoon.

Juan Rodríguez Silvar

G.16
A FROUXEIRA (VALDOVIÑO) LAGOON

A coastal lagoon.

Main species

Residents: Little Grebe, Grey Heron, Mallard, Gadwall, Moorhen, Coot, Reed Bunting.

Summer visitors: Marsh Harrier, Hobby.

Winter visitors: Cormorant, Shoveler, Pochard, Tufted Duck, Golden Plover, Little Stint, Redshank, Turnstone.

Access

From Betanzos take the N-VI or the A-6 motorway (Autopista del Atlántico) to Ferrol. In Ferrol take the C-646 towards Ortigueira. The lagoon is about 17 km from Ferrol and lies to the left of the road.

Description

A Frouxeira is a shallow lagoon lying at right angles to the beach of the same name. It is linked to the sea by a natural outlet. The islet of La Percebelleira acts as a natural dyke, forming the mouth of the outlet. Vegetation consists of marshland with reedbeds in the southern third of the lagoon, which is succeeded by a stand of alder and willow. A dune system, severely damaged by sand extraction operations, closes off the lagoon to the north. Human presence affects the area, particularly in summer. It is a Game Refuge.

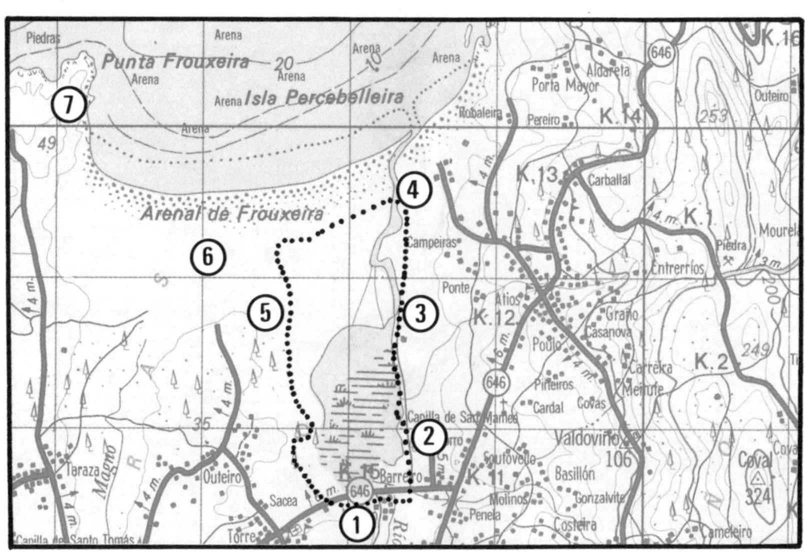

Recommended routes

500 m before the junction with the Cedeira road there is a poultry slaughterhouse. Opposite this an unsurfaced but passable track leads off and runs along the eastern shore of the lagoon. This could be the starting point of a route on which you will see the transition to hydrophytic vegetation and associated fauna.

In the waterside fields and woods commanded by point 1 you will see Snipe and small passerines. Point 2, next to the reedbeds and rushes, is a good spot for seeing Marsh Tit, warblers, etc. Points 3, 4 and 5 give views of the open water of the lagoon, which are frequented by Coot and ducks. The ducks tend to move away during the day to the sea, returning at dusk. Thus it is easier to see them by using a telescope and positioning yourself on the sand bar (6). The sand bar also enables you to see small groups of waders and, in winter, Stone Curlew and Snow Bunting. Punta Frouxeira (7) is a promontory from which, between late August and November, you can watch the passage of sea birds, particularly Gannet, scoters and shearwaters.

Accommodation

There are several hostels and a couple of campsites in Valdoviño. Ferrol also offers accommodation.

Comments

The best time of year for visiting Valdoviño is from October to March, coinciding with the presence of wintering birds. Migration periods, September to October and March to May, are also very rewarding.

Juan Rodríguez Silvar

G.17 RÍA OF ORTIGUEIRA

An Atlantic estuary significant in terms of wintering water birds.

Main species

Residents: Shag.

Summer visitors: Kentish Plover.

Winter visitors: Mallard, Widgeon, Shoveler, Oystercatcher, Curlew (500 individuals), Dunlin (1,000 individuals), Ringed Plover, Grey Plover, Bar-tailed Godwit.

On passage: waders.

Access

Take the C-642 from Ferrol to Ortigueira (54 km).

Description

An Atlantic estuary lying between the headlands of Ortegal and Estaca de Bares. The outer part is deep with beaches and stretches of rock and cliffs. The inner part is sheltered and somewhat shallower. It has intertidal flats stretching for a little more than 1,000 ha, extensive salt marshes and 3 km of beach with a string of stabilized dunes. The estuary banks are relatively unspoiled with water meadows and plantations of pine and eucalyptus. It is a Game Refuge and included in the Ramsar Convention.

Recommended routes

A single route to be undertaken by car. It starts at the harbour in Espasante and finishes at the lighthouse on the Ortegal headland, taking an estimated 6-8 hours.

Begin at the village of Espasante (point 1). From the beach groups of ducks at rest can be seen, particularly Mallard, Widgeon and small groups of Common Scoter.

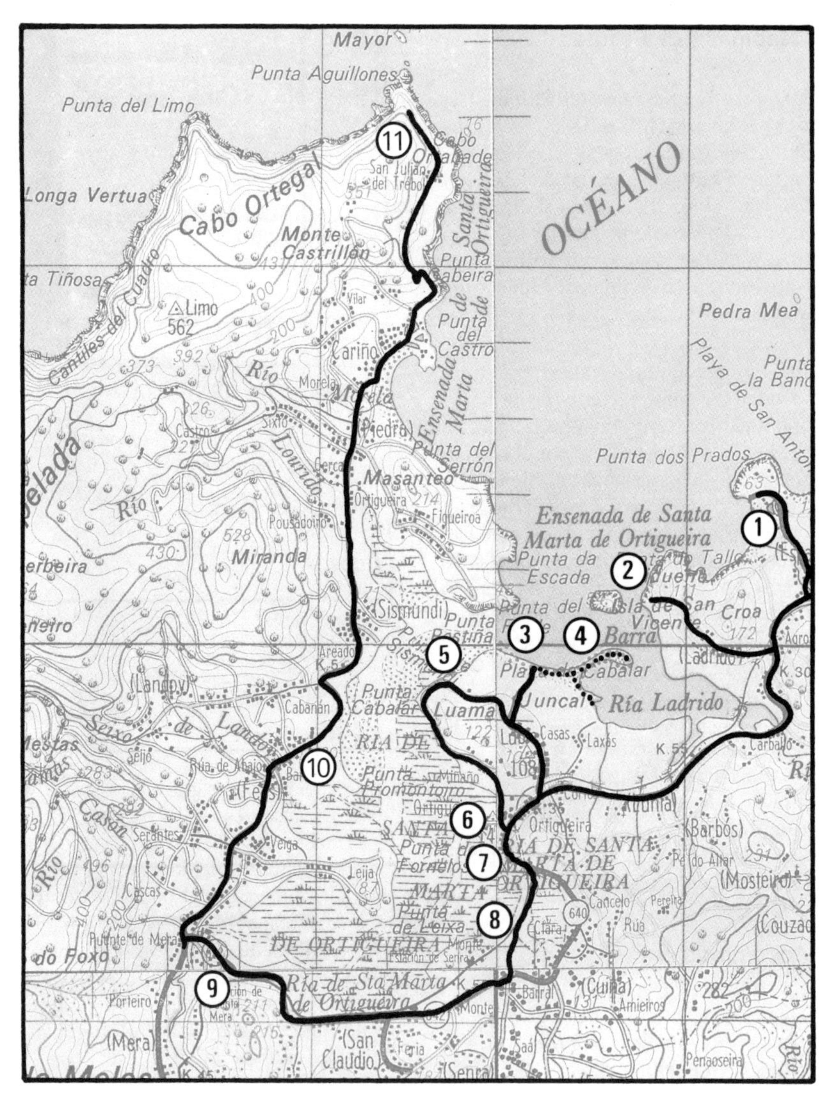

To reach point 2, take the road to the village of Ladrido and go down to the harbour breakwater which commands most of the inlet. At low tide you will see waders feeding, which at high tide congregate in resting places.

Continue along the road to Ortigueira. As you come into the village take the road leading off to the right down to the beach. From here (3) you can see the open water with the occasional diver and other sea birds such as Gannet, Shag and auks. Walk through the dunes to the shore of the Ladrido inlet (4), where waders can be seen feeding or resting.

Leave the beach and continue along the road skirting the estuary and returning to Ortigueira. Opposite the far western end of the beach (5) high tide will bring sightings of groups of resting waders, particularly Oystercatcher and Curlew.

Continue to Ortigueira and go to the harbour (6). At low tide many waders can be seen feeding, along with herons and ducks such as Mallard, Teal and Shoveler.

Leave Ortigueira in the direction of Ferrol. Stop near the petrol station located on the edge of the town (7) to watch ducks and waders on the intertidal flats. Point 8 is a high observation point reached by a very narrow track leading up from Telleira. From it you can see most of the inner part of the estuary.

Continuing towards Ferrol, stop opposite the La Ría discotheque (9) from where you can see waders and ducks, particularly at low tide.

Then turn right for Cariño. The road to Cariño skirts the estuary; make stops (10) for good sightings of various waders.

In Cariño ask someone for the track leading to Cabo Ortegal. The way is not marked and is therefore a little confusing. It is a dirt track in good conditions, suitable for cars. From the lighthouse (11), you can see the islets of Os Aguillóns de Cabo Ortegal. During the breeding season you will see the nests of Shag and Yellow-legged Gull on the islets. In winter you may see various sea birds such as shearwaters, Gannet, Common Scoter and auks.

Accommodation

There is not much accommodation available in the area; a hotel in Cariño and a couple of hostels in Ortigueira. There are no campsites near the estuary, although you can camp in the pine wood lying beside the Cabalar beach. Facilities are basic.

Comments

It is worth visiting the area in winter or during the migration periods.

Jesús Domínguez Conde
and Antonio Fernández-Cordeiro

■ G.18 CAPE OF BARES

A granite headland, the northernmost point in the Iberian Peninsula. The area is well-known for the observation of sea birds on post-breeding migration between late August and late September.

Main species

On passage: Gannet, shearwaters (Cory's, Manx, Yelkouan and Sooty) Common Scoter, skuas (Pomarine, Arctic and Great), gulls, terns and marsh terns.

Access

Take the C-642 from Ferrol to Viveiro and Foz. After about 70 km you will come across O Barqueiro, where you turn left onto a local road (at the junction there is a sign for the *Estación Ornitológica* or bird observatory). Continue for 7 km, passing through Villa de Bares and, after some tight bends, take a left turn which after 2 km will bring you to a wind generator station. Turn right and, having passed a telecommunications station, turn left. Leave your vehicle at the top and walk down to the Estación Ornitológica.

Description

The Cabo de Estaca de Bares separates the estuaries of O Barqueiro and Ortigueira. The landscape is very attractive although somewhat spoilt by intensive plantings of eucalyptus and open cast mining.

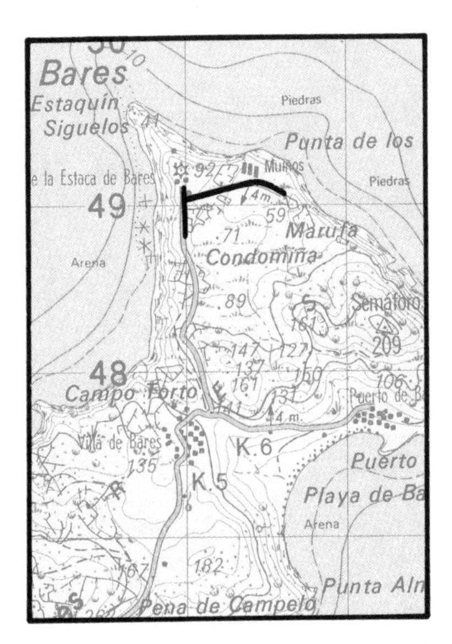

The Estación Ornitológica was opened in October 1988 for the purpose of facilitating observation of sea birds on migration. It is a small stone building with a hide on its upper floor. There are 4 bunk beds and a fireplace, although at present there is no water or electricity.

Recommended routes

Patience is the key to seawatching, so we recommend that you make yourself comfortable and enjoy it.

Accommodation

There are hostels, fondas and the occasional hotel in Ortigueira, Vicedo and Viveiro. However the best place to stay is the Estación Ornitológica. Applications to stay there should be sent to the following address: Estación Ornitológica de Estaca de Bares, Edificio Múltiple Ministerial, Consellería de Agricultura, Servicio de Medio Ambiente Natural (planta 5), c/ Monelos s/n, A Coruña.

Ramón F. Ramón

■ G.19 RÍA OF FOZ

A small, shallow estuary with extensive sand banks and intertidal zones.

Main species

Residents: Shag, Grey Heron, Curlew, Oystercatcher.

Winter visitors: Whimbrel, godwits, Dunlin, various plovers, Avocet.

On passage: Gannet, shearwaters, Grey Heron, Little Egret, Spoonbill, Common Scoter, Great Skua, terns.

Access

From the N-VI take the N-634 which goes through Villalba and Mondoñedo. About 18 km from Mondoñedo turn left on to the C-642 for Foz and after about 500 m you will come to A Espiñeira at the head of the estuary.

Description

The Foz estuary, with the river Masma emptying into it, provides perfect conditions for waders. There are gravel works on the right bank which, while still operative, have partially returned to their natural state and are quite interesting. It is a Game Refuge.

The open sea around the mouth of the estuary and the beaches, cliffs and other small estuaries are of special interest for those watching the passage of sea birds.

Recommended routes

The road from A Espiñeira to Foz runs parallel to the left bank of the estuary. It is quite high up, providing a first general impression. Several tracks lead down to the estuary shores (point 1) from the road.

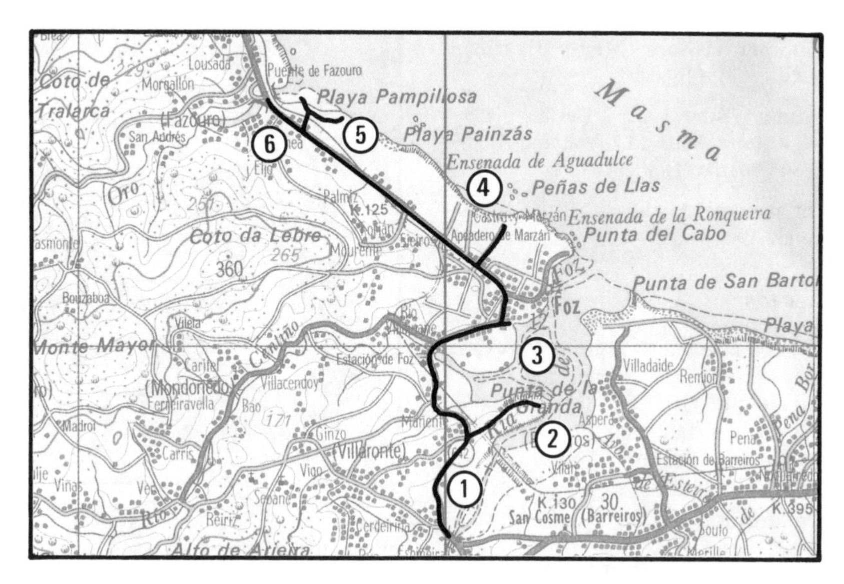

At the top of the climb, in the hamlet of Mañente, turn right onto an unmarked track, unsurfaced but passable, which goes to Punta Frondal, a promontory creating a natural observatory commanding the extensive sand banks at the entrance to the estuary as well as the mudflats and rushes within the estuary (2).

The harbour at Foz provides a new vantage point over the mouth of the estuary. Take the road running along the coast to the beaches of A Rapadoira and Llás. From the road you can see the open sea. The small cliffs lying parallel to the road are good observation points, being particularly rewarding during the migration periods (points 3 and 4).

In Foz take the C-642 towards Viveiro. The road runs parallel to the coastline with cliffs and small estuaries (Fazouro, Lieiro, etc.) (points 5 and 6). Also interesting are the various islets which can be seen from the road. These include Os Farallons, which lies just off San Ciprián, about 25 km from Foz.

Accommodation

Foz is a traditional summer holiday resort with plenty of rooms available in pensions and private houses, although all accommodation may be taken in July and August. The Hotel Leytón is highly recommended.

Comments

The best times of year for visiting the area are during the autumn migration period (second half of August onwards) and during the winter, from December to February.

Jorge de Vivero Pérez
and Xoan Carlos Castro Laxe

■ G.20 COSPEITO LAGOONS

A series of small lagoons interspersed with extensive open pastureland.

Main species

Residents: Little Grebe, Mallard, Moorhen, Lapwing, Curlew.

Summer visitors: Marsh Harrier, Hobby, Little Bustard.

Winter visitors: Grey Heron, ducks (especially Mallard, Teal and Widgeon), Merlin, Golden Plover.

On passage: Garganey, Ruff, Black Tern.

Access

In Lugo take the N-VI towards A Coruña. At Rábade turn onto the C-641 signed for Villalba. As you leave Rábade turn right onto the minor road for Cospeito (27 km).

Description

The original lagoon of Cospeito used to cover about 70 ha but was drained in the 1960s. Today about 5 ha have been recovered, making it the most interesting wetland area in the Terrachá region. This region is characterized by its flatness and abundance of lagoons, ponds and fertile river plains which are individually of little interest but as a whole are quite remarkable. The significance of the area lies in that, along with some large grasslands, it is one of the few wetland areas in all of Galicia.

Recommended routes

It is worthwhile visiting the Cospeito lagoon and surrounding pastureland. It can be reached from the town of A Feira do Monte, main centre of the Cospeito municipality. There is a turning next to the Guardia Civil houses, and after 300 m you will come across a hide commanding the lagoon and surrounding meadows and woodland. Various tracks run across the fields, which are very interesting in their own right.

The other lagoons and *veigas* (fertile flood plains) in the region are severely affected by human presence because

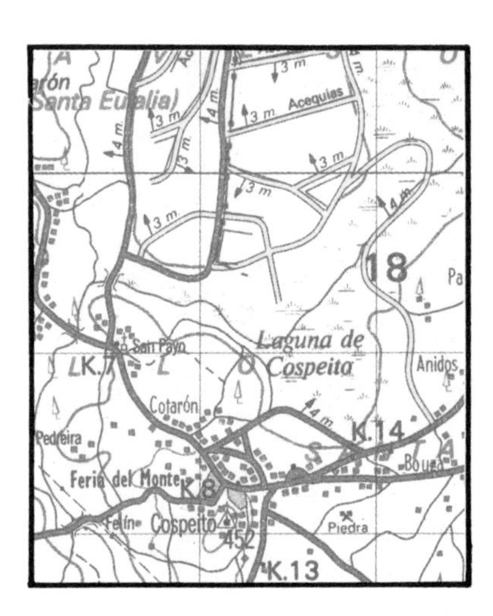

they are small and do not avail of facilities for visitors.

Accommodation

In A Feira do Monte the only accommodation available is in private houses. However, in Villalba there is a Parador Nacional and some hotels, among which the Hotel Villamartín is recommended.

Comments

The best times of year for visiting the area are from March to June and over the winter, from December to mid-February.

Xoan Carlos Castro Laxe
and Jorge de Vivero Pérez

■ G.21 ANCARES RANGE

A mountain area at the far western end of the Cantabrian range, with interesting areas of deciduous woodland.

Main species

Residents: Hen Harrier, Capercaillie, Grey Partridge, Woodcock, Black

Woodpecker, Water Pipit, Alpine Accentor, Goldcrest, Marsh Tit, Bullfinch.

Summer visitors: Honey Buzzard, Short-toed Eagle, Wryneck, Rock Thrush, Red-backed Shrike.

Access

There are two means of access which are easy to follow but, in places, dangerous (see below). The first involves entering the area from the south; come off the N-VI at Ambasmestas (province of Leon) and take the minor road to Balboa, Ponte de Doiras and Degrada, starting points for the routes (30 km). To enter the area from the north, come off the N-VI at Becerreá (province of Lugo). In the town centre take the minor road signed for Navia de Suarna. You will reach the hamlet of Liber, from where you can get to Degrada either via Ponte de Doiras or via San Román de Cervantes (30 km).

In winter, ask someone in Ambasmestas to find out whether the Portelo pass is open.

Description

The Sierra de los Ancares forms the western part of the range separating the provinces of Lugo and León. The range reaches heights of 1,900 m and the deep valleys, running down to the river Navia, are forested with oak, birch, holly, hazel, etc. on the northern sides, while the southern sides are largely taken up by heath and oak woodland.

Population in the area is very low and villages are of great ethnographical and architectural interest. It is a National

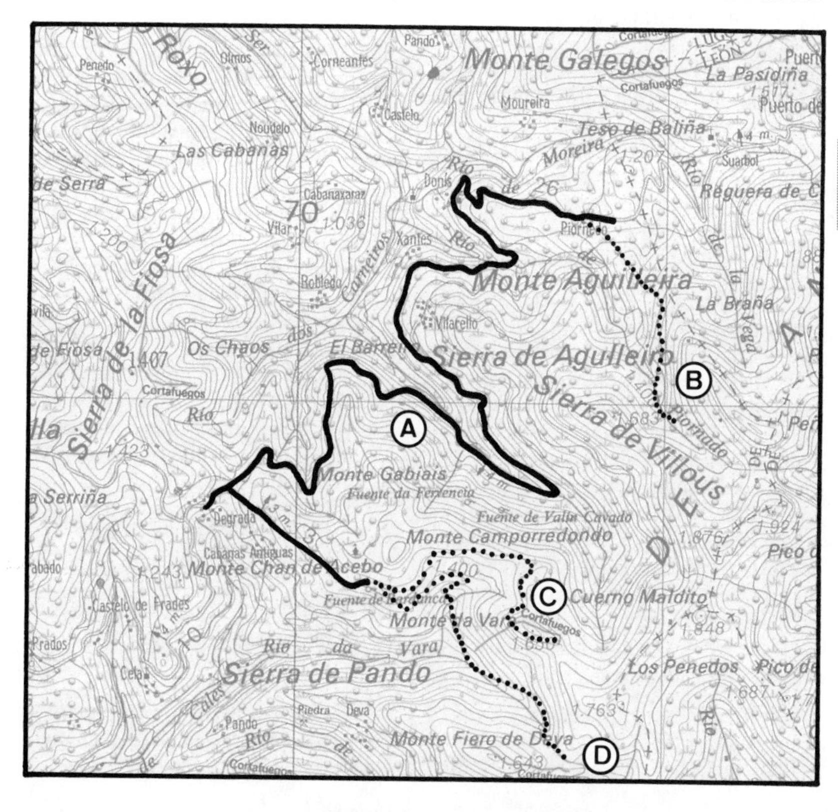

Game Refuge (8,000 ha) and has been declared a place of aesthetic merit.

Recommended routes

Route A involves a drive, starting from Degrada and taking you along the road to Donis until you reach the village of Piornedo. Make a stop on the bridge over the river Ser a little before the turning for Vilarello and at other points, road width permitting, so as to take short walks in the woodland.

Route B starts from the village of Piornedo and takes you to the Campa de Camporredondo and the lower slopes of Mustallar, running along a glacial valley between rocky cliffs and scrubland. The path, well trodden to begin with, starts at the chapel in the village and continues upwards to die out at the bottom of the cirque of peaks, from where you can climb up to the summit of Mustallar or any other mountain in the range. Apart from various birds of prey you will also see Alpine Accentor, Water Pipit and Grey Partridge. This walk can last between 2 hours and a whole day, depending on the length of the route you choose for the ascent. It is very tiring when there is powder snow on the ground.

Route C leaves Degrada on the road known as Tres Obispos. Continue until reaching the first turn to the right which takes you to the Cabanavella valley, where you can leave your vehicle. The route crosses heath and woodland typical of north- and south-facing slopes to reach Campa de Brego, an area surrounded by birch and holly. You will see all of the interesting woodland birds and, in winter, Capercaillie. From the point where you left your car the route will take 3½ to 4 hours there and back, and up to 5 with snow.

Route D starts at the place where you leave your car for Route C. Walk to the end of the Tres Obispos road, from where you will get a good view of the cirque of peaks. This will take a couple of hours, 3 with snow, and will provide the opportunity of seeing various raptors: Hen Harrier, Honey Buzzard, etc.

Accommodation

Villafranca del Bierzo is recommended for large groups or visitors without financial restrictions. Closer to the area, accommodation is available in Ponte de Doiras, San Román de Cervantes and Degrada, although it is worth telephoning to book in advance. You can also use the Club Ancares youth hostel near Degrada, where facilities are a combination of mountain refuge and modest hostel. Camping is not allowed within the National Game Refuge area.

Comments

It is worth visiting the area in winter, autumn or early spring. Avoid the summer months. The climate in Ancares is very changeable, and you should be well equipped against the cold in winter and against rain all year round. It is also recommended that you do not visit the area during the frequent periods when the mist descends —you should ask in the villages beforehand or survey the mountains from the N-VI (Puerto de Manzanal, a pass, or near Becerreá). After heavy snow, the best sites are too far away to be reached on foot from the valleys. It has to be said that Ancares is much more rewarding in terms of birdwatching if you are able to stay for a long period of time.

Jorge Vivero and José Guitián

■ G.22 CAUREL RANGE

A mountain area with very complex contours and some areas of deciduous woodland.

Main species

Residents: Goshawk, Golden Eagle, Hen Harrier, Grey Partridge, Dipper, Goldcrest, Nuthatch, Bullfinch.

Summer visitors: Short-toed Eagle, Montagu's Harrier, Hobby, Red-backed Shrike, Rock Thrush.

Access

Come off the N-VI in Pedrafita do Cebreiro and take the minor road to Sarria (Camino de Santiago). Shortly before the hamlet of Hospital, turn left onto the road for Quiroga and stop in Seoane de Caurel, starting point for the various routes (30 km). You can also reach the area from the south via Quiroga, located on the C-533, where you take the turning for Seoane de Caurel (34 km). This is a mountain route and can be dangerous when temperatures drop below freezing.

Description

The region of Caurel, located in the far southwest of the province of Lugo, is the link between two very distinct areas: the high ground of Cebreiro and the Sil valley.

The landscape, a succession of valleys and peaks with very steep slopes, perfectly reflects this position between the northern and Mediterranean environments. If we add to this the variety of substrates and differences in height, we gain an idea of the diversity of habitats present in this region: peaks and scrubland (above all heath), limestone cliffs and holm oak woods; woodland typical of north-facing slopes (*devesas*) with beech, oak, yew and maple; riverside woodland consisting of chestnut;

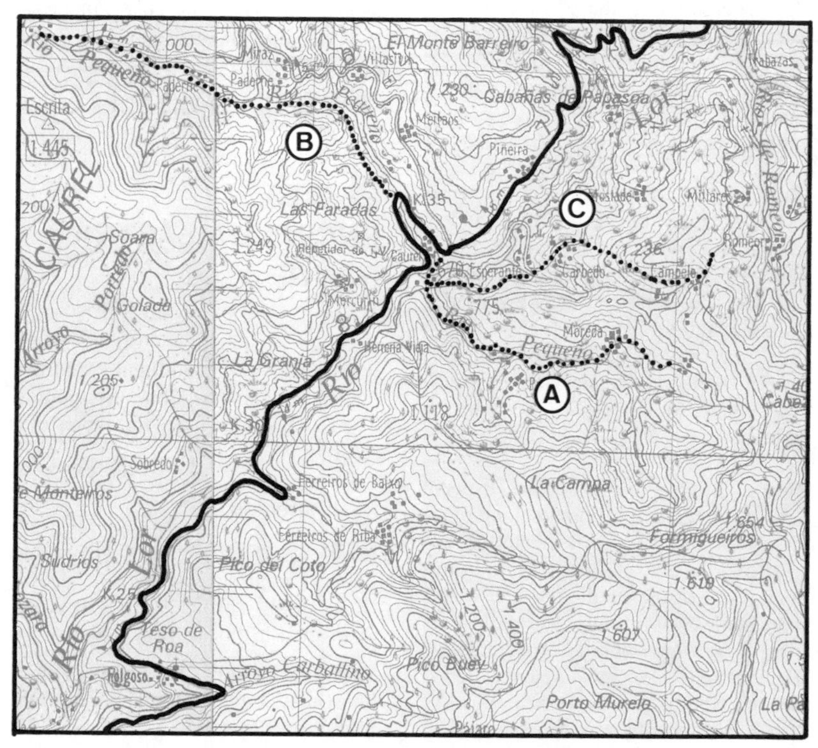

and gushing rivers bordered by plentiful vegetation.

Recommended routes

It is recommended that you first drive along the road running between Quiroga, Seoane de Caurel and Hospital in order to gain a general impression of the area, making stops at the highest points. The routes described below are walks.

The starting point for **Route A** is Seoane de Caurel, from where you take a well-marked shortcut to La Ferrería, on the banks of the river Lor. From here follow the track to the village of Moreda, from where, in the woodland in the lower part of the village, a track climbs up towards the Rogueira woods and subsequently works its way up a very steep slope through the woods to the upper limit of the treeline. Here, among other woodland-dwelling birds, you may see Goshawk and Goldcrest. This route takes an estimated 3 to 5 hours, depending on how long you require to climb up through the wood.

Route B runs from Seoane to the villages of Paderne and Pedrafita do Caurel, following the old road which runs next to the river. The return journey can be done on the new road, running halfway up the valley side. You may have sightings of Golden Eagle, Dipper, Nuthatch and Bullfinch. The whole route takes some 4 or 5 hours.

Route C takes you to Seoane, Esperante, Carbedo and Campelo along old, disused roads; for this reason it is worthwhile asking the way as you leave each of these villages. The walk lasts some 5 or 6 hours, and will give rise to sightings of Short-toed Eagle, Hen Harrier, Montagu's Harrier, Red-backed Shrike and Bullfinch. If you can, avoid recently constructed roads.

Accommodation

Quiroga is recommended for groups because it has several establishments with good facilities; also recommended is the hospice at Cebreiro, located in a beautiful spot beside the Camino de Santiago or pilgrims' route. Accommodation is also available in Seoane and Folgoso, as are excellent restaurants, although the number of rooms available is very low.

Camping in the area is not strictly controlled, although it is difficult to find flat places to set up more than one tent.

Comments

It is worth visiting this area in autumn and late spring. Take waterproof clothing. The weather is very bad in winter with frequent rain, mist and wind.

The length of unplanned walks should be carefully calculated since climbs are considerable, whichever direction you go in.

Jorge Vivero and José Guitián

■ G.23 ENCINA DA LASTRA RANGE

A mountain range of average height with holm oak woodland, Mediterranean scrubland and limestone gorges. The route also includes the shores of a reservoir.

Main species

Residents: Golden Eagle, Bonelli's Eagle, Peregrine Falcon, Rock Dove, Blue Rock Thrush, Chough, Rock Sparrow, Bullfinch, Hawfinch.

Summer visitors: Egyptian Vulture, Short-toed Eagle, Montagu's Harrier, Red-rumped Swallow.

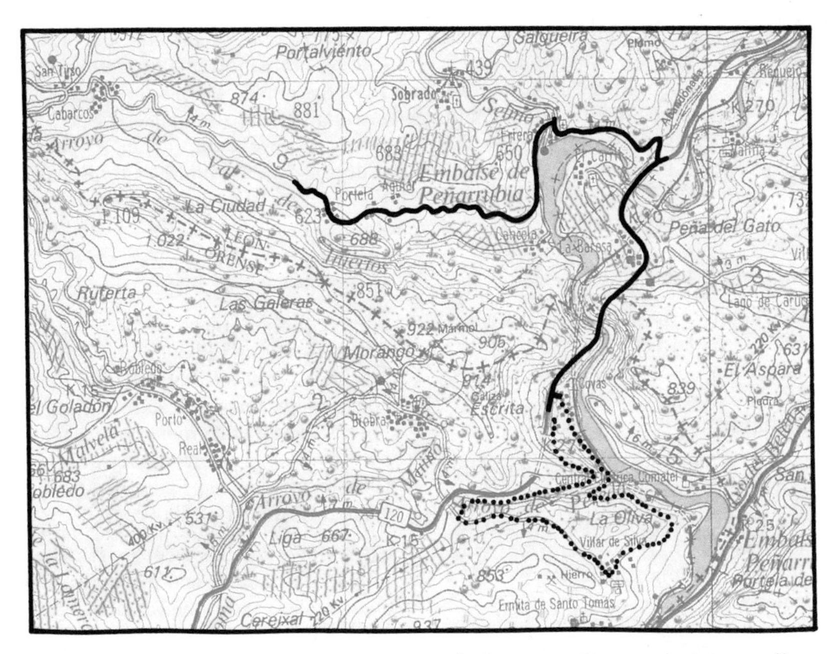

Winter visitors: Wallcreeper.

Access

Take the N-VI and between Villafranca del Bierzo and Ponferrada, take the new road to Galicia via Toral de los Vados (province of León). The recommended starting point for the routes is the petrol station located between the viaduct over the river Sil and the entrance to the first of the tunnels along the road to Galicia (25 km). The road running from the N-VI to O Barco de Valdeorras does not pass through any villages and it is necessary to turn off this road if you wish to ask for information.

Description

The region, lying within the valley of the river Sil, is one of the westernmost sites for Mediterranean habitats in Spain. The area is dominated by limestone cliffs, holm oak woodland and areas of Mediterranean scrub. It includes part of a reservoir as well as farmland and chestnut groves.

Recommended routes

It is worth making a short car journey, starting from the petrol station mentioned above and travelling in the direction of Villafranca del Bierzo. Before reaching Villafranca, turn off for Friera and, once in the village, turn left by the bridge over the river Selmo towards Cabarcos, or alternatively to Sobrado, on the road running beside the river. It is worth making stops and going for short walks on both sides of the road where the width of the road allows. This is a good route for seeing riverside birds: Dipper, Kingfisher, Golden Oriole, etc. The whole can be undertaken in a couple of hours.

The walk has its starting point at the turning for the village of Covas, immediately after coming out of the second tunnel going towards O Barco de Valdeorras. Walk along the track to Covas and from there take the old road to

Vilar da Silva, returning by the same route or alternatively by the road which joins this village with the main road (avoid the tunnel by taking the old track to Covas). You will probably see Golden Eagle, Peregrine Falcon, Egyptian Vulture, Chough, Red-rumped Swallow and Rock Dove.

Accommodation

Any hotel or hostel in Toral de los Vados or Villafranca del Bierzo is recommended, since they suit all budgets.

Comments

Spring is the best time of year for undertaking bird-watching trips to the area. Please be careful on and around the roads leading off from the main road near the tunnels, which is a particularly dangerous area.

José Guitián

■ G.24 PEÑA TREVINCA MOUNTAINS AND THE SEGUNDEIRA RANGE

A sparsely populated high mountain area with relicts of original woodland.

Main species

Residents: Hen Harrier, Goshawk, Golden Eagle, Peregrine Falcon, Grey Partridge, Water Pipit, Bluethroat, Blue Rock Thrush, Chough.

Summer visitors: Short-toed Eagle, Rock Thrush.

Access

From Ponferrada, on the N-VI, take the N-120 in the direction of O Barco de Valdeorras and turn left at Sobradelo onto the local road for Casaio, starting point for the routes (50 km).

The area is part of an extensive mountain region which can also be reached from the N-525, taking the turning for Porto in the village of A Canda. A third —more complicated— possibility is via the village of La Baña in the province of León (Cabrera region).

Description

A large massif consisting of a succession of rolling hillsides and valleys reaching 1,700 m in height. The outer edges of the massif feature cliffs and gorges. The high ground is occupied by low-growing scrubland and small permanent lagoons. Snow lies on the ground for much of the year.

The valleys are very steep, with inhospitable stony sides and the occasional area of woodland in the valley bottoms. The valley of San Xil is remarkable for its large areas of yew.

This area is excellent for sighting large birds of prey, and a lot of big game is resident in the area, as are wolves.

Recommended routes

Route A leaves Casaio on the road to La Baña, allowing you to visit the yew wood in San Xil. A few kilometres after leaving the village, take the track which leads up beyond the new chapel, visible from afar. Leave your vehicle by the mine buildings and continue on foot, firstly along a track and then along a path, bringing you to the wood. It is more convenient if you have a four-wheel drive vehicle but an ordinary car will suffice if you drive with care. You will see various birds of prey, Grey Partridge, rock thrushes, etc. The whole route takes about 4 hours.

Route B takes you up to Trevinca Norte, a peak at 2,124 m. The route starts at the Fonte da Cova mountain refuge on the road from Casaio to La

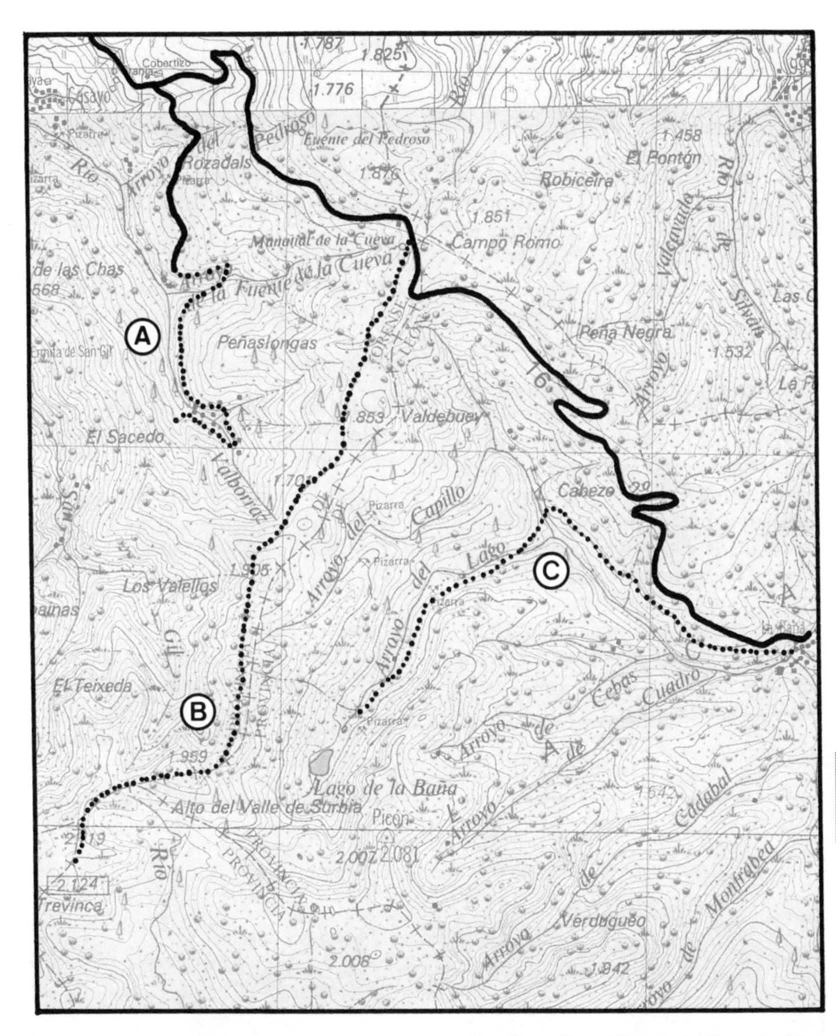

Baña. From there take the well-trodden track towards the peaks; on higher levels this track becomes a path. You will see rock thrushes, wheatears, Golden Eagle, Short-toed Eagle, Peregrine Falcon, Water Pipit, etc.

Route C has its starting point in La Baña, in the province of León, from where a narrow track which subsequently becomes a path takes you to the lakes, which lie at the foot of an attractive cirque. You should see raptors, Grey Partridge and Chough. The route takes some 3 or 4 hours, and it is worthwhile asking someone for information in Casaio with reference to the state of the road running up to the mountain refuge. For information about the track leading up to the lakes, ask someone in La Baña.

Accommodation

Casaio has a comfortable hostel, although it is worth telephoning to book in advance. For those on a small budget, there is the Fonte da Cova mountain refuge (information in O Barco de Valdeorras and Casaio).

Otherwise, there is suitable accommodation available in O Barco de Valdeorras, lying 1 hour away from the site by car.

Comments

The area adjoins the mountains of the provinces of Zamora and León and offers endless possibilities in terms of routes on the high ground. Since there are very few villages in a very large area, trips should be planned carefully, especially in winter when weather conditions are extremely harsh. The best time of year for visiting the area is late spring. Do not be discouraged by the landscape, which has been destroyed by slate mining, visible from roads leading into the area.

José Guitián

G.25 SAN MAMEDE RANGE, QUEIXA RANGE AND INVERNADEIRO FOREST

An extensive and largely deforested mountain area.

Main species

Residents: Hen Harrier, Grey Partridge, Water Pipit, Dipper, Goldcrest, Bullfinch.

Summer visitors: Short-toed Eagle, Hobby, Bluethroat.

Access

There are three ways of reaching the area. The first is to come off the N-VI in Ponferrada and take the N-120 to Puebla de Trives, where you turn off for the ski resort of Cabeza de Manzaneda (103 km).

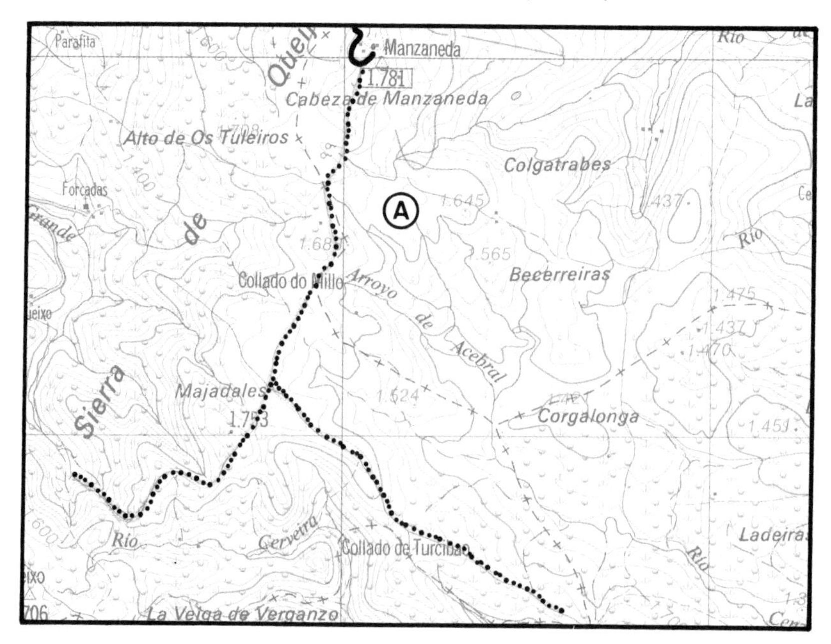

From Ourense, take the N-120 towards Ponferrada and then turn right after the village of Vilariñofrío onto the minor road for Montederramo (45 km).

The third option is to enter the area from the south on the N-525, taking the minor road to Campobecerros from Verín (33 km).

Description

A large region lying mostly at over 1,000 m and dominated by extensive areas of heathland. On the high ground, glacial influence can be seen and in the damper valleys there are the remains of deciduous woodland. The rivers running northwards to the basin of the Sil are somewhat altered by the construction of dams.

Population density is low and an extensive network of unmarked forest tracks allow you to work your way around the area with ease. Some of the most interesting areas of this region have been burned down several times since 1970.

Recommended routes

We have chosen three routes to be undertaken on foot, starting from the various points mentioned in the section on access.

Route A begins at the top of the peak of Manzaneda, which can be reached by car from Puebla de Trives via the ski resort (if there is heavy snowfall you may well be able to reach the summit by chair lift). From the top a track runs southwards towards Seixo and Invernadeiro. There are also several tracks running across the upland plain. These tracks are interesting in terms of seeing birds of prey in general, Grey Partridge, Water Pipit and wheatears. The route can be accomplished in 4 or 5 hours.

The starting point for **route B** is Montederramo, where you take the road to

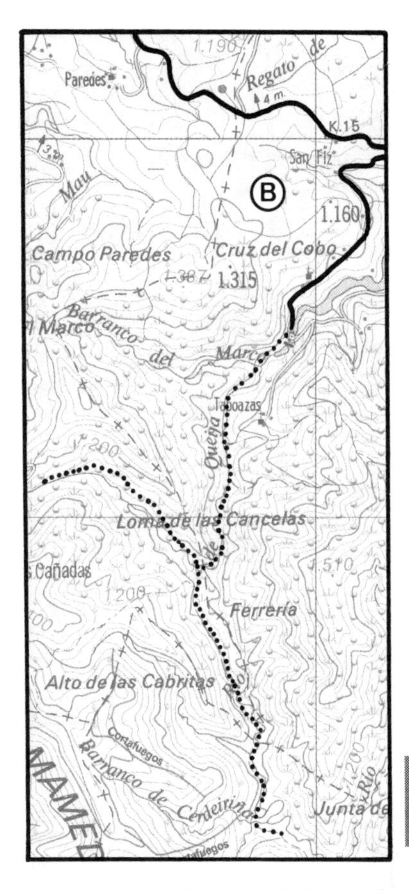

the hamlet of Queixa and there ask somebody for the track running up the river Queixa to the place known as Ferrería. The trip, which can be continued along any of the valleys converging at this point, will give rise to sightings of Goshawk, Sparrowhawk and species living on or by rivers. The route takes approximately 4 or 5 hours.

Route C starts at Campobecerros, from where you can go by car to Invernadeiro estate, a farm (Ribeiras Grande and Ribeiras Pequena). From there walk or drive along the first sections of the track to work your way up to the heads of the valleys through woodland consisting of holly, oak, hazel, etc. An excursion into the woodland starting

from the facilities provided by the Xunta de Galicia (local government body for Galicia), which will take 3 to 5 hours, will allow you to see forest-dwelling birds such as Goldcrest and Bullfinch.

Accommodation

There are some hostels in Puebla de Trives, where it is also possible to rent small houses for short periods over the winter season (rather expensive). To the west there are few possibilities off the N-120, and while Castro Caldelas has some accommodation, it is rather a long way from the area in question. To the south, it is possible to rent a room in Campobecerros, although the only place with hotel accommodation is Verín.

Comments

A very large area which is rather problematic in winter: spring and autumn are the best times of year for a visit. Make sure that you have enough petrol when you take to the tracks in the area. To visit the woodland at the Invernadeiro estate, you should first ask permission from the Consellería de Agricultura (Ministry for Agriculture) in Santiago de Compostela.

José Guitián

■ G.26 LA LIMIA

The old semi-natural lake of Antela, now drained and used for growing crops.

Main species

Residents: Mallard, Marsh Harrier, Hen Harrier, Red Kite, Lapwing, Snipe, Stone Curlew, Kingfisher, Cetti's Warbler.

Summer visitors: White Stork, Black-shouldered Kite (rare), Montagu's Harrier, Black Kite, Short-toed Eagle, Hobby, Quail, Little Ringed Plover, Redshank, Whinchat, Tawny Pipit, Corn Bunting, Golden Oriole.

Winter visitors: Grey Heron, ducks, Merlin, Golden Plover, Dunlin, sandpipers, godwits, pipits, Great Grey Shrike.

On passage: Grey Heron, Little Egret, Garganey, waders, Little Bustard.

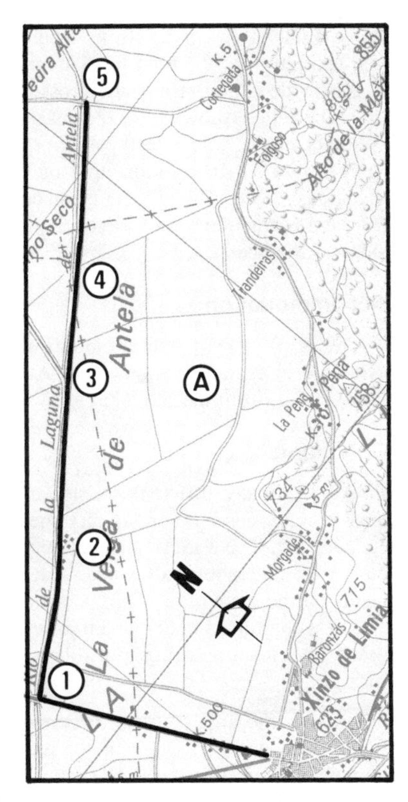

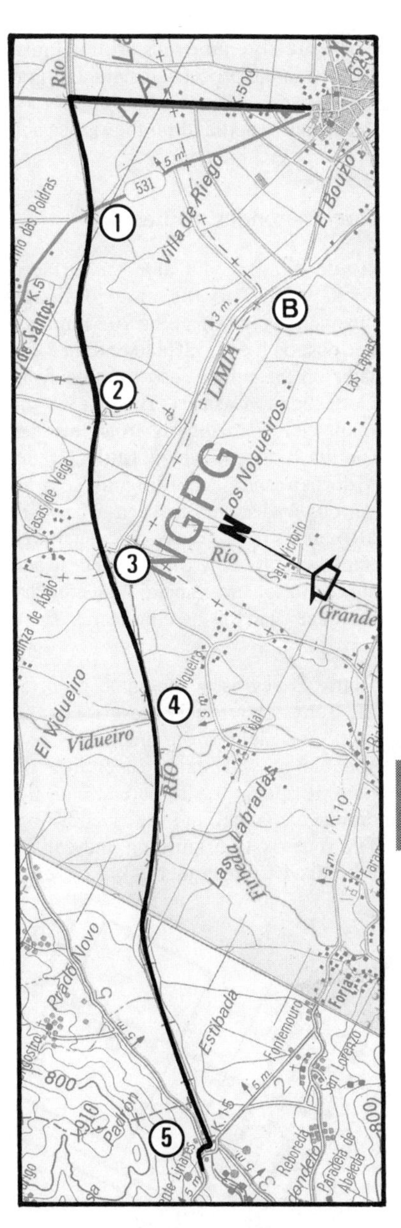

Access

Xinzo de Limia and Sandiás, villages on the N-525 some 40 km from Ourense, are the largest villages in the area. The road crosses the plains, dividing them in two parts, leaving to the northeast the bed of the old lake of Antela and to the southwest the grazing land and oak woodland which originally lined the mouth of the drainage channel and the river Limia.

Description

The draining of the Antela lake, which occupied a Quaternary basin, transformed a previously flooded area measuring some 4,000 ha into fields. Subsequently, the process of farm reallotment, which continues today, increased the area of land for cultivation at the expense of the oak woods and grasslands around the edge of the lake. The drainage channels leading away from the lake and an area of some 500 ha of grazing land with ponds make up the most interesting habitats.

There are also numerous artificial pits, created in the process of sand and gravel extraction, and remains of deciduous woodland on the right bank of the river Limia.

Recommended routes

Route A takes you along a surfaced road parallel to the main drainage channel, beginning at the 202 km marker post on the N-525 and ending 8 km later on the minor road running from Cortegada to Casasoa. You can see the main channel from the road bridges (points 1 to 5), where Little Grebe, Moorhen and, according to season, various waders can be seen. There are also many dirt tracks and surfaced tracks which allow for easy access and surveying of the remaining secondary drainage channels and the plains themselves.

Route B begins at the same point as the route previously described and takes you along a dirt track in a reasonable or bad state, depending on rainfall, along the right bank of the drainage channel and the river Limia. The route is 11.5 km long and can be prolonged for a farther 3 km to reach Ponte Liñares (point 5), from where you can return to the road for Sandiás or Xinzo de Limia. The route crosses several bridges, allowing for the observation of ducks, waders and passerines (points 1 to 4). In addition, the track gives easy access to the shafts made for sand extraction which lie on both sides of the lake.

Accommodation

There is plenty of accommodation available in Xinzo de Limia and Allariz, 10 km from the old lake.

Comments

In Antela, many different species of birds can be seen but none of any special interest. The variety and quantity of ducks, and above all waders, depends on the amount of water present. The best conditions under which to see these species are rainy periods in spring.

In summer the area consists of cereal fields, with harriers, Quail or the extremely rare Great Bustard. All of these species are infrequently seen and populations are declining.

Antonio Villarino Gómez

MADRID

Spanish Imperial Eagle
Aquila adalberti

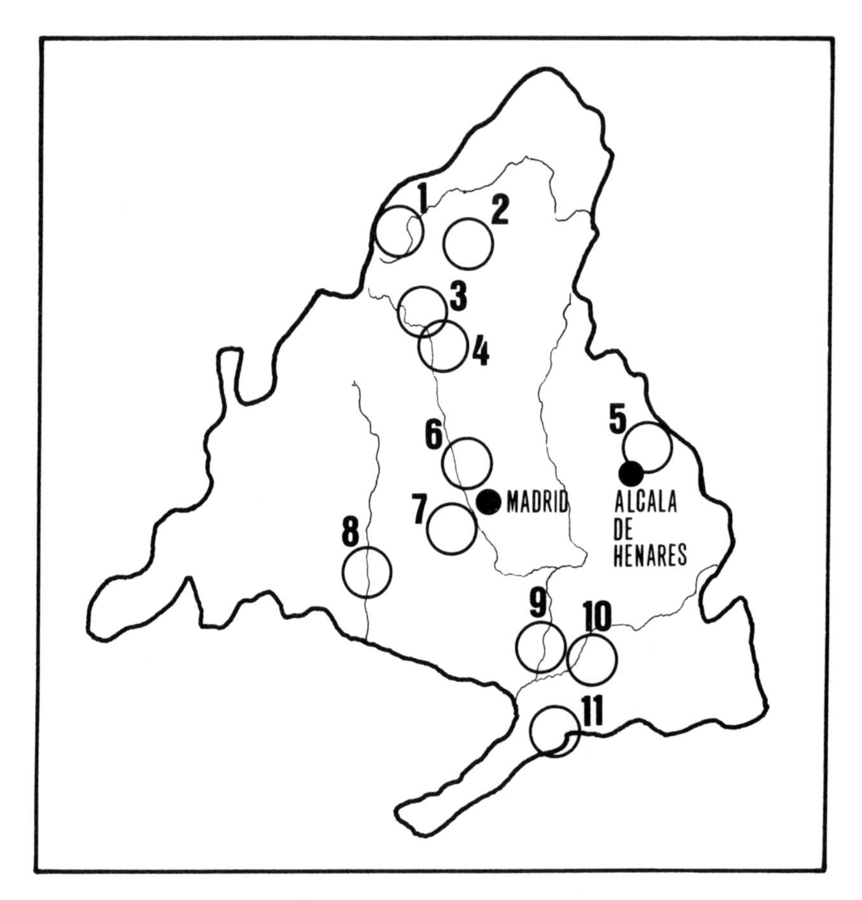

The considerable size of Madrid and its status as capital of Spain mean that it will probably be the starting point for many readers of this book. Fortunately the area around Madrid still offers quite a few opportunities for the birdwatcher; in a short time he or she will gain a very good impression of birdlife in the interior of the Iberian Peninsula in addition to a long list of species. The Comunidad de Madrid lies right in the heart of Spain and stretches from the Guadarrama mountains down to the banks of the river Tajo (Tagus) in Aranjuez. The region lies at an altitude of close to 2,000 m, giving rise to a series of clearly demarcated zones for vegetation (basically consisting of holm oak (*Quercus rotundifolia*), Pyrenean oak (*Quercus pyrenaica*) and Scots pine (*Pinus sylvestris*) woods, with Pyrenean broom (*Cytisus purgans*) and alpine pastures on areas of high ground), each with its individual range of birdlife. Despite dense human population, the traditional methods of forestry, agriculture and animal husbandry have meant that much of the area has remained relatively unspoiled, giving rise to quite high numbers of birds of prey.

We have selected three areas in the mountains around Madrid. The first two take in the mountain passes of Navacerrada and Cotos (M.1) and those of La Morcuera and Canencia (M.2) respectively. These routes provide you with easy access to Pyrenean oak woods, pine woods and high ground. Common woodland-dwelling species include Booted Eagle, Goshawk, Mistle Thrush, Firecrest, Goldcrest, Bonelli's Warbler, Pied Flycatcher, Crossbill and Citril Finch, while on open land you will have no difficulty in seeing Black Vulture, Griffon Vulture, Tawny Pipit, Water Pipit, Bluethroat, Rock Thrush, Chough, Raven, Ortolan Bunting and, near the Peñalara peak (2,430 m), Alpine Accentor. Both routes take in the Lozoya valley, the place with the most rainfall and with the most northern appearance in the province, where you may see species such as Tree Pipit, Song Thrush and Whinchat, albeit in small numbers. The third place is La Pedriza del Manzanares (M.3), remarkable for its spectacular granite cliffs which are the breeding ground of Golden Eagle and Griffon Vulture. Here you will also see Mediterranean species such as Thekla Lark, Red-rumped Swallow, Blue Rock Thrush and Azure-winged Magpie.

At one time holm oak woods probably covered much of the Madrid area, as was also the case with virtually the whole of central and southern Spain. The holm oak woodland at Monte de El Pardo (M.4) has survived the test of time extremely well, being relatively unspoiled thanks to the fact that the area is a hunting ground belonging to the Crown. On the outskirts of the metropolis of Madrid you can therefore see species such as Spanish Imperial Eagle and Black Vulture. Unfortunately you must be content with only visiting a small area open to the public and skirting your way around the rest, but nonetheless this will be enough to see many interesting species. Conversely, holm oak woodland located on open hillsides and dry grazing land in large areas in the southwest of the province have been conserved. This area lies between the N-V and the N-VI, two main roads. We have not selected anywhere specific in this area, but recommend the roads linking Robledo de Chavela, Navas del Rey, Aldea del Fresno and San Martín de Valdeiglesias. The landscape is reminiscent of that of Extremadura and is home to Spanish Imperial Eagle, Booted Eagle, Red Kite, Great Spotted Cuckoo, Red-necked Nightjar, Bee-eater, Roller, Woodlark, Red-rumped Swallow, Woodchat Shrike, Orphean Warbler, Sardinian Warbler, Subalpine Warbler, Azure-winged Magpie, Spanish Sparrow and other species characteristic of the Mediterranean Iberian habitat.

For those without much time or those who are taking up birdwatching for the first time, a trip to the Casa del Campo (M.7) is well worthwhile. This is an urban but relatively natural park full of holm oak and pine. Alternatively there are the banks of the river Guadarrama near Villaviciosa de Odón (M.8).

In marked contrast with the previous regions, the east of the province has been extensively deforested. However, this allows for the presence of another large group of birds. In and around the extensive dry-land cereal crops, Montagu's Harrier, Great Bustard, Little Bustard, Stone Curlew, Black-bellied Sandgrouse, Short-toed Lark and Calandra Lark are common. The best place for seeing these species is between Alcalá de Henares and Torrelaguna (M.5) and also at other locations, such as beside the N-III running between Fuentidueña de Tajo and the provincial border with Cuenca. The rivers (Henares, Jarama, Tajuña and Tajo) give rise to small riverside stands of poplars, irrigated fertile plains, slopes and cliffs, each providing a habitat for new species. In the water courses and riverside woodland you will see Black-winged Stilt, Little Ringed Plover, Scops Owl, Kingfisher, Sand Martin, Cetti's Warbler, Great Reed Warbler, Penduline Tit and Golden Oriole; slopes covered with esparto (*Stipa tenacissima*) grassland or kermes oak (*Quercus coccifera*) will give sightings of Thekla Lark, Great Grey Shrike, Black-eared Wheatear and Spectacled Warbler; on cliffs of marl and gypsum you may see Black Kite, Peregrine Falcon, Stock Dove, Bee-eater, Black Wheatear, Blue Rock Thrush, Rock Sparrow and Chough. Places presenting these habitats and ranges of species include Alcalá de Henares (M.5), the river Jarama from the Arganda road (M.9), the area around the Laguna de San Juan near Chinchón (M.10), and Aranjuez (M.11). The latter also has the attraction of Crown parkland with very mature trees.

Finally we should mention lakeland habitats, which in the Madrid area are virtually always artificial. These include the Santillana (M.4) and El Pardo (M.6) reservoirs, the series of flooded gravel pits dotting the flood plain of the river Jarama (M.9), the small lake at San Juan (M.10) and some reedbeds near Aranjuez (M.11). The lakes are remarkable for wintering grebes, Cormorant, Grey Heron, ducks, Coot and gulls, while the gravel pits and reedbeds are the breeding ground for some interesting aquatic species. These are quite scarce and always occur locally, but include Great Crested Grebe, Little Bittern, Night Heron, Cattle Egret, Marsh Harrier, Red-crested Pochard, Water Rail, Savi's Warbler, Bearded Tit and Avadavat, the last-named having become naturalized in recent years.

■ M.1 NAVACERRADA AND COTOS MOUNTAIN PASSES

Mountain area.

Main species

Residents: Griffon Vulture, Black Vulture, Goshawk, Buzzard, Spanish Imperial Eagle, Golden Eagle, Kestrel, Great Spotted Woodpecker, Alpine Accentor, Dartford Warbler, Goldcrest, Crested Tit, Nuthatch, Chough, Raven, Citril Finch, Crossbill, Rock Bunting.

Summer visitors: White Stork, Red Kite, Black Kite, Short-toed Eagle, Booted Eagle, Water Pipit, Dunnock, Bluethroat, Black Redstart, Wheatear, Rock Thrush, Bonelli's Warbler, Pied Flycatcher, Ortolan Bunting.

Access

The C-604 is the main axis from which the recommended routes run off. It links the Navacerrada mountain pass to the N-I. To reach the Puerto de Navacerrada, leave Madrid on the A-6 motorway and turn off at Villalba onto the N-601, taking you to the pass (61 km). The other option is to take the N-I and after Lozoyuela (67 km), turn left onto the C-604.

Description

The Sierra de Guadarrama constitutes part of the Sistema Central, its main peak being Peñalara (2,430 m). This area of the range has two main ridges, divided by a broad valley along which the river Lozoya and its tributaries run. These granite mountains are rolling in appearance because of periglacial phenomena which also created the mountain lakes of Peñalara and Los Pájaros.

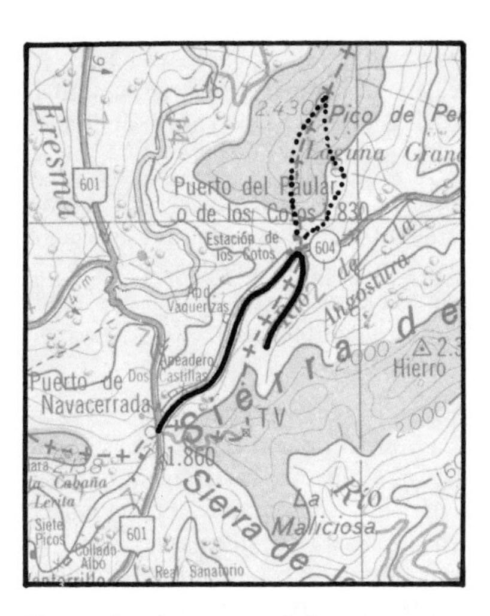

Vegetation is very varied and consists of riverside woodland, ash, oak, pine and areas of scrubland, particularly at higher altitudes.

Recommended routes

This route, some 30 km long, can be done by car and enables you to visit the most interesting areas of the Guadarrama range. It starts at the Navacerrada pass and takes you towards the Cotos pass, running through extensive pine woods in the province of Segovia where access may be difficult because the terrain is very steep. From Cotos you can climb to the summit of Peñalara. This makes for an easy but steep ascent which you can also undertake by travelling in a chair lift, taking you up to 2,100 m. On the way back you can go straight to the Peñalara lake and from there, following the outlet, you will come to a small stone hut from where a track leads off to the area around the pass. The most interesting birds you will see on this route are Griffon Vulture, Black Vulture, Wheatear, Rock Thrush, Alpine Accentor, Bluethroat, Water Pipit, Citril Finch, Crossbill, Chough and Raven.

From the Cotos pass, a road leads off to the right taking you to the Valdesquí ski resort. You do not even have to leave the car park to see Bluethroat, Rock Bunting, Rock Thrush and other scrub-dwelling birds.

The descent to Rascafría takes you through extensive pine forests where you can make detours along the various tracks leading off from the road. The birds in this area will of course be those typical of forest habitats.

A couple of kilometres before Rascafría you will come across the Mirador de Los Robledos, a vantage point distinguished by a monument to a forestry worker. This is an interesting place for watching various birds of prey such as Black Vulture, Short-toed Eagle, Booted Eagle, Red Kite, Goshawk and, with luck, Golden Eagle or Spanish Imperial Eagle.

Accommodation

Although not much accommodation is available, it is possible to stay at the Navacerrada pass, in Lozoya and in Rascafría. In Rascafría there is also the Monasterio de El Paular, a monastery with a hotel.

Comments

The best time of year for visiting the area is during the spring and summer months.

The route can be continued by dropping down the north side of the Navacerrada pass to the village of San Ildefonso-Valsaín (CL.34).

Angel Gómez Manzaneque

M.2 LA MORCUERA AND CANENCIA MOUNTAIN PASSES

Mountain area.

Main species

Residents: Griffon Vulture, Black Vulture, Goshawk, Dartford Warbler, Goldcrest, Crested Tit, Nuthatch, Citril Finch, Crossbill, Rock Bunting.

Summer visitors: Black Kite, Booted Eagle, Skylark, Tawny Pipit, Water Pipit, Crag Martin, Dunnock, Bluethroat, Wheatear, Rock Thrush, Bonelli's Warbler, Pied Flycatcher, Ortolan Bunting.

On passage: Woodpigeon, thrushes, finches.

Access

Leave Madrid on the C-607 (dual carriageway to Colmenar Viejo) and from there continue to Miraflores de la Sierra (50 km). In Miraflores de la Sierra two minor roads will take you respectively to the passes of Canencia and La Morcuera (10 km).

Description

Typical mountain passes of the Sistema Central, located at some 1,700 m in the case of La Morcuera and 1,500 m in the case of Canencia. Here broom and alpine pastures abound with rocky outcrops on the ridges and surrounding peaks. The mountainsides running down from the passes have well-developed woodland consisting of Scots pine and Pyrenean Oak.

Recommended routes

Route A consists of a walk around the area of the Morcuera pass. Near the pass a track runs off to the left (1) and, going down the road towards Rascafría, after a mountain refuge, a dirt track leads off to the right (2). Both tracks lead into the broom expanses and can easily be covered, although you should be aware of free range cattle. The walk, which can take as long as you wish, will allow you to see

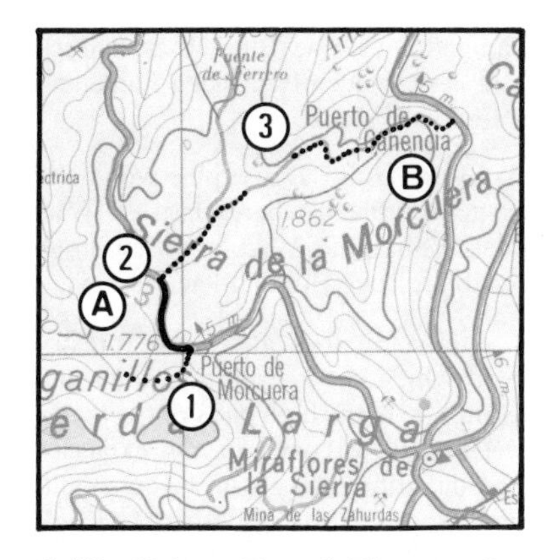

Griffon Vulture, Kestrel, Wheatear, Ortolan Bunting, Bluethroat and Rock Thrush. If you continue along the second track you will come to a mountain saddle (3) which is one of the best places in the Sistema Central for watching the migration of Woodpigeon. Between October and November you will see large groups of these species filtering through between the peaks of Perdiguera and Espartal. There are many shooting butts in this area and for obvious reasons you should avoid days when shooting is taking place.

Route B consists of a walk through the pine woods around the Canencia pass, where you will be able to see birds of prey and other woodland-dwelling birds. Towards the west, a forestry road climbs to the saddle mentioned above (3) through woods of pine and Pyrenean oak. It may also be worthwhile stopping in the Pyrenean oak woodland located on the way up to the pass and in the small clumps of birch encountered as you drop down towards Canencia.

Accommodation

Although accommodation is available in the nearby towns of Miraflores de la Sierra and Manzanares el Real, it is worth returning to Madrid where there is plenty of accommodation to suit all tastes.

Angel Gómez Manzaneque
and Ramón Martí Montes

■ M.3 LA PEDRIZA DEL MANZANARES

Mountain area.

Main species

Residents: Griffon Vulture, Golden Eagle, Eagle Owl, Thekla Lark, Crag Martin, Water Pipit, Dipper, Blue Rock Thrush, Dartford Warbler, Azure-winged Magpie, Chough, Raven, Rock Bunting.

Summer visitors: Bee-eater, Red-rumped Swallow, Bluethroat, Wheatear, Black-eared Wheatear, Rock Thrush, Subalpine Warbler, Woodchat Shrike, Ortolan Bunting.

Winter visitors: Alpine Accentor.

Access

In Madrid take the C-607 (dual carriageway to Colmenar Viejo). Continue in the direction of Miraflores de la Sierra and turn left and left again (both turns are marked) to bring you to Manzanares el Real. Leave the town centre in the direction of Cerceda and after 600 m you will find the road for Pedriza, indicated with a sign saying *Parque Regional. La Pedriza.* In summer traffic on the road within the Pedriza area is one way but on the days when there are a lot of visitors, entrance is restricted to a maximum of 1,500 vehicles.

Description

The granite massif of Pedriza del Manzanares is one of the most picturesque

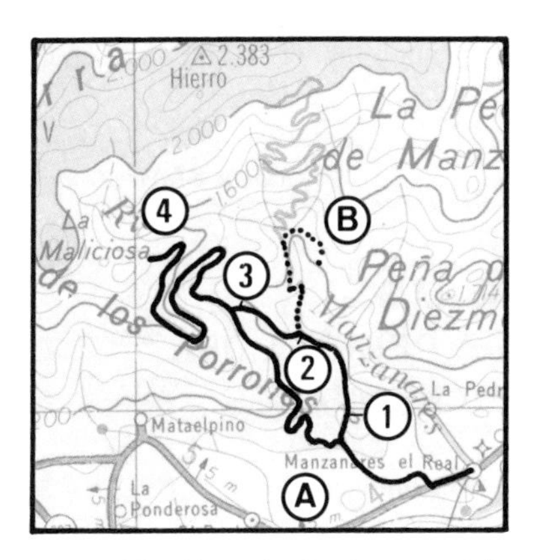

parts of the Sierra de Guadarrama. It is located on the southern side of the range and is a unique example of granite rock formations, where the process of erosion has created a spectacular landscape.

A wide range of habitats is present owing to differences in height, rugged terrain and transformations wrought by man.

The mountain is part of the Parque Regional de la Cuenca Alta del Manzanares (Regional Park of the Upper Manzanares Valley).

Recommended routes

Route A consists of a car journey of some 15 km, beginning and starting at the archway over the entrance to the park. The points of most interest are the following:

1) Collado de Quebrantaherraduras. This mountain saddle offers a broad view over the whole of La Pedriza. The plantations of pine and cypress give rise to observations of many forest-dwelling birds including Azure-winged Magpie, while on the more open land you may see Woodlark, Thekla Lark and Black-eared Wheatear.

2) Canto Cochino. On the surrounding rocky areas you may have sightings of Griffon Vulture, Crag Martin, Red-rumped Swallow, Blue Rock Thrush and, less frequently, Golden Eagle and Peregrine Falcon.

3) El Berzosillo. Dense pine wood and cistus scrubland where Dartford Warbler, Subalpine Warbler, Melodious Warbler, Rock Bunting, etc. abound.

Continue on foot along the forestry road which starts from this point and climbs up to the high parts of the Sierra del Francés (4) with broom expanses and damp meadows where you should see Water Pipit, Bluethroat, Rock Thrush, Chough, etc. This is an easy walk, although a constant climb is involved, which can be done in a couple of hours. Continuing along the road, you will come back to the archway at the entrance.

Route B consists of a walk which is quite hard going because it involves a climb of 500 m. Start at the Canto Cochino car park and having crossed the river Manzanares and passed some forestry houses, take a narrow but well-marked path which coincides with the route of the GR-10, a long-distance footpath. The track climbs up the right bank of the Majadilla riverbed, passing through pine woods and cypress plantations where you may see Azure-winged Magpie, Red-rumped Swallow, etc. Continue by crossing the riverbed and go past the Giner mountain refuge, climbing up the left bank of the Dehesilla riverbed until you reach the mountain saddle of the same name. Here you will leave the GR-10 and take a narrow but well-marked path running in a very round-about way towards the lower slopes of the Yelmo peak. At the foot of the peak there is a meadow with a spring which is a little difficult to find. Here you may see Griffon Vulture, Crag Martin, Rock Thrush, Blue Rock Thrush, Black-eared Wheatear, Rock Bunting, Chough, etc. From this point the path drops down to Manzanares el Real, so if you have left your car in Canto Cochino it is recommended that you take a path running back in that direction. However if you are not very used to finding your way or you do not have maps, it might be a good idea to return by the same route.

Accommodation

Since Madrid is very close by, it is worthwhile making use of the accommodation available in the capital. In any case, accommodation is available in Manzanares el Real and Miraflores de la Sierra. There is also a camping area and two nearby campsites.

Comments

Recently, a motion to close La Pedriza to private traffic was passed, which may make for some changes in the way in which these routes can be undertaken. However, there is a project for a car park and the setting up of a minibus service taking you into the park.

Ramón Martí Montes

■ M.4 SANTILLANA RESERVOIR

Reservoir.

Main species

Residents: White Stork, Gadwall, Thekla Lark, Dartford Warbler, Sardinian Warbler, Azure-winged Magpie, Hawfinch.

Summer visitors: Little Bustard, Black-winged Stilt, Great Spotted Cuckoo, Red-necked Nightjar, Bee-eater, Short-toed Lark, Yellow Wagtail, Fan-tailed Warbler, Melodious Warbler, Subalpine Warbler, Spectacled Warbler, Woodchat Shrike.

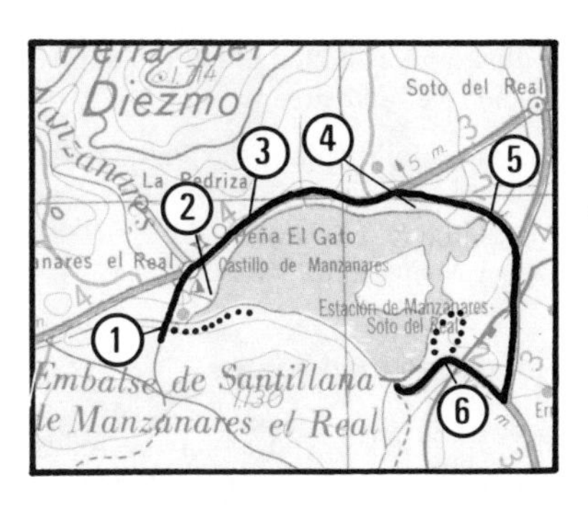

Winter visitors: Black-necked Grebe, Cormorant, Grey Heron, ducks (in large numbers), Black-headed Gull.

On passage: herons, Black Stork, Osprey, waders, marsh terns.

Access

From Madrid take the C-607 (dual carriageway to Colmenar Viejo). Once you have passed the exits for Colmenar, take a little after the 34 km marker post, the turning for Miraflores de la Sierra. At the first junction you come to, turn left and this will bring you to the area around the dam. Another option is to continue a little farther and turn left for Manzanares el Real. This road skirts the reservoir for some 4 km.

Description

The Santillana reservoir is one of the oldest in the province of Madrid and holds the greatest interest in terms of water birds. The river Manzanares and the Samburiel and Mediano streams are the main sources supplying the reservoir. The last two usually dry up in summer, the time of year when the water level in the reservoir is at its lowest. Because of these variations in water level, there is no marsh vegetation on the shores of the reservoir.

The area around the reservoir consists of a patchwork of fields, stands of ash, oak and holm oak and areas of scrubland. There are also substantial willow groves dotted along the course of the river and streams.

The area falls within the Parque Regional de la Cuenca Alta del Manzanares (Regional Park of the Upper Manzanares Valley).

Recommended routes

This route takes you along the roads running round the reservoir. The most interesting places are the following:

1) Arroyo Samburiel. Willows surrounded by a hilly area with holm oak where you may see Dartford Warbler, Sardinian Warbler and Azure-winged Magpie.

2) Mouth of the river Manzanares. A wonderful place for seeing a wide variety of passerines during the migration periods.

3) A good general view of the reservoir with possibilities of seeing Black-necked Grebe, Cormorant, herons and ducks. You may also see Griffon Vulture on the neighbouring mountain of La Pedriza.

4) A small stretch of road taking you to a disused hide. On the shores of the reservoir you will see various water birds including Black-winged Stilt, Little Egret, Black Stork, Garganey and Whiskered Tern.

5) Mouth of the Chozas. An area with gently-sloping banks running down to the stream surrounded by extensive meadows where groups of White Stork, ducks and waders congregate. From July to October there are also groups of Little Bustard.

6) Dam. A deep water area where you should see Black-necked Grebe, Cormorant, ducks and Lesser Black-backed Gull. In the surrounding fields, areas of red lavender and small stands of holm oak, you will see Little Bustard, Stone Curlew, Thekla Lark, Spectacled Warbler, Subalpine Warbler, Azure-winged Magpie and, during the migration periods, Montagu's Harrier and Hobby.

Accommodation

Accommodation is available in Manzanares el Real and Soto del Real. There are also a couple of campsites in each of these towns; the Soto campsite is recommended since it is very close to the reservoir.

Comments

Although access to the reservoir is forbidden, you can easily watch birds from the boundary fence.

Javier Grijalbo, Pedro Molina,
Jaime Ollero and Tomás Velasco

M.5 ALCALÁ DE HENARES – TORRELAGUNA

Plains occupied by grain fields.

Main species

Residents: Marsh Harrier, Hen Harrier, Peregrine Falcon, Little Bustard, Great Bustard, Stone Curlew, Black-bellied Sandgrouse, Pin-tailed Sandgrouse, Calandra Lark, Raven, Dartford Warbler, Penduline Tit.

Summer visitors: White Stork, Montagu's Harrier, Hobby, Lesser Kestrel, Great Spotted Cuckoo, Red-necked Nightjar, Bee-eater, Roller, Short-toed Lark, Black-eared Wheatear.

Winter visitors: Sparrowhawk, Merlin, Short-eared Owl, Rook, small passerines.

Access

Take the N-II from Madrid to Alcalá de Henares (31 km). Alternatively, you can reach the beginning of route B by taking the N-I to Fuente del Fresno and then making for Fuente el Saz, where you join the C-100.

Description

An open area with relatively few trees which is largely occupied by dry-farming. The terrain is quite rolling with a multitude of small hills which usually have relict holm oak woodland and low mountain vegetation. There are also some patches of riverside woodland beside the rivers Torote, Jarama and Henares.

Centres of population are numerous although usually on a small scale. The area is remarkable for the large number of housing developments which have been built in recent years.

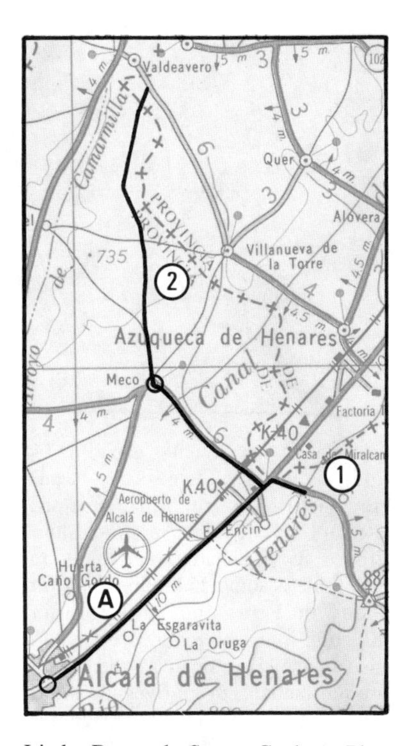

Recommended routes

Route A begins in Alcalá de Henares, where it is worth visiting the old quarter which is the home of a large colony of White Stork and some pairs of Lesser Kestrel. Taking the N-II towards Guadalajara, you will come to the junction with the minor road for Santos de la Humosa which crosses the river Henares at point 1, where there is a good example of riverside woodland and sandy cliffs. Here you may have sightings of Peregrine Falcon, Sparrowhawk, Hobby, Bee-eater, Raven and quite a number of passerines. On the nearby fields you may see some steppe-dwelling birds.

Going back to the N-II, take the minor road to Meco. The church in this village is a nesting place for a colony of Lesser Kestrel. Leave Meco on a farm road leading north and crossing a broad plain occupied by cereal crops (2) where you may see Great Bustard, Little Bustard, Stone Curlew, Pin-tailed Sandgrouse, Black-bellied Sandgrouse, Montagu's Harrier, Hen Harrier, Merlin, Calandra Lark, Short-toed Lark and wheatears. The track comes to an end on the minor road running from Azuqueca de Henares to Valdeavero, the last stop on the route. The approximate length of the route is 32 km, and it can be done in 5 hours.

Route B sets out from Alcalá de Henares on the C-100 running towards Torrelaguna. 31.5 km from Alcalá, shortly after Valdetorres del Jarama, there is a track on the right which crosses a large plain with grain fields and takes you to the ruins of Campoalbillo. Point 3 is a good place for seeing large groups of Great Bustard as well as Montagu's Harrier, Stone Curlew and Black-bellied Sandgrouse. In the ruins you will also see Roller and Bee-eater. From here, take the track which leads northwest towards Talamanca del

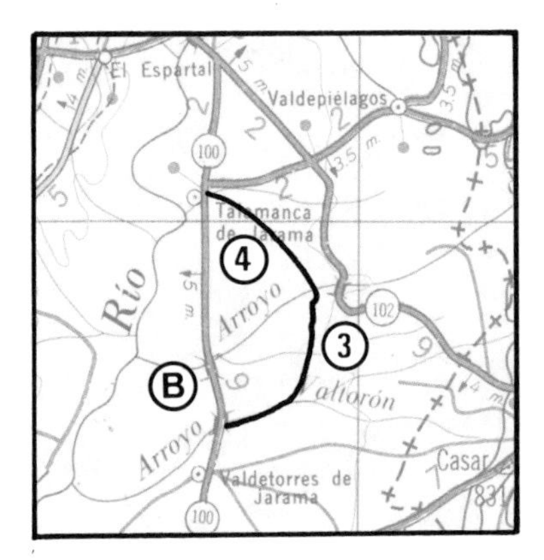

Jarama. On this stretch of the route (4) you may well see three species of harrier, Great Bustard, Little Bustard, Stone Curlew, Black-bellied Sandgrouse and frequently Black Vulture. The route is some 25 km long and finishes in Talamanca del Jarama, although it can be rounded off with a visit to the river Jarama, where there are substantial areas of riverside woodland. These woods may give sightings of Hobby, Sparrowhawk, waders, Bee-eater, Roller and a multitude of passerines including Penduline Tit.

The routes recommended are just two of the many which can be undertaken in this area. There is an extensive network of farm tracks which are excellent for watching birds.

Accommodation

A wide and plentiful range of accommodation is available in Madrid, Alcalá de Henares and Guadalajara. You can also stay in any of the many roadside hostels.

Comments

All of these routes can be undertaken by car although it is wise to be careful on the roads, particularly during the rainy season when many of them may become difficult to drive along. It is worthwhile taking a telescope, especially for watching Great Bustard.

Alfredo Ortega Sirvent
and Susana Casado Campos

■ M.6 MONTE DE EL PARDO

Holm oak woods occupying dry grazing lands located on a plain with large areas of low hills. This is the best conserved area of woodland with these characteristics in central Spain.

Main species

Residents: Grey Heron, Griffon Vulture, Black Vulture, Spanish Imperial Eagle, Eagle Owl, Kingfisher, Blue Rock Thrush, Azure-winged Magpie.

Summer visitors: White Stork, Short-toed Eagle, Booted Eagle, Lesser Kestrel, Black-winged Stilt, Stone Curlew, Great Spotted Cuckoo, Scops Owl, Red-necked Nightjar, Bee-eater, Red-rumped Swallow, Rock Thrush, Great Reed Warbler, Melodius Warbler, Dartford Warbler, Subalpine Warbler.

Winter visitors: Cormorant, ducks (4,000 individuals in January 1990), Black-headed Gull, Lesser Black-backed Gull.

On passage: Night Heron, Black Stork, Crane, Whiskered Tern, Black Tern.

Access

From Madrid, take the N-VI and at the 6 km marker post turn off onto the C-601 for El Pardo (routes A and B). Another possibility (routes C and D) is to take the road running from Colmenar Viejo (the C-607, a dual carriageway) to Torrelodones (29 km marker post on the N-VI).

Description

The Monte de El Pardo is an area of Mediterranean woodland which is surprisingly unspoiled despite its proximity to the urban sprawl of Madrid. It has been Crown property since the time of Carlos I, who used it as a royal hunting ground. It stretches for a little over 15,000 ha and the wall surrounding it is about 99 km long.

It consists of holm oak woodland located on dry grazing lands with gently rolling contours, extensive pastures and huge expanses of low hills. The river Manzanares and its main tributaries (Manina, Trofa, La Zarzuela, Tejada, etc.) give rise to a series of ash groves and riverside woodland running transversely across the area, creating very important habitats. In addition the El Pardo reservoir, located in the middle of the region, is also an important wetland area.

Recommended routes

Access to Monte de El Pardo is strictly forbidden except for a small part delineated by a wire fence which is open to the public. Visits should therefore be limited to these areas and the occasional stop on the periphery.

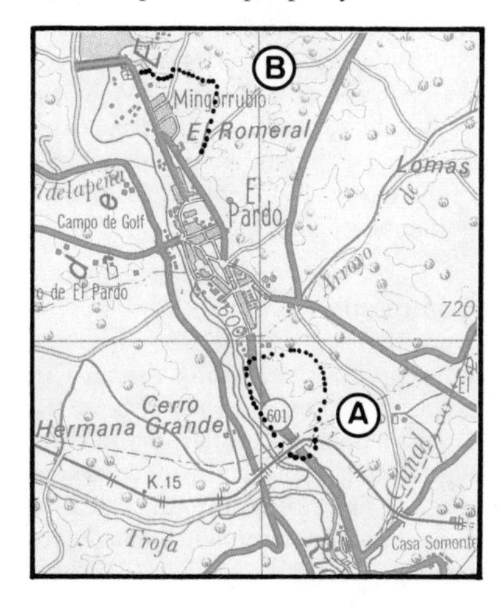

Route A has its starting point in the car park at the 4.2 km marker post on the C-601, lying between the road and the river. Walk up the course of the river Manzanares. Pass under a railway bridge and, after about 2.5 km, having passed a farm with livestock, you will come again to the El Pardo road (C-601). Cross the road and enter a small pine wood. To come back, stay parallel to the road. The route takes you through an area of shrubby oaks and rather steep hills which gradually give way to grazing land with holm oak woods in a reasonable state of conservation. You will come across some hillocks which you can climb and enjoy a general view of the whole area. A little farther on, cross the railway lines and follow them to come back to the departure point.

The first part of the route runs through a riverside area with woodland and beds of rushes where you will be able to see marsh-dwelling birds, waders, and many others coming and going to and from the reservoir, above all in winter. On the far bank are extensive wooded grazing lands where you can see some birds of prey and other species typical of this habitat. However, it will be on the return journey in the area of kermes oak and holm oak where you will be able to find warblers and other characteristic passerines. The walk takes about 3 hours.

Route B. Continue along the road to El Pardo until you reach a junction. At this point continue straight on. At the 9.5 km marker post, just after Colonia Mingorrubio, park in front of the Restaurante El Pinar at the foot of the El Pardo dam. From the fence shutting off the reserved part of the area, you can get a good view of the reservoir and will see many water birds, above all in winter. Follow the fence around to the right on a path running parallel to it, crossing the area where pine woods

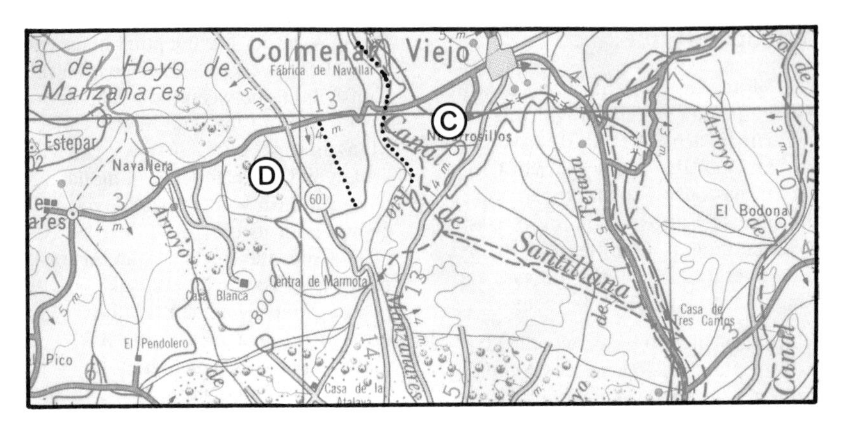

and holm oak growing on dry grazing lands meet —in this area you will see many of the birds typical of holm oak woods and some typical of pine woods. After about 3 km, you will come to a broad track which takes you back to the road and from there to the departure point. If you are at this point half an hour before sunrise between November and February, you will see the spectacular departure of Black-headed Gull making their way to Madrid in search of food.

Route C consists of a walk along the river Manzanares. Leave your car some 25 m before the bridge over the river on the road from Colmenar Viejo to Hoyo de Manzanares. You can walk up- or downstream for some 30 minutes and will have sightings of species such as Blue Rock Thrush, Rock Thrush, Red-rumped Swallow, Crag Martin, etc. It is also worthwhile going into Colmenar Viejo, where the church is a breeding ground for White Stork and Lesser Kestrel.

To undertake **Route D**, continue along the road to Hoyo de Manzanares. You will come to the top of a steep climb, roughly 1.5 km after the bridge; leave your car in the lay-by you will find, where there are two signs. One has been put up by the Agencia de Medio Ambiente de la Comunidad de Madrid (Environmental Department of the Madrid Region), and the second indicates Finca Los Ciervos, a farm. Walk towards this farm for about 2.5 km along a dirt track crossing a broad expanse of pastureland until you come to the holm oak wood at the point where the track forks and the El Cañacerral Integral Reserve begins. From here you have a wonderful view of Monte de El Pardo and will be able to see various birds of prey ranging from Griffon Vulture and Black Vulture to, with luck, Spanish Imperial Eagle.

Accommodation

Since Madrid is close by, it is worthwhile seeking accommodation in the city. However, there is also accommodation available in Colmenar Viejo and Torrelodones. In Hoyo de Manzanares there is a camping area which is part of the Parque Municipal La Cabilda, a public park.

Comments

It is worthwhile visiting the area in spring or winter, when you will see the largest number of species. If you go in winter it is worthwhile undertaking route B first (to see the Black-headed Gulls leaving their roost). On the other hand it is advisable to undertake route

C in the afternoon when the light conditions are most favourable.

A bus services connects the village of El Pardo with Madrid (Moncloa).

Francisco J. Cantos Mengs
and Antonio Fernández Martínez

■ M.7 CASA DE CAMPO

Extensive parkland with holm oak and pine, located on the outskirts of Madrid.

Main species

Residents: Mallard, Moorhen, Stock Dove, Woodpigeon, Little Owl, Green Woodpecker, Great Spotted Woodpecker, Cetti's Warbler, Sardinian Warbler, Long-tailed Tit, Short-toed Treecreeper, Spotless Starling, Serin, Greenfinch, Tree Sparrow.

Summer visitors: Great Spotted Cuckoo, Hoopoe, Nightingale, Melodious Warbler, Subalpine Warbler, Golden Oriole.

Access

Since this area is so close to Madrid access is very easy and fast, both by car and by bus (lines 33, 36, 39 and 65) or underground (stations of El Lago and Batán). Several roads cross the park and there is plenty of parking within the park.

Description

Casa de Campo, the natural continuation of Monte de El Pardo (M.6), is a suburban park taking up some 1,700 ha. Generally speaking the woodland consists of holm oak, although this is interspersed with pine plantations. The main streams contain riverside woodland of some magnitude, constituted by poplar, ash and elm although the numbers of the latter have been severely reduced by Dutch elm disease.

In general terms, the large number of visitors to the area has had a negative effect on the state of conservation of the park, although recently several measures have been taken to regenerate and improve vegetation, restricting wheeled traffic in many areas. Within the Casa de Campo is the zoo, an amusement park and a trade fair complex, as well as many leisure facilities (artificial lake, playing fields and refreshment stalls).

Recommended routes

Route A consists of a quick walk through the main areas of the park which can be undertaken in a couple of hours.

Route B is a walk lasting 4 hours (both ways) leaving from the underground railway stations of Batán or El Lago. For those coming by car it is worth parking in the layby beside the cable car, thus reducing the route to some 3 hours. The route takes you to the least

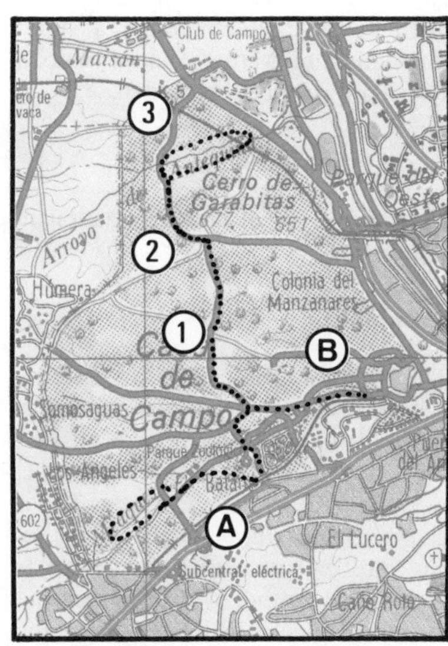

spoiled parts of the park, including the riverside woodland on the Antequina stream and an Ornithological Reserve which can be visited (this only applies to school parties) by contacting the Spanish Ornithological Society in advance.

The points of greatest interest on these routes, which are marked on the map, are the following:

1) Holm oak woods growing on dry grazing lands in which Blue Tit, Great Tit, Magpie and Tree Sparrow abound. You will also have frequent sightings of Hoopoe, Woodpigeon, Sardinian Warbler and Little Owl.

2) Pine plantation. This is the habitat of least ornithological interest, although you will see Green Woodpecker, Great Spotted Woodpecker, Short-toed Treecreeper, Greenfinch and Serin.

3) Riverside woodland. This is the most interesting habitat and will give you sightings of about 20 species including Little Owl, Stock Dove, Great Spotted Cuckoo, Golden Oriole, Cetti's Warbler and Melodious Warbler. At the end of route A you will come across a artificial lake inhabited by a small population of Mallard and Moorhen which are very easy to watch.

Accommodation

There is plenty of accommodation in Madrid.

Comments

The ornithological value of Casa de Campo originates from ease of access, allowing tourists and people passing through to have swift initial contact with the birdlife most representative of central Spain, although there are not any rare or spectacular species. It is highly recommended for beginners and city-dwelling enthusiasts, given the fact that many of the species are present in large numbers and are easy to see.

It is worth going to the area early in the morning on weekdays, since in the afternoon and at weekends a lot of people come to the area and will cause disturbance. The area located between the lake and the zoo is that most frequented by visitors, and therefore should whenever possible be avoided.

Alejandro Sánchez

■ M.8 RIVER GUADARRAMA AT VILLAVICIOSA DE ODÓN

A stretch of river with marsh vegetation and ash groves.

Main species

Residents: Little Grebe, Buzzard, Moorhen, Common Sandpiper, Kingfisher, Fan-tailed Warbler, Sardinian Warbler, Penduline Tit.

Summer visitors: Turtle Dove, Great Spotted Cuckoo, Scops Owl, Bee-eater, Roller, Reed Warbler, Great Reed Warbler, Subalpine Warbler, Golden Oriole.

Winter visitors: Snipe, Green Sandpiper, thrushes, Hawfinch.

On passage: Wryneck, swallows and martins, warblers, flycatchers.

Access

The stretch of the river Guadarrama in question lies between the N-V and the C-501, some 25 km from Madrid. A dirt track running parallel to the river joins the two roads and gives access to any point on its banks. In winter, when the track becomes difficult to pass

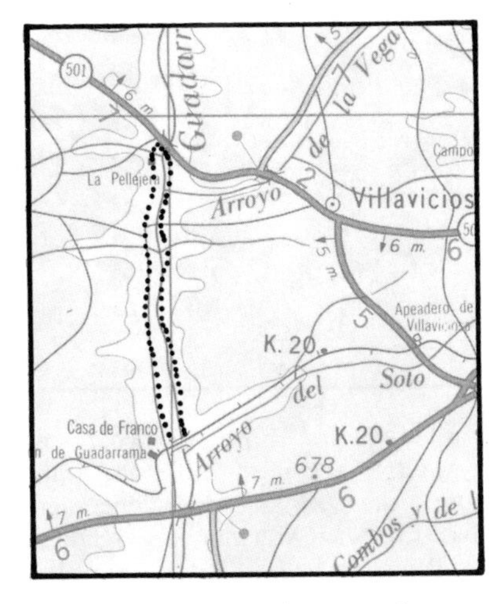

along, you can leave the car at the start of the track and continue on foot.

Description

These are the middle and lower reaches of the river Guadarrama. The riverside woodland has been conserved because it is on the edge of the development work which is so common in the rest of the Madrid area. The surrounding land consists of large fields, some private farms dedicated to extensive stock farming and hunting reserves. Some patches of holm oak woodland still remain.

The area is relatively unspoiled, although there are some problems caused by water pollution, extraction of sand and gravel, tree felling and human presence near the bridges.

Recommended routes

Paths run longitudinally throughout the ash grove. You can start the route either from the C-501 road bridge or from the old railway bridge, 1 km upstream from the N-V road bridge. The trip amounts to a total of 14 km, and it is possible to return along the far bank where there is also a path. In any case, it is worthwhile going down to the riverbanks where you can see, among other birds, Mallard, Kingfisher, Coot, Little Grebe, Penduline Tit and various warblers. It is also worthwhile exploring the gullies running down to the river on both sides if you wish to see Subalpine Warbler, Sardinian Warbler, Buzzard, Red-legged Partridge or Great Grey Shrike. Other species such as Bee-eater, Roller, Golden Oriole, etc. can be seen in and around the ash grove.

Accommodation

This area is near Madrid. There are also hostels in Navalcarnero and along the N-V.

Comments

The best time of year for visiting the area is in spring and summer and during the migration periods, since the area constitutes a migratory passage running from north to south for marsh- and woodland-dwelling birds.

Mario Díaz Esteban

■ M.9 CLIFFS AND GRAVEL PITS ON THE RIVER JARAMA

Main species

Residents: Little Grebe, Great Crested Grebe, Mallard, Pochard, Marsh Harrier, Peregrine Falcon, Water Rail, Kingfisher, Penduline Tit, Bearded Tit, Black Wheatear, Blue Rock Thrush, Dartford Warbler, Chough, Rock Sparrow.

Summer visitors: Little Bittern, Purple Heron, White Stork, Black Kite, Black-winged Stilt, Little Ringed Plover, Bee-eater, Roller, Great Spotted Cuckoo, Sand Martin, Fan-tailed Warbler, Reed Warbler, Great Reed Warbler.

Winter visitors: Cormorant, Grey Heron, Shoveler, Tufted Duck, Ferruginous Duck, Green Sandpiper, Lesser Black-backed Gull, Black-headed Gull, Bluethroat, Reed Bunting.

On passage: Little Egret, Cattle Egret, Gadwall, Pintail, Osprey, Avocet, Redshank, Savi's Warbler, Moustached Warbler.

Access

From Madrid take the N-III to Puente de Arganda, a bridge over the river Jarama (20 km).

Description

The rivers Jarama and Manzanares have carved cliffs of moderate height out of the marl and gypsum deposits present in the area. These cliffs run parallel to the river courses.

In the same area, the extraction of sand and gravel has created a series of flooded gravel pits. Once extraction processes ceased, the shores of the pits were colonized by marsh vegetation. On some stretches of both rivers are remains of riverside woodland, although they have largely been destroyed.

Recommended routes

The route proposed here consists of a walk lasting a couple of hours. Cross the river Jarama on an iron bridge currently in disuse, from where you will be able to see some waders on the riverbanks (1). On the far side you will find the El Campillo gravel pit around which a track runs (2). Ducks abound in the gravel pit, and at the end of the lake, where there are some small islets, you will be able to see grebes, herons and, in the woodland bordering the river Jarama, Penduline Tit. Having

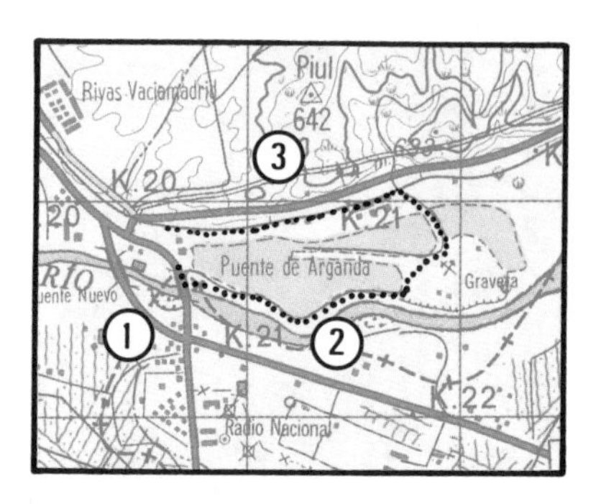

visited the gravel pit, make your way towards the gypsum cliffs and walk along the track running along their base (3), where you may have sightings of Peregrine Falcon, Black Kite, Blue Rock Thrush, Black Wheatear, Rock Sparrow and Chough, among other species.

Accommodation

It is worth staying in Madrid, where a wide range of hotel accommodation is available.

Carlos Palacín Moya

■ M.10 SAN JUAN POND

Wetland area.

Main species

Residents: Little Grebe, Great Crested Grebe, Mallard, Marsh Harrier, Water Rail, Moorhen, Coot, Kingfisher, Fan-tailed Warbler, Dartford Warbler.

Summer visitors: Little Bittern, Black-winged Stilt, Reed Warbler, Great Reed Warbler.

Winter visitors: Gadwall, Teal, Shoveler, Red-crested Pochard, Pochard, Penduline Tit, Starling, Spotless Starling (tens of thousands), Reed Bunting.

On passage: Sedge Warbler.

Access

From the N-IV take the C-404 towards Ciempozuelos and Chinchón. Shortly after crossing the bridge over the river Tajuña, turn right onto a marked dirt track, which after 1.5 km will take you to a car park beside the pond.

Description

The San Juan pond is the result of the artificial excavation of areas which were occasionally flooded when the river Tajuña was in full spate before its course was changed. The water level is regulated by a spring which provides water and also from water filtering through from the river.

In addition to the pond and neighbouring reedbeds, the gypsum cliffs constituting the river terraces should also be mentioned.

The lake is a Game Refuge measuring 25 ha.

Recommended routes

The recommended route consists of a walk leaving the car park and taking you along the track running around the pond. There is a hide by the dam, and by taking the track running round to the far side of the pond you will come to a second hide. Although the hides are not very well maintained and access to them is not concealed with screens, they provide a comfortable place from which to observe most of the birds at large in the area.

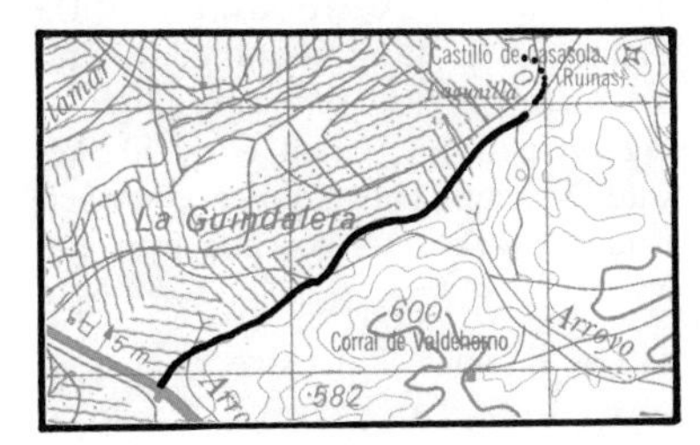

Continuing for another 300 m along the path, you will come across a path turning off to the left and leading up to the top of the cliffs. As you reach the top there is a dolina where you may see Black Wheatear and other species. This point also commands a view over the entire pond and the neighbouring fields.

Accommodation

Madrid, 50 km away, provides many possibilities of accommodation. Chinchón has a pension and a Parador Nacional, and in nearby Arganda del Rey there are several hotels and a campsite.

Ernesto Ferreiro Alcántara

M.11 ARANJUEZ

A stretch of river with irrigated fields, cliffs, riverside woodlands, reedbeds and a park with mature trees.

Main species

Residents: Little Grebe, Cattle Egret, Mallard, Pochard, Marsh Harrier, Peregrine Falcon, Little Bustard, Water Rail, Coot, Stone Curlew, Lapwing, Stock Dove, Pin-tailed Sandgrouse, Calandra Lark, Thekla Lark, Sardinian Warbler, Cetti's Warbler, Penduline Tit, Great Grey Shrike, Reed Bunting (possibly breeding in the area).

Summer visitors: Little Bittern, Night Heron, Purple Heron, White Stork, Black Kite, Hobby, Black-winged Stilt, Little Ringed Plover, Scops Owl, Bee-eater, Roller, Short-toed Lark, Sand Martin, Black-eared Wheatear, Reed Warbler, Great Reed Warbler, Spectacled Warbler, Subalpine Warbler, Golden Oriole, Woodchat Shrike.

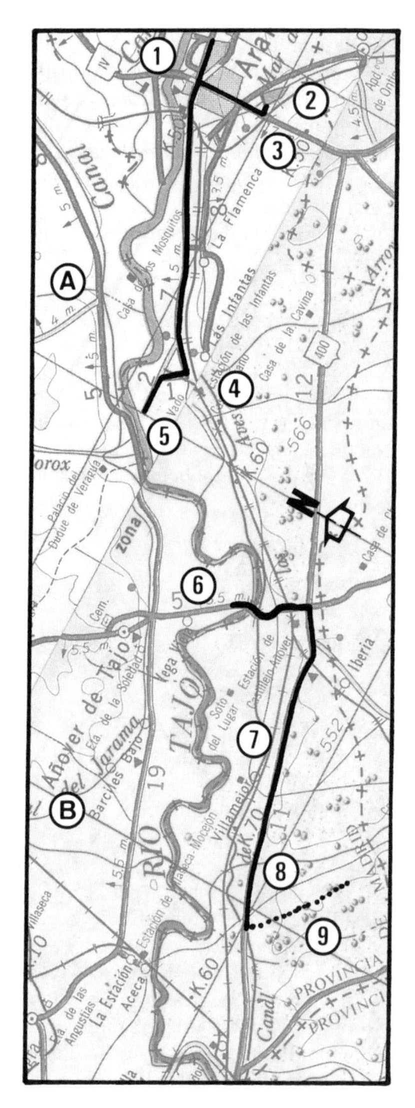

Access

Aranjuez is on the N-IV (E-05 dual carriageway), 65 km south of Madrid.

Description

Large, fertile plains at the confluence of the rivers Jarama and Tajo, lying close to the town of Aranjuez which has extensive Crown parkland featuring mature trees. At some points the riverbanks are well-conserved with alder, white poplar, black poplar, willow, ash and dense undergrowth. The water in the rivers is very contaminated but there are numerous islets and stretches of riverbank with pebbles and mud. There are areas of irrigated farmland and damp pasturelands where fighting bulls graze. A small lake which has been artificially expanded (Mar de Ontígola) and several abandoned meanders, once part of the river Tajo, present thick marshland vegetation.

The flood plains are bordered by gypsum cliffs and hillsides covered with vegetation typical of gypsum substrate as well as cereal crops and fallow land.

Recommended routes

Route A takes you on a car journey to the various points of interests around Aranjuez:

1) Reales Jardines. These are the Crown gardens, lying on the outskirts of the city next to the road for Villaconejos. There are relatively unspoiled areas of riverside woodland and mature trees (Stock Dove, Lesser Spotted Woodpecker?). Opening times for the garden vary during the course of the year.

2) Mar de Ontígola. A small but interesting wetland area where water levels remain relatively constant, giving rise to dense marsh vegetation. There are several breeding species including Little Bittern and Marsh Harrier.

3) Kermes oak woodland at La Flamenca. Rolling countryside with extensive kermes oak scrubland growing on gypsum (Great Grey Shrike, warblers, etc). This is privately-owned land, but access is possible from the N-IV.

4) Las Infantas. Extensive damp pastures used for grazing by large

quantities of livestock. This is a habitual breeding ground for Marsh Harrier, Black-winged Stilt and Lapwing, as well as being a feeding ground for Cattle Egret. During the migration periods various species of waders can be seen.

5) Barca de Añover. A disused landing stage. By taking walks in the surrounding area you will have sightings of Night Heron, Mallard, Pochard, Penduline Tit, Golden Oriole and Roller.

Route B takes you along the N-400 from Aranjuez to Toledo. It is recommended that you stop in the following places:

6) Puente de Añover, a bridge over the river Tajo between the N-400 and the town of Añover de Tajo. Islands with marsh vegetation and well-conserved riverside woodland. A track running along the river course will enable you to walk upstream (Night Heron, Cattle Egret, Hobby, Stock Dove, Cetti's Warbler, Penduline Tit, Golden Oriole).

7) Soto del Lugar. An abandoned meander with marsh vegetation and small areas of open water. Well-surfaced tracks allow you to reach the area from the road and see Purple Heron, Marsh Harrier, Pochard and reed warblers.

8) Carrizal del Villamejor, a reedbed in the basin of the river Martín Román. One of the largest breeding grounds in the Madrid area for Marsh Harrier. Currently steps are being taken to make the area a reserve following severe disturbance of the reedbed.

9) Altos de Valdepastores. Extensive cereal fields with areas of fallow and uncultivated land lying on the border with the province of Toledo. Characteristic steppe-dwelling birds: Little Bustard, Stone Curlew, Pin-tailed Sandgrouse (rare), Calandra Lark, etc.

Accommodation

There is plenty of accommodation available in Aranjuez and Toledo, but it is perfectly possible to undertake these trips from nearby Madrid.

Ramón Martí Montes

MURCIA

Black Wheatear
Oenanthe leucura

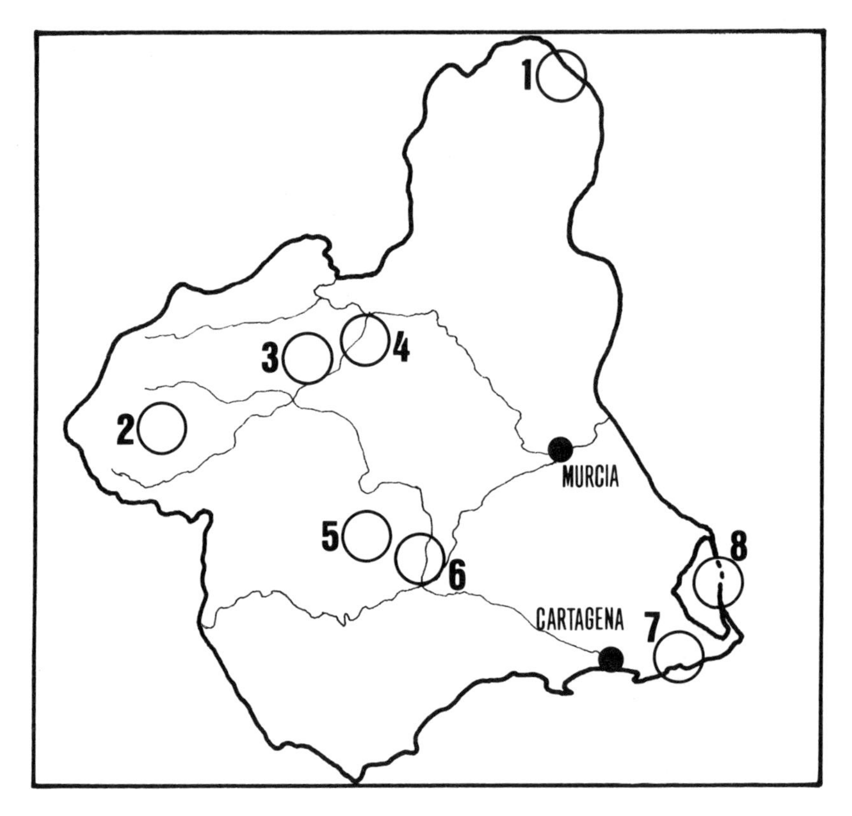

This small Autonomous Region is part of a larger geographical region, that of southeastern Spain, which also comprehends virtually the whole of the provinces of Alicante (País Valenciano) and Almería (Andalusia). Lying in the rain shadow of the Cordilleras Béticas, the area is characterized within the context of Spain by its extreme aridity, with precipitation mostly under 400 mm and many times with an annual average of less than 300 mm. This aridity gives rise to an unusual landscape, North African in appearance with bare mountains and dry expanses of esparto grass (*Stipa tenacissima*) which contrast starkly with the fertile irrigated areas where stands of date palms (*Phoenix dactylifera*) grow. This also accounts for the notable scarcity of fauna, particularly obvious in terms of birds. However, among the few species occurring in these semi-desert habitats, the visiting birdwatcher will find a large proportion of birds which are very rare or occur only locally in Europe and elsewhere in the Iberian Peninsula.

Another feature of the southeast of Spain, and particularly of the Murcia area, is the ruggedness of the terrain. A series of mountain ranges, running parallel from southwest to northeast, drop in height as they approach the coast like a series of giant steps. Greatest heights correspond to the northwestern most corner of the province, where the Sierra de Revolcadores, in fact a spur of the Andalusian massif of Cazorla, Segura and La Sagra (AN.7, AN.8), reaches a little over

2,000 m. In the centre of the province they reach a little over 1,000 m, and rise up like islands from the plain. These include the ranges of El Gigante, Burete, Cambrón, Espuña, Ricote, La Pila, El Carche and others. Beyond the densely populated flood plains of the rivers Guadalentín and Segura, the ranges of Almenara and Carrascoy still have extensive areas lying at over 500 m. Finally a series of small ranges make for a largely rugged coastline from Aguilas and Cabo Cope, via Mazarrón and Cabo Tiñoso, to Cartagena and Cabo de Palos (MU.7). Vegetation in the mountain ranges of Murcia, normally consisting of pine woods, becomes perceptibly sparser as altitude decreases. This is reflected in the birdlife present; typical forest species include Short-toed Eagle, Goshawk, Sparrowhawk, Buzzard, Booted Eagle, Hobby, Tawny Owl, Woodlark, Subalpine Warbler, Orphean Warbler, Bonelli's Warbler, Firecrest, Crested Tit, Coal Tit, Chaffinch and Crossbill. While being common in the Sierra Espuña, a high range of mountains which has been reforested, birds like these become scarcer as the coast is approached, being restricted to some areas of Aleppo pine (*Pinus halepensis*) on the northern slopes of the ranges just inland from the coast and becoming virtually absent on the coast itself. The coast is taken up by spiny scrubland consisting of dwarf fan palm (*Chamaerops humilis*), boxthorn (*Lycium intricatum*), silk-vine (*Periploca laevigata*), *Maytenus senegalensis*, jujube (*Ziziphus lotus*), Barbary arborvitae (*Tetraclinis articulata*) and other interesting Ibero-African species.

Cliff-dwelling birdlife is more resistant to aridity and is present throughout Murcia. Murcia lies on a limestone substrate; the soil is rocky and drastic erosion has occurred, making it possible to see Golden Eagle, Bonelli's Eagle (common), Peregrine Falcon, Alpine Swift, Chough, Raven, Crag Martin, Red-rumped Swallow and particularly Black Wheatear and Blue Rock Thrush, all of which are relatively common, at virtually any altitude. In the Sierra de Cartagena you may also see Trumpeter Finch, a new colonizer.

The only flat areas of any significance are the Campo de Cartagena, a coastal plain, and the area around Yecla, a prolongation of the Meseta. The valleys and depressions lying between the ranges of hills are small and broken up by numerous river gorges and dry river beds. While any land which can be irrigated has been irrigated, unirrigated land has increasingly been taken over by almond groves, since cereal growing in semi-desert areas proved unrewarding. This is perhaps why it is no longer easy to find places such as Yecla (MU.1), Campo de Caravaca (MU.2), El Cagitán (MU.4), La Alcanara (MU.6) and the steppe at Catavientos beside the Mar Menor (MU.8), where typical steppe-dwelling species are well represented (Montagu's Harrier, Little Bustard, Stone Curlew, Black-bellied Sandgrouse, Calandra Lark, Short-toed Lark, Lesser Short-toed Lark...). These sites each have their own individual characteristics, from the high Manchegan plateau of Yecla, predominated by grain crops and vines, to the salt marshes of El Guadalentín or Sangonera, taken up by seablite (*Suaeda* spp.) and other halophytic plants.

Typical dry-farming areas feature a series of gently rolling hillsides and terracing taken up by almond trees. The whole is broken up by ravines and dry river beds of various sizes. Earth screes provide nesting sites for Kestrel, Stock Dove, Bee-eater, Roller, Little Owl, Black Wheatear and Rock Sparrow, while the valley bottoms, taken up by oleander (*Nerium oleander*), tamarisk (*Tamarix* spp.), reeds (*Phragmites australis*) and occasionally palm trees, are the site of Turtle Dove, Nightingale, Melodious Warbler, Olivaceous Warbler and Sardinian Warbler. Fields and areas of scrubland on the hillsides frequently shelter Red-legged Partridge, Great Spotted Cuckoo, Scops Owl, Hoopoe, Thekla Lark (abundant), Rufous Bush Robin, Black-eared Wheatear, Dartford Warbler, Spectacled Warbler, Fan-tailed Warbler, Great Grey Shrike, Woodchat Shrike, Rock Bunting and Corn Bunting, to mention just a few.

The need for water for irrigation and the necessity of combatting the consequences of frequent and devastating flash floods have led to the construction of a series of artificial lakes. Reservoirs important from the ornithological point of view include Argos (MU.3) and Alfonso XIII or Quípar (MU.4). In conjunction with many other smaller pools, these provide a site for nesting water birds such as Little Grebe, Great Crested Grebe, Mallard, Water Rail, Moorhen, Coot, Black-winged Stilt, Reed Warbler and Great Reed Warbler. Of still greater interest is the coastal wetland area of the renowned Mar Menor and the salt pans surrounding it. The first (MU.8) is a huge hypersaline lagoon linked to the Mediterranean. The large number of fish present are enjoyed by wintering Black-necked Grebe, Cormorant and Red-breasted Merganser. The salt pans (San Pedro del Pinatar, Marchamalo, Rasall...; MU.7 and MU.8), although small and nowhere near as interesting as those of La Mata-Torrevieja (VA.16) and Santa Pola (VA.14), nonetheless allow for sightings of Little Egret, Greater Flamingo, Shelduck, Black-winged Stilt, Avocet, Kentish Plover, Slender-billed Gull, Audouin's Gull, Little Tern, Common Tern, Lesser Short-toed Lark, Yellow Wagtail and, during the migration periods, a wide range of waders and gulls. Close to the Mar Menor is Cabo de Palos, a place where you can watch sea birds such as Cory's Shearwater, Gannet, Sandwich Tern and Razorbill.

MU.1 YECLA

A steppe area largely given over to cereal crops.

Main species

Residents: Little Bustard, Stone Curlew, Black-bellied Sandgrouse, Calandra Lark, Lesser Short-toed Lark, Crested Lark, Thekla Lark.

Summer visitors: Short-toed Lark, Black-eared Wheatear.

On passage: Great Bustard.

Access

From Murcia, take the N-340 towards Alicante and 8 km after leaving Murcia turn onto the C-3223 for Yecla, 83 km from Murcia. From Yecla continue towards Almansa (province of Albacete), and after about 10 km you will reach the area in question.

Description

This area measures about 2,500 ha and is largely taken up by cereal crops and vineyards. In some places there are areas of pine woodland and non-irrigated tree plantations. The whole area is surrounded by extensive areas of esparto grass.

Recommended routes

There is one route for this area. It starts 10 km along the road from Yecla to Almansa, where you leave your car and walk along the track leading westwards to the hamlet known as La Teja. Return by a parallel track leading you back to the road. En route you will have sightings of Black-bellied Sandgrouse, Little Bustard, Short-toed Lark, Lesser Short-toed Lark (in the esparto grass), Black-eared Wheatear, Calandra Lark,

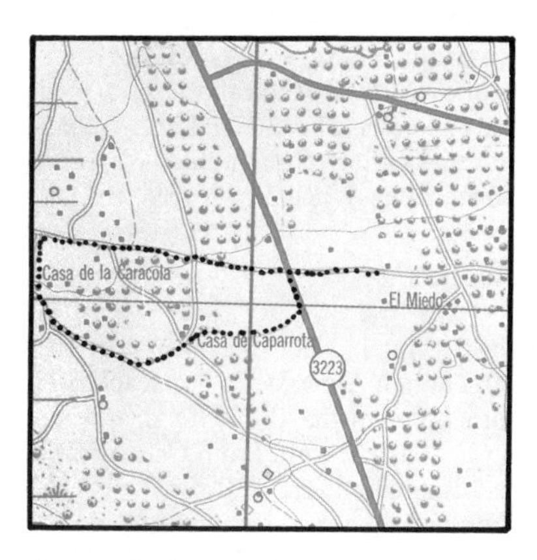

Stone Curlew and, in winter, Great Bustard.

Accommodation

Accommodation is available in Yecla, although it is quite limited.

Comments

The hot summers and harsh winters typical of the area may affect the comfort of your visit. In any case, the best time of year to visit this area is from November to January.

José Francisco Calvo Sendín, Miguel Angel Esteve Selma, Vicente Hernández Gil and Francisco Robledano Aymerich

MU.2 CARAVACA AND LA PUEBLA

Steppe area.

Main species

Residents: Little Bustard, Black-bellied Sandgrouse, Calandra Lark, Thekla Lark, Dartford Warbler, Black Wheatear, Chough, Rock Sparrow.

Summer visitors: Lesser Kestrel, Stone Curlew, Bee-eater, Short-toed Lark, Lesser Short-toed Lark, Subalpine Warbler, Spectacled Warbler, Black-eared Wheatear, Wheatear.

Access

From Murcia, take the N-340 in the direction of Almería and at Alcantarilla turn off onto the C-415 for Caravaca de la Cruz (62 km). From Caravaca de la Cruz, take the C-330 for Puebla de Don Fadrique, 58 km away, and Huéscar, 24 km from Puebla de Don Fadrique. Both of these villages lie in the province of Granada. From any point along this road, it is possible to reach the area via one of the many tracks, few of which are surfaced or marked; it is therefore a good idea only to use the routes described below.

Another way of reaching Caravaca de la Cruz is along the N-301 (Albacete-Murcia); turn off at Venta del Olivo onto the C-3314 going to Cehegín and Caravaca (46 km).

Description

The campos de Caravaca and La Puebla are sedimentary river basins, largely endorreic, located at an average height of 900-1,000 m. They extend for some 200 km^2 and the rolling land is only interrupted by the occasional gully and area of high ground. The depressions are used for growing cereal crops while the hillsides and marginal areas have been taken over by esparto grass and scrubland consisting of thyme (*Thymus* spp.), rosemary (*Rosmarinus officialis*) and broom (*Genista* spp.).

The ploughing which has occurred in order to create new fields and plantations, has caused natural steppe vegetation to decline dramatically.

Recommended routes

Route A consists mainly of a walk starting at the 93.4 km marker post on the C-330, where you turn left onto the road signed for El Moralejo. From the outset you can see large expanses of cereal fields where, in spring, you may be lucky enough to see the occasional group of Little Bustard. About 2 km after the junction, you will see to your left hillsides covered with esparto grassland and intersected by small river courses where you may see Bee-eater, Black Wheatear, Dartford Warbler and Subalpine Warbler. Some of the rush beds are the sites of substantial roosts of Rock Sparrow and Corn Bunting.

Where the road crosses the Junquera gully, leave your car and start walking across country to the Loma de las Pocicas, the highest hill in the area. Throughout the route, which runs between cereal crops, fallow land and steppe, you may have sightings of Calandra Lark, Skylark, Stone Curlew, Thekla Lark, Short-toed Lark and Wheatear. You will also witness the devastating consequences of the cultivation of some North African fodder shrubs such as orache (*Atriplex numularia*) which take up the area once occupied by esparto grassland. From this point, continue northwards

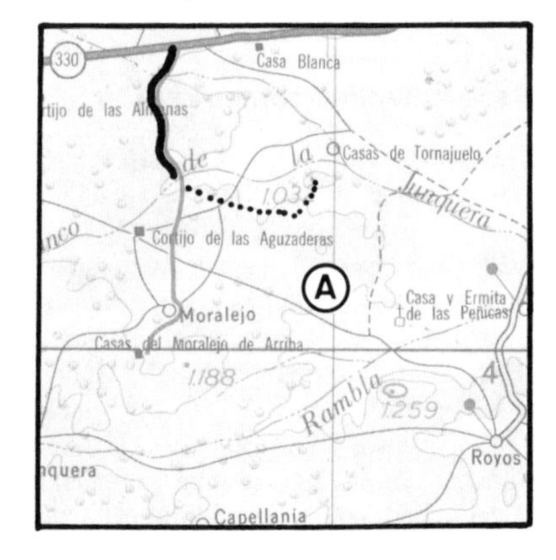

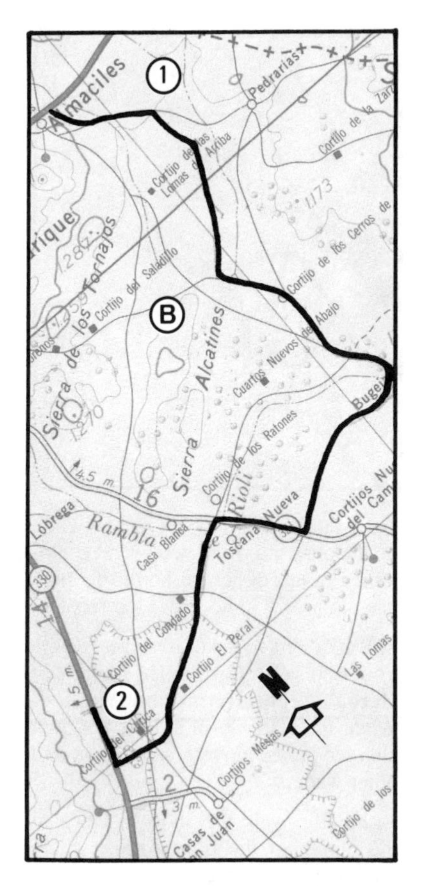

to see Spectacled Warbler, Lesser Short-toed Lark, Black-eared Wheatear and, although not present in large numbers, Black-bellied Sandgrouse.

Route B consists of a car journey some 18 km long running through the Campo of La Puebla. The route starts at the 111 km marker post on the C-330, along a track which leads off to the left from the Almaciles bridge (1). Continue until you reach the farm of El Espino and the hamlet of Bugejar, where you will join the C-321 to Puebla de Don Fadrique. You can continue for some distance along the tracks on the far side of this road running towards Cerro del Curica (2), a nearby hillside. Throughout the route, make stops at will to watch birds inhabiting the grain fields (larks, wheatears, etc.), or alternatively go for a short walk in the surrounding hills (warblers, Black-eared Wheatear, Thekla Lark, etc.). It is worth checking the abandoned farms, since they provide breeding grounds for Lesser Kestrel, Spotless Starling, Black Wheatear, Rock Sparrow and even Chough.

Accommodation

Since there is little tourism in the area, the only places where you will find hostels are Caravaca, Puebla de Don Fadrique or Huéscar. If you require a meal, Bar-Restaurante El Moral, next to the petrol station in the village of El Moral, is recommended.

Comments

The best time of year for visiting the area is spring, and it is worthwhile planning your route so as to avoid the middle of the day. It is also advisable to take a water supply, since springs are few and far between.

It is worth visiting the hamlet of Bugejar, which is very typical of this semi-arid area.

Juan de Dios Morenilla Carrascal

MU

■ MU.3 ARGOS RESERVOIR

Reservoir.

Main species

Residents: Great Crested Grebe, Little Grebe, Grey Heron, Mallard, Water Rail, Moorhen, Black Wheatear, Cetti's Warbler, Sardinian Warbler, Cirl Bunting.

Summer visitors: Night Heron, Purple Heron, Short-toed Eagle, Booted Eagle, Great Spotted Cuckoo, Bee-eater, Wryneck, Red-rumped Swallow, Fan-tailed Warbler, Melodious Warbler, Olivaceous Warbler.

Winter visitors: Shoveler, Merlin, Ringed Plover, Green Sandpiper, Water Pipit, Rock Bunting.

Access

From Murcia, take the N-301 to Venta del Olivo (56 km). At Venta del Olivo, turn left onto the C-3314 for Cehegín and Caravaca de la Cruz. After 30 km you will see the reservoir to your left. The reservoir can be reached by a signed minor road.

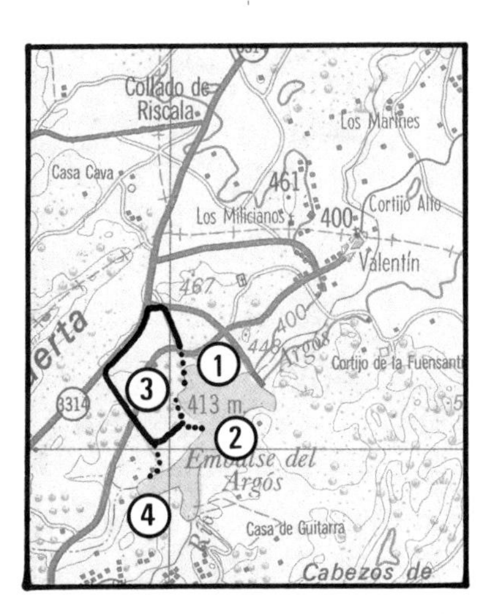

Description

The Argos reservoir, built in 1974, has thick stands of tamarisk on its shores, particularly on the western shore and the various inlets. The other shore, mostly mountainous and steep, is occupied by pine plantations.

Recommended routes

For this area there is one route taking you along the minor road to Canara, which starts near the dam and skirts the reservoir. From this road, you can approach the reservoir at the following points:

1) After a little over 1 km, turn left onto a dirt track leading down to the shore. From here you can reach a small stony point from where, among other species, you will be able to see Grey Heron, Coot and Moorhen.

2) Return to the road and drive for another 1.5 km until you come across another dirt track. This will take you to a small hillock with a stand of pines lying on the shore, where you can leave your car. Climb up to the area of high ground, featuring the ruins of a house, to command a view of the entire reservoir. During the migration periods you may see Cormorant, Little Egret, Little Tern, Pochard and even Osprey, while on the opposite shore you will see wintering groups of herons, some of which use the nearby pine trees as a roost.

3) Walk down to the nearest inlet where you may see Purple Heron, Grey Heron, Night Heron and Mallard. When the water level is low, you will also see pipits, plovers, sandpipers and other waders.

4) Finally, walk the short distance to the mouth of the river Argos, where you may see Water Rail, Moorhen, Cetti's Warbler, Sardinian Warbler, Fan-tailed Warbler, Melodious Warbler, Olivaceous Warbler and Wryneck.

Accommodation

There are pensions and hostels in the villages of Cehegín, Calasparra and Caravaca de la Cruz. There is a bar-restaurant at the foot of the dam itself, although you would be better advised to go to Valentín. There are bars in the village square which provide good food.

Comments

The best time of year for visiting the reservoir is from mid-spring to October.

Juan de Dios Morenilla Carrascal

MU.4 ALFONSO XIII RESERVOIR AND PLAINS AROUND EL CAGITÁN

A reservoir, the most important inland wetland area in the province of Murcia. El Cagitán is an area taken up by dry-farming.

Main species

Residents: Grey Heron, Red-crested Pochard, Golden Eagle, Bonelli's Eagle, Peregrine Falcon, Little Bustard, Stone Curlew, Common Sandpiper, Black-bellied Sandgrouse, Eagle Owl, Kingfisher, Calandra Lark, Thekla Lark, Crag Martin, Black Wheatear, Blue Rock Thrush, Cetti's Warbler, Fan-tailed Warbler, Dartford Warbler, Sardinian Warbler, Chough, Rock Sparrow, Cirl Bunting, Rock Bunting.

Summer visitors: Montagu's Harrier, Black-winged Stilt, Great Spotted Cuckoo, Red-necked Nightjar, Pallid Swift, Alpine Swift, Bee-eater, Roller, Short-toed lark, Red-rumped Swallow, Black-eared Wheatear, Olivaceous Warbler, Melodious Warbler, Spectacled Warbler, Subalpine Warbler, Woodchat Shrike.

Winter visitors: ducks, Hen Harrier, Merlin, Snipe, Green Sandpiper, Penduline Tit.

On passage: herons, Marsh Harrier, Osprey, waders.

Access

From Murcia, take the N-301 to Venta del Olivo (56 km), where you join the C-3314 for Calasparra (24 km). 6.3 km before Calasparra, on the minor road to Bullas and Cieza, you will find a turn to the left for the Alfonso XIII dam (also known as Quípar dam). Continue along this road for some 15 km until you reach the C-330 which, running towards Cieza, skirts around to the east of the El Cagitán plains. All of the junctions and turnings are signposted.

Description

The Alfonso XIII reservoir is brackish. It is fed by the waters of the river Quípar and various other rivers which flow into one end, the site of a dense stand of tamarisk. The shores abound in grasslands and, to a lesser extent, rush beds and small patches of reeds.

At the point where the river Quípar leaves the reservoir it has carved a gorge in the limestone rock. Where the Quípar converges with the river Segura, this gorge merges with a second of similar characteristics (Cañón de Almadenes). The inaccessibility of the area, lying between the ranges of El Molino and La Palera, has allowed for the conservation of one of the best examples of riverside woodland in Murcia. Also worth mentioning is the presence of a small population of Spanish ibex.

The area of El Cagitán is a mosaic of dry-farming and other agricultural areas. It is largely taken up by cereal crops, fallow and uncultivated land.

Recommended routes

Route A takes you along the minor road to the dam. From this road, numerous dirt tracks lead off down to the shores of the reservoir. These tracks also continue onto higher ground, and it is worth climbing the slopes to command a view of the area of tamarisk at the end of the reservoir as well as the opcn water. In the tamarisks it is possible to hear Water Rail, Baillon's Crake and Cetti's Warbler. In winter the tamarisks provide a roost for several thousands of chaffin-

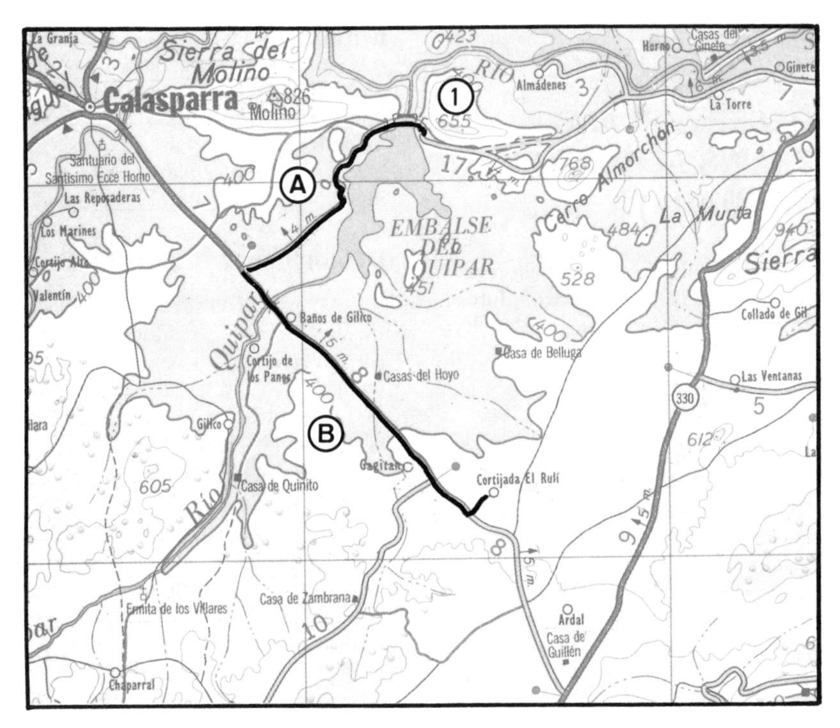

ches, pipits, Corn Bunting, starlings and various corvids. On the open water and on the clear areas of shore you will have sightings of herons, ducks, Great Crested Grebe, Little Grebe, Coot, Moorhen, Black-winged Stilt and other waders. During the autumn migration it is not rare to see Osprey and Marsh Harrier.

The hillsides surrounding the reservoir are the site of Hoopoe, Bee-eater, Roller, Great Spotted Cuckoo, Thekla Lark, Black-eared Wheatear and Woodchat Shrike.

From the dam itself (1) you can command a view of the beginning of the Quípar gorge, although a better general impression of both gorge and reservoir can be had from a vantage point located high on the left side of the gorge, reached via a flight of steps running up from the dam itself. Both dam and lookout point are perfect places for watching birds of prey and other cliff-dwelling species: Golden Eagle, Bonelli's Eagle, Peregrine Falcon, Alpine Swift, Chough, Black Wheatear, Blue Rock Thrush, etc.

Route B takes you to the plains of El Cagitán. Drive along the road from Calasparra to Mula until reaching the junction with the C-330. The whole area is criss-crossed by hundreds of farm tracks, most of which are in dreadful condition. However, there is a surfaced service road which runs across part of the plains. This road, starting about 11 km after the turn for the reservoir and 4 km after the turn onto the regional road, runs through fallow land, grain fields, uncultivated land and stubble fields where you may have sightings of Short-toed Lark, Calandra Lark, Montagu's Harrier, Stone Curlew, Black-eared Wheatear, Spectacled Warbler, Fan-tailed Warbler and, with luck, Black-bellied Sandgrouse and Little Bustard. In winter, Hen Harrier and Merlin are also present.

Accommodation

You can eat and sleep at the Fonda Mari Viti and at La Posada, both of which are in the Plaza del Convento in the village of Calasparra. Outside Mula, on the C-415, is the Venta El Niño de Mula, a well-known establishment with reasonable prices.

Comments

If you are going to visit the reservoir it is worth taking a telescope, since most of the birds congregate on the right shore, which is difficult to reach and therefore not recommended.

During the rainy season, it is better not to drive along unsurfaced roads since they become complete quagmires.

Angel Guardiola Gómez,
Miguel Angel Sánchez Sánchez
and María Pilar Fernández Martín

MU.5 ESPUÑA RANGE

A mountain massif with abundant pine woodland.

Main species

Residents: Goshawk, Sparrowhawk, Buzzard, Golden Eagle, Bonelli's Eagle, Peregrine Falcon, Tawny Owl, Dupont's Lark, Lesser Short-toed Lark, Thekla Lark, Woodlark, Crag Martin, Black Wheatear, Blue Rock Thrush, Dartford Warbler, Sardinian Warbler, Spectacled Warbler, Chough, Crossbill.

Summer visitors: Short-toed Eagle, Booted Eagle, Great Spotted Cuckoo, Bee-eater, Red-rumped Swallow, Subalpine Warbler, Orphean Warbler, Bonelli's Warbler.

On passage: Alpine Accentor, Ring Ouzel.

Access

From Murcia, take the N-340 to Alhama de Murcia (32 km) or Totana (43 km). From these villages, winding roads take you to the heart of the range.

Description

Sierra Espuña is a massif located in the middle of Murcia. It covers over 25,000 ha. Its highest peak is Morrón de Espuña (1,579 m). Generally speaking, cliffs and river gorges abound. Vegetation consists mainly of pine woodland, although there are also areas of scrubby holm oak, scrubland and small fields.

Part of the area (10,000 ha) has been declared a Natural Park.

Recommended routes

Route A: Take the minor road out of Totana for Aledo and Zarzadilla. The first point (1) is El Llano de las Cabras, an extensive area of esparto grassland which you can walk or drive around along badly surfaced tracks. Here you may have sightings of Dupont's Lark, Lesser Short-toed Lark, Spectacled Warbler and Great Spotted Cuckoo. Returning to the road, turn right and make for El Purgatorio (2). From this point you can climb up El Pinillo (3) on foot, passing below the summits of Pedro López and Espuña. Come back via La Carrasca (4) to reach your departure point. En route you may see Golden Eagle, Goshawk, Sparrowhawk, Booted Eagle, Short-toed Eagle, Crossbill, etc.

Route B starts at La Perdiz, a campsite which can be reached from Alhama de Murcia via the C-3315, turning off after 2 km for the forestry house of Huerta Espuña and from there to La Perdiz. From this point (5), you can climb the

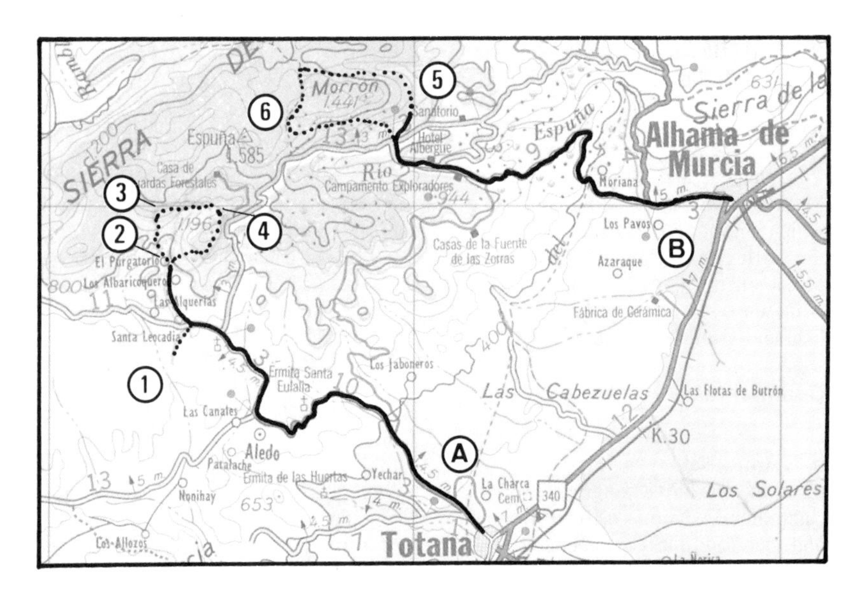

course of the river Leyva to Fuente Blanca and Pozos de la Nieve (6). Return across the hillside known as Morrón Chico to your departure point (3 hours). In addition to numerous forest-dwelling species, you may also see Black Wheatear, Chough, Peregrine Falcon and Blue Rock Thrush.

Accommodation

In the area are 7 campsites, several mountain refuges and a youth hostel accommodating up to 200 people. Permits for using the refuges or the hostel can be obtained from: Agencia para el Medio Ambiente y la Naturaleza (Av. Teniente Flomesta s/n, 30001 Murcia; telephone: 968-216141). Accommodation is available in nearby villages such as Aledo and Mula, although it is advisable to go Totana or Alhama de Murcia, where the range of accommodation available is greater.

Comments

Although Sierra Espuña has been declared a Natural Park, there is as yet no information centre. However, you can ask for some information on the area at the Huerta Espuña house or any of the bars in the village.

The best time of year for visiting the area is from April to June, although you should bear in mind that at weekends a lot of people come to the area.

José Francisco Calvo Sendín,
Miguel Angel Esteve Selma,
Vicente Hernández Gil
and Francisco Robledano Aymerich

■ MU.6 LA ALCANARA (SALT MARSHES ON THE RIVER GUADALENTÍN)

Saline steppe area with cereal crops.

Main species

Residents: Stone Curlew, Black-bellied Sandgrouse, Calandra Lark, Lesser Short-toed Lark, Black Wheatear, Spectacled Warbler, Great Grey Shrike, Rock Sparrow.

Summer visitors: Marsh Harrier, Montagu's Harrier, Quail, Great Spotted Cuckoo, Bee-eater, Roller, Short-toed Lark, Black-eared Wheatear.

Access

From Murcia, take the N-340 towards Almería and stop at Alhama de Murcia (32 km) and Totana (11 km from Alhama de Murcia).

It is possible to reach the area from the minor road linking Murcia to Mazarrón, where you stop at the petrol station located at the 32 km marker post.

Description

An inland salt marsh stretching out for some 2,500 ha on both banks of the river Guadalentín. The salt marshes contain cereal crops and large isolated stands of tamarisks and palm trees.

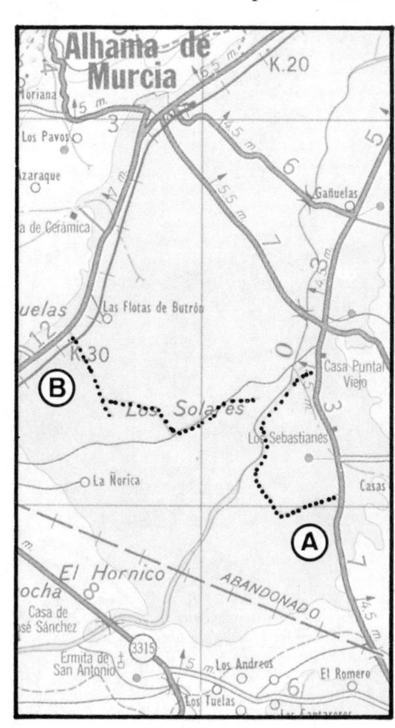

Recommended routes

Route A lasts for 1½ hours and leaves from the petrol station mentioned above (road from Murcia to Mazarrón). From here, take one of the tracks leading off across the salt marshes and fields. You can either retrace your steps to return or walk in a circle, since the extensive network of tracks enables you to improvise at will. En route, you may have sightings of Black-bellied Sandgrouse, Stone Curlew, Calandra Lark, Lesser Short-toed Lark, Short-toed Lark, Spectacled Warbler, Montagu's Harrier, etc.

Route B starts at the 297 km marker post on the N-340 between Alhama de Murcia and Totana. From here, a dirt track leads off to the left, passing close to a stand of palm trees (Roller and Great Spotted Cuckoo may be present in summer) and bringing you to the salt marshes, where a general route will provide sightings of the same species as those mentioned for route A, although in smaller numbers.

The proximity of the course of the river Guadalentín, running between earth screes, makes it worthwhile approaching the river to see Bee-eater, Rock Sparrow, Roller, Black Wheatear, Green Sandpiper, etc.

Accommodation

There is plenty of accommodation available in Alhama de Murcia.

MU

Comments

It is best to visit this area in the early morning; you should remember that temperatures are extremely high at noon over the summer months. It is also worth pointing out that the dirt tracks become virtually impassable after heavy rain.

José Francisco Calvo Sendín,
Miguel Angel Esteve Selma,
Vicente Hernández Gil
and Francisco Robledano Aymerich

MU.7 CARTAGENA RANGE

Coastal range of hills.

Main species

Residents: Bonelli's Eagle, Peregrine Falcon, Stone Curlew, Kentish Plover, Eagle Owl, Lesser Short-toed Lark, Black Wheatear, Blue Rock Thrush, Fan-tailed Warbler, Sardinian Warbler, Long-tailed Tit, Great Grey Shrike, Raven, Rock Sparrow, Trumpeter Finch.

Summer visitors: Shelduck, Black-winged Stilt, Avocet, Little Tern, Turtle Dove, Pallid Swift, Alpine Swift, Bee-eater, Yellow Wagtail, Black-eared Wheatear, Spotted Flycatcher, Golden Oriole, Woodchat Shrike.

Winter visitors: Gannet, Little Egret, Ringed Plover, Little Stint, Dunlin, Snipe, Redshank, Greenshank, Sandwich Tern, Razorbill, Crag Martin, Dartford Warbler, Rock Bunting.

On passage: Cory's Shearwater, Audouin's Gull, Black Tern, passerines.

Access

A good base for visiting this area is Cartagena, on the N-301.

Description

A coastal range of hills scraping a height of about 600 m. The range is divided into small sections running parallel to the coastline, which has many cliffs. There is a dramatic contrast between the northern side of the range, which is gently rolling, and the southern side, which is steep.

Recommended routes

To reach **route A**, near Calblanque, take the road for La Manga del Mar Menor and 2 km after the village of Los Belones, turn onto a surfaced road signed for some car parks (*aparcamientos*), from which the Salinas del Rasall and the beaches can be reached. At the salt pans (1), you will have sightings of Greater Flamingo, Shelduck, Avocet, Black-winged Stilt, terns, etc. From here the fossil dunes and sand flats (2) can be visited, where you will see many larks and finches.

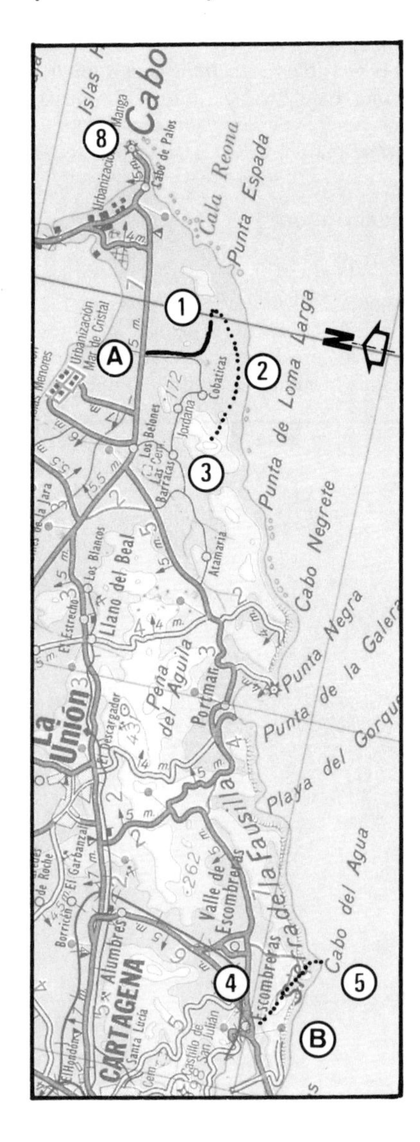

Subsequently climb up to the Cabezo de la Fuente (3), which makes for an excellent vantage point overlooking the pine woods and rock faces.

Route B takes you to the Sierra de Escombreras. Start at the Escombreras pass, some 15 km from Cartagena (take the N-332 to Alumbres and then a minor road). From the pass (4), a dirt track takes you up to a ruined chapel where you can leave your car. Continue on foot along any of the paths until you reach the southern slopes of the range; by walking eastwards you will come to the Cabo de Agua (5), a walk of some 3 hours. En route you will have sightings of Peregrine Falcon, Bonelli's Eagle, Blue Rock Thrush, Raven, Trumpeter Finch, etc.

Route C: Peñas Blancas. From Cartagena, take the N-332 towards Mazarrón and, at Casas de Tallante (15 km), turn left for Rincón de Tallante. From here a dirt track runs all the way along the El Cañar riverbed or *rambla*. From the track, you can walk to the base of Peñas Blancas, limestone cliffs (6), where you may see Bonelli's Eagle, Alpine Swift, Crag Martin, Chough, Rock Sparrow, etc. Work your way down the *rambla* until you reach a spring (7), where you should have sightings of Turtle Dove, Hoopoe, Bee-eater, Nightingale, Black-eared Wheatear, Firecrest, Golden Oriole, etc.

Your visit can be rounded off by going to the Cabo de Palos (8), at the end of the N-332. It is easy to reach the lighthouse, where there is car parking space. From the lighthouse, look out to sea for sightings of Gannet, Razorbill, shearwaters and gulls.

Accommodation

Tourism in the area is highly developed, giving rise to a wide range of hotel accommodation. We recommend Hostal Manolo and Hotel Alfonso XIII in Cartagena, as well as the Villas Caravaning campsite on the road running from Cartagena to La Manga. This campsite is close to some of the recommended routes.

Juan Luis Castanedo García and
Antonio Jesús Hernández Navarro

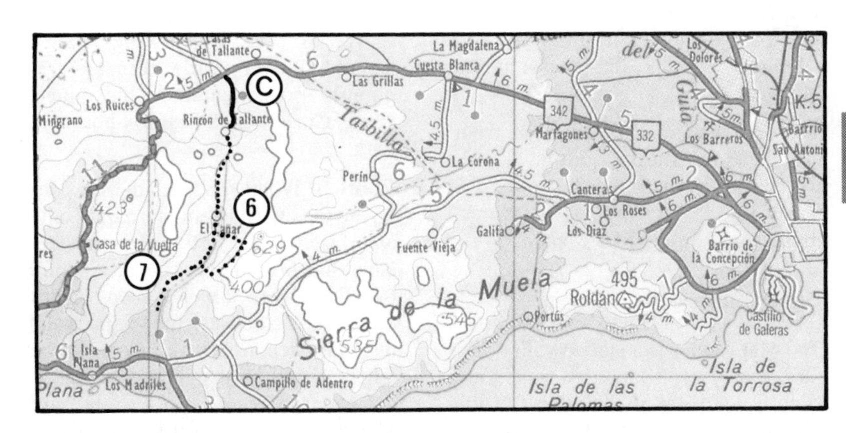

MU.8 MAR MENOR

A coastal lagoon; the largest in Spain and one of the biggest in the Mediterranean.

Main species

Residents: Little Egret, Shelduck, Avocet, Stone Curlew, Kentish Plover, Calandra Lark, Lesser Short-toed Lark, Black Wheatear.

Summer visitors: Black-winged Stilt, Little Tern, Common Tern, Quail, Short-toed Lark, Spectacled Warbler.

Winter visitors: Black-necked Grebe, Cormorant, Grey Heron, Greater Flamingo, Red-breasted Merganser, Audouin's Gull, waders.

Access

Take the N-301 out of Murcia. There are two options: turn off at La Venta de la Virgen onto the C-3319 for San Javier (45 km); or alternatively when you reach El Albujón turn onto the minor road which, after El Algar, will take you to Cabo de Palos and La Manga.

The area can also be reached from Cartagena or Alicante via the N-332, which runs through San Pedro del Pinatar, San Javier and Los Alcázares, towns lying on the Mar Menor.

Description

The Mar Menor is a lagoon with a surface area of 135 km^2. Its waters are slightly more saline than those of the Mediterranean. Over half of its perimeter has been built up and the rest contains salt pans, sand flats, coastal steppe, areas of dry-farming and irrigated areas. There are several islands in the lagoon.

The salt pans at San Pedro del Pinatar (700 ha) have been designated a Protected Natural Area.

Recommended routes

Route A: From San Pedro del Pinatar (1), take the road leading to the port and the salt pans, which is signed as such (*puerto* and *salinas*). The road crosses the salt pans and although you can stop on either side of the road, you are not allowed to walk along the banks separating the pans. When you reach the pine wood, you will find an iron gate (2); leave your car here and walk along a footpath leading off to the left between the pans and the dunes until you reach El Mojón (3), an old fishing village which has now been built up. Cross the fence surrounding the protected area and continue to the left along a footpath taking you through a reedbed, now badly spoiled, back to the road. The route takes a couple of hours and will give sightings of Greater Flamingo (year round except in spring), Black-necked Grebe, Cormorant, Shelduck and the occasional Audouin's Gull. During the breeding season Avocet, Black-winged Stilt, Kentish Plover, Little Tern are frequently present and, in the dunes, Stone Curlew and Lesser Short-toed Lark.

Route B: When you reach the salt pans on the road to El Puerto, turn right onto a surfaced track skirting their western edge and bringing you to a windmill (4). From here turn left along a dirt track running between the salt pans and the Mar Menor. On the lagoon to the left, you will have sightings of Black-necked Grebe, Greater Flamingo, Slender-billed Gull, Little Tern, Common Tern, Avocet, Shelduck and Kentish Plover. The dirt track comes to an end beside another windmill (5); leave your car here and continue on foot to Las Encañizadas (6), a good site

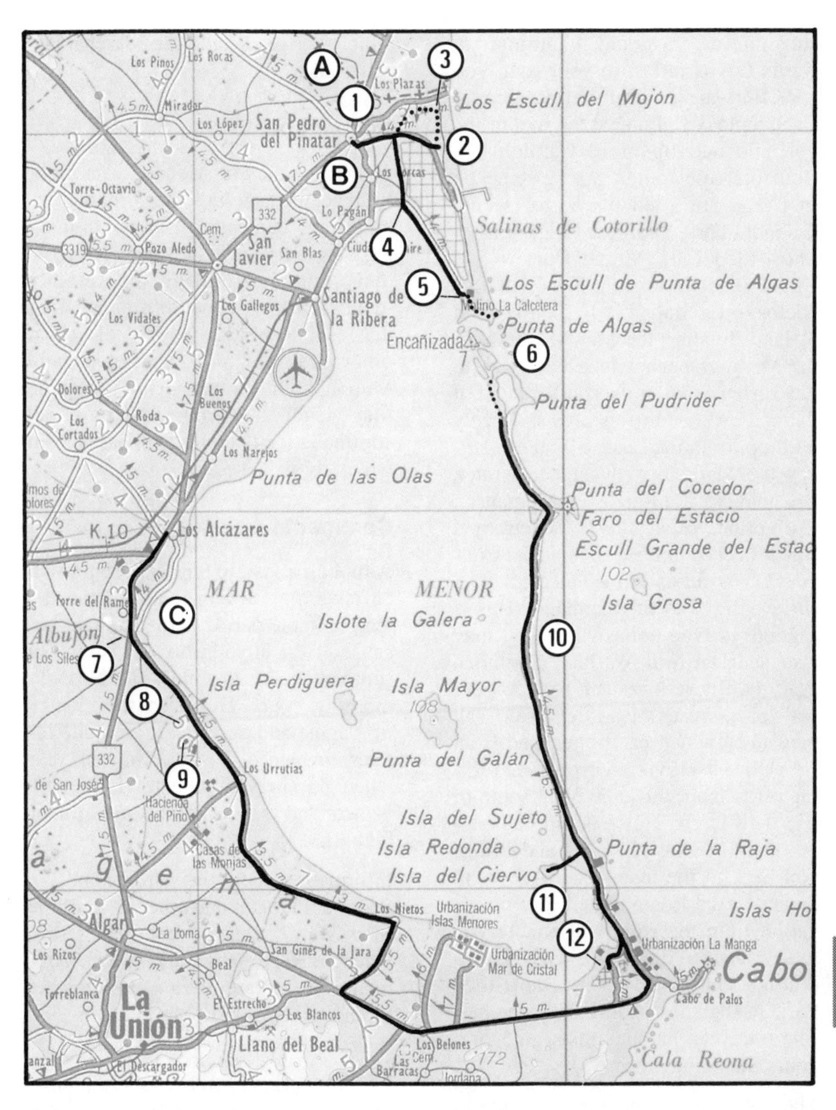

for watching waders and herons in winter and gulls and waders in summer. On the Mar Menor itself you will see wintering Red-breasted Merganser. The route can be extended to the beach at La Llana or Punta de Algas, and can be undertaken in a couple of hours.

Route C: The starting point for this route is Los Alcázares, where you take the N-332 towards El Algar; after 2.5 km, next to a campsite, you will find a left turn for Los Urrutias and Los Nietos. Stop at the crossroads to explore the mouth of the Albujón riverbed (7), which is usually flooded in spring, giving rise to sightings of Black-winged Stilt, Little Ringed Plover and other waders, all of which can also be seen in the numerous irrigation ponds on the

MU

surrounding farmland. Continue towards Los Urrutias; to your right you will find the coastal steppe area of Cataviento (8), lying at the foot of the volcanic outcrop of El Carmolí (9). Both of these routes can be done on foot, and are good places for seeing Calandra Lark, Short-toed Lark, Lesser Short-toed Lark, Stone Curlew and Quail. The route continues via Los Nietos to La Manga (10), the long spit of land dividing the Mar Menor from the Mediterranean. Make your way to Las Encañizadas at the southern end of the spit. Although this area is largely built up, from the sandbar you can survey the Mar Menor where, in winter, you may see Red-breasted Merganser, Cormorant, Great Crested Grebe and Black-necked Grebe. The Isla del Ciervo (11) is an island connected by a surfaced road to the mainland. This is a good vantage point where you may also see Dartford Warbler, Sardinian Warbler, Black Wheatear, etc. On your way back, visit the Marchamalo salt pans (12), which can be reached from La Manga itself via a narrow road turning off to the right some 3 km south of Isla del Ciervo. This road, in bad condition, skirts the salt pans and brings you back to the main road. Access to the salt pans is prohibited, but observation from the edge will enable you to see Greater Flamingo, waders, Audouin's Gull and Lesser Short-toed Lark in the surrounding salt marshes. The route can be undertaken in 5 or 6 hours including stops.

The visit can be extended by going to Cabo de Palos (see above, MU.7) which is right beside the Marchamalo salt pans.

Accommodation

Tourism in the Mar Menor area is highly developed, giving rise to numerous hotels and campsites. It is worth making reservations in advance to avoid disappointment during the summer months. It is also worth remembering that establishments may be closed at other times of year. Cartagena and Murcia, both less than an hour from the Mar Menor, also provide plenty of accommodation and are good bases from which to visit the site.

Comments

Although a visit to the Mar Menor will be rewarding at any time of year, the least suitable period is the summer because of the huge influx of visitors. In summer, make the most of the early morning hours. However, the months of August and September are quite interesting, since it is the time of year when numbers of Greater Flamingo, waders and other migrants are at their highest.

Information about the salt pans of San Pedro del Pinatar and other areas of the Mar Menor can be obtained from: Agencia Regional para el Medio Ambiente y la Naturaleza (Av. Teniente Flomesta s/n, 30001 Murcia).

José Francisco Calvo Sendín,
Miguel Angel Esteve Selma,
Vicente Hernández Gil
and Francisco Robledano Aymerich

NAVARRA

White-backed Woodpecker
Dendrocopos leucotos

Navarra is probably the most varied province in Spain and, for birdwatchers, one of the most exciting. Despite the fact that the province does not actually have a coastline —it nonetheless nudges the coast at its far north-western corner— it includes all possible Iberian habitats. The transition from this north-western corner, a small area of typical Atlantic coastal farmland corresponding to the basins of the rivers Urumea and Bidasoa, to the placid banks of the river Ebro and the semi-desert region of Las Bardenas, represents a near-perfect north to south progression of climates and landscapes. As is also the case with the Basque country, birdlife responds immediately to these changes, making it possible to see many different species from varying biogeographical origins in a small area. In addition, the presence of high mountains and unspoiled woodland throughout the Pyrenees, the range marking the northern boundary of Navarra, and of steppes, lakes and areas of riverside woodland in the south, heavily influence the fact that the range of habitats —and therefore wildlife— in the area is very extensive.

The Pyrenees do not reach great heights in the west of the province, meaning that some alpine species are only present at specific locations in the Roncal valley in the far north-east of Navarra. Examples of this include Ptarmigan, Ring Ouzel, Wallcreeper and Snow Finch. However, lower altitudes make the mountains of Navarra into a major access point for the vast number of different species migrating into Spain in autumn and leaving again in the spring. The autumn migration is the most impressive, featuring large birds such as Black Stork, Osprey, Honey Buzzard, Short-toed Eagle, Booted Eagle, Red Kite, Montagu's Harrier, Greylag Goose and Crane. However, the main body of migrants consists of Woodpigeon and Stock Dove, both traditional targets for hunters, and many passerines including swallows, larks, pipits, wagtails, thrushes, starlings, and finches. Good sites for watching migratory movements are Urkiaga (NA.1), Echalar (near Vera de Bidasoa in the Baztán valley) and Lindux or Lindús (close to Roncesvalles and easily accessible from the Ibañeta pass).

Another attraction of the section of the Pyrenees falling within the province of Navarra is the woodland areas, which are relatively unspoiled and are home to species such as Honey Buzzard, Woodcock, Black Woodpecker, White-backed Woodpecker, Marsh Tit and Treecreeper. Beech predominates, with a fine area of beech woodland at Quinto Real (NA.1), although from Orbaiceta, near Burguete, you can visit the well-known Selva de Irati, a forest consisting of extensive areas of beech (*Fagus sylvatica*) and large numbers of silver fir (*Abies alba*). In the Roncal valley there are also extensive pine woods, the most interesting being the area of mountain pine (*Pinus uncinata*)

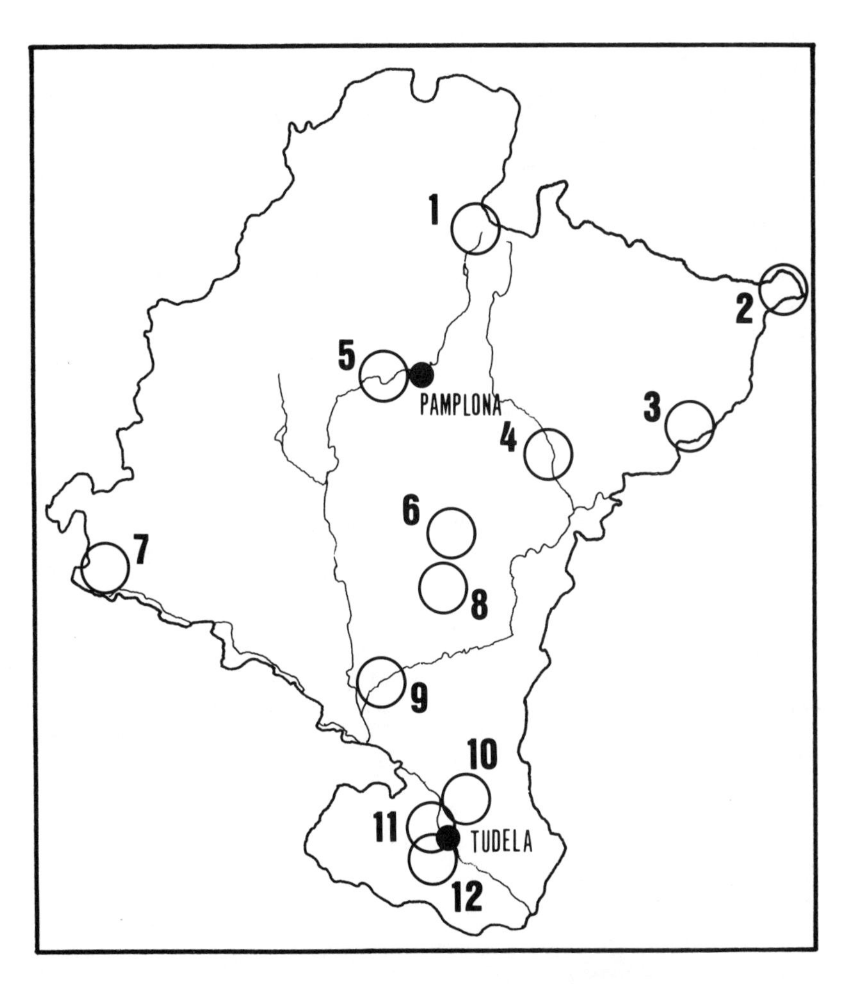

at Belagua-Larra (NA.2). From here you can climb up to the high mountain peaks (Pico de Anie, 2,507 m) with relative ease.

The foothills of the Pyrenees, particularly those lying in the east, provide the greatest range of habitats and of birdlife. Some locations have easily over 100 breeding species. These areas abound in cliffs and river gorges which are nesting sites for birds of prey such as Griffon Vulture (in vast numbers), Egyptian Vulture (very common), Bearded Vulture, Golden Eagle, Peregrine Falcon and Eagle Owl as well as other cliff-dwelling species such as Stock Dove, Alpine Swift, Crag Martin, Blue Rock Thrush, Chough, Raven and Rock Sparrow. Areas with these features include Peñas de Echauri (NA.5), very close to Pamplona, and the gorges or *foces* at Lumbier and Arbayún (NA.4), the latter being truly awe-inspiring.

Passing on to the Mediterranean region of Navarra, a trip to Monte del Conde (NA.6), not far from Tafalla, will bring you a rare example of mature holm oak

(*Quercus rotundifolia*) woodland and the fauna typically associated with this habitat. Of even greater ornithological interest are the treeless expanses of Las Bardenas Reales (NA.10), where birdlife typical of the steppes of the middle reaches of the Ebro valley is to be found, fully represented by Little Bustard, Stone Curlew, Pin-tailed Sandgrouse, Black-bellied Sandgrouse, Red-necked Nightjar, Dupont's Lark, Lesser Short-toed Lark, Black-eared Wheatear, Black Wheatear, Spectacled Warbler and many birds of prey, all in a magnificent but eroded landscape. In riverbeds with growths of tamarisk you may find Olivaceous Warbler, at the northernmost limit of its breeding range.

In marked contrast to Las Bardenas and the agricultural landscape generally found in southern Navarra, the wooded areas along the river banks provide refuge for many birds. Unfortunately there are very few woodland areas of this nature left today which are worth visiting. The best are those on the river Aragón near Caparroso (NA.9), the river Arga between Peralta and Funes, and the river Ebro near Mendavia, Azagra and above all Tudela (NA.11). In these places some of the species which can be seen include Night Heron, Purple Heron, Black Kite, Little Ringed Plover, Common Sandpiper, Scops Owl, Kingfisher, Wryneck, Great Spotted Woodpecker, Sand Martin, Cetti's Warbler, Great Reed Warbler, Long-tailed Tit, Penduline Tit and Golden Oriole. A characteristic feature of the Ebro valley as it runs through Navarra, and indeed throughout the entire length of the valley, are the reservoirs for irrigation such as those at Viana (NA.7), Pitillas (NA.8) and Lor and Pulguer (NA.12). These reservoirs provide nesting sites for new and interesting species living on or near water (Great Crested Grebe, Little Bittern, Little Egret, Red-crested Pochard, Marsh Harrier, Water Rail, Black-winged Stilt, Savi's Warbler, Reed Bunting...) and, during the winter and migration periods, a variety of ducks, waders and passerines on passage.

NA.1 QUINTO REAL AND COLLADO DE URQUIAGA (URKIAGA)

A mountain area with large expanses of forest.

Main species

Residents: Bearded Vulture, Woodcock, White-backed Woodpecker, Black Woodpecker, Water Pipit, Goldcrest, Marsh Tit, Treecreeper, Citril Finch.

Summer visitors: Honey Buzzard.

On passage: Black Stork, Honey Buzzard, Red Kite, Short-toed Eagle, Marsh Harrier, Montagu's Harrier, Osprey, Greylag Goose, Crane, Stock Dove, Woodpigeon, Rook.

Access

From Pamplona take the C-135 to Zubiri (15 km). As you leave Zubiri turn left onto a local road which skirts the Eugui reservoir and heads towards France via Alduides (Les Aldudes). After 16 km you will come to the Collado de Urkiaga, a mountain pass were you can leave your vehicle in a car park on the roadside.

Description

Quinto Real is a forestry area measuring some 6,000 ha, situated atop a gently rolling massif. Vegetation consists of extensive and mature beech woodland giving way on the high ground to pastures with heather and whin.

The area is a National Game Reserve.

Recommended routes

From the Urkiaga pass, set out westwards along a forestry road which will take you up through the beech woods to the plateau at the top. Just within the woods there is a shelter for hunters (1) and a line of butts for pigeon shooting. Continue along the ridge to the peak of Okoro (2), the turning-point for this walk. Retrace your steps to return to your vehicle. The whole of this range of peaks constitutes a wonderful place for watching the autumn migration; you may also have the occasional sighting of Water Pipit and Citril Finch on the pastures and the edges of the woodland.

About 15 m from the hunters' shelter a path branches off and leads south into the beech woods. When you reach a fork, bear left to return to the Urkiaga pass. A wide range of woodland birds can be seen on this last stretch including Honey Buzzard, Woodcock, White-backed Woodpecker, Black Woodpecker and Treecreeper.

Accommodation

Pamplona offers a wide range of accommodation. You can also stay in Eugui, where the Bar-Restaurante Txalot-Enea, next to the village *frontón* court (resembling an outdoor squash court), is highly recommended.

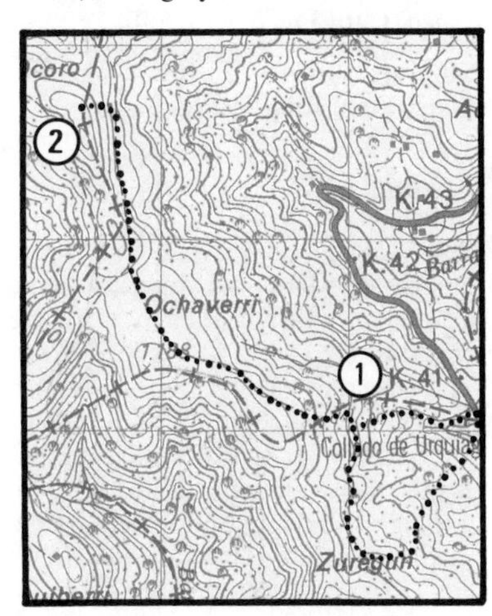

Comments

Quinto Real lies on a sensitive section of the border between Spain and France, so it is a good idea to inform the Guardia Civil stationed nearby that you are going to be in the area.

Alfredo Rueda Díez and
José Carlos Irurzun Santaquiteria

NA.2
LARRA – BELAGUA (RONCAL VALLEY)

A karstic mountain area with woodland consisting of mountain pine, beech and silver fir.

Main species

Residents: Bearded Vulture, Griffon Vulture, Sparrowhawk, Golden Eagle, Peregrine Falcon, Ptarmigan, Capercaillie, Grey Partridge, Woodcock, Tengmalm's Owl, Black Woodpecker, White-backed Woodpecker, Alpine Accentor, Goldcrest, Wallcreeper, Treecreeper, Alpine Chough, Snow Finch, Citril Finch, Crossbill.

Summer visitors: Egyptian Vulture, Water Pipit, Ring Ouzel.

Access

Travel along the N-240 running from Pamplona to Jaca until you reach Venta Carrica (province of Zaragoza), where you take the C-137 to Isaba (35 km). This road runs parallel to the river Esca and crosses the gorges of Sigüés, Burgui (see NA.3), Roncal and Urzainqui. By the petrol station in Isaba take the turning for Belagua and remain on the road until you reach Rincón de Belagua (12 km).

Description

The head of the Roncal valley can be considered as the westernmost edge of the high Pyrenees, therefore influencing the distribution of birds characteristic of the area. Larra has one of the deepest and most extensive karstic complexes in the whole of Europe. The resulting landforms make for extremely rough terrain, enabling the area to remain in its unspoiled state.

At Larra-Belagua two typical valley bottom habitats coexist in a small area; woodland consisting of beech and silver fir and subalpine pine forest, giving rise to a wide variety of birds.

There are three protected areas in the region; the Larra Nature Reserve and the Integral Reserves of Ukerdi and Aztaparreta.

Recommended routes

Route A starts at the 12 km marker post on the road running from Isaba to Arette. From here, before crossing the river Belagua for the last time, take a gravel path leading off to the right towards Rincón de Belagua. The route, some 3 km long and signposted for cross country skiiers, runs along the valley bottom through hayfields and small stands of beech and pine. Throughout the route you may have sightings of Bearded Vulture, Egyptian Vulture, Griffon Vulture, Golden Eagle, Peregrine Falcon, Tree Pipit, Red-backed Shrike, Yellowhammer and, if you are lucky, Sparrowhawk, Black Woodpecker, White-backed Woodpecker and Treecreeper.

The starting point for **Route B** is the Belagua refuge which can be reached by continuing for a farther 6 km along the road to France. The route runs along the Eskilzarra cross country skiing itinerary for 5 km. The itinerary is marked on the map displayed beside the refuge, and the path itself is marked

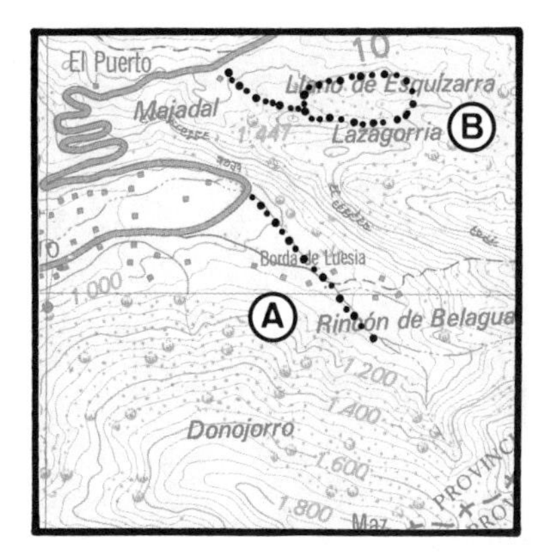

with yellow paint along its entire length. Firstly the path leads down to the Llano de Eskilzarra, a flat area where Bearded Vulture, Water Pipit and Alpine Chough can be seen. It then enters an area of mixed beech and silver fir woodland where you may see Capercaillie, Woodcock, Tengmalm's Owl, Nightjar, Black Woodpecker, White-backed Woodpecker, Goldcrest and Treecreeper. The route offers several alternatives, all of which are signposted.

Route C begins at the *collado* or pass of Ernaz (Piedra de la Sima de San Martín). Take the right-hand path, running close to the edge of the pass, and follow the yellow markings across the mountainside to Fuente de Arlás, a spring. Cross the flanks of the peak of Arlás to reach the Portillo de Pescamou, a small pass, and follow signs for the Portillo de Baticoche. From here the route becomes difficult. Go through the Arriba pass and make for the Anielarra massif. This will bring you to the Anie pass at the base of the peak of the same name. To reach the top of Anie, make your way up the south-west face. To return, retrace your steps. The whole trip, which will take 5-6 hours, is tough. It is a good idea to wear good boots and take compass, map and water supply since there is no water after the Arlás spring. At the beginning of the route there is a pine wood on the right where Ring Ouzel, Citril Finch and Crossbill can usually be seen. After Arlás, pastures predominate where Bearded Vulture, Ptarmigan, Grey Partridge, Water Pipit, Alpine Accentor, Wallcreeper, Alpine Chough and Snow Finch are very occasionally present.

Accommodation

At Isaba you can stay at Hostal Lola or Hotel Isaba. There is also the Belagua mountain refuge, with somewhat sparser comforts, and the Camping Asolaze, a campsite located 6 km from Isaba on the Belagua road. Recommendations for restaurants providing food typical of the area are; the Txamantxoia and the Venta de Juan Pito in the Belagua valley itself, and the Lakora, Hostal Lola and Casa Tapia in Isaba.

Comments

The best time of year for birdwatching in Larra is late spring, during May and June.

Route C becomes hard going after Arlás and it is not advisable to undertake this route in bad weather, particularly if it is misty.

Carmelo Fernández León

NA.3
FOZ DE BURGUI

River gorge.

Main species

Residents: Bearded Vulture, Griffon Vulture (140 pairs), Golden Eagle, Peregrine Falcon, Eagle Owl, Black Woodpecker, Blue Rock Thrush, Chough.

Summer visitors: Egyptian Vulture, Alpine Swift.

Winter visitors: Wallcreeper, Alpine Chough (in their thousands), Alpine Accentor.

Access

The C-137, which joins the N-240 running from Pamplona to Jaca, crosses the gorge.

Description

The Foz de Burgui is a gorge carved by the river Esca in the far south of the Roncal valley lying between the provinces of Navarra and Zaragoza. Stratified cliffs of limestone and dolomite drop from the surrounding mountain crests down to the river, some reaching heights of over 100 m. The sides of the gorge are taken up by immature woodland of pine, beech, lime and maple as well as extensive areas of scrubland consisting of box.

Recommended routes

Apart from the road, there are no practicable routes within the gorge. This means that access to the gorge is limited.

Route A takes you along the road for roughly 3 km. Leave your vehicle at the 13 km marker post and walk. This is quite a flat route, meaning that you can fully appreciate the structure of the

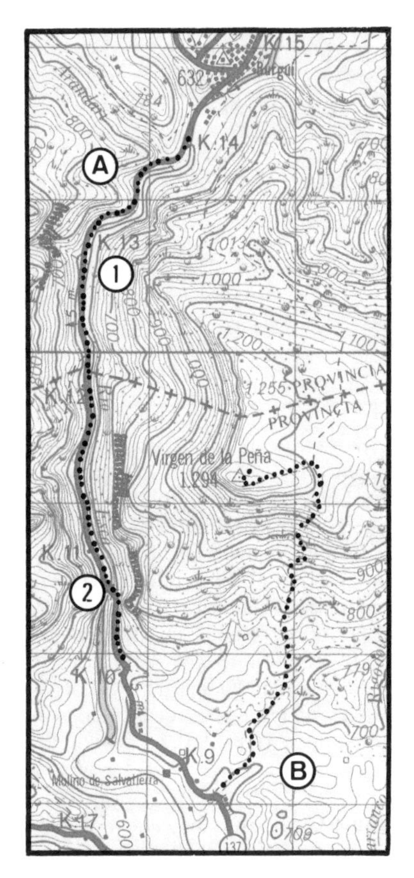

ravine and see most of the birds present. Although anywhere is a good stopping place, the two ends of the route (points 1 and 2) bring you closest to the cliffs and make it easier to spot birds.

Route B consists of a walk up to the chapel or *ermita* of La Virgen de la Peña. The track starts at the 8.5 km marker post on the road and takes you up the right bank of a stream. 1¼ hours' walk will bring you to the chapel. Since this route runs along a south-facing slope you will be able to see, particularly on sunny winter days, large numbers of soaring and gliding birds. From the chapel itself, located on a cliff commanding a view of the gorge in its entirety, you can watch large birds of prey at very close quarters.

An alternative is to reach the chapel by taking a forestry track, 8 km long and only suitable for four-wheel drive vehicles, which starts at the same point on the road as the path.

Accommodation

There are *fondas* and hostels in the larger villages of the Roncal valley, as well as several campsites (wild camping is prohibited). However, in summer accommodation may be difficult to find.

José Antonio Donázar

NA.4 FOZ DE ARBAYÚN AND FOZ DE LUMBIER (LEYRE RANGE)

River gorges.

Main species

Residents: Bearded Vulture, Griffon Vulture, Golden Eagle, Goshawk, Sparrowhawk, Peregrine Falcon, Stock Dove, Eagle Owl, Long-eared Owl, Black Woodpecker, Dipper, Blue Rock Thrush, Sardinian Warbler, Great Grey Shrike, Chough, Citril Finch, Crossbill.

Summer visitors: Egyptian Vulture, Short-toed Eagle, Booted Eagle, Alpine Swift, Crag Martin, Rock Thrush, Red-backed Shrike.

Winter visitors: Wallcreeper, Alpine Chough.

Access

From the N-240 take the C-127 towards Lumbier (3 km). Before reaching the village of Lumbier turn right onto the road signed for the gorge (Foz de Lumbier). The road comes to an end after 2 km, on the edge of the gorge.

To reach the Arbayún gorge, take the local road running out of Lumbier to Navascués and the Salazar valley. Coming down from the Iso pass, turn onto the Bigüezal road after the 96 km marker post. Go through the village of Bigüezal and shortly afterwards take the turning for Arangoiti, a narrow, steep road leading up to a radio mast.

Description

The Leyre range, part of the foothills of the Pyrenees, marks the transition between the beech and pine woods of northern Spain and the Lusitanian oak and scrubby holm oak woodland of southern Spain. The limestone core of the range has been eroded by the rivers Salazar and Irati. These rivers run at right angles to the spine of the Pyrenees and have carved out some impressive gorges, which have remained unspoiled thanks to their inaccessibility.

Three areas have been declared Nature Reserves; Foz de Arbayún, Foz de Lumbier, Acantilados de la Piedra y San Adrián.

Recommended routes

Route A is 1 km long and begins at the entrance to the Lumbier gorge (1), running downstream along the gorge via a track following an old railway line. In spring the nests of vultures and many other cliff-dwelling species such as Egyptian Vulture, Crag Martin, Rock Thrush, Chough and Eagle Owl can easily be seen. In winter you will often encounter Wallcreeper.

Route B, between Bigüezal (2) and Arangoiti, takes you through oak, pine and beech woodland, finally coming out onto scrubland with clumps of broom. En route you may see Short-

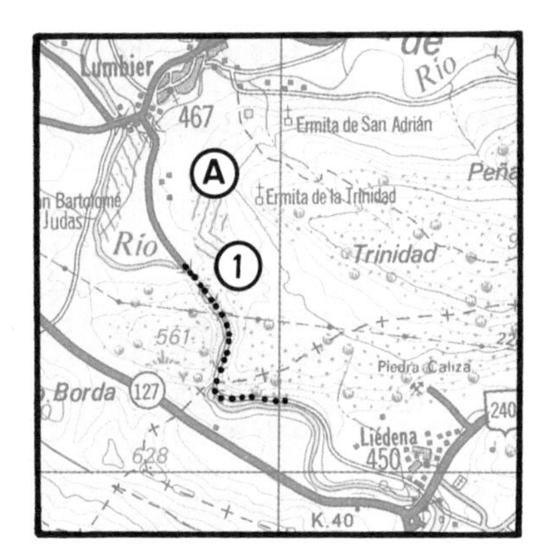

toed Eagle, Booted Eagle, Goshawk, Sparrowhawk, Long-eared Owl, Black Woodpecker, Citril Finch and Crossbill.

In addition to these two routes it is worthwhile making stops at the *mirador* or vantage point at Arbayún (3) and the Arangoiti radio mast (4). The Arbayún vantage point, at the top of the Iso pass, tops a 150 m sheer cliff and commands a view over most of the gorge. From this point you will be able

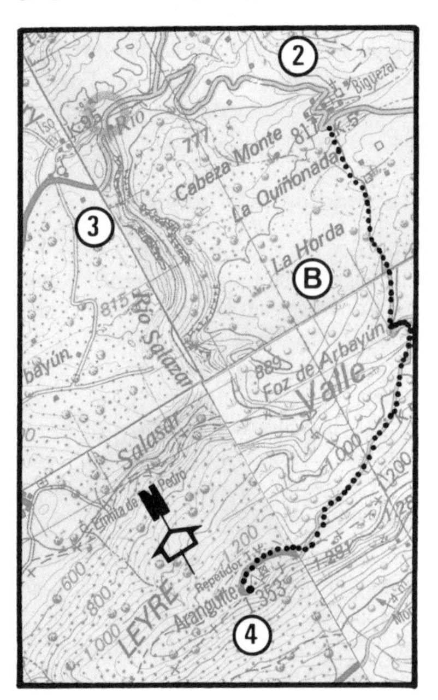

to see large numbers of Griffon Vulture (in 1989, 144 pairs were counted, one of the largest colonies in Spain), Bearded Vulture, Golden Eagle, Egyptian Vulture, Peregrine Falcon, Eagle Owl, Alpine Swift, Blue Rock Thrush, Rock Thrush, Chough, etc. From the Arangoiti radio mast you can see most of the Navarrese Pyrenees; this is also an ideal spot for watching the flight of large birds of prey, who make use of the slope lift and will pass by at very close quarters.

Accommodation

Accommodation can easily be found in Lumbier, Liédena and Sangüesa. If you get hungry while in Arangoiti, you are advised to go to Casa Braco in Navascués, where even the staunchest eaters will leave the table completely sated.

Comments

This area is of great historical and artistic interest. It is well worth visiting Sangüesa and the monastery of Leyre.

Carmelo Fernández León

NA.5 PEÑAS DE ECHAURI

Rocky cliffs.

Main species

Residents: Griffon Vulture, Bonelli's Eagle, Peregrine Falcon, Crag Martin, Blue Rock Thrush, Alpine Chough, Chough, Raven.

Summer visitors: Egyptian Vulture, Short-toed Eagle, Alpine Swift, Wryneck, Rock Thrush, Subalpine Warbler.

Winter visitors: Wallcreeper.

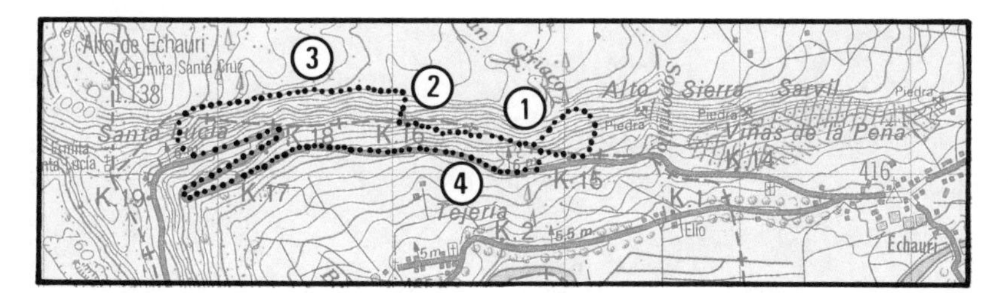

Access

From Pamplona take the minor road to Estella via Ororbia. The village of Echauri is 13 km along this road, and from here the *peñas* or cliffs can be seen. Having passed through the village you begin to climb up to the pass; on reaching the 15.5 km marker post leave your car in a car park to the right of the road.

Description

The Peñas de Echauri, in the southern foothills of the Sierra de Andía, are formed by a limestone escarpment and reach an average height of 200 m.

Recommended routes

The recommended route in this area is a walk. Leading off to the right of the car park, is a track which takes you to the rock face and circles to the right around the base of Kiriako (1), a large monolith separated from the main rock face. Having circled the whole of the base of Kiriako you will come to a climbers' refuge, from where you continue westwards along the base of the cliff until you come to Gradas de Ciriza (2). From here the path leads steeply upwards to the upper edge of the rock face, providing excellent opportunities for seeing Griffon Vulture, Egyptian Vulture, Peregrine Falcon, Crag Martin, Blue Rock Thrush, Rock Thrush, Alpine Chough and Chough.

Continue along the edge of the cliff and you will come to the so-called Cabezón de Echauri (3), the highest summit of the area, from where you descend via a well-marked path to the road running over the pass.

If for some reason you do not feel like undertaking this route, you can walk along the road between the 15 km and 19 km marker posts to get a general view of the area.

Accommodation

There is plenty of accommodation available in nearby Pamplona.

José Carlos Irurzun Santaquiteria
and Alfredo Rueda Díez

■ NA.6 MONTE DEL CONDE (SANSOAIN)

Mediterranean woodland consisting of holm oak and Lusitanian oak.

Main species

Residents: Red Kite, Goshawk, Buzzard, Long-eared Owl, Great Spotted Woodpecker, Firecrest, Rock Sparrow.

Summer visitors: Black Kite, Short-toed Eagle, Booted Eagle, Hobby, Hoopoe, Song Thrush, Orphean Warbler, Subalpine Warbler, Bonelli's Warbler, Woodchat Shrike.

Access

4 km north of Tafalla (Venta del Maño) on the N-121, take the local road to Olleta. After 2 km you will come to the

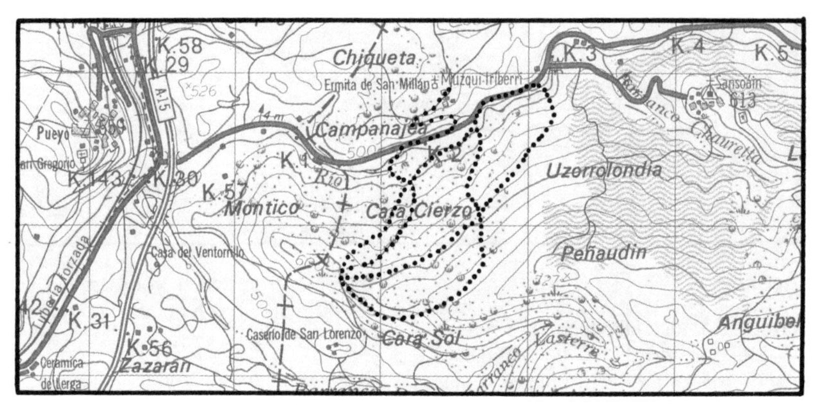

hamlet of Musquer-Iriberri, the starting point for the routes.

Description

Mature, well-conserved woodland made up of holm oak and Lusitanian oak. This is one of the few remaining examples of this kind of woodland, which used to cover a large extent of the central and southern reaches of the province of Navarra. Bordering the woodland is the course of the river Sansoain, while the surrounding valley sides, occupied by kermes oak, are also of great interest.

The Monte del Conde is a Nature Reserve measuring 140 ha.

Recommended routes

Since the wood is quite small, a walk along the network of tracks running through it will be enough to see the most important birds in the area. It is worthwhile covering the edges of the wood and the valley sides covered with kermes oak if you wish to see a wider variety of species.

Accommodation

In addition to the accommodation available in nearby Tafalla, there is a hostel looking out over the valley at Sansoain, 1 km away from the wood.

Anon

NA.7 LAS CAÑAS RESERVOIR (VIANA)

Wetland area: large irrigation reservoir near the river Ebro.

Main species

Residents: Great Crested Grebe, Gadwall, Marsh Harrier, Water Rail, Cetti's Warbler, Reed Bunting.

Summer visitors: Little Bittern, Night Heron, Little Egret, Purple Heron, Red-crested Pochard, Bee-eater, Penduline Tit.

Winter visitors: Cormorant, Bittern, Grey Heron, Shelduck, Teal, Widgeon, Pintail, Shoveler, Pochard, Ferruginous Duck, Jack Snipe.

On passage: Black Stork, Greylag Goose, Garganey, Tufted Duck, Osprey, Black-winged Stilt, Avocet, Ringed Plover, Ruff, Black-tailed Godwit, Curlew, Greenshank, Whiskered Tern, Black Tern.

Access

Take the N-III out of Logroño in the direction of Viana. 3 km before Viana the road runs through a small pine wood. Before entering the wood turn

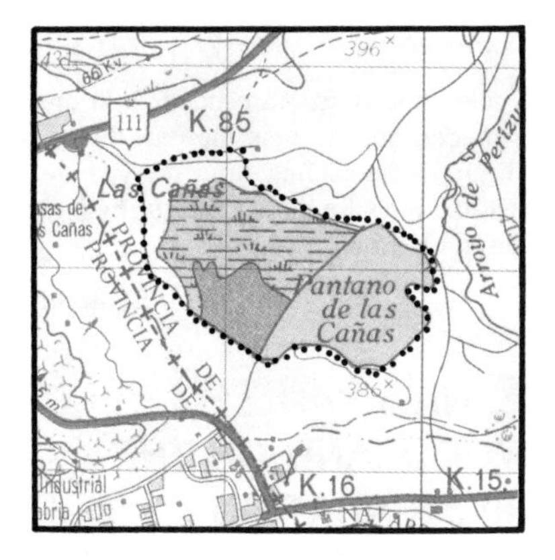

left onto a dirt track which takes you to the foot of a small outcrop planted with cypress trees. Park your car at this point.

Description

The Las Cañas reservoir was originally a natural lake and it has now been damned for agricultural use. For this reason it has a central dyke dividing it into two. Reedbeds abound on the margins of the reservoir, as well as several stands of tamarisk and a small riverside area of poplars. Meadows and cereal crops surround the reservoir.

It is a Nature Reserve.

Recommended routes

The proposed route takes you around the periphery of the reservoir. It is a walk, anti-clockwise round the reservoir, taking about 2½ hours.

The walk will enable you to see the entire reservoir and the birds most characteristic of the site. It is worthwhile climbing the outcrops surrounding the reservoir, which make for excellent observation posts.

Accommodation

Logroño, 5 km away, offers plenty of accommodation as well as a campsite (next to the municipal swimming pools on the banks of the river Ebro). However, accommodation may all be fully booked in the second half of September.

Comments

Spring and autumn are the best times of year for visiting the area.

Jesús Vicente Nalda Saenz-Torre and Francisco Javier Nalda Saenz-Torre

■ NA.8 PITILLAS LAKE

Wetland area

Main species

Residents: Little Grebe, Great Crested Grebe, Grey Heron, Marsh Harrier, Water Rail, Reed Bunting.

Summer visitors: Little Bittern, Purple Heron, Great Reed Warbler.

Winter visitors: Pintail, Widgeon, Teal, Shoveler, Pochard, Tufted Duck.

On passage: Black Stork, Greylag Goose, Shelduck, Garganey, Osprey, Crane, waders, marsh terns.

Access

From Tafalla take the N-121 towards Tudela. After 13 km turn left onto the local road for Pitillas. 3 km after the village of Pitillas a track, indicated by a near-invisible wooden sign, leads to the dyke of the lake where you can leave your vehicle.

Description

The Pitillas lake is a landlocked natural flooded area measuring 300 ha and almost completely occupied by reedbeds. The whole is surrounded by cereal crops and uncultivated land.

Although the lake has natural origins, it has now been increased by a holding

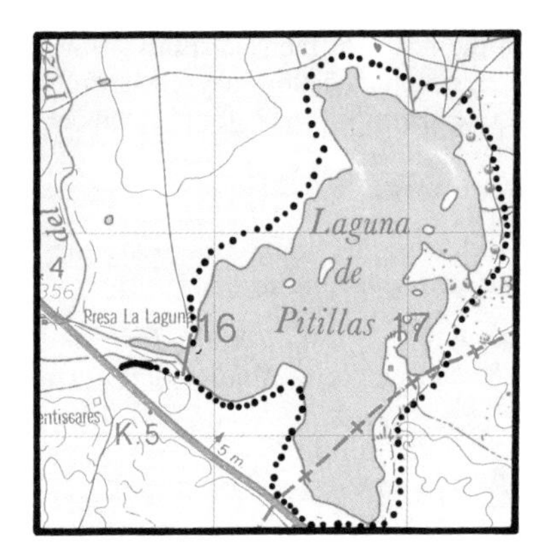

wall which was constructed after the failure of an attempt to cultivate this area. Today the lake and its surroundings are protected as a Nature Reserve. It has been replanted with tamarisk, rosemary, pine and holm oak in order to create a screen of greenery shielding the area from the road, as well as providing nesting places. A wire fence marks the boundary of the protected area, and access to the area is not allowed.

Recommended routes

The recommended route consists of a walk, not more than 5 km long, running around the lake. The terrain is flat, making for easy walking. It is a good idea to walk anti-clockwise around the lake, keeping to the outside of the wire fence at all times.

The route can be complemented by a walk through the adjacent fields, increasing the variety of birds seen with Little Bustard, Stone Curlew, Montagu's Harrier, Black-bellied Sandgrouse, Calandra Lark, Tawny Pipit and other steppe-dwelling birds.

Accommodation

There is a reasonable amount of accommodation available in Tafalla and Olite.

Comments

A telescope is recommended. You are reminded not to cross the wire fence. The most interesting times of year to visit the area are during the spring and autumn migration periods.

Carlos Astrain Massa

■ NA.9 WOODLAND ON THE RIVER ARAGÓN (CAPARROSO)

Riverside woodland.

Main species

Residents: Little Grebe, Great Crested Grebe, Peregrine Falcon, Common Sandpiper, Kingfisher, Fan-tailed Warbler, Long-tailed Tit, Great Grey Shrike, Cirl Bunting.

Summer visitors: Purple Heron, White Stork, Egyptian Vulture, Black Kite, Booted Eagle, Little Ringed Plover, Bee-eater, Wryneck, Sand Martin, Reed Warbler, Great Reed Warbler, Pied Flycatcher, Penduline Tit, Golden Oriole.

Access

Take the N-121 to Caparroso.

Description

This is the most unspoilt stretch of riverside woodland on the river Aragón as it passes through the province of Navarra. Best are the areas of riverside woodland at Lobera and Sotillo (Nature Reserve), López (near Santacara) and particularly the privately-owned woodland at La Requeja (near Murillo el Cuende). Predominating tree cover consists of poplar and willow, although it should be pointed out that these areas of riverside woodland differ from those

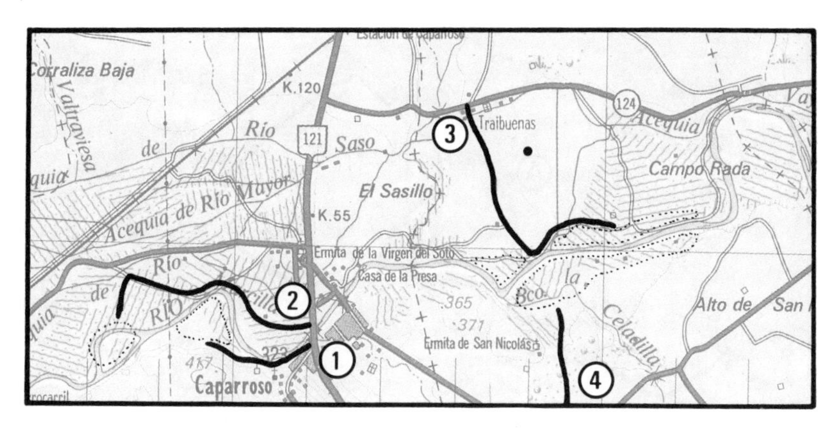

on the river Ebro in both structure and composition. Generally speaking these areas of woodland play an important role as roosts, feeding grounds and areas providing shelter for birds from the nearby reservoirs and lakes such as that at Pitillas (NA.9).

Recommended routes

From Caparroso take a path which runs downstream, parallel to the left bank of the river Aragón, to Sotillo (1). Alternatively, in Caparroso, on the right bank of the river next to the petrol station, there is a series of tracks which cross an area of irrigated farmland and take you to the area of riverside woodland at Lobera (2).

Take the N-121 out of Caparroso towards Pamplona and after 3.5 km turn onto a local road leading to Traibuenas. In the centre of the village take a small road leading down to the river and part of the woodland at La Recueja (3). To get to the other section of woodland, in Caparroso take the local road to Mélida and after 4 km turn left onto a track taking you to this area (4).

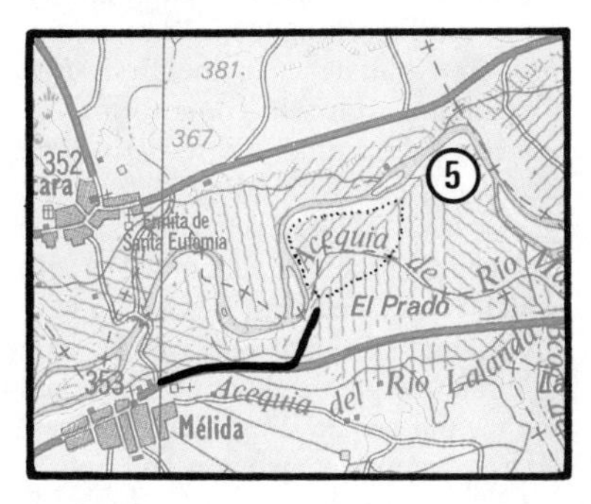

Finally, the riverside woodland at López (5) can be reached by leaving Mélida on the road for Carcastillo. After 1.5 km turn left on to a track.

Given the small dimensions of these riverside woods, a walk within and around them will be enough to show you the birds most characteristic of the area.

Accommodation

Both Tafalla and Tudela have plenty of accommodation and other services available.

Alfredo Rueda Díez

■ NA.10 BARDENAS REALES

Steppe area.

Main species

Residents: Griffon Vulture, Stone Curlew, Black-bellied Sandgrouse, Pin-tailed Sandgrouse, Dupont's Lark,

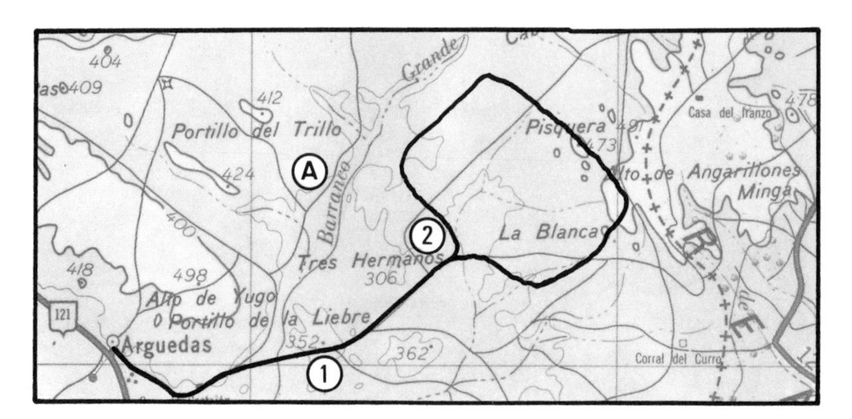

Calandra Lark, Lesser Short-toed Lark, Crested Lark, Thekla Lark, Black Wheatear, Dartford Warbler, Chough, Rock Sparrow.

Summer visitors: Egyptian Vulture, Little Bustard, Red-necked Nightjar, Alpine Swift, Short-toed Lark, Spectacled Warbler, Wheatear, Black-eared Wheatear.

Winter visitors: Merlin, Short-eared Owl.

Access

On the N-134 (N-121 in maps which have not been updated), 1.5 km south of Arguedas, turn right onto an access road for a military base. The base is the starting point for Route A.

To reach the starting point of Route B take the C-125 out of Tudela in the direction of Ejea de los Caballeros.

Description

Las Bardenas Reales constitute one of the most important steppe areas in the Ebro basin. The area consists of flat-topped plateaux with numerous ravines. There is no established human population except an Air Force shooting range set up in 1951.

Despite the predominantly semi-arid climate, nearly half of the area is taken up by cereal crops and asparagus fields. The rest consists of rolling hills and ravines, creating a frequently spectacular landscape sparsely covered with various kinds of scrub. Also worth mentioning are the occasional stands of Aleppo pine with abundant shrubby undergrowth which are to be found on steep slopes, out of reach of the plough.

There are three Nature Reserves within Las Bardenas Reales: Vedado de Eguaras (roughly 500 ha), Rincón del Bu (460 ha) and Caídas de la Negra (1,926 ha). There is a project afoot to turn the whole area into a Natural Park (42,500 ha).

Recommended routes

There are two different routes, both to be undertaken by car.

Route A starts on the N-121 at the turn for the military base. Pass through rice fields until reaching the 6.1 km marker post at Aguilares (1), the first stop. Continuing, you will come to the entrance of the military base (2) where, next to signs forbidding entry, two tracks lead off, one on either side of the road. Take the left-hand track, which is surfaced with gravel and is in good condition, and you will be able to circle the whole shooting range and see the most interesting areas. The best areas of steppe vegetation and one of

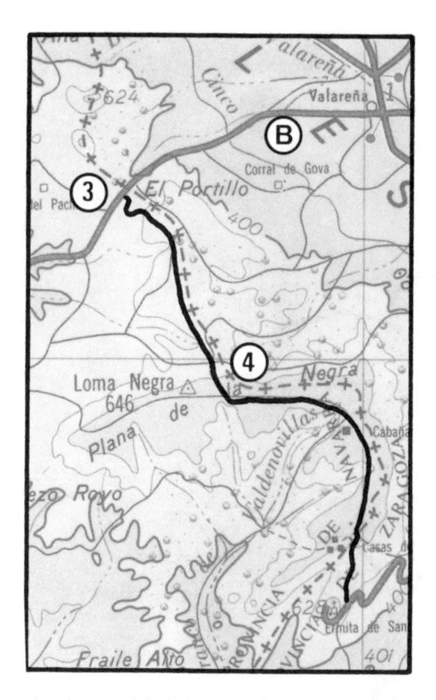

the few artificial ponds in the area both lie within the shooting range, meaning that we have to be content with watching from the track, using suitable optical aids.

Route B starts at the 17.5 km marker post on the C-125, just 1 km away from the provincial boundary line of Navarra. At this point (3) turn right onto a track. After 400 m you will come to a junction with a hut. Take the left-hand track which leads up to the pine woods of La Negra (4) and terminates at the Sancho Abarca chapel. The most interesting parts of this route are the slopes coming down off the plateaux to both the east and the south. The route totals 25 km. Return by the same route.

If you visit the area between May and September it is worthwhile visiting the rice fields at Arguedas if you wish to see a wider range of species.

Accommodation

There is plenty of accommodation in Tudela. Also recommended are Hostal Los Abetos, 7 km out of Arguedas in the direction of Pamplona, and Hostal Hernani in Arguedas itself.

Comments

Visiting the area in summer will not be very rewarding. Do not enter the military zone and do not stray off the marked route since the network of tracks is very complex and the road surfaces bad.

The extremely delicate ecological balance of this area should be stressed. Vegetation is very sparse, so we would ask you to be especially careful.

Alejandro Urmeneta

NA.11 WOODLAND ON THE RIVER EBRO NEAR TUDELA

Areas of riverside woodland.

Main species

Residents: Little Egret, Common Sandpiper, Kingfisher, Cetti's Warbler, Long-tailed Tit, Cirl Bunting.

Summer visitors: Night Heron, Purple Heron, Black Kite, Booted Eagle, Hobby, Little Ringed Plover, Scops Owl, Bee-eater, Sand Martin, Yellow Wagtail, Redstart, Melodious Warbler, Chiffchaff, Penduline Tit, Golden Oriole.

Description

A series of woods constituting the best and most extensive area of riverside woodland on the length of the river Ebro. Both the banks and the islands in the river represent a very mature and highly developed structure featuring poplar, willow, ash, tamarisk and elm.

The areas at Ramalete and La Remonta are Nature Reserves.

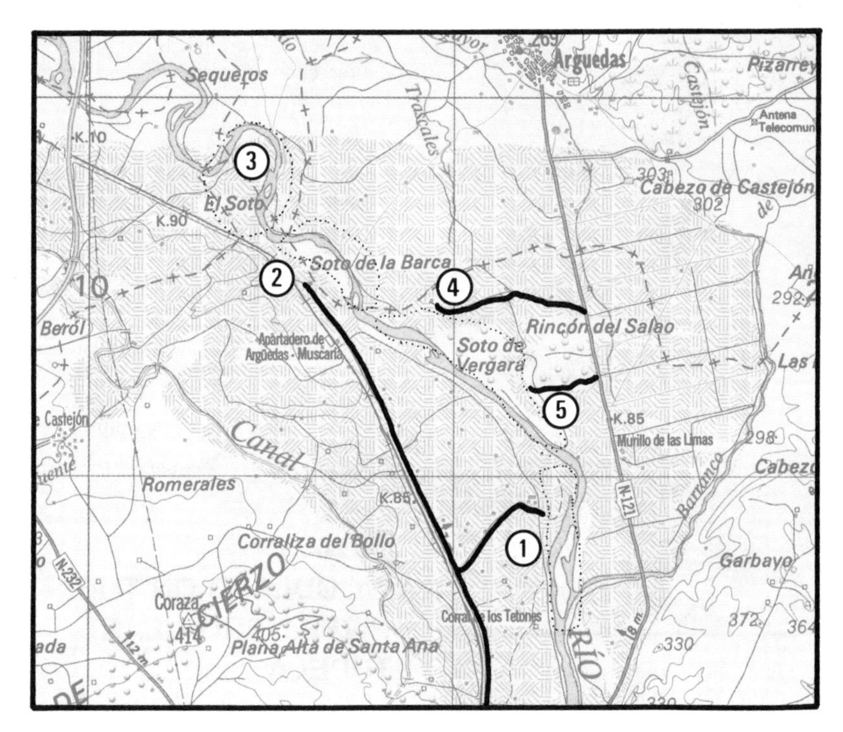

Access

To get to the riverside woodland at La Remonta (1), Arguedas (2) and Ramalete (3), there is a forestry track which begins by the bridge over the Ebro in Tudela and runs parallel to the railway on the right bank of the river. From this track a series of smaller paths lead off, enabling you to get down to the water's edge.

Acess to the riverside woodland at Vergara (4) and Murillo de las Limas (5) is from the N-134. 10 km outside Tudela, travelling towards Pamplona (between the 83 km and 85 km marker posts), several tracks on the left hand side lead down to the woods.

Recommended routes

A walk around and within these areas of riverside woodland is enough to be able to spot the birds characteristic of the area.

Accommodation

Tudela offers plenty of accommodation. The Hotel Remigio is recommended, since it is central and not too expensive.

Alfredo Rueda Díez

■ NA.12 LOR AND PULGUER RESERVOIRS

Wetland area: artificial ponds for irrigation.

Main species

Residents: White Stork, Mallard, Pochard, Coot, Moorhen, Little Grebe, Water Rail, Fan-tailed Warbler.

Summer visitors: Great Crested Grebe, Little Ringed Plover, Great Reed Warbler.

Winter visitors: Grey Heron, Widgeon, Teal, Gadwall, Shoveler, Tufted Duck.

On passage: Greylag Goose, waders, swallows and martins.

Access

Leave Tudela on the minor road for Corella. Having passed under the motorway bridge, take the turning for Fitero-Cintruénigo and after 1 km take the turning for Murchante-Cascante. 2 km farther on you will find a white-painted shed on the right of the road, from where you can see the irrigation reservoir at Pulguer.

To get to the reservoir at Lor continue along the road to Cascante, where you take the turning for Ablitas. After about 3 km you will come across the reservoir to the left of the road.

Description

These two bodies of water form part of a patchwork of small reservoirs in the La Ribera region of Navarra. Pulguer, which is used as a recreation area, has reedbeds and tamarisks while Lor, currently being used solely as a reservoir for irrigation, does not have any vegetation.

Pulguer has been declared a Nature Reserve.

Recommended routes

The reservoir at Pulguer can be seen from the point where you have parked

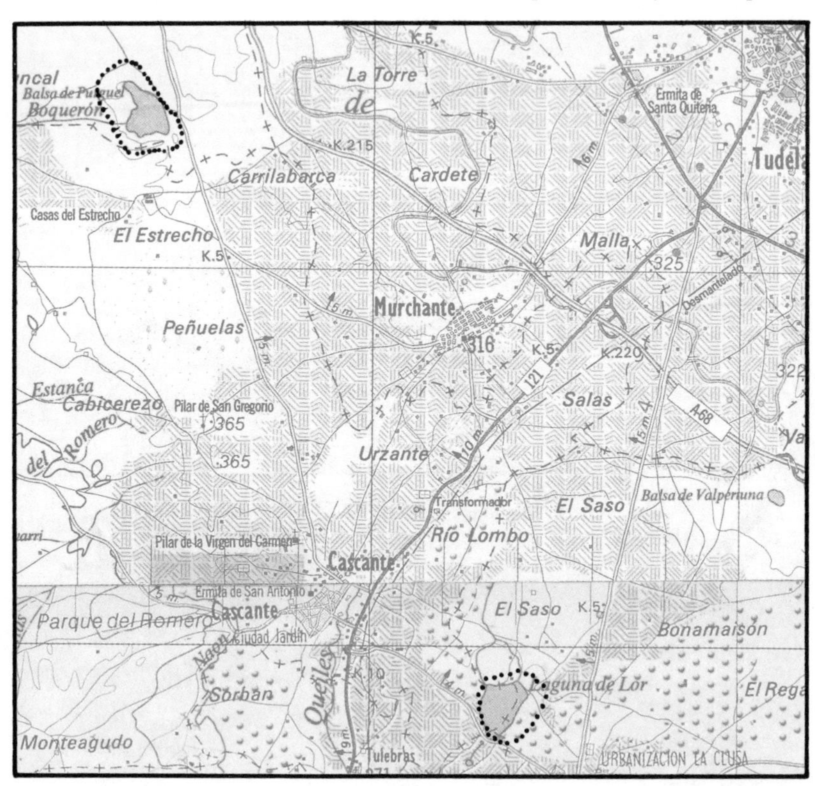

NA

your car. Another good vantage point is the area around the sluice, which can be reached by walking along the containing wall.

You can walk all the way around the Lor reservoir. It is worth taking a telescope.

Accommodation

Tudela is well-equipped to cater for visitors. One recommendation is the Hostal Remigio near the square known as Plaza de los Fueros.

José Antonio Pérez-Nievas Martínez and José Luis Lizarraga Liberal

PAÍS VALENCIANO

Squacco Heron
Ardeola ralloides

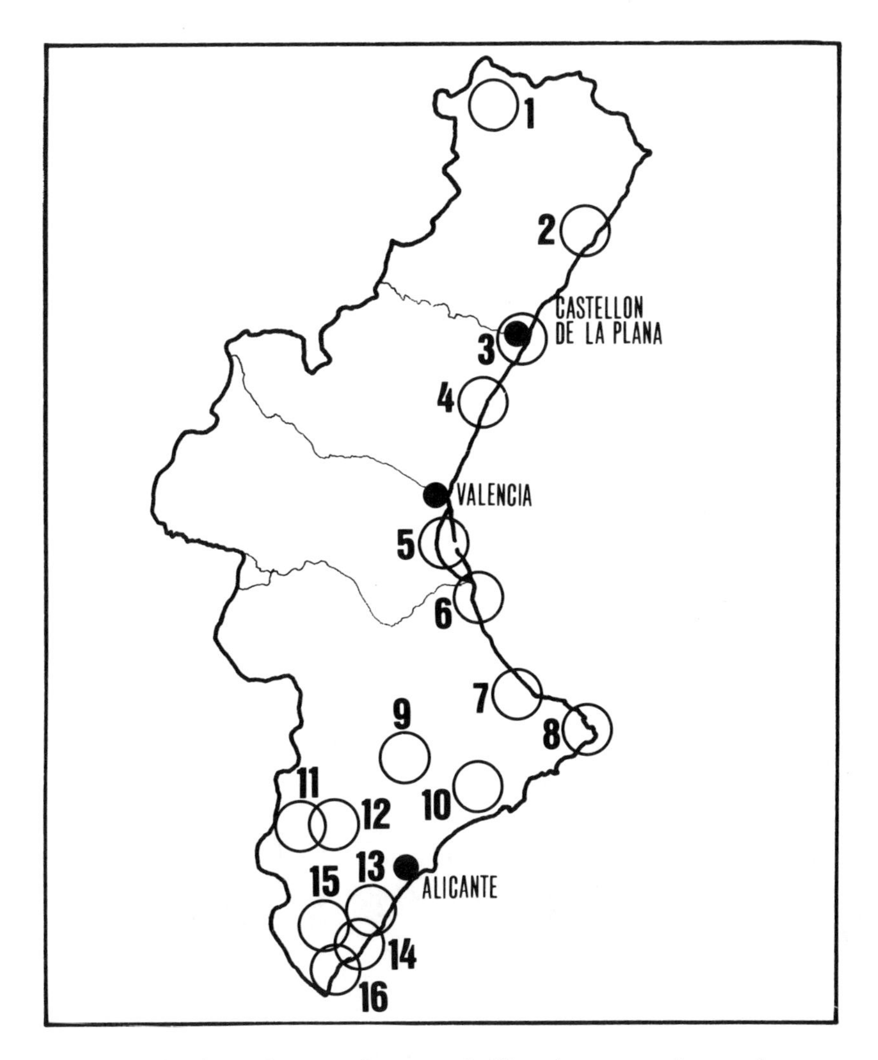

The País Valenciano takes up a large section of the eastern side of the Iberian Peninsula. The region is relatively narrow but stretches for 330 km from north to south, encompassing subhumid regions bordering Aragon and Catalonia and markedly semi-desert areas towards Murcia in the south. Its geography is remarkable for the contrast between a mountainous inland area and a largely flat coastline. The latter, with its wetlands, is the area holding the greatest interest from an ornithological point of view.

The inland mountains belong to two different systems, the Iberian System and the Sierras Béticas. The main bodies of these two systems lie outside the Valencia region, meaning that mountains in the area are quite low, seldom reaching more than 1,100 m or 1,200 m. These are generally limestone ranges with high *muelas* or outcrops and impressive cliffs which have an arid appearance, despite a relatively dense covering of pine forest. The mountains belonging to the Iberian System are generally slightly higher and less dry, giving rise to a wider range of woodland habitats and associated species. To give an idea, some the woodland birds present in inland areas of the province of Castellón (V.1, Ports de Morella and Tinença de Benifassar) and the far north of the province of Valencia are rare or completely absent in the whole of the rest of the País Valenciano. These include Goshawk, Booted Eagle, Nightjar, Great Spotted Woodpecker, Robin, Redstart, Mistle Thrush, Subalpine Warbler, Garden Warbler, Blackcap, Bonelli's Warbler, Chiffchaff, Firecrest, Blue Tit, Nuthatch, Carrion Crow and Citril Finch. Conversely, just a few, such as Sparrowhawk, Tawny Owl, Green Woodpecker, Crested Tit, Coal Tit, Chaffinch and Crossbill are also commonly seen in the Aleppo pine woodland which predominates elsewhere. In the same way, certain species occurring in the *mesetas* or tablelands of the Maestrazgo (Maestrat) and the Ports de Morella, such as Tawny Pipit, Dunnock, Wheatear, Rock Thrush, Whitethroat and Ortolan Bunting, are hardly ever present in the mountains to the south. These species are perhaps the most montane birds in the area.

By contrast, cliff-dwellers are distributed throughout the País Valenciano, with the exception of Griffon Vulture and Egyptian Vulture, now limited to the high ground in the province of Castellón. There are relatively large numbers of Golden Eagle, Bonelli's Eagle, Peregrine Falcon, Rock Dove, Eagle Owl, Alpine Swift, Crag Martin, Black Redstart, Black Wheatear, Blue Rock Thrush, Chough, Raven and Rock Sparrow present on the impressive cliffs carved by the rivers Turia, Júcar (Xúquer) and Cabriel in the west of the province of Valencia. This is also true of parts of the eroded Sierras Béticas, the best example of this being the Sierra Aitana (V.10), followed by the ranges of Salinas (V.11) and Carrascal de Alcoy (V.9). This system takes up much of the southern part of the País Valenciano, which is comprised by the province of Alicante (Alacant). There are some depressions where industrial urban centres have sprung up, in sharp contrast to the unpopulated Iberian mountains.

The mountains in the province of Alicante run northeastwards towards the sea, where the peak of Montgó rises up 760 m virtually on the shore of the Mediterranean. The range gives rise to the only sea cliffs of any significance on the Valencian coast. These include the San Antonio and La Nao capes (V.8), Peñon de Ifach and the Gelada range. Much smaller and more local cliffs are at Peñíscola, Cullera (V.6), and Cabo de Santa Pola (V.13). These cliffs are frequently the home of colonies of Pallid Swift and Yellow-legged Gull, and were once a nesting site for Osprey. They constitute good observation posts for watching the movement of birds such as Cory's Shearwater, Yelkouan Shearwater, Storm Petrel, Shag, Gannet, Great Skua, Arctic Skua, Audouin's Gull, Mediterranean Gull, Kittiwake, Razorbill and Sandwich Tern.

The Sierras Béticas system mentioned above divides the flat coastline into two sections. The largest section lies to the north and comprises extensive irrigated plains largely given over to citrus fruit growing. It might be worth making a couple of visits to the huge orange groves of the Huerta de Valencia (Valencia area) or Plana de Castellón (Castellón area) where, in addition to a vast abundance of small finches, sparrows and Blackbird, other successful species are Turtle Dove, Scops Owl, Little Owl, Hoopoe, Wryneck, Nightingale, Melodious Warbler, Sardinian Warbler, Spotted Flycatcher, Great Tit, Woodchat Shrike and Cirl Bunting. The coastline lying within the province of Alicante is considerably smaller in scale and more rugged. It is of a quite different nature with almond, olive and carob trees and is frequented by a very distinctive bird, the Rufous Bush Robin. It goes without saying that the extensive orchards and cultivated groves of the País Valenciano go some of the way to explaining the very local presence or absence of species such as White Stork, Montagu's Harrier, Lesser Kestrel, Little Bustard, Stone Curlew, Black-bellied Sandgrouse, Roller, Calandra Lark and Short-toed Lark which are so well represented in other areas of Spain.

Where the País Valenciano really comes into its own in terms of birdwatching are the lagoons and marshes which bead the coast from Peñíscola to Torrevieja. This area can also be divided into two sections, north and south. The most important site of the first section, which runs through the provinces of Valencia and Castellón, is La Albufera de Valencia (V.5). This is not so much because of the large lake, once splendid and now ruined by pollution and eutrophication of the water, causing the disappearance of formerly large populations of Little Grebe, Red-crested Pochard, Coot and Whiskered Tern, but because of the surrounding vast areas of rice fields, a wintering ground for many thousands of ducks and a breeding ground for species such as Black-winged Stilt, Common Tern and as many as seven species of the heron family (Little Bittern, Night Heron, Squacco Heron, Cattle Egret, Little Egret, Grey Heron and Purple Heron). Worthwhile sites are El Prat de Cabanes-Torreblanca (V.2), the mouth of the river Mijares or Millars (V.3) and the marshes at Almenara (V.4), El Moro (near Sagunto), Jeresa-Jaraco (Xeresa-Xeraco) and Pego-Oliva (V.7). These are remnants of what used to be a virtually uninterrupted strip of coastal marshland, and are still the breeding ground for small groups of Little Grebe, Little Bittern, Mallard, Red-crested Pochard, Water Rail, Coot, Black-winged Stilt, Little Ringed Plover, Kentish Plover, Savi's Warbler, Moustached Warbler, Reed Warbler, Great Reed Warbler and, sporadically or occasionally, Purple Heron, Collared Pratincole, Whiskered Tern and Bearded Tit.

Possibly even more interesting is the southern sector, falling within the province of Alicante, with the marshland which has been transformed into saltpans (Calpe, Altet, Balsares-Carabassi, Santa Pola, Torrevieja) and some reservoirs farther inland which supply irrigation systems for the areas of Bajo Vinalopó and Bajo Segura. One such reservoir is El Hondo at Elche (V.15) which, together with the extensive saltpans at Santa Pola (V.14) and the lagoon at La Mata, linked to the Torrevieja saltpans (V.16), is remarkable for the birdlife it is home to. Today these sites are the main nesting grounds for certain species in the País Valenciano: Little Grebe, Great Crested Grebe, Red-crested Pochard, Pochard, Coot, Kentish Plover, Gull-billed Tern, Common Tern, Little Tern and Whiskered Tern. There are also the occasional exclusive species such as Black-necked Grebe, Shelduck, Marbled Teal, White-headed Duck, Avocet, Redshank and Slender-billed Gull, although with the exception of Avocet this is only on the basis of counted pairs. Finally, outside the breeding season El Hondo is also remarkable for being a congregation place for ducks, La Mata for wintering Black-necked Grebe and migrating Greater Flamingo and the Santa Pola salt pans also for migrating Greater Flamingo and for numerous species of waders.

V.1
PORTS DE MORELLA – TINENÇA DE BENIFASSAR

Mountain area.

Main species

Residents: Griffon Vulture, Goshawk, Sparrowhawk, Golden Eagle, Bonelli's Eagle, Peregrine Falcon, Stone Curlew, Rock Dove, Eagle Owl, Long-eared Owl, Tawny Owl, Kingfisher, Thekla Lark, Dipper, Dunnock, Black Wheatear, Blue Rock Thrush, Dartford Warbler, Spectacled Warbler, Sardinian Warbler, Firecrest, Chough, Rock Sparrow, Rock Bunting.

Summer visitors: Egyptian Vulture, Short-toed Eagle, Booted Eagle, Hobby, Great Spotted Cuckoo, Scops Owl, Red-necked Nightjar, Alpine Swift, Bee-eater, Wryneck, Short-toed Lark, Crag Martin, Black-eared Wheatear, Rock Thrush, Subalpine Warbler, Orphean Warbler, Olivaceous Warbler.

Winter visitors: Merlin, Alpine Accentor, Fieldfare, Redwing, Wallcreeper, Siskin, Hawfinch.

On passage: Honey Buzzard, Red Kite, Black Kite.

Access

In Vinaroz (Vinaròs), take the N-232 to Morella (64 Km), the main town of the region. From Morella, roads radiate out to communicate the villages in the area.

To reach the subregion of Tinença de Benifassar (route B), continue along the N-232 until reaching the Torre Miró pass, and from there travel on minor roads to the villages of Castell de Cabres, Pobla de Benifassar and Fredes.

Description

The geography of this region is complicated, with heights varying between 700 and 1,300 m. The mountains and hillsides abound in river gorges and rocky cliffs. For this reason and also because of the harsh climate, human population density is very low, allowing the environment to remain unspoiled.

Vegetation consists of holm oak, Lusitanian oak and pine interspersed with large areas of pastureland. In some areas where conditions are less harsh there is beech and holly, and along the rivers there are good examples of riverside woodland. There is also quite a large population of Spanish ibex.

Recommended routes

To reach the starting point of **route A**, take the N-232 out of Morella towards Vinaroz, and after 11 km turn left for Vallibona (16 Km). The route, 17 km long, takes you along a forestry road linking Vallibona with Rosell, following the course of the river Cervol and running between the ranges known as Serra del Mont Turmell and Muntanyes de Benifassà. The whole route can also be done on foot; however, there is the disadvantage that you have to return by the same route, or alternate driving and walking. The route runs through areas of holm oak and Lusitanian oak woodland, taking you past large cliffs inhabited by a wide variety of cliff-dwelling species: Griffon Vulture, Golden Eagle, Bonelli's Eagle, Peregrine Falcon, Alpine Swift, Blue Rock Thrush, Black Wheatear, Rock Sparrow, etc. Roughly halfway along the route you will come across the chapel of Santo Domingo, a very beautiful place of great cultural value. Any of the riverbeds running into the river Cervol are a good way of gaining access to these rugged and isolated spots.

Route B starts in the village of Fredes, where you take the track leading westwards from Font de la Roca, a natural spring. The track runs through pine woods for some 4.5 km, bringing you to a farm (Pinar Pla) located on a wide, flat area of land. Leave your car at the farm and continue walking along the track. After 300 m turn right and after 60 m you will see the red and white markings of the GR-7 (Grandes Routes, part of a network of long-distance footpaths) painted on the rocks.

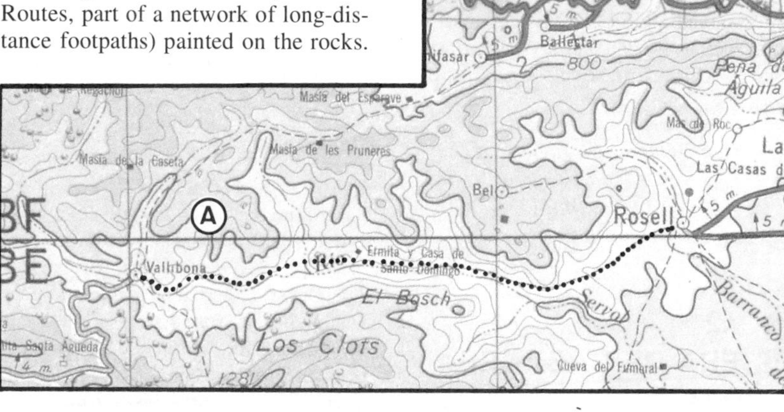

Follow the path and turn left and left again to reach Mas del Peraire, a ruined farm with a fresh water spring. From here you can return by the same route or, if you have come on foot, you can take another path which leads off to the west and takes you to Fredes in 1 hour. The route will allow for sightings of typical forest-dwelling birds, numerous birds of prey and Spanish ibex.

Route C starts in Morella. Take the minor road to Forcall. Before arriving at the village, turn right onto the road for Zorita del Maestrazgo, a village where you can leave your car and take a walk along the most interesting stretch of the river Bergantes. The road runs parallel to the river, enabling you to make your walk as long as you wish or alternatively to combine walking with driving. The most interesting birds to be seen in this area are Griffon Vulture, Egyptian Vulture, Bonelli's Eagle, Booted Eagle, Kingfisher, Dipper, etc.

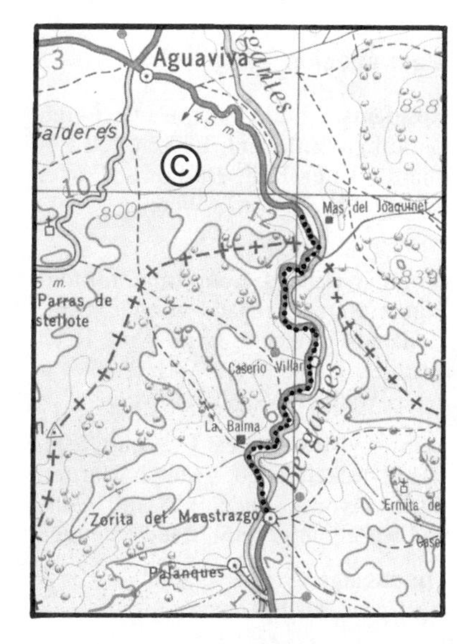

V

In addition to the routes described here, the large area of this region allows for other optional routes which can be planned with the help of a road map.

Accommodation

Morella is a village of great historical and artistic interest. There is a wide range of accommodation available as well as a campsite. You can also find accommodation in other villages in the area, such as Fredes, Pobla de Benifassar, Forcall, Vallibona, Rosell and Zorita.

Isabel Queral, F. Javier Sánchez and Ramón Prades (Colla Ecologista de Castelló)

V.2 RIBERA DE CABANES – PRAT DE TORREBLANCA

A coastal wetland area.

Main species

Residents: Little Grebe, Cattle Egret, Little Egret, Mallard, Red-crested Pochard, Water Rail, Baillon's Crake, Kentish Plover, Cetti's Warbler, Moustached Warbler.

Summer visitors: Little Bittern, Montagu's Harrier, Black-winged Stilt, Collared Pratincole, Little Tern, Reed Warbler, Great Reed Warbler, Olivaceous Warbler, Melodious Warbler.

Winter visitors: Great Crested Grebe, Black-necked Grebe, Marsh Harrier, ducks, Avocet, Audouin's Gull, gulls and waders in general, Reed Bunting.

On passage: Greater Flamingo, Greylag Goose, waders.

Access

From Torreblanca, take the minor road to Torrenostra. After 2 km, turn right onto a dirt track with a sign for the agricultural company Inagrosa. When you come to a small bridge, turn right and after 500 m you will come to a crossroads with a partially ruined hut. Continue straight on, skirting the area until you reach the southern end of the wetland area. However, if you turn left towards the sea you will come to the peat bogs and some artificial lakes created by the extraction of peat.

Description

The Prat de Torreblanca is an old *albufera* or coastal lagoon. It is to a large extent silted up, and is separated from the sea by a series of dune formations. There is still an area of marshland with water all year round, and around this lies pastureland with reedbeds which is flooded from autumn to late spring. There are also some lakes formed by peat extraction, and fields crossed by a large number of channels.

Recommended routes

Route A consists of a walk across the peat bogs. They can be skirted by walking along the banks, where you will see various ducks, waders and herons.

To reach the starting point of **Route B**, in Torrenostra take the track which leads to Boca del Pantano, the place where a series of channels empty out into the sea. Leave the car at this point and walk along a faint path running parallel to a channel, approaching El Prat until you reach the track which runs round its periphery. En route you may have sightings of Montagu's Harrier, Black-winged Stilt, Moustached Warbler and Fan-tailed Warbler.

Route C consists of a trip along the coastline, beginning at the Boca del Pantano. It is a walk of about 7 km.

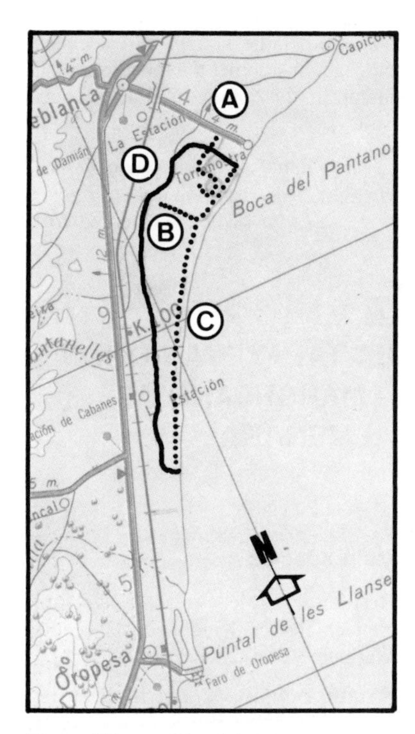

You will see Kentish Plover, Little Tern, Collared Pratincole and, in winter, Marsh Harrier. Be sure to cast an eye over the channels you cross on the way since they are the site of grebes, egrets, ducks, Water Rail, crakes, etc.

Route D takes you along the track running around El Prat. It can be done on foot or by car, making as many stops as you wish. The route is 10 km long.

Accommodation

It is easy to find accommodation in any of the nearby towns and villages. There are also plenty of campsites.

Comments

During autumn and winter the tracks may be impassable for cars because of water and mud. In the months of July and August, the sandy beaches along the coast are much frequented by people, particularly at weekends.

F. Javier Sánchez, Isabel Queral and Ramón Prades (Colla Ecologista de Castelló)

V.3 MOUTH OF THE RIVER MIJARES (MILLARS)

Coastal wetland area.

Main species

Residents: Little Grebe, Mallard, Water Rail, Kentish Plover, Redshank, Cetti's Warbler, Fan-tailed Warbler, Moustached Warbler, Reed Bunting.

Summer visitors: Little Bittern, Black-winged Stilt, Little Ringed Plover, Scops Owl, Lesser Short-toed Lark, Yellow Wagtail, Savi's Warbler, Reed Warbler, Great Reed Warbler.

Winter visitors: Cattle Egret, Little Egret, Grey Heron, ducks, Ringed Plover, Golden Plover, Grey Plover, Dunlin, Ruff, Jack Snipe, Snipe, Common Sandpiper, Sandwich Tern, Kingfisher.

On passage: Night Heron, Squacco Heron, Purple Heron, Marsh Harrier, Osprey, Black-tailed Godwit, Little Gull.

Access

From Castellón de la Plana, take the C-236 towards Burriana. 1 km after Almazora you will come to a bridge across the river Mijares (Millars). You can leave your vehicle near the bridge.

Another road runs from Almazora to the beach; anywhere along this road you can turn right to get down to the left bank of the river.

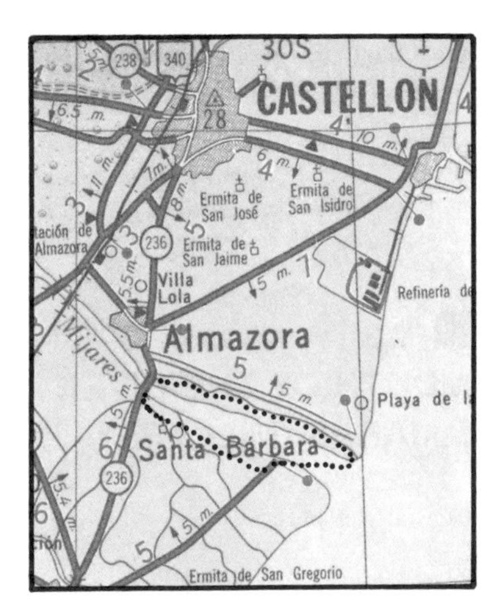

Description

The last 5 km of the river lies in an old delta which is today for the most part cultivated and controlled by the use of channels. All the way along the course of the river are areas of scrubland and ponds surrounded by reeds and reed-mace. The surrounding area is used for citrus fruit growing.

Recommended routes

Just below the bridge where you leave your car, a dirt track runs along the right bank of the river for some 5 km, taking you to the river mouth. This track, which in places becomes a path, runs a few metres above the riverbed, making for easy birdwatching. You can return by the other bank, with the added attraction of finding large groups of plover.

Accommodation

The nearby towns of Castellón de la Plana, Almazora and Burriana offer a wide variety of accommodation in the form of hotels, hostels and campsites.

Comments

The best times of year for visiting this area are autumn and spring, when you will see a large variety of waders on passage. In summer the most important feature is the colony of Black-winged Stilt.

Ramón Prades, Isabel Queral
and F. Javier Sánchez
(Colla Ecologista de Castelló)

■ V.4 LA TALAYOTA PONDS – MARSHLAND AT ALMENARA

Coastal wetland.

Main species

Residents: Little Grebe, Water Rail, Kentish Plover, Kingfisher, Fan-tailed Warbler, Moustached Warbler.

Summer visitors: Little Bittern, Black-winged Stilt, Savi's Warbler, Reed Warbler, Great Reed Warbler, Melodious Warbler.

Winter visitors: Great Crested Grebe, Black-necked Grebe, Cormorant, Cattle Egret, Little Egret, Grey Heron, Greylag Goose, Shelduck, Widgeon, Gadwall, Pintail, Teal, Pochard, Ferruginous Duck, Tufted Duck, Marsh Harrier, Coot, Avocet, Curlew, Dunlin, Little Stint, Redshank, Greenshank, sandpipers, gulls.

On passage: White Stork, Glossy Ibis, Osprey.

Access

From Almenara, a town on the N-340, take the road down to the beach. Having come round the base of a small hill, you will come to a plain which runs down to the sea. The ponds lie to the right of the road, and on both sides of the road are the areas which become flooded in winter.

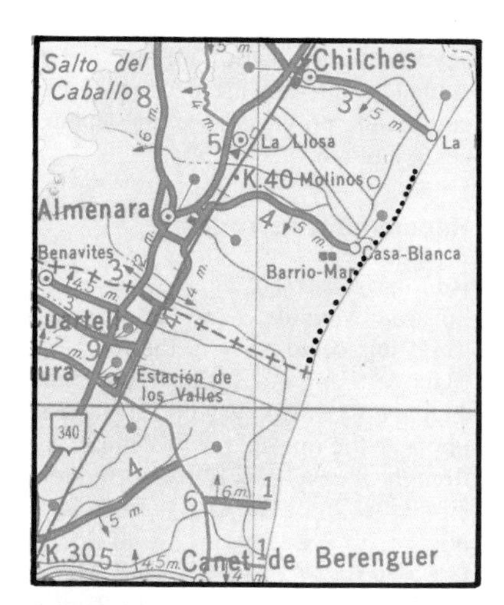

Description

These ponds are formed by the upwelling of underground water issuing from the Sierra de Espadán. Around the ponds, reeds and canes grow.

The ponds are in an area which floods every winter. However, in summer the area is intensively cultivated.

Recommended routes

Apart from visiting the ponds, which are of no great significance, it is not worth describing any route to visit this area. You can see the flooded areas from the road, which are the most important feature of the site from an ornithological point of view. You can take any of the tracks running off to the right or left to approach the ponds.

It is also worthwhile going down to the beach and watching the open sea carefully since large groups of gulls and ducks congregate there.

Accommodation

There is plenty of accommodation available, in the form of hotels and campsites, in the surrounding area (Almenara, Moncófar, Sagunto).

Comments

It is best to visit the area during the winter months when the land is flooded; at other times of year, the area is not of any great interest. It is worth using a telescope. The most interesting places are in the Coto Casablanca, private land to which access is forbidden. However the edges of the Coto, which are adequately indicated by signs, will allow you to watch birds with ease.

Ramón Prades, F. Javier Sánchez
and Isabel Queral
(Colla Ecologista de Castelló)

V.5 ALBUFERA DE VALENCIA

Coastal wetland area of major significance.

Main species

Residents: Great Crested Grebe, Cattle Egret, Little Egret, Red-crested Pochard, Kentish Plover, Audouin's Gull, Sandwich Tern, Moustached Warbler, Sardinian Warbler, Bearded Tit.

Summer visitors: Little Bittern, Night Heron, Squacco Heron, Purple Heron, Black-winged Stilt, Collared Pratincole, Gull-billed Tern, Common Tern, Little Tern, Whiskered Tern, Savi's Warbler.

Winter visitors: Yelkouan Shearwater, Cormorant, ducks in general (40,000 to 70,000 individuals according to year), Shelduck, Marbled Teal, Red-crested Pochard (up to 10,000 individuals), Ferruginous Duck, Marsh Harrier, Golden Plover, Great Skua, Mediterranean Gull, Little Gull, Short-eared Owl.

On passage: Garganey, birds of prey, waders, passerines.

Access

The Albufera is located just to the south of the city of Valencia. The simplest way of getting there is by taking the CV.15 towards El Saler. The motorway ends at the junction with the VV-1041 (Nazaret-Oliva), which runs southwards along the limit or boundary between the Albufera and the Devesa, a long spit of land. The road provides access both to the Devesa and to the Albufera itself (as you leave the village of El Palmar at the 17 km marker post).

If you do not have a car you can take the bus to El Perelló, which leaves from the square or Plaza de la Glorieta in Valencia and will drop you at the El Palmar junction.

Description

The Albufera is a coastal lagoon separated from the sea by a sandy spit, although it is linked to the sea by three canals or *golas* regulated by sluices. Water in the lagoon is fresh and the water level is subject to the irrigation requirements of the surrounding rice fields. Its average depth is of about 1 m.

Around the lake and the islands on the lake large quantities of reedmace, reeds, dense stands of cane and patches of *Cladium mariscus* grow. These marsh communities are also present on the banks of the irrigation ditches and the uncultivated rice fields.

The Devesa, with relatively unspoiled dune structures, presents dense Mediterranean scrubland alternating with occasionally flooded saline hollows surrounded by halophytic vegetation. The area has been changed by an old housing development project, although in recent years a scheme has been put in practice to regenerate the area, with good results.

Two of the main problems encountered in the Albufera are contamination and severe eutrophication of the water. Added to this are the decline of rice cultivation, progressive silting and excessive hunting.

Recommended routes

Route A consists of a car journey starting from Mata del Fang (1). It is best to do this route early in the morning. Mata del Fang is an island containing a large pool of still water and is located opposite the turning for El Palmar. Although access is strictly forbidden, from the shore of the lagoon it is possible to see large groups of ducks, Grey Heron, Cormorant, and Marsh Harrier. Subsequently go to El Palmar, where the route will take you across the rice fields to El Perelló. The route has many bends but it is difficult to get lost. You have to take two left turns which are badly indicated, although you can always ask a passer-by. Make as many stops as you wish along the route, looking out for large groups of herons, waders and gulls in the rice fields. It is also worthwhile taking a walk along the banks of the canals.

On reaching El Perelló, take the VV-1041 southwards and subsequently the VV-1043 towards Sueca, which crosses fields used by large numbers of water birds as wintering grounds. There is also a hide for hunters (only accessible in winter). This is in a little hut to the right of the road. You do not need to go as far as Sueca since you can return to El Perelló via Monte de los Santos (Muntanyeta dels Sants) (2) driving across the rice fields.

Route B consists of a walk along the Devesa. From the *gola* or outlet channel of El Pujol, by the 15 km marker post on the road from Nazaret to Oliva (3) turn off at the sign for L'Estany, which leads you down to the beach. You can leave your car in any of the existing car parks and walk southwards along the track running along the centre of the

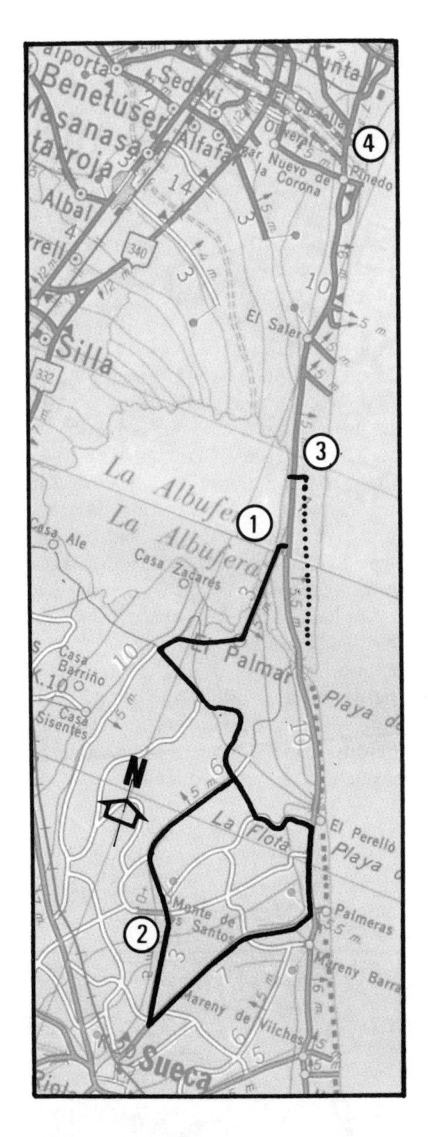

Devesa. The track is about 5 km long, with paths running off it to the beach on one side and the Albufera on the other. The track takes you through areas of scrubland and dunes where you will see warblers, thrushes, larks and buntings. The route is particularly rewarding during the migration periods. Special mention should be made of the Estany del Pujol at the beginning of the route, where you can see waders and Black-necked Grebe. It is also worth having a look at the colony of herons roosting in the pine wood, although they will be some distance away because the area is closed off. Finally go down to the beach to watch gulls, terns, waders and sea ducks.

Another interesting point is 4 km south of the city of Valencia (point 4), namely the mouth of the Nuevo Cauce del Turia (diversion of the river Turia). This is the site of regularly wintering Little Gull and will also give rise to excellent sightings of waders, terns, gulls and marsh terns.

Accommodation

A wide range of plentiful accommodation is available. There are also several campsites.

Comments

If you are thinking of spending several days in the area you could contact the Estación Ornitológica de la Albufera, a bird observatory run by the SEO or Spanish Ornithological Society (Avenida Los Pinares, 106; 46012 Valencia; telephone: 96-1610847) if you would like a detailed description of the area. It is worth taking a telescope.

From October to February the marshes are the site of extensive hunting activities which may spoil your visit.

J. Ignacio Dies Jambrino
and Bosco Dies Jambrino

■ V.6 CULLERA POINT AND THE L'OR RANGE

A headland with cliffs and a small coastal range of hills.

Main species

Residents: Cattle Egret, Kentish Plover, Kingfisher, Fan-tailed Warbler, Dartford Warbler, Sardinian Warbler, Blue Rock Thrush.

Summer visitors: Cory's Shearwater, Little Bittern, Pallid Swift.

Winter visitors: Yelkouan Shearwater, Common Scoter, Great Skua, Mediterranean Gull, Sandwich Tern, Razorbill, Crag Martin, Chough.

On passage: Gannet, Whimbrel, Arctic Skua, Kittiwake, warblers.

Access

The Sierra de l'Or range is located near the town of Cullera, and the Cullera headland can be reached by following signs for the *faro* or lighthouse.

Description

A small area of hills reaching a maximum height of 233 m. Vegetation consists of thyme, mastic tree and pine. The eastern end of the range runs down to the sea, forming a small headland (Punta de Cullera) with gentle cliffs on which a lighthouse has been built. On the north side is a small reservoir known as San Lorenzo, now greatly reduced in size because of changing farming activities. To the south of the range, from the Punta de Cullera to the mouth of the river Júcar, a wide bay runs.

The area is seriously affected by tourism, housing development having taken place in virtually the whole of the bay and a good part of the hillsides. In addition, the area has been subject to several fires.

Recommended routes

Route A has its starting point at the Punta de Cullera. From the lighthouse you can watch the migration of seabirds, the best times of year being March to April and August to October. A walk around the area (point 1) will give sightings of a small breeding colony of Pallid Swift, as well as various passerines. Subsequently, drive or walk to the bay (2) where the patient birdwatcher should be able to see shearwaters, Razorbill, sea ducks and other wintering species.

Route B consists of a car journey. From the lighthouse on Punta de Cullera, take the road which skirts the hills to the north. After a little over 1 km turn left onto a narrow track leading down to the pond or *balsa* of San Lorenzo (3). Continue along the track until you reach the road and, on the way to Cullera, you will find a small turning enabling you to work your way up to the chapel or *ermita* of Los Santos de la Piedra (point 4). This provides a good vantage point over the rice fields to the south of the Albufera as well as being a good spot for watching herons, waders, birds of prey and large groups of wintering ducks.

The route can be extended by climbing the L'Or range, following the signs in Cullera for the Radar Meteorológico or weather station (not signs

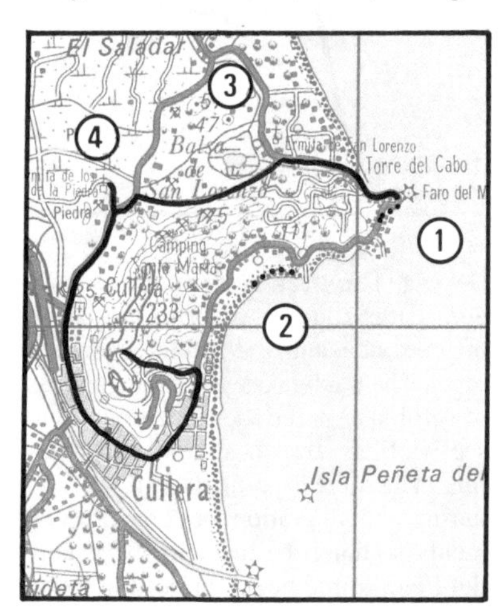

for the *castillo* or castle). A walk along the hilltops will enable you to see a wider range of birds as well as to command a broad view over the Albufera and the sea.

Accommodation

Cullera has plenty of hotels as well as a campsite. Hotels located on the bay are recommended.

Comments

When planning your visit you should bear in mind that during the summer months there are a lot of visitors.

If you wish to watch seabirds from the headland, it is worth going in the evening so as to avoid having the sun in your eyes.

J. Ignacio Dies Jambrino and Bosco Dies Jambrino

V.7 MARSHES AT OLIVA – PEGO

Coastal wetland area.

Main species

Residents: Little Grebe, Kingfisher, Moustached Warbler.

Summer visitors: Little Bittern, Purple Heron, Black-winged Stilt, Kentish Plover, Whiskered Tern, Short-toed Lark.

Winter visitors: Cattle Egret, Little Egret, Grey Heron, ducks, Marsh Harrier, Bluethroat, Cetti's Warbler, Penduline Tit.

On passage: Night Heron, Squacco Heron, Osprey, waders, terns.

Access

From Gandía, take the N-332 towards Alicante and, 7.5 km after Oliva, turn onto the C-3318 to Pego. This road crosses the middle of the marshland, which is located about 500 m from the main road.

Description

These marshes, with an area of approximately 1,000 ha, are the remains of old rice fields now in disuse. The sources of the rivers Bullent and Racons are here. These rivers are formed by numerous small springs, some of which are brackish. A complicated network of drainage channels and irrigation ditches lies between the two rivers, quartering and separating the fields, which remain flooded for most of the year.

Despite drainage and other changes brought by agriculture, the marshes have remained in a good state of conservation. This is largely thanks to the repeated flooding which occurred during 1987.

Apart from the ornithological value of the site, the area is also well-known for the wide variety of freshwater fish it contains, with at least 19 species present.

Recommended routes

Route A consists of a two-hour walk. After taking the road to Pego, cross the bridge over the motorway and, when you come to the third dirt track leading off to the right (1), leave your car and continue on foot. You will go through an area of marshland with extensive beds of reeds and reedmace, a suitable place for watching herons, rails, Penduline Tit and Moustached Warbler. The river Bullent (2) is a good place for watching Little Grebe or Kingfisher. Continue parallel to the river until you come to the confluence with the Salinar tributary. A small hillside next to the

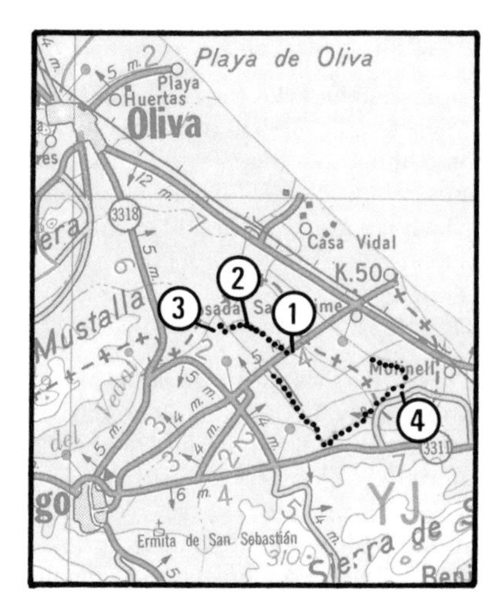

pumping station (3) enables you to get a good view of the entire area.

Route B consists of a three-hour walk starting from the road itself, but this time taking the fourth dirt track after the motorway bridge on the left. The track leads to the river Racons and follows its course. At point 4, next to the Regalaxo canal, there are some fields which, when flooded, are a good place for watching marsh terns, herons, Black-winged Stilt and various waders. In winter you will also see Cetti's Warbler and Bluethroat. The route continues until the point where the track is blocked by the marsh drainage channel leading to the sea.

Accommodation

Some accommodation is available in Oliva but the range is much greater in the nearby towns of Gandía or Denia. However, there are also several campsites a few kilometres from the marshes. In July and August, you may have difficulties in finding somewhere to stay.

Comments

The best time of year to visit the area is from March to October. It is also worth visiting the marshes at Xeresa, located 20 km away on the N-332 going towards Valencia.

Jesús Villaplana Ferrer

■ V.8 SAN ANTONIO AND LA NAO CAPES AND HILLS OF BENITACHELL

A coastal area with sea cliffs.

Main species

Residents: Bonelli's Eagle, Peregrine Falcon, Black Redstart, Black Wheatear, Blue Rock Thrush.

Summer visitors: Cory's Shearwater.

Winter visitors: Yelkouan Shearwater, Great Skua, Mediterranean Gull, Sandwich Tern, Razorbill.

On passage: Gannet, Shag, Arctic Skua, Audouin's Gull.

Access

Whether you are coming from Valencia or Alicante, the turnings off the N-332 for Jávea, Denia or Benitachell will enable you to reach the area. From these roads, minor roads lead respectively to the headlands and the hills.

Description

A coastal plain where isolated mountain plugs reach up to nearly 400 m, on the one side the cape of San Antonio and on the other the cape of La Nao and the hills (*morras*) of Benitachell. Also remarkable for their size are the sea cliffs, which reach some 100 m.

Vegetation is largely composed of scrubland with rosemary, heather and

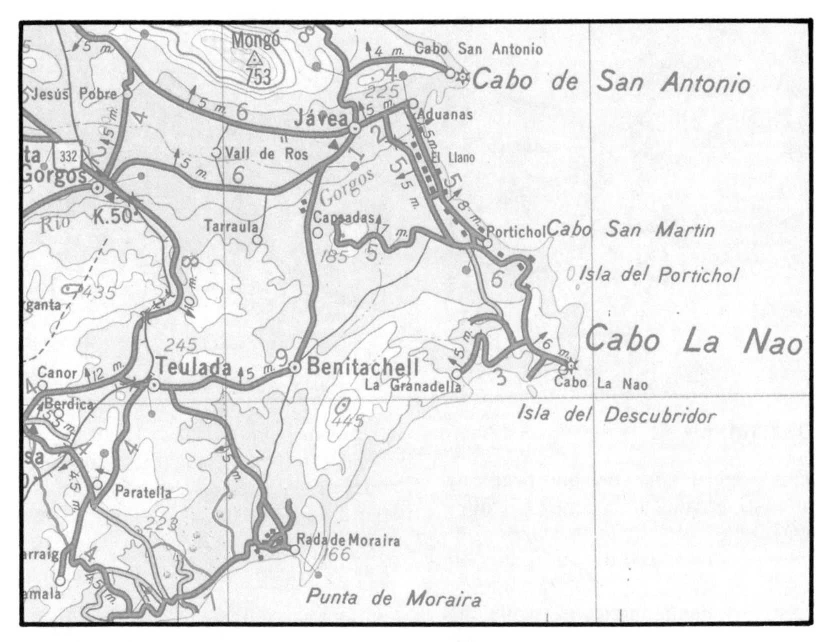

kermes oak interspersed with isolated stands of juniper and holm oak.

Recommended routes

A walk along the upper edge of the sea cliffs will give you a good general impression of the area and its resident birdlife.

Accommodation

Tourism in the nearby towns is highly developed, giving rise to a wide range of hotel accommodation.

Comments

The best time of year for visiting the area coincides with the migration periods. Winter is also good for seabirds.

Very close to the cape San Antonio is the hill of Montgó (763 m) which gives excellent views and is the home of an interesting range of forest-dwelling and cliff-dwelling species.

José Antonio Gil-Delgado Alberti

■ V.9 CARRASCAL DE LA FONT ROJA

A range of hills with interesting woodland areas.

Main species

Residents: Bonelli's Eagle, Crag Martin, Robin, Blue Rock Thrush, Dartford Warbler, Firecrest, Crested Tit, Short-toed Treecreeper.

Summer visitors: Black-eared Wheatear, Subalpine Warbler, Bonelli's Warbler.

Access

Next to the petrol station on the edge of Alcoy, a road leads off to the Santuario de la Font Roja (10 km), a sanctuary. Leave your vehicle in the car park by the sanctuary.

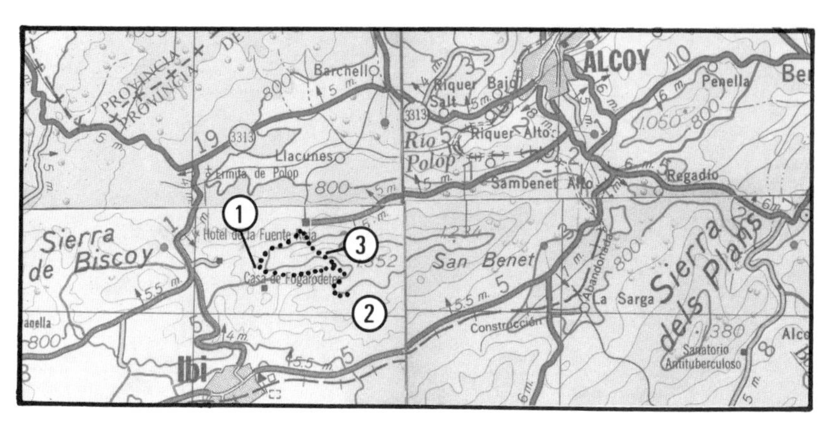

Description

This range of mountains runs from east to west, reaching a maximum height of 1,352 m. There is a noticeable asymmetry between the southern and northern slopes, the former having relatively gentle gradients while the latter is steeper with gorges and screes. Thus vegetation on the southern slopes consists of scrubland with rosemary, whin and the occasional stand of pine, while on the northern slopes, above 1,000 m, there is mixed woodland consisting of holm oak, Lusitanian oak, maple, ash and yew, all of which is exceptionally well-conserved. The lower slopes are occupied by dense pine plantations.

Recommended routes

Next to the car park at Santuario de la Font Roja there is a leisure area from which a forest track leads up to Mas de Tetuán (point 1) and subsequently, on a secondary path, to the top of the range (2). Returning to the main track running along the northern side of the range, after some 200 m you will find a path which runs down to the sanctuary through the holm oak wood. Midway there is a vantage point (3), giving good views over the valley.

You must undertake this route on foot since vehicles are not allowed in the area. The walk will take about 3 or 4 hours. You will be able to see the most interesting forest-dwelling species in the area, with more sightings if you make stops in the pine woods along the road.

Accommodation

The nearby town of Alcoy avails of plenty of accommodation.

Germán López
and Miguel Angel Rodríguez

■ V.10 AITANA RANGE

Mountain area.

Main species

Residents: Golden Eagle, Peregrine Falcon, Eagle Owl, Crag Martin, Black Wheatear, Blue Rock Thrush, Dartford Warbler, Crested Tit, Short-toed Treecreeper, Chough, Rock Sparrow, Rock Bunting.

Summer visitors: Black-eared Wheatear, Woodchat Shrike, Golden Oriole.

Access

In Villajoyosa take the minor road to Orcheta and subsequently to Sella (19 km). Just before reaching Sella, turn right onto a track which leads up to the hills in the area near the Arch gorge.

Continue along the road to reach the Tudons pass; 250 m farther on, in the direction of Alcolecha, a track leads off to the right taking you to the Aitana spring. From the mountain pass itself a road runs up to the TV aerial located on the top of the range.

Description

A limestone massif constituting one of the last spurs of the Cordilleras Béticas. The geography of the area is very steep with high cliffs and deep ravines, reaching a maximum height of 1,558 m with the peak of Aitana.

Vegetation is relatively varied, with holm oak woods and pine woods although large areas are taken up by scrubland. In more hospitable areas there are groves of olive, carob and almond.

Recommended routes

Route A takes you along the track running along the Arch ravine and can be done on foot or by car, although the latter part of the route is only suitable for four-wheel drive vehicles. The track runs under large rock faces, through areas of dry-farming and substantial pine woodland. A couple of hours' walking will be enough to spot the most characteristic species of the area.

Route B takes you along the track running along the northern side of the range and, while it can be undertaken by car, it is better to walk. It will take 2½ hours to reach the spring at Forata. Once there it is worth waiting around to watch the wide variety of birds coming to drink. It is also worthwhile exploring the areas around the old stock enclosures and houses to spot Black Wheatear.

Accommodation

There is plenty of accommodation available in the nearby towns of Villajoyosa and Benidorm. There is also a campsite in Villajoyosa (Hércules) and it is also possible to camp in the mountains (old stock enclosures mentioned in route B).

Comments

The best time of year for visiting the area is spring, since in summer the heat may become unbearable.

Antonio Zaragozí Llenes

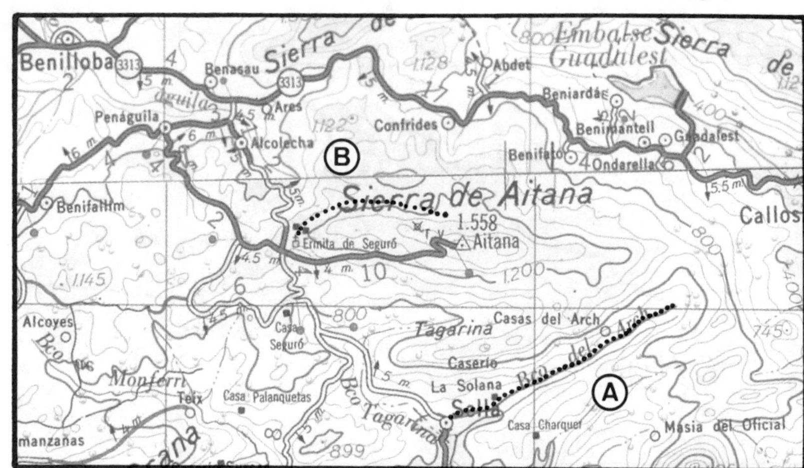

V.11 SALINAS RANGE

A range of mountains with large expanses of pine woodland.

Main species

Residents: Golden Eagle, Bonelli's Eagle, Crag Martin, Black Wheatear, Blue Rock Thrush, Dartford Warbler, Sardinian Warbler, Chough, Rock Sparrow, Crossbill, Rock Bunting.

Summer visitors: Short-toed Eagle, Great Spotted Cuckoo, Scops Owl, Alpine Swift, Bee-eater, Black-eared Wheatear, Olivaceous Warbler, Melodious Warbler, Spectacled Warbler, Subalpine Warbler, Bonelli's Warbler, Woodchat Shrike.

Access

From Villena, take the minor road to Pinoso. By the 13 km marker post, a surfaced track runs off to the left into the hills and bringing you to the hamlet of La Colonia. The track crosses the range at some height, with various paths leading off to different places. The track continues until the hamlet of El Ingeniero, in the province of Murcia, and from there runs down to join the road from Yecla to Pinoso.

Description

The Salinas range, reaching its maximum height with the peak of La Capilla (1,237 m), is part of the Cordilleras Béticas. Fauna consists largely of pine woods, more open and sparse on the southern slopes. The lower slopes of the range as well as some areas within the range have been planted with typical Mediterranean crops: vines, olives, almonds, etc.

Recommended routes

To undertake **Route A**, follow the surfaced track mentioned above until you reach Casas del Alto. A little farther on you will come to La Chola (1), where you take a small path leading off to the right to the Cueva del Lagrimal (2), a cave which is a neolithic archaeological site. The walk can be prolonged by working your way down the ravine to the base of the mountains. Another

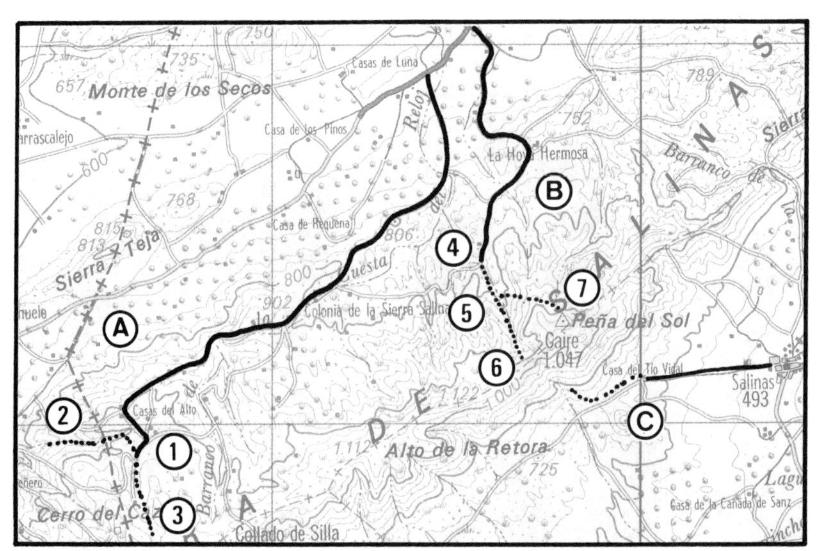

possibility is to climb from La Chola to the summit of La Capilla (3), via the Cañada del Enebral.

Route B consists of taking the dirt track leading off from the minor road about 200 m before the track specified for the beginning of route A. Continue until the forest rangers' hut (4), where you leave your vehicle and continue on foot along the track to the Enmedio spring (5). You can continue up the ravine until you reach Roca de la Manzorrilla (6), although the climb is made difficult by dense vegetation on the lower slopes. Another alternative is to climb up from the forest rangers' hut to the summit of El Caire (7).

The starting point for **Route C** is the village of Salinas (see Access for V.12). From here take the track which leads to Casa del Tío Vidal (8) from where you can walk along the bottom of the range and then climb up any of the ravines on the same side, for instance Barranco del Cura, Barranco Ancho, etc.

Accommodation

The best place for finding accommodation is Villena.

Comments

The routes given here are just an example and can be varied at will since all of the ravines are perfect places for watching birds.

High summer temperatures make it advisable to avoid the midday hours.

Luis Rico Alcaraz
and Angel Sánchez Pardo

■ V.12 SALINAS LAGOON

Inland wetland area.

Main species

Residents: Stone Curlew, Kentish Plover, Calandra Lark, Lesser Short-toed Lark, Fan-tailed Warbler, Dartford Warbler, Great Grey Shrike.

Summer visitors: Little Grebe, Mallard, Marsh Harrier, Black-winged Stilt, Avocet, Little Ringed Plover, Great Spotted Cuckoo, Black-eared Wheatear, Spectacled Warbler.

Winter visitors: Teal, Jack Snipe, Reed Bunting.

On passage: Grey Heron, Greater Flamingo, ducks, waders.

Access

On the N-330 between Elda and Villena, a minor road takes you to Sax and Salinas (8 km). Before reaching the village you will see the lagoon on the left of the road. Leave your car in Salinas and walk to the lagoon, 1.5 km distant, or alternatively take any track from the road leading down to the lagoon.

Description

The natural lagoon of Salinas is located on the middle reaches of the Vinalopó river valley. The main body of the lagoon occasionally floods, and around the lagoon is a margin of halophytic steppe vegetation. This margin varies in width, and also floods as a consequence of heavy rainfall.

Several attempts have been made to drain the lagoon, but none of them have been successful.

Recommended routes

You can circle the lagoon on foot, following the shoreline or the drainage channels. Two dykes cross the lagoon and make for good observation points. However it is recommended that you do not cross the dykes during the

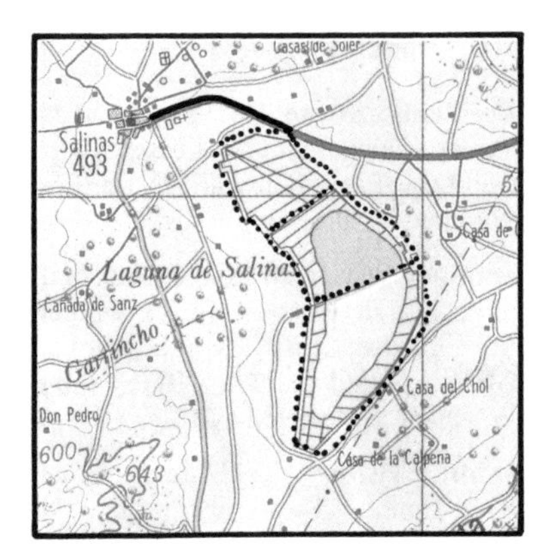

breeding season since they are the nesting ground of some waders.

It is also worthwhile taking in the areas of halophytic vegetation, where you may have sightings of Stone Curlew, Lesser Short-toed Lark, Calandra Lark, Spectacled Warbler, Dartford Warbler and Black-eared Wheatear.

Accommodation

There is no accommodation available in the nearby villages, so you are advised to seek accommodation in Villena, where there are several hostels.

Comments

The best time of year for visiting the lagoon is winter, when it is flooded. However during winter and especially when it is raining, some tracks may be impassable due to flooding.

Luis Enrique Samper Falcó, Juan Ramón Navarro Ganga, Sergio Morán Jover, Eva Mondéjar Verdú and Francisco Mallebrera García

V.13 CAPE SANTA POLA – TABARCA ISLAND

A stretch of coastline.

Main species

Residents: Kentish Plover, Audouin's Gull, Yellow-legged Gull, Black Wheatear, Fan-tailed Warbler, Sardinian Warbler.

Summer visitors: Storm Petrel, Short-toed Lark, Black-eared Wheatear.

Winter visitors: Cory's Shearwater, Yelkouan Shearwater, Gannet, Sandwich Tern, Razorbill, Blue Rock Thrush.

On passage: Shag, Little Egret, Grey Heron, Osprey.

Access

Santa Pola is 14 km from Elche on the C-3317. To reach the headland, take the N-332 towards Alicante and, after 2 km turn right onto a minor road leading to the lighthouse.

To go to the island of Tabarca, passenger boats run from Alicante or Santa Pola, although from Santa Pola the voyage is shorter. The Santa Pola service runs daily, although it is a good idea to check the timetable by ringing the following telephone numbers: 96-5411113 or 96-5412338.

Description

The Santa Pola headland is formed by a series of terraces which have been pushed up out of the sea. They are based on a fossilized coral reef of great geological interest. The whole forms a relatively flat surface rising some 100 m above the sea. A cliff drops down and dominates the beach. Vegetation consists of little more than thyme and Mediterranean scrubland with many dwarf fan palm.

Tabarca is an island 4 km off the coast. It is small, flat and surrounded by a series of rocky islets. There is a small walled village, and the most interesting vegetation present is thorny scrub which can reach 2 m in height and grows at the centre of the island. In 1986, the sea

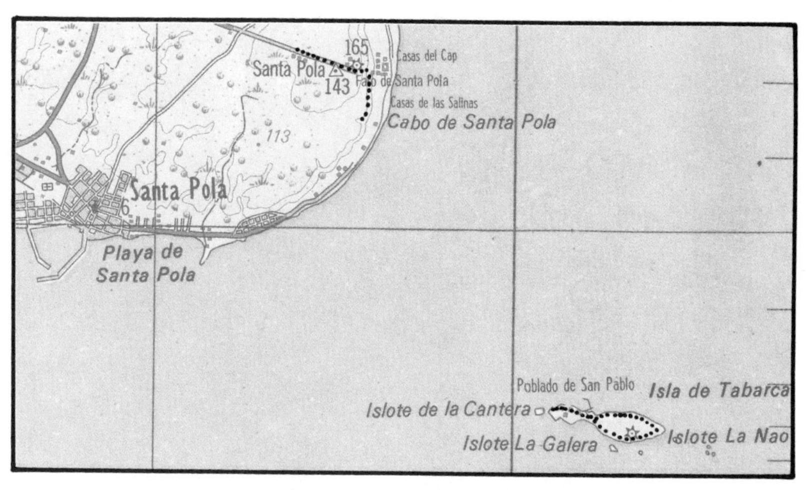

surrounding the area was declared a marine reserve, allowing for considerable recovery of underwater fauna. It should be noted that access to the islet of La Nao, located to the southeast of Tabarca, is restricted.

Recommended routes

From the lighthouse it is possible to cover the entire Santa Pola headland in order to see various passerines, including Black Wheatear and Blue Rock Thrush, on the cliff edges.

When you go to the island of Tabarca, it is worth walking around its shores, which run for some 3 km. Keep a look out for Audouin's gull, which frequents the southern coast of the island.

Accommodation

There is plenty of accommodation available in Santa Pola. Camping is allowed on the island of Tabarca.

Comments

It is better not to visit the island during the months of July and August, since it is overrun by tourists in summer.

German López, Victor Peiró and Just Bayle

V.14 SANTA POLA SALT PANS

Coastal wetland area.

Main species

Residents: Little Egret, Greater Flamingo, Shelduck, Red-crested Pochard, Avocet, Kentish Plover, Yellow-legged Gull, Lesser Short-toed Lark, Fan-tailed Warbler, Moustached Warbler, Bearded Tit.

Summer visitors: Little Bittern, Purple Heron, Marbled Teal, Black-winged Stilt, Common Tern, Gull-billed Tern, Whiskered Tern, Savi's Warbler.

Winter visitors: Black-necked Grebe, Cormorant, Grey Heron, Marsh Harrier, Osprey, ducks, waders, Water Pipit, Reed Bunting.

On passage: Garganey, waders, Slender-billed Gull, Audouin's Gull, Caspian Tern, Black Tern, Kingfisher.

Access

Take the C-3317 from Elche to Santa Pola (14 km). From Santa Pola take the

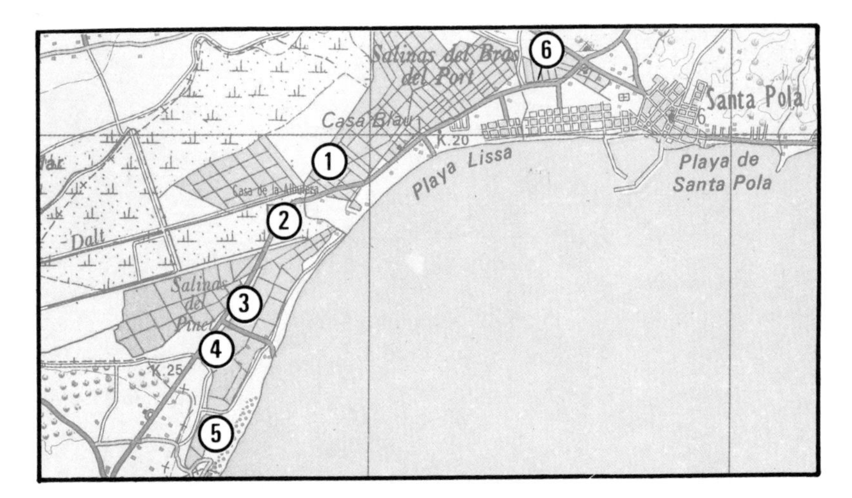

N-332 towards Cartagena, which passes the salt pans.

Description

The *salinas* or salt pans of Santa Pola are located in the former Albufera de Elche, a lagoon at the mouth of the river Vinalopó. The lagoon was drained at the end of the 19th century. The area consists of salt pans, fresh-water ponds with reedbeds, extensive salt marshes and a beach some 5 km long. Several drainage channels cross the landscape, draining through the original outlet of the lagoon into the sea.

The main threats to the area are hunting and encroaching housing development.

Recommended routes

The road itself provides some good observation posts from where you will be able to see between 40 and 50 species of birds in a couple of hours. The most interesting spots are the following:

1) Charca de la Torre (a pond).

2) Canalets – Cuadretas.

3) 4) and 5) Salinas de Bonmatí (salt pans).

6) Ponds lying to the north.

It may also be worthwhile going to the area of the saltwater pond of Charcolís, the freshwater lakes of Santa Fé and the salt marshes. The route, covering the main areas of the salt pans, can be undertaken in some 5 hours although this can be cut down depending on the time that you have (see Comments below).

To finish off your visit, it is worth walking along the beach lying next to the salt pans.

Accommodation

Tourism in the surrounding area is highly developed, giving rise to large numbers of hotels, hostels and campsites, although they may be full over the summer months.

Comments

If you wish to enter the area of the salt pans, you should ask permission from the landowners. It is worthwhile making prior contact with the Agencia de Medio Ambiente de la Generalitat Valenciana, Calle Bailia, 1; 46003 Valencia; telephone: 96-3866350.

It is worth using a telescope.

José D. Navarro Medina

V.15 EL HONDO

A wetland area lying just behind the coast.

Main species

Residents: Cattle Egret, Little Egret, Marbled Teal, Red-crested Pochard, Marsh Harrier, Avocet, Yellow-legged Gull, Fan-tailed Warbler, Moustached Warbler, Bearded Tit, Penduline Tit.

Summer visitors: Little Bittern, Squacco Heron, Purple Heron, Black-winged Stilt, Collared Pratincole, Kentish Plover, Whiskered Tern, Lesser Short-toed Lark, Savi's Warbler.

Winter visitors: Cormorant, Grey Heron, Osprey, ducks (several thousand), Water Pipit, Bluethroat, Cetti's Warbler.

On passage: Night Heron, Greater Flamingo, Garganey, Hobby, large numbers of gulls and waders, Kingfisher, passerines.

Access

Take the N-340 from Elche towards Murcia and just after Crevillente turn onto the C-3321 for Dolores (15 km). Immediately after the railway line you will come across El Realengo, where you turn left through the centre of the village and continue until the road comes to an end (4 km).

Description

Two reservoirs were constructed in an area originally occupied by a marshy lagoon. This was with the aim of regulating supplies of water for the Canal de Levante, an irrigation channel. The reservoirs have large areas of reedbeds, and the surrounding area is taken up by rush beds, salt marshes, some fields and date palm groves. Several other neighbouring ponds have been conditioned for hunting and fishing.

The main problems in terms of conservation are water pollution and excessive hunting.

Recommended routes

Route A takes you along the track between the two reservoirs. It runs for about 6 km and while you will have interesting sightings throughout, it is worthwhile paying special attention to the salt marshes to the north of the Poniente reservoir (1) and the stone marking the boundary line between the Levante reservoir and the Charca Norte (2), where there are good numbers of Bearded Tit. It is also worthwhile climbing the lookout tower (3) from where you can see much of the area and, with the help of a telescope, the heron colony.

Route B takes you along a surfaced track. It is of the same length as route A and can be done by car. Midway you will be able to see a large extent of La Raja (4), where in spring and summer you have a good chance of seeing Squacco Heron, Marbled Teal and Collared Pratincole.

In addition to these routes there are also many other points where birdwatching is good, for example Los Balserones (5), a haunt for waders and Marbled Teal and the Charca Sureste (6), a good place for seeing Collared Pratincole, waders and herons.

Accommodation

Tourism in the surrounding area is highly-developed with a large number of hotels, hostels and campsites. However accommodation may well be full at the height of summer.

Comments

If you wish to enter this area, you should ask permission from the land-

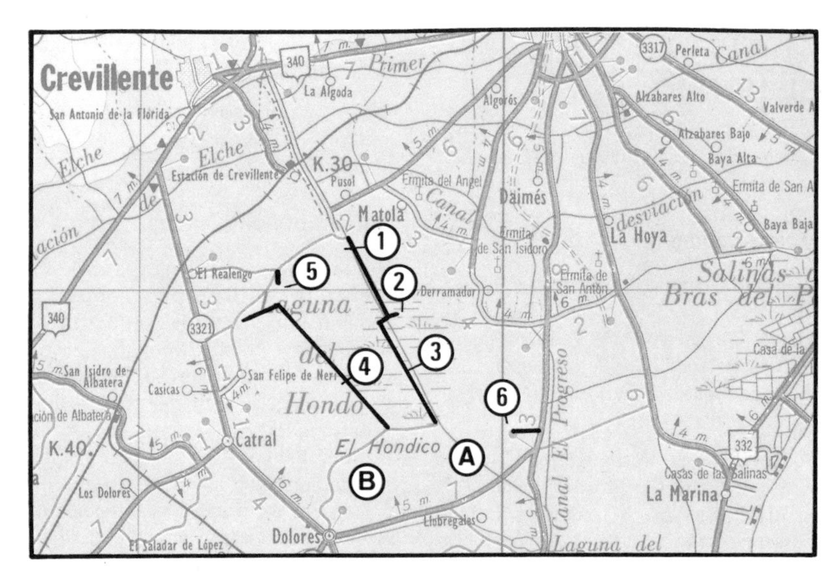

owners. It is worth making prior contact with the Agencia de Medio Ambiente de la Generalitat Valenciana, Calle Bailia, 1; 46003 Valencia; telephone: 96-3866350.

José D. Navarro Medina

V.16 LA MATA LAGOON

A coastal lagoon in a complex of salt marshes.

Main species

Residents: Shelduck, Avocet, Stone Curlew, Kentish Plover, Lesser Short-toed Lark.

Summer visitors: Montagu's Harrier, Black-winged Stilt, Common Tern, Little Tern.

Winter visitors: Black-necked Grebe, ducks, Red-crested Pochard.

On passage: Greater Flamingo, waders.

Access

On the N-332 running from Alicante to Cartagena, at the 42 km marker post near the village of La Mata, turn off onto a dirt track leading down to the lagoon. The track runs along the southern shore of the lagoon and comes out on the C-3321 from Torrevieja to Rojales.

Description

This is a hypersaline lagoon of some 700 ha, lying in a coastal depression. It is used to regulate the water level in the nearby Torrevieja lagoon which is used for salt extraction, causing water levels to vary greatly throughout the year.

The shores of the lagoon run from muddy beaches to beds of reeds and rushes and salt marshes. The surrounding area is taken up by an extensive pine plantation, vineyards and irrigated farmland.

Recommended routes

This is a single route starting on the N-332 and running along the main access track. This is a dirt track which can be travelled along by car, except in the rainy season, but can also be covered on foot. Since it skirts the shore of the lagoon, the whole route is good for bird-watching.

At first the track runs across higher ground giving you a good view of the centre of the lagoon. In winter, particularly when hunting occurs in the nearby wetlands, large groups of duck congregate on the lagoon.

The track finishes near a ruined house beside the channel linking the lagoon to the Torrevieja lagoon. From here you can see a broad expanse of reedbeds and muddy beaches where you can see a large number of birds, particularly waders.

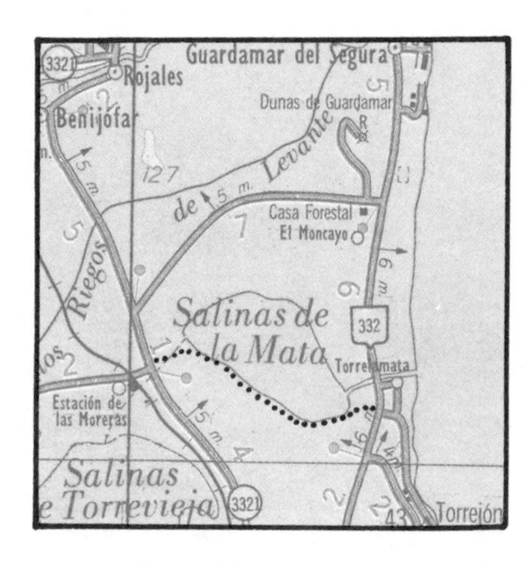

Accommodation

Tourism in the area around Torrevieja has been highly developed, although the number of hotels present is quite low. In summer accommodation may be full; this also applies to the nearby campsites.

José Francisco Calvo Sendín,
Miguel Angel Esteve Selma,
Vicente Hernández Gil
and Francisco Robledano Aymerich

V

PAÍS VASCO (BASQUE COUNTRY)

Bullfinch
Pyrrhula pyrrhula

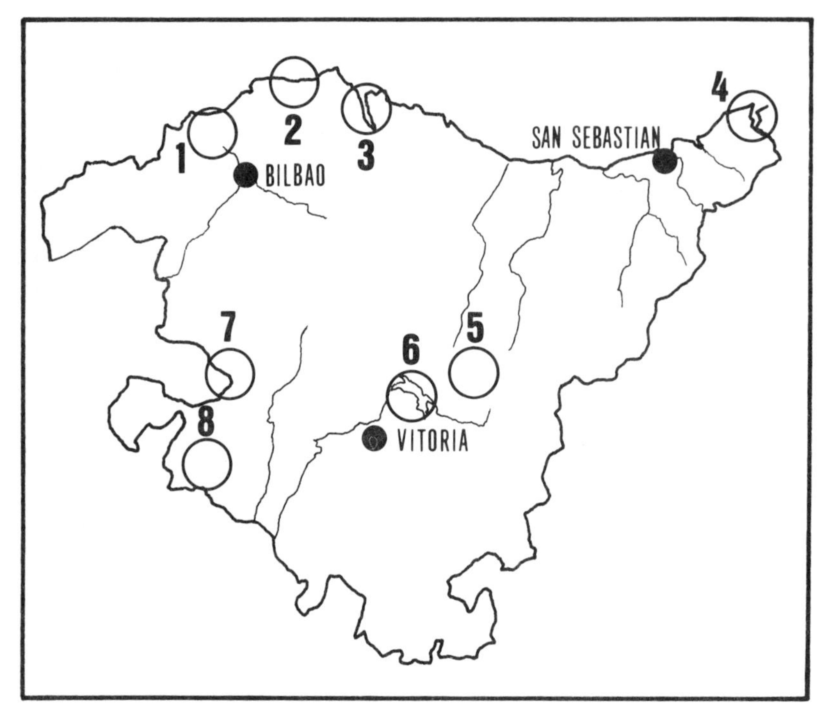

The Basque Country, consists of the provinces of Vizcaya, Guipúzcoa and Alava. Despite its small surface area and high population density, this region is of greater ornithological interest than would at first appear. Positive features include a relatively long coast line as well as mountainous terrain, where a series of tight ranges running from west to east mark the transition from the Pyrenees to the Cantabrian mountains, although the peaks in this area are nowhere near as high as those in either of the adjoining massifs. Climate also plays a part, being mild and rainy in the north and becoming progressively drier and more extreme as one travels inland towards the Ebro basin. The mountain ranges mentioned above run parallel to each other and, despite their low altitude, act as filters which retain moisture from the Atlantic and disperse it as far as the Rioja area in the province of Alava, where the climate and landscape become completely Mediterranean.

Birdlife in the area is clear evidence of this swift climatic transition, which gives rise to numerous species of different biogeographical types in a very small surface. In the northern coastal area, also the most industrialized and spoiled, with widely spread human presence and extensive plantations of non-native conifers, the preponderance of species such as Tree Pipit, Red-backed Shrike, Song Thrush or Yellowhammer is obvious, with opportunities of seeing Lesser Spotted Woodpecker, Grasshopper Warbler and Starling. The spectacular change in landscape which occurs as you travel southwards across the main mountain passes of Orduña, Altube, Barázar or Echegárate is accompanied by the appearance of a whole series of birds previously absent or rarely seen: Black

Kite, Red-legged Partridge, Stock Dove, Hoopoe, Woodlark, Tawny Pipit, Nightingale, Golden Oriole, Great Grey Shrike, Jackdaw, Spotless Starling and Rock Sparrow. This intermediate zone has the city of Vitoria at its centre and is much flatter and more intensively cultivated than the area lying to its north (described above), although it also has low ranges of hills with limestone cliffs and mixed woodland (holm oak, pines, oaks, beech) where it is possible to see a wide range of species in a short space of time. Finally, the small area of the Rioja Alavesa, on the far side of the Toloño and Cantabrian mountain ranges, brings a sudden appearance of birdlife characteristic of the Iberian Mediterranean habitats. Common species include Bee-eater, Crested Lark, Black-eared Wheatear, Subalpine Warbler and Ortolan Bunting.

The main mountain ranges of Aralar (lying largely in Navarra), Aitzkorri (PV.5), Gorbea and Salvada (PV.7), make for what are probably the most fruitful trips, since forest species are well represented in the extensive beech woods as well as interesting mountain species in the cliffs and meadows on the high ground where, at heights which are in fact much lower than elsewhere in Spain, Water Pipit, Alpine Accentor, Rock Thrush, Alpine Chough and Citril Finch are present. These mountains are also home to a number of interesting birds of prey including Griffon Vulture, Egyptian Vulture, Short-toed Eagle, Hen Harrier, Golden Eagle and Peregrine Falcon, among others. The Sierra Salvada and the gorges of the river Ebro at Sobrón (PV.8), both lying partly in the province of Burgos, are by far the best locations for seeing this latter group of species.

The coast, while perhaps not being as interesting as that of Galicia, Asturias or Cantabria, features attractive estuaries at Bilbao (PV.1), Guernica (PV.3) and Fuenterrabia (PV.4) and some interesting sections of cliff such as that running between Cabo Villano and Cabo Machichaco, two headlands (PV.2) very close to Bilbao. Among the birds nesting in this area it is worth mentioning Storm Petrel, Shag, Peregrine Falcon, Yellow-legged Gull, Lesser Black-backed Gull, Rock Dove and Blue Rock Thrush, although the Basque coastline, as is generally the case all along the Cantabrian coast, is of greater ornithological interest in autumn and winter. In autumn, the post-breeding migration of a very wide range of species can be observed. The range runs from sea birds (Cabo Higuer, PV.4; Cabo Machichaco, PV.2), water birds (PV.1, PV.2, PV.4) and land birds, particularly passerines on daytime migration. Within this last group are swallows, pipits, wagtails and finches who, having followed the coast of France for a long way, suddenly find their progress southwards obstructed by the cul-de-sac created by the Bay of Biscay. This results in remarkable concentrations of migrants on many promontories and high points lying next to the sea. Moreover, in winter, albeit in small numbers, various kinds of divers, sea ducks, auks and gulls are present, seldom seen by the inland birdwatcher. Cold spells and storms out at sea naturally increase the possibilities of seeing these birds. Many passerines winter in the Basque Country, above all in the farm and woodland along the coast. However, there are hardly any places where ducks and Coot can be observed, the best site being the large Zadorra reservoir, near Vitoria (PV.6).

PV.1 EL ABRA.

Mouth of the Bilbao estuary.

Main species

Winter visitors: Black-throated Diver, Red-throated Diver, Great Northern Diver, Cormorant, Common Scoter, Velvet Scoter, Eider, Red-breasted Merganser, Purple Sandpiper, Mediterranean Gull, Razorbill, Guillemot.

On passage: Grey Heron, Greylag Goose, ducks, Avocet, Ringed Plover, Grey Plover, Knot, Sanderling, Little Stint, Curlew Sandpiper, Dunlin, Bar-tailed Godwit, Whimbrel, Redshank, Greenshank, Turnstone, Sandwich Tern, Common Tern, Black Tern.

Access

Starting at Bilbao (Bilbo) two routes, both 12 km in length, can be taken. The first runs along the right bank of the estuary via the C-6311 up to the bridge known as Puente de Vizcaya (Guecho). The second runs along the left bank and involves taking the motorway as far as Castro Urdiales, turning off at Portugalete to cross the Puente de Vizcaya. The first route is easier and simpler, although it means crossing the city of Bilbao which may be problematic. The beginning of the route can also be reached by train or bus.

Description

El Abra is the innermost and most secluded part of the Bilbao estuary, lying on the river Nervión. The area is densely populated; human presence is very predominant and there is a high degree of pollution.

Recommended routes

The one and only route begins at the Puente de Vizcaya, better known as the Puente Colgante or suspension bridge. The route consists of a 4.3 km walk along a promenade. It is not necessary to leave the promenade in order to see the birds. A lot of people use the promenade and, if birds come to rest here and are left undisturbed, they become very confident. The most interesting observation points are the following:

1) Churruca wharf. In the migration periods terns can be seen and in winter, if conditions out at sea are very bad, divers, scoters, Redbreasted Merganser and Razorbill come in search of shelter.

2) Las Arenas wharf. At low tide during migration Grey Plover, Whimbrel, Bar-tailed Godwit, Turnstone, Redshank, Greenshank and terns can be seen. You will probably see the occasional Collared Dove from the nearby parks and gardens.

3) La Bola beach. At low tide during the migration periods this is a good place to see the waders mentioned above as well as Dunlin, Knot and Ringed Plover. Nearby rocks provide a favourable spot for Mediterranean Gull; with patience this species can be picked out from the several hundreds of Black-headed and Yellow-legged Gulls also present.

4) Algorta breakwater. This is the most interesting section of the route. The rocks protecting the north side of the breakwater are a feeding ground for Eider and Purple Sandpiper and, from this vantage point, you can see the whole of the bay comprised by the Ereaga beach where divers, scoters, Razorbill and, with luck, the occasional Guillemot can easily be seen. Groups of Avocet are also present, although always at some distance and, during the migration periods, shearwaters, Gannet or skuas, especially if strong winds have been blowing from

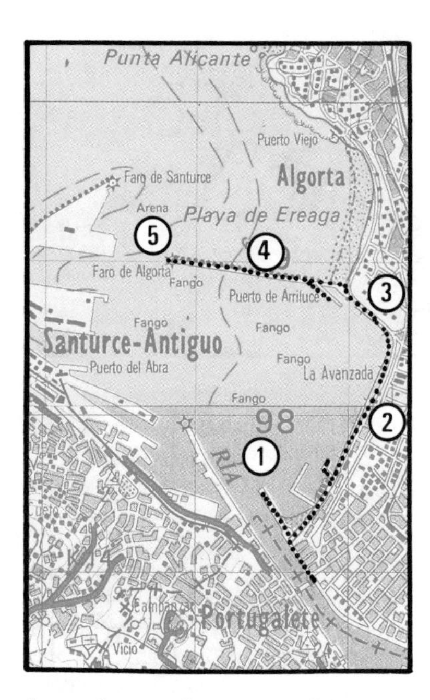

the north or north-west over the course of previous days.

5) Lighthouse on the breakwater. This is the farthest point of the route and, from the lighthouse, gulls and Cormorant can be seen entering and leaving El Abra. In winter this is also a good observation point for Razorbill and divers.

Accommodation

Guecho offers a wide variety of accommodation, but if you are looking for something cheap you might be better off crossing the river and staying in Portugalete.

Comments

This is a good place for observing waders at close quarters during migration. However the winter months are more fruitful, especially on days following big storms when species uncommon in the area can be seen.

Juan Manuel Pérez de Ana

PV.2 MACHICHACO (MATXITXAKO) AND VILLANO (BILLANO) CAPES

Stretch of coast with sea cliffs.

Main species

Residents: Shag, Hen Harrier, Peregrine Falcon, Lesser Spotted Woodpecker, Blue Rock Thrush, Dartford Warbler, Sardinian Warbler, Yellowhammer.

Summer visitors: Short-toed Eagle, Hobby, Wryneck, Red-backed Shrike.

Winter visitors: Manx Shearwater, Gannet, Cormorant, Great Black-backed Gull, Guillemot, Razorbill.

On passage: Sooty Shearwater, ducks, skuas, terns, passerines.

Access

Follow the C-6313 out of Bilbao for 14 km to Munguía. Continue on the same road until reaching Bermeo. In Bermeo take the minor road to Cabo Matxitxako (30 km). From Munguía you can also reach Cabo Villano by taking the C-6320 to Plencia and from there a minor road to Górliz. The headland can be reached via the beach at Górliz (16 km). There is also a winding minor road running for 30 km between the two headlands.

Description

A series of sea cliffs. The original vegetation has been radically changed by extensive plantings of pine and euclapyptus among which small areas of holm oak woodland, pastures and moors with whin still remain.

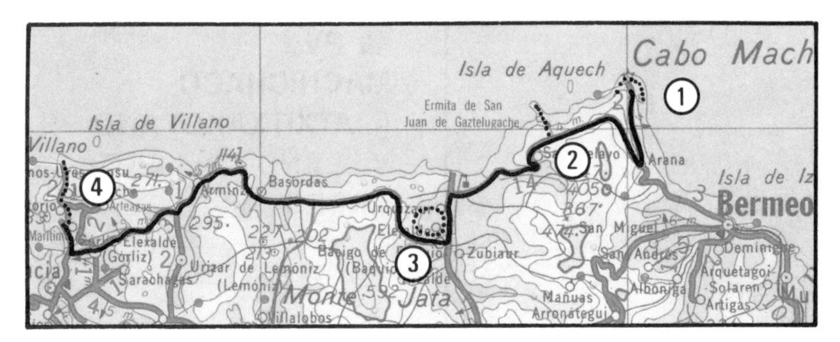

Recommended routes

This single route runs along the road joining the two headlands. Point 1, at Cabo Matxitxako, is a good spot for watching migrating sea birds as well as Peregrine Falcon, Shag, Blue Rock Thrush and other typical scrub-dwelling species.

Continuing westwards we reach point 2, San Juan de Gastelugatxe-Islote de Aketx. The species mentioned above can be seen here in a beautiful setting.

In Bakio (3) there are good stretches of Atlantic-influenced open countryside. A short walk will enable you to see a lot of birds related to this habitat, for instance Red-backed Shrike and Wryneck.

At Cabo Billano (4), walk down to the beach at Górliz via land belonging to the Diputación Foral (local council) and through a gate which is permanently left open. The path, which can be walked in half an hour, crosses pastureland, moors with whin and holm oak woodland where Sardinian Warbler, Dartford Warbler, Short-toed Eagle, Hen Harrier, Red-backed Shrike, Yellowhammer, Lesser Spotted Woodpecker, etc. are to be seen. From the headland itself a wide variety of sea birds can be observed during the migration periods, as well as cliff-dwelling species —Peregrine Falcon, Blue Rock Thrush, etc.

In Plencia (Plentzia) there is a small river estuary which is worth visiting for its wide range of water birds.

Accommodation

Accommodation can be found in any of the coastal towns in the area, although there may be difficulty in finding somewhere during the summer months. Eating places also abound, although campsites are scarce.

Comments

The Lemóniz nuclear power station is located at Basordas, between the towns of Bakio and Armintza. The Guardia Civil guard the entrance and exit to the station and you are not under any circumstances allowed to stop between these two points.

Jon Hidalgo Múgica
(Sociedad Ornitológica Lanius)

■ PV.3 RÍA OF GUERNICA (GERNIKA)

Estuary and stretch of coastline. The second most important marshland area on the Cantabrian coast after the bay of Santoña (CN.4).

Main species

Residents: Shag, Hobby, Peregrine Falcon, Yellow-legged Gull, Lesser Spotted Woodpecker, Blue Rock Thrush, Fan-tailed Warbler.

Summer visitors: Little Ringed Plover, Grasshopper Warbler, Reed Warbler, Great Reed Warbler.

Winter visitors: Cormorant, Little Egret, Grey Heron, Common Scoter, Curlew, Greenshank, Razorbill, Guillemot.

On passage: shearwaters, Gannet, Spoonbill, Red Kite, Whimbrel and waders in general, Sandwich Tern.

Access

Take the A-8 motorway from Bilbao and turn off at the Amorebieta exit onto the C-6315. Continue until reaching Gernika, the starting point for the routes (32 km). Amorebieta can also be reached via the N-634, which follows a similar route.

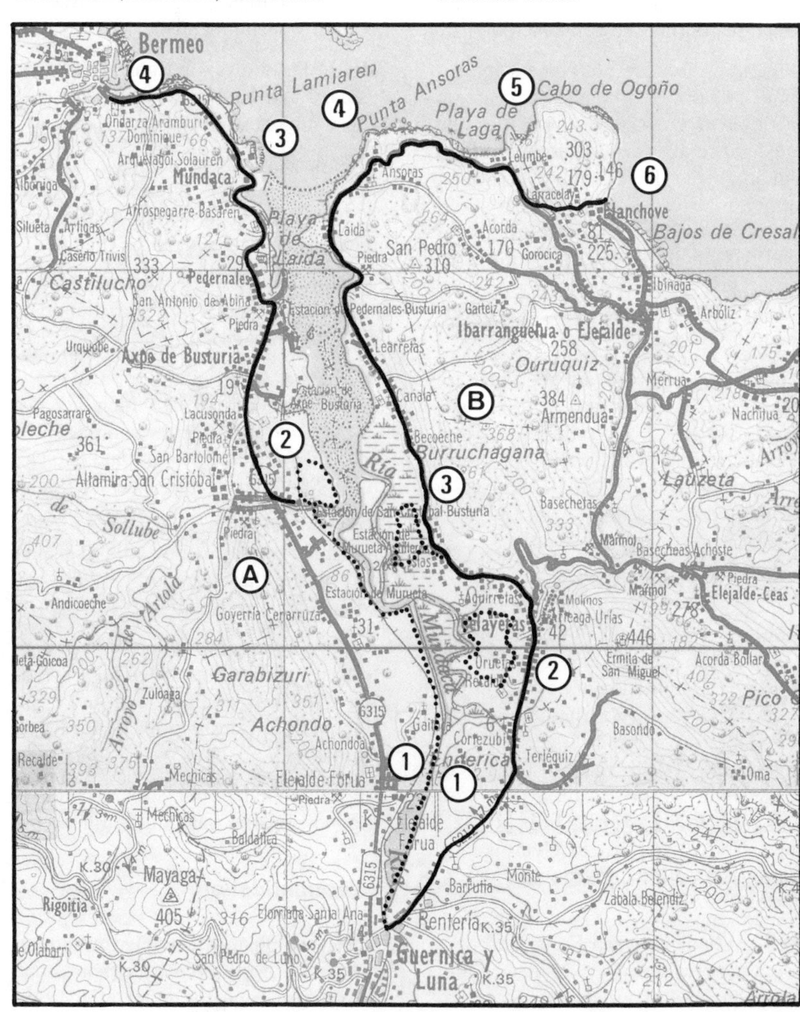

Description

This is a typical Cantabrian estuary with a marshy intertidal zone. The upper part is dominated by reedbeds and partially flooded agricultural land while the estuary mouth features the Ogoño cliffs and the island of Izaro. Around the estuary there are areas of open farmland, conifer plantations and native woodland including extensive areas of Cantabrian holm oak (*Quercus ilex*). The whole area is subject to considerable human presence which increases during the summer months.

Although birds are not present in vast numbers, the geographically strategic position of the estuary occasions the appearance of a great number of different species. The estuary plays an important role as an area providing shelter for wintering birds during cold spells, with the presence of northern birds seldom encountered in Spain (Long-tailed Duck, Velvet Scoter, Brent Goose, etc.).

Both the marshes and the shoreline are Zonas de Especial Protección (Specially Protected Areas) within a Biosphere Reserve covering the entire basin of the river Urdaibai. Hunting is prohibited in the area.

Recommended routes

Route A runs along the left bank of the estuary and can be done on foot, by train or a combination of both. In either case the road from Guernika to Bermeo (C-6315) runs parallel to the route. If you decide to walk, the best thing is to make your way to Busturia (2 hours) and from there take the train to Bermeo. You can return to Guernika by train. The following stopping points are recommended:

1) Reed beds between Forua and Murueta where warblers, buntings and rails can be seen. In winter there are roosts of finches, buntings and starlings.

2) Artificial sand banks at San Cristóbal and Axpe. These allow for access to the most important intertidal zones and constitute an excellent point for observing the waders which assemble on the tide line at high tide.

3) and 4) The fishing ports of Mundaca (Mundaka) and Bermeo. These are good spots for seeing Guillemot, Razorbill, divers, Little Gull and Purple Sandpiper. The jetty at Bermeo is highly recommended.

Route B follows the right bank of the estuary and can be done by car with short stretches on foot.

1) Enderikas. An interesting area of Atlantic-influenced open countryside from where a general view of the upper area of the marshes can be obtained.

2) Castillo de Arteaga. An hour's walk which takes you across marshland and partially flooded meadows.

3) Kanala. Observation point over the intertidal zone, from which herons, ducks and large waders can easily be seen. Between late August and late October Spoonbill can also be seen here.

4) Antzoras. From here you can command a view of the bay and, in winter and during the migration periods, you will see various sea birds.

5) Laga beach. From here you can go to the area of cliffs at Ogoño, a breeding ground for Shag, Storm Petrel, Peregrine Falcon and Blue Rock Thrush.

6) Elantxobe harbour. In winter this is a good spot for watching sea birds.

Accommodation

There are plenty of hotels throughout the area as well as two campsites, one at Mundaca and the other at Ibarrangelua (Laida beach). Highly recommended is the Txope Benta (bed and breakfast), a restored country house in the village of Arteaga (telephone: 94-685 4923).

Comments

The best time of year for a visit is from late August to late November. The least fruitful months are June and July.

Aitor Galarza

■ PV.4 TXINGUDI

Estuary of the river Bidasoa.

Main species

Residents: Peregrine Falcon, Water Rail, Black-headed Gull, Lesser Black-backed Gull, Collared Dove.

Summer visitors: Little Ringed Plover, Savi's Warbler.

Winter visitors: divers, Red-necked Grebe, Cormorant, Shelduck, Eider, Red-breasted Merganser, Purple Sandpiper, auks, Snow Bunting.

On passage: shearwaters, Gannet, Little Egret, Grey Heron, Spoonbill, Black Stork, Osprey, waders (32 species registered), Mediterranean Gull, Caspian Tern, terns, auks, Penduline Tit.

Access

Leave San Sebastian by the A-68 motorway or the N-I and go to Irún and Hondarribia (20 km) which lie on the estuary.

Description

The estuary of the river Bidasoa lies at the bottom of the Bay of Biscay and is a highly populated area in which some marshland areas, intertidal zones and beaches still remain. Some of these areas are gradually being destroyed and a campaign to protect them has been launched.

In some parts —Jaizubía, Playaundi, Islas del Bidasoa (islands in the estuary)— hunting is prohibited.

Recommended routes

Route A passes through the coastal area of the town of Hondarribia (Fuenterrabía) and enables you to see the bay, the beach and the coastline. The whole can be walked in an hour, the most interesting points being the following:

1) Paseo de Butrón, from where most of the bay can be seen. The bay is frequented by divers, Red-necked Grebe, Cormorant, Eider, Little Gull, terns, etc.

2) The breakwater, where Purple Sandpiper can be seen on the rocks.

3) To the left of the breakwater is the Hondarribia beach, a resting place for large groups of gulls and terns.

4) By crossing the beach and retracing your steps you will reach the harbour where divers, auks and gulls, including Mediterranean Gull, can be seen. At migration time this is a good place for seeing skuas and terns.

5) To reach cape Higuer (Higer) take the road leading up the left hand side of the port. The lighthouse becomes visible immediately and from there you can see passing Gannet, shearwaters, sea ducks, gulls, terns, petrels, auks, etc.

Route B, in the Playaundi (Irún) area, can be walked in half an hour and passes through marshland and mud flats (point 6). The path takes you along the side of a rugby pitch where marsh vegetation coexists with old cultivated ground and bramble patches; this area usually accommodates signi-

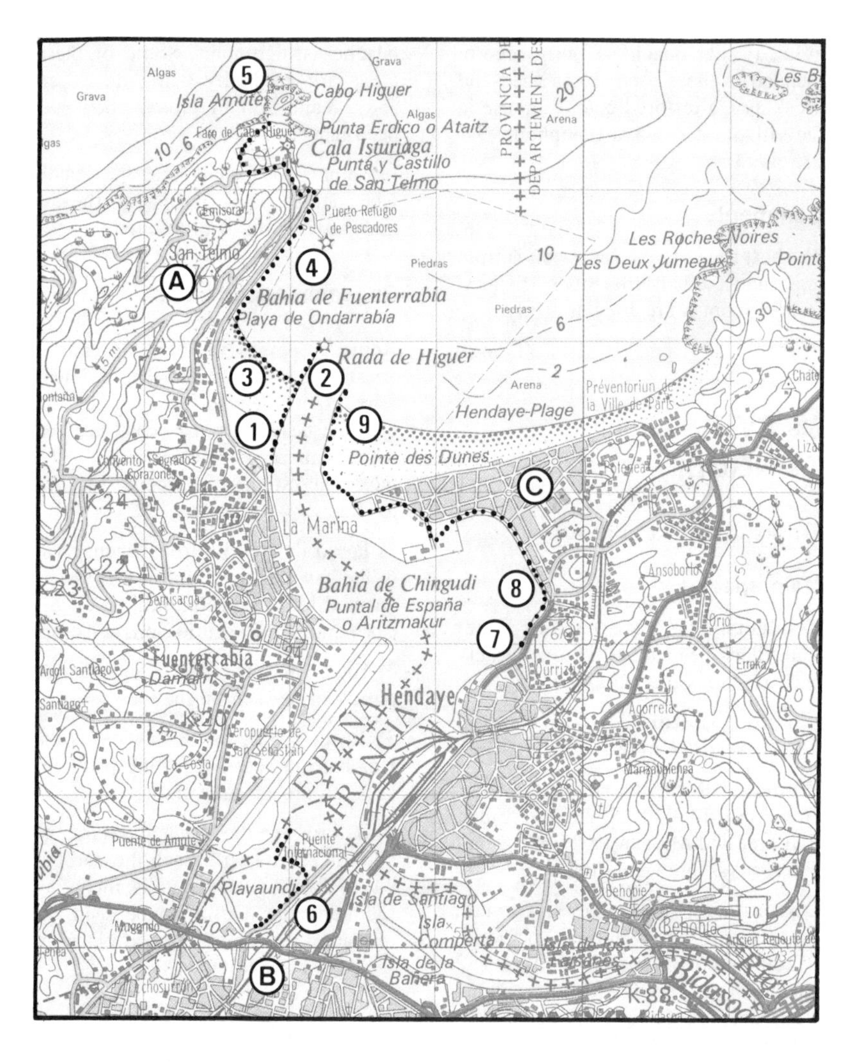

ficant groups of passerines during the autumn passage: warblers of all descriptions, Blue Throat and Penduline Tit. Once past the rugby pitch you will reach the mouth of the Jaizubía irrigation channel from where you can see the mud flats at low tide. This is one of the main feeding grounds in the estuary where egrets, various ducks and a wide range of waders can be found. On the open waters of the bay there are divers, ducks, Cormorant, etc. Playaundi is also a good place for watching the arrival of autumn migrants (herons, Spoonbill, ducks, birds of prey, etc.)

Route C runs along the right shore of the estuary, in other words through Hendaye (France), meaning that you will have to pass through customs. The main points of interest are:

7) Beltzenia promenade, beside the football pitch. From here you can see the Ile des Oiseaux (Bird Island) and, at low tide, a broad mud flat with ex-

panses of eelgrass. This is one of the favourite haunts of waders, egrets, Spoonbill, ducks, Coot, etc. The island frequently accommodates large groups of Cormorant, gulls and terns.

8) Continuing, you will reach a drainage channel where waders can be observed at close quarters. This is a good place for Ringed Plover, Dunlin and Little Stint.

9) Reaching the end of the route with the fishing port of Hendaye on your left, you can continue to the Sokoburu breakwater which is flanked by the remains of the Txingudi dunes, where in winter Snow Bunting can sometimes be found. The far end of Sokoburu provides a good view of the outer bay, a good area for divers, sea ducks and grebes.

Accommodation

Since this is a tourist area there are lots of hotels and a couple of campsites, one of which is next to the lighthouse on cape Higuer. In the high season it is difficult to find accommodation.

Comments

The best time of year for visiting the area is from August to May, coinciding with the winter period and the migration seasons. The times when the tides turn are highly recommended since this is when there is more movement among the birds. A telescope is virtually indispensable, particularly in more open areas.

Gorka Gorospe

■ PV.5 AIZKORRI RANGE

A mountainous area with rocky areas and beech woods.

Main species

Residents: Griffon Vulture, Sparrowhawk, Buzzard, Tawny Owl, Crag Martin, Mistle Thrush, Nuthatch, Alpine Chough, Chough, Citril Finch.

Summer visitors: Egyptian Vulture, Wryneck, Water Pipit, Red-backed Shrike, Alpine Accentor, Wheatear, Rock Thrush.

Winter visitors: Wallcreeper, Brambling.

Access

There are two different access points depending on the route you wish to undertake. For the first leave the main road 5 km south of Beasain to take a local road to Zegama (8 km). Go through the village and continue along the road for 8 km until reaching the Otsuarte pass. Here take the forestry road leading off to the right which, after 2 km of ascent, brings you out on the Collado de Beunda, another pass, as indicated by a large sign. Keep to the road for another 4 km until you reach a 180º bend from where a track leads off. The track is blocked by a chain and takes you, as indicated on a sign, to the *refugio* or mountain refuge of San Adrián. The Otsuarte pass can also be reached by taking the turning for Zegama 7 km outside Alsasua, before the road climbs to the Etxegárate pass (N-I going towards San Sebastian).

The second access point consists of leaving Beasaín on the N-I and after 2 km taking the C-6317 to Zumárraga. Then turn left onto the GI-632 towards Vergara (Bergara). After some 12 km turn right for Oñate (Oñati), a town about 30 km from Beasaín. As you come into the town you will see a square where the way to the Santuario de Arántzazu, a sanctuary, is signposted, 9 km away.

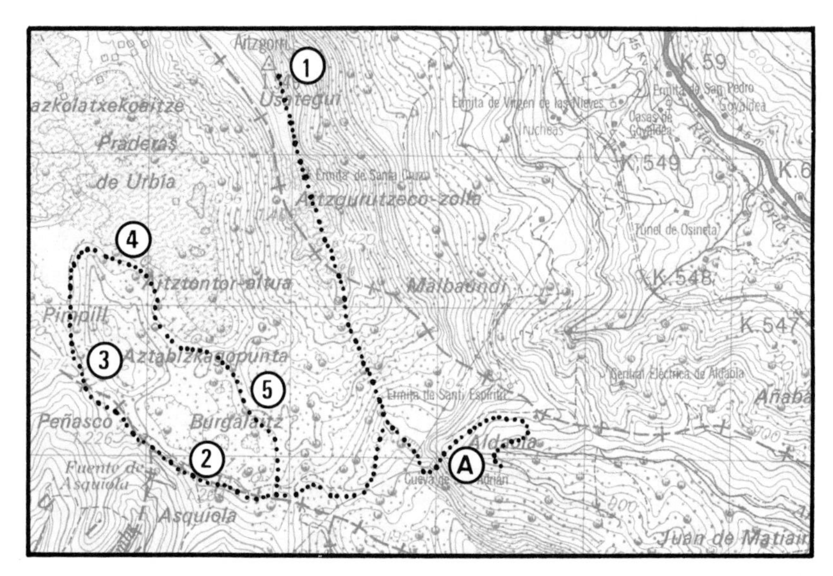

Description

The Aizkorri (or Aitzgorri) range is a limestone massif with the highest peaks in the Basque country (Haitxuri, 1,551 m and Aizkorri, 1,528 m).

The high ground abounds in pastures and, in areas where less grazing occurs, there are areas of heather and whin. The lower slopes are covered with beech woods which form a virtually uninterrupted band of forest.

Recommended routes

Route A is a walk which starts from the San Adrián mountain refuge and goes up to the mountain pass of the same name. In the scrubland you may

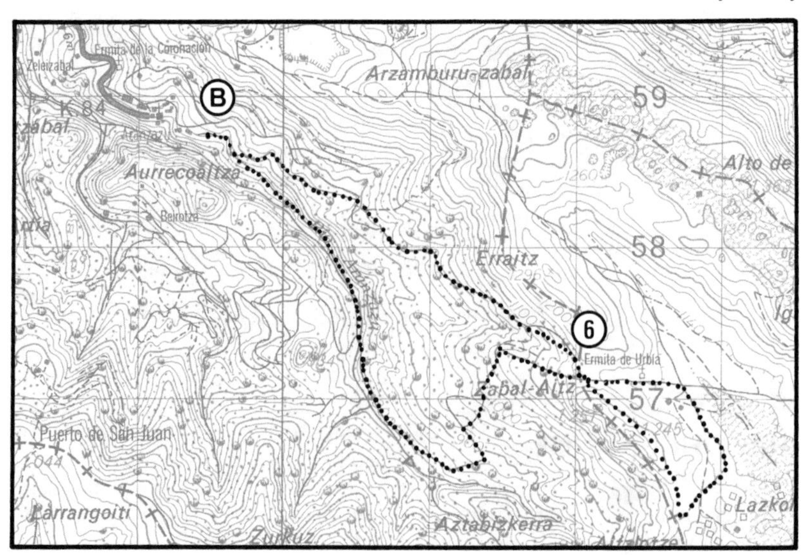

see Dunnock and Stonechat and, on the edges of the beech wood, Citril Finch. Another possibility is to go through the San Adrián tunnel where there is a colony of House Martin and continue along the road for some 200 m until you encounter a sign saying "Aitzgorri" painted in yellow lettering on a rock. Follow the yellow and white markings; the path enters the beech wood and, after an hour's stiff climb, brings you to the summit of Aizkorri (point 1) where you may see Alpine Accentor, Crag Martin, Rock Thrush and Griffon Vulture.

If you are not intending to climb any peaks, you can cover the area on existing tracks and paths. Askiola, Zelaibizkar, Oltza and the beech woodland on the slopes of Mandobide (points 2-5) are highly recommended. The most representative birds to be seen are Wheatear, Mistle Thrush, Black Redstart, Nuthatch and various tits.

Route B starts at the chapel at the Arántzazu sanctuary and takes you along a small road as far as a hostel with a white facade, from where you take a track running off to the left to an irrigation channel. Follow the track for an hour until you reach a pond, from which point you can climb up to the Elorrola pass. By the pond are signs for mountaineering routes (point 6). From here you can either take a path down to Arántzazu or visit the mountain meadows at Urbía. Throughout the route you will have sightings of tits, Jay, woodpeckers, Treecreeper and Nuthatch in forest areas (in autumn also flycatchers, warblers and Brambling). Other birds frequently seen are Citril Finch. Black Redstart, Water Pipit, Wheatear, Chough, Alpine Chough, Egyptian Vulture and Griffon Vulture.

Accommodation

The Refugio de San Adrián (open in summer and at weekends year round) provides food and beds (better to take a sleeping bag). In Arántzazu there are a couple of hostels, and accommodation can also be found in the neighbouring villages of Oñate and Mondragón.

Comments

Since this is a mountain area the possibility of encountering adverse weather conditions should be borne in mind.

During the migration periods it is worth stopping on the Beunda pass to watch birds on passage.

Eduardo Mínguez Díaz

■ PV.6 ZADORRA (ULLÍVARRI) RESERVOIR

A reservoir constituting the main wintering ground for ducks and Coot in the Basque country.

Main species

Residents: Little Grebe, Great Crested Grebe, Grey Heron, Mallard, Moorhen, Coot.

Summer visitors: Little Ringed Plover.

Winter visitors: Cormorant, ducks and Coot (8,600 individuals in January 1988).

On passage: waders (Little Stint, Dunlin, Snipe, Redshank, Greenshank).

Access

The Zadorra reservoir is 11 km from Vitoria (Gasteiz). From Vitoria there are several roads you can take in order to see the whole area.

Take the N-I towards Irún and turn off after 11 km onto the local road for Ozaeta. Between the crossroads and the village of Maturana a series of tracks lead off on the left to Mendijur and Garayo, from where the main inlets of the reservoir can be seen.

An alternative route consists of taking the C-6213 out of Vitoria and after 6 km, having passed through the village of Arróyabe, turn right onto a local road taking you to Nanclares de Gamboa which lies on the shore of the reservoir.

Return to the C-6213 and drive in the direction of Mondragón, enabling you to skirt the deep part of the reservoir. Subsequently pass through Ullívarri-Gamboa to reach the area of Santiagolarra-Playa Barracones.

Description

The Zadorra reservoir, characterized by the diversity of habitats present, has shallow inlets, mudflats, and areas of relatively deep and extremely deep water. The moderate changes in water level have allowed patches of marsh and riverside vegetation (stands of willow) to establish themselves on the shores, particularly in the inlets.

The proximity of the city of Vitoria means that human presence is considerable owing to leisure and recreational activities (fishing, water sports, etc.) conducted around the reservoir.

Recommended routes

Route A covers the ends of the reservoir. Taking the village of Mendijur as a starting point, make your way to a nearby hill topped with a small cemetery. From here (point 1) the two inlets at the end of the reservoir can be

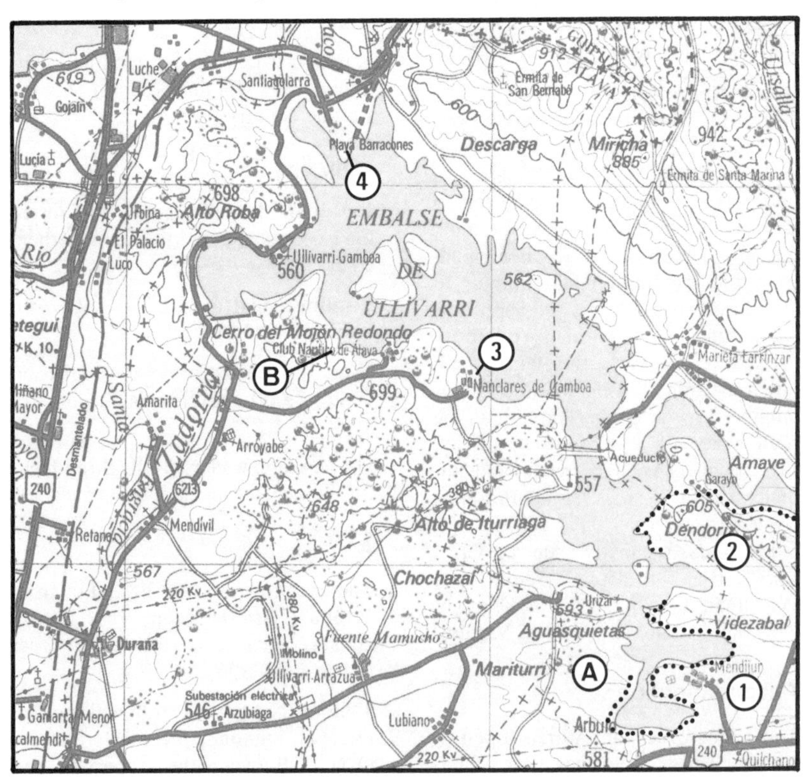

seen. They are dotted with marsh vegetation and willow, and provide nesting sites for Little Grebe, Great Crested Grebe, Mallard and Coot. During the migration periods waders, herons, Osprey and Garganey are present. From this point it takes 1½ hours to work your way around the area.

Near the village of Garayo (2) short routes to different points can be taken in order to see birdlife similar to that outlined above, as well as larger numbers of wintering ducks and Coot.

Route B enables you to survey the open water of the reservoir. The main observation point (3) is on the shore on the same side as the village of Nanclares de Gamboa. In winter and during the migration season there are substantial groups of Mallard, Teal, Pochard, Coot, Cormorant and, in autumn, Red-crested Pochard. Point 4, in the Santiagolarra-Playa Barracones area, provides very similar opportunities.

Accommodation

Vitoria offers a wide range of accommodation to suit all budgets.

Eloy Fernández de Montoya
(Instituto Alavés de la Naturaleza)

PV.7 SALVADA RANGE

A mountain range of medium height with large rock faces.

Main species

Residents: Griffon Vulture, Hen Harrier, Golden Eagle, Peregrine Falcon, Tawny Pipit, Water Pipit, Alpine Accentor, Whinchat, Red-backed Shrike, Citril Finch, Bullfinch.

Summer visitors: Egyptian Vulture, Short-toed Eagle, Alpine Swift, Rock Thrush.

Access

From Bilbao take the N-625 to Orduña (40 km). In order to visit the western end of the range take the C-6318 out of Bilbao for Balmaseda. 1 km after Balmaseda take the C-6210 to Arceniega (12 km), from where you can climb up to the Angulo pass (18 km). For those who like driving on dirt tracks, there is a good network of tracks covering the upper and lower reaches of the range, also taking you up to the crest at the Aro pass.

Description

The Sierra Salvada, forming the northernmost edge of the Meseta, has impressive rock outcrops which in places soar up to 200 m. On the high ground there are areas of moorland with heather and beech woodland, while on the lower slopes and in the valleys are woods of holm oak, beech and oak as well as farmland typical of Cantabria. The area is mainly used for the extensive grazing of sheep, cattle and horses.

Owing to its location, straddling Mediterranean and Eurosiberian regions, flora and fauna are abundant and very varied. It is possible to find many European birds which are not present farther south, and Mediterranean species which are not to be found farther north.

Recommended routes

Route A leaves Orduña going towards the pass of the same name. 1 km after the pass a small road with a very bad surface leads off to the left. For this reason it is advisable to park the car and continue on foot up to the vantage point over the cliffs of the river Nervión. This

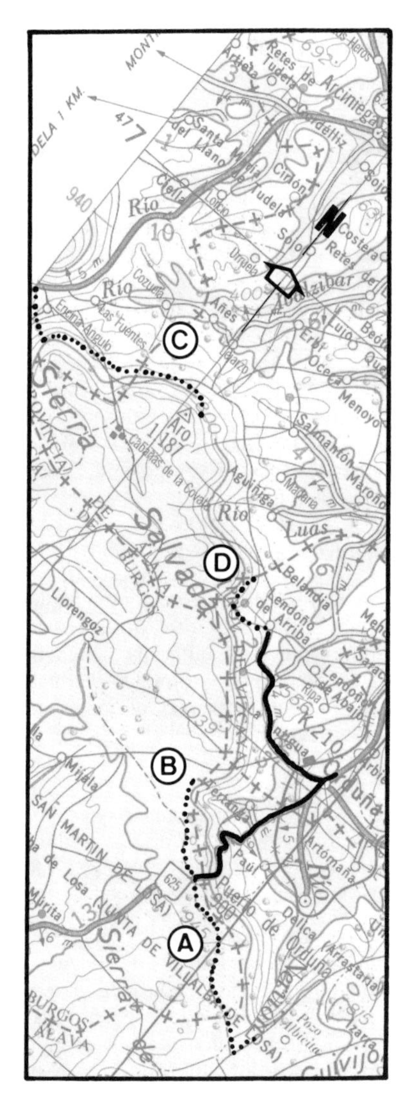

4 km walk takes you through a beech wood where various woodland birds can be seen as well as others living on the moorland and rocky cliffs (look out for the vulture breeding colony).

Route B starts at the Orduña pass and takes you along an unsurfaced track leading off to the right towards La Virgen de la Peña. This route takes you across the high ground of the Tertanga cirque where there is a large colony of Griffon Vulture.

Route C is a walk which leaves the Angulo pass and continues eastwards along the edge of the cliff towards Peña Aro. Returning by the same route, the walk is 14 km long and takes you across heaths and beech wood where Griffon Vulture, Golden Eagle, Alpine Swift and Alpine Accentor can be seen.

The starting point for **Route D** is Orduña, where you take the local road leading to Lendoño de Arriba (5 km). From Lendoño walk through extensive beech woods and subsequently an area of heath up to the summit of Tologorri (1,070 m). The route is 10 km long and involves a climb of 700 m. En route you will see species inhabiting woodland, heath and cliffs. It is also worthwhile walking along the road to Lendoño de Arriba; the road passes through wooded but open countryside where 8 species of birds of prey and 50 further species can be seen in a matter of hours.

Accommodation

In all the main villages of the area there are hostels, pensions and good restaurants. You can also camp on the high ground.

Comments

It may be dangerous to cross high ground on days when there are thunderstorms, since these tend to produce a lot of lightning. Take a water supply if you are going to the high ground in summer.

Luis María Carrascal

■ PV.8 SOBRÓN GORGE

River gorge.

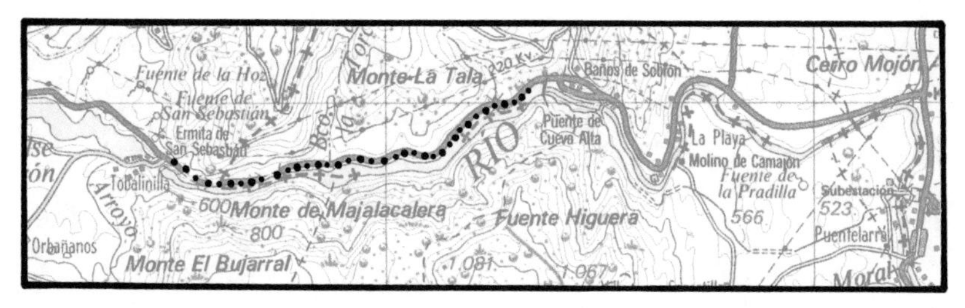

Main species

Residents: Griffon Vulture, Golden Eagle, Bonelli's Eagle, Peregrine Falcon, Raven, Chough.

Summer visitors: Egyptian Vulture, Alpine Swift, Rock Thrush.

Access

1 km north of Puentelarrá on the N-625, turn left for Sobrón (19 km from the junction).

Description

An impressive rocky gorge with the river Ebro running through it and creating the boundary line between the provinces of Burgos and Alava. The steep valley slopes on both sides are thickly wooded with holm oak, Lusitanian oak, Pyrenean oak and strawberry tree which are the habitat of a varied community of passerines. The many limestone cliffs, which reach up to a height of over 500 m, are home to one of the biggest colonies of Griffon Vulture in the Iberian Peninsula as well as several pairs of Golden Eagle, Bonelli's Eagle and Peregrine Falcon.

Recommended routes

The gorge can be followed for 6 km along a narrow road bordering the reservoir. However it is not easy to find places to leave a car and it is therefore advisable to park next to the reservoir dam and continue on foot to the end of the gorge (roughly 4 km).

Accommodation

Accommodation can be found in the nearby villages of Miranda de Ebro and Pancorbo.

Fernando de Juana Aranzana

RIOJA

Griffon Vulture
Gyps fulvus

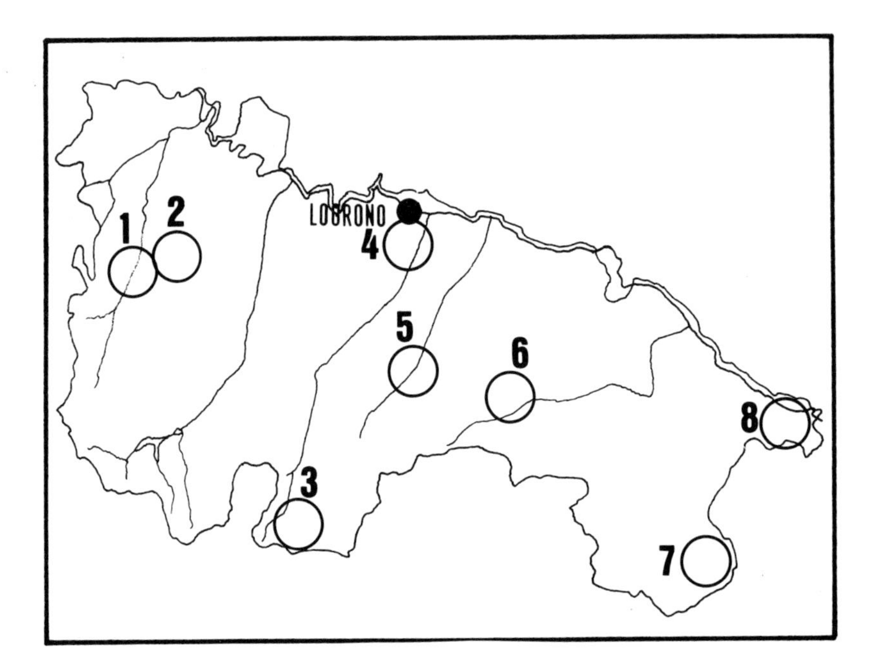

This small province is made up of two main geographical units, the Ebro valley and the mountains of the Northern Iberian System. Each of these areas is clearly defined and has its own characteristic flora and fauna. The latter area is very interesting since the climatological conditions in the mountains, which rise up to over 2,000 m and even 2,200 m, are so different from the conditions prevailing in the surrounding area that they have given rise to an isolated area of Atlantic vegetation in the midst of the dry or Mediterranean region of Spain. This makes it possible for typically central European species of birds, rarely seen farther south, to establish themselves. Examples of these are Honey Buzzard, Hen Harrier, Woodcock, Tree Pipit, Red-backed Shrike, Song Thrush, Marsh Tit, Treecreeper, Bullfinch and Yellowhammer. The southwestern corner of the province, coinciding with the northern slopes of the Demanda, Urbión and Cebollera mountain ranges, is the best place for seeing these species. In these terms the best places of all are the head of the Oja river valley in Ezcaray (R.1), the beech woods at San Millán, Tobía and Valvanera in the basin of the river Najerilla (R.2), and the pine and beech woods on the upper reaches of the river Iregua in the Sierra de Cebollera (R.3). Access to high ground is easy from any of these places, but particularly from the first (Valdezcaray ski resort) and the third (Puerto de Piqueras, a mountain pass). In comparison to the nearby Pyrenees and Cantabrian range, birdlife is sparse, but nonetheless Grey Partridge, Water Pipit, Citril Finch and in certain places Alpine Accentor are present. Some mountain passes, such as those of Santa Inés and Sancho Leza, both in the Sierra de Cebollera, provide a good view of the autumn passage of pigeons, passerines and other types of birds.

To the east of the Piqueras pass altitudes drop off rapidly; as a consequence the moisture level is reduced, as is the amount of woodland and the number of central European species. The valleys of Cidacos and Alhama, in the lee of the Cameros mountains, are completely Mediterranean, in places semi-arid with species such as Thekla Lark, Spectacled Warbler and Black Wheatear. However this section of the mountains of Rioja also has its attractions in the form of a series of cliffs of limestone or conglomerate rock. These are the rugged settings for birds of prey such as Griffon Vulture, present in large numbers, Egyptian Vulture, Golden Eagle, Bonelli's Eagle and Peregrine Falcon. Good sites are at Islallana (R.4), Leza and Jubera (R.5), and Arnedillo, Préjano and Turruncún (R.6).

The section of the Ebro valley lying in Rioja is highly populated and intensely cultivated, meaning that there are few points of special interest. A few areas of riverside woodland remain along the banks of the Ebro, the best example being at Alfaro (R.8), where birdlife identical to that described for the nearby riverside woodland in the region of La Ribera, in the province of Navarra, is present. There are also some small irrigation reservoirs where water birds can be seen, although their presence is nowhere near as significant as that at the Viana or Las Cañas reservoir (NA.7), which is in the province of Navarra but just outside Logroño, the administrative centre of the province of Rioja. Interesting species at large in the open countryside and riverside woodland include White Stork (a large colony at the church in Alfaro), Black Kite, Quail, Scops Owl, Alpine Swift (breeds in the churches of several villages), Bee-eater, Calandra Lark, Tawny Pipit, Great Grey Shrike, Woodchat Shrike, Melodious Warbler, Fan-tailed Warbler, Black-eared Wheatear, Penduline Tit, Ortolan Bunting and, in very localized areas, Olivaceous Warbler and Sardinian Warbler.

R.1 EZCARAY AND PEAK OF SAN LORENZO

A mountain area with extensive woodland.

Main species

Residents: Buzzard, Grey Partridge, Water Pipit, Marsh Tit, Nuthatch, Alpine Accentor, Treecreeper, Bullfinch, Yellowhammer.

Summer visitors: Honey Buzzard, Egyptian Vulture, Short-toed Eagle, Tree Pipit, Bonelli's Warbler, Pied Flycatcher, Red-backed Shrike.

Winter visitors: Red Kite, Woodcock, Brambling.

On passage: Greylag Goose, Red Kite, Crane, Woodpigeon, thrushes, warblers.

Access

Take the N-120 to Santo Domingo de la Calzada and from there the local road to Ezcaray (14 km).

Description

A mountain valley on the northern side of the La Demanda range, topped by peaks of over 2,000 m in height. The valley sides are covered with extensive deciduous woodland and pine woods, while the high ground is occupied by scrubland and pastures which are grazed by stock during the summer.

Tourism throughout the area has developed considerably over the last few years, and includes the building of a ski resort.

Part of the area falls within a National Game Reserve.

Recommended routes

Just before reaching Ezcaray, stop at Peña de San Torcuato (1) from where Egyptian Vulture, Kestrel and Crag Martin can be seen.

Route A starts at the old railway station in Ezcaray. After crossing the bridge over the river Oja, the old road to Turza begins. Walk along this road for 5 km. The route takes you through areas of woodland where, among other species, you may see Nuthatch, Great Spotted Woodpecker, Green Woodpecker, Sparrowhawk and Tree Pipit.

Another option is to drive through the pine wood beside the railway station and take a right turn (2) along a surfaced forestry track which continues for about 6 km.

Route B consists of a drive up towards the Valdezcaray ski resort (3). En route stop in the pine woods flanking the road to see Marsh Tit, Bullfinch, Honey Buzzard and Booted Eagle. Go past the ski resort and continue as far as Cerro Colocobía (4), from where a path will take you up to the summit of San Lorenzo (2,262 m) in about 30 minutes. As you climb you may see Wheatear, Alpine Accentor and Water Pipit. Continuing along the path you will come to the Gitano pass (5); here you may see Grey Partridge, which inhabits the heathland. Farther ahead, near Pico Gatón (6) where there are butts for shooting Woodpigeon, during the migration periods you will see geese, Crane, kites and many passerines on passage. Continue to Cruz de la Demanda (7) where the track meets the road descending the Oja valley to Ezcaray. As you drop down, make stops to see Buzzard, Goldcrest, Firecrest, tits, Yellowhammer, Tree Pipit and Red-backed Shrike.

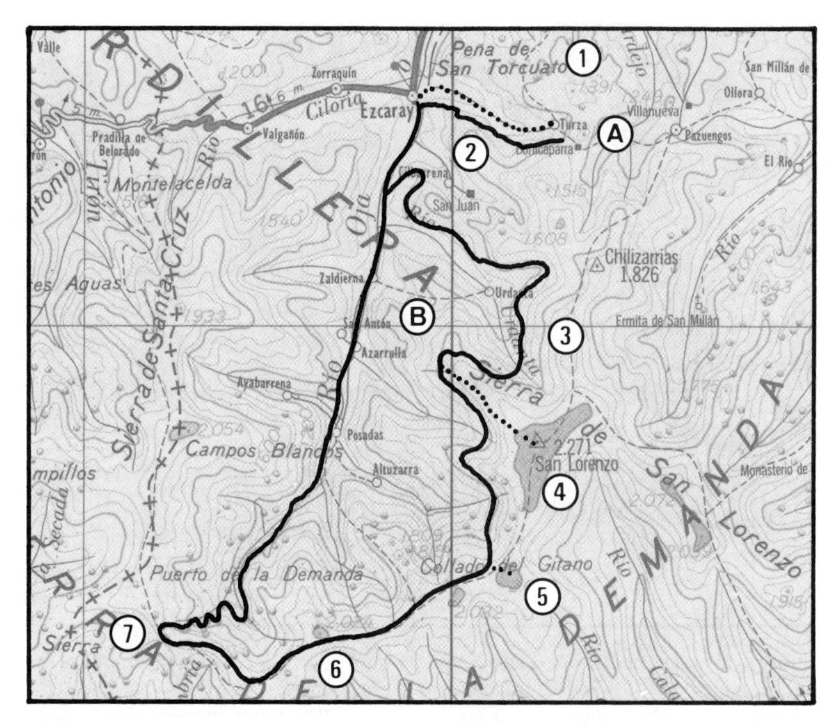

Accommodation

Accommodation is available both in Santo Domingo de la Calzada and Ezcaray. Camping is also allowed in several places.

Alvaro Camiña Cardenal

■ R.2 SAN MILLÁN DE LA COGOLLA, TOBÍA AND VALVANERA

A mountainous area with extensive deciduous woodland.

Main species

Residents: Hen Harrier, Woodcock, Grey Partridge, Crag Martin, Water Pipit, Song Thrush, Pied Flycatcher, Marsh Tit, Treecreeper, Citril Finch, Bullfinch, Yellowhammer.

Summer visitors: Honey Buzzard, Booted Eagle, Short-toed Eagle, Tree Pipit, Bonelli's Warbler, Pied Flycatcher, Red-backed Shrike.

Access

Take the N-120 and at Tricio turn onto the C-113. Continue for 7 km and having crossed the Arenzana bridge take the turn for San Millán de la Cogolla. From here a surfaced track leads to Lugar del Río. 6 km after this hamlet you will come to Los Corrales de Urre, a picnic area with a spring.

To visit the Tobía valley continue along the C-113 and after Bobadilla turn right for Tobía. From here a surfaced track leads up the valley. After 8.5 km you will find a track leading off to the right, taking you to the mountain refuge at El Rajao.

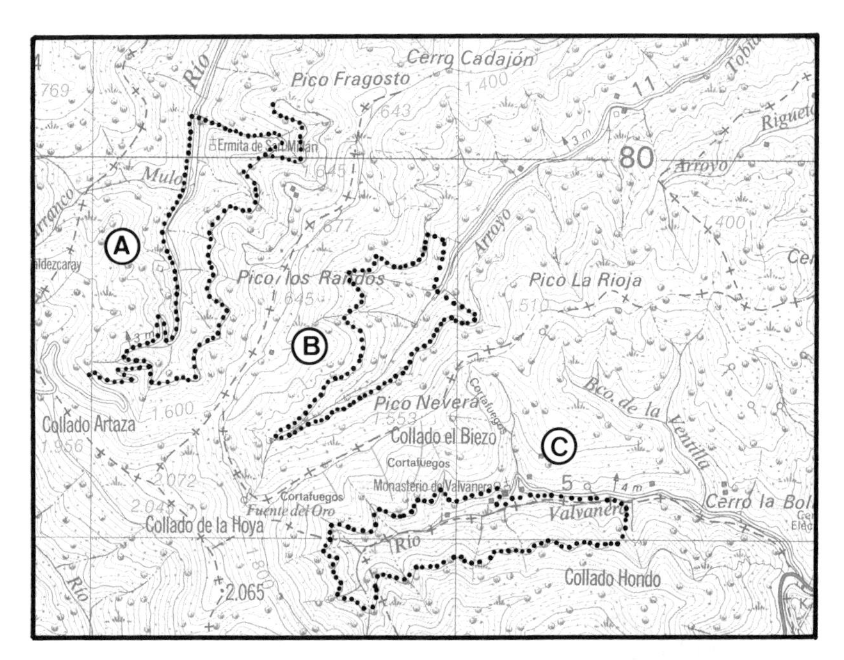

Finally, to reach the Valvanera river valley, take the C-113 and about 9 km after the village of Anguiano you will come to a junction. Turn right for the monastery or Monasterio de Valvanera.

All three points are about 40-60 km from Logroño.

Description

The valleys of San Millán de la Cogolla, Tobía and Valvanera are the most representative and best conserved examples of woodland on the northern side of the Sierra de la Demanda. Beech makes up the main body of this well-formed and structured woodland, although there is also some oak as well as areas of heather and broom.

Recommended routes

Route A runs through the San Millán valley and consists of an 11 km walk lasting 3½ hours. It starts at Corrales de Urre (1) and takes you up a surfaced road to the top of the ravine, passing through beech woods and patches of broom. To come down again, leave the track and make your way down the Fragosto ravine which gives views onto Corrales de Urre. All of the upper part of the ravine is a good site for seeing Treecreeper, Pied Flycatcher, Marsh Tit, Bullfinch, Rock Bunting and Woodcock, although the latter are difficult to see since they are only present in small numbers and tend only to come out at dusk. Migration is intense during September and October, a time of year when you may see Honey Buzzard, Red Kite, Egyptian Vulture and Booted Eagle.

Route B is a circular walk, 7.5 km long, taking in the Tobía valley. It can be undertaken in 2½ hours. Begin at the El Rajao mountain refuge. Work your way upwards through immature Pyrenean oak woodland and cross a small area of dry grazing land with oaks, bringing you out into the beech wood. En route you will be able to see Bonelli's Warbler, Treecreeper, Marsh Tit, Song Thrush, Rock Bunting, Yellowhammer, Tree Pipit and Red-backed Shrike. In autumn you will see birds of prey and Woodpigeon on passage.

Route C is a 10 km walk, taking 3½ hours, through the valley of Valvanera. There are several alternatives, but the most interesting is the route running midway up the side of the valley. Take the wide track leading away from the monastery (3). After 10 minutes you will come to a sharp bend where another, less well-defined track leads off to the left. Take this track and continue. To return, retrace your steps or alternatively use less well-marked paths. Birds seen on this route are the same as for the previous routes, although you will see less migrating birds in this valley.

Tracks and paths leading up to the peaks of Pancrudo can be taken from any of these routes. At Pancrudo you may encounter, among other species, Grey Partridge, Water Pipit and Citril Finch.

Accommodation

There is a hostel at the Monasterio de Valvanera. Accommodation is also available in Anguiano (Hotel El Corzo) and Nájera. There are some campsites in the Tobía and San Millán valleys.

Comments

The best time for visiting the area is the month of June. If you want to see birds on passage, September and October are recommended.

Luis Lopo and Alvaro Camiña

R.3 CEBOLLERA RANGE

A mountain area with dense pine woodland interspersed with areas of oak and Pyrenean oak.

Main species

Residents: Griffon Vulture, Goshawk, Golden Eagle, Grey Partridge, Woodcock, Water Pipit, Alpine Accentor, Marsh Tit, Crested Tit, Treecreeper, Yellowhammer, Citril Finch.

Summer visitors: Honey Buzzard, Egyptian Vulture, Short-toed Eagle, Hen Harrier, Booted Eagle, Crag Martin, Tree Pipit, Red-backed Shrike, Whinchat, Rock Thrush, Bonelli's Warbler.

Winter visitors: Fieldfare, Brambling, Siskin, Hawfinch.

Access

In Logroño take the N-111 for Soria and stop at the Puerto de Piqueras, a mountain pass, after 76 km. The starting point for Route B is 16 km before the pass. Take the turning for Villoslada de Cameros and shortly after this village turn left for the chapel or Ermita de Lomos de Orio.

Description

The Cebollera range, part of the Iberian System, climbs gently, its peaks reaching a little over 2,000 m. The mountain sides are covered with extensive pine forest which is combined in places with woods of oak (Pyrenean oak) and beech. On the high ground, pastures and scrubland predominate.

The area is a National Game Reserve.

Recommended routes

Route A is a 4 km walk which can be undertaken in a couple of hours. It starts from the Piqueras pass itself and takes you up through a pathless expanse of heathland to the peak of El Cabezo, a mountain lying to the west of the pass. From the summit come down on the south side to a saddle with a path crossing it. Turn left onto this path and continue until, after crossing

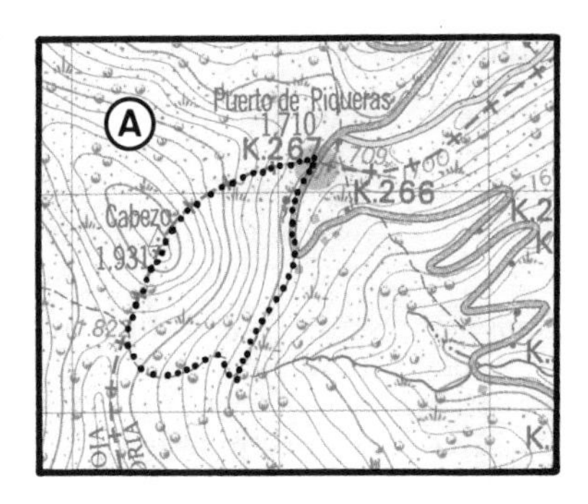

the head of a stream, you come to a mountain refuge actually on the road. From here you can walk back to the pass. The route takes you through heathland, alpine pastures, rocky areas and scattered stands of pine. Birds most characteristic of the area include Hen Harrier, Grey Partridge, Water Pipit, Rock Bunting, Citril Finch and occasionally Golden Eagle, Griffon Vulture, Egyptian Vulture and Alpine Accentor. During the migration periods you may see Crane, geese, thrushes, Bee-eater, birds of prey, etc.

Route B starts shortly after the forestry house of El Achichuelo on the road leading to the chapel or *ermita* at Lomos de Orio. Leave your car at the refuge, which lies in extensive meadows beside the river Iregua. From here, follow the river upstream on tracks and paths through an area of beech and Scots pine, coming back via the chapel. The route is some 10 km long and can be walked in about 4 hours. You may have sightings of Goshawk, Booted Eagle, Woodcock, Marsh Tit, Treecreeper, Brambling (autumn and winter) and Hawfinch.

Accommodation

Although tourism has not been developed in the area it is not hard to find accommodation in Lumbreras, Villoslada or La Póveda and, slightly farther away, in Torrecilla en Cameros. There are also areas where you can camp near El Achichuelo.

Comments

The best time for a visit the area is late spring and, if you want to see the migration, September and October.

Ignacio Gámez Carmona

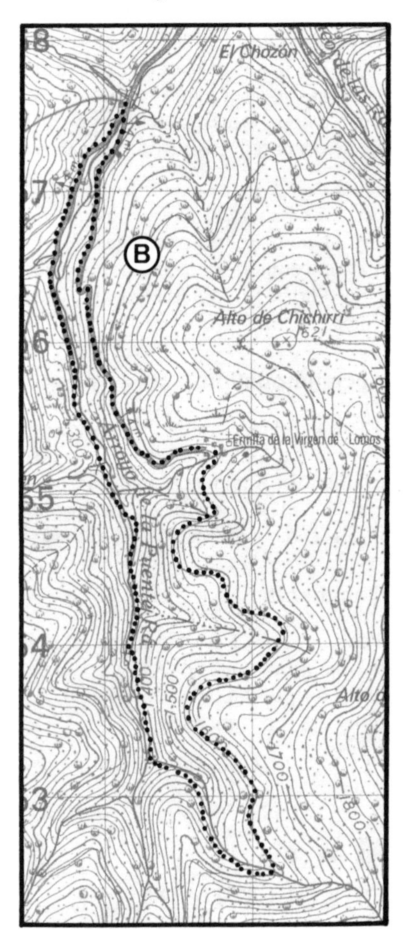

■ R.4
ISLALLANA – VIGUERA

Valley with rocky areas and irrigated land.

Main species

Residents: Griffon Vulture, Crag Martin, Dipper, Chough, Raven, Rock Sparrow, Rock Bunting.

Summer visitors: Egyptian Vulture, Short-toed Eagle, Scops Owl, Alpine Swift, Bee-eater, Wryneck, Golden Oriole.

Access

Take the N-111 out of Logroño towards Soria until you reach the junction with the local road for Nalda (20 km).

Description

Las Peñas de Islallana, as the area is commonly known, consists of a series of large rock formations, composed of conglomerate rock and sandstone, rising up from the banks of the river Iregua. Their picturesque qualities have caused the site to become one of the most popular leisure areas in the Rioja region, leading to the building of numerous holiday houses on the flood-plain of the river.

Recommended routes

The one route in this area is 8 km long and can be covered on foot or by car. On the local road leading to Nalda is a right turn immediately after the bridge over the river Iregua. This track, surfaced for a short distance, is the starting point of the walk. To begin with it runs through vegetable gardens and orchards where Serin, Cirl Bunting, Wryneck and Spotless Starling can be seen. Stay on the track, continue past the village of Islallana and you will reach the first point of interest (1) in terms of seeing cliff-dwelling species. You should see Griffon Vulture, Egyptian Vulture, Crag Martin, Chough and Rock Sparrow. Continue until you come to a bridge over the river (2). Scops Owl, Golden Oriole, Dipper and Cetti's Warbler may be present at this point. From here onwards the surfacing of the track degenerates, making it advisable to park your car and walk on to the village of Viguera, from where you can climb up to a vantage point (3), giving you panoramic views of the valley and the opportunity of seeing Alpine Swift, Short-toed Eagle etc. Return by the same route or alternatively join the N-111 at Viguera.

Accommodation

It is worthwhile taking advantage of accommodation available in Logroño, which is conveniently close to the site.

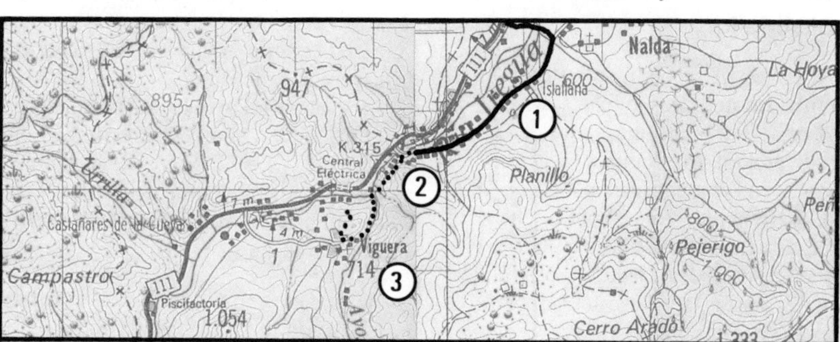

R

Comments

The best time of year for visiting this area is spring.

Javier Ruizolalla

R.5 PEÑAS DE LEZA AND PEÑAS DE JUBERA

River gorge and limestone cliffs.

Main species

Residents: Griffon Vulture, Golden Eagle, Bonelli's Eagle, Eagle Owl, Thekla Lark, Crag Martin, Blue Rock Thrush, Dartford Warbler, Chough, Rock Sparrow.

Summer visitors: Egyptian Vulture, Short-toed Eagle, Booted Eagle, Scops Owl, Alpine Swift, Tawny Pipit, Rock Thrush.

Access

From Logroño take the local road to Laguna de Cameros, stopping after 30 km at Soto en Cameros.

To visit the Peñas de Jubera, take the N-232 out of Logroño towards Zaragoza. After 13 km you will come across a right turn onto a local road for Murillo de Leza and Jubera (35 km).

Description

A series of limestone outcrops and cliffs located at the place where the Ebro valley meets the Sierra de Cameros (part of the Iberian System). Las Peñas de Leza consists of a deep gorge, 4 km in length, carved out by the river Leza, while Las Peñas de Jubera is a similar site but of tectonic origin. The walls of the latter are less impressive and very irregular.

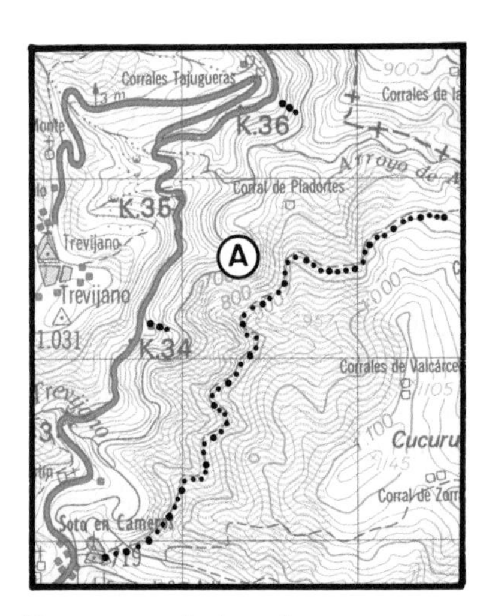

Recommended routes

Route A is a 6 km walk, taking approximately 2 hours, through the area around Las Peñas de Leza. Before setting off it is worthwhile stopping at two interesting vantage points on the roadside, the first 5 km from the Leza turning and the second 2 km from the Trevijano turning. Both are good spots for seeing Griffon Vulture, Egyptian Vulture, Short-toed Eagle, Crag Martin and Blue Rock Thrush.

The route itself begins at Soto en Cameros, where you take the track for Peña La Mora from beside the chapel of Nuestra Señora del Cortijo. To start with the track runs through abandoned fields on terraces covered with scrubland where Red-legged Partridge, Thekla Lark and Dartford Warbler make their home. Subsequently the terrain becomes more rugged, featuring rock walls, until you come to the stock enclosures at Payerne, the turning point of the walk. On this stretch of the route you may see Chough, Rock Thrush, Rock Sparrow, Raven and, though less frequently, Golden Eagle, Bonelli's Eagle and Eagle Owl.

Before starting out on **Route B**, which takes you to Las Peñas de Jubera, it is

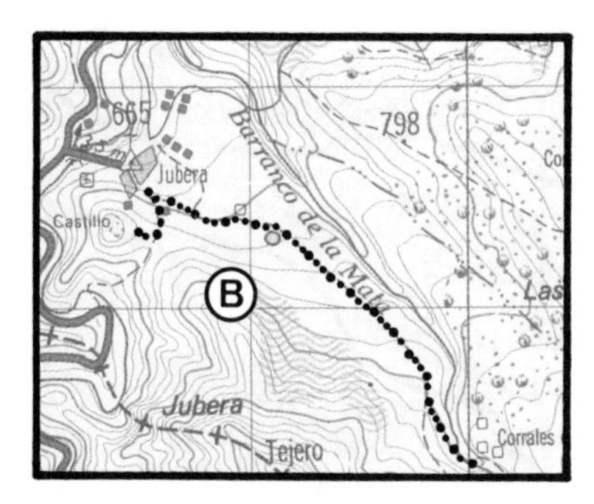

worthwhile climbing up to the castle above the village in order to gain a general impression of the area. You may also see Griffon Vulture, Chough, Egyptian Vulture, Crag Martin, Alpine Swift and Blue Rock Thrush. Return to the village of Jubera and bear right onto the track for La Mata, which continues for another 2 km. This should bring you sightings of Fan-tailed Warbler, Serin, Cirl Bunting and Tawny Pipit. If you are in the poplar groves by the river at dusk, you will hear Scops Owl and may be lucky in seeing the occasional pair of Booted Eagle.

Accommodation

Logroño not only offers a wide range of accommodation but is also close to this area.

Luis Lopo

R.6
CLIFFS AT ARNEDILLO – TURRUNCÚN

An area of cliffs and rocky outcrops.

Main species

Residents: Griffon Vulture, Golden Eagle, Bonelli's Eagle, Peregrine Falcon, Eagle Owl, Thekla Lark, Crag Martin, Black Wheatear, Blue Rock Thrush, Dartford Warbler, Chough, Raven, Rock Sparrow, Rock Bunting.

Summer visitors: Egyptian Vulture, Alpine Swift, Bee-eater, Hoopoe, Tawny Pipit, Black-eared Wheatear, Rock Thrush, Subalpine Warbler, Woodchat Shrike, Ortolan Bunting.

Access

Take the N-232 out of Logroño towards Zaragoza. After 37 km you will come to Villar de Arnedo, where you take the C-123 to Arnedo (12 km), the starting point for the routes.

Description

This is an area of rugged hills which has been extensively deforested. There are many cliffs, largely limestone, of varying size. Vegetation consists largely of various kinds of scrub (whin, rosemary, thyme, etc) with small patches of oak, holm oak, yew, etc. on some slopes.

Recommended routes

To follow **Route A**, take the local road out of Arnedo for Préjano. Approximately 2 km after Préjano, travelling in the direction of Arnedillo, turn left onto a broad, paved track leading up to some mines (point 1). The first part of this track is not suitable for cars. From point 1 you will obtain a good view of the Peñalmonte cliffs where you may see Griffon Vulture, Egyptian Vulture, Chough, Rock Thrush, Blue Rock Thrush and, in the surrounding scrubland, Subalpine Warbler, Dartford Warbler, Tawny Pipit, buntings, etc. Continue along the track and 200 m from the mines a path leads off to the right; this will take you to the upper edge of the mine (2) from where you can enjoy a wonderful view of the whole valley.

Continuing along the road, you will come to Arnedillo where nearby cliffs (3,4) give rise to the presence of a variety of cliff-dwelling species. You can

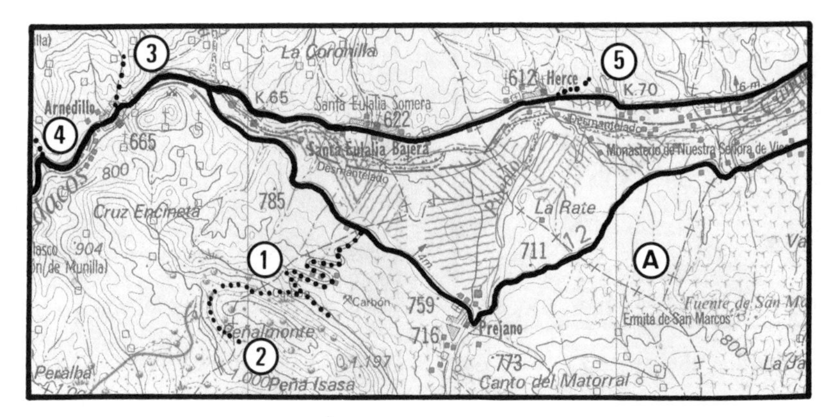

return to Arnedo by taking the C-115, stopping off near Herce (point 5). On the cliffs here you will see Griffon Vulture, Rock Dove and Black Wheatear, and in the surrounding countryside species such as Bee-eater, Ortolan Bunting, Spotless Starling and Woodchat Shrike.

Route B consists of taking the C-123 out of Arnedo towards Cervera del Río Alhama. After passing through the village of Turruncún take the first track on the right. Follow this track, turning left at each crossroads you encounter, until you are again level with the road, to which you will have to return by the same route since it is the only way out of the area. Make stops at will to see Subalpine Warbler, Dartford Warbler, Thekla Lark, Black-eared Wheatear, Black Wheatear, Rock Thrush, Blue Rock Thrush and Crag Martin.

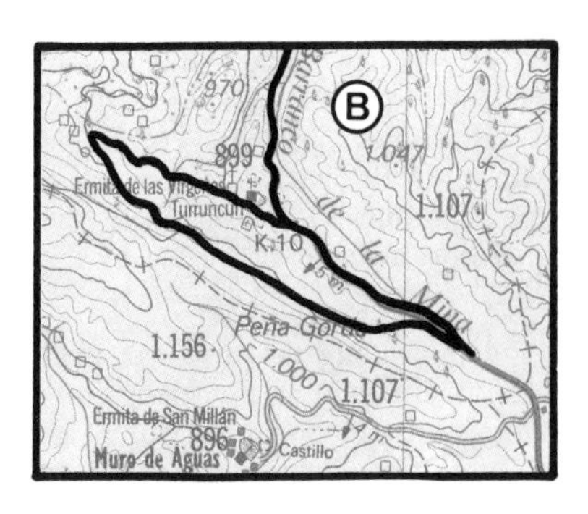

Accommodation

Both Arnedo and Arnedillo avail of accommodation in the form of several fondas and hotels.

Javier Gómez de Francisco and José Luis Gómez de Francisco

■ R.7 FUENTESTRÚN DEL CAJO

A small river gorge.

Main species

Residents: Griffon Vulture, Peregrine Falcon, Thekla Lark, Black-eared Wheatear, Black Wheatear, Blue Rock Thrush, Dartford Warbler, Chough, Raven, Rock Bunting.

Summer visitors: Egyptian Vulture, Alpine Swift, Bee-eater, Wryneck, Crag Martin, Spectacled Warbler, Subalpine Warbler, Golden Oriole, Red-backed Shrike.

Access

Take the N-232 towards Zaragoza and, 4 km from Alfaro, take the C-101 to Valverde. Here turn right on to the C-123 and at the Cabretón crossroads take the surfaced track leading off to the left, signed for Valdegutur (105 km from Logroño). If you are intending to do the route on foot, leave your vehicle in Valdegutur. Alternatively you can drive along the dirt track into the gorge, although the track is not recommended for normal cars.

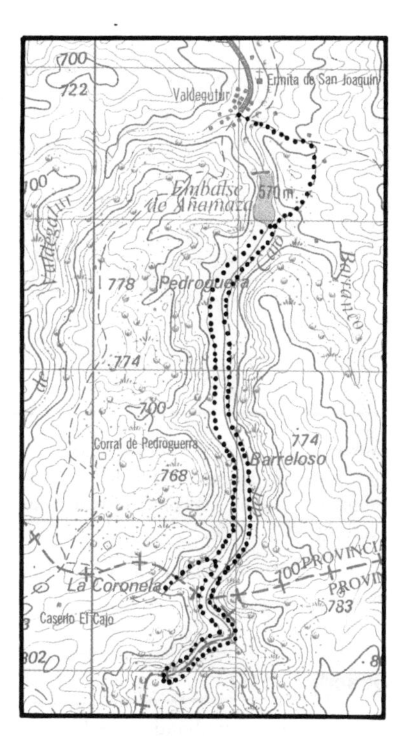

Description

The gorge, carved by the river Fuentestrún del Cajo, is quite narrow with rock walls of varying height. At the valley bottom, crops alternate with groves of poplar and willow. Elsewhere holm oak woods interspersed with Phoenician juniper grow on some hillsides, while the rest of the area is taken up by scrubland.

Recommended routes

This single route consists of working your way along the bottom of the gorge for about 10 km. Return is by the same route, making for a trip lasting about 5 hours. Make stops at will and, if you wish, work your way up some of the ravines running into the main gorge. Cliff-dwelling species are represented by Griffon Vulture, Peregrine Falcon, Egyptian Vulture, Alpine Swift, Chough, Raven, Crag Martin and Black Wheatear, while riverside woodland and scrubland are the home of Red-legged Partridge, Great Spotted Woodpecker, Thekla Lark, Dartford Warbler, Subalpine Warbler, Black-eared Wheatear, Golden Oriole, Red-backed Shrike, Rock Bunting, etc.

Accommodation

Cervera del Río Alhama, 8 km from Valdegutur, offers some accommodation. Fonda La Milagrosa is a reasonably-priced option, as is the welcoming bar Bodegón La Rubia with its lunches and dinners. There is also a wide range of hotels and hostels in the nearby towns of Agreda, Tarazona, Alfaro and Tudela.

Comments

The best times of year for visiting the area are spring and autumn.

Jesús María García García

■ R.8 WOODLAND ON THE RIVER EBRO NEAR ALFARO

Woodland on the banks of the river Ebro.

Main species

Residents: Collared Dove, Kingfisher, Cetti's Warbler, Cirl Bunting.

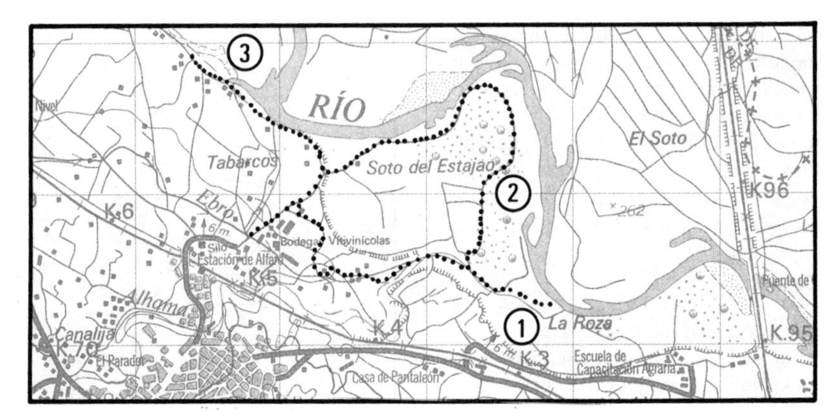

Summer visitors: White Stork, Purple Heron, Night Heron, Black Kite, Bee-eater, Melodious Warbler, Olivaceous Warbler.

Winter visitors and on passage: Cormorant, Grey Heron, ducks, Osprey, waders.

Description

The riverside woodland at Alfaro is what remains of the extensive woodland which used to border the river Ebro. Today these woods have been reduced to small, isolated thickets and lines of trees which flank the river course. The dominant species of tree is black poplar, although there are also some examples of white poplar, tamarisk and willow.

Recommended routes

The starting point of this single route is the old sugar mill to the north of Alfaro. To get to the mill take the road to the train station and, before reaching the station, turn left across the railway tracks to reach the mill. Start by going to the mouth of the river Alhama via the path running alongside the river. On reaching a large poplar plantation leave the path and continue across country. From here to the river mouth (point 1) there is a lot of shrubby vegetation where you may see Night Heron, Cetti's Warbler, Melodious Warbler, Olivaceous Warbler, Cirl Bunting and, in areas without vegetation, various ducks and waders. Retrace your steps to the poplar plantation and return to the path; continue until reaching the wooded area of Soto del Estajao (2). Here the trees are mature and you should see Penduline Tit, Short-toed Treecreeper, Spotless Starling and, with luck, Lesser Spotted Woodpecker.

Continuing farther up the Ebro, you will find areas of gravel and small screes where you may see Black Kite, White Stork, Purple Heron, Kingfisher, Bee-eater and, over winter and during the migration periods, Grey Heron, Cormorant, Osprey and many ducks. The route comes to an end with the Soto Espeso (3), a small wood which is in the process of being reestablished, from where you can go straight back to the sugar mill.

It is also worth visiting the village of Alfaro, a breeding ground for over 50 pairs of White Stork. You may also see Collared Dove in the parks and gardens.

Accommodation

Some accommodation is available in Alfaro. Hotel Palacios Rioja and Hostal Moderno are recommended.

Comments

For further information on this route there is a booklet entitled "Paseos por la Naturaleza" (Nature Walks), published by the Consejería de Medio Ambiente de La Rioja, the Rioja provincial council for the environment.

José María González

LIST OF SPECIES APPEARING IN THE TEXT

Alpine Accentor	*Prunella collaris*
Alpine Chough	*Pyrrhocorax graculus*
Alpine Swift	*Apus melba*
Arctic Skua	*Stercorarius parasiticus*
Arctic Tern	*Sterna paradisaea*
Audouin's Gull	*Larus audouinii*
Avadavat	*Amandava amandava*
Avocet	*Recurvirostra avosetta*
Azure-winged Magpie	*Cyanopica cyana*
Baillon's Crake	*Porzana pusilla*
Bar-headed Goose	*Anser indicus*
Bar-tailed Godwit	*Limosa lapponica*
Barbary Partridge	*Alectoris barbara*
Barn Owl	*Tyto alba*
Barnacle Goose	*Branta leucopsis*
Bean Goose	*Anser fabalis*
Bearded Tit	*Panurus biarmicus*
Bearded Vulture	*Gypaetus barbatus*
Bee-eater	*Merops apiaster*
Bittern	*Botaurus stellaris*
Black Kite	*Milvus migrans*
Black Redstart	*Phoenicurus ochruros*
Black Stork	*Ciconia nigra*
Black Tern	*Chlidonias nigra*
Black Vulture	*Aegypius monachus*
Black Wheatear	*Oenanthe leucura*
Black Woodpecker	*Dryocopus martius*
Blackbird	*Turdus merula*
Blackcap	*Sylvia atricapilla*
Black-bellied Sandgrouse	*Pterocles orientalis*
Black-eared Wheatear	*Oenanthe hispanica*
Black-headed Gull	*Larus ridibundus*
Black-necked Grebe	*Podiceps nigricollis*
Black-shouldered Kite	*Elanus caeruleus*
Black-tailed Godwit	*Limosa limosa*
Black-throated Diver	*Gavia arctica*
Black-winged Stilt	*Himantopus himantopus*
Blue Rock Thrush	*Monticola solitarius*
Blue Tit	*Parus caeruleus*
Bluethroat	*Luscinia svecicus*
Bonelli's Eagle	*Hieraaetus fasciatus*
Bonelli's Warbler	*Phylloscopus bonelli*
Booted Eagle	*Hieraaetus pennatus*
Brambling	*Fringilla montifrigilla*
Brent Goose	*Branta bernicla*
Bullfinch	*Pyrrhula pyrrhula*
Buzzard	*Buteo buteo*
Calandra Lark	*Melanocorypha calandra*
Canada Goose	*Branta canadensis*
Capercaillie	*Tetrao urogallus*
Carrion Crow	*Corvus corone*
Caspian Tern	*Hydroprogne caspia*
Cattle Egret	*Bubulcus ibis*
Cetti's Warbler	*Cettia cetti*
Chaffinch	*Fringilla coelebs*
Chiffchaff	*Phylloscopus collybitus*
Chough	*Pyrrhocorax pyrrhocorax*
Cirl Bunting	*Emberiza cirlus*
Citril Finch	*Serinus citrinella*
Coal Tit	*Parus ater*
Collared Dove	*Streptopelia decaocto*
Collared Pratincole	*Glareola pratincola*
Common Goldeneye	*Bucephala clangula*
Common Gull	*Larus canus*
Common Pheasant	*Phasianus colchicus*
Common Sandpiper	*Actitis hypoleucos*
Common Scoter	*Melanitta nigra*
Common Tern	*Sterna hirundo*
Common Waxbill	*Estrilda astrild*
Coot	*Fulica atra*
Cormorant	*Phalacrocorax carbo*
Corn Bunting	*Emberiza calandra*
Corncrake	*Crex crex*
Cory's Shearwater	*Calonectris diomedea*
Crag Martin	*Hirundo rupestris*
Crane	*Grus grus*
Crested Coot	*Fulica cristata*
Crested Lark	*Galerida cristata*
Crested Tit	*Parus cristatus*
Crossbill	*Loxia curvirostra*
Cuckoo	*Cuculus canorus*
Curlew	*Numenius arquata*
Curlew Sandpiper	*Calidris ferruginea*
Dartford Warbler	*Sylvia undata*
Dipper	*Cinclus cinclus*
Dotterel	*Eudromias morinellus*
Dunlin	*Calidris alpina*
Dunnock	*Prunella modularis*
Dupont's Lark	*Chersophilus duponti*
Eagle Owl	*Bubo bubo*
Egyptian Vulture	*Neophron percnopterus*
Eider	*Somateria mollissima*
Fan-tailed Warbler	*Cisticola juncidis*
Ferruginous Duck	*Aythya nyroca*
Fieldfare	*Turdus pilaris*
Firecrest	*Regulus ignicapillus*
Gadwall	*Anas strepera*
Gannet	*Sula bassana*
Garden Warbler	*Sylvia borin*
Garganey	*Anas querquedula*
Glaucous Gull	*Larus hyperboreus*
Glossy Ibis	*Plegadis falcinellus*

Golden Eagle	*Aquila chrysaetos*
Golden Oriole	*Oriolus oriolus*
Golden Plover	*Pluvialis apricaria*
Goldcrest	*Regulus regulus*
Goldfinch	*Carduelis carduelis*
Goosander	*Mergus merganser*
Goshawk	*Accipiter gentilis*
Grasshopper Warbler	*Locustella naevia*
Great Black-backed Gull	*Larus marinus*
Great Bustard	*Otis tarda*
Great Crested Grebe	*Podiceps cristatus*
Great Grey Shrike	*Lanius excubitor*
Great Northern Diver	*Gavia immer*
Great Reed Warbler	*Acrocephalus arundinaceus*
Great Shearwater	*Puffinus gravis*
Great Skua	*Catharacta skua*
Great Spotted Cuckoo	*Clamator glandarius*
Great Spotted Woodpecker	*Dendrocopos major*
Great Tit	*Parus major*
Great White Egret	*Egretta alba*
Greater Flamingo	*Phoenicopterus ruber*
Green Sandpiper	*Tringa ochropus*
Green Woodpecker	*Picus viridis*
Greenfinch	*Carduelis chloris*
Greenshank	*Tringa nebularia*
Grey Heron	*Ardea cinerea*
Grey Partridge	*Perdix perdix*
Grey Phalarope	*Phalaropus fulicarius*
Grey Plover	*Pluvialis squatarola*
Grey Wagtail	*Motacilla cinerea*
Greylag Goose	*Anser anser*
Griffon Vulture	*Gyps fulvus*
Guillemot	*Uria aalge*
Gull-billed Tern	*Gelochelidon nilotica*
Hawfinch	*Coccothraustes coccothraustes*
Hen Harrier	*Circus cyaneus*
Herring Gull	*Larus cachinnans*
Hobby	*Falco subbuteo*
Honey Buzzard	*Pernis apivorus*
Hoopoe	*Upupa epops*
Horned Grebe	*Podiceps auritus*
House Martin	*Delichon urbica*
House Sparrow	*Passer domesticus*
Jack Snipe	*Lymnocryptes minima*
Jackdaw	*Corvus monedula*
Jay	*Garrulus glandarius*
Kentish Plover	*Charadrius alexandrinus*
Kestrel	*Falco tinnunculus*
Kingfisher	*Alcedo atthis*
Kittiwake	*Rissa tridactyla*
Knot	*Calidris canutus*
Lapwing	*Vanellus vanellus*
Leach's Storm-petrel	*Oceanodroma leucorhoa*
Lesser Black-backed Gull	*Larus fuscus*
Lesser Crested Tern	*Sterna bengalensis*

Lesser Grey Shrike	*Lanius minor*
Lesser Kestrel	*Falco naumanni*
Lesser Short-toed Lark	*Calandrella rufescens*
Lesser Spotted Woodpecker	*Dendrocopos minor*
Linnet	*Carduelis cannabina*
Little Auk	*Alle alle*
Little Bittern	*Ixobrychus minutus*
Little Bustard	*Tetrax tetrax*
Little Button Quail	*Turnix sylvatica*
Little Crake	*Porzana parva*
Little Egret	*Egretta garzetta*
Little Grebe	*Tachybaptus ruficollis*
Little Gull	*Larus minutus*
Little Owl	*Athene noctua*
Little Ringed Plover	*Charadrius dubius*
Little Stint	*Calidris minuta*
Little Tern	*Sterna albifrons*
Long-eared Owl	*Asio otus*
Long-tailed Duck	*Clangula hyemalis*
Long-tailed Skua	*Stercorarius longicaudus*
Long-tailed Tit	*Aegithalos caudatus*
Magpie	*Pica pica*
Mallard	*Anas platyrhynchos*
Manx Shearwater	*Puffinus puffinus*
Marbled Teal	*Marmaronetta angustirostris*
Marmora's Warbler	*Sylvia sarda*
Marsh Harrier	*Circus aeruginosus*
Marsh Sandpiper	*Tringa stagnatilis*
Marsh Tit	*Parus palustris*
Marsh Warbler	*Acrocephalus palustris*
Meadow Pipit	*Anthus pratensis*
Mediterranean Gull	*Larus melanocephalus*
Melodious Warbler	*Hippolais polyglotta*
Merlin	*Falco columbarius*
Middle Spotted Woodpecker	*Dendrocopos medius*
Mistle Thrush	*Turdus viscivorus*
Monk Parakeet	*Myiopsitta monachus*
Montagu's Harrier	*Circus pygargus*
Moorhen	*Gallinula chloropus*
Moustached Warbler	*Acrocephalus melanopogon*
Mute Swan	*Cygnus olor*
Night Heron	*Nycticorax nycticorax*
Nightingale	*Luscinia megarhynchos*
Nightjar	*Caprimulgus europaeus*
Nuthatch	*Sitta europaea*
Olivaceous Warbler	*Hippolais pallida*
Orphean Warbler	*Sylvia hortensis*
Ortoloan Bunting	*Emberiza hortulana*
Osprey	*Pandion haliaetus*
Oystercatcher	*Haematopus ostralegus*
Pallid Swift	*Apus pallidus*
Pectoral Sandpiper	*Calidris melanotos*
Penduline Tit	*Remiz pendulinus*
Peregrine Falcon	*Falco peregrinus*
Pied Flycatcher	*Ficedula hypoleuca*

Pied Wagtail	*Motacilla alba*
Pink-footed Goose	*Anser brachyrhynchus*
Pintail	*Anas acuta*
Pin-tailed Sandgrouse	*Pterocles alchata*
Pochard	*Aythya ferina*
Pomarine Skua	*Stercorarius pomarinus*
Ptarmigan	*Lagopus mutus*
Puffin	*Fratercula arctica*
Purple Gallinule	*Porphyrio porphyrio*
Purple Heron	*Ardea purpurea*
Purple Sandpiper	*Calidris maritima*
Quail	*Coturnix coturnix*
Raven	*Corvus corax*
Razorbill	*Alca torda*
Red Kite	*Milvus milvus*
Redshank	*Tringa totanus*
Redstart	*Phoenicurus phoenicurus*
Redwing	*Turdus iliacus*
Red-backed Shrike	*Lanius collurio*
Red-breasted Merganser	*Mergus serrator*
Red-capped Lark	*Calandrella cinerea*
Red-crested Pochard	*Netta rufina*
Red-footed Falcon	*Falco vespertinus*
Red-legged Partridge	*Alectoris rufa*
Red-necked Nightjar	*Caprimulgus ruficollis*
Red-necked Phalarope	*Phalaropus lobatus*
Red-rumped Swallow	*Hirundo daurica*
Red-throated Diver	*Gavia stellata*
Red-throated Pipit	*Anthus cervinus*
Reed Bunting	*Emberiza schoeniclus*
Reed Warbler	*Acrocephalus scirpaceus*
Ring Ouzel	*Turdus torquatus*
Ring-billed Gull	*Larus delawarensis*
Ringed Plover	*Charadrius hiaticula*
Robin	*Erithacus rubecula*
Rock Bunting	*Emberiza cia*
Rock Dove	*Columba livia*
Rock Partridge	*Alectoris graeca*
Rock Sparrow	*Petronia petronia*
Rock Thrush	*Monticola saxatilis*
Roller	*Coracias garrulus*
Rook	*Corvus frugilegus*
Rose-ringed Parakeet	*Psittacula krameri*
Ruddy Duck	*Oxyura jamaicensis*
Ruddy Shelduck	*Tadorna ferruginea*
Ruff	*Philomachus pugnax*
Rufous Bush Robin	*Cercotrichas galactotes*
Sand Martin	*Riparia riparia*
Sanderling	*Calidris alba*
Sandwich Tern	*Thalasseus sandvicensis*
Sardinian Warbler	*Sylvia melanocephala*
Savi's Warbler	*Locustella luscinioides*
Scaup	*Aythya marila*
Scops Owl	*Otus scops*
Sedge Warbler	*Acrocephalus schoenobaenus*
Serin	*Serinus serinus*
Shag	*Phalacrocorax aristotelis*
Shelduck	*Tadorna tadorna*
Short-eared Owl	*Asio flammeus*
Short-toed Eagle	*Circaetus gallicus*
Short-toed Lark	*Calandrella brachydactyla*
Short-toed Treecreeper	*Certhia brachydactyla*
Shoveler	*Anas clypeata*
Siskin	*Carduelis spinus*
Skylark	*Alauda arvensis*
Slender-billed Gull	*Larus genei*
Snipe	*Gallinago gallinago*
Snow Bunting	*Plectrophenax nivalis*
Snow Finch	*Montifringilla nivalis*
Snow Goose	*Anser caerulescens*
Song Thrush	*Turdus philomelos*
Sooty Shearwater	*Puffinus griseus*
Sooty Tern	*Sterna fuscata*
Spanish Imperial Eagle	*Aquila adalberti*
Spanish Sparrow	*Passer hispaniolensis*
Sparrowhawk	*Accipiter nisus*
Spectacled Warbler	*Sylvia conspicillata*
Spoonbill	*Platalea leucorodia*
Spotless Starling	*Sturnus unicolor*
Spotted Crake	*Porzana porzana*
Spotted Flycatcher	*Muscicapa striata*
Spotted Redshank	*Tringa erythropus*
Squacco Heron	*Ardeola ralloides*
Starling	*Sturnus vulgaris*
Stock Dove	*Columba oenas*
Stone Curlew	*Burhinus oedicnemus*
Stonechat	*Saxicola torquata*
Storm Petrel	*Hydrobates pelagicus*
Subalpine Warbler	*Sylvia cantillans*
Swallow	*Hirundo rustica*
Swift	*Apus apus*
Tawny Owl	*Strix aluco*
Tawny Pipit	*Anthus campestris*
Teal	*Anas crecca*
Temminck's Stint	*Calidris temminckii*
Tengmalm's Owl	*Aegolius funereus*
Thekla Lark	*Galerida theklae*
Tree Pipit	*Anthus trivialis*
Tree Sparrow	*Passer montanus*
Treecreeper	*Certhia familiaris*
Trumpeter Finch	*Bucanetes githagineus*
Tufted Duck	*Aythya fuligula*
Turnstone	*Arenaria interpres*
Turtle Dove	*Streptopelia turtur*
Velvet Scoter	*Melanitta fusca*
Wallcreeper	*Tichodroma muraria*
Water Pipit	*Anthus spinoletta*
Water Rail	*Rallus aquaticus*
Wheatear	*Oenanthe oenanthe*
Whimbrel	*Numenius phaeopus*
Whinchat	*Saxicola rubetra*
Whiskered Tern	*Chlidonias hybrida*
White Stork	*Ciconia ciconia*
Whitethroat	*Sylvia communis*
White-backed Woodpecker	*Dendrocopos leucotos*
White-fronted Goose	*Anser albifrons*

White-headed Duck	*Oxyura leucocephala*
White-rumped Swift	*Apus caffer*
White-winged Black Tern	*Chlidonias leucoptera*
Whooper Swan	*Cygnus cygnus*
Wigeon	*Anas penelope*
Willow Tit	*Parus montanus*
Willow Warbler	*Phylloscopus trochilus*
Wilson's Phalarope	*Phalaropus tricolor*
Wood Sandpiper	*Tringa glareola*
Wood Warbler	*Phylloscopus sibilatrix*
Woodchat Shrike	*Lanius senator*
Woodcock	*Scolopax rusticola*
Woodlark	*Lullula arborea*
Woodpigeon	*Columba palumbus*
Wren	*Troglodytes troglodytes*
Wryneck	*Jynx torquilla*
Yelkouan Shearwater	*Puffinus yelkouan*
Yellow Wagtail	*Motacilla flava*
Yellowhammer	*Emberiza citrinella*
Yellow-legged Gull	*Larus cachinnans*

Other books by the same publisher:
On Observar Ocells a Catalunya (14 authors)
Where to Watch Birds in Catalonia (14 authors)
Els Ocells dels Aiguamolls de l'Empordà (Jordi Sargatal and Josep del Hoyo; colour illustrations by Francesc Jutglar)
Els Ocells del Delta de l'Ebre (A. Martínez-Vilalta and A. Motis; colour illustrations by Francesc Jutglar)
Las Aves de Doñana (C. Llandres and C. Urdiales; colour illustrations by Francesc Jutglar)
Las Aves del P.N. de Las Tablas de Daimiel y Otros Humedales Manchegos (J. Jiménez García-Herrera, A. del Moral, C. Morillo and M.J. Sánchez Soler; colour illustrations by Francesc Jutglar)
Les Oiseaux de Camargue (Jean Boutin; colour illustrations by Francesc Jutglar and Àngels Jutglar)
Los Señores del Bosque –Conservación del lobo, el lince, el oso y el bisonte en Europa– (Christian Kempf)
Els Ocells d'Osona (17 authors)
Alimentación Sana –Combinar placer y salud– (Dr. Josep del Hoyo)
Handbook of The Birds of The World, Volume 1 (J. del Hoyo, A. Elliott and J. Sargatal)

Soon to be published:
Els aucells del Parc de s'Albufera de Mallorca (Joan Mayol)
Las Aves Marinas de la Península Ibérica, Baleares y Canarias (Andrew Paterson)
Els Grans Mamífers de Catalunya (coordinated by Jordi Ruiz-Olmo and Alex Aguilar)
Els Ocells del Delta del Llobregat (Ricard Gutierrez, Pau Esteban and F.X. Santaeufèmia)
Fauna del Parc Natural del Cadí-Moixeró (Jordi Garcia-Petit)